COLLECTABLE
PAPERBACK BOOKS

COLLECTABLE PAPERBACK BOOKS

A New Vintage Paperback Price Reference

JEFF CANJA

SECOND EDITION
Completely revised and expanded

GLENMOOR PUBLISHING
GP

First edition published 2000.
Second edition 2002.

ISBN: 0-9673639-5-0
Library of Congress Control Number: 2002106976

Published by: Glenmoor Publishing
                     P.O. Box 4514
                     East Lansing, MI 48826

Printed in the United States of America

06   05   04   03   5   4   3   2

IMPORTANT NOTICE - DISCLAIMER

The price listings in this book record actual retail sales of paperback books by an established collectable paperback dealer/auction house. Other sellers and buyers might not realize these same prices. The prices of collectable books are determined by real and perceived supply and demand, and can be highly variable. This book is not intended to establish current or future prices, rather, it should be used as a guide by collectors and dealers in making their own determinations of value. Collectors should investigate the market on their own before making any significant buying or selling decisions (see Appendix B for a list of other resources).

Additionally, while great care has been taken to make this book as accurate as possible, there may be mistakes, both typographical and in the content.

The author and publisher shall have no liability nor responsibility for any loss or damage caused, or alleged to be caused, by the information in this book. If you do not wish to be bound by the above, you may return this book to the publisher for a refund.

CONTENTS

Avon 30 (1943)

Dell 17 (1943)

Pocket Books 25 (1939)

Popular Library 15 (1943)

Four early mass-market paperbacks

INTRODUCTION

The modern American mass-market paperback came into existence in 1939 with the release of the first ten titles in the Pocket Books line. Low price, convenient size, attractive cover art, popular authors, and widespread distribution all contributed to make the new books an immediate success and Pocket Books sold more than six million of them in just eighteen months. Soon Avon, Dell, Popular Library, and others had introduced competing paperbacks of their own, and by the early 1940s, the "paperback revolution" was well underway. Over the next three decades, hundreds of publishers joined the paperback bandwagon. Together, they produced an unprecedented assortment of titles, both fiction and non-fiction, reprint editions and original paperbacks alike.

Unlike their hardcovered cousins, which were found primarily in bookstores, paperbacks were sold at newsstands, drugstores, train stations, variety stores, and other high traffic "mass-market" outlets. To attract customers in this new environment, paperback publishers combined the content of their books with the eye-catching packaging and immediate appeal more common to magazines, creating a new medium that reflected the interests of the times in a unique and colorful way. Today these paperbacks of the "vintage" era—running roughly from the late 1930s through the 1960s—are recognized not just as literature, but also as rapidly disappearing artifacts of American popular culture. For both reasons, vintage paperbacks have become sought-after collector's items.

Paperback collecting enjoyed its first significant wave of popularity in the 1960s and 1970s among science fiction and fantasy fans. Since then, the field has greatly expanded and many different genres are now collected. Factors that have contributed to the growing popularity of vintage paperbacks include the resurgence of interest in American crime and detective fiction writers of the vintage era, increased exposure of the classic cover art from this period, and the general interest in the cultural heritage of the recent past. Paperback collecting is now well established in the U.S., and is also popular in Canada and England. In recent years, the visibility of vintage paperbacks on the Internet has greatly increased, and this is another sign that interest in paperback collecting will continue to grow in the years ahead.

ABOUT THIS BOOK

Collectable Paperback Books is the only price guide of its kind and an essential reference for everyone from novice paperback collectors to professional book dealers. In addition to an extensive listing of paperbacks and prices, the book includes over seventy-five pages of useful information on vintage paperbacks and paperback collecting. To supplement the text and aid in identification, almost 1100 illustrations of collectable paperbacks are featured.

The book's content is divided into four main sections. The introductory area covers some of the fundamentals of paperback collecting such as grading and first printings, and will be most useful to new collectors. The second section profiles the major paperback publishers of the vintage era. This section gives a brief history of each publisher, provides information on the various numbering systems used, and identifies a few key books from each publisher that are popular with collectors. Cover art has always been very important to collectors and, accordingly, the third section provides an introduction to one hundred paperback cover artists.

The fourth, and largest, part of this book comprises the price guide. This section presents a consistent and objective view of collectable paperback values. Each of the more than 12,600 price citations is a record of an actual retail sale. There are no "guess-timates" of value or arbitrarily assigned prices, no "asking" (but never realized) prices, and no artificial prices of any kind. Every listing reflects a realized price, that is, a true cash price actually paid for the listed book.

The price information was compiled from the sales records of Modern Age Books, a major national dealer of vintage paperbacks. Modern Age Books conducts competitive telephone and mail-bid auctions of vintage paperbacks, and also issues illustrated fixed-price catalogs. More than one quarter of the listed prices were realized at auction and these are identified by the letter *A* following the dollar amount. The rest of the price data reflect sales from fixed price catalogs and sales lists. Over 95 percent of the prices are drawn from sales during the years 1995–2002, with the balance of the data coming from sales in 1994.

As the listings show, there is now serious collector interest in vintage paperbacks, and prices in excess of $50 or even $100 for desirable titles have become relatively common. For the most part though, vintage paperbacks are still available at prices that any collector can afford. Hopefully the information in this book will prove to be useful to all collectors and will contribute to the growth of this entertaining and rewarding hobby.

PAPERBACK COLLECTING BASICS

WHICH PAPERBACKS ARE COLLECTED?

Vintage paperbacks are collected for many reasons and there are dozens of possible topics or ideas around which a paperback collection can be built. The most popular include:

Collecting by Number – One of the major factors in the growth and popularity of paperback collecting has been the sequential identification numbering used by the vintage paperback publishers. When a collector happens to obtain a copy of Ace D-1 (for example), it is only natural that he or she starts thinking about getting a copy of D-2, or the first ten numbers, or the first one hundred, and so on. Collecting by the number has always been a popular "obsession" with paperback collectors, and this is one of the many factors that distinguish paperbacks from traditional book collecting. Many books that would have little collector value in hardcover form, such as dictionaries or crossword puzzle collections, are often quite valuable as paperbacks simply because they are needed to complete a run of numbers.

Authors – Collecting titles by a favorite author is also very popular. Many paperback authors wrote under various pseudonyms as well as their real name, and accumulating all the works by one of the more prolific authors can be quite a challenge. Some paperback authors who are currently in high demand are (in no particular order): John D. MacDonald, Jim Thompson, Charles Willeford, Louis L'Amour, Harry Whittington, Harlan Ellison, David Goodis, Fredric Brown, Philip K. Dick, Raymond Chandler, Dean Koontz, Richard Matheson, Robert Bloch, A. Merritt, Clyde Allison, and dozens of others.

Cover Artists – Sensational cover art helped propel the mass-market paperback to success and it is not surprising that many people now collect paperbacks featuring their favorite cover artists. At this time, the most popular cover artists include Robert Maguire (Berkley, Monarch, Signet), James Avati (Signet), Paul Rader (Midwood), Earle Bergey (Popular Library), Rudolph Belarski (Popular Library), Bob Stanley (Dell), Robert McGinnis (Dell, Gold Medal), Walter Popp (Graphic), Baryé Phillips (Gold Medal), Norman Saunders (Ace), James Meese (Gold Medal), Mitchell Hooks (Bantam, Gold Medal), Elaine (Brandon House, Gold Medal), Ed "Emsh" Emshwiller (Ace), George Gross (various publishers), Rudy Nappi (various publishers), and others. For more information on cover artists, as well as examples of their work, see "100 Cover Artists" beginning on page 45.

Publishers – Many collectors concentrate on specific publishers or a particular series by a publisher. Always popular are Avon, Gold Medal, Popular Library, Signet, the Ace "D" series, the Dell "mapback" series, and many others. Once ignored but now highly collected are the publishers Beacon and Midwood.

Genres – Some collectors are primarily interested in one or more of the various genres exploited by the vintage paperback publishers, and they collect books that represent high spots in those areas. Some of the genres that are popular with collectors today are crime or "noir" fiction, mystery and detective fiction, westerns, science fiction, books about juvenile delinquent gangs (a very successful genre in the 1950s), adult books, humor or cartoon collections, and others.

Popular Series – As with today's movie sequels, when a vintage paperback publisher or author came up with a winning formula, they would often capitalize on it as long as possible. Almost all the major publishers had one or more long-running series of novels featuring some popular character or hero. Bantam published well over one hundred titles in its *Doc Savage* series, and Richard Prather's *Shell Scott* series was a major success for Gold Medal. Both Bantam and Pyramid put out dozens of Maxwell Grant's *Shadow* novels and Edgar Rice Burroughs's *Tarzan* series was a big seller for both Ace and Ballantine. These books are all favorites with collectors today. Other popular series include *The Phantom Detective* (Corinth Regency), Clyde Allison's *Secret Agent 0008* series, John D. MacDonald's *Travis McGee* series (Gold Medal), and many more.

Three collectable "series" paperbacks

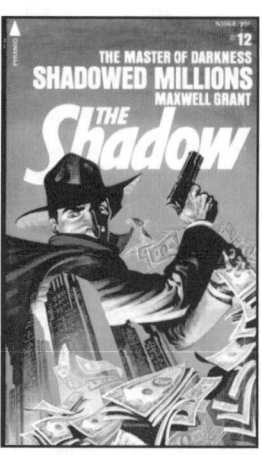

Gold Star 63	Pocket Books 77918	Pyramid 3968
(Hank Janson #15)	(The Baroness #4)	(The Shadow #12)

Other Topics – Movie tie-ins, TV tie-ins, and paperbacks issued with dust-jackets are also widely collected. Of course, many individual collectors have their own favorite subjects as well—paperbacks about Hollywood, paperbacks with nurses on the cover, Civil War novels, and paperbacks published in a particular year are just a few examples.

GRADING

The condition of a book is one of the key determinants of its value. All of the books listed in the price tables were consistently graded in accordance with the following standards:

FINE (F) – Books graded Fine are unused and like new, without any flaws. A Fine book is comparable to a new paperback on a bookstore shelf. Pure white pages are not required for this grade, however, as a slight darkening of the paper with age is usually inevitable.

ABOUT FINE (AF) – Books in this grade are also unread and like new, but have some very minor imperfections, generally due to storage or shelf wear. For example, the book might have slight edgewear, a small chip at the top or base of the spine, light rubbing on the cover, or some other minor flaw. These are extremely high quality books.

VERY GOOD TO FINE (VGF) – Books graded VGF are high quality copies that show minor signs of use. This is the highest grade for any book that appears to have been read. For example, if a book has a light crease down the spine from being opened, but no other significant flaw it would qualify as VGF. Paperbacks that were read carefully one time and then put on a shelf, will generally be in VGF condition. This condition is also used for unread books that are not quite About Fine due to some more noticeable flaw.

VERY GOOD PLUS (VG+) – Books in this grade show more obvious signs of use but still appear to be above average used copies with no significant creasing, spine roll, page browning, or other serious problem.

VERY GOOD (VG) – Books grading VG are typical used books and will exhibit general wear (but not heavy wear). Flaws common to this grade include minor cover creasing, light spine roll, minimal water stains, spine fading (from exposure to sunlight), and peeling cover lamination. This grade covers the widest range of condition and it is to be expected that some books grading VG will appear to be somewhat better than others.

GOOD (G) – Books in this grade will show heavy signs of use but will still be complete and intact, including both covers, spine, and all pages. Also, any book that would be in a higher grade but has some major flaw, such as a clipped corner or a serious cover crease, should generally be downgraded to Good.

GOOD MINUS (G-) – Any truly poor books (i.e., torn, taped, or heavily warped) receive this lowest grade.

Additional plus and minus signs are occasionally used to indicate relative strength within a grade.

MORE ABOUT GRADING AND CONDITION

Although the grading terminology used in this book is somewhat standard, not all dealers and collectors use the same terms. For example, some dealers refer to their top grade as "very fine" or "mint." Others use adjectives such as "solid" and "strong" to modify their basic grades. This can be confusing initially but should not be a problem once you learn how each grade is defined and ranked—ask the seller for details if necessary.

As previously mentioned, the condition of a paperback is one of the most important determinants of its value. Collectors tend to prefer books in better grades, and are generally willing to pay more as the condition approaches Fine. The supply of available books, of course, tends to get smaller as you move up in condition. Most collectable paperbacks are forty to sixty years old, and only a small percent have survived in the highest grades. Consequently, for some paperbacks in top condition, there may be very strong demand but a very limited supply. Such books in Fine or About Fine condition often sell for very large premiums over lower grade copies. At the other extreme, except for very scarce items, paperbacks in the lowest grades generally sell for just a few dollars. The collector demand for such books is much lower and the supply is usually much greater. For example, Gold Medal 347, *Hondo,* is Louis L'Amour's first novel and is generally considered a very desirable item. However, in Good condition it will sell for only about ten dollars (see price listings).

One common condition problem, unique to paperbacks, deserves particular mention. Many early vintage paperbacks have covers laminated with a thin clear sheet of plastic. Over time this lamination can shrink, forcing the spines to bow inward (the lamination separates from the spine and acts like a bowstring), which in turn draws the covers back from the leading edge of the pages. This condition is sometimes called "front-cover pull-back," and unless very minor, is usually considered a significant flaw. Only books with thin cover stock such as Avons and Gold Medals tend to exhibit this problem.

A seller's ink stamp is another flaw often seen on vintage paperbacks. There are actually two types of seller's stamps that may be encountered. The first is a date stamp of the retailer who originally received the book. Arrival dating was not uncommon at outlets like newsstands where dealers were accustomed to selling magazines and wanted regular inventory rotation. These original date stamps are often found on a book's page tops and usually are not considered to be the type of flaw that adversely affects a book's grade. More common and problematic are the ink stamps of used book stores, paperback exchanges, or previous owners. These have to be taken into account in grading a book. If the stamp is small and inconspicuous most collectors will consider it just a minor defect, but larger or multiple stamps may require a significant downgrading.

To place a realistic value on any book you have to make an objective evaluation of its condition. If the book seems to fall between two grades, the conservative practice is to use the lower of the two. When buying by mail or on-line, you should feel free to ask the seller for a detailed description of the condition, and only buy from reputable dealers who provide for returns and refunds.

FIRST PRINTINGS AND REPRINTS

The question of the value of first printings relative to later printings has created a good deal of confusion among paperback collectors and dealers, and a thorough discussion of this topic could take up a small book of its own. As a general rule though, collectors prefer first printings, and these tend to sell for higher prices than subsequent printings of the same book. In some cases, such as with original paperback novels by popular authors, the first printing may be particularly desirable and will sell for a substantial premium over later printings. In most cases though, especially with lower priced books, the differential will be relatively small and later printings often sell for about 60 to 75 percent of the price of a first printing. There is no fixed formula though.

Unless otherwise indicated, the books cited in the price listings were first printings. A few clarifications are in order though:

A) A large percentage of vintage paperbacks had only a single printing.

B) Many publishers assigned new numbers when they reprinted existing titles in their lines. Paperback dealers and collectors generally consider these re-numbered editions to be separate books, rather than subsequent printings of an existing book, and this convention is followed here. For example, Richard Matheson's famous novel *The Shrinking Man* was originally published in 1956 as Gold Medal 577, and was reprinted in 1962 as number 1203. Although the later edition states "second printing" on the copyright page, it is the first printing as Gold Medal 1203 and so will not be designated as a second printing in the price listings.

C) With respect to Avon books, many of the first few hundred titles exist with different cover variations. The back covers of these books would typically advertise other currently available or recently released titles in the Avon line. The cover variations relate to which particular titles are advertised. By inspecting the listed titles, it is possible to tell if one cover variation was printed earlier or later than another. Some collectors consider these cover variations to be different printings and, consequently, the earliest covers may have greater value to some collectors. At this time, though, the matter does not seem to be of great importance to most collectors, and these different cover states are not treated as different printings in the price listings.

D) In some cases, generally with more recent paperbacks, it is not possible to conclusively establish whether or not a paperback is a first printing.

PAPERBACK FORMATS

Almost all vintage paperbacks were published in one of three popular formats, the tall paperback, the short paperback, or the digest format. Pocket Books introduced the short format, which measures a little under 6½ inches tall, while Penguin, and later Signet, favored the tall format, which measures a little over 7 inches. Almost all of the early paperback publishers followed the Pocket Books model, and the short format was the prevailing size through the mid-1950s. Eventually, though, the entire paperback industry converted to the taller Signet format. Pocket Books was one of the last holdouts, but it too adopted the tall format in the mid-1960s, and all mass-market paperbacks are this size today.

The digest format is similar to a small magazine. Digests are somewhat larger and thinner than typical paperbacks. They usually measure about 5¼-by-7½ inches and can have either stapled or glued (flat) spines. The monthly *Mercury Books* (later *Mercury Mysteries*) and Hillman Publication's *Mystery Novel of the Month* were the first modern digest format paperbacks—both imprints dating from the late 1930s. Thousands of paperback novels were published in the digest format and it is still used today for magazines such as *TV Guide*.

Some vintage publishers used non-standard formats. Dell Ten Cent Books were the same size as regular Dell paperbacks but were very thin and bound with two staples. Quick Readers were small enough to fit into a shirt pocket and were also bound with staples, although the covers are cleverly designed to give the appearance of small hardcover volumes. Early Handi-Books were constructed like digests but were only a little bit larger than standard paperbacks, and Royal Giants and Universal Giants were oversized paperbacks. All of these odd format books are very collectable today.

Pocket Books 7

Signet 720

Early short and tall format paperbacks

CARING FOR A COLLECTION

There are several common sense steps you can take to preserve the condition of a paperback collection. Damage to paperbacks often occurs when the books are not properly stored or when they are being handled or moved. To prevent this you should place high-grade books on a shelf as soon as possible. Most commercially available bookshelves are designed to accommodate large hardcover volumes and do not protect or display paperbacks effectively so you may want to design and/or build your own shelves. The books should be placed upright on the shelf with the spines facing outward. They should be pressed firmly together, but not wedged in so tightly as to put stress on the bindings (see the photo on the front cover of this book for example). Do not put warped books or books with gritty or tacky covers alongside higher condition copies—use a separate shelf or a box for lower grade copies of this type. The shelves should not be exposed to direct sunlight as this will quickly fade the spines and darken the pages of your books.

Some people store paperbacks in boxes, and if properly done this can also be an acceptable method. A major problem with boxes, though, is that they generally do not provide completely flat support, which is necessary to prevent warping or waving. Additionally, finding a particular book in a box often involves digging through many others, and this increases the potential for damage. There are some boxes specially designed for paperback storage, these each hold a single row of paperbacks and are sturdy enough to provide sufficient support and protection (see Appendix B for more information). Some cardboard boxes may also be acidic, which can adversely affect paperback covers over long periods of time.

Regardless of your storage method, you should keep your books in a dry and relatively bug-free location. In damp conditions such as old basements, paperbacks are very susceptible to mold and mildew and can quickly take on a musty smell that is very hard to eliminate. In garages or attics, exposed paperbacks can be damaged by bookworms (insect larvae that feed on paper).

Several types and sizes of plastic bags are available for paperbacks and these can provide excellent short-term protection against moisture, bumps, bugs, and general wear. You can use these bags any time a book is going to be frequently handled, shipped, or temporarily stored in a box. However, you generally should not use plastic bags for permanent or long-term storage of high-grade books. Over time chemicals in the plastic can dull the finish of paperback covers. This is most noticeable with glossy laminated covers as on Avons, Dells, Signets, or early Gold Medals. Mylar bags are inert and will not create this problem, which is why they are widely used for comic book storage. However, mylar bags have some problems of their own—they are relatively expensive, not available in all paperback sizes, and some are too thin and flimsy to provide substantial protection against bumping and handling. For valuable books you may want to consider this option, though.

In addition to these basic considerations, anyone with a major collection might want to consult with an archivist or a library for advice on humidity, temperature, lighting, insect control, and other storage conditions.

Pocket  Books

A DELL BOOK

ACE 25¢ BOOKS

LION LIBRARY 35¢

CARDINAL  EDITIONS

PERMA BOOKS
BOOKS·TO·KEEP

POPULAR
LIBRARY

Bantam

AVON

PENGUIN BOOKS

Major paperback imprints of the vintage era

PUBLISHER PROFILES

INTRODUCTION

The following pages present brief profiles of some of the larger paperback publishers of the vintage era from a collector's point of view. Although each of these publishers was unique and found its own market niche, for a preliminary perspective it is interesting to divide them into two basic groups. The first group consists of publishers having their roots in hardcover publishing. This group includes Ballantine, Bantam, Penguin, Perma, Pocket Books, and Signet. The second group consists of publishers rooted primarily in the magazine business, such as Ace, Avon, Beacon, Berkley, Dell, Gold Medal, Lion, Monarch, Popular Library, and most of the others.

As a general rule, publishers in the first group were oriented in favor of traditional publishing values such as reader enrichment and conventional notions of literary merit. Consistent with this, their primary business was the reprinting of books that had already achieved some mainstream acceptance in hardcover form. This group generally produced sturdy, well constructed paperbacks with tasteful and moderate cover art. Finally, with only a few exceptions, these publishers numbered all their books in single, long running series.

In contrast, publishers in the magazine group were most interested in mass-market appeal rather than critical merit. Accordingly, they were partial to sensational subject matter, alluring cover art, and provocative cover blurbs. As a group, these publishers were also primarily reprinters, however, they were equally at home with pulp fiction, and account for the bulk of all original (non-reprint) paperbacks. The magazine based publishers produced virtually all of the digest format paperbacks, and their regular paperbacks are more likely to be cheaply constructed. Finally, perhaps reflecting the tendency in the magazine business to always offer something new, these publishers were more likely to periodically introduce new short running series, and often had two or more series ongoing at the same time.

Publishers from both groups went on to achieve lasting success in the publishing world, however, among paperback collectors, the magazine group is somewhat favored. The same factors that made the books from these publishers stand out at the newsstand tend to appeal to collectors today. Of course, this is a broad generalization—exceptions are easy to find and almost all of the vintage publishers have many avid collectors.

The profiles that follow highlight some of the history and strengths of the major vintage publishers. For most of the publishers, several particular paperbacks are noted. This is not intended to be a complete account of each publisher's most valuable paperbacks, but simply to provide a sample of the types of books collectors are interested in. For reference purposes, the titles of these books are usually followed by the publisher's number in parenthesis, and many are illustrated in the price guide section of this book.

ACE

Ace is one of the most well known of the vintage paperback publishers. The long running Ace "D" series (so called because most books in the series were numbered with a *D* prefix) was launched in 1952 and introduced the double novel—two novels bound back-to-back in the same volume. The Ace doubles were an immediate success with value-minded readers, and their distinctive format continues to make them popular today.

Ace Books was the creation of magazine and book publisher A. A. Wyn. Wyn had published pulp magazines since the late 1920s (*Ace Sports*, *Western Aces*, *Secret Agent X*, etc.), and the pulp influence on the D series is easy to see. Like Wyn's pulps, these early Ace paperbacks featured bold primary colors, dramatic cover art, and striking graphics. Subject matter was almost exclusively confined to four well established pulp genres—western, mystery, science fiction, and adventure. Even the concept of two novels in one book continued a pulp tradition of packing as much fiction as possible into each issue. For example, two popular Wyn pulps were *Ten Story Love* and *Ten Detective Aces*.

An early Ace double, D-10

Among collectors, the Ace D series has long been a favorite. Arrayed on a shelf, the spines make a very attractive display. Mysteries are black, yellow, and red; westerns are green, red, and white; science fiction is red, white, and blue; and the adventure titles are assorted colors. Ace employed leading cover artists and each double novel has two "front" covers. Adding to their value, most books in the D series contain at least one original novel, and many highly regarded authors are represented. The D series also includes traditional single novels. Many of these were numbered with an *S* prefix (for "single") or a *G* prefix (for "giant"), however, after number 275 the S prefix was discontinued.

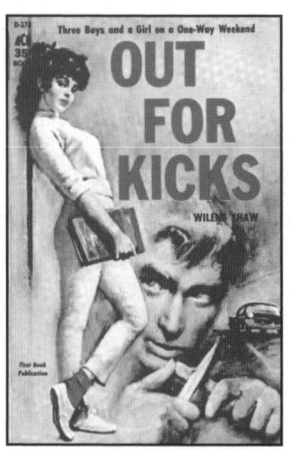

Ace D-378

Three key titles in the D series are D-1, the first paperback double novel; D-13, which includes the first science fiction novel in the series, Theodore S. Drachman's *Cry Plague!*; and D-15, which features William S. Burroughs's first novel, *Junkie* (written under the pseudonym William Lee). Other important titles include all of the novels by Philip K. Dick, Robert Bloch, Harlan Ellison, Harry Whittington, and Louis L'Amour (including those written under his pseudonym Jim Mayo). Additionally, Ace published a number of lurid juvenile delinquent novels in the 1950s that are very collectable, such as D-343, *The Young Wolves* by Edward De Roo and D-378, *Out for Kicks* by Wilene Shaw.

The basic D series cover price was thirty-five cents, but the thinner *S* prefix titles were a quarter. The series ran until 1965, ending with D-599. In 1961 Ace began simultaneously publishing its forty cent "F" series. Like the D series, the F series includes both double and single novels, and paperback originals along with reprints. Science fiction, westerns, mysteries, and nurse romance novels account for most of the titles. The F series also includes Ace's well known reprints of the *Tarzan* novels of Edgar Rice Burroughs.

Ace F-133
(one side of a double novel)

Compared to the D series, the F series is very inexpensive, making it a good project for collectors on a budget. This is even more true of Ace's subsequent "M" series, which includes only sixty-six books—most of which are science fiction or western double novels.

In 1959 Ace launched its Ace Star, or "K", series to cover reprints of serious fiction and nonfiction. These were Ace's first tall format paperbacks, and carried a cover price of fifty cents. The first Star title, K-100, reprinted Richard Wright's *The Long Dream*. Other key titles in the series are K-160, *The Werewolf of Paris* by Guy Endore and K-202, *Junkie*—a reprint of D-15.

Also of interest to collectors are the "G" series, which features many science fiction doubles as well as the first 16 of Ace's 23 *Man From U.N.C.L.E.* TV tie-in novels; the "H" series, which includes Dean R. Koontz's first novel *Star Quest* (H-70); and the "A" series, which includes the first U.S. editions of J.R.R. Tolkien's *Lord of The Rings* trilogy. In 1968 Ace began intermittently publishing its Science Fiction Specials. This series features debut novels from several popular authors including both William Gibson and Lucius Shepard.

Three collectable paperbacks from Ace's later series

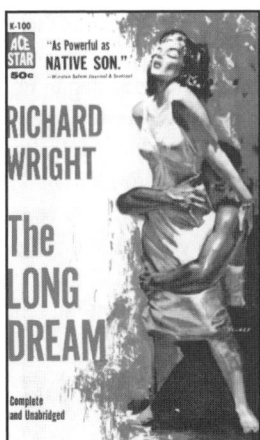

Ace A-4   Ace H-70   Ace K-100

AVON

Avon Pocket-Size Books was established in 1941 by publisher Joseph Myers with the backing of the American News Company (ANC). Prior to forming Avon, Myers's primary business was the Illustrated Editions Company, a publisher of inexpensive hardcover reprints. He was also a co-owner of J. S. Ogilvie Publications Co., which published popular paperback literature sold at train stations and newsstands. ANC was the leading distributor of magazines in the U.S., and operated a retail arm, the Union News Company. Earlier that year, Pocket Books had abandoned ANC in favor of independent distributors. ANC competed directly with the independents and needed a rival paperback line to fill the void left by Pocket Books' departure.

The new company was quickly established and Avon released its first twelve titles in late 1941. The early Avons were somewhat similar in appearance to the existing paperbacks of Pocket Books, resulting in an immediate and largely ineffective lawsuit by that company. Despite this superficial similarity, though, from early on, Myers differentiated Avon by placing an emphasis on popular appeal rather than loftier concepts of literary merit. Murder mysteries, ghost stories, and racy love novels were a substantial part of the Avon list, and provocative covers with eye-catching graphics soon became the norm. As a result, collectors today tend to value Avons more highly than the stodgy (by comparison) Pocket Books.

The first Avon paperback

Avon's first series of books had a fixed price of twenty-five cents and ultimately included more than 875 titles. The first 40 of these were not numbered and are generally referred to as no#1, no#2, etc. First printings of the first 16 of the un-numbered books can be identified by a large illustration of an old fashioned map of the world inside the front and back covers of the book. These so-called "globe endpaper" editions are prized by Avon collectors.

Key titles in the twenty-five cent series include all the books by A. Merritt, which feature outstanding fantasy cover art; *The Big Sleep* by Raymond Chandler (No# 38); the very rare *Avon Book of Complete Crosswords and Cryptograms* (162); *Europa* by Robert Briffault (272), which was issued with two different covers; *An Earthman on Venus* by Ralph M. Farley (285); and many others. Avon also published two twenty-five cent Avon Fantasy Novels. *The Princess of the Atom* by Ray Cummings was number 1 and *The Green Girl* by Jack Williamson was number 2. Both have classic vintage cover art and are very collectable.

In 1953, Avon launched its thirty-five cent "T" series, which began with AT-51 and ran for over seven hundred titles. The T series continued Avon's emphasis on strong mass-market appeal, and included many popular movie tie-ins and sensational juvenile delinquent novels such as *Reformatory Girls* (T-417), *Gang Rumble* (T-262), *High-School Confidential* (T-257), *Teen-Age Jungle* (T-241), and others. Science fiction and mysteries were also well represented.

Avon's fifty cent "G" (for "giant") series is also popular with collectors. The series began in 1951 with number 1001 (although the *G* prefix was not added until number 1003), and by 1969 included about 350 titles. Initially, these books were labeled "Double-Size Books" and ran to more than six hundred pages. Later books in the series are of normal thickness, though. Key titles include the *All-American Fiction Reader* (G1002); *Maggie Cassidy* (G1035), an original novel by Jack Kerouac; and the very scarce *Avon Webster English Dictionary* (G1007).

Avon published a large number of digest format paperbacks, and these often rank among the company's most valuable titles. *Murder Mystery Monthly*, Avon's first digest series, was launched in 1942 and ran for 49 issues. Featuring outstanding pulp magazine style cover art and authors such as Raymond Chandler, James M. Cain, and A. Merritt, the series is very collectable today. Avon's second digest line, *Modern Short Story Monthly,* ran for 50 issues. The first 34 of these have plain text-only covers and are not highly valued. Beginning with number 35 the books had illustrated covers, and these later issues are much more desirable.

In 1947 Donald A. Wolheim, who later founded DAW Books, joined Avon to edit the *Avon Fantasy Readers*, a new digest format anthology series featuring sensational cover art and authors such as A. Merritt and Robert E. Howard. The series ran for eighteen issues and all are very collectable—as are the similar *Avon Science Fiction Readers* and *Avon Science Fiction and Fantasy Readers*.

Between 1947 and 1950 Avon brought out the *Avon Bedside Readers*, *Avon Book Dividends*, *Avon Love Book Monthlies*, and *Avon Specials*. These digests feature risqué romance fiction with glamorous pin-up style cover art, and all have significant collector value. Other important Avon digests include the *Romance Novel Monthlies, Western Novel Monthlies,* and *Avon Monthly Novels*.

Avon produced Eton paperbacks from 1951 to 1953. Only 32 Etons were published but the line is quite popular with collectors. The most valuable Eton title is *The Marijuana Mob* by James Hadley Chase (116). Avon was also behind Novel Library paperbacks, and Broadway and Diversey digests. All three of these imprints are widely collected today.

Three vintage Avon digests

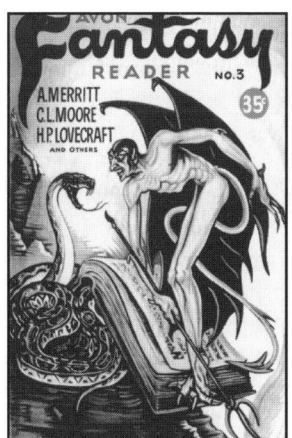
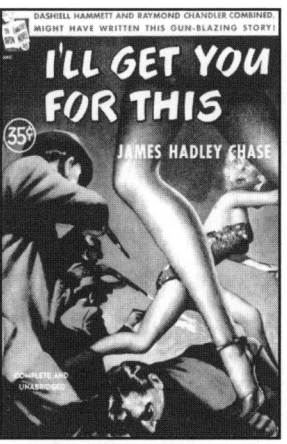
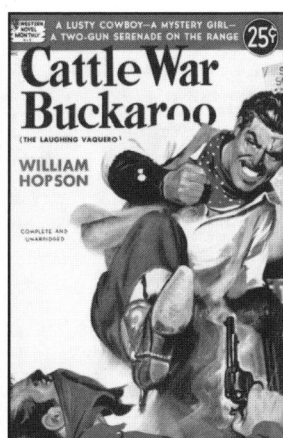

Avon Fantasy Reader 3   Avon Monthly Novel 18   Western Novel Monthly 2

BALLANTINE

In 1952 publisher Ian Ballantine left Bantam and started his own paperback firm, Ballantine Books. Ballantine's original plan was to work in league with hardcover publishers and simultaneously release hardcover and paperback editions of new titles, rather than having the hardcover edition precede the paperback. He believed this system would result in greater total sales, which would benefit both publishers, and also allow for higher royalty payments to authors.

Executive Suite by Cameron Hawley, Ballantine's first book, was co-published in this way with Houghton Mifflin. The book became a best-seller and helped to insure the new company's success. The co-publishing plan itself was not as successful, though. Only a few other publishers signed on and it was eventually discontinued. Ballantine self-published hardcover editions of several of its early paperbacks and today these books are quite scarce and are popular with hardcover and paperback collectors alike.

Three early Ballantines

Ballantine 1   Ballantine 10   Ballantine 41

Ballantine put out a broad line of relatively high quality reading material and was especially strong in westerns and science-fiction, publishing many well regarded novels in both genres. Abstract futuristic covers by Richard Powers helped give the science fiction titles a distinct identity. Ballantine also published many non-fiction paperbacks dealing with World War II.

Initially, Ballantine numbered all its books in a single series that began with number 1. The books were tall format paperbacks and the basic cover price was thirty-five cents. An *F* prefix indicated a fifty cent price and an *S* prefix was used for seventy-five cent books. In 1963, after almost 800 titles, Ballantine discontinued its first series and initiated the "U" series, which began with U-1001 for forty cent books and U-2001 for fifty cent books. The *Tarzan* novels of Edgar Rice Burroughs were extremely popular at that time, and the first two dozen fifty cent titles in the U series are all Tarzan reprints. The U series lasted until the late 1960s, and subsequent Ballantines carry various four and five digit numbers.

Also of interest to collectors is the Ballantine Adult Fantasy series, which began in 1969 and featured authors such as H. P. Lovecraft and H. Rider Haggard. These books are not sequentially numbered, but many have a unicorn head colophon on the cover. Ballantine was well regarded in the fantasy field because it had published the first authorized U.S. editions of J.R.R. Tolkein's *Lord of the Rings* trilogy. Ace Books had exploited a defect in Tolkein's copyright to publish its earlier versions, and in response Tolkein agreed to let Ballantine issue the authorized editions—which are still big sellers.

The most valuable Ballantine paperback may be the dust jacketed edition of *Concannon* (10), an original western by Frank O'Rourke that was also issued in a Ballantine hardcover edition. Other key titles include Elmore Leonard's first novel, *The Bounty Hunters* (54); *Farenheit 451* (41) and *The October Country* (139), both by Ray Bradbury; the original novels of Hal Ellson; and the various *Mad Magazine* tie-in paperbacks of the 1950s.

In the Adult Fantasy series, *The Man Who Was Thursday* by G. K. Chesterton (2305) is generally regarded as the key title. Among later Ballantines, *A Werewolf Among Us* by Dean R. Koontz (3005) and *Bid Time Return* by Richard Matheson (24810) are both very collectable.

Ballantine Adult Fantasy
2305

Three paperbacks from Ballantine's "U" series

Ballantine U2010   Ballantine U2140   Ballantine U2191

BANTAM

Bantam Books, which became one of the giants of the publishing business, was established in 1945 by publisher Ian Ballantine with the backing of hardcover publishing house Grosset & Dunlap and magazine publisher Curtis Publishing Company, which were the company's two majority owners. Ballantine had earlier run the American operations of Penguin, and would later go on to found his own firm, Ballantine Books. Bantam's first twenty titles were released in early 1946, and with the established distribution system of Curtis, the company was successful from the start.

Like Penguin, Bantam published reprints rather than original novels, and favored very low-key cover art. Consequently, collector demand for typical early Bantams is not great, and the books generally sell for relatively low prices. Ironically, though, the drab covers indirectly brought about production of some of the most valuable Bantam paperbacks. In order to stimulate sales on several of its slower moving titles, the publisher retrofitted the books with dust jackets having much catchier cover art. These dust jacketed editions are very scarce today, especially in the higher grades.

Bantam 22 before and after dust jacketing

Bantam numbered all its books consecutively in a single series, and by 1960 more than two thousand titles had been released. The books were initially short format paperbacks but the company converted to the tall format in 1953. The basic price was a quarter, and extra lengthy titles, such as *The Underworld* by Ira Wolfert (A798), were thirty-five cents and numbered with an *A* prefix. Later, Bantam added forty cent titles (*J* prefix), fifty cent titles (*F* prefix), and other price and prefix combinations.

In addition to the dust jacketed editions, key Bantams include *Behold This Woman* by David Goodis (407), and all the novels of Fredric Brown, Louis L'Amour, and Dean R. Koontz. The *Doc Savage* series by Kenneth Robeson and the *Shadow* series by Maxwell Grant are also very popular with collectors. Bantam produced the Pennant paperback line in the U.S. and established Corgi in Great Britain, and continues to be a leading paperback imprint today.

BEACON, AWARD, and UNIVERSAL PUBLISHING

Beacon was one of several imprints of the Universal Publishing and Distributing Corporation. Universal was founded in 1947 by Arnold E. Abramson, and initially published various special interest or hobby magazines such as *Smart Knitting* and *Family Handyman*. The company made its initial foray into the paperback market in the early 1950s, with Uni Books and Universal Giants.

Uni Books were digest format novels that featured racy stories and cover art. *Hoyden of the Hills* and *Passion in the Pines*, were typical of the titles. The series began with number 3 and ran to number 78. Uni Books were priced at thirty-five cents, and a substantial number were original novels.

Universal Giants were oversized paperbacks similar in theme to the Uni Books. This series ran from number 1 to number 11 and was then renamed "Royal Books Giant Editions" and continued from number 12 to 29. These "giant" books sold for fifty cents and almost half were double novels. Universal was also behind several other digest imprints of the early 1950s. These are all comparable to Uni Books and include Intimate Novels, Stallion Books, Fiesta Novels, and others.

Scarcity, sensational cover art, popular authors, and a touch of notoriety make almost all the early paperbacks from Universal very collectable. Of special interest is Royal Giant 20, a double volume that includes *High Priest of California,* the first novel by mystery author Charles Willeford.

Three early paperbacks from Universal Publishing

Uni Book 36   Universal Giant 1   Royal Giant 18

In 1954 Universal launched Beacon, its first line of regular size paperbacks. The initial cover price was thirty-five cents, and numbering began with 101. The first few Beacons can be found in both short and tall variants, but by number 109 the tall format had become the standard. Beacon developed into a very long-running and successful line for Universal. Beginning in 1961, the imprint went through a series of name changes that included "Beacon-Signal," "Signal," and "Signal Beam." Finally, at about number 800, the name "Softcover Library" was adopted. Continuous numbering was maintained throughout these name changes, though, and all the books in the series are generally referred to as Beacons.

Along with Midwood, Beacon was one of the leading adult publishers of the vintage era. Although the content of these books was tame by today's standards, the cover blurbs and artwork suggested the most extravagant kind of stories. Beacon authors could find an adult angle to even seemingly innocent activities, for example, *The Scuba Set* (B730) promised to "unmask today's aqualung elite," and 1963's *Change Partners* (B568) put a salacious spin on doing the twist. Big business came in for revealing scrutiny in *The Office Game* (B447) and *Faithful for 8 Hours* (B596), and exposés of life in suburbia such as *Commuter Widow* (B426) and *The Split-Level Game* (B888), comprised an entire sub-genre.

Not every Beacon was about sex, though. The company published a short story anthology, *31 Short Short Stories from Collier's* (249); two anthologies of war stories: *Highlights from Yank* (B113) and *Combat* (B199); several adventure novels, such as Talbot Mundy's *King of the Khyber Rifles* (B105); and a series of eleven science fiction novels under an arrangement with Galaxy Publishing Company. Beacon also published one movie tie-in, *Girl in Trouble* (B717).

Beacon B169   Beacon B199   Beacon B568

Beacons are all collected, even into the Softcover Library period. The cover art on most of the early books has a classic vintage look, but after about number 350, begins to take on a more modern appearance, somewhat less desirable to most collectors. Typical titles above number 500 should not be expensive, and this becomes more true as you go higher in the numbering. Key Beacons include all the novels by Charles Willeford (including the Softcover Library reprint editions); titles written by Peter Rabe under the pseudonym Marco Malaponte (originals and reprints); all the Galaxy science fiction novels (these can be identified in the listings because they were numbered without a *B* prefix); and novels by Harry Whittington and Orrie Hitt. Additionally, *Rock 'N Roll Gal* (131) and *Marijuana Girl* (328), and their later reprints, are very popular with collectors.

In 1961 Universal started its Beacon Envoy line. Envoys had their own numbering sequence and were identified with an *E* prefix. Only about ten titles were published, though, and the series is too obscure to attract any substantial collector interest.

In 1964 Universal launched Award, a mainstream paperback line that became its most successful imprint. The first Award, number 101, premiered the Nick Carter *Killmaster* secret agent series, which ran for hundreds of titles. Award had several other popular series, and was also very strong in movie and TV tie-ins, with titles such as *McCloud*, *Adam 12*, *Gunsmoke*, *Planet of the Apes*, and others. Awards are still relatively common and inexpensive, making this a good publisher for low-budget collectors. Universal also published Nova paperbacks for young readers, but that imprint has not developed a significant collector following yet.

Three later paperbacks from Universal Publishing

Beacon Envoy E103   Award 101   Nova 116

BELMONT

A relative latecomer to the paperback market, Belmont Productions, Inc. was formed in 1960 by Archie Comic Publications and released its first twenty-one titles that same year. The company published a diverse assortment of fiction and nonfiction, both originals and reprints, with an emphasis on popular appeal. Included are a number of science fiction and western double novels that are quite collectable and not particularly expensive. Initially, Belmonts were short format paperbacks, but the publisher converted to the tall format in 1961.

Belmont published several series of paperbacks and its numbering system is somewhat complex. In general, the company started a new numeric series for each change in cover price. The first series included books with cover prices of thirty-five or forty cents, and began with number 201. The early titles in this series were numbered without a prefix, but later books had a *91* or *90* prefix. Belmont's second series covered fifty cent titles and began with number 501. Prefixes in this series included *L*, *L92*, *92*, and *B50*. Subsequent series covered other price levels and had their own prefixes. For example, the "B60" series consisted of sixty cent titles. In 1969, Belmont merged with Tower Publications (see Midwood), and a few years later the imprint was renamed "Belmont-Tower." Belmont-Tower paperbacks have five digit numbers with a *BT* prefix.

Key Belmonts include *Nightmares* (233), *More Nightmares* (L92-530), *Yours Truly, Jack The Ripper* (L92-527), and *Ladies Day/This Crowded Earth* (B60-080), all by Robert Bloch; Charles Willeford's *The Machine in Ward Eleven* (90-286); *Marilyn Monroe* by George Carpozi (L508); *The Penultimate Truth* by Philip K. Dick (92-603); and *From The Land of Fear* by Harlan Ellison (B60-069). Belmont also published a number of secret agent and spy-spoof series that are popular with collectors such as the *Miss From S.I.S.* novels by Bob Tralins.

Belmont 221   Belmont B50-704   Belmont B50-759

BERKLEY

Berkley Publishing was established in 1954 and published its first paperbacks the following year. The company was founded and run by former Avon executives and the Avon mass-market approach is reflected in the Berkley line. The early books are attractive, well designed short format paperbacks featuring eye-catching covers by Robert Maguire, Charles Copeland, Rudy Nappi, and other top artists.

Berkley published a broad assortment of general fiction. Mysteries, westerns, science fiction anthologies, and cartoon books were all well represented, and racy love novels added spice to the list. Non-fiction titles consisted primarily of books about World War II. Early Berkleys were almost entirely reprint editions, with only an occasional paperback original.

The company initially established two paperback series, a twenty-five cent line, and a line of thirty-five and fifty cent editions numbered with *G* or *BG* prefixes respectively. The twenty-five cent line began with numbers 101 through 112, then jumped to number 313 and continued sequentially to number 386. The higher priced line began with G-1 and ran for thousands of titles. The *G* prefix stood for "giant" but the books were giant only in comparison to their very skinny twenty-five cent counterparts. Fifty cent *BG* titles were a little thicker yet than a standard "G." In 1957 Berkley discontinued its twenty-five cent line and all new titles went into the G series, which was no longer reserved exclusively for giant editions. A few years later the company retired the BG prefix, replaced it with an *F* prefix for the fifty cent titles, and began adding other price and prefix combinations.

In late 1959 the G series underwent a makeover. New titles were designated "Berkley Medallion Books," and given an updated version of the company's *fleur-de-lis* insignia. At the same time, Berkley began converting to the tall paperback format and its cover art took on a more modern look. The following years also saw science fiction and original novels assume greater prominence.

From the collector's standpoint, the early short format editions are generally more desirable than the later tall format titles. Superior cover art and a classic vintage look make many of the early titles very collectable. Key Berkleys in the twenty-five cent line include *They Shoot Horses Don't They?* (108) and *I Should Have Stayed Home* (328), both by Horace McCoy; *Torture Garden* by Ocatve Mirbeau (111), which has an outstanding surrealist cover; and *We Too Are Drifting* by Gale Wilhelm (327). Favorites in the G (or "letter-prefix") series include *If He Hollers Let Him Go* by Chester Himes (G-6); *Burn, Witch, Burn* (F-621) by Fritz Leiber (the movie tie-in version of *Conjure Wife*); *One for the Money* (Y658) by Elliot Chaze (a re-titled reprint of Gold Medal 296, *Black Wings Has My Angel*); Clyde Allison's *Have Nude, Will Travel* (Y705); and *Counter-Clock World*, an original science fiction novel by Philip K. Dick (X1372).

Berkley published several spy and pulp-hero series that are very collectable. These include *The Spider* by Grant Stockbridge, *G8 and His Battle Aces* by Robert J. Hogan, *The Girl From Pussycat* by Ted Mark, and the *Burns Bannion* series by Earl Norman (*Kill Me In Shimbashi*, *Kill Me in Yoshiwara*, etc.)

Berkley also published the Berkley Diamond line of thirty-five cent short format paperbacks, which is sometimes called the "D" series. This imprint had a short life, beginning with D-2001 in 1959, and ending the following year with D-2043. Berkley Diamonds are very similar in appearance to Berkley's early twenty-five cent titles and are somewhat scarcer than the publisher's other books. Key titles in the Diamond line include the various novels by Harry Whittington, Day Keene, and William Ard.

Three vintage Berkley paperbacks

Berkley 361   Berkley G-116   Berkley D-2037

CREST

Crest was established in 1955 by magazine and Gold Medal publisher Fawcett Publications. In 1945 Fawcett had entered into a ten year contract to distribute paperbacks for Penguin (and later Signet). The terms of the agreement precluded Fawcett from competing in the field of paperback reprints. Even so, just five years into the agreement, Fawcett made a major entry into the paperback market with Gold Medal, which published original paperbacks only, rather than reprints. When the Signet distribution contract expired, Fawcett launched Crest as its paperback reprint line.

Crest went on to reprint many notable hardcover books, including best-sellers by James A. Michener and Mario Puzo, as well as William L. Shirer's massive *Rise and Fall of the Third Reich,* the first mass-market paperback priced over one dollar. The imprint was not entirely limited to reprints, though, and of greater interest to collectors are Crest's original mystery and suspense novels by such authors as Gil Brewer, William Campbell Gault, and Day Keene.

Crest cover art is very similar to that of Gold Medal, and leading artists such as Baryé Phillips, Mitchell Hooks, Robert McGinnis, and Stanley M. Zuckerberg are well represented. In 1976 Crest came up with a novel concept for the cover of *This Suitcase is Going to Explode* by Tom Ardies (2778). Billed as the first (and apparently the last) to use the "Xograph" process, the cover is made of plastic and displays one of two alternating images depending on the viewing angle. This book makes an interesting conversation piece but is not particularly scarce.

Crests are all numbered consecutively in a single series that started with number 114. The basic cover price was twenty-five cents and letter prefixes indicate higher prices. Crest used the same price and prefix system as Gold Medal. Key titles include *Saturday Night Town* by Harry Whittington (151); *A Stir of Echoes* by Richard Matheson (308); *Little Tramp* (173), *Wild* (229), *The Vengeful Virgin* (238) and *The Red Scarf* (310), all by Gil Brewer; the five *Joe Puma* mystery novels by William Campbell Gault; *Dead Dolls Don't Talk* by Day Keene (286), and many others. Two popular Crest movie tie-ins are Robert Bloch's *Psycho* (385), and the Elvis Presley MTI, *Flaming Lance* by Clair Huffaker (421).

Crest 309   Crest 310   Crest 385

DELL

Dell Publishing Company was founded in the early 1920s by George T. Delacorte, Jr. Over the next twenty-five years it became the country's largest publisher of newsstand material with an evolving line of magazines, pulps, and comic books. *Modern Screen, Inside Detective,* and *Walt Disney's Comics* were just a few of Dell's publications. By 1942 Delacorte had decided to add paperbacks to his product line and Dell entered into a production agreement with its comic book printer, Western Printing and Lithographing Company. Western had some previous paperback experience—in 1940 it produced the short lived Bantam of Los Angeles paperbacks. The L.A. Bantams were sold through vending machines for ten cents each and are now highly prized by collectors.

Dell and Western developed a very close working arrangement under which Western handled not only printing, but most title selection, cover art, and editorial work as well. Dell approved the books and handled all distribution.

The first Dell paperbacks were released in 1943. Like Pocket Books, they were well-made short format books with sturdy covers and protective lamination. Several features gave the imprint a distinct identity, though. Dell covers featured bold lettering and a prominent eye-in-a-keyhole colophon. The artwork, characterized by large central figures and geometric designs, was executed with an airbrush, resulting in vivid color and a somewhat animated look. Equally distinctive were Dell's back covers which, beginning with number 5, featured a map illustrating an area where some part of the story takes place. With mysteries this typically included the scene of the crime. The back cover map was very popular with readers and remains popular with collectors—like the Ace doubles, the Dell "mapbacks" are among the most well known vintage paperbacks.

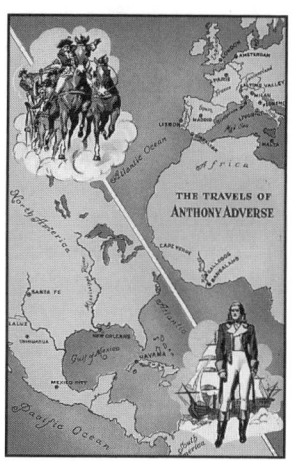

A back cover map
Dell 281

Dell's first series of books, which includes the mapbacks, began with number 1, and by 1960 exceeded number 1000. Books in the first series were priced at twenty-five cents and were almost entirely reprints rather than original novels. Mysteries accounted for about half the titles, while westerns and romances comprised the next largest categories. Second printings of some of the books were renumbered by adding 1000 to the original number—for example, number 367 was reprinted as number 1367. In the early 1950s, as series numbering reached the 400s, Dell began updating the appearance of its books. Initially, the simple, stylized front cover art was phased out in favor of covers featuring more realistic action scenes. Soon after, beginning in 1951, the back cover maps began to be gradually replaced with conventional text and "blurb" covers.

In 1952 Dell launched its thirty-five cent "D" series and soon after, the fifty cent "F" series. Of more interest to collectors, though, are two other Dell series introduced at about the same time, Dell First Editions and Dell Ten Cent Books.

Dell First Editions, as the name implies, consisted of original novels rather than reprints. These books competed with Gold Medal, the first all-original paperback imprint. There are several numeric sequences within the First Editions line. The first of these began with number 1 and ran for over two hundred titles. In this series, books numbered without a prefix or with an *A* prefix were twenty-five cents, while thirty-five cent titles had a *D* prefix, and an *F* prefix indicated a fifty cent cover price. The second First Editions series consisted entirely of thirty-five cent titles numbered with a *B* prefix. Higher priced *C*, *K*, and *R* series followed.

The Dell Ten Cent series consisted of thirty-six "vestpocket size" books. These books had the same dimensions as standard Dell paperbacks but were much thinner (just sixty-four pages each), and had stapled spines. Like Dell's other books, the Ten Cent series consisted primarily of popular genre fiction, including mysteries, westerns, science fiction, and romances.

For paperback collectors, Dell is a rich storehouse of material. All of the mapbacks are collected, especially the mysteries and the first one hundred titles. Perhaps the most valuable Dell paperbacks are the two scarce crossword puzzle collections, (205 and 278). Other key titles include a David Goodis mapback, *Dark Passage* (221), and all the mapbacks by Dashiell Hammett. In 1947 Dell published two un-numbered paperbacks based on newspaper comic strips, *Blondie and Dagwood in Footlight Folly* and *Dick Tracy and the Woo Woo Sisters*. Both of these are quite scarce and very popular with collectors today.

The D and F series feature some excellent covers by artists such as Robert McGinnis and Robert Stanley but in terms of price, these books are generally not in the same league as the mapbacks. One exception is D-114, *Go Down to Glory* by Richard Warren Hatch, which was issued with a dust jacket.

In the Ten Cent series, the most valuable titles are *Marijuana* by William Irish (11), *The Case of the Dancing Sandwiches* by Fredric Brown (33), *Superstition Farm* by Perry Stowe (35), and *Universe* by Robert A. Heinlein (36). Key titles in the Dell First Editions include all the novels by John D. MacDonald and Charles Williams, *Madball* by Fredric Brown (2E), *The Nothing Man* by Jim Thompson (22), *Last Stand at Saber Ridge* by Elmore Leonard (A184), and many others.

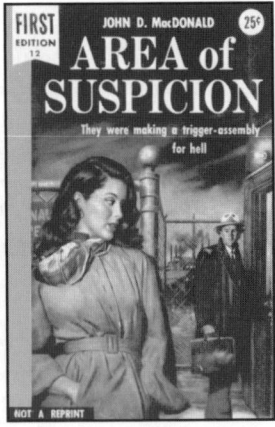

| Dell 72 | Dell First Edition 12 | Dell Ten Cent 30 |

GOLD MEDAL

Like Ace, Gold Medal is one of the most familiar of the vintage paperback publishers, and its distinctive bright yellow books can still be regularly spotted on used bookstore shelves. Gold Medal was founded in 1950 by magazine publisher Fawcett Publications. Fawcett had been distributing paperbacks for Penguin and Signet since 1945 and sought to start its own paperback line. At that time paperback publishing was primarily a reprint business. Books were expected to appear first in a hardcover edition and the paperback publishers would subsequently obtain the reprint rights from the hardcover publisher. Fawcett, however, had agreed not to compete in the field of paperback reprints for the ten year life of its distribution contract. Original paperback novels were not covered by the agreement, though, and Gold Medal was established as an originals-only paperback line. The company contracted directly with authors for new novels and to attract talent offered a minimum royalty of $2000. The concept was successful and first printings of 250,000 copies or more soon became common.

Paperback originals, of course, had been produced earlier on a sporadic basis by other publishers, but it was Gold Medal's success that established the original novel as a staple of the paperback industry, and almost every other paperback publisher subsequently adopted the original novel to a greater degree. Today, as a general rule, collectors value paperback originals more highly than reprints of hardcover books, and this is one of the primary reasons why Gold Medals tend to be worth more than typical Bantams, Signets, or Pocket Books.

In early 1950, prior to launching Gold Medal, Fawcett tested the market with two prototype paperbacks: *The Best From True*, a collection of stories from Fawcett's *True* magazine for men, and *What Today's Woman Should Know About Marriage and Sex*, a collection of articles taken from *Today's Woman* magazine. Both books are popular with Gold Medal collectors. Perhaps the *True* collection outperformed *Marriage and Sex* because the subsequent Gold Medal line was clearly geared for a male audience.

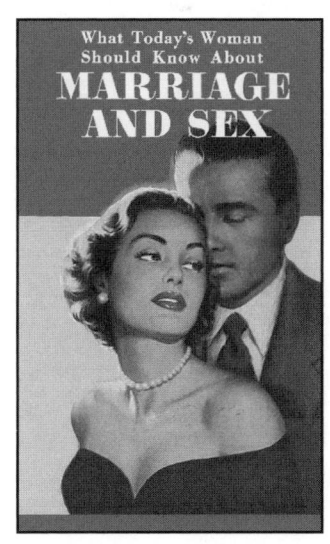

The two prototype Gold Medal paperbacks from 1950

Westerns, mysteries and adventure novels with titles such as *Come Murder Me*, *Nude in Mink*, and *War Bonnet Pass* were the standard Gold Medal fare. John D. MacDonald's *Travis McGee* series, Richard S. Prather's *Shell Scott* series, and Donald Hamilton's *Matt Helm* series were all developed for Gold Medal and all three were very successful. Other popular Gold Medal authors included Gil Brewer, David Goodis, Jim Thompson, Sax Rohmer, Charles Williams, John McPartland, Louis L'Amour, Peter Rabe, Bruno Fischer, and dozens of others.

Gold Medal published all its books in a single series that began with number 101. The two test titles were un-numbered, but are often referred to as numbers 99 and 100. Gold Medals are tall format paperbacks that carried a basic cover price of twenty-five cents. To accommodate novels too lengthy to sell for a quarter, Fawcett created the thirty-five cent Red Seal label in 1952. Red Seals look similar to Gold Medals but are substantially thicker and most have red, rather than yellow, covers. Twenty-three Red Seals, numbered 7 to 29, were released before the imprint was discontinued in 1953. Following Red Seal's demise, thirty-five cent titles were included within the Gold Medal line and numbered with a *G* (and later an *S*) prefix. The first fifty cent *D*-prefix Gold Medal appeared in 1954, and other price and prefix combinations were added as time went on.

Red Seal 26

Key Gold Medals are too numerous to list, but one unusual title worth noting is *Mansion of Evil* (129), a comic book style paperback with color illustrations that is now very scarce and quite valuable. The price tables list more than 1500 Gold Medal citations, which is a testament to the popularity among collectors of this ground-breaking publisher.

Three vintage Gold Medal paperbacks

Gold Medal G-205   Gold Medal s-549   Gold Medal 654

LANCER

Lancer Books was founded in 1961 by Irwin Stein and Walter Zacharius. The two published several nationally distributed magazines such as *H.Q.* (later *Dapper*) and *Infinity Science Fiction*. Lancer was in business for over a decade, but in late 1973 filed a major breach of contract suit against its distributor and shortly thereafter ceased operations. A year or two later, the company briefly re-emerged as Magnum Books, and many Lancer titles can be found in almost identical Magnum reprint editions.

Lancer paperbacks run the gamut from romance to horror, and non-fiction to science fiction. Both original novels and reprints are well represented. Collectable titles include double novels, movie and TV tie-ins, secret agent series novels, and others. Lancer published many books in its "Easy-Eye" large-print format and also published the Domino line of adult paperbacks. Domino was a 1963 offshoot of Lancer, and the books are similar to Beacon paperbacks.

Lancer had a separate series, identified by a numeric prefix, for each of its various cover prices. For example, the "70" series consisted of forty cent titles, while the "72" series was reserved for fifty cent titles. Domino numbers were intermixed with Lancer numbers, and used the same prefixes. Key titles for collectors include all the original science fiction novels by Dean R. Koontz such as *The Dark Symphony* (74-621) and *Hell's Gate* (74-656), as well as the original gothic romance novels Koontz wrote under his Deanna Dwyer pseudonym. These include *Legacy of Terror* (75-256), *Children of the Storm* (75-365), *The Dark of Summer* (75-393), and others. Mrs. Dean Koontz, Gerda A. Cerra, also wrote an original Lancer gothic, *A Darker Heritage* (75-294), which is fairly common in its Magnum reprint edition.

Other popular Lancers include *Who has Wilma Lathrop?/Murder on the Side,* a double novel by Day Keene (72-633); *Slaves of Sleep*, by L. Ron Hubbard (73-573); the gruesome horror movie tie-ins such as *Premature Burial* (71-313) and *The Masque of the Red Death* (72-725); and the various secret agent novels of Ted Mark. The company also published a number of collectable comic book style paperbacks in the 1960s featuring Marvel Comics characters.

The three related Lancer paperback imprints

| Domino 72-712 | Lancer 74-621 | Magnum 75-309 |

LION

Lion Books was founded in 1949 by pulp, magazine, and Marvel Comics publisher Martin Goodman. One of Goodman's companies was Red Circle Magazines, and his first seven paperbacks were designated "Red Circle Books." The imprint was then renamed Lion, and the first four Lion titles were numbered 8 through 11. Numbers 12 and 13 in the sequence were assigned to the last two Red Circle paperbacks, and all subsequent titles were published as Lions. Goodman also published under the Atlas name, and the various Atlas mystery digests of the 1940s were Goodman publications.

During its eight year life, Lion published almost four hundred books, in two different series. The principal series featured a lion's head colophon and consisted entirely of short format paperbacks numbered without a prefix and priced at twenty-five cents. Titles in the second series were designated either "Lion Library" or "Lion Books" editions and numbered with an *LL* or *LB* prefix respectively. Lion Library titles were tall format paperbacks that sold for thirty-five cents, while Lion Books titles sold for a quarter and included both tall and short format editions. Many titles originally published in Lion's first series were subsequently reprinted in Lion Library or Lion Books editions.

Red Circle 3

The three Lion imprints

Lion 154

Lion Library LL-5

Lion Books LB-129

In 1957 Goodman sold Lion to New American Library, the publisher of Signet paperbacks, which brought the imprint to an end. The deal included the publishing rights to works in progress, and some of these pending Lion titles were eventually published as Signets.

Although Lion was not regarded as a major force in the publishing business, among collectors it ranks near the top in importance. Lion published paperback originals and reprints in several genres, notably westerns, science fiction, and contemporary adult fiction, but its real claim to fame are its original crime novels by such authors as Jim Thompson, David Goodis, Robert Bloch, and Richard Matheson. In the mid-1980s, this Lion crime fiction began to be rediscovered, and the authors, Jim Thompson and David Goodis most notably, have since received much critical acclaim. Today, their paperbacks frequently sell for hundreds of dollars. The cachet of these key crime titles has rubbed off on the rest of the line to some extent and almost any high-grade original novel from Lion's first series can now bring a respectable price.

Key Lion titles from the first series are too numerous to list, but include all the novels by the authors mentioned above, and many others. In the second series, some popular titles include *Desperate Asylum* (LL44) and *The Brass Bed* (LL87), two original novels by Fletcher Flora; *Nightfall* by David Goodis (LB131); and the three Jim Thompson reprints: *Recoil* (LB124), *A Hell of a Woman* (LB138), and *The Kill Off* (LL142). The nine Red Circle paperbacks are all quite scarce and that entire series is very collectable.

MONARCH

Monarch Books was founded in 1958 with the backing of magazine and comic book publisher Charlton Publications and its affiliated Capital Distributing Company. The company was run by Charles N. Hecklemann, previously editor-in-chief of Popular Library, and Frederick Fell, who owned a hardcover publishing firm. Monarch entered the business at a time of intense competition among paperback publishers for newsstand space. In response, the company produced a line of books with strong mass-market appeal that is a favorite with collectors today. Monarchs are very colorful, eye-catching books with dramatic titles such as *America's Major Air Disasters* and *I Am a Teen-Age Drug Addict*. Cover art was never neglected, and some of the best work by Robert Maguire, Harry Barton, Tom Miller, Rafael de Soto, Ralph Brillhart, and Ray Johnson can be found on Monarch paperbacks. Many of the books have adult themes, but the company also published westerns, science fiction, historical novels, and mysteries. Non-fiction was an important part of the line as well, original biographies in particular.

From 1958 to 1965 Monarch published over six hundred books, primarily in a single series numbered between 101 and 563. Included in this sequence are Monarch Americana titles, numbered with an *MA* prefix, and Monarch Human Behavior titles, which have an *MB* prefix. Secondary series include Monarch Movie Books (numbered MM600 to MM607), the "MS" series, consisting of non-fiction titles with political themes, and the "K" series, which includes biographies and other non-fiction. Gold Star Books was an affiliated paperback imprint.

Key titles for collectors include the *Lou Largo* detective novels by William Ard; the original novels of Gil Brewer; Marion Zimmer Bradley's novels written under the pseudonyms Morgan Ives and Miriam Gardner; and the three monster movie tie-ins (*Gorgo, Konga, and Reptilicus*). Outstanding cover art and sensational subject matter make many other Monarch titles very collectable.

MIDWOOD and TOWER PUBLICATIONS

Midwood was one of the leading adult paperback imprints of the vintage era. Like Beacon, Midwood published relatively high quality original novels that could be sold alongside paperbacks from the more mainstream publishers. The early history of the company is somewhat obscure, but Midwood Enterprises and Tower Publications were apparently established no later than 1957 or 1958 by Harry Shorten, who is best known for the popular syndicated newspaper cartoon *There Oughta Be A Law*, which he co-authored with Al Fagaly. Michael Avallone, who wrote several novels for Midwood in the early 1960s, recounted in a 1993 article that Shorten ran the entire Midwood operation.

The first Midwoods are paperback collections of Shorten and Fagaly's cartoons. Midwood 4 is a 1958 collection. It was preceded by a similar but un-numbered collection in 1957. Following number 4, Midwood published two un-numbered fiction titles in 1958: *I Take What I Want,* an original juvenile delinquent novel by Hal Ellson, and *Call Me Mistress,* a racy love novel by Tomlin Rede. These early books were short format paperbacks apparently designed to test the market.

Midwood hit its stride with its next book *Love Nest,* which was designated number 7. The book was the publisher's first tall format paperback and the first to be identified on the title page as a Midwood-Tower (rather than Midwood) publication. The book featured prominent graphics, a risqué cover illustration by artist Rudy Nappi, and a blurb that promised "an unblushing tale of a man's indiscretions—and his so willing women!" It was written by Robert Silverberg under the pseudonym Loren Beauchamp.

Love Nest set out the basic Midwood formula that would last for the next ten years—pin-up style cover art, eye-catching graphics, provocative blurbs, credible writing, and stories centered on relationships—with enough sex to keep readers returning. Beginning with number 8, artist Paul Rader painted hundreds of covers for Midwood and his distinctive style helped to set the publisher apart from its competition. With number 29, Midwood adopted a clover leaf colophon and this served to further distinguish its books.

Early Midwoods

Midwood 4

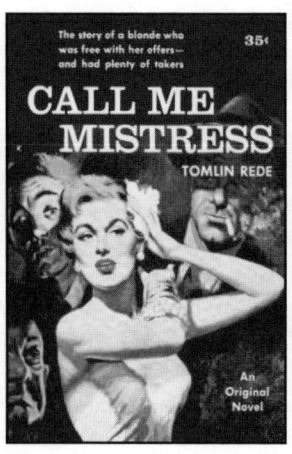

Midwood No# 6

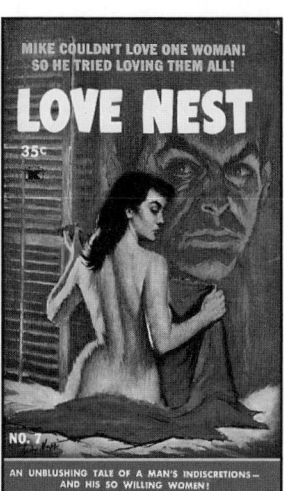

Midwood 7

Midwood numbered all its books sequentially in a single series. The early titles were thirty-five cents and numbered without a prefix. Beginning with number 63, the company introduced fifty cent editions numbered with an *F* prefix. Other letter and price combinations were added later. At number 395, Midwood converted to a numeric prefix system using a *32* prefix for fifty cent titles, *33* for sixty cent titles, *34* for seventy-five cent titles, and *35* for ninety-five cent titles.

In 1963 Tower Publications launched a new line of general interest paperbacks called Tower Books. Tower paperbacks shared the same numerical sequence used by Midwood, but had prefixes in the 40s rather than the 30s. For example, Midwood 32-527 is followed by Tower 43-528.

For collectors, desirable Midwoods can be distinguished by artists as well as authors. With respect to artists, Paul Rader is a perennial favorite. Midwoods with his covers, especially the earlier titles, are very collectable. The same is true of Robert Maguire and Robert McGinnis. Additionally, Midwood published a number of double novels that include interior illustrations by well known artists, and these are all popular. Particularly noteworthy is number D-231, Midwood's first double novel, which features illustrations by Frank Frazetta. As for authors, several collectable authors, in addition to Robert Silverberg, wrote for Midwood using pseudonyms, and a few, such as Avallone and Ellson, wrote under their real names.

Midwood 207 (Rader cover)

The Tower paperback line is not as well known as Midwood, but it includes several notable titles. Two in particular are *Five Day Nightmare* by Fredric Brown (42-502) and *Dracula's Curse* by Bram Stoker (43-970). Tower Publications also published comic books, and in 1966 the company released a few comic book style paperbacks, such as *Noman* (42-672) and *Menthor* (42-674), that are popular with comic book and paperback collectors alike.

Tower 43-430

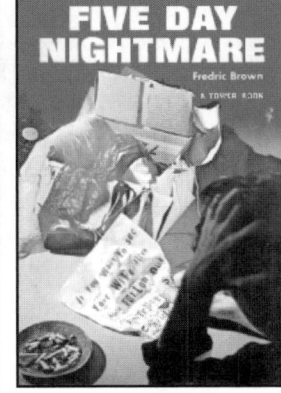

Tower 42-502

Tower 42-672

PAPERBACK LIBRARY

Paperback Library was founded in 1961 by magazine publishers Hy Steirman of *Bluebook* and Morris S. Latzen. The company's early titles covered a broad spectrum of interests—science fiction, non-fiction, westerns, gothic romance, and nurse romance novels were all well represented. Interestingly though, crime and mystery fiction were almost completely ignored.

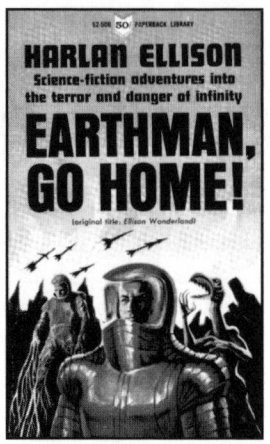

The publisher added TV tie-ins to its list in 1966, with the first of over thirty *Dark Shadows* novels. Subsequent tie-ins were based on *The Rat Patrol*, *Gunsmoke, Bonanza, The Six Million Dollar Man*, and other popular shows. Series novels based on popular characters were also strong sellers and included Donald A. Wolheim's *Mike Mars* series, Kenneth Robeson's *Avenger* series, Ron Goulart's *Vampirella* series, and many others.

In 1972 Warner Communications acquired Paperback Library and changed the company's name—first to Warner Paperback Library and finally to Warner Paperbacks. Warner continues to publish paperbacks today as part of media conglomerate AOL Time Warner.

Paperback Library 52-508

Paperback Library had a relatively complicated numbering system. The first few titles were numbered with a *B, S,* or *G* prefix, reflecting the publisher's initial plan of marketing titles at three price levels—Bronze Editions were priced at thirty-five cents, Silver Editions were fifty cents and Gold Editions were seventy-five cents. This three tiered pricing/prefix system, however, soon gave way to a more flexible multi-tiered system that used numeric prefixes, rather than letters, to identify the various price levels. For example, thirty-five cent books were numbered with a *51* prefix, and fifty cent books (which continued to carry the "Silver Edition" designation) were identified with a *52* prefix. Regardless of the price and prefix, these books were all part of a single numeric sequence. The numbers in the sequence were not always used in chronological order, though. Number 968, for example, was published prior to number 568. When all numbers up to 1000 had been exhausted, a new series was started using prefixes in the 60s. Other series followed, with prefixes in the 70s, 80s and 90s.

Key titles for collectors include *Ellison Wonderland* by Harlan Ellison (52-149), as well as its re-titled reprint *Earthman Go Home* (52-508 and 53-727); *Anti-Man*, an original science fiction novel by Dean Koontz (63-384); *A Maze of Death* by Philip K. Dick (64-636); *Army Girl* (51-173) and *Lisa* (52-816), both written under pseudonyms by Harry Whittington; the two *House of Mystery* comic book tie-ins (75-226 and 75-256); and *Sneak Preview,* an original novel by Robert Bloch (64-660). The series novels mentioned above are also very collectable, particularly the *Vampirella* and *Dark Shadows* titles.

PERMA

Permabooks was created in 1949 as a mass-market imprint of hardcover publisher Doubleday & Company. The first Perma titles were not true paperbacks, though. Although these books were of paperback size, they had stiff laminated cardboard covers intended to provide greater durability. A standard Perma cover blurb of the time read "books of permanent value for permanent use." The company's first 101 titles were published in this paperback/hardcover hybrid format and numbered with a *P* prefix. They sold for thirty-five cents each. These early books were primarily non-fiction, and while they make interesting curiosities, they do not have significant collector value today.

In 1951 Perma abandoned the stiff cardboard covers and continued the P series as a true paperback line. The books were much thicker than average, though, apparently to justify the continuation of the thirty-five cent price. Permas from this period have attractive, sometimes outstanding cover art and many are reprints of historical novels. In 1953 the publisher converted to the tall format and began to include thinner books in its line—these were priced at a quarter, while the more weighty volumes were priced at thirty-five or fifty cents. Some of the most attractive and collectable Permas are the thin twenty-five cent titles from 1953 and 1954, which were designated "Perma Stars," and identified with a five-pointed star on the spine and back cover.

In August 1954 Perma was merged with Pocket Books, which quickly phased out the P series and introduced the long running "M" series. M series titles are short format paperbacks very similar in appearance to the Pocket Books of the time. The acquisition proved a success and over the next ten years Pocket Books sold about 100 million paperbacks under the Perma imprint.

For collectors, key P series and Star titles include *Women in Prison* (239); two anthologies, *In The Grip of Terror* (P117) and *As Tough as They Come* (P118); and the two *Ed Noon* mysteries by Michael Avallone (244 and 289). In the M series, key titles include *The Best From Manhunt* (M3111); all of the original Ed McBain novels; and the three James Bond titles by Ian Fleming: *Live and Let Die* (M3048), *Too Hot to Handle* (M3070), and *Diamonds are Forever* (M3084).

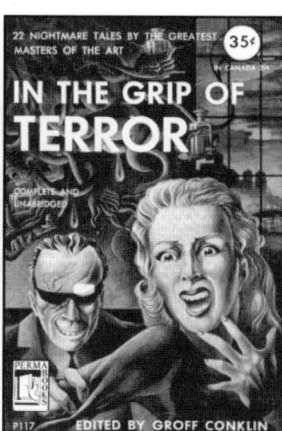

Perma P-41	Perma P-117	Perma 239
A paperback/hardcover hybrid	An early Perma paperback	A Perma Star

POCKET BOOKS and CARDINAL

Pocket Books originated the modern mass-market paperback in the United States, and quickly became so identified with the paperback format that for years all paperbacks, regardless of publisher, were often generically referred to as Pocket Books. The company was founded in 1938 by Robert de Graff, with the backing of hardcover publisher Simon and Schuster. De Graff got his start in the publishing business in 1922 with Doubleday, Page & Co. where he created the Star Dollar Books, a very successful line of low-priced hardcover reprints. In 1936 he left Doubleday to head Blue Ribbon Books, another hardcover firm. Blue Ribbon's line included the Triangle Books—reprints of popular novels that sold at Woolworth's for just thirty-nine cents each.

Despite his success with hardcover reprints, de Graff was more intrigued by the idea of even cheaper paperbound editions, similar to the Penguins, which had achieved great success in England. In 1938 he left Blue Ribbon to pursue that goal. After conducting an encouraging market survey, he approached Simon and Schuster with a partnership proposal. The hardcover firm was receptive to his idea, and Pocket Books, Inc. was established with de Graff as the majority stockholder. In the fall of 1938, his fledgling company test-marketed a prototype edition of *The Good Earth* by Pearl Buck. Only about two thousand copies of the test version were produced and it is generally considered the rarest and most valuable vintage paperback. However, there has not been a copy on the market for the last ten years so its actual value is unknown. The prototype edition is similar in appearance to Pocket Books' later reprint of *The Good Earth* (number 11), but can be easily distinguished because it is un-numbered and has no cover price.

The first ten Pocket Books went on sale in June 1939. Initial print runs were approximately ten thousand copies each—a small number by later mass-market standards, and the books were distributed only in the New York metropolitan area. Consequently, the first printings of these ten books are very scarce, and they are highly valued by collectors. The books were also very popular with the public—reorders started coming in immediately, and Pocket Books was on its way to becoming a major force in American publishing.

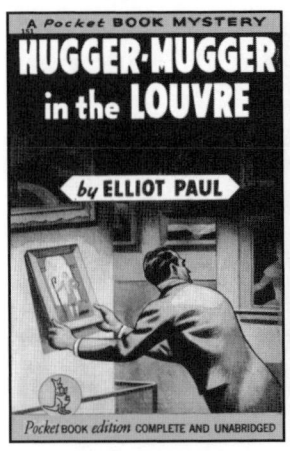

Pocket Books 151

Pocket Books 283

Pocket Books 285

Pocket Books' formula for success included attractive illustrated covers, convenient size, and careful title selection—virtually all Pocket Books were reprints of titles that had recently sold well in hardcover editions. Affordability was also a major factor, Pocket Books established the twenty-five cent price, which remained the paperback standard for almost two decades. De Graff's most important innovation, though, may have been in the area of distribution. Rather than relying on bookstores, he distributed Pocket Books through drugstores, department stores, "five and tens," and similar retail outlets. Newsstands were another key element of the distribution scheme. Initially, de Graff relied on a single wholesaler, the American News Company (ANC), to reach this market, but, dissatisfied with ANC, in 1941 he switched to independent magazine distributors, or "IDs." The IDs serviced thousands of retailers in addition to newsstands, and by the mid-1940s, an extensive ID network was handling the bulk of the company's production.

Pocket Books were numbered sequentially in a single series. Reprints of existing titles, though, were often renumbered by adding 2000 to the original number. These reprints are sometimes called the "2000" series. To accommodate cover prices higher than a quarter, Pocket Books established the Cardinal imprint in 1950. Regular Cardinals (*C* prefix) were priced at thirty-five cents and Giant Cardinal Editions (*GC* prefix) were priced at fifty cents.

Within the Pocket Books line itself, the twenty-five cent price barrier was broken in 1960. New thirty-five cent Pocket Books were given numbers beginning with 6001, while fifty cent titles were numbered 7001 and higher. Later, forty-five cent titles were introduced and were assigned numbers 4001 and up. Twenty-five cent titles continued to be released and were numbered in continuity with the existing sequence, which was then at about 1300. At the same time, the company introduced a new design scheme for its three major imprints. Pocket Books were given new silver spine straps to match Cardinal's existing gold design, and Perma, which Pocket had acquired in 1954, was distinguished with a bronze spine color.

Pocket Books published three other imprints that are of interest to collectors. In 1948 the company introduced Comet Books, a line of digest size paperbacks for young readers. Beginning with number 35 the line was renamed "Pocket Books Jr." and the books were reformatted as standard size paperbacks very similar to regular Pocket Books. These colorful books make an attractive collection and are not expensive. Pocket Books also produced the Reader's League of America paperbacks, which were special reprints of Pocket Book titles. The original cover art was used but the books were not numbered, and were designated Reader's League editions rather than Pocket Books. About 30–40 different titles have been identified and they are all relatively scarce.

Pocket Books Jr. J-50

Despite the publisher's prominent historical role, most vintage Pocket Books are not expensive, and typical titles above number 200 can be very easy to collect. These books were printed in huge quantities and can still often be found at bookstores, garage sales, and flea markets for a dollar or two. Of course there are also many Pocket Books that are quite valuable. In addition to the first ten titles previously mentioned, Pocket Books issued four paperbacks with dust jackets, and all are scarce and desirable. Pocket Book 259, *Halfway House* by Ellery Queen was published in an odd experimental edition bound at the bottom edge rather than along the side. This scarce variant edition is also very collectable. Other key titles include *The Pocket Book of Science Fiction* (214), *Rendezvous in Black* by Cornell Woolrich (570), *Of Missing Persons* by David Goodis (833), and all of the novels by Raymond Chandler and Dashiell Hammett.

Key titles in the Cardinal line include *The Blackboard Jungle* (C187) and *Quartet in "H"* (C236) by Evan Hunter; *Will Acting Spoil Marilyn Monroe?* by Pete Martin (C248); *Playback* by Raymond Chandler (C375); and the dust jacketed edition of Nelson Algren's *The Man With the Golden Arm* (C31).

Readers League No#   Pocket Books 2696   Cardinal C-375

POPULAR LIBRARY

Part of the first wave of paperback publishers to follow Pocket Books into the mass-market, Popular Library was founded in 1942 by Pines Publications, which was a leading pulp and magazine publisher of the time. Four of the company's most successful pulp magazines were *Popular Detective, Thrilling Detective, Popular Western,* and *Thrilling Western,* so it isn't surprising that detective and western titles made up a large part of Popular Library's list. In fact, of the first two hundred titles, only about fifteen were not mysteries or westerns. The early titles are almost exclusively reprints, but beyond number 500, original novels appeared more frequently.

Popular Library is well known for its cover art, which was very distinctive and went through several stages. The first stage ran through number 137 and was defined by the work of artist/designers H. Lawrence Hoffman and Saul Immerman. These covers usually depict one or two large central objects in a simple but effective style that is somewhat similar to early Dell cover art.

Popular Library 138 featured a cover by artist Rudolph Belarski, and this roughly marks the beginning of the second stage, which was characterized by sensational pulp magazine style covers. In addition to Belarski, pulp artists Earle Bergey, George Rozen, and Samuel Cherry all produced outstanding covers for Popular Library during this period. For some books, rather than commissioning a new painting, Pines would re-use a suitable cover that had previously appeared on one of its pulp magazines. Virtually all of the paperbacks with these dramatic pulp art covers are very collectable—especially the mysteries.

By number 400 Popular Library had begun to phase in a more realistic style of cover art. This roughly coincided with a conversion to the tall format, and the two changes combined to give the books a more modern look.

Three stages of Popular Library cover art

Popular Library 18 (1943)   Popular Library 173 (1949)   Popular Library 621 (1954)

Popular Library produced several different series of paperbacks. Its first series, priced at twenty-five cents, included over 830 titles, the first three of which are not numbered. Second printings of many of these books were re-numbered by adding 1000 to the original number. In 1952 Popular Library launched its *G* (for "giant") series, which consisted of thicker books priced at thirty-five cents. The following year the company started a second line of twenty-five cent books, designated "Popular Library Eagle Books," and numbered with an *EB* prefix. Eagle Books were tall format paperbacks and had wrap-around cover art. Subsequent series from the publisher included *K*, *PC*, *SP*, and others.

For collectors, key twenty-five cent titles include *The Private Life of Helen of Troy* (147), and *Gentlemen Prefer Blondes* (221), both of which have classic Earle Bergey covers; *The Doll's Trunk Murder* (211) which features a notorious cover by Rudolph Belarski; *Tales of Chinatown* (217) by Sax Rohmer; and all the novels of William Irish and John D. MacDonald. Among later titles, *Cry Scandal* by William Ard (G236), *The Man in the High Castle* by Philip K. Dick (SP-250), and the three original Jim Thompson novels: *Ironside* (60-2244), *The Undefeated* (60-8104), and *Nothing But a Man* (60-8116) are all very collectable.

PYRAMID

Pyramid was the paperback imprint of the Almat Publishing Company. Almat was founded in 1949, and its name comes from a combination of the first names of the company's founders. Pyramid paperbacks were Almat's primary business but the company branched off into magazine publishing as well, with periodicals such as *Challenge For Men* and *Man's Magazine*.

Pyramid 70

Early Pyramids were almost exclusively reprints but original novels later became an important part of the line. Westerns, mysteries, racy adult romances such as *Reckless Passion* (12), and sensational newsstand titles such as T*een-Age Vice!* (G43), were all well represented. Pyramid later became very strong in science fiction as well. The company was partial to eye-catching cover art with strong mass-market appeal. Early Pyramid covers have a classic vintage look, and many of the later titles, from the mid-1950s through the early 1960s feature outstanding covers by leading artists such as Robert Maguire, John Schoenherr, Harry Schaare, Lou Marchetti, William Rose, Tom Miller, and others.

Pyramid initially published a single series of books that began with number 11. The early titles were short format paperbacks with a basic cover price of twenty-five cents. Giant editions numbered with a *G* prefix were priced at thirty-five cents, and subsequent cover prices included forty cents (*F* prefix), and fifty cents (*R* prefix). Beginning in 1956 the short format was phased out, and beyond number 200, Pyramids are almost entirely tall format paperbacks. In 1957 the company launched its Pyramid Royal line, which consisted primarily of non-fiction and classics. By 1963, though, only about forty Pyramid Royal titles had been published, and the series is of little collector interest.

In contrast to the Royals, Pyramid's sensational juvenile delinquent and narcotics titles such as *I Was a Drug Addict* (122), *The Junk Pusher* (126), and *The Young Punks* (G271) have proven very popular with collectors. Other key titles include *Fire in My Blood* (G462), which features a classic cover by Robert Maguire; J*ourney Into Violence* (G578), an original novel by Harry Whittington; two paperback originals by Day Keene, *His Father's Wife* (138) and *Dead in Bed* (G448); and many others. Pyramid also published the *Fu Manchu* novels by Sax Rohmer, the *Shadow* series by Maxwell Grant, and the *Honey West* novels by G.G. Fickling. All of these series are very collectable.

In 1975 Pyramid was acquired by hardcover publisher Harcourt Brace Jovanovich, and in 1977 Harcourt renamed the line "Jove." The original long-running numerical sequence was continued, though, as were popular Pyramid series such as *The Shadow*, and *Weird Heroes*. New series continued to be initiated in the Jove era, such as the *M.I.A. Hunter* combat novels, and the *Longarm, Gunsmith,* and *Slocum* western series, each of which ran for hundreds of titles in the 1980s and 1990s.

SIGNET, PENGUIN, and NEW AMERICAN LIBRARY

Penguin, of Great Britain, pre-dated Pocket Books and pioneered the publishing of inexpensive modern paperbacks. British Penguins featured text-only covers, though, rather than the illustrated covers favored in the U.S., and the company never fully exploited American style mass-market distribution. Even so, Penguin was very influential on American paperback publishing, and helped to spawn not just the U.S. branch of Penguin, but Bantam, Signet, and Ballantine as well.

Penguin was founded by Allen Lane, whose idea was to produce inexpensive paper editions of good literature that would be sold through bookstores and variety stores such as Woolworth's. The first ten Penguins were published in the summer of 1935 and were an immediate success. In October of that year Lane released ten more, and by the spring of 1937, the Penguin list exceeded one hundred titles. In three years Penguin sold over 25 million books. The British Penguins had dust jackets with plain text covers, and subject matter determined the color—green for mystery, orange for general fiction, red for drama, blue for biography, and yellow for miscellaneous topics.

In 1939 Lane hired Ian Ballantine to open a U.S. branch of Penguin. Initially the U.S. branch simply distributed Penguins that were imported from England. By 1941, though, many of the English titles were being printed in America. In 1942 the U.S. branch began publishing its own list of titles and, to further accommodate American taste, added illustrated covers as well. Between 1942 and 1945 the American branch also produced and distributed wartime paperbacks in joint ventures with both the *Infantry Journal* and the Military Services Publishing Company (Superior Reprints).

The U.S. Penguins are numbered from 500 to 659, and almost all are reprints rather than paperback originals. Initial print runs were about 25,000 copies, fewer than average for mass-market paperbacks and accordingly, these books are scarcer than paperbacks from larger publishers such as Pocket Books. Penguins are primarily tall format paperbacks but the short format was also used. Cover art was very subdued and much of it was executed by Robert Jonas.

Penguin 38
A British Penguin

Penguin 589
An American Penguin

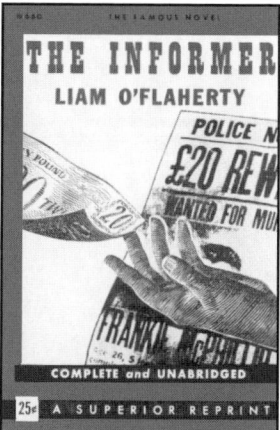

Superior Reprint 650
A wartime paperback

Six U.S. Penguins were issued with dust jackets, and for collectors these are the most valuable books in the series. Other key titles include the novels by James M. Cain, Wade Miller, and Frank Gruber. British Penguins are not heavily collected in the U.S. but, of course, they are popular with collectors in England.

In 1945, following editorial differences with Lane, Ian Ballantine left Penguin, taking the wartime joint venture business with him. Later that year he helped found Bantam Books. After Ballantine's departure, the U.S. Branch was managed by Kurt Enoch and Victor Weybright, but friction again developed as the new managers, like Ballantine before them, wanted to take Penguin further in the mass-market direction than the conservative Lane would accept. To resolve the situation, in 1948 Enoch and Weybright purchased all the assets of the U.S. branch and renamed the company "New American Library" (NAL).

The new owners also changed the name of their paperback line, first to "Penguin-Signet" and soon after to "Signet." The numbering sequence was continued, though, and the first Penguin-Signet was numbered 660. Along with Penguin's other assets, NAL obtained a distribution contract with magazine publisher Fawcett Publications (see Gold Medal), and over the next ten years the company became a major figure in the publishing business.

Like Penguin, NAL/Signet published almost entirely reprints and leaned towards serious literature, with titles by Joseph Conrad, Herman Melville, Thomas Mann, Richard Wright, Ayn Rand, D.H. Lawrence, and many other highly regarded authors. The company did not neglect popular taste, though, and mysteries and westerns made up a good portion of the Signet list. Erskine Caldwell of *Tobacco Road* fame and Mickey Spillane, creator of *Mike Hammer*, were the publisher's strongest selling authors.

In contrast to the Penguin period, Signet soon began emphasizing its cover art. The Jonas covers were discontinued after about number 700 and replaced primarily with covers by James Avati. Avati's covers, often depicting brooding figures against dark backgrounds, brought a new level of realism and emotional

Three vintage Signet paperbacks

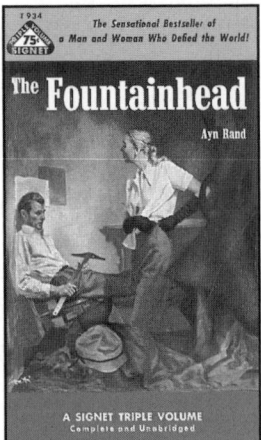

| Signet S1174 | Signet D1198 | Signet T934 |
| *A Signet Giant* | *A Signet Double Volume* | *A Signet Triple Volume* |

depth to the field. His work gave Signet's paperbacks a modern look that was intriguing and recognizable, and very distinct from the more sensational cover art favored by other publishers. In the mid-1950s Robert Maguire became another important new cover artist for the publisher.

Signets are all numbered in a single continuous series. The books are tall format paperbacks and the basic initial cover price was twenty-five cents. "Signet Giants" were numbered with an *S* prefix and priced at thirty-five cents. "Double-Volumes" carried a cover price of fifty cents and were numbered with a *D* prefix. These books were simply thicker than normal, not true double novels. "Triple-Volumes" (*T* prefix) were thicker still, and priced at seventy-five cents. NAL also published Mentor paperbacks, which featured serious literature and scholarly writing, and a nonfiction line, the Signet Key Books.

Collectable Signet titles include the novels of Horace McCoy, Chester Himes, James M. Cain, and Lionel White; first printings of Ian Fleming's *James Bond* novels; three original novels by Jim Thompson: *Wild Town* (1461), *The Getaway* (1584), and *The Transgressors* (2034); the four original horror novels written by Stephen King under his Richard Bachman pseudonym; and many others. Mentors are not widely collected, but *New World Writing #7* (MD130) includes a short piece by Jack Kerouac written under the pseudonym Jean-Louis, making it popular with many collectors.

Three paperback imprints of New American Library

Mentor M92

Signet 879

Signet Key Ks 360

New York

BALLANTINE BOOKS

PENGUIN **SIGNET** BOOKS
Complete and Unabridged

INTRODUCTION

Cover art is one of the major attractions of paperback collecting, and covers by top artists can add significant value to a paperback. At the same time, many lesser known artists are just beginning to develop followings and their paperbacks are often available at bargain prices. This section provides some capsule information on one hundred assorted paperback cover artists, along with representative examples of their work. For many of the artists, additional covers are noted that can be seen in the price guide section. Most of the artists who are popular with collectors can be found here, along with many who are not as well known. Because of space limitations, though, some worthy artists had to be left out.

1) Avon 864

1. Robert K. Abbett
During the late 1950s and early 1960s, Abbett painted covers for most of the major publishers, notably Avon, Ballantine, Dell, Gold Medal, Perma, and Pocket Books.

2. James Avati
Famous for defining the Signet look in the 1950s. Avati was one of the most important paperback cover artists of his era and his style was frequently imitated.

2) Signet 754

3) Bantam 3067

3. James Bama
In the late 1960s and early 1970s Bama regularly painted covers for Bantam, including dozens of *Doc Savage* paperbacks. He also did covers and illustrations for men's adventure magazines.

4. Walter M. Baumhofer
A highly regarded pulp artist, Baumhofer is well known for his covers on the early issues of Street & Smith's *Doc Savage* magazine. His work can also be seen on a few Crests and Gold Medals of the mid-1950s.

4) Gold Medal 728

5) Popular Library 362

5. Rudolph Belarski

A leading pulp artist of the 1930s through the 1950s, Belarski is well known among paperback collectors for his classic Popular Library covers. He also did a number of digest covers in the early 1950s. (See Carnival 918 illustrated in the price listings.)

6. Harry Bennett

Bennett painted many covers for Gold Medal, Perma, Pocket Books, Dell, and others during the early 1960s. His haunting work often features isolated, lonely-looking figures.

6) Gold Medal 1277

7) Popular Library 273

7. Earle Bergey

Like Rudolph Belarski, Bergey was an accomplished pulp artist who also did paperback covers for Popular Library. Beautiful women and science fiction were two of his specialties (also see Popular Library 147 and 221 in the price listings).

8. Charles Binger

Best known for his Bantam and Pennant covers from the mid-1950s, Binger had a realistic style for general fiction or mysteries, and a more abstract futuristic style for science fiction.

8) Bantam 1241

9) Bantam 751

9. Herman E. Bischoff

Painted a few covers for both Bantam and Gold Medal in the early 1950s. Bischoff had his own unique style and his covers are always interesting. (Also see Bantam 835 and Gold Medal 438 in the price listings.)

10. Carl Bobertz

In the early to mid-1950s Bobertz painted covers for Dell, Signet, Gold Medal, and others. He had a dramatic style well suited to mysteries and suspense novels.

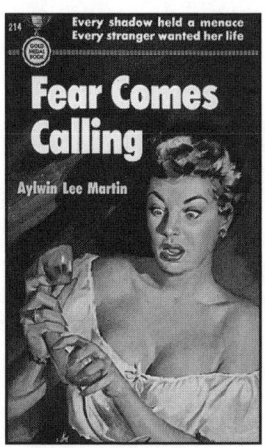

10) Gold Medal 214

11) Newsstand U132

11. Robert Bonfils
Painted hundreds of covers in the 1960s, and is best known for his distinctive pin-up style work for such publishers as Newsstand Library and Playtime. Bonfils also did the covers for Corinth Regency's various series of pulp-hero novels.

12. Stanley Borack
From the mid-1950s, through the 1960s, Borack painted covers for Dell, Lion, Monarch, and others. Westerns were a specialty, but he also did covers for other fiction genres.

12) Lion Books LB70

13) Monarch 270

13. Ralph Brillhart
Brillhart painted science fiction covers in an animated futuristic style. He is probably best known for his classic Monarch covers of the early 1960s, but he worked for Ballantine and Belmont as well. (Also see Monarch 354 in the price listings.)

14. Milton Charles
Charles painted Gold Medal and Crest covers in a style similar to that of Baryé Phillips. He had a large flowing signature that is easy to recognize.

14) Gold Medal 814

15) Popular Library 324

15. Samuel Cherry
Another outstanding artist who made the transition from pulp magazines to paperbacks for Popular Library. Westerns were a Cherry specialty but he also did crime and mystery fiction.

16. L. B. Cole
Known primarily as a comic book artist, Cole also painted mystery and romance paperback covers in a classic vintage style. He did a number of Croydon covers from 1945 to 1950, as well as two covers for Stork digests.

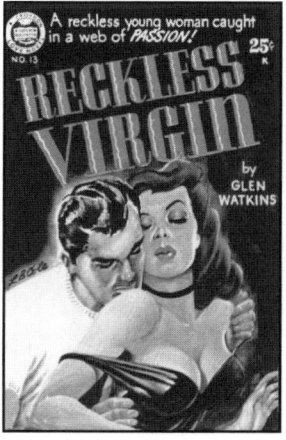

16) Croydon 13

17) Lion Library LL128

17. Charles Copeland
Copeland's work can be seen on paperbacks of the late 1950s and early 1960s from publishers such as Berkley, Lion Library, and Paperback Library.

18. Frank Cozzarelli
During the second half of the 1950s Cozzarelli painted covers for Signet and Pyramid. He also did covers for the mystery digests *Manhunt* and *Murder*.

18) Pyramid 126

19) Lion Books LB108

19. Mel Crair
Primarily known for his western covers, Crair worked for several publishers during the 1950s and 1960s including Ballantine, Lion, Pennant, and Pyramid. He also painted martial arts covers for Berkley in the mid 1970s.

20. Rafael M. DeSoto
A prolific pulp artist, famous for his portrayals of *The Spider*, DeSoto painted paperback covers for publishers such as Popular Library, Monarch, Ace, Dell, and Lion. He also did a number of classic digest covers.

20) Monarch 420

21) Gold Medal 1146

21. Leo and Diane Dillon
Throughout the 1960s and 1970s, the Dillons painted covers for many publishers, including Gold Medal and Regency. Their work is easy to recognize and features flowing abstract figures with heavy use of the color black.

22. Willard Downes
One of the earliest Gold Medal cover artists, Downes also did covers for Readers Choice, Lion, Popular Library, and Manhunt. (Also see Lion 68 and Gold Medals 103 and 133 in the price listing illustrations.)

22) Readers Choice 39

23) Novel Library 18

23. Peter Driben
Famous for his glamorous pin-up style magazine covers of the 1940s, Driben also did a number of paperback and digest covers.

24. Tom Dunn
Dunn painted many covers for Pocket Books and Cardinal during the second half of the 1950s. He was often used for leading authors such as Raymond Chandler, James M. Cain, and Evan Hunter.

24) Pocket Books 389

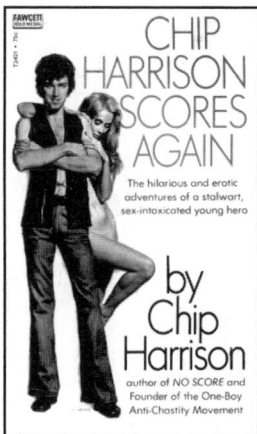

25) Gold Medal 2421

25. Elaine
Popular with collectors for her very sexy Brandon House covers of the mid-1960s, Elaine also worked for other publishers such as Ace, and Gold Medal—where she did the covers for Lawrence Block's *Chip Harrison* novels.

26. Ed "Emsh" Emshwiller
A science fiction artist well known for his Ace covers. Emshwiller often hid his "Emsh" signature in an obscure part of the futuristic machinery frequently depicted in his work.

26) Ace F-301

27) Pyramid 719

27. Mort Engel
Engel painted a number of covers for Pyramid in the late 1950s and early 1960s. He also worked for other publishers such as Avon and Lancer, and did mystery and western digest covers as well.

28. George T. Erickson
Erickson painted many covers from 1950 to 1955 for publishers such as Avon, Gold Medal, Lion, and Signet. His work has been compared to that of James Avati.

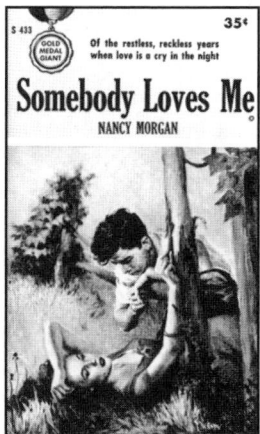

28) Gold Medal 433

29) MacFadden 60-277

30) Pyramid 1192

29. Jack Faragasso
Faragasso worked for several publishers during the 1950s and 1960s. He was versatile enough to go from pin-up style covers for Beacon to science fiction covers for MacFadden.

30. Virgil Finlay
A very well known pulp artist who specialized in weird fantasy art, Finlay's work can also be seen on a few paperbacks.

31) Gold Medal 369

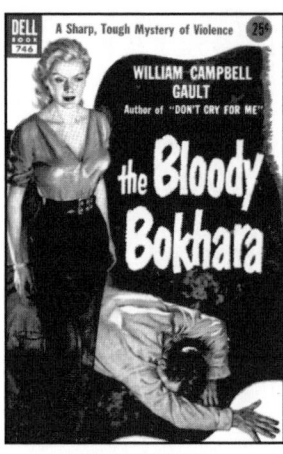

32) Dell 746

31. John J. Floherty Jr.
Floherty worked for a number of publishers in the 1950s, but was most active at Gold Medal where he painted covers for novels by Ann Aldrich, Wade Miller, Peter Rabe, Theodore Pratt, and many others.

32. Griffith Foxley
Foxley painted covers for Dell in the mid-1950s. His best known cover may be Dell First Edition 2E, *Madball* by Fredric Brown (illustrated in the price listings).

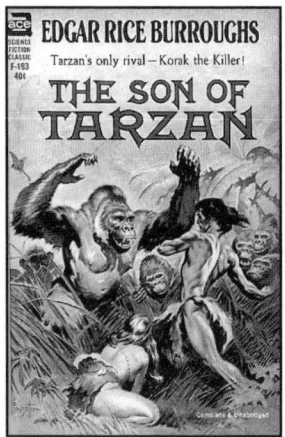

33) Ace F-193

34) Astounding 4/54

33. Frank Frazetta
Famous for "swords and sorcery" style fantasy art, Frazetta is well known by paperback collectors for his many Ace *Tarzan* covers. He also did *Conan* covers in a similar style for Lancer and other publishers.

34. Kelly Freas
A popular science fiction artist with a distinctive and somewhat animated style, Freas painted the covers for all 57 Laser paperbacks. He also worked for Ace, Astounding, Lancer, and others.

35) Ace G-576

35. Jack Gaughan
A very active science fiction and fantasy artist for Ace, Gaughan painted the covers for all three books in Ace's early edition of the *Lord of the Rings* trilogy. He also worked for Pyramid and other publishers.

36. William George
Active throughout the 1950s, George worked for Pocket Books and Bantam, but is better known for his Dell covers, including Dell First Editions and Dell's *Zane Grey's Western Magazine.*

36) Bantam 1610

37) Ace D-43

37. George Geygan
In the 1950s, Geygan did covers for several Universal Publishing imprints, including Beacon, Uni Books, and Intimate Novels. He also did sensational covers for Ace, Bantam, and others.

38. Gerald Gregg
A master of the airbrush with color illustration, Gregg's covers helped to give the early Dell paperbacks a distinct identity.

38) Dell 22

39) Exotic Novels 6

39. George Gross
A well known pulp artist who painted most of the covers for *Jungle Stories,* Gross is popular among paperback collectors for his sensational "bad girl" and western digest covers. (Also see Ecstasy 4 and Exotic 19 in the listings.)

40. Reginald Heade
One of the most famous British cover artists, Heade's work can be seen on digests from publishers such as Leisure Library, Archer, and Harborough. He also worked under the name Cy Webb.

40) Archer 96

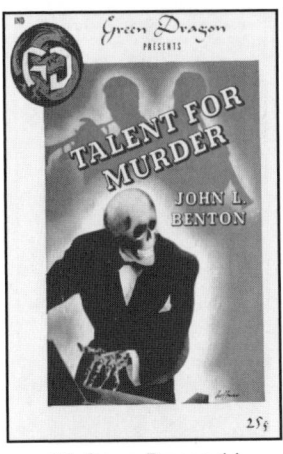

41) Green Dragon 14

41. H. Lawrence Hoffman

Best known for his early work at Popular Library, Hoffman also painted covers for many other mystery paperbacks and digests in the 1940s (for example, see Vulcan 4 and Pocket Books 214 illustrated in the listings).

42. Mitchell Hooks

A very active artist who worked for most of the major publishers, Hooks is probably best known for his Gold Medal covers, which include *Rockabilly* (1161) and *The Shrinking Man* (577).

42) Gold Medal 703

43) Gold Medal 473

43. Clark Hulings

Another prolific artist, Hulings worked for publishers from Avon to Zenith. He had a tense and dramatic style very well suited to thrillers and suspense novels.

44. Ray Johnson

Over a long career that extended from the late 1940s into at least the 1970s, Johnson worked for many of the major publishers, most notably, Popular Library, Gold Medal, and Monarch. (Also see Monarch 101, 262, and 487 in the price listings.)

44) Monarch 487

45) Penguin 604

45. Robert Jonas

Had a simple but effective style that is easy to recognize on early Penguins, Signets and Mentors.

46. Victor Kalin

A very versatile artist, Kalin did covers for mysteries, westerns, science fiction, horror novels, romance novels, and more. Some of his best work can be seen on Avon and Dell paperbacks.

46) Dell Ten Cent 2

47) Beacon 179

47. Owen Kampen
Kampen worked for publishers such as Gold Medal, Beacon, and Popular Library. Two of his most well known covers are Gold Medal 189, *Cassidy's Girl,* and Beacon 131, *Rock 'N Roll Gal* (see illustrations in the price listings).

48. Van Kaufman
Kaufman did a small number of covers for Bantam, Lion and Dell. He had a whimsical style used for humorous or lighthearted titles.

48) Bantam 469

49) Crest 115

49. Lou Kimmel
In the mid-1950s, Kimmel painted many covers for Crest and Gold Medal. His work was frequently used for tough crime novels by authors such as Peter Rabe, Wade Miller, and Gil Brewer.

50. Roy Krenkel
Like Frank Frazetta, Krenkel is well known for his work on Ace's popular Edgar Rice Burroughs novels. He also painted other covers for Ace in the same genre.

50) Ace F-157

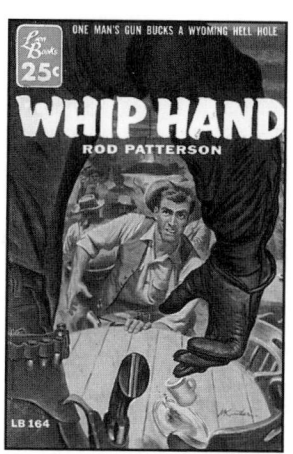

51) Lion Books LB164

51. Mort Kunstler
Kunstler painted several western and crime novel covers for Lion Library in the 1950s. He also worked for Pyramid and Zenith, and did magazine illustration.

52. Ron Lesser
From the late 1950s, through the 1960s, Lesser worked for many of the larger publishers including Ace, Avon, Ballantine, Berkley, Gold Medal, Lancer, Midwood, Pyramid, and Crest.

52) Pyramid 740

53) Pyramid 462

53. Robert Maguire

One of the most widely collected cover artists, Maguire is known for his sensational portrayals of beautiful women. Some of his best work appears on Berkley, Signet, Pyramid, and Monarch books, but he worked for several other publishers as well.

54. Leo Manso

Best known for his many Pocket Books covers from the 1940s. Manso's covers are usually very striking, and often feature large central objects such as faces.

54) Avon SF & Fantasy 1

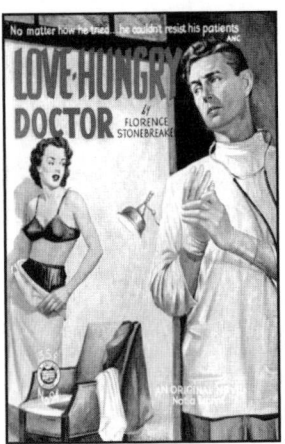

55) Croydon 24

55. Lou Marchetti

From the late 1940s, into the 1960s, Marchetti did hundreds of covers for a broad range of publishers. Impressive examples of his work can be seen on digests such as Accused, Croydon, and Pursuit.

56. Earl Mayan

Primarily a Bantam artist, Mayan also did the cover of Pennant #1. His best known cover may be Bantam 943, the Fredric Brown novel *Here Comes a Candle* (see illustration in the price listings).

56) Bantam 1081

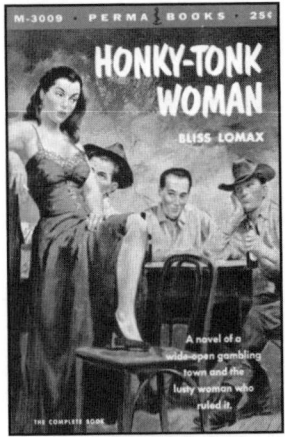

57) Perma M3009

57. George Mayers

Throughout the first half of the 1950's, Mayers painted covers for Gold Medal, Popular Library, Pocket Books, Perma, and Dell, including three of the Dell Ten Cent Books.

58. Frank McCarthy

A very active artist in the 1950s, and well known for his Gold Medal western covers, McCarthy also painted mystery covers for Pocket Books, and worked for Dell in the 1960s.

58) Gold Medal 411

59) Crest 413

60) Crest 142

59. Robert McGinnis
A prolific and highly collected artist who has received much recent acclaim, McGinnis painted beautiful women in an elegant, modern style.

60. James Meese
Meese had a striking style much in demand from the mid-1950s through the early 1960s. He painted hundreds of covers for Crest, Gold Medal, Dell, Signet, Pocket Books, and others. (Also see Gold Medals 472, 546, 687 & 734 illustrated in the listings.)

61) Beacon 280

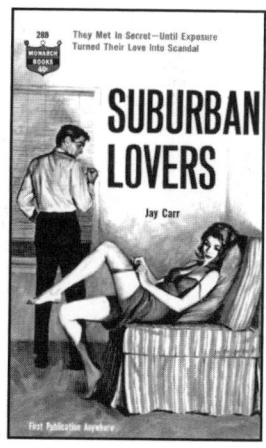

62) Monarch 288

61. Micarelli
Almost exclusively a Beacon artist, Micarelli painted covers from the late 1950s, on into the 1960s. A well known example of his work is Beacon 175, an early novel by Charles Willeford (see illustration in the price listings).

62. Tom Miller
Best known for risqué Monarch covers of the early 1960s, Miller also worked for Pyramid and Dell (see Monarch 189, 227, and 238 illustrated in the price listings).

63) Midwood 225

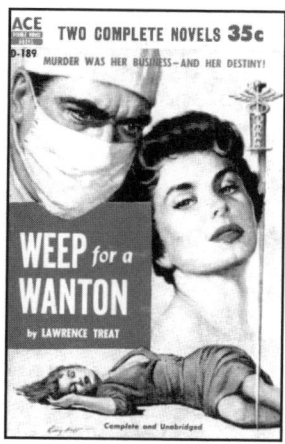

64) Ace 189

63. Bruce Minney
An illustrator of men's adventure magazines since the mid-1950s, Minney also painted paperback covers during the 1960s and 1970s. (Also see Pinnacle 694 in the price listings.)

64. Rudy Nappi
Very active throughout the 1950s and into the 1960s, Nappi painted hundreds of covers for publishers from Ace to Zenith. Some of his best work appears on digests of publishers such as Cameo, Venus, Falcon, Carnival, Original, and Rainbow.

65) Ace D57

66) Pyramid 92

65. Victor Olson

Olson worked throughout the 1950s and '60s for publishers such as Gold Medal, Ace, and Avon. He also did pin-up style covers for Beacon and Midwood. Gold Medal 348, *The Moon in the Gutter,* is a well known example of his work.

66. Julian Paul

Painted covers for Pyramid and Lion during the early 1950s in a classic vintage style. A good example of Paul's work can be seen on Pyramid 122, *I Was a Drug Addict.*

67) Carnival 911

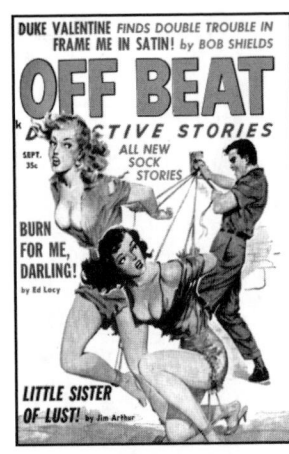

68) Off Beat 9/60

67. Ray Pease

In the early 1950s Pease painted digest covers for publishers such as Cameo, Carnival, Venus, and Star (see Star 751 illustrated in the price listings). He also did paperback covers for Popular Library, Signet, and Lion.

68. Carl Pfeufer

A shock-value specialist, Pfeufer drew lurid covers during the late 1950s and early 1960s for the crime digests *Keyhole Detective*, *Off Beat Detective Stories,* and *Sure Fire Detective Stories*.

69) Gold Medal 476

70) Beacon 563

69. Barye Phillips

Perhaps the most prolific of all cover artists, Phillips produced hundreds of covers for Gold Medal and was also an important artist for Bantam, Crest, Signet, and several other publishers. He signed his work Baryé.

70. Jerome Podwil

From at least as early as 1961, Podwil painted covers for many publishers including Ace, Crest Belmont, Midwood, Gold Medal, Beacon, and Chariot. He usually signed his full name.

71) Graphic 215

72) Graphic 152

71. Samson Pollen

Pollen painted several covers for Lion Library and also worked for Galaxy, Graphic, and Zenith. He apparently did only a limited amount of paperback work.

72. Walter Popp

Very popular with collectors for his Graphic and Beacon covers of the 1950s, which typically featured beautiful but dangerous women, Popp also did western covers for Ace, pulp covers, and magazine illustration. He was still working into the 1990s.

73) Gold Medal 693

74) Ballantine 472

73. Jerry Powell

In the second half of the 1950s Powell produced covers for Dell, Gold Medal, Pocket Books, and Pyramid.

74. Richard Powers

A prominent science fiction artist with an abstract futuristic style, Powers worked for most of the major publishers but is probably best known for his Ballantine covers. One of the most active paperback artists. (Also see Pocket Books 1222 illustrated in the price listings.)

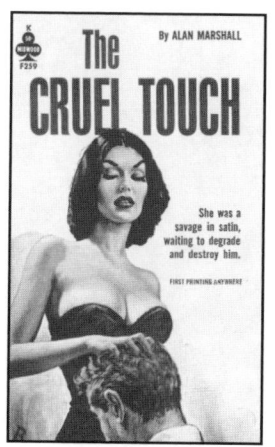

75) Midwood 259

76) Ecstasy Novel 3

75. Paul Rader

Although he worked for other publishers, Rader is identified with Midwood, where he painted hundreds of covers from 1958 to 1968. (Also see Midwood 65, 101, 248, 271, and most of the others illustrated in the listings.)

76. Rodewald

One of the earlier vintage era artists, Rodewald painted racy romance digest covers in the late 1940s and early 1950s. (Also see Astro 2, Stork 6, and Romantic Novels *The Loves of a Harlot*, illustrated in the price listings.)

77) Pyramid 298

77. William Rose
In the mid-1950s, Rose did covers for a number of publishers, such as Avon, Berkley, Cardinal, Dell, Gold Medal, Perma and Pyramid. (Also see Perma 3084 illustrated in the price listings.)

78. A. Leslie Ross
A prominent western artist, Ross worked for Gold Medal, Hillman, Popular Library, and others. He also painted western pulp covers. Ross cowboys are extremely lean, with an almost elongated look.

78) Hillman 43

79) Beacon 195

79. Al Rossi
Rossi did covers for publishers such as Avon, Lion, Bantam, and Signet in the mid-1950s, and later painted quite a few covers for Beacon.

80. George Rozen
A top pulp artist, well known for his work on Street & Smith's *Shadow* magazine, Rozen also painted many covers for Popular Library including western covers for Popular Library's *Thrilling Novels* digest imprint.

80) Popular Library 291

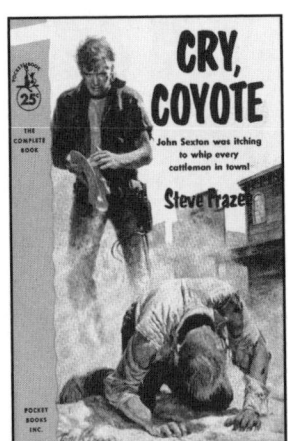

81) Pocket Books 1101

81. Tom Ryan
Primarily a western artist, Ryan painted covers for Pocket Books, Dell, Perma, and Pyramid during the second half of the 1950s. His work can also be seen on the digests *Western* and *Three-Book Western*.

82. Bernard Safran
Painted several covers for Pocket Books in the late 1940s but is probably better known for his digest work of the early 1950s, which included covers for Uni Book, Cosmos, and Croydon.

82) Cosmos 2

83) Readers Choice 4

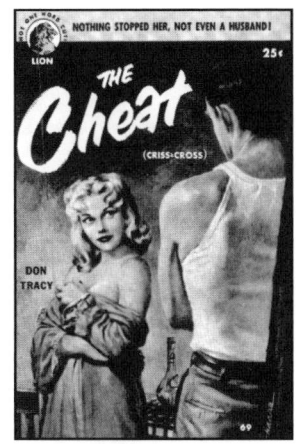

84) Lion 69

83. Norman Saunders
A top pulp artist, Saunders also did many paperback covers in the late 1940s and early 1950s. Among paperback collectors, his Ace covers are probably the most well known (see Ace D1, D3, and D7 illustrated in the listings).

84. Harry Schaare
A very active artist, Schaare painted hundreds of covers from 1949 on. Some of his best work was done for Bantam, Monarch, and Lion (also see Pyramid 448 illustrated in the listings).

85) Pyramid 658

86) Popular Library 236

85. John Schoenherr
A science fiction and fantasy artist, Schoenherr painted covers for Pyramid, Ace, and Monarch throughout the 1960s. In the early 1970s he did covers for Ace and Daw.

86. Alex Schomburg
Although best known for science fiction pulp and digest covers (see Rocket Stories 1-2), Schomburg also did a few paperback covers for Popular Library in 1950.

87) Ace D-468

88) Gold Medal 307

87. Robert E. Schulz
A very versatile and productive artist, Schulz did sci-fi covers for Ace, western covers for Gold Medal and Lion, pin-up style covers for Beacon and Midwood, and World War II covers for Dell and Ballantine. He also painted mystery and digest covers.

88. Amos Sewell
Painted a few covers for Gold Medal in the early 1950s. *Witch of Salem*, at right, is one of his best, but also see Gold Medal 331 illustrated in the price listings.

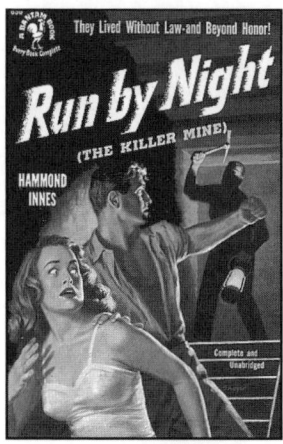

89) Bantam 890

89. William Shoyer
In the late 1940s and early 1950s, Shoyer painted a number of covers for Pocket Books, Bantam, and Lion.

90. Paul Stahr
Responsible for many of Avon's outstanding early covers on titles by authors such as A. Merritt, James M. Cain, and Raymond Chandler. Stahr's cover for Avon 38, *The Big Sleep*, is generally considered to be a classic.

90) Avon M.M.M. 34

91) Zane Grey Western 12/52

91. Robert Stanley
Best known for his many Dell covers, including much of the Dell Ten Cent series, Stanley also did western covers for Lion and Graphic, and science fiction covers for several novels in the Beacon/Galaxy series.

92. Isador N. Steinberg
The first mass-market paperback artist, Steinberg painted covers for many of the early Pocket Books, including numbers 1, 2, and 3.

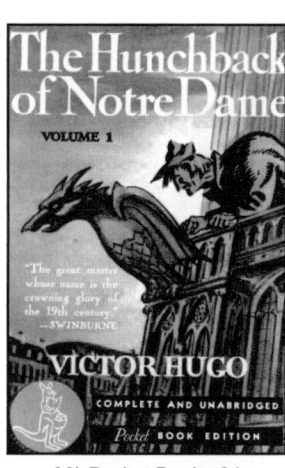

92) Pocket Books 31

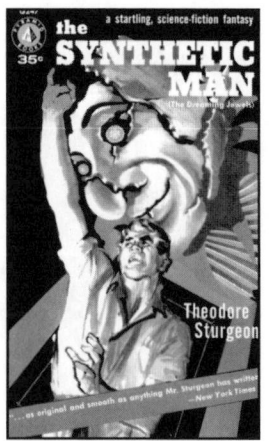

93) Pyramid 247

93. Arthur Sussman
Sussman painted science fiction and mystery covers for several publishers. He had an abstract style similar to that of Richard Powers, giving many of his covers a sketchy, somewhat unfinished look.

94. Saul Tepper
Active as a magazine and ad illustrator, Tepper also painted paperback covers for Gold Medal and Signet in the mid-1950s (also see Gold Medal 434 illustrated in the price listings).

94) Signet 1089

95) Beacon 497

95. Jack Thurston
Worked for publishers such as Monarch, Beacon, Berkley, and Ballantine in the late 1950s and early 1960s. In 1964 and 1965 Thurston did the covers for Pyramid's series of *Toff* novels by John Creasey.

96. Verne Tossey
During the 1950s Tossey worked for several publishers, but may be best known for his Ballantine and Ace covers. (Also see Ace D-234, Ballantine 54, and Signet 1076 illustrated in the listings.)

96) Ace S-104

97) Prize Love Novel 23

97. Bill Wenzel
Although known mainly for his "girlie" cartoons, Wenzel did a few paperback and digest covers. (Also see Pyramid 861, Prize Love 24, and Candid Love 22 illustrated in the price listings.)

98. Wallace Wood
Well known as a comic book artist, Wood also did some paperback covers—notably, the final six Galaxy Science Fiction Novels (numbers 30–35).

98) Galaxy 33

99) Avon T-203

99. George Ziel
Did a few covers for Pyramid, Pocket Books, and Avon during the mid 1950s. Ziel apparently had a relatively small paperback output.

100. Stanley Zuckerberg
An outstanding artist of the Avati school, Zuckerberg worked for several publishers from the mid-1950s, through the 1960s. His best work includes his Signet covers of 1954–55.

100) Signet 1129

PONY BOOKS

A HANDI-BOOK
WESTERN

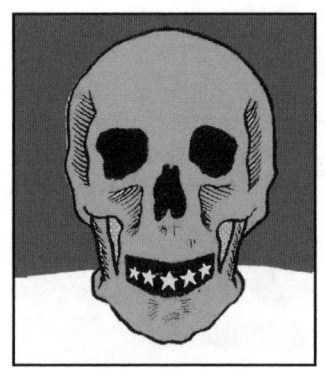

Five Star Mystery

HOW TO USE THE PRICE LISTINGS

Unlike the traditional hardcover collecting practice, in which books are identified or listed by author and title, the predominant method used to identify paperbacks is to specify the publisher and the sequential number that the publisher assigned to the book. The price listings that follow are organized around this publisher and number convention. Shown below are several sample entries from the listings. Please take a minute to familiarize yourself with all the features of this guide:

1 PUBLISHER	2 PUB. #	3 TITLE	4 DATE	5 AUTHOR	6 COND.	7 TYPE	8 PRICE
ACE	D 15	Junkie *Narcotic Agent*	1953	Lee, W.* *Helbrant, M.*	VG-	DBL	$181.00 A
BANTAM	356	Sorry, Wrong Number	1948	Ullman, A.	VGF	MTI	$9.00
BROADWAY NOVEL	9	Dangerous Love	1950	Woodford, J.	AF	Digest	$73.00 A
DELL	F 84	The Beat Generation	1959	Anthology	AF		$26.00 A
GOLD MEDAL	489	Blood Alley	1955	Fleischman, A.S.	VG+	MTI	$33.00 A
GOLD MEDAL	s 1164	The Defenders	1961	Aarons, E.S.	VGF	TVTI	$10.00

1. *Publisher* – Publishers are listed alphabetically. In some cases publishers' names have been abbreviated due to space limitations.

2. *Publisher's Number* – This field (Pub. #) consists of two parts, a prefix and a number. Vintage paperback publishers almost always numbered their books sequentially for identification purposes. The number can generally be found on the spine and/or front cover of a book. In some cases books were not numbered and this is shown in the listings by the abbreviation "No#."

In addition to the basic number, many publishers used a letter or numeric prefix to designate different series of books (such as the Ace "D" series or the Avon "T" series). In the price listings, with a few exceptions, if a publisher had more than one series, they are listed in alphabetical or numeric order, and within each series the books are listed numerically. In many cases, publishers assigned prefixes that do not designate a series, but simply indicate different cover prices. See the Gold Medal listings for an example of this. In the case of periodical digests such as *Manhunt* or *Ellery Queen's Mystery Magazine,* the prefix indicates the volume, for example, **1 4** would mean volume 1, number 4.

3. *Title* – In some cases titles have been shortened or abbreviated due to space limitations. The abbreviation "TCOT" stands for "The Case Of The" and "Science Fiction" is frequently shortened to "Sci-Fi." The letters "d.j." after a title identify a dust jacketed edition. A second title in italics underneath a primary listing indicates that the book is a double novel. See paragraph 7A below for more information on double novels.

4. *Date* – Almost all the listed books have been dated to provide an additional identification reference, and also for historical interest. As a general rule, the dates given in the listings correspond to the year the listed book originally went on sale—this is what is usually considered to be the publishing date. However, not all paperback publishers established actual publication dates, and the source of the dating information varies by publisher.

Many publishers, such as Bantam, Gold Medal, Pocket Books, and Signet, regularly reported in their books the printing date or date published. When so provided, this information was used in the listings. If neither of these dates were given, the copyright date was generally used in the case of new books, that is, original or newly revised titles, but not if the paperback was a reprint of an earlier edition. With new books, the copyright date usually coincides with the year the book went on sale, but it may be a year earlier or later—this can happen with books released near the beginning or end of a year.

In cases where the publisher included no useful information within the book itself, some books have been dated through outside sources such as *Publishers Weekly* magazine, which often reported scheduled release dates of mass-market paperbacks. In other cases, a book's relative position in a numerical sequence provided enough information to date it with sufficient accuracy. The abbreviation "n/d" stands for "no date" and indicates the book could not be reliably dated.

The great majority of the listed books (over 93%) date from the late 1930s through the 1960s, but many non-vintage books are also collected and are included here. For example, some popular series such as *Doc Savage* and *The Shadow* were published throughout the 1970s and 1980s. Additionally, the publishers Daw, Laser, and Black Lizard are popular with collectors and are included in the listings even though they did not publish at all prior to 1970.

5. *Author* – In most cases co-authors have not been listed due to space limitations. Names followed by asterisks are pseudonyms (see Appendix A for a listing of the various authors and pseudonyms). The author index at the end of this book can be used to find all the listed paperbacks by any particular author.

6. *Cond*. – The condition or grade of the book. See pages 5–6 for more information on condition and grading.

7. *Type* – This field lists additional information on many of the books. There are four possible entries in this column:

A) *DBL* – This indicates that the book is a double novel or "double," that is, two novels published together under the same cover. The Ace doubles are the best known examples but many other publishers also issued doubles. For examples, see Belmont, Lancer, and Midwood. In almost all cases the first listing for any particular double will include both of the titles and authors, and will take up two lines (the second line will be in italics). Subsequent listings for the same book include only one title and author, and occupy just a single line. (Listings for some later Midwood doubles, and a few Midwood triples, include just one title and author.)

B) *Digest* – This indicates that the book is in digest format. For more information on digests see "Paperback Formats" on page 8.

C) *MTI* – This code indicates that the book is a movie tie-in. When an existing book is made into a movie, publishers often release a new edition exploiting the movie connection. In other cases, original novelizations of current or upcoming movies are published to capitalize on a movie's publicity or popularity. In either case, movie tie-ins often feature the names and photos of the movie's stars on the cover, and many include photos of movie scenes within the book. Most of the major publishers and many smaller ones have published movie tie-ins. The price listings include over 450 MTIs.

D) *TVTI* – Television tie-ins are similar to movie tie-ins but are associated with TV shows rather than movies. Hundreds of popular TV shows of the 1950s and 1960s were the subject of paperback novelizations and some shows spawned lengthy series of original novels based on the show's characters. For example, see the Ace *Man From U.N.C.L.E.* series (23 titles) or the Paperback Library *Dark Shadows* series (over 30 titles). The listings include nearly 200 TVTIs.

8. *Price* – As mentioned in the introduction, these listings are records of actual retail sales and each price reflects a true cash amount actually paid for the listed book. There are no estimated prices, no Internet "asking" prices, and no artificial prices of any kind. The letter *A* following a price indicates an auction sale. For consistency, auction prices that included cents have been rounded to whole dollar amounts.

Avon Monthly Novel 4

Handi-Book 33

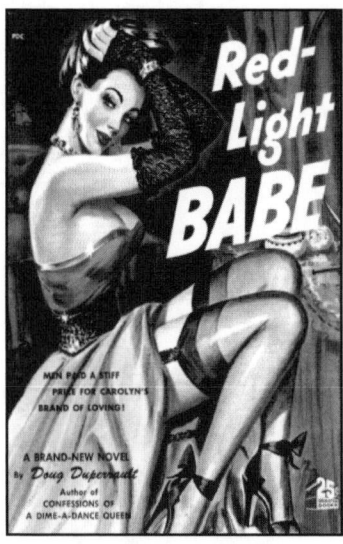

Quarter Book 77

Readers Choice 14

Four collectable vintage digests

Ace D-1 VG+ $220   Ace D-3 VG+ $18   Ace D-5 VG- $24

PUBLISHER	PUB. #	TITLE	DATE	AUTHOR	COND.	TYPE	PRICE
ACE	D 1	The Grinning Gismo	1952	Taylor, S.W.	VG+	DBL	$220.00 A
		Too Hot For Hell		Vining, K.			
ACE	D 1	The Grinning Gismo	1952	Taylor, S.W.	VGF	DBL	$208.00 A
ACE	D 2	Bloody Hoofs	1952	Leithead, J.E.	VG	DBL	$17.00 A
		Bad Man's Return		MacDonald, W.C.			
ACE	D 2	Bloody Hoofs	1952	Leithead, J.E.	G	DBL	$10.00
ACE	D 3	The Big Fix	1952	Colton, M.	VG+	DBL	$18.00 A
		Twist The Knife Slowly		Clugston, K.			
ACE	D 4	Rimrock Rider	1952	Tompkins, W.A.	VGF	DBL	$33.00 A
		Massacre At White River		Patten, L.B.			
ACE	D 4	Rimrock Rider	1952	Tompkins, W.A.	G	DBL	$10.00
ACE	D 5	Drawn To Evil	1952	Whittington, H.	VG-	DBL	$24.00
		The Scarlet Spade		Goldthwaite, E.K.			
ACE	D 6	Plunder Valley	1952	Nye, N.	VG	DBL	$12.00
		The Branded Lawman		Vance, W.E.			
ACE	D 7	So Dead My Love!	1953	Whittington, H.	VG	DBL	$30.00 A
		I, The Executioner		Ransome, S.			
ACE	D 7	So Dead My Love!	1953	Whittington, H.	G+	DBL	$22.00
ACE	D 7	So Dead My Love!	1953	Whittington, H.	G	DBL	$20.00
ACE	D 8	Terror Rides The Range	1953	Echols, A.K.	G	DBL	$8.00
		Gunsmoke Gold		West, T.			
ACE	D 9	Decoy	1953	Morgan, M.	VGF	DBL	$35.00 A
		If I Die Before I Wake		King, S.			
ACE	D 9	Decoy	1953	Morgan, M.	G	DBL	$12.00
ACE	D 10	The Brazos Firebrand	1953	Scott, L.	VG+	DBL	$17.00 A
		Hell On Hoofs		Young, G.			
ACE	D 11	Mrs. Homicide	1953	Keene, D.	VG+	DBL	$27.00 A
		Dead Ahead		Stuart, W.L.			
ACE	D 11	Mrs. Homicide	1953	Keene, D.	VG	DBL	$20.00
ACE	D 13	Cry Plague!	1953	Drachman, T.S.	VGF	DBL	$85.00 A
		The Judas Goat		Edgley, L.			
ACE	D 15	Junkie	1953	Lee, W.*	VG-	DBL	$181.00 A
		Narcotic Agent		Helbrant, M.			
ACE	D 16	Crime d'Amour	1953	Bourget, P.	VG+	DBL	$12.00
		Germinie		De Goncourt, E.			
ACE	D 17	Shakedown	1953	Scott, R.	VG-	DBL	$10.00
		The Darkness Within		Ericson, W.			
ACE	D 18	The Lead Slingers	1953	Leithead, J.E.	VGF	DBL	$14.00
		The Hanging Hills		Ward, B.			
ACE	D 18	The Lead Slingers	1953	Leithead, J.E.	VG+	DBL	$11.00
ACE	D 18	The Lead Slingers	1953	Leithead, J.E.	VG	DBL	$9.00
ACE	D 19	Never Kill A Cop	1953	Colton, M.	G	DBL	$7.00
		Fear No More		Edgley, L.			
ACE	D 21	Nightshade	1953	Makris, J.N.	VG+	DBL	$27.00 A
		High Stakes		Dent, L.			

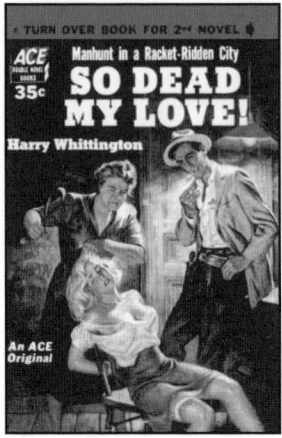

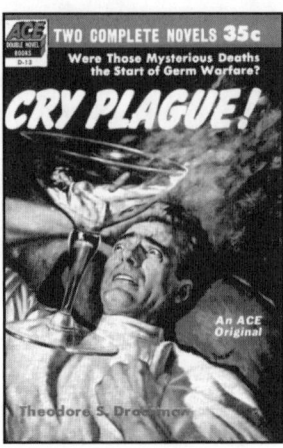

Ace D-7 VG $30　　　　Ace D-11 VG+ $27　　　　Ace D-13 VGF $85

PUBLISHER	PUB. #	TITLE	DATE	AUTHOR	COND.	TYPE	PRICE
ACE	D 22	Mavericks Of The Plains	1953	Lomax, B.	VGF	DBL	$20.00
		Badlands Masquerader		Scott, L.			
ACE	D 22	Mavericks Of The Plains	1953	Lomax, B.	VG	DBL	$20.00 A
ACE	D 23	Passing Strange	1953	Sale, R.	AF	DBL	$18.00 A
		Bring Back Her Body		Brock, S.			
ACE	D 23	Passing Strange	1953	Sale, R.	VG	DBL	$12.00
ACE	D 24	The Sidewinders	1953	Callahan, J.	VGF	DBL	$11.00 A
		Vulture Valley		West, T.			
ACE	D 26	The Impotent General	1953	Pettit, C.	AF	DBL	$39.00 A
		Love In A Junk		Acton, H.			
ACE	D 26	The Impotent General	1953	Pettit, C.	VGF+	DBL	$22.00 A
ACE	D 27	The Fingered Man	1953	Fischer, B.	AF	DBL	$33.00 A
		Double Take		Colton, M.			
ACE	D 27	The Fingered Man	1953	Fischer, B.	VG+	DBL	$22.00
ACE	D 28	Avenger From Nowhere	1953	Vance, W.E.	VG+	DBL	$12.00
		Gunsmoke Kingdom		Evan, P.			
ACE	D 29	The Fast Buck	1953	Laurence, R.	VG+	DBL	$16.00
		Dead Man Friday		Hutton, J.F.			
ACE	D 29	The Fast Buck	1953	Laurence, R.	VG+	DBL	$15.00
ACE	D 29	The Fast Buck	1953	Laurence, R.	VG	DBL	$10.00
ACE	D 29	The Fast Buck	1953	Laurence, R.	G+	DBL	$7.00
ACE	D 30	Johnny Sundance	1953	Ward, B.	AF	DBL	$18.00 A
		South To Sante Fe		Kilrain, G.			
ACE	D 31	Universe Maker	1953	Van Vogt, A.E.	VG	DBL	$7.00
		The World Of Null A		Van Vogt, A.E.			
ACE	D 32	Cookbook For Beginners	1953	Malone, D.	VG+		$8.00
ACE	D 33	About Face	1953	Kane, F.	AF	DBL	$35.00
		Murder By The Pack		Hodges, C.G.			
ACE	D 33	About Face	1953	Kane, F.	VGF	DBL	$23.00 A
ACE	D 33	About Face	1953	Kane, F.	VG+	DBL	$15.00
ACE	D 33	About Face	1953	Kane, F.	VG-	DBL	$8.00
ACE	D 34	Hellion's Hole	1953	Murray, K.	AF	DBL	$18.00 A
		Feud In Piney Flats		Murray, K.			
ACE	D 34	Hellion's Hole	1953	Murray, K.	VG+	DBL	$12.00
ACE	D 37	The Drowning Wire	1953	Claire, M.	VGF	DBL	$44.00 A
		Departure Delayed		Oursler, W.			
ACE	D 37	The Drowning Wire	1953	Claire, M.	VG+	DBL	$17.00 A
ACE	D 37	The Drowning Wire	1953	Claire, M.	VG	DBL	$9.00
ACE	D 38	Showdown At Yellow Butte	1953	Mayo, J.*	VGF	DBL	$206.00 A
		Outlaw River		Lomax, B.			
ACE	D 38	Showdown At Yellow Butte	1953	Mayo, J.*	VG-	DBL	$30.00
ACE	D 38	Showdown At Yellow Butte	1953	Mayo, J.*	G+	DBL	$20.00
ACE	D 39	Quantrell's Raiders	1953	Gruber, F.	VGF	DBL	$47.00 A
		Rebel Road		Gruber, F.			
ACE	D 39	Quantrell's Raiders	1953	Gruber, F.	VG	DBL	$9.00

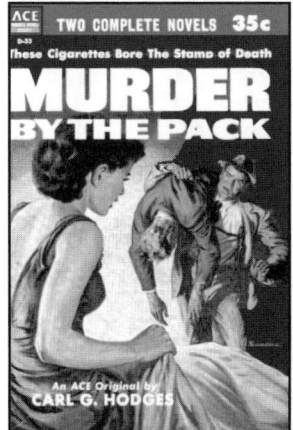

Ace D-21 VG+ $27   Ace D-33 AF $35   Ace D-38 VGF $206

PUBLISHER	PUB. #	TITLE	DATE	AUTHOR	COND.	TYPE	PRICE
ACE	D 39	Quantrell's Raiders	1953	Gruber, F.	G+	DBL	$6.00
ACE	D 40	Waltz Into Darkness	1954	Irish, W.*	VG+	DBL	$32.00 A
		Scylla		Bishop, M.G.			
ACE	D 40	Waltz Into Darkness	1954	Irish, W.*	G	DBL	$16.00
ACE	D 40	Waltz Into Darkness	1954	Irish, W.*	G	DBL	$10.00
ACE	D 42	One Against A Bullet Horde	1954	Tompkins, W.A.	VG+	DBL	$16.00 A
		Law For Tombstone		Martin, C.M.			
ACE	D 43	Salome	1954	Viereck, G.S.	VG+		$33.00 A
ACE	D 44	The Ultimate Invader	1954	Anthology	VGF-	DBL	$20.00
		Sentinels Of Space		Russell, E.F.			
ACE	D 45	Death Hitches A Ride	1954	Weiss, M.L.	VG	DBL	$44.00 A
		Tracked Down		Edgley, L.			
ACE	D 46	Vengeance Valley	1954	Manning, R.	VG	DBL	$12.00
		Law From Back Beyond		Martin, C.			
ACE	D 47	Kiss And Kill	1954	Barry, J.	VG+	DBL	$18.00 A
		On The Hook		Powell, R.			
ACE	D 47	Kiss And Kill	1954	Barry, J.	VG-	DBL	$10.00
ACE	D 48	Utah Blaine	1954	Mayo, J.*	VG	DBL	$110.00 A
		Desert Showdown		Ward, B.			
ACE	D 48	Utah Blaine	1954	Mayo, J.*	AF-	DBL	$82.00 A
ACE	D 49	Tongking!	1954	Cushman, D.	AF	DBL	$88.00 A
		Golden Temptress		Grayson, C.			
ACE	D 49	Tongking!	1954	Cushman, D.	VG	DBL	$10.00
ACE	D 50	Bad 'Un	1954	Grant, O.	VGF+	DBL	$35.00 A
		The Mating Call		Shaw, W.			
ACE	D 51	Over The Edge	1954	Treat, L.	VGF	DBL	$11.00 A
		Switcheroo		McDowell. E.			
ACE	D 52	Crossfire Trail	1954	L'Amour, L.	VGF	DBL	$175.00 A
		Boomtown Bucaneers		MacDonald, W.C.			
ACE	D 52	Crossfire Trail	1954	L'Amour, L.	VG+	DBL	$60.00 A
ACE	D 53	Gateway To Elsewhere	1954	Leinster, M.	VGF	DBL	$53.00 A
		The Weapon Shops Of Isher		Van Vogt, A.E.			
ACE	D 53	Gateway To Elsewhere	1954	Leinster, M.	VGF	DBL	$18.00 A
ACE	D 56	Ambush At Coffin Canyon	1954	Lomax, B.	VGF	DBL	$17.00 A
		Hellbent For A Hangrope		Hardin, C.			
ACE	D 56	Ambush At Coffin Canyon	1954	Lomax, B.	VG+	DBL	$9.00
ACE	D 56	Ambush At Coffin Canyon	1954	Lomax, B.	VG	DBL	$7.00
ACE	D 57	Treachery In Trieste	1954	Leonard, C.L.	VG+	DBL	$16.00 A
		Counterspy Express		Fleischman, A.S.			
ACE	D 57	Treachery In Trieste	1954	Leonard, C.L.	VG	DBL	$8.00
ACE	S 58	Vice, Inc.	1954	Joesten, J.	VGF		$23.00 A
ACE	S 58	Vice, Inc.	1954	Joesten, J.	VGF		$22.00 A
ACE	D 59	Spiderweb	1954	Bloch, R.	VGF	DBL	$51.00 A
		The Corpse In My Bed		Alexander, D.			
ACE	D 59	Spiderweb	1954	Bloch, R.	VG+	DBL	$36.00 A

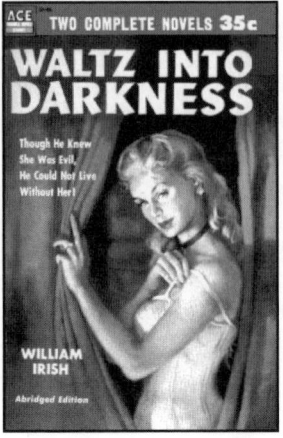

Ace D-40 VG+ $32   Ace D-48 VG $110   Ace D-49 AF $88

PUBLISHER	PUB. #	TITLE	DATE	AUTHOR	COND.	TYPE	PRICE
ACE	D 59	Spiderweb	1954	Bloch, R.	VG	DBL	$33.00 A
ACE	S 60	Marshall Of Medicine Bend	1954	Ward, B.	VG+		$5.00
ACE	D 61	Cosmic Manhunt	1954	De Camp, L.S.	VGF	DBL	$57.00 A
		Ring Around The Sun		Simak, C.D.			
ACE	D 61	Cosmic Manhunt	1954	De Camp, L.S.	VG+	DBL	$18.00
ACE	D 63	You'll Die Next!	1954	Whittington, H.	VG+	DBL	$73.00 A
		Drag The Dark		Davis, F.C.			
ACE	D 63	You'll Die Next!	1954	Whittington, H.	VG	DBL	$15.00
ACE	D 63	You'll Die Next!	1954	Whittington, H.	G	DBL	$7.00
ACE	D 64	Bullets Don't Bluff	1954	Lehman, P.E.	VG+	DBL	$12.00
		Under The Mesa Rim		Whipple, C.			
ACE	D 65	Night Fire	1954	Kimbrough	VG+	DBL	$12.00
		Tornado		Osborne, J.			
ACE	S 66	Return To Tomorrow	1954	Hubbard, L.R.	AF-		$40.00 A
ACE	S 66	Return To Tomorrow	1954	Hubbard, L.R.	VG+		$14.00
ACE	S 66	Return To Tomorrow	1954	Hubbard, L.R.	G+		$7.00
ACE	S 67	The Will To Kill	1954	Bloch, R.	VG		$44.00 A
ACE	S 67	The Will To Kill	1954	Bloch, R.	VG-		$30.00 A
ACE	D 69	Daybreak-2250 A.D.	1954	Norton, A.	VG+	DBL	$10.00
		Beyond Earth's Gates		Padgett, L.			
ACE	D 69	Daybreak-2250 A.D.	1954	Norton, A.	VG	DBL	$7.00
ACE	D 71	Drop Dead!	1954	Ashe, G.	VG	DBL	$10.00
		TCOT Hated Senator		Scherf, M.			
ACE	D 72	The Devil's Saddle	1954	Fox, N.A.	VGF	DBL	$12.00 A
		Nightrider Deputy		Perry, R.R.			
ACE	D 72	The Devil's Saddle	1954	Fox, N.A.	VG	DBL	$7.00
ACE	D 73	Adventures In The Far Future	1954	Anthology	VGF	DBL	$12.00 A
		Tales Of Outer Space		Anthology			
ACE	S 74	Heat Lightning	1954	Shaw, W.	VG+		$10.00
ACE	S 74	Heat Lightning	1954	Shaw, W.	VG		$7.00
ACE	D 77	Catch The Brass Ring	1954	Marlowe, S.	VG	DBL	$12.00
		Stranger At Home		Sanders, G.			
ACE	D 78	The One-Shot Kid	1954	Nye, N.	VGF	DBL	$12.00
		Lobo Legacy		West, T.			
ACE	D 78	The One-Shot Kid	1954	Nye, N.	VG-	DBL	$7.00
ACE	D 79	Atta	1954	Bellamy, F.R.	VGF	DBL	$15.00
		The Brain Stealers		Leinster, M.			
ACE	D 79	Atta	1954	Bellamy, F.R.	VG+	DBL	$8.00
ACE	S 80	The Fear And The Guilt	1954	Shaw, W.	VGF		$35.00 A
ACE	S 80	The Fear And The Guilt	1954	Shaw, W.	VG+		$18.00 A
ACE	D 81	Liability Limited	1954	Saxon, J.A.	VGF	DBL	$22.00
		Too Many Sinners		Stark, S.			
ACE	S 82	Kilkenny	1954	L'Amour, L.	VG		$121.00 A
ACE	S 82	Kilkenny	1954	L'Amour, L.	VG+		$110.00 A
ACE	S 83	The Steel Noose	1954	Drake, A.	VG		$8.00

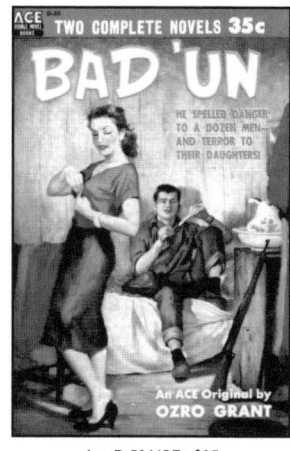

| Ace D-50 VGF+ $35 | Ace D-52 VGF $175 | Ace D-53 VGF $53 |

PUBLISHER	PUB. #	TITLE	DATE	AUTHOR	COND.	TYPE	PRICE
ACE	D 84	The Rebellious Stars *An Earth Gone Mad*	1954	Asimov, I. *Dee, R.*	VGF+	DBL	$17.00
ACE	D 84	The Rebellious Stars	1954	Asimov, I.	VGF-	DBL	$14.00
ACE	D 86	Shoot-Out At Sentinel Peak *Tangled Trail*	1954	Brister, R. *Manning, R.*	VG	DBL	$10.00
ACE	S 87	Why I Am So Beat	1954	Miller, N.	VG		$5.00
ACE	D 88	The 7-Day System	1955	Davis, D.	VG+		$7.00
ACE	D 89	Death Watch *Turn Left For Murder*	1955	Wilson, R. *Marlowe, S.*	VG+	DBL	$13.00
ACE	D 89	Death Watch	1955	Wilson, R.	VG	DBL	$8.00
ACE	S 90	The Chaos Fighters	1955	Williams, R.M.	VGF		$25.00 A
ACE	S 90	The Chaos Fighters	1955	Williams, R.M.	VG+		$12.00
ACE	S 93	Modern Casanova's Handbook	1955	Elmo, H.T.	VG+		$9.00
ACE	D 94	The Other Side Of Here *One Against Eternity*	1955	Leinster, M. *Van Vogt, A.E.*	VGF	DBL	$16.00
ACE	S 95	The Naked Jungle	1955	Whittington, H.	VG+		$20.00
ACE	S 95	The Naked Jungle	1955	Whittington, H.	G		$8.00
ACE	D 96	The Last Planet *A Man Obsessed*	1955	Norton, A. *Nourse, A.E.*	VGF	DBL	$16.00
ACE	D 96	The Last Planet	1955	Norton, A.	VGF	DBL	$15.00
ACE	D 96	The Last Planet	1955	Norton, A.	VG	DBL	$8.00
ACE	D 99	Conquest Of The Space Sea *The Galactic Breed*	1955	Williams, R.M. *Brackett, L.*	VGF	DBL	$17.00
ACE	D 99	Conquest Of The Space Sea	1955	Williams, R.M.	VGF	DBL	$12.00
ACE	D 101	Point Of No Escape *Knock 'Em Dead*	1955	Colton, M. *Karney, J.*	VGF+	DBL	$54.00 A
ACE	S 102	Oath Of Seven	1955	Glay, G.A.	AF		$28.00 A
ACE	S 102	Oath Of Seven	1955	Glay, G.A.	VG		$8.00 A
ACE	D 103	Solar Lottery *The Big Jump*	1955	Dick, P.K. *Brackett, L.*	VG	DBL	$45.00 A
ACE	D 103	Solar Lottery	1955	Dick, P.K.	G+	DBL	$10.00
ACE	S 104	Left Bank Of Desire	1955	Cassill, R.V.	VG+		$10.00
ACE	S 104	Left Bank Of Desire	1955	Cassill, R.V.	VG+		$8.00
ACE	S 105	The Fires Of Youth	1955	De Roo, E.	VG		$17.00 A
ACE	D 106	Lawman Without A Badge *Four Texans North*	1955	Bonar, D.L. *Floren, L.*	VG	DBL	$6.00
ACE	S 107	The Gilded Hideaway	1955	Twist, P.	VGF		$14.00 A
ACE	S 108	Lie Like A Lady	1955	Cody, C.S.	VG+		$8.00
ACE	S 108	Lie Like A Lady	1955	Cody, C.S.	VG		$8.00
ACE	D 109	Mambo To Murder *I See Red*	1955	Clark, D. *Noel, S.*	VG+	DBL	$14.00
ACE	D 109	Mambo To Murder	1955	Clark, D.	VG	DBL	$10.00
ACE	D 109	Mambo To Murder	1955	Clark, D.	VG-	DBL	$7.00
ACE	D 110	The 1,000 Year Plan *No World Of Their Own*	1955	Asimov, I. *Anderson, P.*	AF-	DBL	$20.00

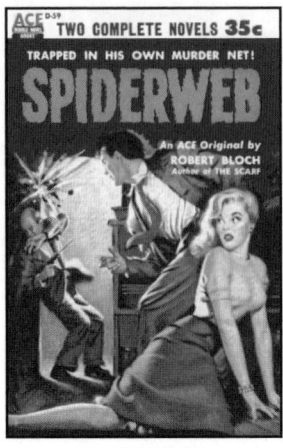

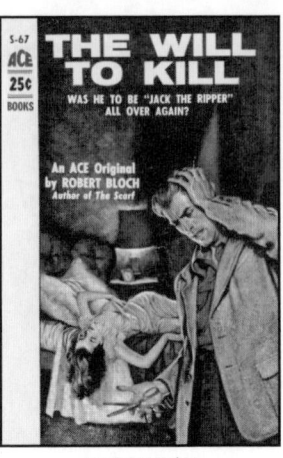

Ace D-59 VGF $51   Ace D-63 VG+ $73   Ace S-67 VG $44

PUBLISHER	PUB. #	TITLE	DATE	AUTHOR	COND.	TYPE	PRICE
ACE	D 110	The 1,000 Year Plan	1955	Asimov, I.	VG+	DBL	$10.00
ACE	S 111	The Smoldering Fire	1955	Kroll, H.H.	G-		$2.00
ACE	D 113	One In 300	1955	McIntosh, J.T.	AF	DBL	$17.00
		The Transposed Man		*Swain, D.V.*			
ACE	D 115	One Got Away	1955	Whittington, H.	VG+	DBL	$44.00 A
		Shady Lady		*Adams, C.F.*			
ACE	S 116	Words Fail Me	1955	House, B., ed.	VG+		$8.00
ACE	D 118	The Paradox Men	1955	Harness, C.L.	VG+	DBL	$9.00 A
		Dome Around America		*Williamson, J.*			
ACE	D 118	The Paradox Men	1955	Harness, C.L.	VG	DBL	$6.00
ACE	S 119	The Driven Flesh	1955	Easton, L.	VGF		$41.00 A
ACE	S 119	The Driven Flesh	1955	Easton, L.	VG		$7.00
ACE	D 121	The Stars Are Ours!	1955	Norton, A.	AF	DBL	$17.00
		Three Faces Of Time		*Merwin, S.*			
ACE	D 121	The Stars Are Ours!	1955	Norton, A.	VGF	DBL	$15.00
ACE	S 122	The Preying Streets	1955	Baker, L.	AF		$49.00 A
ACE	S 122	The Preying Streets	1955	Baker, L.	G		$7.00
ACE	D 123	The Squeeze	1955	Brewer, G.	VG	DBL	$16.00 A
		Love Me To Death		*Diamond, F.*			
ACE	S 124	House Of Deceit	1955	Loomis, R.	VG+		$12.00
ACE	S 126	Washington Bachelor	1955	Berzen, A.H.	VG+		$10.00
ACE	D 128	High Saddle	1955	Hopson, W.	VG+	DBL	$8.00
		Way Station West		*Vance, W.E.*			
ACE	D 128	High Saddle	1955	Hopson, W.	VG+	DBL	$7.00
ACE	D 129	The Dangling Carrot	1955	Keene, D.	VG+	DBL	$24.00 A
		The Silenced Witness		*Rosenthal, N.C.*			
ACE	D 129	The Dangling Carrot	1955	Keene, D.	G+	DBL	$10.00
ACE	S 130	Backlash	1955	Weissman, S.	VG		$8.00
ACE	S 132	Cartoon Annual #2	1955	House, B., ed.	VG		$10.00
ACE	S 133	Adventures On Other Planets	1955	Anthology	VGF		$8.00
ACE	S 133	Adventures On Other Planets	1955	Anthology	VG+		$7.00
ACE	D 134	Tornado On Horseback	1955	Nye, N.	VG+	DBL	$10.00
		The Outsiders		*Olson, G.*			
ACE	D 135	Maid For Murder	1955	Ozaki, M.K.	VG	DBL	$22.00 A
		Dead Ringer		*Chase, J.H.*			
ACE	S 136	A Taste Of Sin	1955	Cassill, R.V.	VGF		$15.00
ACE	S 136	A Taste Of Sin	1955	Cassill, R.V.	VG		$12.00
ACE	S 137	Violent Night	1955	Jackson, R.	AF		$25.00 A
ACE	D 139	Alien From Arcturus	1956	Dickson, G.R.	VGF	DBL	$20.00 A
		Atom Curtain		*Williams, N.B.*			
ACE	D 139	Alien From Arcturus	1956	Dickson, G.R.	AF-	DBL	$17.00
ACE	D 139	Alien From Arcturus	1956	Dickson, G.R.	AF	DBL	$15.00
ACE	D 139	Alien From Arcturus	1956	Dickson, G.R.	VGF	DBL	$12.00
ACE	S 141	Blood On The Branches	1956	Crawford, O.	VG		$8.00
ACE	S 141	Blood On The Branches	1956	Crawford, O.	VG		$7.00

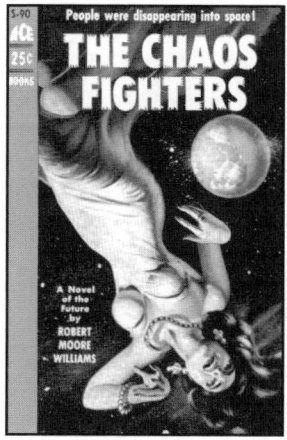

Ace D-77 VG $12   Ace S-82 VG $121   Ace S-90 VGF $25

PUBLISHER	PUB. #	TITLE	DATE	AUTHOR	COND.	TYPE	PRICE
ACE	D 144	A Killer Comes Riding	1956	Patterson, R.	VG	DBL	$8.00
		The Man From Stony Lonesome		*Albert, J.*			
ACE	D 146	The Forgotten Planet	1956	Leinster, M.	AF	DBL	$16.00
		Contraband Rocket		*Correy, L.*			
ACE	D 146	The Forgotten Planet (special ed.)	1956	Leinster, M.	VGF		$15.00
ACE	S 148	The Man From Andersonville	1956	Ward, B.	VG		$6.00
ACE	D 149	A Run For The Money	1956	Clark, D.	G+	DBL	$7.00
		The Thin Edge Of Mania		*Macklin, M.*			
ACE	D 150	The World Jones Made	1956	Dick, P.K.	AF	DBL	$38.00 A
		Agent Of The Unknown		*St. Clair, M.*			
ACE	D 150	The World Jones Made	1956	Dick, P.K.	VGF-	DBL	$38.00 A
ACE	D 150	The World Jones Made	1956	Dick, P.K.	VGF	DBL	$30.00 A
ACE	D 150	The World Jones Made	1956	Dick, P.K.	VGF	DBL	$29.00 A
ACE	D 150	The World Jones Made	1956	Dick, P.K.	VG+	DBL	$18.00 A
ACE	S 152	Medic Mirth	1956	Felsen, H.	VG+		$8.00
ACE	S 152	Medic Mirth	1956	Felsen, H.	VG+		$7.00 A
ACE	S 153	The Wild Seed	1956	Whitney, H.*	G		$8.00
ACE	S 153	The Wild Seed	1956	Whitney, H.*	G		$7.00
ACE	S 153	The Wild Seed	1956	Whitney, H.*	G-		$7.00
ACE	D 154	Voyage To Somewhere	1956	Wilson, S.	VG+		$7.00
ACE	D 155	Journey To Center Of Earth	1956	Verne, J.	AF		$12.00
ACE	D 156	The Naked Range	1956	Lawrence, S.C.	VG+	DBL	$10.00
		Thruway West		*Floren, L.*			
ACE	D 157	Never Say No To A Killer	1956	Gant, J.	VGF	DBL	$40.00 A
		Stab In The Dark		*Trimble, L.*			
ACE	S 158	Golden Girl	1956	Darien, K.	VGF-		$15.00 A
ACE	S 158	Golden Girl	1956	Darien, K.	VG+		$8.00
ACE	S 159	She Shark	1956	Farr, J.	AF		$15.00
ACE	S 159	She Shark	1956	Farr, J.	VGF		$13.00
ACE	D 162	The Mars Monopoly	1956	Sohl, J.	VGF	DBL	$11.00
		The Man Who Lived Forever		*Miller, R.D.*			
ACE	D 164	Mankind On The Run	1956	Dickson, G.R.	VG+	DBL	$10.00
		The Crossroads Of Time		*Norton, A.*			
ACE	S 165	Love And Hisses	1956	House, B., ed.	VG+		$15.00 A
ACE	D 167	Never Say Die	1956	Ozaki, M.K.	VG	DBL	$8.00
		Destroying Angel		*Creighton, J.*			
ACE	D 167	Never Say Die	1956	Ozaki, M.K.	VG-	DBL	$7.00
ACE	S 168	Riverboat Girl	1956	Hoover, P.A.	G+		$6.00
ACE	D 169	Star Bridge	1956	Williamson, J.	VGF+		$14.00
ACE	D 169	Star Bridge	1956	Williamson, J.	VG+		$8.00
ACE	D 170	Flight By Night	1956	Keene, D.	G	DBL	$10.00
		Black Fire		*Goldman, L.*			
ACE	D 170	Flight By Night	1956	Keene, D.	G	DBL	$7.00
ACE	D 172	Johnny No-Name	1956	Smith, B.	VG+	DBL	$8.00 A
		Stage South		*Steelman, R.*			

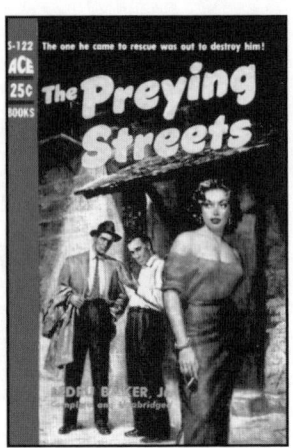

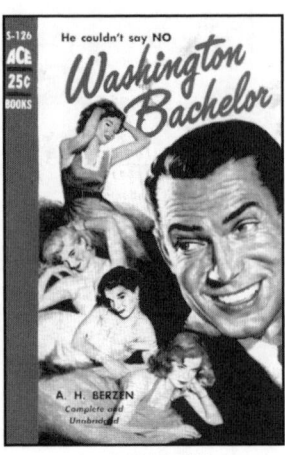

Ace D-109 VG+ $14　　　　Ace S-122 AF $49　　　　Ace S-126 VG+ $10

PUBLISHER	PUB. #	TITLE	DATE	AUTHOR	COND.	TYPE	PRICE
ACE	D 173	Overlords From Space	1956	Kelleam, J.E.	VGF	DBL	$14.00
		The Man Who Mastered Time		Cummings, R.			
ACE	S 174	B-Girl	1956	Novak, R.	VGF		$25.00
ACE	S 174	B-Girl	1956	Novak, R.	AF		$24.00
ACE	D 175	Best Television Humor	1956	Anthology	VGF		$8.00
ACE	D 175	Best Television Humor	1956	Anthology	VG+		$6.00
ACE	D 176	3 Thousand Years	1956	McClary, T.C.	AF	DBL	$17.00
		The Green Queen		St. Clair, M.			
ACE	D 176	3 Thousand Years	1956	McClary, T.C.	AF	DBL	$15.00
ACE	D 177	The Girl In The Cop's Pocket	1956	Turner, R.	VG+	DBL	$10.00
		Violence Is Golden		Thames, C.H.			
ACE	D 177	The Girl In The Cop's Pocket	1956	Turner, R.	VG	DBL	$7.00
ACE	D 178	The Savage City	1956	Paradise, J.	VG		$8.00
ACE	S 179	Squelches	1956	House, B., ed.	VG+		$8.00 A
ACE	S 179	Squelches	1956	House, B., ed.	VG		$8.00
ACE	D 181	New Exploits Of S. Holmes	1956	Carr, J.D.	VGF		$7.00
ACE	D 181	New Exploits Of S. Holmes	1956	Carr, J.D.	VG		$6.00
ACE	D 182	Shame	1956	Zola, E.	VG+	DBL	$8.00
		Therese Raquin		Zola, E.			
ACE	D 182	Shame	1956	Zola, E.	G	DBL	$5.00
ACE	D 184	The Big Ivy	1956	McCague, J.	VG+		$8.00
ACE	D 185	The Humming Box	1956	Whittington, H.	VGF	DBL	$36.00 A
		Build My Gallows High		Homes, G.			
ACE	D 185	The Humming Box	1956	Whittington, H.	VG+	DBL	$27.00 A
ACE	D 185	The Humming Box	1956	Whittington, H.	VG	DBL	$17.00
ACE	D 186	Ex-Marshall	1956	Hogan, R.	VG+	DBL	$10.00
		Steel Horizon		Churchill, E.			
ACE	D 186	Ex-Marshall	1956	Hogan, R.	VG	DBL	$7.00
ACE	D 187	The Pawns Of Null A	1956	Van Vogt, A.E.	AF		$8.00
ACE	D 189	Weep For A Wanton	1956	Treat, L.	VG+	DBL	$14.00 A
		Dead On Arrival		Marlowe, S.			
ACE	D 189	Weep For A Wanton	1956	Treat, L.	VG+	DBL	$10.00
ACE	S 190	The Golden Couch	1956	Nixon, H.L.	VG+		$9.00
ACE	D 191	Apalachee Gold	1956	Slaughter, F.G.	VGF+		$14.00
ACE	D 192	Bad Blood At Black Range	1956	Callahan, J.	VG+	DBL	$12.00
		Beware Of This Tenderfoot		Manning, R.			
ACE	D 193	The Man Who Japed	1956	Dick, P.K.	AF	DBL	$25.00 A
		The Space Born		Tubb, E.C.			
ACE	D 193	The Man Who Japed	1956	Dick, P.K.	VG+	DBL	$22.00
ACE	D 193	The Man Who Japed	1956	Dick, P.K.	G+	DBL	$7.00
ACE	D 194	Moscow	1956	Plievier, T.	AF		$15.00
ACE	D 195	The Deep End	1956	Dudley, O.	VGF+	DBL	$42.00 A
		The Quaking Widow		Colby, R.			
ACE	D 195	The Deep End	1956	Dudley, O.	VG+	DBL	$16.00
ACE	D 195	The Deep End	1956	Dudley, O.	VG	DBL	$7.00

Ace D-129 VG+ $24   Ace S-136 VGF $15   Ace S-174 VGF $25

PUBLISHER	PUB. #	TITLE	DATE	AUTHOR	COND.	TYPE	PRICE
ACE	D 196	The Highwayman	1956	Gruber, F.	VG+	DBL	$8.00
		The Night Branders		Coburn, W.			
ACE	D 196	The Highwayman	1956	Gruber, F.	VG	DBL	$7.00
ACE	D 197	TNT For Two	1956	Byron, J.	VGF	DBL	$33.00 A
		Counterfeit Corpse		Findley, F.			
ACE	D 197	TNT For Two	1956	Byron, J.	G+	DBL	$6.00
ACE	S 198	Tokyo Intrigue (Signed)	1956	Bender, W.	VGF-		$37.00 A
ACE	S 198	Tokyo Intrigue	1956	Bender, W.	F		$10.00 A
ACE	S 198	Tokyo Intrigue	1956	Bender, W.	VG		$5.00
ACE	D 199	Star Guard	1956	Norton, A.	VGF-	DBL	$12.00
		Planet Of No Return		Anderson, P.			
ACE	D 199	Star Guard	1956	Norton, A.	VGF	DBL	$10.00
ACE	D 200	The Report On UFOs	1956	Ruppelt, E.J.	VGF		$7.00
ACE	D 200	The Report On UFOs	1956	Ruppelt, E.J.	VG		$5.00
ACE	D 201	Across That River	1956	Whittington, H.	VG	DBL	$16.00
		Saturday Mountain		Jones, N.E.			
ACE	D 201	Across That River	1956	Whittington, H.	VG	DBL	$10.00
ACE	D 203	Uneasy Lies The Head	1957	Rohde, W.L.	VG+	DBL	$15.00
		Cain's Girl Friend		Grote, W.			
ACE	D 203	Uneasy Lies The Head	1957	Rohde, W.L.	VG+	DBL	$9.00 A
ACE	D 204	John Law, Keep Out!	1957	Durst, P.	VG+	DBL	$5.00
		The Desperate Donigans		Donalds, G.			
ACE	D 206	Great Day In The Morning	1957	Andrews, R.H.	VG		$6.00
ACE	D 207	Hollywood Doctor	1957	Grayson, C.	AF		$14.00
ACE	D 209	Three Times A Victim	1957	Wallace, F.L.	AF	DBL	$27.00 A
		A Night For Treason		Jakes, J.			
ACE	D 210	The Lion At Morning	1957	Longstreet, S.	VGF		$8.00
ACE	D 211	Eye In The Sky	1957	Dick, P.K.	VG+		$33.00 A
ACE	D 211	Eye In The Sky	1957	Dick, P.K.	VG		$14.00
ACE	D 213	How To Stop Killing Yourself	1957	Steinchrohn, P.	G		$5.00
ACE	D 214	Hate Alley	1957	Weiss, M.L.	VG		$37.00 A
ACE	D 215	Three To Conquer	1957	Russell, E.F.	VGF+	DBL	$20.00
		Doomsday Eve		Williams, R.M.			
ACE	D 215	Three To Conquer	1957	Russell, E.F.	AF	DBL	$17.00
ACE	D 215	Three To Conquer	1957	Russell, E.F.	VG	DBL	$8.00
ACE	D 217	Downwind	1957	McKnight, B.	VGF-	DBL	$18.00 A
		A Rage To Kill		Lovell, B.E.			
ACE	D 218	Tigrero!	1957	Siemel, S.	VGF-		$14.00
ACE	S 219	Backwater Woman	1957	Hoover, P.A.	VGF		$52.00 A
ACE	D 221	You've Bet Your Life	1957	Ashe, G.	VG	DBL	$8.00
		The Terror Package		Chavis, R.			
ACE	D 221	You've Bet Your Life	1957	Ashe, G.	VG	DBL	$7.00
ACE	D 222	First On The Rope	1957	Frison-Roche, R.	VG		$6.00
ACE	D 223	The 13th Immortal	1957	Silverberg, R.	VGF	DBL	$17.00
		This Fortress World		Gunn, J.E.			

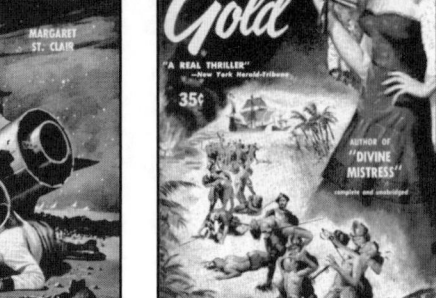

Ace D-176 AF $17   Ace D-191 VGF+ $14   Ace D-211 VG+ 33

PUBLISHER	PUB. #	TITLE	DATE	AUTHOR	COND.	TYPE	PRICE
ACE	D 225	Loser By A Head	1957	Giddings, H.	VG	DBL	$8.00
		A Lonely Walk		*Chaber, M.E.*			
ACE	D 226	Doc Colt	1957	Peeples, S.A.	VG	DBL	$5.00
		Showdown At Warbird		*Booth, E.*			
ACE	D 227	Crisis In 2140	1957	Piper, H.B.	VG+	DBL	$10.00
		Gunner Cade		*Judd, C.*			
ACE	D 227	Crisis In 2140	1957	Piper, H.B.	VG	DBL	$7.00
ACE	D 228	We Die Alone	1957	Howarth, D.	VGF		$10.00
ACE	D 229	Take It Out In Trade	1957	Whitney, W.	VGF+		$30.00 A
ACE	D 231	Point Of Peril	1957	Ronns, E.*	VG+	DBL	$36.00 A
		Murder For Charity		*Dudley, O.*			
ACE	D 233	First On Mars	1957	Gordon, R.	VGF		$8.00
ACE	D 233	First On Mars	1957	Gordon, R.	VG		$6.00
ACE	D 234	Look Of The Eagle	1957	Scott, R.L.	VGF		$9.00
ACE	D 235	The Lady And The Snake	1957	Farr, J.	VGF-	DBL	$12.00
		Nothing To Lose But My Life		*Trimble, L.*			
ACE	D 237	Master Of Life And Death	1957	Silverberg, R.	VGF+	DBL	$17.00
		The Secret Visitors		*White, J.*			
ACE	D 237	Master Of Life And Death	1957	Silverberg, R.	VGF-	DBL	$12.00
ACE	D 237	Master Of Life And Death	1957	Silverberg, R.	VG	DBL	$8.00
ACE	D 238	Go	1957	Holmes, C.	VGF		$70.00 A
ACE	D 238	Go	1957	Holmes, C.	VG		$20.00
ACE	D 238	Go	1957	Holmes, C.	VG		$16.00 A
ACE	D 239	Earth Satellites	1957	Stine, G.H.	VGF+		$7.00
ACE	D 241	One Deadly Dawn	1957	Whittington, H.	VG	DBL	$20.00
		The Hired Target		*Tucker, W.*			
ACE	D 242	Empire Of The Atom	1957	Van Vogt, A.E.	VGF	DBL	$14.00
		Space Station #1		*Long, F.B.*			
ACE	D 242	Empire Of The Atom	1957	Van Vogt, A.E.	VG+	DBL	$8.00
ACE	D 243	The Roving Eye	1957	Wells, M.	AF		$38.00 A
ACE	D 243	The Roving Eye	1957	Wells, M.	VGF		$28.00 A
ACE	D 244	Night Raider Of The Atlantic	1957	Robertson, T.	AF		$12.00
ACE	D 245	Off On A Comet	1957	Verne, J.	AF		$15.00
ACE	D 245	Off On A Comet	1957	Verne, J.	VG		$7.00
ACE	D 246	The Magnate	1957	Harriman, J.	AF		$8.00
ACE	D 247	Look Out Behind You	1957	Lewis, K.	F	DBL	$37.00 A
		Not So Evil As Eve		*Creighton, J.*			
ACE	D 247	Look Out Behind You	1957	Lewis, K.	VG+	DBL	$10.00
ACE	D 247	Look Out Behind You	1957	Lewis, K.	VG	DBL	$10.00
ACE	D 249	The Cosmic Puppets	1957	Dick, P.K.	AF	DBL	$42.00 A
		Sargasso Of Space		*North, A.*			
ACE	D 249	The Cosmic Puppets	1957	Dick, P.K.	VGF	DBL	$36.00 A
ACE	D 249	The Cosmic Puppets	1957	Dick, P.K.	VGF-	DBL	$25.00 A
ACE	D 250	The Terrible Swift Sword	1957	Steuer, A.	VGF		$8.00
ACE	D 251	Windward Passage	1957	Cochran, H.	VG+		$8.00

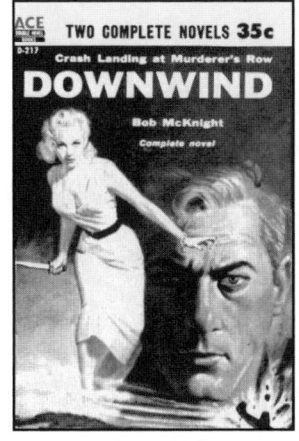

Ace D-214 VG $37   Ace D-217 VGF- $18   Ace S-219 VGF $52

PUBLISHER	PUB. #	TITLE	DATE	AUTHOR	COND.	TYPE	PRICE
ACE	D 253	Marked Down For Murder	1957	Dean, S.	VG	DBL	$5.00
		The Buried Motive		Cassiday, B.			
ACE	D 255	City Under The Sea	1957	Bulmer, K.	AF	DBL	$17.00
		Star Ways		Anderson, P.			
ACE	D 255	City Under The Sea	1957	Bulmer, K.	VG	DBL	$7.00
ACE	D 258	The Long Walk	1957	Rawicz, S.	VGF		$7.00
ACE	D 259	TCOT Violent Virgin	1957	Avallone, M.	VG+	DBL	$25.00
		TCOT Bouncing Betty		Avallone, M.			
ACE	D 260	The Saddle Wolves	1957	Floren, L.	AF	DBL	$10.00
		Land Of The Strangers		Hogan, R.			
ACE	D 261	The Variable Man	1957	Dick, P.K.	VGF		$54.00 A
ACE	D 261	The Variable Man	1957	Dick, P.K.	VGF		$28.00 A
ACE	D 261	The Variable Man	1957	Dick, P.K.	VG+		$21.00
ACE	S 262	Attack!	1957	Jamieson, L.	VG+		$8.00
ACE	S 262	Attack!	1957	Jamieson, L.	VG+		$6.00
ACE	S 263	See How They Run	1957	Shaw, W.	VG+		$15.00
ACE	S 263	See How They Run	1957	Shaw, W.	VGF		$13.00
ACE	S 263	See How They Run	1957	Shaw, W.	VG+		$11.00 A
ACE	S 263	See How They Run	1957	Shaw, W.	VG+		$10.00
ACE	D 266	Twice Upon A Time	1958	Fontenay, C.L.	AF	DBL	$17.00
		The Mechanical Monarch		Tubb, E.C.			
ACE	D 266	Twice Upon A Time	1958	Fontenay, C.L.	VG	DBL	$7.00
ACE	D 267	Speed Demon	1958	Bosworth, J.	VGF		$20.00 A
ACE	D 267	Speed Demon	1958	Bosworth, J.	VG+		$10.00
ACE	D 267	Speed Demon	1958	Bosworth, J.	VG		$10.00
ACE	D 268	Lincoln's Wit	1958	Lincoln, A.	VGF+		$12.00
ACE	D 269	Death In The South Atlantic	1958	Powell, M.	VGF	MTI	$8.00
ACE	D 269	Death In The South Atlantic	1958	Powell, M.	VGF	MTI	$7.00
ACE	D 270	D For Delinquent	1958	Clifton, B.	G		$10.00
ACE	D 271	Lovers And Libertines	1958	Howe, C.	VGF		$8.00
ACE	D 272	Backlash At Cajon Pass	1958	Hopson, W.	VG	DBL	$13.00
		Riders In The Night		Floren, L.			
ACE	S 275	Cartoon Annual #3	1958	House, B., ed.	VG		$7.00
ACE	D 277	Men On The Moon	1958	Anthology	VGF+	DBL	$17.00
		City On The Moon		Leinster, M.			
ACE	D 277	Men On The Moon	1958	Anthology	VG+	DBL	$8.00
ACE	D 277	Men On The Moon	1958	Anthology	VG+	DBL	$7.00
ACE	D 277	Men On The Moon	1958	Anthology	VG	DBL	$7.00
ACE	D 278	This Bright Sword	1958	Chidsey, D.B.	VG+		$7.00
ACE	D 279	Bye Bye, Baby	1958	Bond, J.H.	VG	DBL	$14.00
		Murder Mutual		McNight, B.			
ACE	D 282	Scoundrels, Fiends, Monsters	1958	Howe, C.	VGF		$7.00
ACE	D 283	City	1958	Simak, C.D.	VGF		$8.00
ACE	D 284	The Man Who Killed Tex	1958	Booth, E.	VGF	DBL	$10.00
		The Guns Of Hammer		Cord, B.			

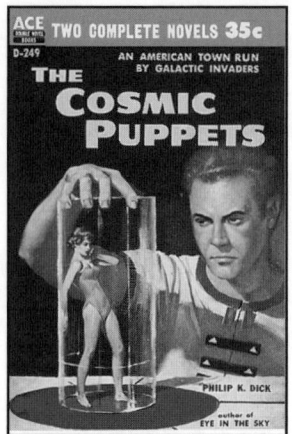

Ace D-234 VGF $9   Ace D-238 VGF $70   Ace D-249 AF $42

PUBLISHER	PUB. #	TITLE	DATE	AUTHOR	COND.	TYPE	PRICE
ACE	D 285	Odd Woman Out	1958	Linklater, J.	VGF	DBL	$18.00
		The Brass Shroud		*Cassiday, B.*			
ACE	D 286	Invaders From Earth	1958	Silverberg, R.	VGF	DBL	$13.00
		Across Time		*Grinnell, D.*			
ACE	D 286	Invaders From Earth	1958	Silverberg, R.	VGF	DBL	$10.00
ACE	D 287	Coral And Brass	1958	Smith, H.M.	VGF+		$8.00
ACE	D 287	Coral And Brass	1958	Smith, H.M.	VGF		$8.00
ACE	D 289	This'll Slay You	1958	Payne, A.	VG	DBL	$8.00
		Violent City		*Hawkins, J.*			
ACE	D 290	A Woman Called Trouble	1958	Hoover, P.A.	AF		$23.00 A
ACE	D 290	A Woman Called Trouble	1958	Hoover, P.A.	VG-		$6.00
ACE	D 291	People Minus X	1958	Gallun, R.Z.	VG	DBL	$7.00
		Lest We Forget Thee, Earth		*Knox, C.M.*			
ACE	D 292	The Insiders	1958	Mooney, B.	VGF		$12.00
ACE	D 292	The Insiders	1958	Mooney, B.	VG		$6.00
ACE	D 293	The Unknown Soldier	1958	Linna, V.	VGF		$7.00
ACE	D 293	The Unknown Soldier	1958	Linna, V.	VG		$7.00
ACE	D 294	Bad Bunch Of The Brasada	1958	Latham, J.H.	G+	DBL	$5.00
		Beyond The Wild Missouri		*Coburn, W.*			
ACE	D 295	Big Planet	1958	Vance, J.	VGF	DBL	$10.00
		Slaves Of The Klau		*Vance, J.*			
ACE	D 295	Big Planet	1958	Vance, J.	VG+	DBL	$8.00
ACE	D 296	Run The River Gauntlet	1958	Clagett, J.	VGF-		$8.00
ACE	D 297	The Cut Of The Whip	1958	Rabe, P.	VGF	DBL	$18.00 A
		Kill One, Kill Two		*Kelston, R.H.*			
ACE	D 297	The Cut Of The Whip	1958	Rabe, P.	VG	DBL	$15.00
ACE	D 297	The Cut Of The Whip	1958	Rabe, P.	G	DBL	$4.00
ACE	D 299	Star Born	1958	Norton, A.	VG+	DBL	$9.00
		A Planet For Texans		*Piper, H.B.*			
ACE	D 299	Star Born	1958	Norton, A.	VG	DBL	$8.00
ACE	D 300	The Dance Merchants	1958	Small, J.W.	AF		$11.00 A
ACE	D 300	The Dance Merchants	1958	Small, J.W.	VGF+		$10.00
ACE	D 301	Murder Isn't Funny	1958	Bond, J.H.	VGF	DBL	$45.00 A
		The Deadly Combo		*Farr, J.*			
ACE	D 302	The Iron King	1958	Druon, M.	VGF		$8.00
ACE	D 306	All Shook Up	1958	Antholz, P.	VG		$30.00 A
ACE	D 309	The Island Of Dr. Moreau	1958	Wells, H.G.	VG+		$7.00
ACE	D 310	Mocambu	1958	Spinelli, M.	VG		$8.00
ACE	D 311	Stepsons Of Terra	1958	Silverberg, R.	AF	DBL	$17.00
		A Man Called Destiny		*Wright, L.*			
ACE	D 311	Stepsons Of Terra	1958	Silverberg, R.	VGF	DBL	$15.00
ACE	D 312	The Deadly Streets	1958	Ellison, H.	VG		$143.00 A
ACE	D 313	Design For Dying	1958	Krasney, S.A.	VG+	DBL	$10.00
		The Deadly Boodle		*Flynn, J.M.*			
ACE	D 314	Deeds Of Darkness	1958	Ashton, B.	VG		$6.00

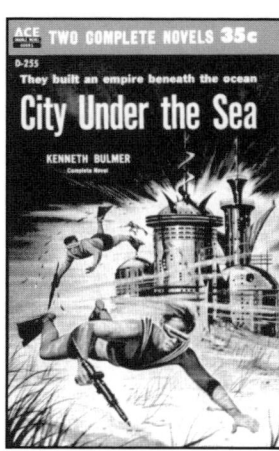

Ace D-255 AF $17   Ace D-267 VGF $20   Ace D-279 VG $14

PUBLISHER	PUB. #	TITLE	DATE	AUTHOR	COND.	TYPE	PRICE
ACE	D 315	The Space Willies	1958	Russell, E.F.	VGF	DBL	$10.00
		Six Worlds Yonder		Russell, E.F.			
ACE	D 315	The Space Willies	1958	Russell, E.F.	VG-	DBL	$6.00
ACE	D 316	Mesquite Johnny	1958	Cord, B.	AF	DBL	$10.00
		A Time For Guns		Patterson, R.			
ACE	D 316	Mesquite Johnny	1958	Cord, B.	VG+	DBL	$8.00
ACE	D 317	The Big Bite	1958	Travis, G.	VGF	DBL	$17.00
		The Wayward Blonde		Creighton, J.			
ACE	D 318	Captain Crossbones	1958	Chidsey, D.B.	AF		$8.00
ACE	D 319	The Man With Three Faces	1958	Meissner, H.O.	F		$10.00
ACE	D 319	The Man With Three Faces	1958	Meissner, H.O.	VG+		$7.00
ACE	D 321	Trial By Perjury	1958	Creighton, J.	VG+	DBL	$14.00
		The Smell Of Trouble		Trimble, L.			
ACE	D 322	The Blue Atom	1958	Williams, R.M.	VG+	DBL	$9.00
		The Void Beyond		Williams, R.M.			
ACE	D 324	Brigands Of The Moon	1958	Cummings, R.	VGF		$8.00
ACE	D 324	Brigands Of The Moon	1958	Cummings, R.	VG		$7.00
ACE	D 325	July, 1863	1958	Werstein, I.	AF		$10.00
ACE	D 326	Battling The Bombers	1958	Johnen, W.	AF		$7.00
ACE	D 327	First On The Moon	1958	Sutton, J.	VGF		$14.00
ACE	D 327	First On The Moon	1958	Sutton, J.	VGF		$10.00
ACE	D 327	First On The Moon	1958	Sutton, J.	VG+		$6.00
ACE	D 328	The Fourth Gunman	1958	Costiner, M.	AF	DBL	$14.00
		Slick On The Draw		West, T.			
ACE	D 328	The Fourth Gunman	1958	Costiner, M.	VG+	DBL	$10.00
ACE	D 329	Three For The Gallows	1958	McDowell, E.	VG	DBL	$6.00
		Stamped For Death		McDowell, E.			
ACE	D 330	Muscle Boy	1958	Clifton, B.	AF		$28.00 A
ACE	D 330	Muscle Boy	1958	Clifton, B.	VG+		$12.00
ACE	D 330	Muscle Boy	1958	Clifton, B.	VG		$8.00
ACE	D 331	Beyond The Vanishing Point	1958	Cummings, R.	VGF	DBL	$15.00
		The Secret Of Zi		Buler, K.			
ACE	D 331	Beyond The Vanishing Point	1958	Cummings, R.	VGF+	DBL	$12.00
ACE	D 331	Beyond The Vanishing Point	1958	Cummings, R.	VGF+	DBL	$10.00
ACE	D 332	Blood On Boot Hill	1959	Welles, K.	VG-	DBL	$6.00
		Stranger In Sundown		Smith, B.			
ACE	D 333	Scream Street	1959	Brett, M.	VG+	DBL	$12.00
		Stranglehold		Creighton, J.			
ACE	D 334	Queen Of The Flat-Tops	1959	Johnston, S.	AF		$8.00
ACE	D 335	The War Of Two Worlds	1959	Anderson, P.	AF	DBL	$11.00
		Threshold Of Eternity		Brunner, J.			
ACE	D 340	Solar Lottery	1959	Dick, P.K.	VG+		$15.00
ACE	D 340	Solar Lottery	1959	Dick, P.K.	VG-		$7.00
ACE	D 341	The Marina Street Girls	1959	Loomis, R.	F		$15.00
ACE	D 341	The Marina Street Girls	1959	Loomis, R.	AF		$12.00

Ace D-300 AF $11   Ace D-306 VG $30   Ace D-331 VGF $15

PUBLISHER	PUB. #	TITLE	DATE	AUTHOR	COND.	TYPE	PRICE
ACE	D 342	Queen's Blade	1959	Gorham, N.	VGF		$8.00
ACE	D 343	The Young Wolves	1959	De Roo, E.	VG+		$48.00 A
ACE	D 345	Voodoo Planet	1959	North, A.	AF	DBL	$16.00
		Plague Ship		North, A.			
ACE	D 345	Voodoo Planet	1959	North, A.	VGF	DBL	$12.00
ACE	D 346	Sheriff Of Big Hat	1959	Cord, B.	AF	DBL	$10.00
		Wanted: Alive!		Hogan, R.			
ACE	D 347	Play For Keeps	1959	Whittington, H.	VG+	DBL	$15.00 A
		The Corpse Without A Country		Trimble, L.			
ACE	D 347	Play For Keeps	1959	Whittington, H.	VG+	DBL	$14.00
ACE	D 347	Play For Keeps	1959	Whittington, H.	G+	DBL	$10.00
ACE	D 347	Play For Keeps	1959	Whittington, H.	G	DBL	$9.00
ACE	D 349	The Guilty Bystander	1959	Brett, M.	VG+	DBL	$14.00
		Kill Me With Kindness		Bond, J.H.			
ACE	D 349	The Guilty Bystander	1959	Brett, M.	VG	DBL	$7.00
ACE	D 350	Red Alert	1959	Bryant, P.	VGF		$8.00
ACE	D 350	Red Alert	1959	Bryant, P.	VGF		$7.00
ACE	D 351	The Sun Smasher	1959	Hamilton, E.	AF	DBL	$17.00
		Starhaven		Jorgenson, I.			
ACE	D 351	The Sun Smasher	1959	Hamilton, E.	VGF	DBL	$10.00
ACE	G 352	Fire And Morning	1959	Leary, F.	VG+		$7.00
ACE	D 353	The Macabre Reader	1959	Anthology	VGF		$13.00
ACE	D 353	The Macabre Reader	1959	Anthology	AF		$10.00
ACE	D 354	The Hidden Planet	1959	Anthology	VGF		$8.00
ACE	D 354	The Hidden Planet	1959	Anthology	VG+		$6.00
ACE	D 355	The Beachhead Spies	1959	Strutton, B.	AF-		$8.00
ACE	D 355	The Beachhead Spies	1959	Strutton, B.	VG		$5.00
ACE	D 357	Lady In Peril	1959	Dent, L.	AF	DBL	$73.00 A
		Wired For Scandal		Wallace, F.			
ACE	D 357	Lady In Peril	1959	Dent, L.	VGF	DBL	$25.00 A
ACE	D 358	The Plot Against Earth	1959	Knox, C.M.	AF	DBL	$17.00
		Recruit For Andromeda		Lesser, M.			
ACE	D 358	The Plot Against Earth	1959	Knox, C.M.	VG+	DBL	$8.00
ACE	D 359	The Haunted Strangler	1959	Cooper, J.C.	VG+	MTI	$7.00
ACE	D 359	The Haunted Strangler	1959	Cooper, J.C.	G	MTI	$5.00
ACE	D 360	Johnny Sixgun	1959	Latham, J.	AF	DBL	$12.00
		War In Peaceful Valley		Cord, B.			
ACE	D 361	Dangerous To Know	1959	Duff, J.P.	VG-	DBL	$5.00
		Murder Mistress		Colby, R.			
ACE	D 362	Edge Of Time	1959	Grinnell, D.	F	DBL	$15.00
		The 100th Millennium		Brunner, J.			
ACE	D 362	Edge Of Time	1959	Grinnell, D.	VG+	DBL	$7.00
ACE	D 363	The Rapist	1959	Krasney, S.A.	VGF		$40.00 A
ACE	D 363	The Rapist	1959	Krasney, S.A.	G		$6.00
ACE	D 364	The Pipes Are Calling	1959	Chidsey, D.B.	VG+		$7.00

Ace D-340 VG+ $15   Ace D-343 VG+ $48   Ace D-345 AF $16

PUBLISHER	PUB. #	TITLE	DATE	AUTHOR	COND.	TYPE	PRICE
ACE	D 365	MIG Alley	1959	Eunson, R.	VGF		$8.00
ACE	D 366	The Invaders Are Coming	1959	Nourse, A.E.	AF		$15.00
ACE	D 366	The Invaders Are Coming	1959	Nourse, A.E.	VGF		$8.00
ACE	D 367	Till Death Do Us Part	1959	Trimble, L.	VGF	DBL	$15.00
		Negative Of A Nude		*Fritch, C.E.*			
ACE	D 367	Till Death Do Us Part	1959	Trimble, L.	VG+	DBL	$14.00
ACE	D 369	The Changeling Worlds	1959	Bulmer, K.	VGF	DBL	$15.00
		Vanguard From Alpha		*Aldiss, B.W.*			
ACE	D 369	The Changeling Worlds	1959	Bulmer, K.	VGF	DBL	$10.00
ACE	G 371	Berlin	1959	Plievier, T.	VGF+		$8.00
ACE	D 374	The Thoroughbred And The Tramp	1959	Leonard, B.	F		$12.00
ACE	D 374	The Thoroughbred And The Tramp	1959	Leonard, B.	AF		$10.00
ACE	D 375	Fire In The Heavens	1959	Smith, G.O.	VG+	DBL	$10.00
		Masters Of Evolution		*Knight, D.*			
ACE	D 377	Bombs In Orbit	1959	Sutton, J.	VGF		$8.00
ACE	D 377	Bombs In Orbit	1959	Sutton, J.	AF		$7.00
ACE	D 378	Out For Kicks	1959	Shaw, W.	VGF		$20.00 A
ACE	D 378	Out For Kicks	1959	Shaw, W.	VG-		$14.00
ACE	D 381	Secret Of The Lost Race	1959	Norton, A.	AF	DBL	$12.00
		One Against Herculum		*Sohl, J.*			
ACE	D 381	Secret Of The Lost Race	1959	Norton, A.	VG+	DBL	$10.00
ACE	D 381	Secret Of The Lost Race	1959	Norton, A.	VG	DBL	$6.00
ACE	G 382	The Willing Maid	1959	Ritchie, C.T.	VG+		$8.00
ACE	D 383	The Murder Specialist	1959	Clifton, B.	VGF		$49.00 A
ACE	D 383	The Murder Specialist	1959	Clifton, B.	G+		$5.00
ACE	G 386	The Sulu Sword	1959	O'Connor, R.	VGF		$10.00
ACE	D 387	The Bikini Bombshell	1959	McKnight, B.	VG	DBL	$8.00
		Fare Prey		*Fisher, L.*			
ACE	D 388	When The Sleeper Wakes	1959	Wells, H.G.	AF		$16.00
ACE	D 389	No Entry	1959	Coles, M.	AF		$12.00
ACE	D 389	No Entry	1959	Coles, M.	VG+		$8.00
ACE	D 391	Siege Of The Unseen	1959	Van Vogt, A.E.	AF	DBL	$14.00
		The World Swappers		*Brunner, J.*			
ACE	D 391	Siege Of The Unseen	1959	Van Vogt, A.E.	VG+	DBL	$10.00
ACE	D 394	The Flaming Island	1959	Chidsey, D.B.	AF		$8.00
ACE	D 394	The Flaming Island	1959	Chidsey, D.B.	VG		$6.00
ACE	D 395	Thunder At Harper's Ferry	1959	Keller, A.	VGF+		$12.00
ACE	D 397	Journey To Center Of Earth	1959	Verne, J.	VGF		$8.00
ACE	D 398	Why I Am So Beat	1959	Miller, N.	AF		$50.00 A
ACE	D 398	Why I Am So Beat	1959	Miller, N.	VGF		$33.00 A
ACE	D 400	Shadow Of A Gunman	1959	Shirreffs, G.D.	AF-	DBL	$14.00
		Last Chance At Devil's Canyon		*Cord, B.*			
ACE	D 401	Obit Deferred	1959	Trimble, L.	VG	DBL	$7.00
		I Want Out		*Thomey, T.*			
ACE	D 401	Obit Deferred	1959	Trimble, L.	VG	DBL	$5.00

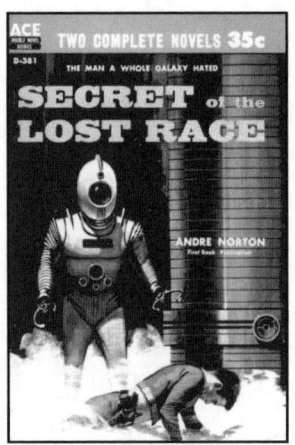

Ace D-357 AF $73   Ace D-381 AF $12   Ace D-427 AF $17

PUBLISHER	PUB. #	TITLE	DATE	AUTHOR	COND.	TYPE	PRICE
ACE	G 402	Kiboko	1959	Mannix, D.P.	AF		$14.00 A
ACE	G 402	Kiboko	1959	Mannix, D.P.	VG+		$12.00
ACE	D 403	The Pirates Of Zan	1959	Leinster, M.	AF	DBL	$14.00
		The Mutant Weapon		*Leinster, M.*			
ACE	D 403	The Pirates Of Zan	1959	Leinster, M.	VG	DBL	$7.00
ACE	D 405	First To The Stars	1959	Gordon, R.	VG+		$8.00
ACE	D 405	First To The Stars	1959	Gordon, R.	VG+		$7.00
ACE	D 406	Go, Man, Go	1959	De Roo, E.	VG		$35.00 A
ACE	D 407	The Planet Killers	1959	Silverberg, R.	VGF	DBL	$8.00
		We Claim These Stars!		*Anderson, P.*			
ACE	D 407	The Planet Killers	1959	Silverberg, R.	VG-	DBL	$2.50
ACE	D 411	Swamp Sanctuary	1959	McKnight, B.	VG		$10.00
ACE	D 413	The Man With Nine Lives	1960	Ellison, H.	VGF	DBL	$30.00 A
		A Touch Of Infinity		*Ellison, H.*			
ACE	D 415	Dead Certain	1960	Sterling, S.	VGF	DBL	$22.00 A
		Fire On Fear Street		*Sterling, S.*			
ACE	D 415	Dead Certain	1960	Sterling, S.	VG+	DBL	$16.00
ACE	D 416	The Big Question	1960	Kenneth, J.	VG		$7.00
ACE	D 418	Nothing But My Gun	1960	West, T.	VG+	DBL	$9.00
		The Quiet Ones		*Park, C.S.*			
ACE	D 419	Open Season	1960	Thielen, B.	VGF	DBL	$10.00
		A Slice Of Death		*McKnight, B.*			
ACE	D 419	Open Season	1960	Thielen, B.	VG	DBL	$8.00
ACE	D 420	The Angry Ones	1960	Williams, J.A.	VG		$29.00 A
ACE	D 421	Dr. Futurity	1960	Dick, P.K.	AF-	DBL	$21.00 A
		Slavers Of Space		*Brunner, J.*			
ACE	D 421	Dr. Futurity	1960	Dick, P.K.	G	DBL	$5.00
ACE	D 422	Best From Fantasy & Sci-Fi #3	1960	Anthology	AF		$8.00
ACE	D 422	Best From Fantasy & Sci-Fi #3	1960	Anthology	VGF		$7.00
ACE	D 423	Tidal Wave	1960	Norton, B.	VG+		$5.00
ACE	D 424	Shoot-Out At The Way Station	1960	Richards, L.	VG+	DBL	$8.00
		Wild Justice		*McCaig, R.*			
ACE	D 425	Dig Her A Grave	1960	Kruger, P.	VG+	DBL	$9.00
		A Half Interest In Murder		*Creighton, J.*			
ACE	D 426	Penal Colony	1960	Close, R.S.	VGF		$27.00 A
ACE	D 426	Penal Colony	1960	Close, R.S.	VG		$12.00
ACE	D 427	World Of The Masterminds	1960	Williams, R.M.	AF	DBL	$17.00
		To The End Of Time		*Williams, R.M.*			
ACE	D 427	World Of The Masterminds	1960	Williams, R.M.	VG+	DBL	$7.00
ACE	D 428	Scowtown Woman	1960	Hoover, P.A.	VG+		$28.00 A
ACE	D 428	Scowtown Woman	1960	Hoover, P.A.	G+		$5.00
ACE	D 429	The Anatomy Of Violence	1960	Runyon, C.	VG		$8.00
ACE	D 429	The Anatomy Of Violence	1960	Runyon, C.	G+		$6.00
ACE	D 431	Earth's Last Fortress	1960	Van Vogt, A.E.	VGF	DBL	$13.00
		Lost In Space		*Smith, G.O.*			

Ace D-431 VGF $13   Ace D-446 VGF $34   Ace D-452 VG $18

PUBLISHER	PUB. #	TITLE	DATE	AUTHOR	COND.	TYPE	PRICE
ACE	D 432	Convention Queen	1960	Broward, D.	VGF		$8.00
ACE	D 432	Convention Queen	1960	Broward, D.	G-		$3.00
ACE	D 433	If Hate Could Kill	1960	Bradley, J.	VG	DBL	$8.00
		The Smasher		*Powell, T.*			
ACE	D 433	If Hate Could Kill	1960	Bradley, J.	VG	DBL	$7.00
ACE	D 434	Purchase Of The North Pole	1960	Verne, J.	VGF		$7.00
ACE	D 436	The Challenger	1960	Lutz, G.A.	AF	DBL	$14.00
		The Phantom Pistoleer		*West, T.*			
ACE	D 436	The Challenger	1960	Lutz, G.A.	VGF	DBL	$12.00
ACE	D 437	And Then The Town Took Off	1960	Wilson, R.	AF	DBL	$14.00
		The Sioux Spaceman		*Norton, A.*			
ACE	D 437	And Then The Town Took Off	1960	Wilson, R.	VGF	DBL	$12.00
ACE	D 438	The Panic Button	1960	Fogg, C.	AF		$8.00 A
ACE	G 440	Letter Of Marque	1960	Hepburn, A.	VG+		$8.00
ACE	D 441	Skip Bomber	1960	Olson, L.E.	VG+		$6.00
ACE	D 442	Killer's Paradise	1960	Bickham, J.M.	VGF	DBL	$6.00
		Riders Of The Rincon		*Patterson, R.*			
ACE	D 443	Bow Down To Nul	1960	Aldiss, B.W.	AF	DBL	$10.00
		The Dark Destroyers		*Wellman, M.W.*			
ACE	D 443	Bow Down To Nul	1960	Aldiss, B.W.	VG+	DBL	$10.00
ACE	D 444	Desire Island	1960	Rifkin, S.	VGF		$16.00 A
ACE	D 445	In At The Kill	1960	McDowell, E.	VG+	DBL	$10.00
		Bloodline To Murder		*McDowell, E.*			
ACE	D 446	Flight 685 Is Overdue	1960	Moore, E.	VGF		$34.00 A
ACE	D 446	Flight 685 Is Overdue	1960	Moore, E.	VG		$7.00
ACE	D 447	The Hot Chariot	1960	Flynn, J.M.	VG	DBL	$8.00
		Kiss The Babe Goodbye		*McKnight, B.*			
ACE	D 447	The Hot Chariot	1960	Flynn, J.M.	VG	DBL	$6.00
ACE	D 449	Time To Teleport	1960	Dickson, G.R.	AF	DBL	$15.00
		The Genetic General		*Dickson, G.R.*			
ACE	D 451	Odds Against Linda	1960	Ward, S.	VGF	DBL	$22.00
		A Key To The Morgue		*Martin, R.*			
ACE	D 451	Odds Against Linda	1960	Ward, S.	VGF-	DBL	$10.00
ACE	D 452	The Color Of Hate	1960	Hensley, J.L.	VG		$18.00 A
ACE	D 453	The Games Of Neith	1960	St. Clair, M.	VGF	DBL	$12.00
		The Earth Gods Are Coming		*Bulmer, K.*			
ACE	D 453	The Games Of Neith	1960	St. Clair, M.	VGF	DBL	$8.00
ACE	D 455	Best From Fantasy & Sci-Fi #4	1960	Boucher, A.	VGF		$7.00
ACE	D 455	Best From Fantasy & Sci-Fi #4	1960	Boucher, A.	VG+		$7.00
ACE	D 456	Danger Trail	1960	Booth, E.	VG+	DBL	$7.00
		The Desperate Dude		*Booth, E.*			
ACE	D 457	Vulcan's Hammer	1960	Dick, P.K.	VG+	DBL	$25.00 A
		The Skynappers		*Brunner, J.*			
ACE	D 458	Womanhunt	1960	Derby, M.	VGF		$10.00
ACE	D 458	Womanhunt	1960	Derby, M.	VG+		$8.00

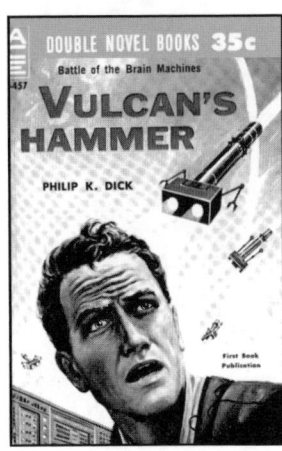

Ace D-457 VG+ $25   Ace D-469 VG+ $36   Ace D-472 VG $75

PUBLISHER	PUB. #	TITLE	DATE	AUTHOR	COND.	TYPE	PRICE
ACE	D 458	Womanhunt	1960	Derby, M.	VG		$7.00
ACE	D 459	The Hot Diary	1960	Olmsted, H.J.	VG+	DBL	$9.00
		Ring Around A Rogue		Flynn, J.M.			
ACE	D 461	The Time Traders	1960	Norton, A.	VG		$5.00
ACE	D 463	Dying Room Only	1960	Sterling, S.	VG+	DBL	$12.00
		The Body In The Bed		Sterling, S.			
ACE	D 464	Tame The Wild Flesh	1960	Shaw, W.	VG		$7.00
ACE	D 465	The Atlantic Abomination	1960	Brunner, J.	AF	DBL	$15.00
		The Martian Missile		Grinnell, D.			
ACE	D 466	Wild Bill Hickock	1960	O'Connor, R.	VGF		$12.00
ACE	D 467	5,4,3,2,1-Pfftt	1960	Anderson, W.C.	VG+		$8.00 A
ACE	D 468	Sentinels Of Space	1960	Russell, E.F.	AF		$18.00 A
ACE	D 468	Sentinels Of Space	1960	Russell, E.F.	VGF		$8.00
ACE	D 468	Sentinels Of Space	1960	Russell, E.F.	VG-		$6.00
ACE	D 469	Man-Killer	1960	Powell, T.	VG+	DBL	$36.00 A
		Running Scared		McKnight, B.			
ACE	D 471	Sanctuary In The Sky	1960	Brunner, J.	VGF+	DBL	$14.00
		The Secret Martians		Sharkey, J.			
ACE	D 471	Sanctuary In The Sky	1960	Brunner, J.	VGF+	DBL	$13.00
ACE	D 471	Sanctuary In The Sky	1960	Brunner, J.	VG+	DBL	$9.00
ACE	D 471	Sanctuary In The Sky	1960	Brunner, J.	VG	DBL	$6.00
ACE	D 472	A Night For Screaming	1960	Whittington, H.	VG		$75.00 A
ACE	D 473	The Greatest Adventure	1960	Taine, J.	VGF		$6.00
ACE	D 477	The Duchess Of Skid Row	1960	Trimble, L.	VG	DBL	$8.00
		Love Me And Die		Trimble, L.			
ACE	D 478	Spacehive	1960	Sutton, J.	VGF		$7.00
ACE	D 479	To The Tombaugh Station	1960	Tucker, W.	AF	DBL	$14.00
		Earthman, Go Home!		Anderson, P.			
ACE	D 479	To The Tombaugh Station	1960	Tucker, W.	VGF	DBL	$13.00
ACE	D 479	To The Tombaugh Station	1960	Tucker, W.	AF	DBL	$12.00
ACE	G 480	The Strong Men	1960	Brick, J.	VGF		$8.00
ACE	G 480	The Strong Men	1960	Brick, J.	AF		$7.00
ACE	G 480	The Strong Men	1960	Brick, J.	VG		$6.00
ACE	D 481	The Biggest Holdup	1960	Dinneen, J.F.	VGF		$8.00
ACE	D 482	The Weapon Shops Of Isher	1961	Van Vogt, A.E.	AF-		$8.00
ACE	D 482	The Weapon Shops Of Isher	1961	Van Vogt, A.E.	VGF		$8.00
ACE	D 483	The Corpse In Picture Window	1961	Cassiday, B.	VG	DBL	$7.00
		If Wishes Were Hearses		Bond, J.H.			
ACE	D 485	The Angry Espers	1961	Biggle, L.	AF	DBL	$15.00
		The Puzzle Planet		Lowndes, R.			
ACE	D 485	The Angry Espers	1961	Biggle, L.	VGF	DBL	$12.00
ACE	D 486	The Little Caesars	1961	De Roo, E.	VGF		$22.00 A
ACE	D 488	Third Time Down	1961	Brennan, D.	VG		$4.00
ACE	D 489	Dally With A Deadly Doll	1961	Miles, J.	VG	DBL	$10.00
		Somebody's Walking Over My Grave		Arthur, R.			

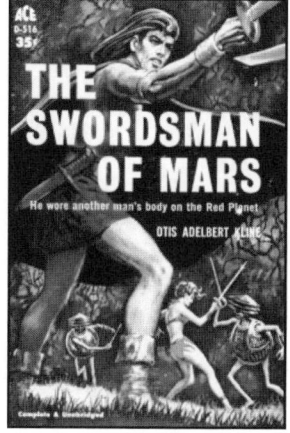

Ace D-499 VGF $41   Ace D-503 VG+ 12   Ace D-516 AF $15

PUBLISHER	PUB. #	TITLE	DATE	AUTHOR	COND.	TYPE	PRICE
ACE	D 492	Winter Drive	1961	Hopson, W.	VG+	DBL	$8.00
		The Wild Quarry		*Lutz, G.A.*			
ACE	D 493	The Queen's Awards	1961	Queen, E.	VGF		$5.00
ACE	D 494	Log Jam	1961	White, L.T.	AF		$10.00
ACE	D 494	Log Jam	1961	White, L.T.	G+		$6.00
ACE	D 496	With Blood In Their Eyes	1961	Lawrence, S.G.	VG+	DBL	$8.00
		Killer's Canyon		*West, T.*			
ACE	D 497	Wandl The Invader	1961	Cummings, R.	VGF	DBL	$12.00
		I Speak For Earth		*Woodcott, K.*			
ACE	D 497	Wandl The Invader	1961	Cummings, R.	VG+	DBL	$8.00
ACE	D 498	Galactic Derelict	1961	Norton, A.	AF		$7.00
ACE	D 499	High Heel Homicide	1961	Davis, F.C.	VGF	DBL	$41.00 A
		Night Drop		*Davis, F.C.*			
ACE	D 499	High Heel Homicide	1961	Davis, F.C.	VG+	DBL	$12.00
ACE	D 499	High Heel Homicide	1961	Davis, F.C.	VG+	DBL	$10.00
ACE	D 499	High Heel Homicide	1961	Davis, F.C.	VG	DBL	$6.00
ACE	D 501	Let Him Go Hang	1961	Clifton, B.	VG+		$12.00
ACE	D 503	The Girl In The Death Seat	1961	Nichols, F.	VG+		$12.00
ACE	D 503	The Girl In The Death Seat	1961	Nichols, F.	VG-		$7.00
ACE	D 504	Master Of The World	1961	Verne, J.	AF	MTI	$8.00
ACE	D 504	Master Of The World	1961	Verne, J.	VGF	MTI	$6.00
ACE	D 504	Master Of The World	1961	Verne, J.	VG+	MTI	$6.00
ACE	D 505	The Surfside Caper	1961	Trimble, L.	VGF	DBL	$12.00
		In A Vanishing Room		*Colby, R.*			
ACE	D 505	The Surfside Caper	1961	Trimble, L.	VG	DBL	$8.00
ACE	D 507	Beyond The Silver Sky	1961	Bulmer, K.	VGF+	DBL	$12.00
		Meeting At Infinity		*Brunner, J.*			
ACE	D 507	Beyond The Silver Sky	1961	Bulmer, K.	VGF	DBL	$12.00
ACE	D 507	Beyond The Silver Sky	1961	Bulmer, K.	G	DBL	$4.00
ACE	D 508	More Macabre	1961	Anthology	AF-		$13.00
ACE	D 508	More Macabre	1961	Anthology	VGF		$10.00
ACE	D 508	More Macabre	1961	Anthology	VG+		$8.00
ACE	D 509	The Beast Master	1961	Norton, A.	AF	DBL	$15.00
		Star Hunter		*Norton, A.*			
ACE	D 509	The Beast Master	1961	Norton, A.	VGF+	DBL	$12.00
ACE	D 509	The Beast Master	1961	Norton, A.	VG	DBL	$7.00
ACE	D 510	The Searching Rider	1961	Whittington, H.	VGF	DBL	$15.00
		Hangman's Territory		*Bickham, J.M.*			
ACE	D 510	The Searching Rider	1961	Whittington, H.	VG	DBL	$6.00
ACE	D 511	One For The Death House	1961	Flynn, J.M.	VGF	DBL	$14.00
		Drop Dead, Please		*McKnight, B.*			
ACE	D 515	Kill Me A Fortune	1961	Colby, R.	VG+	DBL	$8.00
		Five Alarm Funeral		*Sterling, S.*			
ACE	D 516	The Swordsman Of Mars	1961	Kline, O.A.	AF		$15.00 A
ACE	D 516	The Swordsman Of Mars	1961	Kline, O.A.	VGF+		$11.00

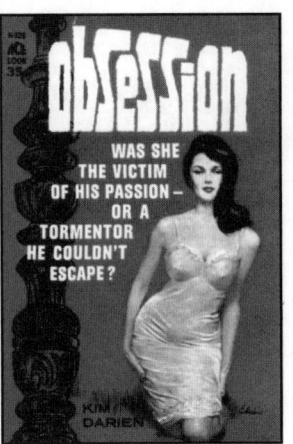

Ace D-518 VG+ $28   Ace D-526 VG+ $10   Ace D-533 VG+ $10

PUBLISHER	PUB. #	TITLE	DATE	AUTHOR	COND.	TYPE	PRICE
ACE	D 517	Bring Back Yesterday	1961	Chandler, A.B.	VGF	DBL	$15.00
		The Trouble With Tycho		Simster, C.D.			
ACE	D 518	Nightmare Cruise	1961	Miller, W.	VG+		$28.00 A
ACE	D 518	Nightmare Cruise	1961	Miller, W.	G+		$6.00
ACE	D 519	Air Rescue!	1961	Glines, C.V.	VGF		$8.00
ACE	D 520	One Foot In Hell	1961	Shaw, W.	AF		$10.00 A
ACE	D 520	One Foot In Hell	1961	Shaw, W.	VG+		$10.00
ACE	D 522	A Nest Of Fear	1961	Ellson, H.	VG+		$12.00 A
ACE	D 523	Strike The Black Flag	1961	Scotland, J.*	G+		$6.00
ACE	D 525	This World Is Taboo	1961	Leinster, M.	AF		$10.00
ACE	D 525	This World Is Taboo	1961	Leinster, M.	VG		$5.00
ACE	D 526	Obsession	1961	Darien, K.	VG+		$10.00
ACE	D 531	The Outlaws Of Mars	1961	Kline, O.A.	VG		$6.00
ACE	D 533	Mad. Ave.	1961	Elmo, H.T.	VG+		$10.00
ACE	D 535	The Shadow Girl	1962	Cummings, R.	VG+		$5.00
ACE	D 540	School Nurse	1962	Hale, A.	AF		$6.00
ACE	D 541	Scavengers In Space	1962	Nourse, A.E.	VGF		$7.00
ACE	D 541	Scavengers In Space	1962	Nourse, A.E.	VG+		$6.00
ACE	D 541	Scavengers In Space	1962	Nourse, A.E.	VG		$5.00
ACE	D 543	Small Town Nurse	1962	Myers, H.K.*	VGF		$14.00
ACE	D 543	Small Town Nurse	1962	Myers, H.K.*	VG+		$10.00
ACE	D 544	Space Station #1	1962	Long, F.B.	VG+		$7.00
ACE	D 547	The Super Barbarians	1962	Brunner, J.	VG+		$7.00
ACE	D 549	Spotlight On Nurse Thorne	1962	Adams, T.	VGF		$6.00
ACE	D 551	Red Alert	1962	Bryant, P.	VGF		$7.00
ACE	D 553	The House On The Borderland	1962	Hodgson, W.H.	VGF		$8.00
ACE	D 555	The Trial Of Terra	1962	Williamson, J.	AF		$7.00
ACE	D 560	Medic In Love	1962	Boylan, R.	AF		$7.00
ACE	D 560	Medic In Love	1962	Boylan, R.	AF		$6.00
ACE	D 563	Leave It To Nurse Kathy	1962	Hale, A.	VG+		$6.00
ACE	D 564	Prodigal Nurse	1963	Myers, H.K.*	VGF		$10.00
ACE	D 564	Prodigal Nurse	1963	Myers, H.K.*	VG-		$4.00
ACE	D 568	Star Ways	1963	Anderson, P.	VG+		$5.00
ACE	D 570	Spanish Grant	1963	Foreman, L.L.	VGF		$8.00
ACE	D 571	Princess Of White Starch	1963	McComb, K.	VGF		$6.00
ACE	D 592	Gunslick Mountain	1964	Nye, N.	VGF		$6.00
ACE	A 4	The Fellowship Of The Ring	1966	Tolkien, J.R.R.	VG+		$8.00
ACE	A 5	The Two Towers	1966	Tolkien, J.R.R.	VG+		$8.00
ACE	A 5	The Two Towers	1966	Tolkien, J.R.R.	VG		$7.00
ACE	A 5	The Two Towers	1966	Tolkien, J.R.R.	VG-		$6.00
ACE	A 6	The Return Of The King	1966	Tolkien, J.R.R.	VGF		$10.00
ACE	A 6	The Return Of The King	1966	Tolkien, J.R.R.	VG+		$7.00
ACE	A 6	The Return Of The King	1966	Tolkien, J.R.R.	VG		$6.00
ACE	A 16	Rite Of Passage	1968	Panshin, A.	AF		$8.00
ACE	A 27	The Great Radio Heroes	1968	Harmon, J.	VG		$7.00

Ace A-5 VG+ $8   Ace F-101 VG $8   Ace F-103 VGF $16

PUBLISHER	PUB. #	TITLE	DATE	AUTHOR	COND.	TYPE	PRICE
ACE	A 29	A Torrent Of Faces	1968	Blish, J.	AF		$7.00
ACE	F 101	Calling Dr. Merryman	1961	Howe, M.	VG	DBL	$8.00
		Cruise Nurse		*Sargent, J.*			
ACE	F 102	Never Forget, Never Forgive	1961	Fox, C.	VGF	DBL	$7.00
		The Flying Eye		*McKnight, B.*			
ACE	F 103	A Trap For Sam Dodge	1961	Whittington, H.	VGF	DBL	$16.00
		High Thunder		*Floren, L.*			
ACE	F 103	A Trap For Sam Dodge	1961	Whittington, H.	VGF	DBL	$15.00
ACE	F 104	Mayday Orbit	1961	Anderson, P.	VGF	DBL	$10.00
		No Man's World		*Bulmer, K.*			
ACE	F 104	Mayday Orbit	1961	Anderson, P.	VGF	DBL	$7.00
ACE	F 105	Best From Fantasy & Sci-Fi #5	1961	Boucher, A.	VG+		$6.00
ACE	F 107	Scratch A Thief	1961	Trinian, J.	VG+	DBL	$9.00
		My Pal, The Killer		*Warwick, C.*			
ACE	F 108	The Sun Saboteurs	1961	Knight, D.	VGF	DBL	$7.00
		The Light Of Lilith		*Wallis, G.M.*			
ACE	F 111	The Girl From Las Vegas	1961	Flynn, J.M.	VGF	DBL	$10.00
		To Have And To Kill		*Martin, R.*			
ACE	F 112	Fashions For Carol	1961	Dean, N.M.	VGF	DBL	$7.00
		Barbara Ames Private Secretary		*Judson, J.*			
ACE	F 113	200 Years To Christmas	1961	McIntosh, J.T.	AF	DBL	$8.00
		Rebels Of The Red Planet		*Fontenay, C.L.*			
ACE	F 113	200 Years To Christmas	1961	McIntosh, J.T.	VGF+	DBL	$8.00
ACE	F 114	The Bird Of Time	1961	West, W.	VGF		$7.00
ACE	F 115	Killing Cousins	1961	Flora, F.	VG+	DBL	$7.00
		The Blonde Cried Murder		*Creighton, J.*			
ACE	F 115	Killing Cousins	1961	Flora, F.	VG	DBL	$6.00
ACE	F 115	Killing Cousins	1961	Flora, F.	VG-	DBL	$3.00
ACE	F 117	The Door Through Space	1961	Bradley, M.Z.	AF	DBL	$8.00
		Rendevous On A Lost World		*Chandler, A.B.*			
ACE	F 117	The Door Through Space	1961	Bradley, M.Z.	VGF	DBL	$7.00
ACE	F 117	The Door Through Space	1961	Bradley, M.Z.	VG	DBL	$7.00
ACE	F 118	Making Profits In The Stock Market	1961	Kamm, J.O.	AF		$5.00
ACE	F 119	Spacial Delivery	1961	Dickson, G.R.	VG+	DBL	$7.00
		Delusion World		*Dickson, G.R.*			
ACE	F 120	Gunmen Can't Hide	1961	Bickham, J.M.	VGF	DBL	$8.00
		Come In Shooting		*Callahan, J.*			
ACE	F 122	Calling Nurse Linda	1961	Stone, P.	VGF	DBL	$7.00
		Dr. Kilbourne Comes Home		*Worley, D.*			
ACE	F 123	Collision Course	1961	Silverberg, R.	AF	DBL	$7.00
		The Nemesis From Terra		*Brackett, L.*			
ACE	F 124	Slattery	1961	Lawrence, S.G.	VGF	DBL	$8.00
		Bullet Welcome For Slattery		*Lawrence, S.G.*			
ACE	F 125	Deep Six	1961	Flynn, J.M.	AF	DBL	$14.00
		The Widow Maker		*Diamond, F.*			

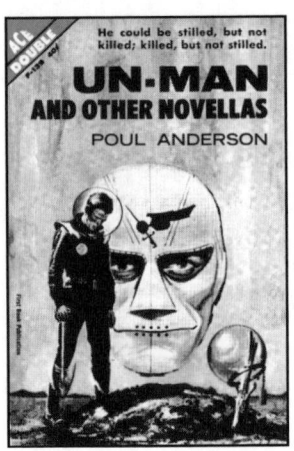

Ace F-104 VGF $10	Ace F-139 VGF $7	Ace F-151 AF $40

PUBLISHER	PUB. #	TITLE	DATE	AUTHOR	COND.	TYPE	PRICE
ACE	F 127	Worlds Of The Imperium	1962	Laumer, K.	VGF	DBL	$7.00
		Seven From The Stars		Bradley, M.Z.			
ACE	F 129	The Three Suns of Amara	1962	Temple, W.F.	AF	DBL	$8.00
		The Automated Goliath		Temple, W.F.			
ACE	F 130	The Screaming Cargo	1962	Flynn, J.M.	VG+	DBL	$4.00
		The Bullet-Proof Martyr		Howard, J.A.			
ACE	F 131	Best From Fantasy & Sci-Fi #6	1962	Anthology	VGF		$6.00
ACE	F 133	The Rim Of Space	1962	Chandler, A.B.	AF	DBL	$10.00
		Secret Agent Of Terra		Brunner, J.			
ACE	F 139	Un-Man And Other Novellas	1962	Anderson, P.	VGF	DBL	$7.00
		The Makeshift Rocket		Anderson, P.			
ACE	F 141	The Ladder In The Sky	1962	Woodcott, K.	AF	DBL	$7.00
		The Darkness Before Tomorrow		Williams, R.M.			
ACE	F 143	End Of A Big Wheel	1962	Fox, C.	VGF	DBL	$10.00
		A Stone Around Her Neck		McNight, B.			
ACE	F 143	End Of A Big Wheel	1962	Fox, C.	VG	DBL	$7.00
ACE	F 145	The Seed Of Earth	1962	Silverberg, R.	AF	DBL	$7.00
		Next Stop The Stars		Silverberg, R.			
ACE	F 146	Sir Scoundrel	1962	Scotland, J.*	AF		$10.00
ACE	F 147	Sea Siege	1962	Norton, A.	AF	DBL	$8.00
		Eye Of The Monster		Norton, A.			
ACE	F 148	Wild Sky	1962	Whittington, H.	VGF	DBL	$9.00
		Dead Man's Double Cross		West, T.			
ACE	F 148	Wild Sky	1962	Whittington, H.	VG	DBL	$6.00
ACE	F 149	Cosmic Checkmate	1962	DeVet, C.V.	VG+	DBL	$7.00
		King Of The Fourth Planet		Williams, R.M.			
ACE	F 151	Reformatory Girls	1962	Tyre, N.	AF		$40.00 A
ACE	F 151	Reformatory Girls	1962	Tyre, N.	VGF		$20.00
ACE	F 151	Reformatory Girls	1962	Tyre, N.	VG		$12.00
ACE	F 155	A Death At Sea	1962	White, L.	VG	DBL	$7.00
		The Time Of Terror		White, L.			
ACE	F 157	The Moon Maid	1962	Burroughs, E.R.	VG+		$6.00
ACE	F 161	Times Without Number	1962	Brunner, J.	VGF	DBL	$7.00
		Destiny's Orbit		Grinnell, D.			
ACE	F 163	Doctor Ellen	1962	De Leeuw, A.	AF		$5.00
ACE	F 166	Maigret And The Reluctant Witness	1962	Simenon, G.	AF	DBL	$10.00
		Maigret Has Scruples		Simenon, G.			
ACE	F 169	Tarzan And The Lost Empire	1962	Burroughs, E.R.	VGF		$6.00
ACE	F 173	Second Ending	1962	White, J.	VGF	DBL	$7.00
		The Jewels Of Aptor		Delany, S.R.			
ACE	F 181	The Mastermind Of Mars	1963	Burroughs, E.R.	VGF		$6.00
ACE	F 185	The Dragon Masters	1963	Vance, J.	VGF	DBL	$7.00
		The Five Gold Bands		Vance, J.			
ACE	F 187	Alpha Centauri Or Die	1963	Brackett, L.	VGF	DBL	$7.00
		Legend Of Lost Earth		Wallis, G.M.			

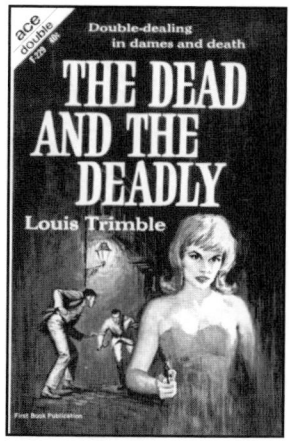

Ace F-157 VG+ $6   Ace F-199 VGF $7   Ace F-229 VGF $9

PUBLISHER	PUB. #	TITLE	DATE	AUTHOR	COND.	TYPE	PRICE
ACE	F 189	Tarzan The Invincible	1963	Burroughs, E.R.	VGF+		$7.00
ACE	F 193	The Son Of Tarzan	1963	Burroughs, E.R.	VGF		$8.00
ACE	F 194	Tarzan Triumphant	1963	Burroughs, E.R.	VGF		$6.00
ACE	F 195	The Silent Invaders	1963	Silverberg, R.	AF	DBL	$7.00
		Battle On Venus		Temple, W.F.			
ACE	F 196	Drygulch Town	1963	Whittington, H.	VG	DBL	$8.00
		Prarie Raiders		Whittington, H.			
ACE	F 196	Drygulch Town	1963	Whittington, H.	VG	DBL	$6.00
ACE	F 199	The Psionic Menace	1963	Woodcott, K.	VGF	DBL	$7.00
		Captives Of The Flames		Delany, S.R.			
ACE	F 203	The Beasts Of Tarzan	1963	Burroughs, E.R.	VGF		$7.00
ACE	F 204	Tarzan And The Jewels Of Opar	1963	Burroughs, E.R.	VGF		$6.00
ACE	F 205	Tarzan And The City Of Gold	1963	Burroughs, E.R.	VGF+		$6.00
ACE	F 206	Jungle Tales Of Tarzan	1963	Burroughs, E.R.	VGF+		$6.00
ACE	F 209	Wizard Of Starship Poseidon	1963	Bulmer, K.	VGF	DBL	$8.00
		Let The Spacemen Beware		Anderson, P.			
ACE	F 209	Wizard Of Starship Poseidon	1963	Bulmer, K.	VGF	DBL	$5.00
ACE	F 211	Planet Of Peril	1963	Kline, O.A.	AF		$6.00
ACE	F 215	The Rebellers	1963	Roberts, J.	VG	DBL	$6.00
		Listen! The Stars		Brunner, J.			
ACE	F 220	The People That Time Forgot	1963	Burroughs, E.R.	AF		$7.00
ACE	F 221	Lost On Venus	1963	Burroughs, E.R.	AF		$7.00
ACE	F 221	Lost On Venus	1963	Burroughs, E.R.	VGF		$6.00
ACE	F 223	Envoy To New Worlds	1963	Laumer, K.	AF	DBL	$7.00
		Flight From Yesterday		Williams, R.M.			
ACE	F 226	Huon Of The Horn	1963	Norton, A.	F		$7.00
ACE	F 227	The Space-Time Juggler	1963	Brunner, J.	VGF	DBL	$7.00
		The Astronauts Must Not Land		Brunner, J.			
ACE	F 229	Homicide Handicap	1963	McKnight, B.	VGF	DBL	$9.00
		The Dead And The Deadly		Trimble, L.			
ACE	F 229	Homicide Handicap	1963	McKnight, B.	VG+	DBL	$5.00
ACE	F 233	Out Of Time's Abyss	1963	Burroughs, E.R.	VGF		$7.00
ACE	F 237	Beyond The Galactic Rim	1963	Chandler, A.B.	AF	DBL	$7.00
		The Ship From Outside		Chandler, A.B.			
ACE	F 249	The Search For Zei	1963	De Camp, L.S.	VG+	DBL	$6.00
		The Hand Of Zei		De Camp, L.S.			
ACE	F 251	The Game Players Of Titan	1963	Dick, P.K.	VG		$7.00
ACE	F 253	One Of Our Asteroids Is Missing	1964	Knox, C.M.	VGF	DBL	$7.00
		The Twisted Men		Van Vogt, A.E.			
ACE	F 257	Alien Planet	1964	Pratt, F.	AF		$7.00
ACE	F 258	The Cave Girl	1964	Burroughs, E.R.	F		$7.00
ACE	F 261	The Lunar Eye	1964	Williams, R.M.	VGF+	DBL	$8.00
		The Towers of Toron		Delany, S.R.			
ACE	F 267	Best From Fantasy & Sci-Fi #9	1964	Anthology	VGF		$6.00
ACE	F 269	Quest Of The Dawn Man	1964	Rosny, J.H.	AF		$7.00

Ace F-251 VG $7   Ace F-253 VGF $7   Ace F-309 VGF $22

PUBLISHER	PUB. #	TITLE	DATE	AUTHOR	COND.	TYPE	PRICE
ACE	F 273	Falcons Of Narabedla	1964	Bradley, M.Z.	VGF	DBL	$7.00
		The Dark Intruder		Bradley, M.Z.			
ACE	F 274	The Cosmic Computer	1964	Piper, H.B.	VGF		$6.00
ACE	F 275	No Truce With Terra	1964	High, P.E.	VGF	DBL	$8.00
		The Duplicators		Leinster, M.			
ACE	F 277	To Conquer Chaos	1964	Brunner, J.	VGF+		$6.00
ACE	F 278	Patty Goes To Washington	1964	Leighton, F.S.	G+	TVTI	$5.00
ACE	F 281	Atlantida	1964	Benoit, P.	AF		$6.00
ACE	F 283	The Day The World Ended	1964	Rohmer, S.	AF		$10.00
ACE	F 283	The Day The World Ended	1964	Rohmer, S.	VGF+		$8.00
ACE	F 285	The Million Year Hunt	1964	Bulmer, K.	VGF	DBL	$7.00
		Ships To The Stars		Leiber, F.			
ACE	F 289	Demons' World	1964	Bulmer, K.	VGF	DBL	$7.00
		I Want The Stars		Purdom, T.			
ACE	F 295	The World Of Nul-A	1964	Van Vogt, A.E.	VG		$5.00
ACE	F 296	Gulliver Of Mars	1964	Arnold, E.L.	AF		$8.00
ACE	F 299	The Arsenal Of Miracles	1964	Fox, G.F.	AF	DBL	$7.00
		Endless Shadow		Brunner, J.			
ACE	F 301	The Simulacra	1964	Dick, P.K.	F		$31.00 A
ACE	F 301	The Simulacra	1964	Dick, P.K.	AF		$28.00 A
ACE	F 307	Warrior Of Llarn	1964	Fox, G.F.	AF		$8.00
ACE	F 309	Clans Of The Alphane Moon	1964	Dick, P.K.	VGF		$22.00
ACE	F 310	Galactic Derelict	1964	Norton, A.	AF		$5.00
ACE	F 312	The Radio Planet	1964	Farley, R.M.	VGF		$7.00
ACE	F 319	Crashing Suns	1964	Hamilton, E.	AF		$7.00
ACE	F 320	The Martian Sphinx	1965	Woodcott, K.	AF		$6.00
ACE	F 326	The Wizard Of Lemuria	1965	Carter, L.	AF		$6.00
ACE	F 326	The Wizard Of Lemuria	1965	Carter, L.	VGF		$6.00
ACE	F 330	What Strange Stars & Skies	1965	Davidson, A.	AF		$6.00
ACE	F 334	The Insect Warriors	1965	Levie, R.D.	VGF		$6.00
ACE	F 335	The Second Atlantis	1965	Williams, R.M.	AF		$6.00
ACE	F 335	The Second Atlantis	1965	Williams, R.M.	VGF		$5.00
ACE	F 337	Dr. Bloodmoney	1965	Dick, P.K.	VGF-		$15.00
ACE	F 337	Dr. Bloodmoney	1965	Dick, P.K.	VG-		$7.00
ACE	F 347	The Last Hope Of Earth	1965	Wright, L.	VGF		$6.00
ACE	F 363	Tama Of The Light Country	1965	Cummings, R.	VGF		$6.00
ACE	F 367	The Maker Of Universes	1965	Farmer, P.J.	VG+		$7.00
ACE	F 373	The Sword Of Lankor	1966	Cory, H.L.	F		$6.00
ACE	F 377	The Crack In Space	1966	Dick, P.K.	VGF-		$10.00
ACE	F 377	The Crack In Space	1966	Dick, P.K.	VG		$8.00
ACE	F 391	The Crossroads Of Time	1966	Norton, A.	VG+		$6.00
ACE	F 391	The Crossroads Of Time	1966	Norton, A.	VG		$3.00
ACE	F 399	Thief Of Llarn	1966	Fox, G.F.	AF		$7.00
ACE	F 416	Utopia Minus X	1966	Gordon, R.	F		$6.00
ACE	F 420	The Planet Of The Double Sun	1967	Jones, N.R.	F		$6.00

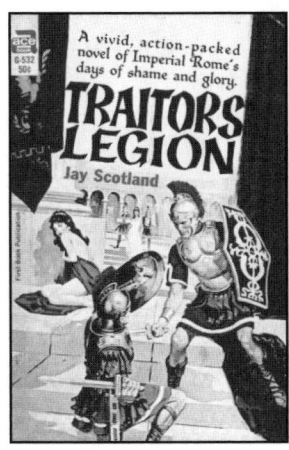

Ace G-532 VGF+ $8   Ace G-618 AF $6   Ace G-632 VG+ $5

PUBLISHER	PUB. #	TITLE	DATE	AUTHOR	COND.	TYPE	PRICE
ACE	F 422	The Sword Of Rhiannon	1967	Brackett, L.	AF		$6.00
ACE	F 429	The World Jones Made	1967	Dick, P.K.	VGF		$15.00
ACE	F 429	The World Jones Made	1967	Dick, P.K.	VG		$8.00
ACE	G 502	Pat Garrett	1963	O'Connor, R.	VGF		$6.00
ACE	G 510	TCOT Weird Sisters	1963	Armstrong, C.	AF		$7.00
ACE	G 518	The Opening Door	1963	Reilly, H.	F	DBL	$8.00
		Follow Me		*Reilly, H.*			
ACE	G 522	The Firebrand	1963	Challis, G.	VG+		$7.00
ACE	G 526	The Mark Of The Hand	1963	Armstrong, C.	AF	DBL	$8.00
		The Dream Walker		*Armstrong, C.*			
ACE	G 532	Traitors' Legion	1963	Scotland, J.*	VGF+		$8.00
ACE	G 534	Kill Joy	1963	Holding, E.S.	AF-	DBL	$8.00
		Speak Of The Devil		*Holding, E.S.*			
ACE	G 543	They Buried A Man	1964	Davis, M.	F	DBL	$8.00
		The Dark Place		*Davis, M.*			
ACE	G 553	The Man From U.N.C.L.E. #1	1965	Avallone, M.	VGF	TVTI	$5.00
ACE	G 560	The Doomsday Affair	1965	Whittington, H.	VG+	TVTI	$5.00
ACE	G 564	The Copenhagen Affair	1965	Oram, J.	VGF	TVTI	$5.00
ACE	G 571	The Dagger Affair	1965	McDaniel, D.	AF-	TVTI	$5.00
ACE	G 571	The Dagger Affair	1965	McDaniel, D.	VGF	TVTI	$5.00
ACE	G 574	Rocannon's World	1966	LeGuinn, U.K.	VG+	DBL	$6.00
		The Kar-Chee Reign		*Davidson, A.*			
ACE	G 574	Rocannon's World	1966	LeGuinn, U.K.	VG	DBL	$5.00
ACE	G 576	Danger From Vega	1966	Rackham, J.	AF	DBL	$7.00
		Clash Of Star Kings		*Davidson, A.*			
ACE	G 576	Danger From Vega	1966	Rackham, J.	VG	DBL	$5.00
ACE	G 580	Dawnman Planet	1966	Reynolds, M.	AF	DBL	$7.00
		Inherit The Earth		*Nunes, C.*			
ACE	G 585	The Ultimate Weapon	1966	Campbell, J.W.	VG	DBL	$6.00
		The Planeteers		*Campbell, J.W.*			
ACE	G 588	The Off-Worlders	1966	Baxter, J.	VGF	DBL	$7.00
		The Star Magicians		*Carter, L.*			
ACE	G 590	The Vampire Affair	1966	McDaniel, D.	VG	TVTI	$4.00
ACE	G 600	The Radioactive Camel Affair	1966	Leslie, P.	VGF+	TVTI	$5.00
ACE	G 602	The Unteleported Man	1966	Dick, P.K.	VG-	DBL	$8.00
		The Mind Monsters		*Cory, H.L.*			
ACE	G 605	The Flying Saucer Gambit	1966	Maddock, L.	VG+		$7.00
ACE	G 606	Time To Live	1966	Rackham, J.	VGF	DBL	$7.00
		The Man Without A Planet		*Carter, L.*			
ACE	G 609	Contraband From Outerspace	1967	Chandler, A.B.	AF	DBL	$7.00
		Reality Forbidden		*High, P.E.*			
ACE	G 613	The Monster Wheel Affair	1967	McDaniel, D.	VGF	TVTI	$5.00
ACE	G 614	Envoy To The Dog Star	1967	Shaw, F.L.	VG+	DBL	$6.00
		Shock Wave		*Richmond, W.*			
ACE	G 617	The Diving Dames Affair	1967	Leslie, P.	VGF	TVTI	$5.00

Ace G-637 VG+ $8   Ace G-699 VGF $7   Ace H-22 AF $7   Ace H-34 VG+ $6

PUBLISHER	PUB. #	TITLE	DATE	AUTHOR	COND.	TYPE	PRICE
ACE	G 618	The Stolen Sun	1967	Petaja, E.	AF	DBL	$6.00
		The Ship From Atlantis		*Munn, H.W.*			
ACE	G 620	The Golden Goddess Gambit	1967	Maddock, L.	VGF		$7.00
ACE	G 623	These Savage Futurians	1967	High, P.E.	VGF	DBL	$7.00
		The Double Invaders		*Rackham, J.*			
ACE	G 632	Nebula Alert	1967	Chandler, A.B.	VG+	DBL	$5.00
		The Rival Rigellians		*Reynolds, M.*			
ACE	G 634	War Of The Wing Men	1967	Anderson, P.	VGF		$6.00
ACE	G 636	The Assassination Affair	1967	Holly, J.H.	VGF	TVTI	$6.00
ACE	G 637	The Ganymede Takeover	1967	Dick, P.K.	VG+		$8.00
ACE	G 639	The Weapon From Beyond	1967	Hamilton, E.	F		$7.00
ACE	G 644	The Emerald Elephant Gambit	1967	Maddock, L.	VGF		$7.00
ACE	G 645	The Invisibility Affair	1967	Stratton, T.	VGF	TVTI	$6.00
ACE	G 667	The Arsenal Out Of Time	1967	McDaniel, D.	VG		$4.00
ACE	G 670	The Rainbow Affair	1967	McDaniel, D.	VGF	TVTI	$6.00
ACE	G 689	The Cross Of Gold Affair	1968	Davies, F.	VGF	TVTI	$8.00
ACE	G 699	The Bride Wore Black	1968	Woolrich, C.	VGF		$7.00
ACE	G 701	The Closed Worlds	1968	Hamilton, E.	AF		$6.00
ACE	G 718	Solar Lottery	1968	Dick, P.K.	VG		$6.00
ACE	G 725	The Littlest Rebels	1968	Johnston, W.	VGF	TVTI	$6.00
ACE	G 729	The Utopia Affair	1968	McDaniel, D.	AF	TVTI	$5.00
ACE	G 752	The Splintered Sunglasses Affair	1968	Leslie, P.	AF	TVTI	$7.00
ACE	H 7	The Restless Land	1962	Culp, J.H.	VG+		$3.00
ACE	H 19	The IF Reader Of Sci-Fi	1966	Anthology	VGF		$7.00
ACE	H 20	The Key To Irunium	1967	Bulmer, K.	AF	DBL	$7.00
		The Wandering Tellurian		*Schwartz, A.*			
ACE	H 21	The Last Castle	1967	Vance, J.	VGF	DBL	$7.00
		World Of The Sleeper		*Wayman, T.R.*			
ACE	H 22	Lord Of The Green Planet	1967	Petaja, E.	AF	DBL	$7.00
		Five Against Arlane		*Purdom, T.*			
ACE	H 27	The Winds Of Gath	1967	Tubb, E.C.	VGF	DBL	$7.00
		Crisis On Cheiron		*Coulson, J.*			
ACE	H 29	The Road To The Rim	1967	Chandler, A.B.	VG-	DBL	$5.00
		The Lost Millenium		*Richmond, W.*			
ACE	H 30	City	1967	Simak, C.D.	AF		$5.00
ACE	H 32	Games	1967	Ellson, H.	VG+	MTI	$7.00
ACE	H 34	Computer War	1967	Reynolds, M.	VG+	DBL	$6.00
		Death Is A Dream		*Tubb, E.C.*			
ACE	H 36	The Wrecks Of Time	1967	Moorcock, M.	VG	DBL	$6.00
		Tramontane		*Petaja, E.*			
ACE	H 39	Eye In The Sky	1968	Dick, P.K.	VGF		$15.00
ACE	H 39	Eye In The Sky	1968	Dick, P.K.	VG+		$12.00
ACE	H 40	Alien Sea	1968	Rackham, J.	VGF	DBL	$7.00
		C.O.D. Mars		*Tubb, E.C.*			
ACE	H 41	Into The Niger Bend	1968	Verne, J.	AF		$7.00
ACE	H 42	Why Call Them Back From Heaven	1967	Simak, C.D.	VGF		$5.00
ACE	H 48	The Youth Monopoly	1968	Wobig, E.	VGF	DBL	$5.00
		The Pictures Of Pavanne		*Wright, L.*			

Ace H-65 AF $7	Ace K-107 VG $6	Ace K-112 VGF $8	Ace K-160 AF $15

PUBLISHER	PUB. #	TITLE	DATE	AUTHOR	COND.	TYPE	PRICE
ACE	H 57	Rendezvous In Black	1968	Woolrich, C.	VGF		$7.00
ACE	H 65	Mercenary From Tomorrow	1968	Reynolds, M.	AF	DBL	$7.00
		The Key To Venudine		*Bulmer, K.*			
ACE	H 66	The Black Path Of Fear	1968	Woolrich, C.	VGF		$7.00
ACE	H 67	The Village In The Treetops	1968	Verne, J.	AF		$7.00
ACE	H 70	Star Quest	1968	Koontz, D.R.	AF	DBL	$33.00 A
		Doom Of The Green Planet		*Petaja, E.*			
ACE	H 70	Star Quest	1968	Koontz, D.R.	VGF	DBL	$25.00 A
ACE	H 70	Star Quest	1968	Koontz, D.R.	VG+	DBL	$12.00
ACE	H 70	Star Quest	1968	Koontz, D.R.	G-	DBL	$6.00
ACE	H 77	Derai	1968	Tubb, E.C.	VGF	DBL	$7.00
		The Singing Stones		*Coulson, J.*			
ACE	H 85	Destination Saturn	1968	Grinnell, D.	VGF	DBL	$7.00
		Invader On My Back		*High, P.E.*			
ACE	H 90	Swords In The Mist	1968	Leiber, F.	VG+		$6.00
ACE	H 102	Subspace Explorers	1968	Smith, E.E.	VGF		$8.00
ACE	H 103	The Age Of Ruin	1968	Faucette, J.M.	VGF	DBL	$7.00
		Code Duello		*Reynolds, M.*			
ACE	H 109	The Man With Three Chins	1968	Ames, D.	VG		$5.00
ACE	K 100	The Long Dream	1959	Wright, R.	VGF		$8.00
ACE	K 107	The Cross On The Drum	1959	Cave, H.B.	VG		$6.00
ACE	K 108	The Three Days	1959	Robertson, D.	AF		$7.00
ACE	K 112	The Royal City	1960	Savage, L.	VGF		$8.00
ACE	K 113	Tall Short Stories	1959	Anthology	VGF+		$5.00
ACE	K 129	Conscience Of The King	1960	Duggan, A.	AF		$7.00
ACE	K 136	Hoaxes	1960	MacDougall, C.D.	VGF		$6.00
ACE	K 137	Private World Of C. Powers	1960	Bluestone, G.	VGF+		$5.00
ACE	K 143	The Twelfth Physician	1961	Gibbs, W.	AF		$5.00
ACE	K 148	The Chicago Underworld	1962	Asbury, H.	VG+		$6.00
ACE	K 150	Lady Chatterly's Daughter	1962	Robins, P.	VGF		$6.00 A
ACE	K 151	The Great Adventure	1960	Fredericks, P.G.	VGF		$5.00
ACE	K 160	The Werewolf Of Paris	1962	Endore, G.	AF		$15.00
ACE	K 168	Stranger Than Life	1962	Miller, R.D.	VGF		$5.00
ACE	K 190	Parents Without Partners	1961	Egleson, J.	AF		$5.00
ACE	K 202	Junkie	1964	Burroughs, W.	VGF		$24.00
ACE	K 204	Charlie Chaplin	1964	Payne, R.	VGF		$5.00
ACE	K 223	Corridor Of Whispers	1965	Noone, E.*	AF		$5.00
ACE	K 244	The Gothic Reader	1966	Anthology	AF		$7.00
ACE	M 101	People Of The Talisman	1964	Brackett, L.	F	DBL	$10.00
		The Secret Of Sinharat		*Brackett, L.*			
ACE	M 101	People Of The Talisman	1964	Brackett, L.	AF	DBL	$7.00
ACE	M 102	Trouble At Hangdog Flats	1964	Patterson, R.	VGF	DBL	$8.00
		Hoodoo Guns		*Hogan, R.*			
ACE	M 103	Exile From Xanadu	1964	Wright, L.	AF	DBL	$8.00
		The Golden People		*Saberhagen, F.*			
ACE	M 107	The Coils Of Time	1964	Chandler, A.B.	AF	DBL	$8.00
		Into The Alternate Universe		*Chandler, A.B.*			
ACE	M 107	The Coils Of Time	1964	Chandler, A.B.	VG+	DBL	$5.00

Ace M-101 F $10	Ace M-109 VGF $7	Ace M-123 AF $8

PUBLISHER	PUB. #	TITLE	DATE	AUTHOR	COND.	TYPE	PRICE
ACE	M 109	Stranger Than You Think	1965	Edmondson, G.C.	VGF	DBL	$7.00
		The Ship That Sailed Time...		*Edmondson, G.C.*			
ACE	M 111	Fugitive Of The Stars	1965	Hamilton, E.	VG+	DBL	$5.00
		Land Beyond The Map		*Bulmer, K.*			
ACE	M 113	Off Center	1965	Knight, D.	F	DBL	$8.00
		The Rithian Terror		*Knight, D.*			
ACE	M 113	Off Center	1965	Knight, D.	VGF+	DBL	$6.00
ACE	M 114	Stampede On Farway Pass	1965	Payne, S.	VG-	DBL	$5.00
		Lynch Law Canyon		*Wynne, F.*			
ACE	M 115	Enigma From Tantalus	1965	Brunner, J.	AF	DBL	$6.00
		The Repairmen Of Cyclops		*Brunner, J.*			
ACE	M 117	Our Man In Space	1965	Ronald, B.W.	AF	DBL	$8.00
		Ultimatum In 2050 A.D.		*Sharkey, J.*			
ACE	M 123	Android Avenger	1965	White, T.	AF	DBL	$8.00
		The Altar On Asconel		*Brunner, J.*			
ACE	M 126	Valley Of Savage Men	1965	Whittington, H.	VG	DBL	$10.00
		Brother Badman		*Elliott, B.*			
ACE	M 127	The Water Of Thought	1965	Saberhagen, F.	VGF	DBL	$7.00
		We The Venusians		*Rackham, J.*			
ACE	M 135	Space Captain	1966	Leinster, M.	VGF	DBL	$7.00
		The Mad Metropolis		*High, P.E.*			
ACE	M 137	Best From Fantasy & Sci-Fi #11	1966	Anthology	AF		$8.00
ACE	M 139	Empire Star	1966	Delany, S.R.	VGF	DBL	$7.00
		The Tree Lord Of Imeten		*Purdom, T.*			
ACE	M 141	The Brains Of Earth	1966	Vance, J.	VG	DBL	$6.00
		The Many Worlds Of Magnus R.		*Vance, J.*			
ACE	M 142	Doppelgangers	1966	Heard, H.F.	F		$10.00
ACE	M 147	The Stars Are Ours!	1966	Norton, A.	VG		$5.00
ACE	M 156	Key Out Of Time	1966	Norton, A.	VGF		$5.00
ACE	M 153	The Weapon Makers	1966	Van Vogt, A.E.	VGF		$5.00
ACE	M 165	Worlds Of The Imperium	1966	Laumer, K.	VG		$6.00
ACE	T 137	Basketball For Everyone	1962	Bee, C.	VG		$5.00
ACE	4877	Battlestar Gallactica II	1979	Lee, S.	AF	TVTI	$7.00
ACE	10470	Chisum	1970	Bowie, S.	AF	MTI	$7.00
ACE	11670	The Blade Of Conan	1979	Anthology	VGF		$7.00
ACE	12200	The Crimson Madness	n/d	McShane, M.	AF		$6.00
ACE	13793	Dark Of The Woods	1970	Koontz, D.R.	AF	DBL	$67.00 A
		Soft Come The Dragons		*Koontz, D.R.*			
ACE	13793	Dark Of The Woods	1970	Koontz, D.R.	VG+	DBL	$16.00
ACE	14150	Dead Ringer	n/d	Chase, J.H.	AF		$10.00
ACE	15697	Dr. Futurity	1972	Dick, P.K.	VG	DBL	$6.00
		The Unteleported Man		*Dick, P.K.*			
ACE	18770	Edgar Rice Burroughs	1968	Lupoff, R.A.	AF		$11.00 A
ACE	22600	The Fall Of The Dream Machine	1969	Koontz, D.R.	VGF-	DBL	$12.00
		The Star Ventures		*Bulmer, K.*			

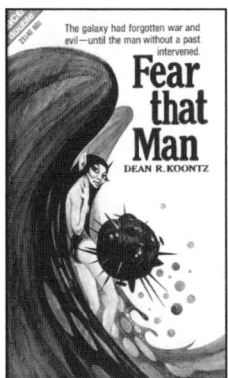

| Ace 23140 F $54 | Ace 30274 VGF $33 | Ace 51375 AF $25 | Ace 51704 AF $18 |

PUBLISHER	PUB. #	TITLE	DATE	AUTHOR	COND.	TYPE	PRICE
ACE	22600	The Fall Of The Dream Machine	1969	Koontz, D.R.	G-	DBL	$7.00
ACE	23140	Fear That Man	1969	Koontz, D.R.	F	DBL	$54.00 A
		Toyman		Tubb, E.C.			
ACE	23775	Final War And Other Fantasies	1969	O'Donnell, K.M.	AF	DBL	$6.00
		Treasure Of Tau Ceti		Rackham, J.			
ACE	25130	The Frankenscience Monster	1969	Ackerman, F.J.	AF	MTI	$7.00
ACE	27310	The Game Players Of Titan	1972	Dick, P.K.	VGF		$7.00
ACE	27346	The Ganymede Takeover	1976	Dick, P.K.	AF		$8.00
ACE	29350	The Glass Teat	1970	Ellison, H.	VG+		$16.00 A
ACE	29375	The Glorious Decade	1971	Thomey, T.	AF		$8.00
ACE	30274	Green Eyes	1984	Shepard, L.	VGF		$33.00 A
ACE	34253	History Of The Acadamy Awards	1973	Fredrik	AF		$6.00
ACE	36394	I Have No Mouth & Must Scream	1983	Ellison, H.	F		$9.00
ACE	36516	The Illustrated Harlan Ellison	1980	Ellison, H.	VGF		$15.00 A
ACE	37421	The Island Of Dr. Moreau	1977	Silva, J.	VGF	MTI	$7.00
ACE	37598	It Takes A Thief #1	1969	Brewer, G.	VG+	TVTI	$7.00
ACE	37599	It Takes A Thief #2	1969	Brewer, G.	VG+	TVTI	$6.00
ACE	37600	It Takes A Thief #3	1970	Brewer, G.	VGF	TVTI	$7.00
ACE	37600	It Takes A Thief #3	1970	Brewer, G.	VG	TVTI	$6.00
ACE	42800	The Bane Of Kanthos	1969	Dain, A.	VGF+	DBL	$6.00
		Kalin		Tubb, E.C.			
ACE	42900	Kar Kaballa	1969	Smith, G.H.	AF	DBL	$7.00
		Tower Of Medusa		Carter, L.			
ACE	42900	Kar Kaballa	1969	Smith, G.H.	VGF	DBL	$7.00
ACE	44470	King Kong	1976	Lovelace, D.W.	VG+		$9.00 A
ACE	44512	Kingdom Of The Spiders	1977	Hurwood, B.J.	AF	MTI	$6.00
ACE	49291	The Lost Continent	1967	Burroughs, E.R.	AF		$5.00
ACE	51375	Lord Of The Trees	1970	Farmer, P.J.	AF	DBL	$25.00 A
		The Mad Goblin		Farmer, P.J.			
ACE	51375	Lord Of The Trees	1970	Farmer, P.J.	AF	DBL	$20.00
ACE	51700	The Hollow Crown Affair	1968	McDaniel, D.	VGF	TVTI	$12.00
ACE	51700	The Hollow Crown Affair	1968	McDaniel, D.	VG+	TVTI	$7.00
ACE	51701	The Unfair Fare Affair	1968	Leslie, P.	AF	TVTI	$10.00
ACE	51702	The Power Cube Affair	1968	Phillifent, J.T.	AF	TVTI	$15.00
ACE	51702	The Power Cube Affair	1968	Phillifent, J.T.	VG+	TVTI	$12.00
ACE	51703	The Corfu Affair	1968	Phillifent, J.T.	G	TVTI	$5.00
ACE	51704	The Thinking Machine Affair	1968	Bernard, J.	AF	TVTI	$18.00
ACE	51704	The Thinking Machine Affair	1968	Bernard, J.	VG	TVTI	$7.00
ACE	51705	The Stone Cold Dead Affair	1968	Oram, J.	AF	TVTI	$18.00
ACE	51705	The Stone Cold Dead Affair	1968	Oram, J.	VGF	TVTI	$15.00
ACE	51706	Finger In The Sky Affair	1968	Leslie, P.	VG+	TVTI	$15.00
ACE	52470	Men On The Moon	1969	Anthology	VGF		$12.00
ACE	53415	Hierarchies	1973	Phillifent, J.T.	VGF	DBL	$6.00
		Mister Justice		Piserchia, D.			
ACE	64400	Our Friends From Frolix 8	1970	Dick, P.K.	AF		$22.00 A
ACE	64400	Our Friends From Frolix 8	1970	Dick, P.K.	VG		$7.00
ACE	66093	The Stolen Spacefleet (P.R. #109)	1977	Darlton, C.	VG+	DBL	$7.00
		Sgt. Robot (Perry Rhodan #110)		Mahr, K.			

All-Picture Mystery 1 VG+ $85   Archer 3 AF $30   Archer 8 VG+ $24

PUBLISHER	PUB. #	TITLE	DATE	AUTHOR	COND.	TYPE	PRICE
ACE	67800	The Preserving Machine	1969	Dick, P.K.	VGF		$20.00
ACE	67901	The Prisoner #2	1969	McDaniel, D.	VG	TVTI	$6.00
ACE	72280	The Rider	n/d	Burroughs, E.R.	AF		$7.00
ACE	76701	The Simulacra	n/d	Dick, P.K.	VGF+		$6.00
ACE	84490	Underground Press Anthology	1972	Anthology	VGF		$6.00
ACE	87718	Web Of The City	1983	Ellison, H.	VGF		$8.00 A
ACE	88077	Whatever Became Of . . . ? #3	1970	Lamparski, R.	AF		$8.00
ACE	88250	Whence All But He Had Fled	1968	Davis, J.L.	AF		$8.00
ACCUSED	1 1	Accused Det. Story Mag. 1/56	1956	Anthology	AF	Digest	$19.00 A
ACCUSED	1 2	Accused Det. Story Mag. 3/56	1956	Anthology	G	Digest	$13.00 A
ACTION CARAVAN	1 1	Action Caravan - 5/51	1951	Anthology	VG	Digest	$20.00 A
ADULT BOOK	AB 418	The Lust Heiress	1968	Dexter, J.	VGF		$31.00 A
ADULT BOOK	AB 418	The Lust Heiress	1968	Dexter, J.	VGF		$20.00 A
ADULT BOOK	AB 440	Charlie Darling	1968	Thomas, A.	AF		$10.00
ADULT BOOK	AB 445	Gay Vista	1968	Lester, L.	AF		$10.00
ADULT BOOK	AB 476	Swap Sweetie	1969	Post, S.	AF-		$13.00 A
ADULT BOOK	AB 1517	Swap At The Top	1970	Aldrich, C.	AF		$15.00 A
ADVENTURE	124 3	Adventure - 2/51	1951	Anthology	VG-	Digest	$8.00
ADVENTURE	124 5	Adventure - 4/51	1951	Anthology	VG	Digest	$8.00
ADVENTURE	124 6	Adventure - 5/51	1951	Anthology	VG	Digest	$8.00
ADVENTURE NVL. CLASSIC	36	The Song Of The Whip	1945	Evans, E.	VG+	Digest	$6.00
AFTER HOURS	AH 108	Three's A Crowd	1964	Conway, B.	VG		$12.00
AFTER HOURS	AH 125	Ball And Chain	1965	Conway, B.	AF		$37.00 A
AFTER HOURS	AH 139	Mixed Up	1966	Benning, C.	AF-		$44.00 A
AFTER HOURS	AH 139	Mixed Up	1966	Benning, C.	AF		$18.00 A
AFTER HOURS	AH 143	Bad Girl	1966	Werner, G.	AF		$10.00 A
AFTER HOURS	AH 152	Name Your Pleasure	1966	Dean, A.	VG		$25.00 A
AFTER HOURS	AH 154	Sob Sister	1966	Hunter, B.	AF		$27.00 A
AIRMONT	M 1	Death Wore Fins	1962	Clark, D.	VGF		$7.00
AIRMONT	CL 40	The Invisible Man	1964	Wells, H.G.	VGF		$5.00
AL BLAKE	No#	Espionage	n/d	Blake, A.	VG	Digest	$12.00
ALFRED HITCHCOCK'S	3 7	A. Hitchcock's Mystery Mag. 7/58	1958	Anthology	AF	Digest	$5.00
ALFRED HITCHCOCK'S	3 9	A. Hitchcock's Mystery Mag. 9/58	1958	Anthology	AF	Digest	$5.00
ALL STAR	AS 21	Passion Fruit	1964	Edge, N.	AF		$10.00
ALL STAR	AS 59	The Sex Thief	1965	Fisher, J.	VGF		$8.00
ALL STAR	AS 68	Hotbed Motel	1965	Grenada, G.	VGF		$8.00
ALL STAR	AS 72	The Hot Canary	1966	Phillips, P.	G		$7.00
ALL STAR	AS 80	Snake Finger	1966	Flaming, I.M.	AF		$51.00 A
ALL STAR	AS 84	A Strange Kind Of Love	1966	Bellaugh, J.	AF		$17.00 A
ALL STAR	AS 85	The Joy Zone	1966	Dare, A.	AF		$12.00
ALL STAR	AS 93	The Night People	1966	Fields, D.	VGF		$18.00 A
ALL STAR	AS 112	Girl From Havana	1966	Colby, E.	VGF		$7.00
ALL STAR	AS 116	The Power And The Passion	1966	Kevin, P.	AF		$12.00
ALL STAR	AS 124	I, A Virgin	1967	Willis, A.M.	AF		$7.00
ALL STAR	AS 501	Girls On Main Street	1961	Roscoe, D.	VGF		$7.00

Archer (U.K.) No# VGF- $50	Archer (U.K.) No# VG+ $50	Armed Services Ed. 1265 VG+ $12

PUBLISHER	PUB. #	TITLE	DATE	AUTHOR	COND.	TYPE	PRICE	
ALL STAR	AS 508	I Want You	1961	Lake, L.	VG+		$7.00	
ALL STAR	AS 518	The Nymph And The Satyr	1962	Farmer, A.	VGF		$5.00	
ALL-PICTURE MYSTERY	1	TCOT Winking Buddha	1950	Stokes, M.L.	VG+	Digest	$85.00	A
AMERICAN AGENT	1 1	American Agent - Spring 1957	1957	Anthology	VGF	Digest	$40.00	A
AMERICAN LIBRARY	No#	Acts Of Black Night	1938	Knight, K.M.	VG		$11.00	A
AMERICAN SPORTS LIB.	101	Sport Sport Sport	1963	Anthology	VGF		$7.00	
ANCHOR EDITIONS	AE 102	Merchant Sinman	1965	Macey, R.	VGF		$7.00	
ANCHOR EDITIONS	AE 104	Devious Turn To Passion	1965	Mace, R.	VGF		$8.00	
APS	6002	Roxana	1965	Defoe, D.	VGF		$7.00	
APS	9500	Hollywood Babylon	1965	Anger, K.	AF		$15.00	A
APS	9503	History Of The Devil	1965	Defoe, D.	VGF		$26.00	A
ARCHER	3	Take It And Like It	1951	Morelli, S.	AF	Digest	$30.00	A
ARCHER	3	Take It And Like It	1951	Morelli, S.	AF	Digest	$23.00	A
ARCHER	5	Dame In My Bed	1951	Storme, M.	AF-	Digest	$50.00	A
ARCHER	5	Dame In My Bed	1951	Storme, M.	AF	Digest	$45.00	A
ARCHER	8	You'll Never Get Me	1952	Morelli, S.	VG+	Digest	$24.00	A
ARCHER	36	Flame	1951	Renin, P.	VG+	Digest	$23.00	
ARCHER	36	Flame	1951	Renin, P.	VG+	Digest	$20.00	
ARCHER	36	Flame	1951	Renin, P.	AF	Digest	$18.00	A
ARCHER	50	Sex	1951	Renin, P.	VGF	Digest	$20.00	
ARCHER	50	Sex	1951	Renin, P.	VGF	Digest	$15.00	
ARCHER	51	Night Haunts Of Paris	1951	Vane, R.	AF-	Digest	$20.00	A
ARCHER	51	Night Haunts Of Paris	1951	Vane, R.	VGF	Digest	$14.00	
ARCHER	51	Night Haunts Of Paris	1951	Vane, R.	VG	Digest	$9.00	
ARCHER	69	Ladies Of The Red Lamp	1951	Vane, R.	AF	Digest	$49.00	A
ARCHER	71	Unlucky Virgin	1951	Storme, M.	AF	Digest	$45.00	A
ARCHER	72	Ladies Sleep Alone	1951	Della, L.	VGF	Digest	$14.00	
ARCHER	84	Make Mine A Harlot	1952	Storme, M.	VGF	Digest	$61.00	A
ARCHER	96	Spoiled Lives	1952	Flammeche, P.	VGF	Digest	$66.00	A
ARCHER	96	Spoiled Lives	1952	Flammeche, P.	AF	Digest	$65.00	A
ARCHER	96	Spoiled Lives	1952	Flammeche, P.	AF	Digest	$47.00	A
ARCHER (U.K.)	No#	Coffin For A Cutie	1950	Morelli, S.	VGF-	Digest	$50.00	A
ARCHER (U.K.)	No#	Sin-Stained	1950	Vane, R.	VG	Digest	$28.00	A
ARCHER (U.K.)	No#	Sultry Love	1950	Cunningham, L.A.	VGF	Digest	$40.00	A
ARCHER (U.K.)	No#	Virus X	1950	Horler, S.	VG+	Digest	$50.00	A
ARMED SERVICES EDITIONS	F 175	Essays Of Charles Lamb	1944	Lamb, C.	VG		$7.00	
ARMED SERVICES EDITIONS	M 29	The Moonstone	1944	Collins, W.	VG		$7.00	
ARMED SERVICES EDITIONS	Q 35	Selected Plays Of Eugene O'Neill	1945	O'Neill, E.	VG		$8.00	
ARMED SERVICES EDITIONS	R 4	Short Stories Of Dorothy Parker	1945	Parker, D.	VG+		$8.00	
ARMED SERVICES EDITIONS	R 33	Sleep No More	1945	Anthology	G		$8.00	
ARMED SERVICES EDITIONS	S 20	After-Dinner Story	1945	Irish, W.*	VG		$9.00	
ARMED SERVICES EDITIONS	T 2	The Time Machine	1945	Wells, H.G.	VG		$10.00	
ARMED SERVICES EDITIONS	T 5	Cannery Row	1945	Steinbeck, J.	VG		$8.00	
ARMED SERVICES EDITIONS	667	To Have And Have Not	1945	Hemingway, E.	VG-		$4.00	
ARMED SERVICES EDITIONS	704	Paul Revere's Ride & Other Stories	1945	Longfellow, H.W.	VG+		$12.00	

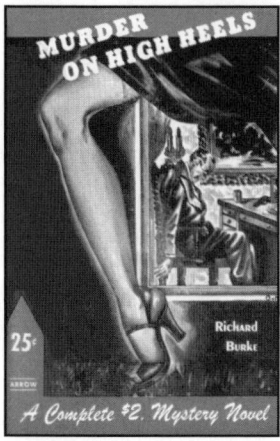

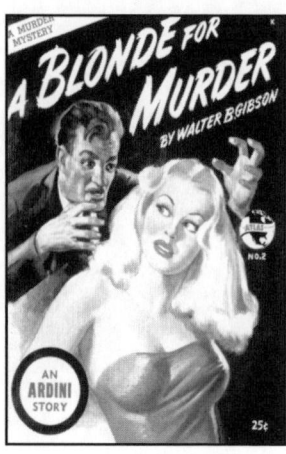

Arrow Mystery 5 VGF $28   Astro 2 VG+ $35   Atlas 2 VGF $36

PUBLISHER	PUB. #	TITLE	DATE	AUTHOR	COND.	TYPE	PRICE
ARMED SERVICES EDITIONS	739	Soldier Art	1945	Anthology	VG		$15.00
ARMED SERVICES EDITIONS	765	Great Tales Of The Sea	1945	Anthology	VG		$5.00
ARMED SERVICES EDITIONS	775	Some Like Them Short	1945	March, W.	VG+		$7.00
ARMED SERVICES EDITIONS	779	On Borrowed Time	1945	Watkin, L.E.	VG		$7.00
ARMED SERVICES EDITIONS	840	The Biscuit Eater & Other Stories	1945	Street, J.	VG+		$10.00
ARMED SERVICES EDITIONS	863	The Gray Champion & Other St.	1945	Hawthorne, N.	VG+		$10.00
ARMED SERVICES EDITIONS	901	The Daniel Jazz & Other Stories	1946	Lindsay, V.	VGF		$8.00
ARMED SERVICES EDITIONS	914	The Lucky Stiff	1946	Rice, C.	VG+		$6.00 A
ARMED SERVICES EDITIONS	920	Jazz	1946	Goffin, R.	VG+		$6.00
ARMED SERVICES EDITIONS	937	The Deadly Dove	1946	King, R.	VGF		$16.00 A
ARMED SERVICES EDITIONS	946	Deadlier Than The Male	1946	Gunn, J.	VGF-		$10.00
ARMED SERVICES EDITIONS	991	Curse Of The Bronze Lamp	1946	Dickson, C.*	G+		$5.00
ARMED SERVICES EDITIONS	1026	The King Is Dead On Queen St.	1946	Bonnamy, F.	VG+		$8.00
ARMED SERVICES EDITIONS	1041	The Lost Weekend	1946	Jackson, C.	VG+		$8.00
ARMED SERVICES EDITIONS	1074	The Sunday Pigeon Murders	1946	Rice, C.	G+		$5.00
ARMED SERVICES EDITIONS	1075	The Murder That Had Everything	1946	Footner, H.	VG		$8.00
ARMED SERVICES EDITIONS	1080	Tales By Tolstoy	1946	Tolstoy, L.	VG		$8.00
ARMED SERVICES EDITIONS	1221	Frontier On The Potomac	1947	Daniels, J.	VGF		$27.00 A
ARMED SERVICES EDITIONS	1223	Strange & Fantastic Stories	1947	Anthology	VG		$10.00
ARMED SERVICES EDITIONS	1231	Death Of A Tall Man	1947	Lockridge, F.	VG		$8.00
ARMED SERVICES EDITIONS	1233	But Look, The Morn	1947	Kantor, M.	VG		$8.00
ARMED SERVICES EDITIONS	1239	Treasure Of The Brasada	1947	Savage, L.	VG+		$12.00
ARMED SERVICES EDITIONS	1264	Gambler's Gold	1947	Field, P.	VGF		$12.00
ARMED SERVICES EDITIONS	1265	Aurora Dawn	1947	Wouk, H.	VG+		$12.00
ARMED SERVICES EDITIONS	1291	Puzzle For Pilgrims	1947	Quentin, P.	VGF+		$8.00 A
ARMED SERVICES EDITIONS	1292	Ghost Of A Chance	1947	Roos, K.	VG		$8.00
ARMED SERVICES EDITIONS	1303	Blood Money	1947	Bellamy, F.R.	VG+		$12.00
ARMED SERVICES EDITIONS	1305	Tomorrow's A Holiday	1947	Loveridge, A.	VGF		$12.00
ARMY FUN	7 9	Army Fun - 4/65	1965	Anthology	VGF	Digest	$6.00
ARMY FUN	9 5	Army Fun - 8/68	1968	Anthology	VGF	Digest	$6.00
ARROW (U.K.)	345	The Devil Rides Out	n/d	Wheatley, D.	VG		$7.00
ARROW MYSTERY	5	Murder On High Heels	1944	Burke, R.	VGF	Digest	$28.00 A
ARROW MYSTERY	6	Murder On Friday	1944	Ashbrook, H.	VG+	Digest	$11.00 A
ARROW MYSTERY	6	Murder On Friday	1944	Ashbrook, H.	VG	Digest	$8.00
ARROW MYSTERY	8	The Kissed Corpse	1944	Baker, A.	VGF	Digest	$9.00
ARROW MYSTERY	9	Invitation To Murder	1944	Long, M.	VG	Digest	$8.00 A
ASIMOV'S SCI-FI	1 1	Isaac Asimov's Sci-Fi Mag.	1977	Anthology	F	Digest	$8.00
ASTOUNDING	39 6	Astounding Sci-Fi - 8/47	1947	Anthology	VG	Digest	$10.00
ASTOUNDING	53 2	Astounding Sci-Fi - 4/54	1954	Anthology	AF	Digest	$7.00
ASTOUNDING	54 1	Astounding Sci-Fi - 9/54	1954	Anthology	VGF	Digest	$8.00
ASTOUNDING	63 6	Astounding Sci-Fi - 8/49	1949	Anthology	VG+	Digest	$15.00
ASTRO	2	Week-End Girl	1948	Clayford, J.	VG+	Digest	$35.00 A
ASTRO	10	Confessions Of A Good-Time Girl	1948	Owen, E.	VGF+	Digest	$33.00 A
ASTRO	12	Shakedown Dame	1948	Herzog, D.	VG	Digest	$10.00
ASTRO	15	Illicit Wife	1948	Clayford, J.	VG	Digest	$15.00

Avon No# 6 VG- $19   Avon No# 38 VG- $60   Avon 63 VG $47

PUBLISHER	PUB. #	TITLE	DATE	AUTHOR	COND.	TYPE	PRICE
ASTRO	18	Strange Mistress	n/d	Clayford, J.	VG	Digest	$15.00
ATLAS	No#	The Corpse Comes Ashore	1945	Mesereau, J.	VG	Digest	$8.00
ATLAS	2	A Blonde For Murder	1948	Gibson, W.B.	VGF	Digest	$36.00 A
ATLAS (MOHAWK)	No#	Kill One, Kill Two	1944	Anderson, W.W.	VGF	Digest	$13.00 A
ATOMIC BOOKS	No#	Billy The Kid	1946	Garrett, P.F.	VGF-	Digest	$11.00 A
ATOMIC BOOKS	No#	Wild Bill Hickock	1946	Buel, J.	VG+	Digest	$6.00 A
AUTOMOTIVE PERIODICALS	No#	The Roaring Road	1957	Anthology	G		$5.00
AVON	No# 1	Elmer Gantry	1941	Lewis, S.	G		$5.00 A
AVON	No# 3	The Big Four	1941	Christie, A.	G		$10.00
AVON	No# 4	Ill Wind	1941	Hilton, J.	G+		$7.00
AVON	No# 5	Dr. Priestley Investigates	1941	Rhode, J.	G		$6.00
AVON	No# 6	The Haunted Hotel & 25 Others	1941	Anthology	VG-		$19.00 A
AVON	No# 6	25 Great Ghost Stories	1943	Anthology	VG-		$16.00
AVON	No# 10	Dr. Thorndyke's Discovery	1941	Freeman, R.A.	G		$8.00
AVON	No# 11	Count Bruga	1941	Hecht, B.	VG		$7.00
AVON	No# 15	Modern Short Stories	1942	Anthology	G+		$3.00
AVON	No# 16	Murder At Midnight	1942	Walling, R.A.J.	G		$5.00
AVON	No# 18	The Man Who Murdered Himself	1942	Homes, G.	G		$7.00
AVON	No# 19	48 Saroyan Stories	1942	Saroyan, W.	G-		$3.00
AVON	No# 22	Red Headed Woman	1942	Brush, K.	G		$3.00
AVON	No# 24	Ashenden Or The British Agent	1943	Maugham, W.S.	VG		$6.00
AVON	No# 26	Seven Footprints To Satan	1943	Merritt, A.	G+		$7.00
AVON	No# 30	Gorgeous Ghoul Murder Case	1943	Babcock, D.V.	VGF		$29.00 A
AVON	No# 30	Gorgeous Ghoul Murder Case	1943	Babcock, D.V.	VGF		$20.00 A
AVON	No# 31	The Doctor's Son	1943	O'Hara, J.	VG		$6.00
AVON	No# 32	Stage Door Canteen	1943	Daves, D.	G+	MTI	$3.00
AVON	No# 33	Corpse In The Waxworks	1943	Carr, J.D.	G+		$10.00
AVON	No# 38	The Big Sleep	1943	Chandler, R.	VG-		$60.00 A
AVON	No# 38	The Big Sleep	1943	Chandler, R.	VG+		$46.00 A
AVON	No# 39	Rage in Heaven	1943	Hilton, J.	VG-		$7.00
AVON	No# 40	In The Teeth Of The Evidence	1943	Sayers, D.	VG+		$5.00 A
AVON	42	The Passionate Year	1944	Hilton, J.	VG		$7.00
AVON	43	Burn Witch Burn	1944	Merritt, A.	G+		$7.00
AVON	44	The Saint In New York	1944	Charteris, L.	VGF-		$15.00
AVON	47	Shoe The Wild Mare	1944	Fowler, G.	VG		$6.00
AVON	48	The Road To Victory	1944	Spellman, F.	VGF		$5.00
AVON	50	Cakes And Ale	1944	Maugham, W.S.	VG+		$7.00
AVON	53	The Mystery Of The Red Triangle	1944	Tuttle, W.C.	VG		$8.00
AVON	58	Winged Victory	1944	Hart, M.	VG+		$15.00
AVON	60	Double Indemnity	1945	Cain, J.M.	VGF		$27.00 A
AVON	63	5 Murderers	1945	Chandler, R.	VG		$47.00 A
AVON	63	5 Murderers	1945	Chandler, R.	G		$18.00
AVON	63	5 Murderers	1945	Chandler, R.	G		$12.00
AVON	71	The Saint Intervenes	1945	Charteris, L.	VG+		$12.00
AVON	73	A Goodly Heritage	1945	Chase, M.E.	G		$6.00

Avon 71 VG+ $12   Avon 165 VGF $25   Avon 178 VG+ $50

PUBLISHER	PUB. #	TITLE	DATE	AUTHOR	COND.	TYPE	PRICE
AVON	78	To Step Aside	1946	Coward, N.	G		$3.00
AVON	81	Bad Girl	1946	Delmar, V.	VG+		$8.00
AVON	85	The Regatta Mystery	1946	Christie, A.	VG+		$11.00 A
AVON	87	Private Affairs Of Bel Ami	1946	De Maupassant, G.	VGF	MTI	$13.00
AVON	88	Five Sinister Characters	1946	Chandler, R.	VG-		$15.00
AVON	88	Five Sinister Characters	1946	Chandler, R.	G		$10.00
AVON	90	Avon Ghost Reader	1946	Anthology	VG		$7.00
AVON	94	Butterfield 8	1946	O'Hara, J.	VG+		$8.00
AVON	96	The Black Angel	1946	Woolrich, C.	VG+		$15.00 A
AVON	99	The Embezzler	1946	Cain, J.M.	AF		$100.00 A
AVON	100	The Secret Adversary	1946	Christie, A.	VG+		$9.00 A
AVON	104	If I Should Die Before I Wake	1946	Irish, W.*	VG		$23.00 A
AVON	106	The Black Path Of Fear	1946	Woolrich, C.	VG+		$27.00 A
AVON	107	The Marriage Racket	1946	Delmar, V.	VG+		$8.00
AVON	108	A Taste For Honey	1946	Heard, H.F.	AF		$23.00 A
AVON	108	A Taste For Honey	1946	Heard, H.F.	VG+		$20.00 A
AVON	112	The Squealer	1946	Wallace, E.	VG+		$11.00
AVON	114	Sinister Errand	1947	Cheyney, P.	VG+		$8.00
AVON	116	Kelly	1947	Clarke, D.H.	AF		$15.00 A
AVON	117	Creep, Shadow, Creep	1947	Merritt, A.	VG+		$15.00
AVON	117	Creep, Shadow, Creep	1947	Merritt, A.	VG		$15.00
AVON	117	Creep, Shadow, Creep	1947	Merritt, A.	VG		$12.00
AVON	119	The Better Taylors	1947	Taylor, R.	VG		$13.00 A
AVON	122	The Unconscious Witness	1947	Freeman, R.A.	VG+		$7.00 A
AVON	124	A Holiday For Murder	1947	Christie, A.	AF-		$20.00
AVON	125	The Door With Seven Locks	1947	Wallace, E.	VG+		$8.00
AVON	125	The Door With Seven Locks	1947	Wallace, E.	VG		$5.00
AVON	127	Eastern Shame Girl	1947	Anthology,	VG+		$8.00
AVON	128	Ten Nights Of Love	1947	Anthology	VG+		$8.00
AVON	128	Ten Nights Of Love	1947	Anthology	G		$3.00
AVON	134	Georgia Boy	1947	Caldwell, E.	VGF		$14.00
AVON	135	Woman And The Puppet	1947	Louys, P.	VGF		$8.00
AVON	137	Double Indemnity	1947	Cain, J.M.	VGF		$137.00 A
AVON	137	Double Indemnity	1947	Cain, J.M.	G		$3.00
AVON	141	Career In C Major	1947	Cain, J.M.	G		$3.00
AVON	145	The Restless Passion	1947	Delmar, V.	AF		$8.00
AVON	145	The Restless Passion	1947	Delmar, V.	VGF		$8.00
AVON	146	The Abortive Hussy	1947	Woodford, J.	VG		$7.00
AVON	148	Love, Health And Marriage	1948	Cowan, J.	G		$2.00
AVON	152	Georgie May	1947	Bodenheim, M.	VG+		$8.00
AVON	154	When She Was Bad	1948	Brush, K.	VGF		$8.00
AVON	160	Casanova's Homecoming	1948	Schnitzler, A.	VG+		$10.00
AVON	161	Love's Lovely Counterfeit	1948	Cain, J.M.	VG		$8.00
AVON	165	The Stone Of Chastity	1948	Sharp, M.	VGF		$25.00 A
AVON	165	The Stone Of Chastity	1948	Sharp, M.	G		$6.00

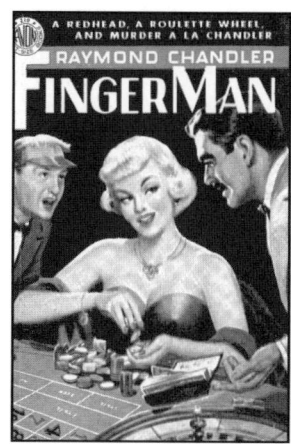

Avon 191 VGF $10   Avon 212 VGF+ $71   Avon 219 VG+ $34

PUBLISHER	PUB. #	TITLE	DATE	AUTHOR	COND.	TYPE	PRICE
AVON	168	Virtuous Girl	1948	Bodenheim, M.	VGF		$16.00
AVON	168	Virtuous Girl	1948	Bodenheim, M.	AF		$12.00 A
AVON	169	The Amboy Dukes	1948	Shulman, I.	VGF		$15.00
AVON	169	The Amboy Dukes (MTI ed.)	1949	Shulman, I.	VG	MTI	$7.00
AVON	171	Amourous Philandre	1948	De Bibiena, J.G.	VG+		$6.00
AVON	172	Bubu Of Montparnasse	1948	Philippe, C.L.	VG+		$7.00
AVON	173	On The Spot	1948	Wallace, E.	VGF		$10.00
AVON	174	Sinful Woman	1948	Cain, J.M.	F		$49.00 A
AVON	174	Sinful Woman	1948	Cain, J.M.	VGF		$20.00 A
AVON	174	Sinful Woman	1948	Cain, J.M.	VG-		$5.00
AVON	177	Midsummer Passion	1948	Caldwell, E.	VG+		$7.00
AVON	178	Fast One	1948	Cain, P.	VG+		$50.00 A
AVON	178	Fast One	1948	Cain, P.	AF		$32.00 A
AVON	178	Fast One	1948	Cain, P.	VGF-		$30.00 A
AVON	180	French Summer	1948	Gilpatric, G.	VGF		$14.00 A
AVON	182	New Avon Bedside Companion	1949	Anthology	VGF		$7.00
AVON	183	Burial Of The Fruit	1948	Dortort, D.	VG		$4.00
AVON	186	Night Cry	1949	Stuart, W.L.	VGF		$15.00
AVON	186	Night Cry	1949	Stuart, W.L.	VG		$7.00
AVON	189	The Daughter Of Fu Manchu	1949	Rohmer, S.	VG		$20.00 A
AVON	190	Modern Mister Bluebeard	1949	Greene, W.	G+		$5.00
AVON	191	Replenishing Jessica	1949	Bodenheim, M.	VGF		$10.00
AVON	197	Son Of The Grand Eunuch	1949	Pettit, C.	VG+		$12.00
AVON	198	Yvette And Other Stories	1949	De Maupassant, G.	VG		$7.00
AVON	202	From Gags To Riches	1949	Adams, J.	VGF		$5.00 A
AVON	205	The Last Frontier	1949	Fast, H.	VGF		$15.00
AVON	207	Virgie Goodbye	1949	Rothman, N.	VG		$6.00
AVON	207	Virgie Goodbye	1949	Rothman, N.	G		$3.00
AVON	212	Iron Man	1949	Burnett, W.R.	VGF+		$71.00 A
AVON	213	Nina	1949	Clarke, D.H.	VGF		$8.00
AVON	214	The Fox Woman	1949	Merritt, A.	AF		$37.00 A
AVON	214	The Fox Woman	1949	Merritt, A.	VG+		$20.00
AVON	214	The Fox Woman	1949	Merritt, A.	VG		$17.00
AVON	215	All The Brothers Were Valiant	1949	Williams, B.A.	VGF+		$8.00
AVON	217	Miss Jill From Shanghai	1950	Hahn, E.	VGF		$8.00
AVON	219	Finger Man	1950	Chandler, R.	VG+		$34.00 A
AVON	219	Finger Man	1950	Chandler, R.	G+		$10.00
AVON	221	Don Juan	1950	Lewisohn, L.	VGF		$11.00 A
AVON	225	Anyone Can Have A Great Vocab.	1950	Stephenson, J.L.	VGF		$5.00
AVON	226	I Can Get It Wholesale	1949	Weidman, J.	VG+		$7.00
AVON	229	All About Girls	1950	Anthology	VG+		$12.00
AVON	233	The Servant	1950	Maugham, R.	VGF		$10.00
AVON	233	The Servant	1950	Maugham, R.	VG+		$7.00
AVON	234	The Old Goat	1950	Thayer, T.	VG+		$7.00
AVON	235	Seven Footprints To Satan	1950	Merritt, A.	G		$7.00

Avon 281 VGF $38   Avon 285 AF $66   Avon 307 VG+ $27

PUBLISHER	PUB. #	TITLE	DATE	AUTHOR	COND.	TYPE	PRICE
AVON	236	Venus Of The Counting House	1950	Zola, E.	VG		$6.00
AVON	237	Tawny	1950	Clarke, D.H.	VGF+		$8.00
AVON	239	Bad Girl From Maine	1950	Brush, K.	VGF+		$220.00 A
AVON	240	End As A Man	1950	Willingham, C.	VG		$3.00
AVON	241	What's In It For Me?	1950	Weidman, J.	VGF+		$15.00
AVON	244	Cry Tough!	1950	Shulman, I.	G		$2.00
AVON	248	Love Among The Haystacks	1950	Lawrence, D.H.	AF-		$9.00
AVON	249	It Happens Every Spring	1950	Davies, V.	VGF		$8.00
AVON	252	A Hell Of A Good Time	1950	Farrell, J.T.	VGF+		$12.00
AVON	255	Tropical Passions	1950	Anthology	VG-		$7.00
AVON	261	The Avon Improved Cook Book	1950	Metzelthin, P.V.	F		$23.00
AVON	263	The Gangs Of New York	1950	Asbury, H.	AF		$40.00 A
AVON	268	Seven Slayers	1950	Cain, P.	G		$10.00
AVON	270	The Chastity Of Gloria Boyd	1950	Clarke, D.H.	VGF		$8.00
AVON	272	Europa ("map" cover)	1950	Briffault, R.	F		$48.00 A
AVON	272	Europa ("map" cover)	1950	Briffault, R.	VG		$8.00
AVON	272	Europa (whipping cover)	1950	Briffault, R.	VG+		$15.00
AVON	272	Europa (whipping cover)	1950	Briffault, R.	VG		$14.00
AVON	276	Madwoman?	1951	Harvin, E.	AF		$53.00 A
AVON	277	Perelandra	1950	Lewis, C.S.	AF		$28.00 A
AVON	277	Perelandra	1950	Lewis, C.S.	VGF		$25.00
AVON	278	A Killer Is Loose Among Us	1950	Terrall, R.	VG+		$7.00
AVON	281	Into Plutonium Depths	1950	Coblentz, S.A.	VGF		$38.00 A
AVON	281	Into Plutonium Depths	1950	Coblentz, S.A.	VG+		$24.00 A
AVON	282	Lovely Lady, Pity Me	1951	Huggins, R.	VGF		$25.00 A
AVON	282	Lovely Lady, Pity Me	1951	Huggins, R.	VG		$10.00
AVON	284	Madam Is Dead	1951	Terrall, R.	VG+		$8.00
AVON	285	An Earth Man On Venus	1951	Farley, R.M.	AF		$66.00 A
AVON	285	An Earth Man On Venus	1951	Farley, R.M.	VG+		$25.00
AVON	285	An Earth Man On Venus	1951	Farley, R.M.	VG+		$22.00 A
AVON	290	Gas-House McGinty	1950	Farrell, J.T.	AF		$14.00
AVON	291	Call Her Savage	1951	Thayer, T.	VGF+		$14.00
AVON	291	Call Her Savage	1951	Thayer, T.	AF		$13.00
AVON	292	Four Boys A Girl And A Gun	1951	Weiner, W.	VGF		$31.00 A
AVON	292	Four Boys A Girl And A Gun	1951	Weiner, W.	G		$3.00
AVON	293	Hellbox	1950	O'Hara, J.	AF		$17.00
AVON	296	A Modern Lover	1950	Lawrence, D.H.	AF		$20.00 A
AVON	300	Amboy Dukes (reclining cover)	1950	Shulman, I.	AF		$17.00 A
AVON	300	Amboy Dukes (standing cover)	1951	Shulman, I.	VG		$8.00
AVON	302	Perversity	1950	Carco, F.	AF		$10.00
AVON	303	Dream Street	1950	Sylvester, R.	AF		$59.00 A
AVON	303	Dream Street	1950	Sylvester, R.	VG+		$6.00
AVON	305	God Wears A Bow Tie	1950	Stuart, L.	VG		$7.00
AVON	305	God Wears A Bow Tie	1950	Stuart, L.	VG		$6.00
AVON	306	Gone To Texas	1950	Thomason, J.W.	VG+		$7.00

Avon 315 AF $45   Avon 370 AF $60   Avon 376 VG+ $45

PUBLISHER	PUB. #	TITLE	DATE	AUTHOR	COND.	TYPE	PRICE
AVON	307	Big League Baseball	1951	Anthology	VG+		$27.00 A
AVON	308	Musk, Hashish And Blood	1951	France, H.	VG+		$13.00 A
AVON	308	Musk, Hashish And Blood	1951	France, H.	G+		$7.00
AVON	312	Mysterious Affair At Styles	1951	Christie, A.	VG		$7.00
AVON	313	The Ugly Duchess	1951	Feuchtwanger, L.	AF		$15.00
AVON	314	Nigger Heaven	1951	Van Vechten, C.	AF		$75.00 A
AVON	314	Nigger Heaven	1951	Van Vechten, C.	VG+		$25.00
AVON	315	The Metal Monster	1951	Merritt, A.	AF		$45.00 A
AVON	315	The Metal Monster	1951	Merritt, A.	AF		$38.00 A
AVON	315	The Metal Monster	1951	Merritt, A.	VGF		$38.00 A
AVON	315	The Metal Monster	1951	Merritt, A.	VG+		$15.00
AVON	318	Dear Sir (4th)	1951	Lowell, J.	VG		$7.00
AVON	319	Along The Broadway Beat	1951	Sobol, L.	VGF-		$13.00
AVON	319	Along The Broadway Beat	1951	Sobol, L.	VG+		$6.00
AVON	322	Slipping Beauty	1951	Weidman, J.	AF		$18.00
AVON	323	The Furies In Her Body	1951	Endore, G.	VGF-		$10.00
AVON	323	The Furies In Her Body	1951	Endore, G.	VG+		$8.00
AVON	324	The Ship Of Ishtar	1951	Merritt, A.	VGF-		$24.00
AVON	324	The Ship Of Ishtar	1951	Merritt, A.	VGF		$20.00
AVON	324	The Ship Of Ishtar	1951	Merritt, A.	VG		$14.00
AVON	325	Ill Wind	1951	Hilton, J.	VGF+		$8.00
AVON	327	One Man Show	1951	Thayer, T.	VG		$8.00
AVON	328	Strong Poison	1951	Sayers, D.L.	VG+		$7.00
AVON	330	Desperate Men	1951	Horan, J.D.	VGF		$8.00
AVON	330	Desperate Men	1951	Horan, J.D.	VG		$6.00
AVON	331	Trio	1951	Maugham, W.S.	AF		$10.00
AVON	333	Line On Ginger	1951	Maugham, R.	AF		$20.00 A
AVON	333	Line On Ginger	1951	Maugham, R.	AF+		$12.00 A
AVON	335	In The Teeth Of The Evidence	1951	Sayers, D.	VGF		$9.00
AVON	336	The Housekeeper's Daughter	1951	Clarke, D.H.	VGF		$20.00 A
AVON	337	The Agony Column	1951	Biggers, E.D.	VG+		$10.00
AVON	338	Hollywood Bedside Reader	1951	Anthology	AF		$27.00 A
AVON	339	Terror Of The Leopard Men	1951	Kennerley, J.	VGF+		$14.00 A
AVON	342	The Woman Aroused	1951	Lacey, E.	AF		$67.00 A
AVON	342	The Woman Aroused	1951	Lacey, E.	VG+		$35.00 A
AVON	344	The Chinese Parrot	1951	Biggers, E.D.	VG+		$15.00
AVON	344	The Chinese Parrot	1951	Biggers, E.D.	VG		$10.00
AVON	345	I Lost My Girlish Laughter	1951	Allen, J.	VG		$15.00 A
AVON	346	Possess Me Not	1951	Nichols, F.	AF		$23.00 A
AVON	346	Possess Me Not	1951	Nichols, F.	VG+		$16.00
AVON	347	The Saint At The Thieves Picnic	1951	Charteris, L.	AF		$10.00
AVON	348	Jealous Woman	1951	Cain, J.M.	AF		$43.00 A
AVON	351	Millie's Daughter	1951	Clarke, D.H.	VG+		$6.00
AVON	352	Ninth Avenue	1951	Bodenheim, M.	VG+		$7.00
AVON	352	Ninth Avenue	1951	Bodenheim, M.	VG+		$6.00

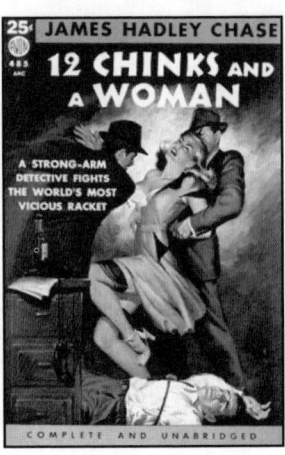

| Avon 392 AF $22 | Avon 415 F $59 | Avon 485 VGF $43 |

PUBLISHER	PUB. #	TITLE	DATE	AUTHOR	COND. TYPE	PRICE
AVON	354	The Werewolf Of Paris	1951	Endore, G.	AF	$36.00 A
AVON	357	All About Girls	1951	Anthology	VG+	$12.00
AVON	357	All About Girls	1951	Anthology	VG	$7.00
AVON	360	As They Reveled	1951	Wylie, P.	VGF	$8.00
AVON	362	Calamity Jane	1951	Hueston, E.	VG	$6.00
AVON	364	The Point Of Honor	1951	Maugham, W.S.	AF	$9.00
AVON	366	They'll Do It Every Time	1951	Hatlo, J.	VGF	$10.00
AVON	368	All The Girls He Wanted	1951	O'Hara, J.	VGF+	$20.00
AVON	370	The Moon Pool	1951	Merritt, A.	AF	$60.00 A
AVON	370	The Moon Pool	1951	Merritt, A.	VGF+	$44.00 A
AVON	372	Cry Tough!	1951	Shulman, I.	VGF	$12.00
AVON	373	The Blue Negro	1951	Payne, R.	AF	$25.00
AVON	376	Home To Harlem	1951	McKay, C.	VG+	$45.00 A
AVON	377	Taffy	1951	Kaye, P.B.	AF	$30.00 A
AVON	377	Taffy	1951	Kaye, P.B.	VGF	$16.00
AVON	378	The Marshall Of Deer Creek	1951	Cody, A.	VGF	$17.00 A
AVON	378	The Marshall Of Deer Creek	1951	Cody, A.	VG+	$7.00
AVON	382	Tough Kid From Brooklyn	1951	Mende, R.	VG+	$15.00
AVON	382	Tough Kid From Brooklyn	1951	Mende, R.	VG	$6.00
AVON	383	The Untamed Wife Of Louis Scott	1951	Munro, W.C.	VGF	$11.00
AVON	389	Post Fantasy Stories	1951	Anthology	VGF	$29.00 A
AVON	391	Maidens In The Midden	1951	Anderson, O.	VG+	$6.00
AVON	392	Burn Witch Burn	1951	Merritt, A.	AF	$22.00 A
AVON	392	Burn Witch Burn	1951	Merritt, A.	VGF	$20.00 A
AVON	396	His First Million Women	1952	Weston, G.	VGF	$30.00 A
AVON	397	Nina	1952	Clarke, D.H.	AF-	$8.00
AVON	397	Nina	1952	Clarke, D.H.	VG+	$7.00
AVON	399	. . . Plus Blood In Their Veins	1952	Smith, R.P.	VGF	$10.00
AVON	399	. . . Plus Blood In Their Veins	1952	Smith, R.P.	VG	$7.00
AVON	400	Jule: Alabama Boy In Harlem	1952	Henderson, G.W.	VGF+	$15.00
AVON	400	Jule: Alabama Boy In Harlem	1952	Henderson, G.W.	VGF	$14.00
AVON	401	Perversity	1952	Carco, F.	VGF	$33.00 A
AVON	401	Perversity	1952	Carco, F.	VG+	$8.00
AVON	402	Dangerous Love	1952	Woodford, J.	AF	$17.00 A
AVON	406	Two Beds For Roxanne	1952	Longstreet, S.	VGF+	$8.00
AVON	406	Two Beds For Roxanne	1952	Longstreet, S.	VG+	$7.00
AVON	407	Strange Brother	1952	Niles, B.	VGF+	$20.00
AVON	410	The Secret Adversary	1952	Christie, A.	AF	$13.00 A
AVON	413	Dwellers In The Mirage	1952	Merritt, A.	AF	$37.00 A
AVON	413	Dwellers In The Mirage	1952	Merritt, A.	AF-	$29.00 A
AVON	413	Dwellers In The Mirage	1952	Merritt, A.	VGF	$20.00 A
AVON	415	Musk, Hashish And Blood	1952	France, H.	F	$59.00 A
AVON	415	Musk, Hashish And Blood	1952	France, H.	AF	$51.00 A
AVON	417	Star Lust	1952	Hanley, J.	AF	$50.00 A
AVON	419	Never Come Morning	1952	Algren, N.	F	$18.00 A

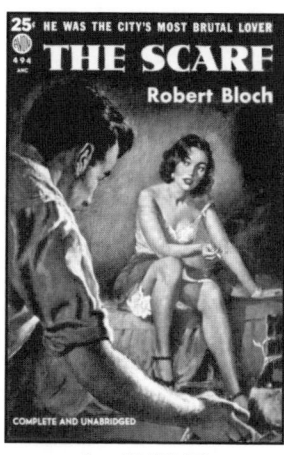

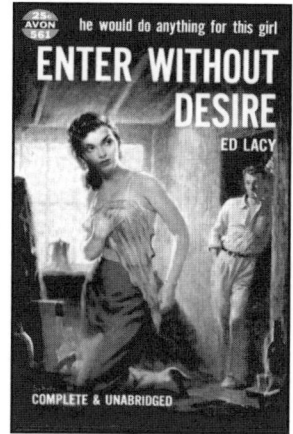

Avon 494 VGF $38   Avon 538 VGF- $31   Avon 561 F $72

PUBLISHER	PUB. #	TITLE	DATE	AUTHOR	COND.	TYPE	PRICE
AVON	421	Love's Lovely Counterfeit	1952	Cain, J.M.	AF		$41.00 A
AVON	421	Love's Lovely Counterfeit	1952	Cain, J.M.	F		$37.00 A
AVON	429	The Price Is Right	1952	Weidman, J.	AF		$10.00
AVON	437	Battle At Apache Pass	1952	Conrad, H.	G-	MTI	$4.00
AVON	438	Confidential	1952	Clarke, D.H.	AF		$10.00
AVON	438	Confidential	1952	Clarke, D.H.	VGF		$8.00
AVON	444	Four Boys A Girl And A Gun	1952	Weiner, W.	VGF		$15.00
AVON	446	Outcasts Of Poker Flat	1952	Harte, B.	VGF	MTI	$9.00
AVON	448	The Last Of Mr. Norris	1952	Isherwood, C.	AF-		$8.00
AVON	452	Red Bone Woman	1952	Tillery, C.	VGF+		$9.00
AVON	454	The Challenge Of Smoke Wade	1952	Hogan, R.J.	VGF		$7.00
AVON	455	The Root Of His Evil	1952	Cain, J.M.	VG		$10.00
AVON	466	Gas-House McGinty	1952	Farrell, J.T.	VGF		$8.00
AVON	467	Hell-Bent With Jake	1952	La Due, R.	VGF		$7.00
AVON	468	A Hell Of A Good Time	1952	Farrell, J.T.	AF		$10.00
AVON	468	A Hell Of A Good Time	1952	Farrell, J.T.	VGF		$10.00
AVON	469	Roaring Guns At Apache Landing	1952	Hogan, R.J.	VG		$6.00
AVON	470	Low Company	1952	Benney, M.	VGF		$10.00
AVON	473	The Saint's Getaway	1952	Charteris, L.	G		$3.00
AVON	476	The Bride Of Newgate	1952	Carr, J.D.	VG+		$7.00
AVON	478	A Bullet For Billy The Kid	1952	Nye, N.	AF-		$8.00
AVON	479	Jealous Woman	1952	Cain, J.M.	AF		$54.00 A
AVON	479	Jealous Woman	1952	Cain, J.M.	VG+		$8.00
AVON	481	The Hucksters	1952	Wakeman, F.	VGF		$8.00
AVON	483	A Lady Named Lou	1952	Clarke, D.H.	AF		$50.00 A
AVON	483	A Lady Named Lou	1952	Clarke, D.H.	VG		$5.00
AVON	485	12 Chinks And A Woman	1952	Chase, J.H.	VGF		$43.00 A
AVON	485	12 Chinks And A Woman	1952	Chase, J.H.	VG		$24.00 A
AVON	485	12 Chinks And A Woman	1952	Chase, J.H.	VG		$24.00 A
AVON	489	The Saint Meets His Match	1952	Charteris, L.	VG+		$7.00
AVON	494	The Scarf	1952	Bloch, R.	VGF		$38.00 A
AVON	494	The Scarf	1952	Bloch, R.	VG+		$33.00 A
AVON	494	The Scarf	1952	Bloch, R.	VG		$20.00 A
AVON	496	Fast One	1952	Cain, P.	VG+		$10.00
AVON	497	A Night With Mr. Primrose	1952	Cook, W.	VG		$7.00
AVON	499	Chorus Of Cuties	1952	Campbell, E.S.	VG-		$8.00
AVON	506	Nonce	1953	Brandon, M.	VGF		$14.00
AVON	513	Bachelor's Joke Book	1953	Guild, L.	AF		$8.00
AVON	513	Bachelor's Joke Book	1953	Guild, L.	VGF		$8.00 A
AVON	513	Bachelor's Joke Book	1953	Guild, L.	VGF		$7.00
AVON	518	The Avenging Saint	1953	Charteris, L.	AF		$12.00
AVON	519	Dennis The Menace	1953	Ketcham, H.	AF		$7.00
AVON	520	Scratch The Surface	1953	Schiddel, E.	AF		$10.00
AVON	525	Guns Blaze At Sundown	1952	Cody, A.	VG+		$5.00
AVON	528	Kiss The Killer	1953	Shallit, J.	VG		$30.00 A

Avon 621 VGF $15　　　　Avon 630 VGF $14　　　　Avon 649 VG+ $7

PUBLISHER	PUB. #	TITLE	DATE	AUTHOR	COND.	TYPE	PRICE
AVON	529	Gunshot Empire	1953	Wells, L.E.	AF		$12.00
AVON	530	Impatient Virgin	1953	Clarke, D.H.	VG		$5.00
AVON	534	Time And The Place	1953	Smith, R.P.	AF		$11.00 A
AVON	534	Time And The Place	1953	Smith, R.P.	VG		$5.00
AVON	535	Dead As A Dinosaur	1953	Lockridge, F.	AF		$12.00
AVON	A 538	Dope, Inc.	1953	Joesten, J.	VGF-		$31.00 A
AVON	A 538	Dope, Inc.	1953	Joesten, J.	VGF-		$23.00 A
AVON	A 538	Dope, Inc.	1953	Joesten, J.	VG		$15.00
AVON	541	Burial Of The Fruit	1953	Dortort, D.	VG-		$6.00
AVON	A 542	Call Me Killer!	1953	Carter, M.	AF		$17.00 A
AVON	548	Away And Beyond	1953	Van Vogt, A.E.	AF		$10.00
AVON	A 549	Tales Of Love And Fury	1953	Anthology	VGF+		$5.00 A
AVON	550	Renegade Guns	1953	Hogan, R.J.	VGF		$8.00
AVON	552	Man On The Tightrope	1953	Paterson, N.	VG+		$10.00 A
AVON	553	Rusty Desmond	1954	January, S.	VG		$13.00
AVON	554	I'll Call Every Monday	1954	Hitt, O.	VG-		$6.00
AVON	555	Rue Pigalle	1954	Carco, F.	AF		$25.00 A
AVON	561	Enter Without Desire	1954	Lacy, E.	F		$72.00 A
AVON	561	Enter Without Desire	1954	Lacy, E.	AF		$44.00 A
AVON	563	The Creepers	1954	Creasey, J.	AF		$8.00
AVON	564	Every Bet's A Sure Thing	1954	Dewey, T.B.	VG		$7.00
AVON	564	Every Bet's A Sure Thing	1954	Dewey, T.B.	VG-		$3.00
AVON	577	Jule: Alabama Boy In Harlem	1954	Henderson, G.W.	VG		$7.00
AVON	578	Girl On The Left Bank	1954	Shepherd, J.	VG+		$7.00
AVON	579	Rebel Ranger	1954	MacDonald, W.C.	AF		$15.00
AVON	580	The Guy From Coney Island	1954	Hanley, J.	VGF		$21.00 A
AVON	583	Death Has A Small Voice	1954	Lockridge, F.	VG+		$7.00
AVON	584	Few Die Well	1954	Noel, S.	VGF		$10.00
AVON	588	Saint Errant	1954	Charteris, L.	VG+		$7.00
AVON	589	The Other Side Of The Night	1954	Schiddel, E.	AF		$13.00 A
AVON	589	The Other Side Of The Night	1954	Schiddel, E.	VG+		$8.00
AVON	590	The Figure In The Dusk	1954	Creasey, J.	F		$10.00
AVON	590	The Figure In The Dusk	1954	Creasey, J.	VG		$3.00
AVON	593	Nina	1954	Clarke, D.H.	VGF		$7.00
AVON	594	The Pennycross Murders	1954	Proctor, M.	AF		$12.00
AVON	595	How Brave We Live	1954	Monash, P.	AF		$10.00
AVON	599	Sinful Woman	1954	Cain, J.M.	VG+		$6.00
AVON	601	Love For A Stranger	1954	McCoy, J.P.	VG		$5.00
AVON	605	Death Hits The Jackpot	1954	Tiger, J.	AF		$10.00
AVON	609	French Postcards	1954	Anthology	AF-		$8.00 A
AVON	610	The Saint Steps In	1954	Charteris, L.	AF		$10.00
AVON	611	The Saint In Europe	1954	Charteris, L.	AF		$8.00
AVON	613	Break-Up	1954	Schiddel, E.	AF		$10.00 A
AVON	614	And Dream Of Evil	1954	Thomey, T.	VG+		$5.00
AVON	617	Battle Of The Sexes	1955	Anthology	VG		$7.00

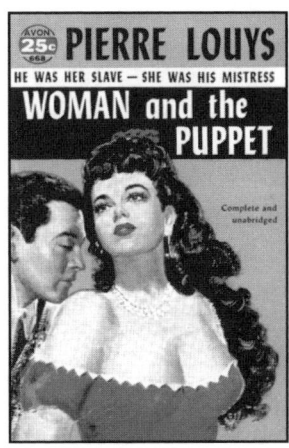

Avon 668 VGF $6   Avon 691 AF $12   Avon 695 AF $8

PUBLISHER	PUB. #	TITLE	DATE	AUTHOR	COND.	TYPE	PRICE
AVON	620	Death In The Desert	1955	Wells, L.E.	VG		$5.00
AVON	621	It Walks By Night	1954	Carr, J.D.	VGF		$15.00 A
AVON	624	The Stone Of Chastity	1955	Sharp, M.	AF		$8.00
AVON	628	The Monk & Hangman's Daughter	1955	Bierce, A.	AF-		$14.00
AVON	630	20 Great Ghost Stories	1955	Anthology	VGF		$14.00
AVON	632	Jet Pilot	1955	Thomey, T.	AF		$12.00
AVON	634	Miss Lonelyhearts	1955	West, N.	F		$12.00
AVON	635	The Saint Goes West	1955	Charteris, L.	F		$12.00
AVON	638	Tropical Passions	1955	Anthology	VG		$10.00
AVON	640	The Man Who Never Was	1955	Montagu, E.	VGF+		$8.00
AVON	641	TCOT Acid Throwers	1955	Creasey, J.	F		$10.00
AVON	643	South Sea Cartoons	1955	Anthology	VGF		$13.00 A
AVON	649	Nudist Cartoons	1955	Anthology	VG+		$7.00
AVON	651	Murder In Las Vegas	1955	Waer, J.	VGF		$7.00
AVON	660	Wake Up To Murder	1955	Keene, D.	VG+		$60.00 A
AVON	660	Wake Up To Murder	1955	Keene, D.	VGF		$27.00 A
AVON	660	Wake Up To Murder	1955	Keene, D.	VG+		$12.00
AVON	660	Wake Up To Murder	1955	Keene, D.	VG		$8.00
AVON	661	Stories Of Venial Sin	1955	O'Hara, J.	F		$7.00
AVON	668	The Woman And The Puppet	1955	Louys, P.	VGF		$6.00
AVON	668	The Woman And The Puppet	1955	Louys, P.	VG		$4.00
AVON	669	Sensualite	1955	LaFouchardiere, G.	AF		$6.00
AVON	673	Henry Morgan's Jokebook	1955	Morgan, H.	VG+		$7.00
AVON	675	Room In Berlin	1955	Birkenfeld, G.	AF		$7.00
AVON	676	White Barrier	1955	Clad, N.	VG		$8.00
AVON	676	White Barrier	1955	Clad, N.	G+		$5.00
AVON	684	The Passion Murders	1955	Keene, D.	VG		$8.00
AVON	685	Alibi Baby	1955	Sterling, S.	VGF		$10.00
AVON	691	Sappho	1956	Daudet, A.	AF		$12.00
AVON	691	Sappho	1956	Daudet, A.	AF		$8.00
AVON	695	The Jungle Of Love	1956	Maugham, R.	AF		$8.00
AVON	698	Smoking Room Joke Book	1956	Anthology	VG+		$12.00
AVON	699	Counterspy Murders	1956	Cheyney, P.	AF		$7.00
AVON	699	Counterspy Murders	1956	Cheyney, P.	VG+		$6.00
AVON	710	The Wound Of Love	1956	Cassill, R.V.	F		$8.00
AVON	711	Experiment In Crime	1956	Wylie, P.	VG+		$8.00
AVON	712	The Man Nobody Saw	1956	Cheyney, P.	AF		$34.00 A
AVON	717	How Rough Can It Get?	1956	Weiss, J.	VGF		$23.00 A
AVON	718	Enter The Saint	1956	Charteris, L.	VGF		$8.00
AVON	720	Give A Man A Gun	1956	Creasey, J.	AF		$8.00
AVON	728	Safari To Dishonor	1956	Schiddel, E.	VG+		$7.00
AVON	730	TCOT Hypnotized Virgin	1956	Roeburt, J.	AF		$10.00
AVON	734	TCOT Dark Hero	1956	Cheyney, P.	VG		$7.00
AVON	742	KKK	1956	Walsh, P.E.	VG		$5.00 A
AVON	745	Martinis And Murder	1956	Kane, H.	VGF		$8.00

Avon 774 VG $8   Avon 847 AF $39   Avon G-1004 VG+ $35

PUBLISHER	PUB. #	TITLE	DATE	AUTHOR	COND.	TYPE	PRICE
AVON	750	Southern Daughter	1956	White, D.	VG		$6.00
AVON	751	Murder Of The Park Ave. Playgirl	1956	Kane, H.	VG+		$7.00
AVON	752	Death By Moonlight	1956	Innes, M.	F		$12.00
AVON	752	Death By Moonlight	1956	Innes, M.	AF		$8.00
AVON	753	The Passionate Seekers	1956	Matthiessen, P.	AF		$22.00 A
AVON	761	Death On The Double	1957	Kane, H.	VGF-		$5.00 A
AVON	762	The Hotel Murders	1957	Sterling, S.	AF		$12.00
AVON	763	Vice-Squad Cop	1957	Carey, M.	VG+		$7.00
AVON	764	Dark Street Murders	1957	Cheyney, P.	VG+		$5.00
AVON	766	The Poisoned Playboy	1957	Lockridge, F.	VG		$6.00
AVON	771	The Saint On Spanish Main	1957	Charteris, L.	AF		$12.00
AVON	774	Gunfight At The O.K. Corral	1957	Frazee, S.	VG	MTI	$8.00
AVON	774	Gunfight At The O.K. Corral	1957	Frazee, S.	VG	MTI	$6.00
AVON	775	The Tall T	1957	Leonard, E.	VG	MTI	$10.00
AVON	777	Kiss And Kill	1957	McCary, R.	VGF		$8.00
AVON	778	Tales Of Midsummer Passion	1957	Anthology	AF		$7.00
AVON	780	The Lonely Man	1957	Turner, R.	VGF	MTI	$15.00
AVON	781	Calypso Murders	1957	Mulholland, P.H.	VG+		$7.00
AVON	782	Gun Feud At Stampede Valley	1957	Peeples, S.A.	AF		$8.00
AVON	783	Hot Rod Gang Rumble	1957	Dolinsky, M.	VGF	MTI	$33.00 A
AVON	786	Murder, My Love	1957	Atiyah, E.	AF		$8.00
AVON	787	TCOT Murdered Model	1957	Dewey, T.B.	AF		$12.00
AVON	790	My Business Is Murder	1957	Kane, H.	AF		$8.00
AVON	794	The Ripper Murders	1957	Procter, M.	AF		$12.00
AVON	794	The Ripper Murders	1957	Procter, M.	VG		$6.00
AVON	797	Cocktails And The Killer	1957	Cheyney, P.	VGF-		$8.00
AVON	802	Murder In Baracoa	1958	Walsh, P.E.	AF		$7.00 A
AVON	803	Featuring The Saint	1958	Charteris, L.	VGF		$10.00
AVON	811	Let Me Kill You, Sweetheart!	1958	Flora, F.	VGF		$8.00
AVON	816	Thunderbolt Range	1958	Lehman, P.E.	AF		$7.00
AVON	817	The Doctor's Woman	1958	Koenig, H.P.	F		$12.00
AVON	818	Alias The Saint	1958	Charteris, L.	F		$10.00
AVON	823	Cry Killer!	1958	Fearing, K.	AF		$12.00
AVON	827	The Saint On Guard	1958	Charteris, L.	F		$8.00
AVON	828	Tall In The Saddle	1958	Martin, C.	AF		$7.00
AVON	830	The Bitch	1958	Brewer, G.	VGF		$31.00 A
AVON	831	Renegade Marshall	1958	Lehman, P.E.	VGF		$7.00
AVON	835	Too Hot To Kill	1958	Sterling, S.	AF		$5.00 A
AVON	836	Unfaithful	1958	Baxter, J.	F		$10.00
AVON	836	Unfaithful	1958	Baxter, J.	VG+		$5.00
AVON	839	Leave Her To Hell	1958	Flora, F.	VG+		$7.00
AVON	841	Day Of Vengeance	1959	Martin, C.	AF		$7.00
AVON	847	My Name Is Violence	1959	Matthews, J.D.	AF		$39.00 A
AVON	848	The Saint Cleans Up	1959	Charteris, L.	VG+		$8.00
AVON	860	Caveman Cartoons	1959	Anthology	VGF		$8.00

Avon G-1035 F $53	Avon G-1100 AF $24	Avon F105 F $8	Avon S-384 VGF $10

PUBLISHER	PUB. #	TITLE	DATE	AUTHOR	COND.	TYPE	PRICE
AVON	864	The Deadly Game	1959	Daniels, N.	VG		$6.00
AVON	866	Angel	1960	Brewer, G.	VGF+		$33.00 A
AVON	867	Killer Behind A Badge	1959	Cook, W.	AF		$7.00
AVON	1001	Jew Suss	1951	Feuchtwanger, L.	VG		$14.00
AVON	1001	Jew Suss	1951	Feuchtwanger, L.	VGF		$10.00
AVON	1002	All-American Fiction Reader	1951	Anthology	AF		$43.00 A
AVON	1002	All-American Fiction Reader	1951	Anthology	VGF		$32.00
AVON	1002	All-American Fiction Reader	1951	Anthology	VG		$10.00
AVON	G 1004	Giant Mystery Reader	1951	Anthology	VG+		$35.00 A
AVON	G 1004	Giant Mystery Reader	1951	Anthology	VGF		$32.00
AVON	G 1007	Avon Webster English Dictionary	1951		AF-		$181.00 A
AVON	G 1010	Out Of This World To Tibet	1954	Thomas, L.	VGF		$7.00
AVON	G 1016	Modern Writing #2	1954	Anthology	F		$7.00
AVON	G 1035	Maggie Cassidy	1959	Kerouac, J.	F		$53.00 A
AVON	G 1035	Maggie Cassidy	1959	Kerouac, J.	VGF+		$18.00 A
AVON	G 1068	Dempsey	1960	Considine, B.	AF		$7.00
AVON	G 1100	Women Without Morals	1962	Gallagher, R.F.	AF		$24.00 A
AVON	G 1100	Women Without Morals	1962	Gallagher, R.F.	VG		$7.00
AVON	G 1124	Other Worlds Of Clifford Simak	1962	Simak, C.D.	AF		$6.00
AVON	G 1151	Queer Patterns	1962	Brock, L.	G		$15.00 A
AVON	G 1154	Space Plague	1963	Smith, G.O.	AF		$5.00
AVON	G 1159	The Quintessence Of Queen	1963	Anthology	VG+		$6.00
AVON	G 1166	Fee, Fei, Fo, Fum	1963	Aylesworth, J.	VGF		$5.00
AVON	G 1217	The Man On A Nylon String	1964	Masterson, W.	VGF		$7.00
AVON	G 1237	The Munsters	1964	Cooper, M.	VG	TVTI	$10.00
AVON	G 1281	Beat Not The Bones	1966	Jay, C.	F		$7.00
AVON	G 1307	The Man From Avon	1967	Avallone, M.	VGF		$7.00
AVON	G 1346	The Cage	1969	Powell, T.	AF		$6.00
AVON	F 105	The Self Starting Wheel	1961	Murray, W.	F		$8.00
AVON	F 118	Little Fuzzy	1962	Piper, H.B.	VG+		$10.00
AVON	F 118	Little Fuzzy	1962	Piper, H.B.	VG		$10.00
AVON	F 150	No Mother To Guide Her	1962	Loos, A.	VG		$5.00
AVON	F 155	Meredith Blake, M.D.	1962	Gaddis, P.	F		$6.00
AVON	F 156	The Five Faces Of Murder	1962	Flynn, J.	VG		$6.00
AVON	N 250	They Shoot Horses, Don't They?	1969	McCoy, H.	F	MTI	$7.00
AVON	S 107	The Goddam White Man	1960	Lytton, D.	VGF		$5.00
AVON	S 127	The Hugo Winners	1962	Anthology	VGF+		$7.00
AVON	S 129	From The Back Of The Bus	1962	Gregory, D.	VGF-		$5.00
AVON	S 145	That Kid	1964	Gehman, R.	VGF	MTI	$15.00 A
AVON	S 194	Kilo 40	1966	Tripp, M.	VG+		$5.00
AVON	S 304	Privilege	1967	Burke, J.	VG	MTI	$4.00
AVON	S 325	Thieves Like Us	1968	Alter, R.E.	VG		$7.00
AVON	S 341	The Double Man	1968	Maxfield, H.S.	VGF	MTI	$7.00
AVON	S 354	The Thomas Crown Affair	1968	Heyman, E.L.	AF	MTI	$6.00
AVON	S 379	Burden's Mission	1968	Whittington, H.	VG+		$10.00
AVON	S 380	Path To Savagery	1969	Alter, R.E.	VGF		$8.00
AVON	S 380	Path To Savagery	1969	Alter, R.E.	VG+		$6.00
AVON	S 384	Avon Fantasy Reader	1969	Anthology	VGF		$10.00

Avon T-170 AF $40	Avon T-177 VG+ $8	Avon T-181 AF $49

PUBLISHER	PUB. #	TITLE	DATE	AUTHOR	COND.	TYPE	PRICE
AVON	S 397	A Walk With The Beast	1969	Anthology	VG-		$3.00
AVON	AT 61	Stories In The Modern Manner	1953	Anthology	VG		$6.00
AVON	AT 65	Sex Habits Of American Women	1953	Wittels, F.	VGF		$7.00
AVON	AT 66	Modern Writing	1953	Anthology	VG+		$6.00
AVON	AT 68	I, Claudius	1953	Graves, R.	AF		$8.00
AVON	AT 69	Intimacy	1953	Sartre, J.P.	AF-		$7.00
AVON	AT 70	Turn Back The River	1953	Hardy, W.G.	F		$10.00
AVON	T 80	No Time Like The Future	1954	Bond, N.	AF		$8.00 A
AVON	T 80	No Time Like The Future	1954	Bond, N.	VGF		$8.00
AVON	T 85	Gone To Texas	1954	Thomason, J.W.	AF		$7.00
AVON	T 86	Savage Holiday	1954	Wright, R.	VG-		$4.00
AVON	T 91	The Dark Journey	1954	Green, J.	VG		$6.00
AVON	T 92	Belly Laughs	1955	Anthology	VGF		$8.00
AVON	T 93	What D'ya Know For Sure	1955	Zinberg, L.	VGF-		$7.00
AVON	T 94	Diary Of A Chamber Maid	1955	Mirbeau, O.	VG+		$6.00
AVON	T 97	I Can Get It Wholesale	1955	Wiedman, J.	VGF		$8.00
AVON	T 97	I Can Get It Wholesale	1955	Weidman, J.	VG+		$6.00
AVON	T 105	Juvenile Delinquents	1955	Kaufman, L.	VG		$10.00
AVON	T 105	Juvenile Delinquents	1955	Kaufman, L.	VG		$9.00 A
AVON	T 108	Never Come Morning	1955	Algren, N.	VGF		$10.00 A
AVON	T 113	Stories Of Scarlet Women	1955	Anthology	VGF		$7.00
AVON	T 115	Seven Footprints To Satan	1956	Merritt, A.	AF		$17.00
AVON	T 115	Seven Footprints To Satan	1956	Merritt, A.	AF-		$15.00
AVON	T 123	Girls For Men Only	1956	Adams, J.P.	VG		$5.00
AVON	T 125	Neon Wilderness	1956	Algren, N.	VG		$4.00
AVON	T 132	Naked Acre	1956	Mitchell, F.	AF		$7.00
AVON	T 137	Bride Comes To Yellow Sky	1956	Crane, S.	VGF		$7.00
AVON	T 138	The Amboy Dukes	1956	Shulman, I.	VG		$6.00
AVON	T 142	Murder In Port Afrique	1956	Dryer, B.V.	VG+	MTI	$7.00
AVON	T 143	Burial Of The Fruit	1956	Dortort, D.	VG+		$7.00
AVON	T 144	Coming Up For Air	1956	Orwell, G.	AF		$12.00
AVON	T 144	Coming Up For Air	1956	Orwell, G.	VGF		$8.00
AVON	T 145	Diary Of A Chamber Maid	1956	Mirbeau, O.	VGF+		$7.00
AVON	T 146	21st Century Sub	1956	Herbert, F.	VGF		$7.00
AVON	T 151	Hannibal	1956	Dolan, M.	VGF		$7.00
AVON	T 152	The Ship Of Ishtar	1956	Merritt, A.	VG+		$6.00
AVON	T 156	Bride Of Violence	1957	Gray, H.	VG		$4.00
AVON	T 161	Face In The Abyss	1957	Merritt, A.	VG+		$6.00
AVON	T 162	Teen-Age Mobster	1957	Appel, B.	AF		$24.00
AVON	T 162	Teen-Age Mobster	1957	Appel, B.	VGF		$20.00
AVON	T 165	Boy On A Dolphin	1957	Divine, D.	VG+	MTI	$100.00 A
AVON	T 170	Juvenile Hoods	1957	Shallit, J.	AF		$40.00 A
AVON	T 170	Juvenile Hoods	1957	Shallit, J.	VGF		$27.00 A
AVON	T 172	The Metal Monster	1957	Merritt, A.	VGF		$7.00
AVON	T 172	The Metal Monster	1957	Merritt, A.	VG+		$5.00

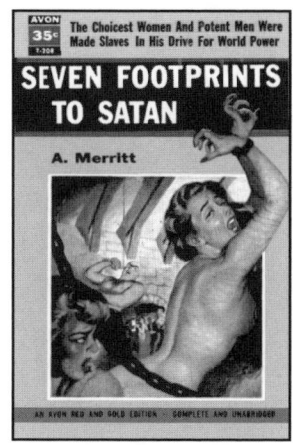

Avon T-208 AF $20	Avon T-241 AF $22	Avon T-257 AF $20

PUBLISHER	PUB. #	TITLE	DATE	AUTHOR	COND.	TYPE	PRICE
AVON	T 173	Naked Morning	1957	Cassill, R.V.	AF		$8.00
AVON	T 174	The Young Killers	1957	Weiner, W.	VG+		$15.00
AVON	T 174	The Young Killers	1957	Weiner, W.	VG+		$12.00
AVON	T 177	Man On Fire	1957	Aherne, O.	VG+	MTI	$8.00
AVON	T 178	Beyond Mombasa	1957	Hilton, J.	AF	MTI	$8.00
AVON	T 179	Cry Slaughter!	1957	Tiempo, E.K.	AF		$7.00
AVON	T 180	Space Plague	1957	Smith, G.O.	VGF		$6.00
AVON	T 181	Pickup Alley	1957	Ronns, E.*	AF	MTI	$49.00 A
AVON	T 185	The Jungle	1957	Algren, N.	AF		$13.00 A
AVON	T 185	The Jungle	1957	Algren, N.	VGF		$12.00
AVON	T 196	Man In The Shadow	1957	Whittington, H.	F	MTI	$30.00 A
AVON	T 196	Man In The Shadow	1957	Whittington, H.	VG	MTI	$12.00
AVON	T 197	Panzer Ghost Division	1957	Goethals, T.	AF		$5.00
AVON	T 199	The Saint Vs. Scotland Yard	1957	Charteris, L.	AF		$12.00
AVON	T 202	The Planet Explorer	1957	Leinster, M.	AF		$7.00
AVON	T 203	Les Girls	1957	Tomkinson, C.	AF		$10.00
AVON	T 203	Les Girls	1957	Tomkinson, C.	VGF		$7.00
AVON	T 208	Seven Footprints To Satan	1957	Merritt, A.	AF		$20.00
AVON	T 208	Seven Footprints To Satan	1957	Merritt, A.	AF		$15.00
AVON	T 208	Seven Footprints To Satan	1957	Merritt, A.	VG		$8.00
AVON	T 211	The Tortured Planet	1957	Lewis, C.S.	VGF+		$7.00
AVON	T 214	Hot Spell	1958	Coleman, L.	VG+	MTI	$6.00
AVON	T 219	Juvenile Jungle	1957	Counsel, F.	VG+	MTI	$20.00
AVON	T 222	Officer's Plot To Kill Hitler	1958	Fitzgibbon, C.	VGF		$7.00
AVON	T 223	Never Come Morning	1958	Algren, N.	VGF		$10.00
AVON	T 225	Earthman, Come Home	1958	Blish, J.	AF		$8.00
AVON	T 227	Belly Laughs Annual	1958	Anthology	VG+		$7.00
AVON	T 228	The Lady Takes A Flyer	1958	Ronns, E.*	VG-	MTI	$6.00
AVON	T 230	Cry Baby Killer	1958	Hilton, J.	VG+	MTI	$13.00 A
AVON	T 230	Cry Baby Killer	1958	Hilton, J.	VG	MTI	$7.00
AVON	T 234	The Saint In Miami	1958	Charteris, L.	F		$12.00
AVON	T 234	The Saint In Miami	1958	Charteris, L.	VGF		$7.00
AVON	T 237	The High Cost Of Loving	1958	Golightly, B.	F	MTI	$10.00
AVON	T 239	D-Day	1958	Gunther, J.	VGF		$7.00
AVON	T 241	Teen-Age Jungle	1958	Whittington, H.	AF		$22.00 A
AVON	T 244	Naked Sin	1958	Clark, G.	F		$8.00
AVON	T 244	Naked Sin	1958	Clark, G.	VGF		$7.00
AVON	T 248	Chattels Of Eldorado	1958	Bracco, E.J.	AF		$7.00
AVON	T 250	The Saint In England	1958	Charteris, L.	AF		$12.00
AVON	T 250	The Saint In England	1958	Charteris, L.	AF		$8.00
AVON	T 251	The Young Who Sin	1958	Haase, J.	F		$8.00
AVON	T 252	The Mind Cage	1958	Van Vogt, A.E.	AF		$7.00
AVON	T 253	Breathe No More, My Lady	1958	Lacy, E.	AF		$14.00
AVON	T 253	Breathe No More, My Lady	1958	Lacy, E.	VG+		$10.00
AVON	T 257	High School Confidential	1958	Cooper, M.	AF	MTI	$20.00 A

Avon T-287 AF $21　　　　　Avon T-288 F $64　　　　　Avon T-311 AF $22

PUBLISHER	PUB. #	TITLE	DATE	AUTHOR	COND.	TYPE	PRICE
AVON	T 257	High School Confidential	1958	Cooper, M.	G	MTI	$10.00
AVON	T 262	Gang Rumble	1958	Ronns, E.*	F		$17.00 A
AVON	T 262	Gang Rumble	1958	Ronns, E.*	G-		$6.00
AVON	T 264	Trinity In Violence	1958	Kane, H.	AF		$8.00
AVON	T 266	Vice Trap	1958	Gilbert, E.	VGF+		$5.00 A
AVON	T 267	Naked Tide	1958	Hastings, R.	VG		$6.00
AVON	T 268	ESPer	1958	Blish, J.	F		$7.00
AVON	T 269	Mitsou	1958	Colette	AF	MTI	$8.00
AVON	T 272	I Am A Marked Woman	1958	Anonymous	VGF		$8.00
AVON	T 277	Sinful	1958	Frame, B.	VGF-		$7.00
AVON	T 280	Death Hits The Jackpot	1958	Wager, W.	F		$10.00
AVON	T 284	Cry Horror!	1958	Lovecraft, H.P.	VGF		$10.00
AVON	T 284	Cry Horror!	1958	Lovecraft, H.P.	VG+		$7.00
AVON	T 287	The Death Dealers	1958	Asimov, I.	AF		$21.00 A
AVON	T 287	The Death Dealers	1958	Asimov, I.	AF		$18.00
AVON	T 288	Shakedown For Murder	1958	Lacy, E.	F		$64.00 A
AVON	T 289	BR-R-R-R-!	1959	Anthology	AF		$15.00
AVON	T 289	BR-R-R-R-!	1959	Anthology	AF		$15.00 A
AVON	T 296	Over My Dead Body	1959	Stout, R.	VG		$7.00
AVON	T 300	Confidential	1959	Clarke, D.H.	AF		$7.00
AVON	T 302	The Subterraneans	1959	Kerouac, J.	AF		$16.00 A
AVON	T 302	The Subterraneans	1959	Kerouac, J.	VG		$8.00
AVON	T 303	Cry Tough! (11th)	1958	Shulman, I.	VG-	MTI	$6.00
AVON	T 305	The Naked Sword	1959	Chidsey, D.B.	VG+		$6.00
AVON	T 307	Doorway To Death	1959	Marlowe, D.	AF-		$22.00 A
AVON	T 307	Doorway To Death	1959	Marlowe, D.	AF		$10.00
AVON	T 310	Beat Girl	1959	Golightly, B.	VG+		$9.00
AVON	T 311	Anything For Kicks	1959	Cooper, M.	AF		$22.00 A
AVON	T 314	Undressed To Kill	1959	Cheyney, P.	VG+		$5.00
AVON	T 323	Pnin	1959	Nabokov, V.	AF-		$6.00
AVON	T 324	The Jungle	1959	Algren, N.	VG+		$15.00 A
AVON	T 327	Gun For Sale	1959	Wells, L.E.	AF		$7.00
AVON	T 328	The Real Cool Killers	1959	Himes, C.	VG		$14.00
AVON	T 328	The Real Cool Killers	1959	Himes, C.	G+		$7.00
AVON	T 337	The Tragedy Of Y	1959	Queen, E.	VG-		$5.00
AVON	T 341	Iron Lover	1959	Fox, G.F.	AF		$7.00
AVON	T 343	Find Eileen Hardin – Alive!	1959	Frazer, A.	VGF		$7.00
AVON	T 345	Monsters And Such	1959	Leinster, M.	F		$15.00 A
AVON	T 345	Monsters And Such	1959	Leinster, M.	F		$12.00
AVON	T 347	Strange Bargain	1959	Whittington, H.	VG+		$44.00 A
AVON	T 347	Strange Bargain	1959	Whittington, H.	F		$25.00 A
AVON	T 349	Killer With A Key	1959	Marlowe, D.	VG		$7.00
AVON	T 350	Love For A Stranger	1959	McCoy, J.P.	VGF		$6.00
AVON	T 351	Murder Is An Art	1959	Innes, M.	F		$8.00
AVON	T 354	Beyond The Night	1959	Woolrich, C.	AF		$49.00 A

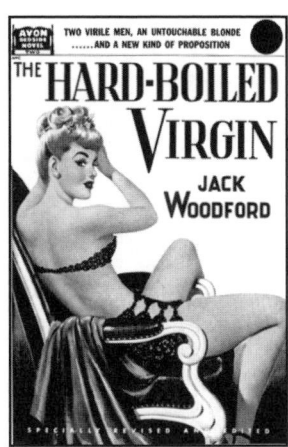

Avon Bedside Novel 2 AF $110	Avon Bedside Novel 3 VG+ $121	Avon Book Dividend 3 AF $55

PUBLISHER	PUB. #	TITLE	DATE	AUTHOR	COND.	TYPE	PRICE
AVON	T 354	Beyond The Night	1959	Woolrich, C.	VGF		$17.00
AVON	T 354	Beyond The Night	1959	Woolrich, C.	G+		$8.00
AVON	T 359	Rusty Desmond	1959	January, S.	AF		$24.00 A
AVON	T 361	Run, Killer, Run	1959	White, L.	VG		$7.00
AVON	T 363	The Pagan Queen	1959	Treece, H.	VGF		$8.00
AVON	T 365	The Terrible Night	1959	Cheyney, P.	VG+		$7.00
AVON	T 367	Avon Bedside Companion	1959	Anthology	VG+		$7.00
AVON	T 371	Planet In Peril	1959	Christopher, J.	AF		$7.00
AVON	T 372	The Long Night	1959	Demaris, O.	VG+		$5.00 A
AVON	T 376	Beat Not The Bones	1959	Jay, C.	F		$10.00
AVON	T 376	Beat Not The Bones	1959	Jay, C.	VG+		$6.00
AVON	T 380	The Bastard Of Orleans	1960	Fox, G.F.	AF		$12.00
AVON	T 383	Addicted To Murder	1960	Drachman, T.S.	VG		$5.00
AVON	T 387	Swamp Tease	1960	Kempton, E.	AF		$18.00 A
AVON	T 390	The Subterraneans	1960	Kerouac, J.	VG+	MTI	$14.00
AVON	T 392	Doom Service	1960	Marlowe, D.	VG		$7.00
AVON	T 392	Doom Service	1960	Marlowe, D.	VG		$5.00
AVON	T 397	Voyage From Lesbos	1960	Robertiello, R.C.	F		$9.00 A
AVON	T 400	The Invaders	1960	Treece, H.	VG+		$7.00
AVON	T 403	Rebel Woman	1960	Whittington, H.	VG		$7.00 A
AVON	T 403	Rebel Woman	1960	Whittington, H.	G		$7.00
AVON	T 405	Stop-Over	1960	Cooper, M.	F		$8.00
AVON	T 405	Stop-Over	1960	Cooper, M.	VG		$5.00
AVON	T 407	Power Play	1960	Goeney, W.M.	VGF		$7.00
AVON	T 410	Out Of The Silent Planet	1960	Lewis, C.S.	AF		$7.00
AVON	T 413	Cargo: Trouble	1960	Thomas, P.	AF		$6.00
AVON	T 417	Reformatory Girls	1960	Morrison, R.	VG		$8.00
AVON	T 419	The Fall Of Marty Moon	1960	Frazer, A.	AF		$7.00
AVON	T 430	Run For The Money	1960	Colby, R.	VG+		$7.00
AVON	T 438	Life With Fiorello	1960	Cuneo, E.	VG		$6.00
AVON	T 440	Oh Careless Love	1960	Zolotow, M.	VG		$6.00
AVON	T 448	The Golden Cage	1960	Torres, T.	VG		$7.00
AVON	T 450	Die, Lover	1960	Whittington, H.	VG		$12.00
AVON	T 450	Die, Lover	1960	Whittington, H.	VG		$10.00
AVON	T 452	The Fatal Frails	1960	Marlowe, D.	VG+		$7.00
AVON	T 458	A Day To Die	1960	Frazee, S.	VGF		$11.00
AVON	T 458	A Day To Die	1960	Frazee, S.	VG+		$10.00
AVON	T 458	A Day To Die	1960	Frazee, S.	VG		$7.00
AVON	T 459	The Brimstone Bed	1960	Keene, D.	VGF		$40.00 A
AVON	T 459	The Brimstone Bed	1960	Keene, D.	VG+		$15.00
AVON	T 459	The Brimstone Bed	1960	Keene, D.	VG		$10.00
AVON	T 462	The Gold Plated Sewer	1960	Demaris, O.	VG+		$6.00
AVON	T 463	A Scent Of White Poppies	1960	Christopher, J.	F		$28.00 A
AVON	T 468	Teen-Age Mobster	1960	Appel, B.	VGF		$14.00
AVON	T 469	Girl On A Slay Ride	1960	Trimble, L.	VG+		$7.00

Avon Book Dividend 6 VG+ $60　　　Avon Fantasy Reader 7 VGF $39　　　Avon Fantasy Reader 14 VGF $34

PUBLISHER	PUB. #	TITLE	DATE	AUTHOR	COND.	TYPE	PRICE
AVON	T 469	Girl On A Slay Ride	1960	Trimble, L.	G+		$5.00
AVON	T 472	Rogue Sword	1960	Anderson, P.	VG+		$8.00
AVON	T 480	Prisoners Of Tordesillas	1960	Schoonover, L.	AF		$6.00
AVON	T 489	Beatville U.S.A.	1961	Mandel, G.	AF-		$12.00 A
AVON	T 491	Shake A Crooked Town	1961	Marlowe, D.	AF		$28.00 A
AVON	T 491	Shake A Crooked Town	1961	Marlowe, D.	VG+		$16.00
AVON	T 491	Shake A Crooked Town	1961	Marlowe, D.	G		$5.00
AVON	T 492	Bitter Water	1961	Thompson, T.	AF		$6.00
AVON	T 495	Suburban Wife	1961	Martin, K.	AF		$7.00
AVON	T 499	The Long Trail Back	1961	Ballard, T.	AF		$8.00
AVON	T 513	The Babe And I	1961	Ruth, B., Mrs.	VG		$10.00 A
AVON	T 528	An American Romance	1961	Koningsberger, H.	AF		$20.00 A
AVON	T 531	Survive!	1961	Heyman, E.L.	VGF		$5.00
AVON	T 634	Miss Lonelyhearts	1959	West, N.	VGF-		$8.00
AVON	V 2044	The Smut Peddlers	1962	Kilpatrick, J.	VG+		$6.00
AVON	V 2056	Stranger In A Strange Land	1962	Heinlein, R.A.	VGF		$30.00 A
AVON	V 2150	The Lion Of Lucca	1966	Fox, G.F.	VG		$7.00
AVON	V 2239	For Love Of Ivy	1968	Smith. C.S.	AF	MTI	$7.00
AVON	W 213	Custer Died For Your Sins	1970	Deloria, V.	AF		$7.00
AVON	14894	The Golden Circle (Phantom #5)	1973	Falk, L.	VGF		$7.00
AVON	17731	Killer's Town (Phantom #9)	1973	Falk, L.	VGF		$8.00
AVON	18184	Goggle-Eyed Pirates (Phant. #10)	1974	Falk, L.	AF		$10.00
AVON	18416	Thieves Like Us	1974	Anderson, E.	AF	MTI	$8.00
AVON	18515	The Lion Men Of Mongo	1974	Raymond, A.	VGF+		$7.00
AVON	19166	The Plague Of Sound	1974	Raymond, A.	VG+		$6.00
AVON	19695	The Space Circus	1974	Raymond, A.	VGF-		$6.00
AVON	20446	The Time Trap Of Ming XIII	1974	Raymond, A.	AF		$9.00
AVON	20446	The Time Trap Of Ming XIII	1974	Raymond, A.	VGF		$6.00
AVON	20495	Cockfighter	1974	Willeford, C.	VG-	MTI	$5.00
AVON	21378	The Witch Queen Of Mongo	1974	Raymond, A.	AF		$9.00
AVON	21378	The Witch Queen Of Mongo	1974	Raymond, A.	VGF		$6.00
AVON	22335	The War Of The Cybernauts	1975	Raymond, A.	VGF		$9.00
AVON	22335	The War Of The Cybernauts	1975	Raymond, A.	VG		$5.00
AVON	23085	The Island Of Dogs (Phantom #13)	1975	Falk, L.	F		$8.00
AVON	23283	The Assassins (Phantom #14)	1975	Falk, L.	AF		$10.00
AVON	68429	The Elmore Leonard Reader	1983	Leonard, E.	AF		$6.00
AVON	75216	Shadowfires	1987	Nichols, L.*	AF		$12.00
AVON ANNUAL	1	18 Great Stories Of Today	1944	Anthology	VG+	Digest	$20.00 A
AVON BEDSIDE NOVEL	2	The Hard-Boiled Virgin	1950	Woodford, J.	AF	Digest	$110.00 A
AVON BEDSIDE NOVEL	3	Queer Patterns	1951	Brock, L.	VG+	Digest	$121.00 A
AVON BEDSIDE NOVEL	5	Male And Female	1951	Woodford, J.	VG	Digest	$50.00 A
AVON BEDSIDE NOVEL	7	Millie	1952	Clarke, D.G.	VG	Digest	$39.00 A
AVON BOOK DIVIDEND	2	Star Lust	1951	Woodford, J.	G+	Digest	$8.00
AVON BOOK DIVIDEND	3	New York Madness	1951	Bodenheim, M.	AF	Digest	$55.00 A
AVON BOOK DIVIDEND	4	Grounds For Divorce	1951	Woodford, J.	AF	Digest	$50.00 A

Modern Short Story Monthly 48 VG $24

Avon Monthly Novel 9 VG+ $82

Avon Monthly Novel 21 G- $7

PUBLISHER	PUB. #	TITLE	DATE	AUTHOR	COND.	TYPE	PRICE
AVON BOOK DIVIDEND	5	Her Private Passions	1951	Holland, M.	AF	Digest	$25.00
AVON BOOK DIVIDEND	6	Teach Me To Love	1951	Woodford, J.	VG+	Digest	$60.00 A
AVON BOOK DIVIDEND	7	Tropical Passions	1951	Anthology	AF	Digest	$45.00 A
AVON FANTASY NOVELS	1	The Princess Of The Atom	1950	Cummings, R.	VGF		$41.00 A
AVON FANTASY NOVELS	1	The Princess Of The Atom	1950	Cummings, R.	VG+		$40.00 A
AVON FANTASY NOVELS	1	The Princess Of The Atom	1950	Cummings, R.	VGF+		$30.00 A
AVON FANTASY READER	1	Avon Fantasy Reader #1	1947	Anthology	VG	Digest	$8.00
AVON FANTASY READER	2	Avon Fantasy Reader #2	1947	Anthology	VGF+	Digest	$16.00 A
AVON FANTASY READER	3	Avon Fantasy Reader #3	1947	Anthology	AF	Digest	$16.00 A
AVON FANTASY READER	3	Avon Fantasy Reader #3	1947	Anthology	VG	Digest	$7.00
AVON FANTASY READER	4	Avon Fantasy Reader #4	1947	Anthology	VG+	Digest	$22.00 A
AVON FANTASY READER	5	Avon Fantasy Reader #5	1947	Anthology	VG	Digest	$5.00
AVON FANTASY READER	6	Avon Fantasy Reader #6	1948	Anthology	VG+	Digest	$27.00 A
AVON FANTASY READER	6	Avon Fantasy Reader #6	1948	Anthology	VGF	Digest	$20.00
AVON FANTASY READER	7	Avon Fantasy Reader #7	1948	Anthology	VGF	Digest	$39.00 A
AVON FANTASY READER	7	Avon Fantasy Reader #7	1948	Anthology	VGF	Digest	$27.00 A
AVON FANTASY READER	8	Avon Fantasy Reader #8	1948	Anthology	VGF+	Digest	$29.00 A
AVON FANTASY READER	8	Avon Fantasy Reader #8	1948	Anthology	VGF	Digest	$22.00
AVON FANTASY READER	8	Avon Fantasy Reader #8	1948	Anthology	VG+	Digest	$22.00 A
AVON FANTASY READER	8	Avon Fantasy Reader #8	1948	Anthology	VG+	Digest	$16.00
AVON FANTASY READER	9	Avon Fantasy Reader #9	1949	Anthology	VG+	Digest	$16.00
AVON FANTASY READER	9	Avon Fantasy Reader #9	1949	Anthology	VG+	Digest	$12.00 A
AVON FANTASY READER	10	Avon Fantasy Reader #10	1949	Anthology	VGF-	Digest	$30.00 A
AVON FANTASY READER	10	Avon Fantasy Reader #10	1949	Anthology	AF	Digest	$29.00 A
AVON FANTASY READER	10	Avon Fantasy Reader #10	1949	Anthology	VGF	Digest	$20.00
AVON FANTASY READER	11	Avon Fantasy Reader #11	1949	Anthology	VGF	Digest	$20.00 A
AVON FANTASY READER	11	Avon Fantasy Reader #11	1949	Anthology	VGF	Digest	$17.00 A
AVON FANTASY READER	12	Avon Fantasy Reader #12	1950	Anthology	VGF	Digest	$34.00 A
AVON FANTASY READER	12	Avon Fantasy Reader #12	1950	Anthology	VGF	Digest	$28.00 A
AVON FANTASY READER	13	Avon Fantasy Reader #13	1950	Anthology	VGF-	Digest	$33.00 A
AVON FANTASY READER	13	Avon Fantasy Reader #13	1950	Anthology	AF	Digest	$20.00 A
AVON FANTASY READER	14	Avon Fantasy Reader #14	1950	Anthology	VGF	Digest	$34.00 A
AVON FANTASY READER	14	Avon Fantasy Reader #14	1950	Anthology	VG+	Digest	$28.00 A
AVON FANTASY READER	15	Avon Fantasy Reader #15	1951	Anthology	VG+	Digest	$44.00 A
AVON FANTASY READER	15	Avon Fantasy Reader #15	1951	Anthology	VG+	Digest	$22.00 A
AVON FANTASY READER	16	Avon Fantasy Reader #16	1951	Anthology	VGF	Digest	$41.00 A
AVON FANTASY READER	16	Avon Fantasy Reader #16	1951	Anthology	VGF	Digest	$19.00 A
AVON FANTASY READER	17	Avon Fantasy Reader #17	1951	Anthology	VGF	Digest	$33.00 A
AVON FANTASY READER	17	Avon Fantasy Reader #17	1951	Anthology	AF	Digest	$25.00 A
AVON FANTASY READER	18	Avon Fantasy Reader #18	1952	Anthology	VGF-	Digest	$24.00 A
AVON FANTASY READER	18	Avon Fantasy Reader #18	1952	Anthology	AF	Digest	$22.00
AVON IF YOU WERE BORN	No#	If You Were Born In January	1952		VG+		$7.00
AVON M.S.S.M.	1	W.S. Maugham's Cosmopolitans	1943	Maugham, W.S.	VG	Digest	$7.00
AVON M.S.S.M.	9	Steinbeck 13 Great Stories	1943	Steinbeck, J.	G+	Digest	$4.00
AVON M.S.S.M.	18	Ah King	1944	Maugham, W.S.	VG	Digest	$8.00

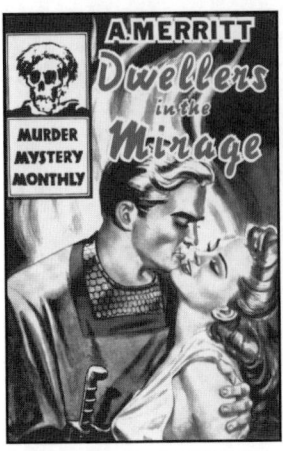

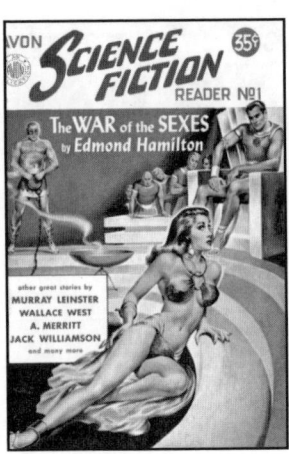

Murder Mystery Monthly 24 VG+ $20   Avon Sci-Fi Reader 1 VGF $29   Avon Special 4 VG+ $100

PUBLISHER	PUB. #	TITLE	DATE	AUTHOR	COND.	TYPE	PRICE
AVON M.S.S.M.	21	Great Stories By Farrell	1945	Farrell, J.T.	VG	Digest	$4.00
AVON M.S.S.M.	35	The Trembling Of A Leaf	1946	Maugham, W.S.	VG	Digest	$7.00
AVON M.S.S.M.	38	Great Stories Of Love & Intrigue	1947	Maugham, W.S.	VG+	Digest	$30.00 A
AVON M.S.S.M.	39	Stories Of Venial Sin	1947	O'Hara, J.	VGF	Digest	$22.00 A
AVON M.S.S.M.	40	Marianne In India	1947	Feuchtwanger, L.	VG+	Digest	$10.00
AVON M.S.S.M.	43	East Of Suez	1948	Maugham, W.S.	G+	Digest	$7.00
AVON M.S.S.M.	45	Hellbox	1949	O'Hara, J.	AF	Digest	$22.00 A
AVON M.S.S.M.	46	Love Among The Haystacks	1949	Lawrence, D.H.	VGF	Digest	$9.00 A
AVON M.S.S.M.	48	Night Club	1949	Brush, K.	VG	Digest	$24.00 A
AVON M.S.S.M.	50	All The Girls He Wanted	1949	O'Hara, J.	AF	Digest	$50.00 A
AVON M.S.S.M.	50	All The Girls He Wanted	1949	O'Hara, J.	VGF	Digest	$27.00 A
AVON MONTHLY NOVEL	4	The Villan And The Virgin	1948	Chase, J.H.	VG+	Digest	$25.00 A
AVON MONTHLY NOVEL	9	The Scarf Of Passion	1948	Bloch, R.	VG+	Digest	$82.00 A
AVON MONTHLY NOVEL	18	I'll Get You For This	1951	Chase, J.H.	VG	Digest	$29.00 A
AVON MONTHLY NOVEL	18	I'll Get You For This	1951	Chase, J.H.	VG+	Digest	$26.00 A
AVON MONTHLY NOVEL	21	Tomcat In Tights	1951	Hanley, J.	G-	Digest	$7.00
AVON M.M.M.	1	Seven Footprints To Satan	1942	Merritt, A.	G+	Digest	$10.00
AVON M.M.M.	4	The French Key Mystery	1942	Gruber, F.	G	Digest	$6.00
AVON M.M.M.	5	Burn Witch Burn!	1942	Merritt, A.	VG	Digest	$8.00
AVON M.M.M.	5	Burn Witch Burn!	1942	Merritt, A.	VG	Digest	$7.00
AVON M.M.M.	6	The Postman Rings Twice	1942	Cain, J.M.	G	Digest	$10.00
AVON M.M.M.	11	Creep Shadow Creep	1943	Merritt, A.	VG+	Digest	$60.00 A
AVON M.M.M.	11	Creep Shadow Creep	1943	Merritt, A.	G+	Digest	$6.00
AVON M.M.M.	12	Hungry Dog Murders	1943	Gruber, F.	G	Digest	$6.00
AVON M.M.M.	13	If The Shroud Fits	1943	Roos, K.	VG+	Digest	$17.00 A
AVON M.M.M.	14	Whose Body?	1943	Sayers, D.L.	VG	Digest	$8.00
AVON M.M.M.	15	Premeditated Murder	1943	Cheyney, P.	VG	Digest	$11.00
AVON M.M.M.	17	Who Killed Chloe?	1943	Allingham, M.	VG	Digest	$7.00
AVON M.M.M.	18	The Moon Pool	1943	Merritt, A.	VG+	Digest	$39.00 A
AVON M.M.M.	20	The Embezzler	1944	Cain, J.M.	VG-	Digest	$10.00
AVON M.M.M.	21	The Counter Spy Murders	1944	Cheyney, P.	G+	Digest	$7.00
AVON M.M.M.	24	Dwellers In The Mirage	1944	Merritt, A.	VG+	Digest	$20.00 A
AVON M.M.M.	24	Dwellers In The Mirage	1944	Merritt, A.	G-	Digest	$5.00
AVON M.M.M.	29	The Face In The Abyss	1945	Merritt, A.	VGF	Digest	$14.00 A
AVON M.M.M.	29	The Face In The Abyss	1945	Merritt, A.	VG-	Digest	$6.00
AVON M.M.M.	30	Farewell To The Admiral	1945	Cheyney, P.	VGF	Digest	$40.00 A
AVON M.M.M.	31	If I Should Die Before I Wake	1945	Irish, W.*	VG-	Digest	$14.00 A
AVON M.M.M.	34	The Ship Of Ishtar	1945	Merritt, A.	VGF	Digest	$20.00 A
AVON M.M.M.	34	The Ship Of Ishtar	1945	Merritt, A.	VG-	Digest	$7.00
AVON M.M.M.	41	The Metal Monster	1946	Merritt, A.	VG+	Digest	$55.00 A
AVON M.M.M.	41	The Metal Monster	1946	Merritt, A.	AF-	Digest	$36.00 A
AVON SCI. FI. READER	1	Avon Science Fiction Reader #1	1951	Anthology	VGF	Digest	$29.00 A
AVON SCI. FI. READER	1	Avon Science Fiction Reader #1	1951	Anthology	VG+	Digest	$24.00 A
AVON SCI. FI. READER	1	Avon Science Fiction Reader #1	1951	Anthology	VG	Digest	$9.00
AVON SCI. FI. READER	1	Avon Science Fiction Reader #1	1951	Anthology	G	Digest	$5.00

| Award 131 AF $7 | Award 278 VG+ $8 | Award 493 AF $15 | Badger CS 2 AF $36 |

PUBLISHER	PUB. #	TITLE	DATE	AUTHOR	COND.	TYPE	PRICE
AVON SCI. FI. READER	2	Avon Science Fiction Reader #2	1952	Anthology	VGF-	Digest	$25.00 A
AVON SCI. FI. READER	2	Avon Science Fiction Reader #2	1952	Anthology	VGF	Digest	$22.00
AVON SCI. FI. READER	3	Avon Science Fiction Reader #3	1952	Anthology	VGF-	Digest	$25.00 A
AVON SCI. FI. READER	3	Avon Science Fiction Reader #3	1952	Anthology	VGF	Digest	$22.00
AVON SF & FANT. READER	1 1	Avon Sci-Fi & Fantasy Reader #1	1953	Anthology	VGF	Digest	$25.00 A
AVON SF & FANT. READER	1 2	Avon Sci-Fi & Fantasy Reader #2	1953	Anthology	VGF	Digest	$22.00 A
AVON SPECIAL	4	Night Club Girl	1951	Wilstach, J.	VG+	Digest	$100.00 A
AVON WESTERN NOVEL	1	The Gun-Wolf Of Tubac	1949	Nye, N.	G-	Digest	$7.00
AVON WESTERN NOVEL	2	Cattle War Buckaroo	1950	Hopson, W.	VGF	Digest	$24.00 A
AVON WESTERN NOVEL	2	Cattle War Buckaroo	1950	Hopson, W.	G+	Digest	$6.00
AWARD	A 101	Run, Spy, Run	1964	Carter, N.	VGF-		$7.00
AWARD	A 101	Run, Spy, Run	1964	Carter, N.	VGF		$6.00
AWARD	A 124	The Night Walker	1964	Bloch, R.	VG-	MTI	$6.00
AWARD	A 125	Vein Of Violence	1965	Gault, W.C.	AF		$9.00
AWARD	A 131	Savage Holiday	1965	Wright, R.	AF		$7.00
AWARD	A 131	Savage Holiday	1965	Wright, R.	VG		$4.00
AWARD	A 132	A Shot In The Dark	1965	Powell, R.	F		$5.00
AWARD	A 133	Shadow Of A Lady	1965	Roth, H.	F		$4.00
AWARD	A 145	Detour At Night	1965	Endore, G.	AF		$5.00
AWARD	A 146	People vs Withers & Malone	1965	Rice, C.	AF		$5.00
AWARD	A 154	Comrade Spy	1965	Ovalov, L.	AF		$6.00
AWARD	A 212	The Man From T.O.M.C.A.T.	1967	Knight, M.T.	VG		$3.00
AWARD	A 236	For A Few Dollars More	1967	Millard, J.	VGF		$6.00
AWARD	A 249	The Man From TOMCAT #3	1967	Knight, M.T.	G+		$3.00
AWARD	A 278	The Man From TOMCAT #4	1967	Knight, M.T.	VG+		$8.00
AWARD	A 327	Carmen, Baby	1968	Grant, S.	VGF	MTI	$6.00
AWARD	A 379	A Dollar To Die For	1968	Fox, B.	AF		$6.00
AWARD	A 426	Secret Ceremony	1968	Hughes, W.	VGF	MTI	$4.00
AWARD	A 431	A History Of Torture	1969	Swain, J.	VGF		$4.00
AWARD	A 452	Tell Them Willie Boy Is Here	1969	Lawton, H.	VGF	MTI	$6.00
AWARD	A 454	For A Few Dollars More (2nd)	1969	Millard, J.	VGF		$6.00
AWARD	A 493	Friends And Lovers	1969	Marsh, L.	AF	MTI	$15.00
AWARD	A 494	The Libertine	1969	Massimo, J.	F	MTI	$10.00
AWARD	A 512	This Woman Is Death	1969	Frances, S.	VGF		$5.00
AWARD	A 539	The Peking Pornographer	1969	Knight, M.T.	VGF		$7.00
AWARD	A 663	Performance	1970	Hughes, W.	VG	MTI	$6.00
AWARD	A 811	Fear Today - Gone Tomorrow	1971	Bloch, R.	VG+		$7.00
AWARD	A 918	The Good, The Bad & The Ugly	1971	Millard, J.	G+		$5.00
AWARD	AN 1069	Dr. Phibes Rises Again	1972	Goldstein, W.	F	MTI	$6.00
AWARD	AN 1174	Adam 12 - The Hostages	1974	Stratton, C.	VG+	TVTI	$6.00
AWARD	AQ 1185	Duke:The Story Of J. Wayne	1974	Ramer, J.	F		$7.00
AWARD	AN 1195	Hate Is For The Hunted	1974	Frances, S.	F		$5.00
AWARD	AN 1241	Conquest Of Planet Of Apes	1974	Jakes, J.	AF	MTI	$3.00
AWARD	AN 1283	Gunsmoke #1, The Renegades	1974	Flynn, J.	VGF	TVTI	$6.00
AWARD	AQ 1351	The Nickel Ride	1974	Kaufman, M.T.	VG	MTI	$6.00
AWARD	AQ 1438	Police Woman #1	1975	Trevor, L.	VGF	TVTI	$7.00
AWARD	AN 1444	The Hunting Party	1975	Millard, J.	VG	MTI	$7.00
AWARD	AQ 1452	Police Woman #2	1975	Trevor, L.	VG	TVTI	$6.00

Badger CS 8 VGF- $22　　Badger SF 57 VGF $18　　Badger SF 115 VGF $20　　Badger SN 46 VG+ $35

PUBLISHER	PUB. #	TITLE	DATE	AUTHOR	COND.	TYPE	PRICE
AWARD	AQ 1463	Park Avenue Executioner	1975	Wilson, D.	AF	TVTI	$6.00
AWARD	AQ 1468	The Wind And The Lion	1975	Milius, J.	VG+	MTI	$5.00
AWARD	AN 1469	Fear Today - Gone Tomorrow	1975	Bloch, R.	VGF		$6.00
AWARD	AD 1482	The Jaqueline Susann Story	1975	Ventura, J.	VG		$6.00
AWARD	AQ 1505	Psycho	1975	Bloch, R.	VG+		$6.00
BACHELOR BOOK	501	The Adultress	1966	Sanders, N.	AF		$8.00
BACHELOR BOOK	515	Sex On Campus	1966	Canning, S.	AF		$8.00
BACHELOR BOOK	516	The Warm Flesh	1966	Keith, V.	AF		$9.00
BACHELOR BOOK	519	Perfume Of Lust	1966	Clifton, R.	VGF		$7.00
BACHELOR BOOK	527	The Yes Girls	1966	Farley, A.A.	VGF		$7.00
BACHELOR BOOK	528	Warm And Willing	1966	Rey, L.	VGF+		$8.00
BACKGROUND BOOKS	No#	Not For The Squeamish	1948	Scott-Moncrieff, D.	VG+	Digest	$29.00 A
BADGER	CS 2	Murder Be My Mistress	1958	Storm, M.	AF		$36.00 A
BADGER	CS 3	The Long Silence	1959	Costello, P.	VG+		$37.00 A
BADGER	CS 4	The Tight Corner	1959	Ross, S.	VGF		$33.00 A
BADGER	CS 8	The Big Frame	n/d	Baxter, J.K.	VGF-		$22.00 A
BADGER	CS 13	The Set Up	n/d	Baxter, J.K.	VG+		$24.00 A
BADGER	S 3	The Unidentified	1960	Barker, G.	VGF		$11.00 A
BADGER	SF 13	Twilight Zone	n/d	La Salle, V.	VG+		$20.00 A
BADGER	SF 36	Hydrosphere	n/d	Merak, A.J.	AF		$16.00 A
BADGER	SF 40	Exit Humanity	n/d	Brett, L.	VGF		$10.00
BADGER	SF 40	Exit Humanity	n/d	Brett, L.	VGF		$8.00
BADGER	SF 44	Hand Of Doom	n/d	Fanthorpe, R.L.	VG+		$8.00 A
BADGER	SF 45	World Of The Gods	n/d	Torro, P.	AF-		$9.00 A
BADGER	SF 46	Last Man On Earth	n/d	Fane, B.	VGF		$10.00
BADGER	SF 48	Search The Dark Stars	n/d	Muller, J.E.	VGF+		$14.00 A
BADGER	SF 52	The Synthetic Ones	n/d	Roberts, L.	VGF+		$20.00
BADGER	SF 57	The Uninvited	n/d	Muller, J.E.	VGF		$18.00 A
BADGER	SF 58	The Mind Makers	n/d	Muller, J.E.	AF		$10.00 A
BADGER	SF 58	The Mind Makers	n/d	Muller, J.E.	VG		$6.00
BADGER	SF 58	The Mind Makers	n/d	Muller, J.E.	VG-		$6.00
BADGER	SF 60	Crimson Planet	n/d	Muller, J.E.	VGF		$6.00 A
BADGER	SF 64	Night Of The Black Horror	n/d	Norwood, V.	VG		$10.00
BADGER	SF 67	Uranium 235	n/d	Muller, J.E.	VGF		$16.00 A
BADGER	SF 67	Uranium 235	n/d	Muller, J.E.	VG		$6.00
BADGER	SF 69	Orbit One	n/d	Muller, J.E.	AF		$10.00 A
BADGER	SF 69	Orbit One	n/d	Muller, J.E.	AF-		$10.00
BADGER	SF 70	Micro Infinity	n/d	Muller, J.E.	VG+		$7.00
BADGER	SF 76	In The Beginning	n/d	Muller, J.E.	VGF		$12.00 A
BADGER	SF 76	In The Beginning	n/d	Muller, J.E.	VG+		$7.00
BADGER	SF 77	Space Fury	n/d	Fanthorpe, R.L.	VG		$7.00
BADGER	SF 81	Zero Minus X	n/d	Zeigfreid, K.	AF		$20.00 A
BADGER	SF 83	Radar Alert	n/d	Zeigfreid, K.	VGF+		$9.00
BADGER	SF 87	Formula 29X	n/d	Torro, P.	VGF+		$14.00 A
BADGER	SF 93	The Last Astronaut	n/d	Torro, P.	VG+		$7.00
BADGER	SF 94	The Alien Ones	n/d	Brett, L.	AF		$20.00 A
BADGER	SF 95	Power Sphere	n/d	Brett, L.	AF		$15.00 A
BADGER	SF 96	Reactor XK9	n/d	Muller, J.E.	VG+		$8.00

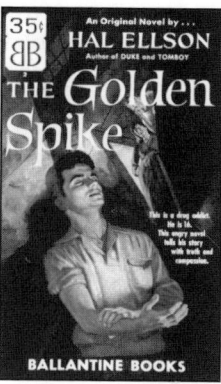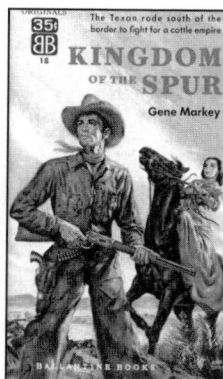

Badger SN 76 AF $22	Ballantine 2 VGF $86	Ballantine 8 VGF $70

Ballantine 18 AF $12

PUBLISHER	PUB. #	TITLE	DATE	AUTHOR	COND.	TYPE	PRICE
BADGER	SF 102	Suspension	n/d	Fane, B.	VG+		$5.00 A
BADGER	SF 103	Projection Infinity	n/d	Zeigfreid, K.	AF		$16.00 A
BADGER	SF 103	Projection Infinity	n/d	Zeigfreid, K.	VGF+		$10.00 A
BADGER	SF 106	Space No Barrier	n/d	Torro, P.	AF		$11.00 A
BADGER	SF 110	Force 97X	n/d	Torro, P.	VGF		$15.00 A
BADGER	SF 111	The Man From Beyond	n/d	Muller, J.E.	VG+		$8.00
BADGER	SF 112	Beyond The Void	n/d	Muller, J.E.	VG+		$5.00
BADGER	SF 114	The Girl From Tomorrow	n/d	Zeigfreid, K.	VGF		$10.00 A
BADGER	SF 115	U.F.O. 517	n/d	Fane, B.	VGF		$20.00 A
BADGER	SF 115	U.F.O. 517	n/d	Fane, B.	VG		$15.00 A
BADGER	SF 118	The Watching World	n/d	Fanthorpe, R.L.	VG+		$7.00
BADGER	SN 23	Mermaid Reef	1959	Fanthorpe, R.L.	VG+		$22.00 A
BADGER	SN 37	Werewolf At Large	1960	Fanthorpe, R.L.	VG		$15.00 A
BADGER	SN 40	The Last Valkyrie	1961	Roberts, L.	AF-		$18.00 A
BADGER	SN 44	Black Infinity	1961	Brett, L.	VG+		$21.00 A
BADGER	SN 46	Flame Goddess	1961	Roberts, L.	VG+		$35.00 A
BADGER	SN 47	Devil From The Depths	1961	Fanthorpe, R.L.	VGF		$15.00 A
BADGER	SN 51	The Grip Of Fear	1961	Fanthorpe, R.L.	VGF+		$18.00 A
BADGER	SN 52	Return Of Zeus	1962	Muller, J.E.	VGF		$8.00 A
BADGER	SN 55	Supernatural Stories #55	1962	Anthology	VG+		$6.00
BADGER	SN 56	The Eye Of Karnak	1962	Muller, J.E.	VG+		$12.00 A
BADGER	SN 65	Curse Of The Totem	1962	Fanthorpe, R.L.	VG+		$8.00
BADGER	SN 65	Curse Of The Totem	1962	Fanthorpe, R.L.	AF-		$9.00 A
BADGER	SN 76	The Timeless Ones	1963	Torro, P.	AF		$22.00 A
BADGER	SN 76	The Timeless Ones	1963	Torro, P.	VGF		$15.00 A
BADGER	SN 83	Roman Twilight	1963	Trent, O.	VG		$5.00
BADGER	SN 93	Supernatural Stories #93	1964	Anthology	AF		$10.00 A
BADGER	SN 94	The Exorcists	1965	Muller, J.E.	AF-		$14.00 A
BADGER	SN 100	Out Of The Night	1965	Muller, J.E.	VG		$7.00
BADGER	SN 101	The Sealed Sarcophagus	1965	Fanthorpe, R.L.	VGF		$13.00 A
BADGER	SN 102	The Unconfined	1966	Fanthorpe, R.L.	VGF		$15.00 A
BADGER	SN 104	The Shadow Man	1966	Barton, L.	AF-		$15.00 A
BADGER	SN 105	Curse Of The Khan	1966	Fanthorpe, R.L.	AF		$16.00 A
BADGER	SN 109	Supernatural Stories # 109	1967	Chartair, M.	VG-		$8.00 A
BADGER	SP 6	Twelve Hours To Destiny	n/d	Robertson, M.K.	VGF		$8.00
BALLANTINE	2	The Golden Spike	1952	Ellson, H.	VGF		$86.00 A
BALLANTINE	2	The Golden Spike	1952	Ellson, H.	VG		$20.00
BALLANTINE	7	Blood On The Land	1952	Bonham, F.	VGF-		$13.00 A
BALLANTINE	8	The World Of Li'l Abner	1953	Capp, A.	VGF		$70.00 A
BALLANTINE	8	The World Of Li'l Abner (2nd)	1953	Capp, A.	VG+		$5.00
BALLANTINE	10	Concannon	1952	O'Rourke, F.	VGF+		$9.00
BALLANTINE	10	Concannon (hardcover edition)	1952	O'Rourke, F.	VGF		$87.00 A
BALLANTINE	11	War Bonnet	1952	Fisher, C.	VGF		$8.00
BALLANTINE	12	Heyday	1953	Spackman, W.M.	VGF		$7.00
BALLANTINE	13	First Blood	1953	Schaefer, J.	VG		$7.00
BALLANTINE	15	The Wheel And The Hearth	1953	Moore, L.	VGF		$7.00
BALLANTINE	18	Kingdom Of The Spur	1953	Markey, G.	AF		$12.00
BALLANTINE	22	The Big Range	1953	Schaefer, J.	VGF+		$8.00

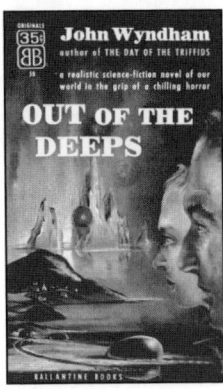

| Ballantine 50 AF $10 | Ballantine 54 VG- $55 | Ballantine 78 VG- $8 | Ballantine 89 VGF $7 |

PUBLISHER	PUB. #	TITLE	DATE	AUTHOR	COND.	TYPE	PRICE
BALLANTINE	27	Summer Street	1953	Ellson, H.	AF-		$24.00 A
BALLANTINE	28	The Secret Masters	1953	Kersh, G.	VG		$7.00
BALLANTINE	33	Childhood's End (2nd)	1953	Clarke, A.C.	AF		$6.00
BALLANTINE	36	Earthly Creatures	1953	Jackson, C.	AF		$11.00 A
BALLANTINE	39	New Poems	1953	Anthology	VG+		$5.00
BALLANTINE	41	Fahrenheit 451	1953	Bradbury, R.	VG		$16.00 A
BALLANTINE	45	The Canyon	1953	Schaefer, J.	AF-		$6.00
BALLANTINE	48	The Burl Ives Songbook	1953	Ives, B.	VGF		$8.00
BALLANTINE	50	Out Of The Deeps	1953	Wyndham, J.	AF		$10.00
BALLANTINE	54	The Bounty Hunters	1953	Leonard, E.	VG-		$55.00 A
BALLANTINE	54	The Bounty Hunters	1953	Leonard, E.	G		$20.00
BALLANTINE	58	Riders To The Stars	1953	Siodmak, C.	VG+	MTI	$5.00
BALLANTINE	63	New Short Novels	1954	Anthology	VGF+		$8.00
BALLANTINE	68	Prelude To Space	1954	Clarke, A.C.	G		$2.50
BALLANTINE	70	Broken Wagon	1954	Fox, N.A.	VGF		$6.00 A
BALLANTINE	73	Untouched By Human Hands	1954	Sheckley, R.	VG+		$7.00
BALLANTINE	78	The Real Story Of Lucille Ball	1954	Harris, E.	VG-		$8.00
BALLANTINE	89	Star Short Novels	1954	Anthology	VGF		$7.00 A
BALLANTINE	92	A Life For A Life	1954	Fanger, H.	VGF		$7.00
BALLANTINE	93	The Mad Reader	1954	Kurtzman, H.	VGF+		$20.00 A
BALLANTINE	95	Brave Harvest	1954	Cargoe, R.	VGF		$5.00 A
BALLANTINE	96	Star Sci-Fi Stories #3	1954	Anthology	VGF-		$20.00 A
BALLANTINE	98	Violence At Sundown	1955	O'Rourke, F.	VGF		$7.00
BALLANTINE	99	Of All Possible Worlds	1955	Tenn, W.	VG		$4.00
BALLANTINE	100	Young	1955	Colwell, M.	AF		$25.00
BALLANTINE	100	Young	1955	Colwell, M.	VG+		$14.00 A
BALLANTINE	101	The Dam Busters	1955	Brickhill, P.	VGF+		$7.00
BALLANTINE	103	Rock	1955	Ellson, H.	VG+		$24.00 A
BALLANTINE	103	Rock	1955	Ellson, H.	VG+		$18.00 A
BALLANTINE	103	Rock	1955	Ellson, H.	VG		$11.00 A
BALLANTINE	105	How To Play With Your Child	1955	Arnold, A.	VG+		$5.00
BALLANTINE	111	Car Deal!	1955	O'Rourke, F.	VGF		$15.00 A
BALLANTINE	115	The Power Of Negative Thinking	1955	Price, R.	VG		$5.00
BALLANTINE	117	The Girls From Planet 5	1955	Wilson, R.	VGF-		$8.00
BALLANTINE	122	No Boundaries	1955	Kuttner, H.	VG		$5.00
BALLANTINE	132	In One Head And Out The Other	1956	Price, R.	VG+		$6.00
BALLANTINE	135	Reach For Tomorrow	1956	Clarke, A.C.	VGF		$6.00
BALLANTINE	F 139	The October Country	1955	Bradbury, R.	VGF		$24.00
BALLANTINE	F 139	The October Country	1955	Bradbury, R.	VG-		$16.00
BALLANTINE	140	New Short Novels 2	1956	Anthology	VG		$8.00
BALLANTINE	144	Presidential Year	1956	Pohl, F.	AF		$53.00 A
BALLANTINE	152	I'm For Me First	1956	Price, R.	VGF		$5.00
BALLANTINE	171	The Wild Reader	1956	Anthology	AF		$22.00 A
BALLANTINE	180	James Dean	1956	Bast, W.	VGF		$28.00 A
BALLANTINE	180	James Dean	1956	Bast, W.	AF		$25.00 A
BALLANTINE	187	Buffalo Wagons	1956	Kelton, E.	VG		$8.00
BALLANTINE	189	Fire Mission	1957	Mulvihill, W.	VGF		$7.00
BALLANTINE	F 201	Zero!	1956	Okumiya, M.	VG+		$6.00

Ballantine 100 AF $25   Ballantine 103 VG+ $24   Ballantine 139 VGF $24   Ballantine 171 AF $22

PUBLISHER	PUB. #	TITLE	DATE	AUTHOR	COND.	TYPE	PRICE
BALLANTINE	202	Yellowhorse	1956	Brown, D.	AF		$7.00
BALLANTINE	F 204	Best Am. Short Stories 1956	1956	Anthology	VG		$8.00
BALLANTINE	211	Legend In The Dust	1957	O'Rourke, F.	AF		$8.00
BALLANTINE	212	Gun Hand	1957	O'Rourke, F.	VGF+		$6.00
BALLANTINE	213	Violence At Sundown	1957	O'Rourke, F.	AF		$6.00
BALLANTINE	214	High Vengeance	1957	O'Rourke, F.	AF		$6.00
BALLANTINE	219	Spanish Ridge	1957	Halleran, E.E.	AF		$7.00
BALLANTINE	220	The Deep South Says Never	1957	Martin, J.B.	VG		$6.00
BALLANTINE	226	New Poems #2	1957	Anthology	AF		$8.00
BALLANTINE	F 231	The 85 Days	1957	Thompson, R.W.	VGF		$7.00
BALLANTINE	235	Best TV Humor Of 1957	1957	Anthology	F		$10.00
BALLANTINE	236	Gunsmoke	1957	Ward, D.	G	TVTI	$7.00
BALLANTINE	239	The Wild Sweet Wine	1957	Anthology	F		$7.00
BALLANTINE	247	Barbed Wire	1957	Kelton, E.	VGF		$8.00
BALLANTINE	F 248	Samurai!	1957	Sakai, S.	AF		$7.00
BALLANTINE	250	The Big Boxcar	1957	Maund, A.	AF		$18.00 A
BALLANTINE	250	The Big Boxcar	1957	Maund, A.	VGF		$10.00
BALLANTINE	257	The Graveyard Reader	1958	Anthology	AF		$10.00
BALLANTINE	265	Inside Mad (5th)	1958	Gaines, W.M.	AF		$8.00
BALLANTINE	267	The Brothers Mad	1958	Gaines, W.M.	VG+		$15.00 A
BALLANTINE	267	The Brothers Mad	1958	Gaines, W.M.	VG		$7.00 A
BALLANTINE	268	On An Odd Note	1958	Kersh, G.	VGF		$7.00
BALLANTINE	272	Star Sci-Fi Stories #4	1958	Anthology	VGF		$18.00 A
BALLANTINE	F 273	V-2	1958	Dornberger, W.	F		$7.00
BALLANTINE	279	Tomorrow's Gift	1958	Cooper, E.	VG+		$5.00
BALLANTINE	281	The Old Copper Collar	1958	Cushman, D.	AF		$10.00
BALLANTINE	282	Colorado Gold	1958	Merriman, C.	F		$7.00
BALLANTINE	284	After The Rain	1959	Bowen, J.	AF		$5.00
BALLANTINE	287	How To Succeed With Women	1959	Mead, S.	VGF		$6.00
BALLANTINE	288	The Bright Road To Fear	1959	Stern, R.M.	F		$8.00
BALLANTINE	F 291	Battle For The Rhine	1959	Thompson, R.W.	AF		$7.00
BALLANTINE	294	Apache Wells	1959	Steelman, R.	AF		$7.00
BALLANTINE	299	The Midwich Cuckoos	1959	Wyndham, J.	AF		$10.00
BALLANTINE	302	The Beast	1959	Mannix, D.P.	AF		$20.00
BALLANTINE	302	The Beast	1959	Mannix, D.P.	VG+		$8.00
BALLANTINE	304	Shadow Of A Star	1959	Keelton, E.	VGF		$7.00
BALLANTINE	F 307	Air Spy	1959	Smith, C.B.	AF		$5.00
BALLANTINE	308	Star Sci-Fi Stories #5	1959	Anthology	VGF		$16.00 A
BALLANTINE	317	Kamikaze	1959	Kuwahara, Y.	AF		$7.00
BALLANTINE	319	Stairway To Nowhere	1959	Ellson, H.	VG+		$10.00
BALLANTINE	F 323	Thunderbolt	1959	Caidin, M.	VGF		$7.00
BALLANTINE	326	Deals With The Devil	1959	Anthology	VGF+		$9.00
BALLANTINE	338	Jungle Book	1959	Kurtzman, H.	VGF-		$22.00 A
BALLANTINE	343	Stampede	1959	Merriman, C.	AF-		$6.00
BALLANTINE	350	The World Of Li'l Abner	1959	Capp, A.	VG+	MTI	$10.00
BALLANTINE	308	Star Sci-Fi Stories #6	1959	Anthology	VGF		$14.00 A
BALLANTINE	354	The Hell Fire Club	1959	Mannix, D.P.	AF		$16.00
BALLANTINE	354	The Hell Fire Club	1959	Mannix, D.P.	F		$11.00 A

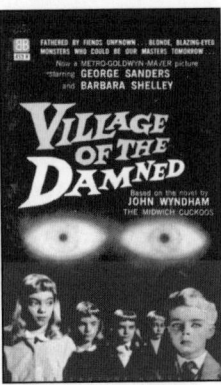

Ballantine 267 VG+ $15   Ballantine 302 AF $20   Ballantine 338 VGF- $22   Ballantine 453 VGF $18

PUBLISHER	PUB. #	TITLE	DATE	AUTHOR	COND.	TYPE	PRICE
BALLANTINE	F 359	The Night Hamburg Died	1960	Caidin, M.	AF		$7.00
BALLANTINE	F 363	The Jazz Word	1960	Anthology	VG+		$9.00
BALLANTINE	370	Zacherley's Midnight Snacks	1960	Anthology	AF		$12.00
BALLANTINE	370	Zacherley's Midnight Snacks	1960	Anthology	VGF		$7.00
BALLANTINE	377	The Sound Of His Horn	1960	Sarban	AF		$11.00 A
BALLANTINE	377	The Sound Of His Horn (2nd)	1960	Sarban	AF		$25.00 A
BALLANTINE	380	Tales To Be Told In The Dark	1960	Anthology	AF		$8.00
BALLANTINE	382	Farenheit 451	1960	Bradbury, R.	VGF		$5.00
BALLANTINE	F 384	Stalingrad	1960	Schroter, H.	AF		$7.00
BALLANTINE	392	The American Slave Trade	1960	Spears, J.R.	VG		$6.00
BALLANTINE	401	Invisible Men	1960	Anthology	AF		$7.00
BALLANTINE	401	Invisible Men	1960	Anthology	VGF		$7.00
BALLANTINE	406	The Climacticon	1960	Livingston, H.	VGF		$5.00
BALLANTINE	407	Of All Possible Worlds	1960	Tenn, W.	VG		$3.00
BALLANTINE	410	The Hurricane	1960	Robertson, T.	AF		$6.00
BALLANTINE	417	Zacherly's Vulture Stew	1960	Anthology	F		$15.00 A
BALLANTINE	417	Zacherly's Vulture Stew	1960	Anthology	VGF		$12.00
BALLANTINE	423	Re-Birth	1960	Wyndham, J.	AF		$7.00
BALLANTINE	F 425	A Torch To The Enemy	1960	Caidin, M.	AF		$7.00
BALLANTINE	F 428	The Call Girl	1960	Greenwald, H.	VG	MTI	$5.00
BALLANTINE	431	The Doll Maker	1960	Sarban	VGF		$13.00 A
BALLANTINE	F 450	The Shocking History Of Drugs	1960	Mathison, R.	VG+		$4.00
BALLANTINE	453	Village Of The Damned	1960	Wyndham, J.	VGF	MTI	$18.00 A
BALLANTINE	453	Village Of The Damned	1960	Wyndham, J.	AF	MTI	$15.00
BALLANTINE	F 457	Japanese Destroyer Captain	1961	Hara, T.	VG+		$6.00
BALLANTINE	465	So Close To Home	1961	Blish, J.	AF		$6.00
BALLANTINE	476	Turn Left At Thursday	1961	Pohl, F.	VGF		$7.00
BALLANTINE	480	The Other Passenger	1961	Cross, J.K.	VGF		$6.00
BALLANTINE	483	Strangers From Earth	1961	Anderson, P.	VGF		$6.00
BALLANTINE	497	Bypass To Otherness	1961	Kuttner, H.	VGF		$7.00
BALLANTINE	498	Ringstones	1961	Sarban	VGF		$13.00
BALLANTINE	508	Night's Black Agents	1961	Leiber, F.	VGF		$8.00
BALLANTINE	512	England Under Hitler	1961	Clarke, C.	AF		$7.00
BALLANTINE	522	Tales Of Love & Horror	1961	Anthology	VGF		$6.00
BALLANTINE	531	The Clock Strikes 12	1961	Wakefield, H.R.	AF		$8.00
BALLANTINE	540	Sardonicus	1961	Russell, R.	VG+	MTI	$7.00
BALLANTINE	S 541	College Parodies	1961	Anthology	VGF		$7.00
BALLANTINE	542	Not Long For This World	1961	Derleth, A.	AF		$12.00
BALLANTINE	542	Not Long For This World	1961	Derleth, A.	VGF		$8.00
BALLANTINE	545	Out Of The Deeps	1961	Wyndham, J.	VGF		$5.00
BALLANTINE	551	Paris Blues	1961	Flender, H.	VGF	MTI	$7.00
BALLANTINE	552	And Some Were Human	1961	Del Rey, L.	VGF		$5.00
BALLANTINE	563	Alone By Night	1961	Anthology	AF		$7.00
BALLANTINE	577	Shadows With Eyes	1962	Leiber, F.	VGF		$7.00
BALLANTINE	579	After Doomsday	1962	Anderson, P.	VGF		$6.00
BALLANTINE	F 581	Satan's Disciples	1962	Goldston, R.	VG+		$5.00
BALLANTINE	587	Nine Horrors And A Dream	1962	Brennan, J.P.	AF		$5.00
BALLANTINE	F 596	H.M.S. Defiant	1962	Tilsley, F.	VGF	MTI	$8.00

Ballantine U1022 VGF $28	Ballantine U2106 AF $22	Ballantine 3055 AF $50	Ballantine 34947 AF $15

PUBLISHER	PUB. #	TITLE	DATE	AUTHOR	COND.	TYPE	PRICE
BALLANTINE	F 606	The Big Clock	1962	Fearing, K.	VG		$3.00
BALLANTINE	F 609	Telepath	1962	Sellings, A.	VGF		$5.00
BALLANTINE	F 619	Return To Otherness	1962	Kuttner, H.	AF		$7.00
BALLANTINE	629	The Survivor	1962	Lovecraft, H.P.	AF		$18.00 A
BALLANTINE	F 641	The Fiend In You	1962	Anthology	VGF		$12.00
BALLANTINE	F 641	The Fiend In You	1962	Anthology	VG+		$7.00
BALLANTINE	F 648	Citizen In Space	1962	Sheckley, R.	VGF		$5.00
BALLANTINE	F 657	Sometime, Never	1962	Anthology	AF		$5.00
BALLANTINE	671	Sun Dance	1962	Grove, F.	VGF		$7.00
BALLANTINE	F 680	The Frankenstein Reader	1962	Anthology	AF		$15.00 A
BALLANTINE	F 680	The Frankenstein Reader	1962	Anthology	VGF-		$8.00
BALLANTINE	F 687	The First Man In The Moon	1963	Wells, H.G.	VGF		$6.00
BALLANTINE	F 704	Sweet Daddy	1963	Rubin, T.I.	VG+		$7.00
BALLANTINE	F 712	All The Way Down	1962	Riccio, V.	VGF		$10.00 A
BALLANTINE	F 724	Mutant	1963	Kuttner, H.	F		$6.00
BALLANTINE	F 725	The Food Of The Gods	1963	Wells, H.G.	AF		$5.00
BALLANTINE	X 743	Allan Quartermain	1963	Haggard, H.R.	AF		$7.00
BALLANTINE	U 1020	High Fury	1964	Whittington, H.	VG		$10.00
BALLANTINE	U 1022	Wild Lonesome	1965	Whittington, H.	VGF		$28.00 A
BALLANTINE	U 1022	Wild Lonesome	1965	Whittington, H.	VG		$8.00
BALLANTINE	U 1051	Massacre At Goliad	1965	Kelton, E.	VG+		$6.00
BALLANTINE	U 2001	Tarzan Of The Apes (TVTI ed.)	1966	Burroughs, E.R.	VG+	TVTI	$7.00
BALLANTINE	U 2106	Tales From The Crypt	1964	Anthology	AF		$22.00 A
BALLANTINE	U 2140	Tales Of The Incredible	1965	Anthology	AF-		$10.00
BALLANTINE	U 2141	The Autumn People	1965	Bradbury, R.	VG+		$10.00
BALLANTINE	U 2191	Martian Time Slip	1965	Dick, P.K.	VGF		$12.00
BALLANTINE	U 2191	Martian Time Slip	1965	Dick, P.K.	AF		$9.00 A
BALLANTINE	U 2192	Inside Outside	1964	Farmer, P.J.	AF		$8.00
BALLANTINE	U 2193	Dare	1965	Farmer, P.J.	AF		$8.00
BALLANTINE	U 2307	After The Bugles	1967	Kelton, E.	G		$5.00
BALLANTINE	U 5032	A Clockwork Orange	1965	Burgess, A.	VG+		$6.00
BALLANTINE	U 5050	The 10th Victim	1965	Sheckley, R.	VGF	MTI	$5.00
BALLANTINE	U 5056	Hombre (4th)	1967	Leonard, E.	VG	MTI	$6.00
BALLANTINE	U 5065	The Leather Boys	1967	Freeman, G.	G		$5.00
BALLANTINE	U 5070	The Bogeyman	1967	Forster, M.	VG+		$5.00
BALLANTINE	U 5090	I Couldn't Smoke The Grass...	1967	Chaplin, M.	VG		$7.00
BALLANTINE	U 6026	The Destruction Of Dresden	1965	Irving, D.	VGF		$6.00
BALLANTINE	U 6033	Japanese Destroyer Captain	1965	Hara, T.	AF		$6.00
BALLANTINE	U 6054	The Battle For Guadalcanal	1966	Griffith, S.B.	AF		$6.00
BALLANTINE	U 6063	The Bridge At Remagen	1966	Hechler, K.	VGF		$6.00
BALLANTINE	U 6084	Torpedo Bomber!	1967	Barker, R.	VG+		$6.00
BALLANTINE	U 6088	The Ragged Rugged Warriors	1967	Caidin, M.	VGF		$6.00
BALLANTINE	U 6090	Men And Waves	1967	Dixon, P.L.	VG+		$6.00
BALLANTINE	U 6106	Night Fighter	1967	Rawnsley, C.F.	AF		$6.00
BALLANTINE	U 6108	Restoree	1967	McCaffrey, A.	VG		$10.00
BALLANTINE	U 6125	Tarzan And The Valley Of Gold	1967	Leiber, F.	VG+	MTI	$7.00
BALLANTINE	U 6234	Battle For The Rhine	1967	Thompson, R.W.	VGF		$6.00
BALLANTINE	U 6238	Secret Weapons Of WWII	1967	Pawle, G.	AF		$6.00

Banner Mystery 2 VG+ $24   Banner B60-106 VG $52   Bantam 12 VG+ $8

PUBLISHER	PUB. #	TITLE	DATE	AUTHOR	COND.	TYPE	PRICE
BALLANTINE	U 7011	Pornography And The Law	1964	Kronhausen, E.	VGF		$5.00
BALLANTINE	U 7089	Bob Dylan - Don't Look Back	1968	Pennebaker, D.A.	VG		$6.00
BALLANTINE	2038	Do It!	1970	Rubin, J.	VGF		$16.00 A
BALLANTINE	2038	Do It!	1970	Rubin, J.	VG		$5.00
BALLANTINE	2305	The Man Who Was Thursday	1971	Chesterton, G.K.	VG+		$20.00 A
BALLANTINE	2396	The Long Goodbye (3rd)	1973	Chandler, R.	AF	MTI	$7.00
BALLANTINE	2424	Fork-Tailed Devil	1971	Caidin, M.	VG+		$5.00
BALLANTINE	2818	Super Fly	1972	Fenty, P.	VGF	MTI	$13.00 A
BALLANTINE	3055	A Werewolf Among Us	1973	Koontz, D.R.	AF		$50.00 A
BALLANTINE	3126	Captain's Rangers	1973	Kelton, E.	VG+		$4.00
BALLANTINE	3337	A Confederate General ...	1973	Brautigan, R.	AF		$6.00
BALLANTINE	24426	Help I Am Being Held Prisoner	1975	Westlake, D.E.	F		$5.00
BALLANTINE	24810	Bid Time Return	1975	Matheson, R.	AF		$50.00 A
BALLANTINE	24810	Bid Time Return	1975	Matheson, R.	VG+		$20.00 A
BALLANTINE	25140	Dragonfly	1976	Dwyer, K.R.*	VG+		$16.00
BALLANTINE	25140	Dragonfly	1975	Dwyer, K.R.*	VG+		$15.00
BALLANTINE	25158	A Week As Andrea Benstock	1977	Emerson, J.*	VG-		$5.00 A
BALLANTINE	25224	Martian Time-Slip	1976	Dick, P.K.	VGF		$6.00
BALLANTINE	25719	I Am Not Spock	1977	Nimoy, L.	VG		$5.00
BALLANTINE	30638	Somewhere In Time	1982	Matheson, R.	VG	MTI	$7.00
BALLANTINE	34947	Sideswipe	1988	Willeford, C.	AF		$15.00 A
BALLANTINE	70703	Captain's Rangers	1969	Kelton, E.	VGF		$8.00
BALLANTINE	70703	Captain's Rangers	1969	Kelton, E.	VG		$8.00
BANNER	B50 101	Way Out	1967	Charbonneau, L.	VG		$15.00 A
BANNER	B50 103	Get Dumm!	1967	Brewer, J.	VG		$5.00
BANNER	B50 105	The Girl On Crown Street	1967	Karp, D.	VGF+		$14.00 A
BANNER	B50 112	Six Graves To Munich	1967	Cleri, M.	G		$4.00
BANNER	B50 113	The Brotherhood Of Velvet	1967	Karp, D.	VG		$7.00
BANNER	B50 113	The Brotherhood Of Velvet	1967	Karp, D.	VG		$6.00
BANNER	B50 115	Plunder Canyon	1967	Bonner, P.	VG		$4.00
BANNER	B50 116	Incident At Butler's Station	1967	Wyler, R.	VGF		$5.00
BANNER	B60 106	Doomsday Mission	1967	Whittington, H.	VG		$52.00 A
BANNER	B60 108	The Devious Defector	1967	Saber, W.J.	VGF		$5.00
BANNER	B60 108	The Devious Defector	1967	Saber, W.J.	VG		$5.00
BANNER	B60 111	Somebody's Done For	1967	Goodis, D.	VG		$36.00 A
BANNER MYSTERY	1	The Sunday Pigeon Murders	1945	Rice, C.	G	Digest	$7.00
BANNER MYSTERY	2	Death Goes To School	1945	Patrick, Q.	VG+	Digest	$24.00 A
BANNER VOLUME	104	The Strangest Way Of Love	1964	Kurts, A.	AF		$7.00
BANNER VOLUME	104	The Strangest Way Of Love	1964	Kurts, A.	VG		$6.00
BANTAM	No#	Puppy And Dog Care	1956	Miller, H.	VG-		$6.00
BANTAM	No#	Roosevelt And Hopkins Vol. 1	1950	Sherwood, R.E.	VGF+		$5.00
BANTAM	No#	Roosevelt And Hopkins Vol. 2	1950	Sherwood, R.E.	VGF		$5.00
BANTAM	No#	The Bantam Story	1970	Petersen, C.	AF		$16.00 A
BANTAM	No#	The Bantam Story (revised ed.)	1975	Petersen, C.	VGF		$8.00 A
BANTAM	3	Nevada	1945	Gray, Z.	VG+		$3.00

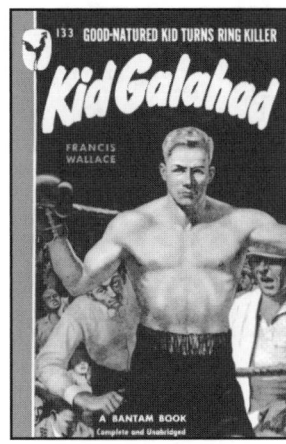

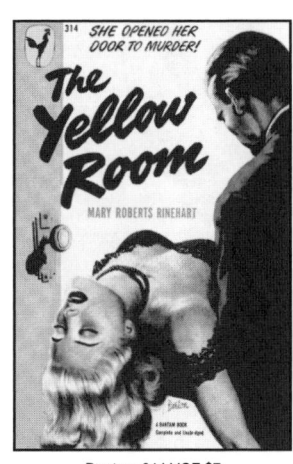

Bantam 133 VG+ $7   Bantam 302 VG+ $20   Bantam 314 VGF $7

PUBLISHER	PUB. #	TITLE	DATE	AUTHOR	COND.	TYPE	PRICE
BANTAM	9	Rogue Male (2nd)	1946	Household, G.	VG+		$3.00
BANTAM	12	Then There Were Three	1945	Homes, G.	VG+		$8.00 A
BANTAM	12	Then There Were Three	1945	Homes, G.	VG		$5.00
BANTAM	12	Then There Were Three (3rd)	1946	Homes, G.	G		$6.00
BANTAM	21	Men, Women And Dogs	1946	Thurber, J.	VG		$3.00
BANTAM	22	Babbitt (dust jacket)	1946	Lewis, S.	VGF		$111.00 A
BANTAM	22	Babbitt (dust jacket)	1946	Lewis, S.	VG+		$45.00 A
BANTAM	24	Valliant Is The Word For Carrie (d.j.)	1946	Benefield, B.	VG+		$20.00
BANTAM	33	The Prisoner Of Zenda	1946	Hope, A.	VGF		$7.00
BANTAM	36	Trail Boss	1946	Dawson, P.	VGF		$6.00
BANTAM	46	Escape The Night	1946	Eberhart, M.G.	VG		$3.00
BANTAM	54	The Love Letters	1946	Massie, C.	F		$6.00
BANTAM	62	Dead Center	1946	Collins, M.	VG		$5.00
BANTAM	63	Green Mansions	1946	Hudson, W.H.	VGF		$6.00
BANTAM	70	Lay That Pistol Down (2nd)	1946	Powell, R.	VGF		$5.00
BANTAM	74	Halo In Blood	1946	Evans, J.*	VG		$5.00
BANTAM	74	Halo In Blood	1946	Evans, J.*	G		$2.00
BANTAM	76	Drink To Yesterday (2nd)	1947	Coles, M.	AF		$5.00
BANTAM	81	Puzzles, Quizes & Games	1947	Fraser, P.	AF		$18.00 A
BANTAM	94	The Crimson Horseshoe	1947	Dawson, P.	VG+		$6.00
BANTAM	100	The Cautious Amorist	1947	Lindsay, N.	VGF		$7.00
BANTAM	102	Range Rider	1947	Kent, W.H.B.	VGF		$5.00
BANTAM	104	Powder Valley Pay-Off	1947	Field, P.	VG		$3.00
BANTAM	113	Riders Of The Night	1947	Cunningham, E.	VGF		$20.00 A
BANTAM	116	Stories From The Sat. Eve. Post	1947	Anthology	VGF		$4.00
BANTAM	123	A Treasury Of Folk Songs	1948	Kolb, S.	VGF+		$8.00
BANTAM	126	Quality	1947	Sumner, C.R.	VG+		$5.00
BANTAM	131	The Pearl	1947	Steinbeck, J.	VGF	MTI	$7.00
BANTAM	133	Kid Galahad	1947	Wallace, F.	VG+		$7.00
BANTAM	134	Hell For Breakfast	1947	LeMay, A.	VGF		$5.00
BANTAM	135	Mama's Bank Account	1947	Forbes, K.	VG	MTI	$6.00
BANTAM	158	The Sign Of The Ram (2nd)	1948	Ferguson, M.	VGF	MTI	$8.00
BANTAM	207	Short Grass	1948	Blackburn, T.W.	AF		$5.00
BANTAM	208	Dead Man's Range	1948	Hopkins, T.J.	VGF-		$5.00
BANTAM	213	Hell Or High Water	1949	Pearce, D.	VGF		$5.00
BANTAM	214	Rio Grande Kid	1949	Hankins, R.M.	VG+		$4.00
BANTAM	251	Relentless	1948	Perkins, K.	VGF		$5.00
BANTAM	252	Barbed Wire	1948	Foster, B.	VG		$2.00
BANTAM	254	The Border Bandit	1948	Evans, E.	VG+		$3.00
BANTAM	255	Badlands	1948	Foster, B.	VGF		$5.00
BANTAM	302	The Fabulous Clipjoint	1948	Brown, F.	VG+		$20.00
BANTAM	306	The Day He Died	1948	Padgett, L.	VG		$3.00
BANTAM	307	The Bride Saw Red	1948	Carson, R.	VG		$3.00
BANTAM	310	Murder In The Glass Room	1948	Rolfe, E.	VGF		$4.00
BANTAM	314	The Yellow Room	1949	Rinehart, M.R.	VGF		$7.00

Bantam 317 VGF $7　　　Bantam 360 (DJ) VGF $83　　　Bantam 407 VG $24

PUBLISHER	PUB. #	TITLE	DATE	AUTHOR	COND.	TYPE	PRICE
BANTAM	317	Murder Is Cheap	1949	Gilbert, A.	VGF		$7.00
BANTAM	351	The Lying Ladies	1948	Finnegan, R.	VG		$4.00
BANTAM	354	San Francisco Murders	1948	Anthology	VG+		$4.00
BANTAM	355	The Man Within (dust jkt.)	1948	Greene, G.	VGF		$66.00 A
BANTAM	355	The Man Within	1948	Greene, G.	AF		$7.00
BANTAM	356	Sorry, Wrong Number	1948	Ullman, A.	VGF	MTI	$9.00
BANTAM	360	One More Unfortunate (dust jkt.)	1949	Lustgarten, E.	VGF		$83.00 A
BANTAM	361	The Dead Ringer	1949	Brown, F.	VGF+		$41.00 A
BANTAM	363	Many A Monster	1949	Finnegan, R.	VG		$7.00
BANTAM	400	Winter Meeting	1948	Vance, E.	AF	MTI	$14.00
BANTAM	402	The Red Pony	1948	Steinbeck, J.	VGF-	MTI	$8.00
BANTAM	406	Mickey	1948	Goodin, P.	VG	MTI	$3.00
BANTAM	407	Behold This Woman	1948	Goodis, D.	VG		$24.00
BANTAM	407	Behold This Woman	1948	Goodis, D.	VG		$23.00 A
BANTAM	407	Behold This Woman	1948	Goodis, D.	G		$10.00
BANTAM	410	The Grass Is Always Greener	1948	Smith, G.M.	G+		$2.00
BANTAM	420	Illusion	1949	Corliss, A.	VG+		$6.00
BANTAM	459	Joan Of Arc	1948	Winwar, F.	AF	MTI	$7.00
BANTAM	459	Joan Of Arc	1948	Winwar, F.	VGF	MTI	$7.00
BANTAM	461	Back Home	1948	Mauldin, B.	VGF		$7.00
BANTAM	462	What Became Of Anna Bolton? (d.j.)	1948	Bromfield, L.	VG+		$55.00 A
BANTAM	469	Lady Godiva And Master Tom	1949	Faure, R.C.	AF		$8.00
BANTAM	474	Hazard	1949	Chanslor, R.	VG+		$5.00
BANTAM	476	Road Show	1949	Hatch, E.	VG+		$5.00
BANTAM	500	My Greatest Day In Baseball	1948	Carmichael, J.P.	VG		$5.00
BANTAM	554	Hot Leather	1948	Millhauser, B.	VG+		$5.00
BANTAM	556	The Brooklyn Dodgers	1949	Barber, R.	VG+		$15.00 A
BANTAM	557	Jack Dempsey	1949	Fleischer, N.	VG		$5.00
BANTAM	701	Dead As A Dummy	1949	Homes, G.	G		$6.00
BANTAM	708	The Captive Women	1949	Edmonds, W.D.	VG+		$5.00
BANTAM	725	Blackleg Range	1949	Foster, B.	F		$7.00
BANTAM	733	The Valley Of Fear	1950	Doyle, A.C.	VG+		$8.00
BANTAM	733	The Valley Of Fear	1950	Doyle, A.C.	VG		$6.00
BANTAM	737	The Darker Brother	1949	Moon, B.	VGF		$10.00 A
BANTAM	737	The Darker Brother	1949	Moon, B.	VG		$7.00
BANTAM	743	Twelve O'Clock High (3rd)	1950	Lay, B.	VG	MTI	$6.00
BANTAM	750	Thieves' Market	1950	Bezzerides, A.I.	VG		$7.00
BANTAM	751	Shot In The Dark (2nd)	1950	Anthology	AF		$17.00 A
BANTAM	770	The Whip	1950	Mason, S.E.	AF		$6.00
BANTAM	774	Heritage Of The River	1950	Elwood, M.	VG+		$6.00
BANTAM	776	Only The Valiant (2nd)	1950	Warren, C.M.	VGF		$7.00
BANTAM	783	The Bloody Moonlight	1950	Brown, F.	G		$6.00
BANTAM	794	Angels Camp	1950	Morrison, R.	VG+		$17.00 A
BANTAM	797	The 3rd Man	1950	Greene, G.	VG+	MTI	$7.00
BANTAM	A 798	The Underworld	1950	Wolfert, I.	VG+		$5.00

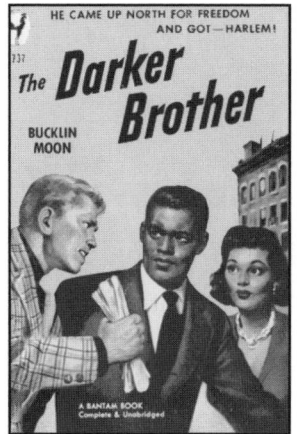

Bantam 462 (DJ) VG+ $55   Bantam 737 VGF $10   Bantam 774 VG+ $6

PUBLISHER	PUB. #	TITLE	DATE	AUTHOR	COND.	TYPE	PRICE
BANTAM	813	Sailor Town	1950	Fox, P.	VGF		$5.00
BANTAM	A 815	A Lion In The Streets	1950	Langley, A.L.	VGF		$6.00
BANTAM	819	Donovan's Brain	1950	Siodmak, C.	VGF		$12.00
BANTAM	819	Donovan's Brain	1950	Siodmak, C.	VG		$8.00
BANTAM	819	Donovan's Brain	1950	Siodmak, C.	VG-		$4.00
BANTAM	825	A Private Killing	1950	Benet, J.	VG+		$7.00
BANTAM	831	The Screaming Mimi	1950	Brown, F.	VGF		$76.00 A
BANTAM	831	The Screaming Mimi	1950	Brown, F.	G-		$5.00
BANTAM	835	What Mad Universe	1950	Brown, F.	VGF		$41.00 A
BANTAM	835	What Mad Universe	1950	Brown, F.	VG+		$24.00 A
BANTAM	835	What Mad Universe	1950	Brown, F.	G+		$6.00
BANTAM	839	Mission: Danger	1950	Orsborne, D.	VGF		$5.00
BANTAM	845	How To Survive An Atomic Bomb	1950	Gerstell, R.	VG		$4.00
BANTAM	848	The Queen Bee	1950	Lee, E.	VG		$6.00
BANTAM	857	The Haters	1950	Strauss, T.	VGF		$9.00
BANTAM	857	The Haters	1950	Strauss, T.	G		$3.00
BANTAM	875	Something For Nothing	1951	Dixon, H.V.	VG		$2.00
BANTAM	876	Compliments Of A Fiend	1951	Brown, F.	VG+		$15.00
BANTAM	878	Ticket To Oblivion	1951	Parker, R.	VGF		$7.00
BANTAM	882	Lone Hand	1951	Evans, E.	VG		$5.00
BANTAM	896	He Who Whispers	1951	Carr, J.D.	VG+		$7.00
BANTAM	A 902	The Flames Of Time	1951	Kendrick, B.	VGF		$10.00
BANTAM	907	The Case Against Myself	1951	Tree, G.	VGF		$7.00
BANTAM	913	Saturday Review Reader	1951	Anthology	VG		$2.50
BANTAM	A 914	Stories For Here And Now	1951	Anthology	VG		$2.50
BANTAM	923	Hot Rod	1951	Felsen, H.G.	VG+		$14.00 A
BANTAM	923	Hot Rod	1951	Felsen, H.G.	G		$5.00
BANTAM	934	Blues For The Prince	1951	Spicer, B.	VG+		$7.00
BANTAM	942	Romelle	1951	Burnett, W.R.	VG		$6.00
BANTAM	943	Here Comes A Candle	1951	Brown, F.	VGF		$46.00 A
BANTAM	943	Here Comes A Candle	1951	Brown, F.	VG		$15.00
BANTAM	A 944	Timeless Stories	1952	Anthology	VG+		$8.00
BANTAM	945	Tomboy	1951	Ellson, H.	VG		$5.00
BANTAM	959	The Best Go First	1952	O'Malley, F.	VG		$3.00
BANTAM	962	The Trees	1951	Richter, C.	VG		$5.00
BANTAM	967	A Man Without Friends	1952	Echard, M.	AF		$7.00
BANTAM	968	Dig Me A Grave	1951	Spain, J.	VGF		$8.00
BANTAM	976	The Gambler	1952	Krasner, W.	VGF		$8.00
BANTAM	A 979	Model Railroading	1951	Lionel	VG		$5.00
BANTAM	990	Night Of The Jabberwock	1952	Brown, F.	VG-		$9.00
BANTAM	998	Tomorrow's Another Day	1952	Burnett, W.R.	G		$5.00
BANTAM	1012	Murder On The Left Bank	1952	Paul, E.	VG		$6.00
BANTAM	1020	Theresa	1952	Zola, E.	VGF		$5.00
BANTAM	1026	Big Shot	1952	Treat, L.	AF		$7.00
BANTAM	1032	The Second Confession	1952	Stout, R.	VG+		$6.00

Bantam 835 VGF $41   Bantam 896 VG+ $7   Bantam 907 VGF $7

PUBLISHER	PUB. #	TITLE	DATE	AUTHOR	COND.	TYPE	PRICE
BANTAM	1040	Death Has Many Doors	1952	Brown, F.	VGF		$29.00 A
BANTAM	1040	Death Has Many Doors	1952	Brown, F.	VG+		$27.00 A
BANTAM	1040	Death Has Many Doors	1952	Brown, F.	VG		$18.00 A
BANTAM	1040	Death Has Many Doors	1952	Brown, F.	VG-		$15.00
BANTAM	1046	The Farmers Hotel	1952	O'Hara, J.	VG+		$6.00
BANTAM	A 1051	The Disenchanted	1952	Schulberg, B.	VGF-		$5.00
BANTAM	1054	Cage Of Darkness	1952	Masson, R.	VG+		$8.00
BANTAM	1054	Cage Of Darkness	1952	Masson, R.	VG+		$7.00
BANTAM	1077	Space On My Hands	1952	Brown, F.	VG+		$11.00 A
BANTAM	1077	Space On My Hands	1952	Brown, F.	G		$6.00
BANTAM	A 1089	Coronado's Children	1953	Dobie, J.F.	VG+		$6.00
BANTAM	A 1106	Fancies And Goodnights	1953	Collier, J.	VG-		$6.00
BANTAM	1126	The Long Green	1953	Spicer, B.	AF		$9.00 A
BANTAM	1128	Thin Edge Of Violence	1953	O'Farrell, W.	VG+		$4.00
BANTAM	1133	The Far Cry	1953	Brown, F.	VG-		$8.00
BANTAM	1134	The Fabulous Clipjoint	1953	Brown, F.	VG		$16.00
BANTAM	1134	The Fabulous Clipjoint	1953	Brown, F.	G+		$6.00
BANTAM	1143	Mountain Meadow	1953	Buchan, J.	VG+		$5.00
BANTAM	1147	A Cry Of Children	1953	Burns, J.H.	VG		$7.00
BANTAM	1148	The Price Of Salt	1953	Morgan, C.*	VGF		$24.00
BANTAM	1148	The Price Of Salt	1953	Morgan, C.*	VG+		$15.00
BANTAM	1148	The Price Of Salt	1953	Morgan, C.*	VG		$8.00
BANTAM	1148	The Price Of Salt	1953	Morgan, C.*	VG		$5.00
BANTAM	1149	Gold Under Skull Peak	1953	O'Rourke, F.	VG		$5.00
BANTAM	F 1165	Flee The Angry Strangers	1953	Mandel, G.	VG		$4.00
BANTAM	1173	In The Best Families	1953	Stout, R.	VG+		$7.00
BANTAM	1176	We All Killed Grandma	1953	Brown, F.	VG		$100.00 A
BANTAM	1179	Four Steps To The Wall	1953	Webb, J.E.	VGF		$7.00
BANTAM	A 1181	Wait For Tomorrow	1953	Wilder, R.	F		$17.00 A
BANTAM	A 1181	Wait For Tomorrow	1953	Wilder, R.	VGF		$10.00
BANTAM	A 1181	Wait For Tomorrow	1953	Wilder, R.	VGF-		$7.00
BANTAM	A 1201	Manhattan	1954	Anthology	AF		$7.00
BANTAM	1215	The Deep End	1954	Brown, F.	G+		$6.00
BANTAM	1215	The Deep End	1954	Brown, F.	VG-		$4.00
BANTAM	1216	The Dead Ringer	1954	Brown, F.	VG		$9.00
BANTAM	1216	The Dead Ringer	1954	Brown, F.	VG		$7.00
BANTAM	1226	Blood Will Tell	1954	Bagby, G.	AF		$9.00
BANTAM	F 1233	Eyeless In Gaza	1954	Huxley, A.	VG+		$5.00
BANTAM	A 1234	Suleiman The Magnificent	1954	Lamb, H.	VG		$5.00
BANTAM	A 1241	Golden Apples Of The Sun	1954	Bradbury, R.	AF		$16.00 A
BANTAM	A 1241	Golden Apples Of The Sun	1954	Bradbury, R.	AF		$15.00
BANTAM	A 1241	Golden Apples Of The Sun	1954	Bradbury, R.	AF		$15.00 A
BANTAM	A 1241	Golden Apples Of The Sun	1954	Bradbury, R.	VG-		$5.00
BANTAM	A 1245	A Good Man	1954	Young, J.	F		$4.00
BANTAM	A 1249	The Sun Also Rises	1954	Hemingway, E.	VGF		$4.00

Bantam 923 VG+ $14   Bantam 943 VGF $46   Bantam 1040 VGF $29

PUBLISHER	PUB. #	TITLE	DATE	AUTHOR	COND.	TYPE	PRICE
BANTAM	1251	Line To Tomorrow	1954	Padgett, L.	AF		$10.00
BANTAM	1253	What Mad Universe	1954	Brown, F.	VGF		$8.00 A
BANTAM	1253	What Mad Universe	1954	Brown, F.	VG		$4.00
BANTAM	A 1262	Utopia 14	1954	Vonnegut, K.	VGF-		$15.00
BANTAM	1271	The Venus Death	1954	Benson, B.	VGF		$7.00
BANTAM	1278	Costigan's Needle	1954	Sohl, J.	VGF		$8.00
BANTAM	1278	Costigan's Needle	1954	Sohl, J.	AF		$7.00
BANTAM	F 1279	Battle Cry	1954	Uris, L.	VG+		$3.00
BANTAM	1285	The Lights In The Sky Are Stars	1954	Brown, F.	AF-		$12.00 A
BANTAM	1285	The Lights In The Sky Are Stars	1954	Brown, F.	VG		$4.00
BANTAM	1286	Shakedown	1954	Ellington, R.	VGF		$5.00
BANTAM	A 1292	War With The Newts	1955	Capek, K.	VGF		$7.00
BANTAM	A 1292	War With The Newts	1955	Capek, K.	VG+		$5.00
BANTAM	1294	Third From The Sun	1955	Matheson, R.	VGF		$17.00
BANTAM	1294	Third From The Sun	1955	Matheson, R.	VG		$7.00
BANTAM	1294	Third From The Sun (Signed)	1955	Matheson, R.	VGF		$22.00
BANTAM	1308	Drop Dead	1955	Bagby, G.	AF		$7.00
BANTAM	1315	Murder Points A Finger	1955	Alexander, D.	VGF		$7.00
BANTAM	A 1319	The Enchanted Cup	1955	Roberts, D.J.	VGF+		$7.00
BANTAM	1323	Target In Taffeta	1955	Benson, B.	AF		$8.00
BANTAM	1327	The Schirmer Inheritance	1955	Ambler, E.	AF		$6.00 A
BANTAM	1328	Frontiers In Space	1955	Anthology	VG+		$6.00
BANTAM	1330	But That's Unprintable (6th)	1955	Anthology	VG+		$5.00
BANTAM	1334	Strange As It Seems	1955	Hix, E.	VG-		$5.00
BANTAM	1343	Man From Tomorrow	1955	Tucker, W.	AF		$10.00
BANTAM	1371	The Seven Year Itch (2nd)	1955	Axelrod, G.	VG+	MTI	$10.00
BANTAM	1376	Giveaway	1955	Fisher, S.	AF-		$12.00
BANTAM	1376	Giveaway	1955	Fisher, S.	VG		$6.00
BANTAM	1400	Time:X	1955	Tucker, W.	VGF		$7.00
BANTAM	A 1412	Sweet Thursday	1956	Steinbeck, J.	G+		$2.50
BANTAM	1423	Star Shine	1956	Brown, F.	VG-		$5.00
BANTAM	1423	Star Shine (2nd)	1956	Brown, F.	VG+		$7.00
BANTAM	1436	His Name Was Death	1956	Brown, F.	G		$7.00
BANTAM	1436	His Name Was Death	1956	Brown, F.	G		$4.00
BANTAM	1437	Street Rod (2nd)	1956	Felsen, H.G.	VG		$7.00
BANTAM	1438	Violent Saturday	1956	Heath, W.L.	AF		$8.00
BANTAM	1468	The Silver Cobweb	1956	Benson, B.	VG		$5.00
BANTAM	1486	The Burning Hills	1956	L'Amour, L.	AF		$87.00 A
BANTAM	F 1510	Waterfront	1956	Schulberg, B.	VGF		$7.00
BANTAM	1534	Paint The Town Black	1956	Alexander, D.	AF		$8.00
BANTAM	1538	Rag Top	1956	Felsen, H.G.	VGF		$13.00 A
BANTAM	1546	Martians, Go Home	1956	Brown, F.	VGF		$17.00
BANTAM	1559	The Rainmaker	1957	Nash, N.R.	AF	MTI	$8.00
BANTAM	1565	The Wench Is Dead	1957	Brown, F.	VG+		$38.00 A
BANTAM	1565	The Wench Is Dead (2nd)	1957	Brown, F.	VG-		$4.00

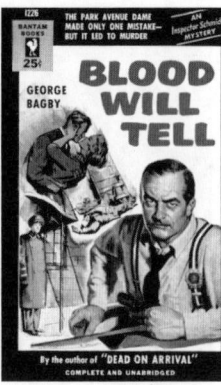

Bantam 1148 VGF $24   Bantam 1181 F $17   Bantam 1216 VG $9   Bantam 1226 AF $9

PUBLISHER	PUB. #	TITLE	DATE	AUTHOR	COND.	TYPE	PRICE
BANTAM	1571	The Shores Of Space	1957	Matheson, R.	VG+		$12.00
BANTAM	1577	The Tough Die Hard	1957	Martin, R.	VG		$7.00
BANTAM	1602	Square In The Middle	1957	Gault, W.C.	VGF-		$18.00 A
BANTAM	1610	The Gun	1957	Forester, C.S.	VG	MTI	$7.00
BANTAM	A 1615	Science Fiction Carnival	1957	Anthology	VG		$7.00
BANTAM	1623	Mating Manual	1957	Keller, R.	AF		$6.00
BANTAM	1638	Day Of The Ram	1957	Gault, W.C.	VG+		$10.00
BANTAM	1638	Day Of The Ram	1957	Gault, W.C.	VG		$7.00
BANTAM	1638	Day Of The Ram	1957	Gault, W.C.	G		$3.00
BANTAM	A 1653	Will Success Spoil Rock Hunter?	1957	Axelrod, G.	AF	MTI	$10.00
BANTAM	1681	Silver Canyon	1957	L'Amour, L.	VGF		$30.00 A
BANTAM	1681	Silver Canyon	1957	L'Amour, L.	VG+		$8.00
BANTAM	A 1701	Rogue In Space	1957	Brown, F.	VGF		$8.00
BANTAM	F 1707	The Big War	1957	Myrer, A.	VG+	MTI	$3.00
BANTAM	1712	The Lenient Beast	1958	Brown, F.	VG		$8.00
BANTAM	1712	The Lenient Beast	1958	Brown, F.	G+		$4.00
BANTAM	A 1713	Sitka	1958	L'Amour, L.	VG+		$60.00 A
BANTAM	1726	Tales Of Wells Fargo	1958	Gruber, F.	AF	TVTI	$7.00
BANTAM	1728	Halo In Blood	1958	Evans, J.*	AF		$6.00
BANTAM	1729	Halo For Satan	1958	Evans, J.*	AF		$6.00
BANTAM	1729	Halo For Satan	1958	Evans, J.*	AF		$6.00
BANTAM	1757	The Screaming Mimi	1958	Brown, F.	VGF	MTI	$16.00 A
BANTAM	A 1759	Yonder	1958	Beaumont, C.	AF-		$11.00 A
BANTAM	A 1759	Yonder	1958	Beaumont, C.	VG		$6.00
BANTAM	A 1759	Yonder	1958	Beaumont, C.	G		$5.00
BANTAM	A 1812	Honeymoon In Hell	1958	Brown, F.	VG+		$6.00
BANTAM	A 1831	The Price Of Salt	1958	Morgan, C.*	AF		$16.00
BANTAM	A 1842	Bell, Book And Candle	1958	Van Druten, J.	VGF	MTI	$7.00
BANTAM	1853	Radigan	1958	L'Amour, L.	VG		$82.00 A
BANTAM	A 1868	The Journey	1958	Tabori, G.	AF	MTI	$7.00
BANTAM	A 1892	Hot Rod	1958	Felsen, H.G.	VG+		$8.00
BANTAM	1893	Rio Bravo	1959	Brackett, L.	G	MTI	$5.00
BANTAM	1893	Rio Bravo (3rd)	1959	Brackett, L.	VGF	MTI	$14.00
BANTAM	A 1917	The Hunger And Other Stories	1959	Beaumont, C.	AF		$24.00 A
BANTAM	A 1917	The Hunger And Other Stories	1959	Beaumont, C.	VG		$7.00
BANTAM	1927	The Convertible Hearse	1959	Gault, B.	AF		$16.00 A
BANTAM	1927	The Convertible Hearse	1959	Gault, B.	AF-		$13.00 A
BANTAM	1927	The Convertible Hearse	1959	Gault, B.	G+		$5.00
BANTAM	A 1957	Blue Denim	1959	Herlihy, J.L.	VG+	MTI	$3.00
BANTAM	A 1957	Blue Denim (3rd)	1959	Herlihy, J.L.	AF	MTI	$7.00
BANTAM	1965	The Beat Generation	1959	Zugsmith, A.	VGF	MTI	$18.00 A
BANTAM	1965	The Beat Generation	1959	Zugsmith, A.	VG	MTI	$10.00
BANTAM	1965	The Beat Generation (3rd)	1959	Zugsmith, A.	VGF	MTI	$14.00
BANTAM	A 1966	Middle Of The Night	1959	Chayefsky, P.	AF	MTI	$7.00
BANTAM	1977	Taggart	1959	L'Amour, L.	VG		$69.00 A
BANTAM	A 1982	The Mouse That Roared	1959	Wibberley, L.	VGF	MTI	$6.00
BANTAM	A 1983	Ask Any Girl (4th)	1959	Wolfe, W.	VGF	MTI	$4.00
BANTAM	F 1987	The Detroiters	1959	Livingston, H.	VGF+		$6.00

Bantam 1278 VGF $8   Bantam 1285 AF- $12   Bantam 1294 VGF $17   Bantam 1546 VGF $17

PUBLISHER	PUB. #	TITLE	DATE	AUTHOR	COND.	TYPE	PRICE
BANTAM	1990	One For The Road	1959	Brown, F.	VG+		$15.00
BANTAM	1990	One For The Road	1959	Brown, F.	VG		$10.00
BANTAM	A 2028	Rafferty	1960	White, L.	VGF		$8.00
BANTAM	A 2028	Rafferty	1960	White, L.	VG		$7.00
BANTAM	A 2029	Signal Thirty-Two (2nd)	1960	Kantor, M.	F		$7.00
BANTAM	2030	The Late Lamented	1960	Brown, F.	AF		$60.00 A
BANTAM	A 2046	Stories From Twilight Zone	1960	Serling, R.	VG+	TVTI	$3.00
BANTAM	A 2048	The Stars Are Too High	1960	Bahnson, A.H.	VGF		$4.00
BANTAM	A 2060	Sink The Bismark	1959	Forester, C.S.	AF	MTI	$5.00
BANTAM	A 2075	Once There Was A War	1960	Steinbeck, J.	AF		$6.00
BANTAM	A 2076	Crash Club	1960	Felsen, H.G.	VG+		$10.00
BANTAM	A 2087	Night Ride And Other Journeys	1960	Beaumont, C.	AF		$10.00 A
BANTAM	A 2087	Night Ride And Other Journeys	1960	Beaumont, C.	VGF		$8.00
BANTAM	A 2087	Night Ride And Other Journeys	1960	Beaumont, C.	G+		$5.00
BANTAM	A 2088	Our Troubled Youth	1960	Mayer, F.	VG-		$5.00
BANTAM	A 2112	Let's Make Love	1960	Andrews, M.	G	MTI	$6.00
BANTAM	F 2122	The Divine Wind	1960	Inoguchi, N.	AF		$6.00
BANTAM	A 2153	Flint	1960	L'Amour, L.	VG		$119.00 A
BANTAM	A 2171	Marines!	1960	Leckie, R.	AF		$6.00
BANTAM	A 2190	No House Limit	1961	Fisher, S.	VG		$6.00
BANTAM	J 2204	Splendor In The Grass	1961	Inge, W.	VGF	MTI	$7.00
BANTAM	A 2216	Calibre .50	1961	Sheckley, R.	AF		$9.00
BANTAM	A 2240	Dead Run	1961	Sheckley, R.	VG		$7.00
BANTAM	A 2247	The Merriweather File	1961	White, L.	VGF		$10.00
BANTAM	A 2247	The Merriweather File	1961	White, L.	VGF+		$8.00
BANTAM	H 2279	In Dubious Battle	1961	Steinbeck, J.	F		$7.00
BANTAM	F 2285	The Amboy Dukes	1961	Shulman, I.	VG		$4.00
BANTAM	A 2296	Nightmares And Geezenstacks	1961	Brown, F.	AF		$18.00 A
BANTAM	J 2296	Nightmares And Geezenstacks	1961	Brown, F.	G+		$5.00
BANTAM	A 2297	Twenty Plus Two	1961	Gruber, F.	VGF	MTI	$7.00
BANTAM	A 2315	Road Rocket	1961	Felsen, H.G.	VGF		$12.00
BANTAM	F 2317	No High Ground	1961	Knebel, F.	AF		$6.00
BANTAM	A 2325	Shalako	1962	L'Amour, L.	VG-		$7.00
BANTAM	J 2362	I Thank A Fool	1962	Lindop, A.E.	VG+	MTI	$5.00
BANTAM	A 2412	New Stories From The Twilight Zone	1962	Serling, R.	VGF	TVTI	$7.00
BANTAM	J 2467	Third From The Sun	1962	Matheson, R.	AF		$12.00
BANTAM	J 2467	Third From The Sun	1962	Matheson, R.	AF		$10.00 A
BANTAM	J 2467	Third From The Sun	1962	Matheson, R.	VG		$6.00
BANTAM	J 2490	A Loss Of Roses	1968	Inge, W.	VGF	MTI	$6.00
BANTAM	A 2494	Lando	1962	L'Amour, L.	VG+		$14.00
BANTAM	A 2494	Lando	1962	L'Amour, L.	VG		$8.00
BANTAM	F 2495	Two For Seesaw /The Seesaw Log	1962	Gibson, W.	VGF	DBL	$5.00
BANTAM	A 2512	Fallon	1963	L'Amour, L.	VG-		$7.00
BANTAM	H 2528	Mignon	1963	Cain, J.M.	VG		$6.00
BANTAM	J 2552	Message From Sirius	1963	Jenkins, C.	AF		$6.00
BANTAM	J 2553	Opium Flower	1963	Cushman, D.	VGF		$6.00
BANTAM	J 2578	The Lights In The Sky Are Stars	1963	Brown, F.	VG-		$5.00
BANTAM	J 2578	The Lights In The Sky Are Stars	1963	Brown, F.	VG		$4.00

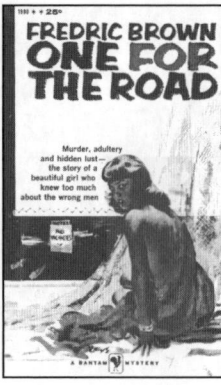

Bantam 1565 VG+ $38   Bantam 1892 VG+ $8   Bantam 1965 VGF $18   Bantam 1990 VG+ $15

PUBLISHER	PUB. #	TITLE	DATE	AUTHOR	COND.	TYPE	PRICE
BANTAM	J 2614	Mi Amigo	1963	Burnett, W.R.	VGF		$6.00
BANTAM	F 2629	Seven Men At Daybreak	1963	Burgess, A.	AF		$4.00
BANTAM	H 2630	Something Wicked This Way Comes	1963	Bradbury, R.	AF-		$8.00 A
BANTAM	S 2642	Big Sur	1963	Kerouac, J.	AF		$22.00
BANTAM	S 2642	Big Sur	1963	Kerouac, J.	VG+		$14.00
BANTAM	J 2650	Honeymoon In Hell	1963	Brown, F.	VGF+		$8.00 A
BANTAM	HZ 2850	The True Story Of The Beatles	1964	Shepard, B.	VG+		$6.00
BANTAM	J 2902	The High Graders	1965	L'Amour, L.	VG-		$6.00
BANTAM	S 2906	The Mark Of The Swastika	1965	Hagen, L.	VGF		$4.00
BANTAM	F 2929	Psychedelic-40	1965	Charbonneau, L.	AF		$4.00
BANTAM	J 2967	The Sackett Brand	1965	L'Amour, L.	VG		$74.00 A
BANTAM	S 3018	Save Them For Pallbearers	1965	Garrett, J.	VGF+		$6.00
BANTAM	H 3029	Only Lovers Left Alive	1965	Wallis, D.	VG		$6.00
BANTAM	E 3055	Mustang Man	1966	L'Amour, L.	VGF		$62.00 A
BANTAM	F 3067	Tomboy (9th)	1967	Ellson, H.	VGF		$6.00
BANTAM	F 3067	Tomboy (9th)	1967	Ellson, H.	VG		$3.00
BANTAM	F 3084	That Darn Cat (3rd)	1965	Gordons, The	VGF	MTI	$6.00
BANTAM	F 3093	King Kong	1965	Wallace, E.	VGF	MTI	$10.00
BANTAM	J 3098	The Broken Gun	1966	L'Amour, L.	AF		$20.00
BANTAM	J 3098	The Broken Gun	1966	L'Amour, L.	VG+		$15.00 A
BANTAM	E 3146	Fear Cay	1966	Robeson, K.	VG+		$4.00
BANTAM	N 3153	Desolation Angels	1966	Kerouac, J.	VG+		$12.00
BANTAM	F 3252	Kilrone	1966	L'Amour, L.	VG+		$14.00
BANTAM	S 3264	Golden Boy	1966	Odets, C.	F	MTI	$5.00
BANTAM	S 3335	Tobruk	1967	Rabe, P.	VG+	MTI	$10.00
BANTAM	H 3353	The Happening	1967	Curry, E.	VG+	MTI	$6.00
BANTAM	H 3353	The Happening	1967	Curry, E.	VG	MTI	$6.00
BANTAM	H 3424	Hitler And Nazism	1967	Lynder, L.L.	VGF		$4.00
BANTAM	N 3480	The Life Of Ian Fleming	1967	Pearson, J.	AF		$10.00
BANTAM	F 3580	Down The Long Hills	1968	L'Amour, L.	AF		$20.00
BANTAM	F 3640	Plague From Space	1968	Harrison, H.	VGF		$5.00
BANTAM	F 3716	Fortress Of Solitude	1968	Robeson, K.	VG+		$4.00
BANTAM	F 3722	Two Tales & Eight Tomorrows	1968	Harrison, H.	AF		$5.00
BANTAM	F 3780	The Great Gold Steal	1968	White, T.	VG		$5.00
BANTAM	F 3782	The Green Eagle	1968	Robeson, K.	VGF		$6.00
BANTAM	F 3839	The Deadly Dwarf	1968	Robeson, K.	VGF		$6.00
BANTAM	F 3885	The Annihilist	1968	Robeson, K.	AF		$6.00
BANTAM	F 3885	The Annihilist	1968	Robeson, K.	VG+		$5.00
BANTAM	F 3936	The Shores Of Space	1969	Matheson, R.	F		$7.00
BANTAM	RG 4053	Cowboy Kate & Other Stories	1969	Haskins, B.	VGF		$8.00
BANTAM	H 4056	Eyes Of The Shadow (Shadow #2)	1969	Grant, M.*	VGF		$8.00
BANTAM	H 4402	The Lonely Men	1969	L'Amour, L.	VGF		$15.00
BANTAM	H 4402	The Lonely Men	1969	L'Amour, L.	VG+		$6.00 A
BANTAM	H 4463	The Living Shadow (Shadow #1)	1969	Grant, M.*	VGF		$7.00
BANTAM	H 4463	The Living Shadow (Shadow #1)	1969	Grant, M.*	VG		$5.00
BANTAM	H 4707	Hex	1969	Robeson, K.	VGF		$6.00
BANTAM	H 4730	The Gold Ogre	1969	Robeson, K.	AF		$5.00
BANTAM	H 4761	The Man Who Shook The Earth	1969	Robeson, K.	VGF		$6.00

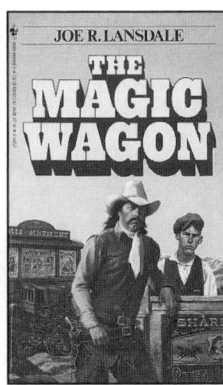

Bantam 2467 AF $12	Bantam 2650 VGF+ $8	Bantam 14156 AF $8	Bantam 27365 VGF $21

PUBLISHER	PUB. #	TITLE	DATE	AUTHOR	COND.	TYPE	PRICE
BANTAM	H 4770	The Death Tower (The Shadow #4)	1969	Grant, M.*	VGF		$6.00
BANTAM	H 4884	Hidden Death-The Shadow #6	1970	Grant, M.*	AF		$7.00
BANTAM	PS 5200	US #2	1969	Anthology	VG+		$6.00
BANTAM	Q 5205	US #3	1970	Anthology	VGF		$20.00 A
BANTAM	H 5309	Land Of Long Ju Ju	1970	Robeson, K.	VGF		$6.00
BANTAM	H 5329	The Ghost Makers (Shadow #5)	1970	Grant, M.*	VG		$7.00
BANTAM	H 5406	The Sea Angel	1970	Robeson, K.	AF		$5.00
BANTAM	H 5413	Gangdom's Doom (Shadow #7)	1970	Grant, M.*	VG+		$7.00
BANTAM	H 5450	Devil On The Moon	1970	Robeson, K.	VGF		$6.00
BANTAM	H 5482	Haunted Ocean	1970	Robeson, K.	VGF		$6.00
BANTAM	H 5536	The Vanisher	1970	Robeson, K.	VGF		$6.00
BANTAM	H 5652	The Golden Peril	1970	Robeson, K.	AF		$6.00
BANTAM	S 5674	Beneath The Planet Of Apes	1970	Avallone, M.	VGF	MTI	$6.00
BANTAM	N 5760	The Drug Scene	1970	Louria, D.B.	VG		$4.00
BANTAM	S 5871	Black Mark	1971	Kane, G.	VG		$6.00
BANTAM	Q 6352	The Man Of Bronze	1975	Robeson, K.	VGF	MTI	$7.00
BANTAM	Q 6419	The Stone Man	1976	Robeson, K.	VGF		$5.00
BANTAM	Q 6424	The Boss Of Terror	1976	Robeson, K.	VGF		$6.00
BANTAM	S 6977	The Flesh In The Furnace	1972	Koontz, D.R.	VGF+		$27.00 A
BANTAM	S 6992	Quest Of The Spider	1972	Robeson, K.	F		$6.00
BANTAM	Q 7003	Veronica (3rd)	1972	Lake, V.	VGF		$8.00
BANTAM	S 7035	The Mystery On The Snow	1972	Robeson, K.	F		$6.00
BANTAM	N 7190	Demon Seed	1973	Koontz, D.R.	VGF		$14.00
BANTAM	SP 7203	Night Gallery 2	1972	Serling, R.	VGF	TVTI	$6.00
BANTAM	S 7229	The Metal Master	1973	Robeson, K.	AF		$5.00
BANTAM	S 7282	Ride The Dark Trail	1972	L'Amour, L.	VGF		$12.00
BANTAM	T 7332	Tarantula	1972	Dylan, B.	VG+		$5.00
BANTAM	S 7439	Tales From The Crypt	1972	Oleck, J.	VGF	MTI	$7.00
BANTAM	S 7571	The South Pole Terror	1974	Robeson, K.	AF		$6.00
BANTAM	N 7592	The Getaway	1973	Thompson, J.	VG-	MTI	$7.00
BANTAM	Q 7613	Binary	1973	Lange, J.*	VGF		$7.00
BANTAM	N 7643	Sleuth	1972	Shaffer, A.	VGF	MTI	$6.00
BANTAM	S 7719	The Land Of Fear	1973	Robeson, K.	AF		$6.00
BANTAM	Q 7739	Drug Of Choice	1974	Lange, J.*	AF		$12.00
BANTAM	Q 7739	Drug Of Choice	1974	Lange, J.*	VG		$5.00
BANTAM	Q 7745	Zero Cool	1973	Lange, J.*	VG-		$5.00
BANTAM	S 7790	The Magic Island	1977	Robeson, K.	F		$6.00
BANTAM	Q 7884	Scratch One	1974	Lange, J.*	VG		$5.00
BANTAM	Q 8076	The Last Tomb	1974	Lange, J.*	VG+		$5.00
BANTAM	S 8305	The Black Spot	1974	Robeson, K.	VGF		$5.00
BANTAM	T 8324	Grave Descend	1973	Lange, J.*	VGF		$5.00
BANTAM	S 8367	The Crimson Serpent	1974	Robeson, K.	AF		$6.00
BANTAM	Q 8441	WestWorld	1974	Crichton, M.	AF	MTI	$7.00
BANTAM	Q 8717	Star Trek 11	1975	Blish, J.	VG+	TVTI	$3.00
BANTAM	Q 8765	The Female Man	1975	Russ, J.	VGF		$10.00
BANTAM	S 8772	The Devil Genghis	1974	Robeson, K.	VGF		$6.00
BANTAM	Q 8834	Doc Savage His Apocalyptic Life	1975	Farmer, P.J.	VGF		$12.00
BANTAM	Q 8834	Doc Savage His Apocalyptic Life	1975	Farmer, P.J.	VG+		$8.00

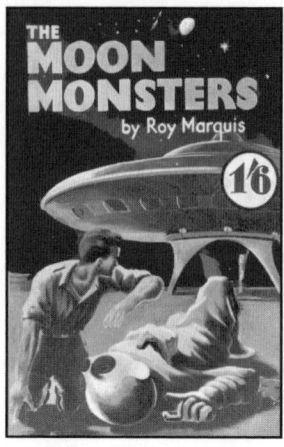

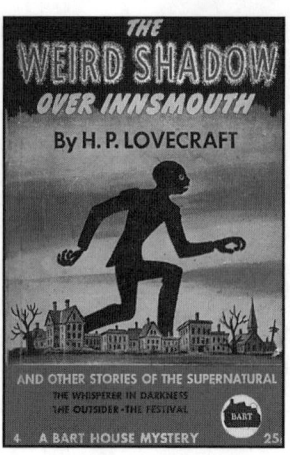

Barrington Gray No# VG $17   Bart House 4 VG $25   Bart House 6 VGF $27

PUBLISHER	PUB. #	TITLE	DATE	AUTHOR	COND.	TYPE	PRICE
BANTAM	10075	The Spotted Men	1977	Robeson, K.	AF		$5.00
BANTAM	10237	Eaters Of The Dead	1977	Crichton, M.	VG		$6.00
BANTAM	10402	UBIK	1977	Dick, P.K.	VGF		$6.00
BANTAM	10586	The 3 Stigmata Of P. Eldrich	1977	Dick, P.K.	AF-		$7.00
BANTAM	10930	Demon Seed	1977	Koontz, D.R.	VG+	MTI	$36.00 A
BANTAM	11116	The Purple Dragon	1978	Robeson, K.	AF		$6.00
BANTAM	11190	The Flying Goblin	1977	Robeson, K.	AF		$5.00
BANTAM	11191	Tunnel Terror	1979	Robeson, K.	VGF		$6.00
BANTAM	11346	Where No Man Has Gone Before	1977	Peeples, S.A.	VG+	TVTI	$7.00
BANTAM	11349	Star Trek Fotonovel #5	1978	Coon, G.L.	VG+	TVTI	$7.00
BANTAM	11382	Star Trek #12	1977	Blish, J.	VGF	TVTI	$6.00
BANTAM	11382	Star Trek #12	1977	Blish, J.	VGF	TVTI	$5.00
BANTAM	11418	Logan's World	1977	Nolan, W.F.	VGF		$6.00
BANTAM	11898	The Vision	1978	Koontz, D.R.	VGF		$8.00
BANTAM	11950	Rogue In Space	1978	Brown, F.	VG		$5.00
BANTAM	12021	Star Trek Fotonovel #9	1978	Mandala	AF	TVTI	$9.00
BANTAM	12456	Nightmares And Geezenstacks	1979	Brown, F.	VG		$5.00
BANTAM	12706	Conan The Liberator	1979	De Camp, L.S.	VGF+		$5.00
BANTAM	12780	The Hate Genius	1979	Robeson, K.	AF		$5.00
BANTAM	13158	Goldilocks	1979	McBain, E.*	VGF		$6.00
BANTAM	13421	Doc Savage #97 & 98	1980	Robeson, K.	VG+	DBL	$8.00
BANTAM	13421	Doc Savage #97 & 98	1980	Robeson, K.	VG	DBL	$4.00
BANTAM	14156	Valis	1981	Dick, P.K.	AF		$8.00
BANTAM	14348	Doc Savage # 99 & 100	1980	Robeson, K.	VGF	DBL	$10.00
BANTAM	14615	Doc Savage #101 & 102	1981	Robeson, K.	AF	DBL	$10.00
BANTAM	14616	Doc Savage #103 & 104	1981	Robeson, K.	VGF	DBL	$8.00
BANTAM	14916	Doc Savage #105 & 106	1981	Robeson, K.	VGF	DBL	$10.00
BANTAM	14916	Doc Savage #105 & 106	1981	Robeson, K.	VGF	DBL	$7.00
BANTAM	20573	Doc Savage #109 & 110	1982	Robeson, K.	VG	DBL	$5.00
BANTAM	20578	Forty Lashes Less One (2nd)	1981	Leonard, E.	AF		$6.00
BANTAM	20606	Buckskin Run	1981	L'Amour, L.	VG+		$8.00
BANTAM	20752	Honeymoon In Hell	1982	Brown, F.	VGF		$4.00
BANTAM	22610	Doc Savage #111 & 112	1982	Robeson, K.	AF	DBL	$10.00
BANTAM	22755	Doc Savage #113 & 114	1982	Robeson, K.	VGF+	DBL	$10.00
BANTAM	23364	Doc Savage #115 & 116	1983	Robeson, K.	AF	DBL	$10.00
BANTAM	23364	Doc Savage #115 & 116	1983	Robeson, K.	VG	DBL	$6.00
BANTAM	23648	Doc Savage #26 & 27	1983	Robeson, K.	VG+	DBL	$6.00
BANTAM	23851	Doc Savage #117 & 118	1984	Robeson, K.	AF	DBL	$10.00
BANTAM	24528	Doc Savage #121 & 122	1984	Robeson, K.	VG+	DBL	$8.00
BANTAM	25947	Doc Savage Omnibus #1	1986	Robeson, K.	AF		$12.00
BANTAM	26207	Doc Savage Omnibus #2	1987	Robeson, K.	AF		$12.00
BANTAM	26738	Doc Savage Omnibus #3	1987	Robeson, K.	F		$12.00
BANTAM	26802	Doc Savage Omnibus #4	1987	Robeson, K.	F		$14.00
BANTAM	26802	Doc Savage Omnibus #4	1987	Robeson, K.	VGF		$10.00
BANTAM	26996	Doc Savage Omnibus #5	1988	Robeson, K.	F		$13.00

Bart House 9 VGF $19   Bart House 15 VG+ $8   Beacon B105 AF $20

PUBLISHER	PUB. #	TITLE	DATE	AUTHOR	COND.	TYPE	PRICE
BANTAM	27215	Doc Savage Omnibus #6	1988	Robeson, K.	VGF-		$10.00
BANTAM	27365	The Magic Wagon	1988	Lansdale, J.R.	VGF		$21.00 A
BANTAM	27861	Doc Savage Omnibus #8	1989	Robeson, K.	F		$13.00
BANTAM	28000	Doc Savage Omnibus #9	1989	Robeson, K.	F		$12.00
BANTAM	28000	Doc Savage Omnibus #9	1989	Robeson, K.	VGF+		$10.00
BANTAM	28325	Doc Savage Omnibus #10	1989	Robeson, K.	AF		$12.00
BANTAM	28389	Doc Savage Omnibus #11	1990	Robeson, K.	AF		$12.00
BANTAM	28389	Doc Savage Omnibus #11	1990	Robeson, K.	VGF+		$10.00
BANTAM	28510	Doc Savage Omnibus #12	1990	Robeson, K.	VGF		$13.00
BANTAM	28510	Doc Savage Omnibus #12	1990	Robeson, K.	VGF		$10.00
BANTAM	28563	Savage Season	1990	Lansdale, J.R.	VGF		$10.00
BANTAM	28626	Doc Savage Omnibus #13	1990	Robeson, K.	AF		$12.00
BANTAM	28626	Doc Savage Omnibus #13	1990	Robeson, K.	VGF		$10.00
BANTAM	28626	Doc Savage Omnibus #13	1990	Robeson, K.	VG		$7.00
BANTAM	29553	The Jade Ogre	1992	Robeson, K.	AF		$8.00
BANTAM	29554	The Whistling Wraith	1993	Robeson, K.	AF		$12.00
BANTAM (LOS ANGELES)	5	How To Make Friends Easily	1940	Currie, S.	G+		$14.00 A
BANTAM (LOS ANGELES)	21	The Shadow & The Voice Of Murder	1940	Grant, M.*	VG		$315.00 A
BANTAM (LOS ANGELES)	22	The Green Death (pictorial cvr.)	1940	Hutton, B.	G		$50.00 A
BARCLAY HOUSE	7377	Gang Wars Of The 20's	1974	Allen, T.	VG+		$7.00
BARRINGTON GRAY	No#	The Moon Monsters	n/d	Marquis, R.	VG	Digest	$17.00 A
BART HOUSE	1	The Hand In The Cobbler's Safe	1944	Bailey, S.	VG		$8.00
BART HOUSE	2	The Delinquent Ghost	1944	Hatch, E.	VG-		$7.00
BART HOUSE	3	The Spy Trap	1944	Gilman, W.	VG		$6.00
BART HOUSE	4	Weird Shadow Over Innsmouth	1944	Lovecraft, H.P.	VG		$25.00
BART HOUSE	4	Weird Shadow Over Innsmouth	1944	Lovecraft, H.P.	G		$9.00 A
BART HOUSE	5	John Smith Hears Death Walk	1944	Blassingame, W.	VGF		$35.00 A
BART HOUSE	6	Rebirth	1944	McClary, T.C.	VGF		$27.00 A
BART HOUSE	6	Rebirth	1944	McClary, T.C.	VG-		$11.00
BART HOUSE	7	The Shivering Bough	1944	Burke, N.	G		$5.00
BART HOUSE	9	The Waltz Of Death	1944	Maxon, P.B.	VGF		$19.00 A
BART HOUSE	10	The Devil Drives	1944	Markham, V.	VG		$7.00
BART HOUSE	11	Murder Meets Mephisto	1945	Mario, Q.	VG+		$15.00 A
BART HOUSE	11	Murder Meets Mephisto	1945	Mario, Q.	G		$5.00
BART HOUSE	13	4 Feet In The Grave	1945	Long, A.R.	G		$5.00
BART HOUSE	15	Three Short Biers	1945	Starr, J.	VG+		$8.00
BART HOUSE	15	Three Short Biers	1945	Starr, J.	G		$5.00
BART HOUSE	18	Terry	1945	Comstock, H.T.	VG-		$6.00
BART HOUSE	19	Said With Flowers	1945	Nash, A.	VG+		$6.00
BART HOUSE	20	Motionless Shadows	1945	Norris, K.	G		$4.00
BART HOUSE	23	Roughly Speaking	1946	Pierson, L.R.	VG+	MTI	$12.00
BART HOUSE	33	A Smattering Of Ignorance	1946	Levant, O.	VGF		$8.00
BART HOUSE	33	A Smattering Of Ignorance	1946	Levant, O.	VG+		$6.00
BART HOUSE	36	Murder Among Friends	1946	Lewis, L.	VGF		$5.00 A
BART HOUSE	39	Can You Top This?	1947	Ford, S.	VG		$6.00

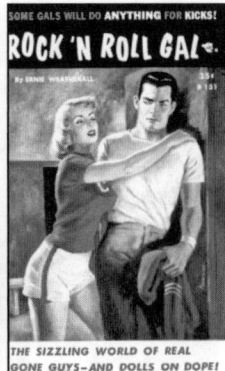

Beacon B109 VG $75   Beacon B112 VG+ $27   Beacon B130 VG $67   Beacon B131 VG+ $54

PUBLISHER	PUB. #	TITLE	DATE	AUTHOR	COND.	TYPE	PRICE
BART HOUSE	101	"Mr. Ace"	1946	Christie, H.	VGF	MTI	$10.00 A
BEACON	B 102	Pawn	1954	Nichols, F.	F		$16.00
BEACON	B 102	Pawn	1954	Nichols, F.	VGF		$12.00
BEACON	B 102	Pawn	1954	Nichols, F.	VG		$7.00
BEACON	B 103	Rooming House	1954	Malloy, F.	VG		$5.00
BEACON	B 104	Shabby Street	1954	Hitt, O.	VG+		$23.00 A
BEACON	B 104	Shabby Street	1954	Hitt, O.	VG+		$20.00
BEACON	B 105	King Of The Khyber Rifles	1954	Mundy, T.	AF		$20.00 A
BEACON	B 105	King Of The Khyber Rifles	1954	Mundy, T.	VG+		$10.00 A
BEACON	B 107	Stable Boy	1954	Rebel, A.	F		$40.00 A
BEACON	B 107	Stable Boy	1954	Rebel, A.	VG+		$20.00 A
BEACON	B 108	Gutter Gang	1954	De Bekker, J.	VG		$11.00
BEACON	B 108	Gutter Gang	1954	De Bekker, J.	VG		$7.00 A
BEACON	B 109	Pick-Up	1955	Willeford, C.	VG		$75.00 A
BEACON	B 110	Keyhole Peeper	1955	De Bekker, J.	VGF+		$17.00 A
BEACON	B 111	Liz	1955	Kane, F.	VG+		$30.00 A
BEACON	B 111	Liz	1955	Kane, F.	VGF		$10.00
BEACON	B 112	Lady Cop	1955	Pritchard, J.T.	VG+		$27.00 A
BEACON	B 112	Lady Cop	1955	Pritchard, J.T.	VGF		$15.00 A
BEACON	B 113	Highlights From Yank	n/d	Anthology	G		$4.00
BEACON	B 114	Scandalous Lady	n/d	Nichols, F.	F		$15.00
BEACON	B 116	Hired Girl	n/d	Taylor, V.	VGF		$15.00
BEACON	B 120	Confessions Of A Psychiatrist	n/d	Nixon, H.L.	AF		$22.00 A
BEACON	B 121	Warped Women (3rd)	n/d	Pritchard, J.	G-		$4.00
BEACON	B 122	Dolly	n/d	Nichols, F.	AF		$10.00
BEACON	B 122	Dolly	n/d	Nichols, F.	VGF		$8.00
BEACON	B 124	Honey	n/d	Woodford, J.	AF		$12.00
BEACON	B 125	Swamp Hoyden	n/d	Woodford, J.	VG+		$9.00
BEACON	B 126	Unfaithful Wives	1956	Hitt, O.	VGF		$12.00
BEACON	B 126	Unfaithful Wives	1956	Hitt, O.	VG+		$9.00
BEACON	B 127	Savage Eve	1956	Woodford, J.	AF-		$10.00 A
BEACON	B 128	Witch On Wheels	1956	Boltin, W.	VGF-		$10.00
BEACON	B 129	Bayou Girl	1956	Thompson, J.	VG+		$12.00 A
BEACON	B 129	Bayou Girl	1956	Thompson, J.	VG		$7.00
BEACON	B 130	High Priest Of California	1956	Willeford, C.	VG		$67.00 A
BEACON	B 131	Rock 'N Roll Gal	1957	Weatherall, E.	VG+		$54.00 A
BEACON	B 131	Rock 'N Roll Gal	1957	Weatherall, E.	VGF+		$41.00 A
BEACON	B 131	Rock 'N Roll Gal	1957	Weatherall, E.	G		$6.00
BEACON	B 134	Twisted	1957	Jones, G.	VG		$13.00
BEACON	B 135	Queer Affair	1957	Emery, C.	F		$74.00 A
BEACON	B 136	Shack Baby	1957	Williams, L.	AF		$13.00 A
BEACON	B 140	Sugar Doll	1957	Thompson, J.B.	VG+		$24.00 A
BEACON	B 141	Love Peddler	1957	Weiss, J.	AF		$15.00
BEACON	B 142	The Promoter	1957	Hitt, O.	VG+		$10.00
BEACON	B 142	The Promoter	1957	Hitt, O.	VG		$7.00
BEACON	B 143	Shock Treatment	1957	Williams, W.	AF		$19.00 A
BEACON	B 144	Girls Of The French Quarter	1957	Thompson, J.B.	VG		$7.00
BEACON	B 145	Passion Blues	1957	Weiss, J.	VG		$5.00

Beacon B134 VG $13   Beacon B135 F $74   Beacon B160 VG- $120   Beacon B165 VGF $47

PUBLISHER	PUB. #	TITLE	DATE	AUTHOR	COND.	TYPE	PRICE
BEACON	B 146	Ladies' Man	1957	Hitt, O.	G		$2.50
BEACON	B 148	Lovely Fraud	1957	Weiss, J.	VGF-		$14.00
BEACON	B 149	Call Her Wanton	1957	Williams, L.	VG		$9.00
BEACON	B 149	Call Her Wanton	1957	Williams, L.	VG		$7.00
BEACON	B 151	Dolls And Dues	1957	Hitt, O.	VG+		$13.00
BEACON	B 152	Adam And Two Eves	1957	Anonymous	AF-		$28.00 A
BEACON	B 153	Trailer Tramp	1957	Hitt, O.	VGF		$14.00
BEACON	B 155	Gang Girl	1957	Weiss, J.	VGF+		$27.00 A
BEACON	B 155	Gang Girl	1957	Weiss, J.	VG-		$10.00
BEACON	B 156	Twilight Women	1957	Scott, L.	VGF-		$16.00
BEACON	B 156	Twilight Women	1957	Scott, L.	VG+		$12.00
BEACON	B 158	Teaser	1958	Hitt, O.	AF		$14.00 A
BEACON	B 158	Teaser	1958	Hitt, O.	VG+		$13.00
BEACON	B 159	Ellie's Shack	1958	Hitt, O.	VG		$8.00
BEACON	B 160	Honey Gal	1958	Willeford, C.	VG-		$120.00 A
BEACON	B 160	Honey Gal	1958	Willeford, C.	VG-		$70.00
BEACON	B 161	Back Of Town	1958	Pruett, H.	VGF		$14.00
BEACON	B 163	Hell Bent	1958	Ames, H.B.	VG+		$8.00
BEACON	B 164	Suburban Wife	1958	Hitt, O.	VG+		$11.00 A
BEACON	B 165	Gutter Gang	1958	De Bekker, J.	VGF		$47.00 A
BEACON	B 165	Gutter Gang	1958	De Bekker, J.	F		$40.00 A
BEACON	B 165	Gutter Gang	1958	De Bekker, J.	G		$8.00
BEACON	B 166	Private Pleasures Of Mary Linton	1958	Arthur, W.	F		$16.00 A
BEACON	B 166	Private Pleasures Of Mary Linton	1958	Arthur, W.	VG+		$5.00 A
BEACON	B 167	Play For Pay	1958	Williams, W.	AF-		$8.00
BEACON	B 169	Wild Oats	1958	Hitt, O.	AF		$18.00 A
BEACON	B 169	Wild Oats	1958	Hitt, O.	VGF		$15.00 A
BEACON	B 169	Wild Oats	1958	Hitt, O.	VG+		$15.00
BEACON	B 172	The Woman He Wanted	1958	Winston, D.	AF		$14.00
BEACON	B 175	Lust Is A Woman	1958	Willeford, C.	VG-		$110.00 A
BEACON	B 175	Lust Is A Woman	1958	Willeford, C.	G		$47.00
BEACON	B 176	Call South 3300: Ask For Molly	1958	Hitt, O.	AF-		$15.00 A
BEACON	B 176	Call South 3300: Ask For Molly	1958	Hitt, O.	VGF		$15.00 A
BEACON	B 177	Hill Hellion!	1958	Williams, L.	F		$22.00 A
BEACON	B 178	Fair Game	1958	Wood, C.	VG		$7.00
BEACON	B 179	The Girl In The Black Chemise	1958	Scott, L.	VGF		$14.00
BEACON	B 181	Back Alley	1958	Smith, F.	VGF		$30.00 A
BEACON	B 181	Back Alley	1958	Smith, F.	VG+		$8.00
BEACON	B 182	Fast Girl	1958	West, T.	AF		$14.00
BEACON	B 183	The Naked And The Fair	1958	Moore, H.	F		$16.00
BEACON	B 184	Confessions Of A Psychiatrist	1958	Nixon, H.L.	VGF		$18.00
BEACON	B 185	Rooming House	1958	Malloy, F.	VGF+		$12.00
BEACON	B 185	Rooming House	1958	Malloy, F.	VG		$5.00
BEACON	B 188	I Made My Bed	1958	Hye, C.	VGF+		$22.00 A
BEACON	B 188	I Made My Bed	1958	Hye, C.	VG+		$16.00 A
BEACON	B 190	Three Women	1958	Hastings, M.	AF		$24.00 A
BEACON	B 190	Three Women	1958	Hastings, M.	VG-		$6.00
BEACON	B 191	Girls' Dormitory	1958	Hitt, O.	VGF		$50.00 A

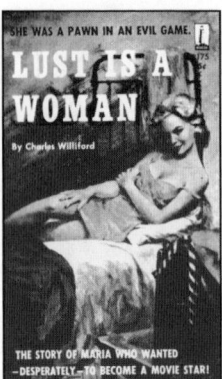
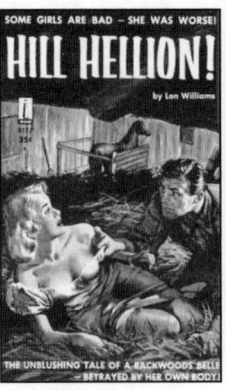

Beacon B175 VG- $110   Beacon B177 F $22   Beacon B217 AF $27   Beacon B228 VG+ $25

PUBLISHER	PUB. #	TITLE	DATE	AUTHOR	COND.	TYPE	PRICE
BEACON	B 192	Forbidden	1958	Priest, J.C.	AF		$22.00 A
BEACON	B 192	Forbidden	1958	Priest, J.C.	AF		$21.00 A
BEACON	B 193	The Other Stranger	1958	Winston, D.	VGF		$10.00 A
BEACON	B 195	She Got What She Wanted	1958	Hitt, O.	AF		$9.00 A
BEACON	B 195	She Got What She Wanted	1958	Hitt, O.	VGF		$9.00 A
BEACON	B 195	She Got What She Wanted	1958	Hitt, O.	VG-		$7.00
BEACON	B 196	The Mistress	1958	Ross, C.	AF		$10.00
BEACON	B 197	Woman Hunt	1958	Hitt, O.	AF		$16.00 A
BEACON	B 197	Woman Hunt	1958	Hitt, O.	VG+		$7.00
BEACON	B 199	Combat	1958	Anthology	VGF		$10.00
BEACON	B 201	Keyhole Peeper	1958	De Bekker, J.	F		$20.00 A
BEACON	B 201	Keyhole Peeper	1958	De Bekker, J.	AF		$16.00 A
BEACON	B 202	School For Girls	1958	Kramer, G.	AF		$17.00 A
BEACON	B 203	Hot Cargo	1958	Hitt, O.	AF		$15.00 A
BEACON	B 206	The Cheat	1958	Hitt, O.	VG+		$8.00
BEACON	B 207	Circle Of Sin	1958	Hastings, M.	AF		$30.00 A
BEACON	B 207	Circle Of Sin	1958	Hastings, M.	VG+		$8.00
BEACON	B 210	The Dispossessed	1959	Wagner, G.	F		$15.00
BEACON	B 210	The Dispossessed	1959	Wagner, G.	VGF		$12.00
BEACON	B 211	Sheba	1959	Hitt, O.	VGF		$18.00 A
BEACON	B 213	Hitch-Hike Hussy	1959	Thompson, J.B.	VGF		$28.00 A
BEACON	B 214	Adulteress	1959	Williams, L.	VGF		$9.00
BEACON	B 215	Passionate Land	1959	Wagner, G.	F		$8.00
BEACON	B 217	Slave Ship	1959	Drake, H.B.	AF		$27.00 A
BEACON	B 217	Slave Ship	1959	Drake, H.B.	VG+		$10.00
BEACON	B 218	Strumpet's Seed	1959	Malloy, F.	VGF-		$30.00 A
BEACON	B 220	Scandalous Lady	1959	Nichols, F.	VGF		$12.00 A
BEACON	B 220	Scandalous Lady	1959	Nichols, F.	AF-		$11.00 A
BEACON	B 221	The Hussy	1959	Williams, I.	AF		$15.00
BEACON	B 221	The Hussy	1959	Williams, I.	VG+		$7.00
BEACON	B 223	Chris (2nd)	1959	Salem, R.	VG+		$12.00
BEACON	B 223	Chris (2nd)	1959	Salem, R.	G		$7.00
BEACON	B 224	Half-Caste	1959	Thompson, J.B.	VGF		$15.00
BEACON	B 224	Half-Caste	1959	Thompson, J.B.	G-		$2.00
BEACON	B 226	The Strange Ones	1959	Travis, B.	VG+		$5.00
BEACON	B 227	Add Flesh To The Fire	1959	Hitt, O.	AF		$24.00 A
BEACON	B 228	Nude In The Mirror	1959	Viereck, G.	VG+		$25.00
BEACON	B 228	Nude In The Mirror	1959	Viereck, G.	VGF		$17.00 A
BEACON	B 228	Nude In The Mirror	1959	Viereck, G.	VG		$12.00
BEACON	B 229	Alcoholic Woman	1959	Walsh, R.M.	VGF		$7.00
BEACON	B 230	Odd Girl	1959	Smith, A.	VG		$20.00 A
BEACON	B 232	Private Club	1959	Hitt, O.	VG		$7.00
BEACON	B 233	Turncoat	1959	Fox, R.	AF		$15.00 A
BEACON	B 233	Turncoat	1959	Fox, R.	VGF+		$12.00
BEACON	B 234	Night Of Shame	1959	Lester, L.	VGF		$16.00 A
BEACON	236	Odd John	1959	Stapledon, O.	VG+		$42.00 A
BEACON	B 238	Carnival Girl	1959	Hitt, O.	AF-		$22.00 A
BEACON	B 239	The Peeper	1959	Hitt, O.	VGF		$10.00 A

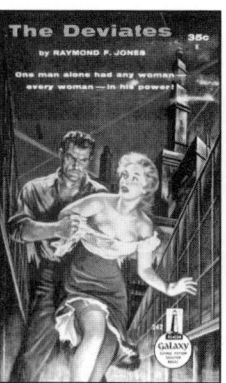

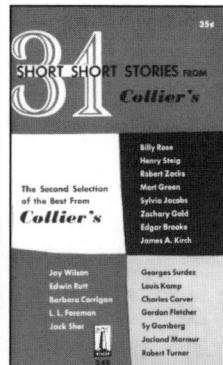

Beacon 236 VG+ $42	Beacon 242 VGF $27	Beacon B245 VGF+ $49	Beacon 249 AF $27

PUBLISHER	PUB. #	TITLE	DATE	AUTHOR	COND.	TYPE	PRICE
BEACON	B 241	Street Walker	1959	Seeley, E.S.	AF		$20.00 A
BEACON	242	The Deviates	1959	Jones, R.F.	VGF		$27.00 A
BEACON	242	The Deviates	1959	Jones, R.F.	VG+		$15.00
BEACON	B 243	Hell Cat	1959	Clark, D.	F		$17.00 A
BEACON	B 244	The Virgin	1959	Morro, D.	AF		$13.00 A
BEACON	B 245	The Young Hoods	1959	Castro, J.	VGF+		$49.00 A
BEACON	B 246	The Divorcées	1959	Stone, S.	VGF+		$30.00 A
BEACON	B 247	Too Many Women	1959	Devlin, B.	AF		$36.00 A
BEACON	B 248	Margo	1959	Stone, S.	F		$12.00 A
BEACON	B 248	Margo	1959	Stone, S.	VG+		$10.00
BEACON	249	31 Short Short Stories	1959	Anthology	AF		$27.00 A
BEACON	249	31 Short Short Stories	1959	Anthology	AF		$24.00 A
BEACON	249	31 Short Short Stories	1959	Anthology	VGF		$18.00
BEACON	B 250	Too Hot To Handle	1959	Hitt, O.	VGF		$48.00 A
BEACON	B 251	One Kind Of Woman	1959	Dean, R.	VGF+		$15.00 A
BEACON	256	Troubled Star	1959	Smith, G.O.	VGF+		$20.00 A
BEACON	256	Troubled Star	1959	Smith, G.O.	VG		$10.00
BEACON	B 257	Shack Woman	1959	Reed, K.	VGF-		$20.00 A
BEACON	B 258	Wild Blonde	1959	Kelly, J.	AF		$15.00
BEACON	B 259	Queer Patterns	1959	Addams, K.*	VGF+		$17.00
BEACON	B 259	Queer Patterns	1959	Addams, K.*	VG+		$12.00
BEACON	B 262	Danielle	1959	Foster, J.	VG+		$6.00
BEACON	263	Pagan Passions	1959	Garrett, R.	VGF		$25.00 A
BEACON	B 264	Strange Thirsts	1959	Norday, M.	AF		$50.00 A
BEACON	B 264	Strange Thirsts	1955	Norday, M.	VG+		$7.00
BEACON	B 266	Private Life Of A Strip-Tease Girl	1959	Anton, C.	VGF		$29.00 A
BEACON	B 268	The Third Sex	1959	Smith, A.	VG+		$28.00 A
BEACON	B 268	The Third Sex	1959	Smith, A.	G+		$7.00
BEACON	B 269	Private School	1959	Priest, J.C.	VG		$8.00
BEACON	B 271	Naked Desire	1959	Nixon, H.L.	VGF		$8.00
BEACON	B 273	Of G-Strings And Strippers	1959	Tryon, M.	VG+		$25.00 A
BEACON	B 275	Mimi	1959	Morell, L.	VGF		$10.00
BEACON	B 276	Triangle Of Sin	1959	Stokes, M.	VG+		$7.00
BEACON	B 279	Convention Girl	1959	Lucas, R.	VG		$7.00
BEACON	B 280	Warped	1959	Norday, M.	VGF		$33.00 A
BEACON	B 280	Warped	1959	Norday, M.	VG+		$10.00
BEACON	B 281	Strange Circle	1959	Sydney, G.	VGF		$13.00
BEACON	B 282	Mavis	1960	Kent, J.	VGF		$12.00
BEACON	B 282	Mavis	1960	Kent, J.	VGF		$11.00 A
BEACON	284	The Sex War	1960	Merwin, S.	AF		$18.00 A
BEACON	B 285	Ex-Mistress	1960	Stone, T.	VGF		$8.00
BEACON	B 287	Pound Of Flesh	1960	Albert, S.	VGF+		$12.00
BEACON	B 287	Pound Of Flesh	1960	Albert, S.	VGF		$9.00
BEACON	B 289	Warped Desire	1960	Addams, K.*	VGF		$50.00 A
BEACON	B 289	Warped Desire	1960	Addams, K.*	VGF		$30.00 A
BEACON	B 290	Scarlet City	1960	Barry, W.	VG		$4.00
BEACON	B 293	Station Wagon Wives	1960	Pritchard, J.	VGF		$7.00
BEACON	B 294	The Torrid Teens	1960	Hitt, O.	VGF-		$20.00 A

Beacon B251 VGF+ $15	Beacon 256 VGF+ $20	Beacon 263 VGF $25	Beacon B266 VGF $29

PUBLISHER	PUB. #	TITLE	DATE	AUTHOR	COND.	TYPE	PRICE
BEACON	B 297	Summer Resort Women	1960	Semple, G.	VG+		$5.00
BEACON	298	The Mating Cry	1960	Van Vogt, A.E.	VG+		$50.00 A
BEACON	298	The Mating Cry	1960	Van Vogt, A.E.	VGF		$45.00
BEACON	B 299	Ask For Therese	1960	Wall, E.	AF		$15.00
BEACON	B 300	Lingerie Ltd.	1960	Dean, R.	VGF		$12.00
BEACON	B 300	Lingerie Ltd.	1960	Dean, R.	VGF		$8.00
BEACON	B 303	Restless Women	1960	Lucas, R.	AF		$8.00
BEACON	B 303	Restless Women	1960	Lucas, R.	VG+		$5.00
BEACON	B 304	From Door To Door	1960	Hitt, O.	VGF		$12.00
BEACON	B 304	From Door To Door	1960	Hitt, O.	VG		$10.00
BEACON	B 304	From Door To Door	1960	Hitt, O.	VG		$6.00
BEACON	B 306	Gutter Girl	1960	Rifkin, L.	VG		$12.00
BEACON	B 306	Gutter Girl	1960	Rifkin, L.	G		$7.00
BEACON	B 307	Pleasure Alley	1960	Carter, R.	AF		$10.00
BEACON	B 311	Different	1960	Clark, D.	VG		$7.00
BEACON	B 315	She Learned The Hard Way	1960	Stone, S.	VGF		$7.00
BEACON	B 324	She Made Her Bed	1960	McKnight, E.	AF		$14.00
BEACON	B 327	Play Girl	1960	De Forest, B.	VG+		$8.00
BEACON	B 334	The Resort	1960	Day, M.	VGF		$12.00
BEACON	B 337	Prime Sucker	1960	Whittington, H.	VG-		$13.00
BEACON	B 337	Prime Sucker	1960	Whittington, H.	VG-		$11.00
BEACON	B 345	Young Widow	1960	Harding, M.	AF		$10.00
BEACON	B 346	Girl On The Beach	1960	Day, M.	AF		$12.00
BEACON	B 346	Girl On The Beach	1960	Day, M.	VG+		$6.00
BEACON	B 350	Strip The Town Naked	1960	Harrison, W.*	VG		$15.00
BEACON	B 350	Strip The Town Naked	1960	Harrison, W.*	VG		$15.00 A
BEACON	B 351	Scandal High	1960	Pruett, H.O.	AF		$24.00 A
BEACON	B 352	Waterfront Blonde	1960	Semple, G.	AF		$8.00
BEACON	B 352	Waterfront Blonde	1960	Semple, G.	VGF		$8.00
BEACON	B 353	Stranger In My Bed	1960	Lutz, G.A.	F		$8.00
BEACON	B 355	Cafe Society Sinner	1960	Manning, B.	AF		$17.00 A
BEACON	B 356	Sexurbia County	1960	Hitt, O.	AF		$27.00 A
BEACON	B 357	Loves Of A Girl Wrestler	1960	West, B.	VGF		$30.00 A
BEACON	B 357	Loves Of A Girl Wrestler	1960	West, B.	VGF		$20.00 A
BEACON	B 359	Girl Artist	1960	West, B.	AF-		$20.00 A
BEACON	B 362	The Other Woman	1960	Burgess, C.	VGF		$7.00
BEACON	B 362	The Other Woman	1960	Burgess, C.	VG+		$7.00
BEACON	B 363	The Sisters	1960	Bligh, N.	AF		$8.00
BEACON	B 363	The Sisters	1960	Bligh, N.	VGF		$8.00
BEACON	B 364	Suzy	1960	Sherman, J.	F		$7.00
BEACON	B 365	All Woman	1960	Harding, M.	AF		$15.00
BEACON	B 367	Wild Fruit	1960	Sherman, J.	AF		$12.00
BEACON	B 367	Wild Fruit	1960	Sherman, J.	VGF		$8.00
BEACON	B 369	Cheating Woman	1960	Gooch, M.S.	AF		$7.00
BEACON	B 370	The Sucker	1960	Hitt, O.	AF-		$17.00
BEACON	B 371	Honey	1961	Woodford, J.	VGF+		$12.00
BEACON	B 372	Gang Girl	1961	Weiss, J.	VGF+		$14.00 A
BEACON	B 374	They Couldn't Say No	1961	Harding, M.	AF		$8.00

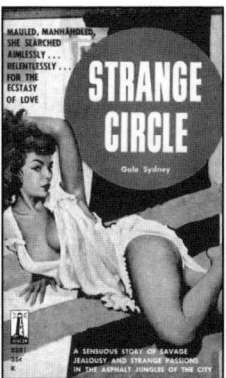

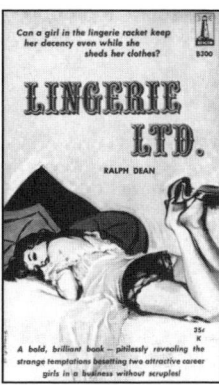

Beacon B268 VG+ $28   Beacon B281 VGF $13   Beacon 298 VG+ $50   Beacon B300 VGF $12

PUBLISHER	PUB. #	TITLE	DATE	AUTHOR	COND.	TYPE	PRICE
BEACON	B 377	Queer Affair	1961	Emery, C.	VG+		$20.00 A
BEACON	B 379	Rock 'N Roll Gal	1961	Weatherall, E.	VG		$20.00
BEACON	B 387	Pads Are For Passion	1961	Lord, S.*	VG+		$10.00 A
BEACON	B 388	Kept Sisters	1961	Stonebraker, F.	VG+		$7.00
BEACON	B 390	Twilight Girl	1961	Martin, D.	VG+		$15.00
BEACON	B 391	Side Street	1961	Williams, W.	AF		$7.00
BEACON	B 395	Ladies' Man	1961	Hitt, O.	AF		$16.00 A
BEACON	B 403	Lusting Women	1961	Balmer, J.	AF		$9.00
BEACON	B 403	Lusting Women	1961	Balmer, J.	VGF		$6.00
BEACON	B 407	Sensual Woman	1961	Hale, L.	VG+		$7.00
BEACON	B 408	After Hours	1961	Munroe, V.	AF-		$10.00
BEACON	B 414	The Development	1961	McCoy, D.	VGF-		$8.00
BEACON	B 415	Dirt Farm	1961	Hitt, O.	VGF		$20.00
BEACON	B 416	A Woman Possessed	1961	Harrison, W.*	VG		$16.00
BEACON	B 423	Weekend Wife	1961	Elliott, B.	AF-		$9.00
BEACON	B 423	Weekend Wife	1961	Elliott, B.	VG+		$7.00
BEACON	B 426	Commuter Widow	1961	Lorraine, L.	AF		$12.00
BEACON	B 427	The Lash Of Lust	1961	Evens, H.	VGF		$9.00 A
BEACON	B 428	Chip's Girls	1961	Demaris, O.	VG-		$3.00
BEACON	B 430	Tomorrow's Call Girls	1961	Somervill, J.W.	VGF		$10.00
BEACON	B 431	Weekend	1961	Carr, J.	VGF		$7.00
BEACON	B 434	The Love Season	1961	Hitt, O.	AF		$14.00
BEACON	B 436	Lessons In Lust	1961	Hale, L.	VGF		$7.00
BEACON	B 438	The Barn	1961	Low, G.	VGF		$7.00
BEACON	B 439	House Party	1961	Napier, D.	AF		$12.00
BEACON	B 441	Squeeze Play	1961	Balmer, J.	VG		$7.00
BEACON	B 446	Community Of Women	1961	Lord, S.*	VG+		$9.00
BEACON	B 452	Party Wives	1961	Layne, J.	AF		$10.00
BEACON	B 454	Cry Rape	1961	Viletti, M.	VG+		$7.00
BEACON	B 455	The Motel	1961	Carr, J.	VG+		$6.00
BEACON	B 458	Blonde Dynamite	1961	Lorraine, L.	F		$7.00
BEACON	B 459	Naked Lens	1961	Gregory, P.	AF		$7.00
BEACON	B 460	Sexbound	1961	McCoy, D.	AF		$15.00
BEACON	B 460	Sexbound	1961	McCoy, D.	VGF		$8.00
BEACON	B 461	A Woman's Need	1962	Williams, S.	AF		$12.00
BEACON	B 464	Woman Chaser	1962	Turner, R.	VGF		$7.00
BEACON	B 465	Dial "M" For Man	1962	Hitt, O.	F		$13.00
BEACON	B 465	Dial "M" For Man	1962	Hitt, O.	VG		$6.00
BEACON	B 471	Man Crazy	1962	Holmes, R.	AF		$7.00
BEACON	B 474	The Golden Girls	1962	Barry, K.	VG+		$7.00
BEACON	B 477	The Bed At The Top	1962	Beck, C.	VGF		$14.00
BEACON	B 483	Faithful To None	1962	Ammons, P.	AF		$6.00
BEACON	B 485	Hot Summer	1962	Harrison, T.	AF		$12.00
BEACON	B 486	Doctor's Women	1962	Sorrell, P.	VG+		$7.00
BEACON	B 487	Strange Embrace	1962	Christopher, B.	G-		$2.00
BEACON	B 491	The Third Way	1962	Lord, S.*	VGF		$28.00 A
BEACON	B 493	Bachelor Nurse	1962	March, K.	VGF		$8.00
BEACON	B 497	Motel Mismates	1962	Roberts, H.	AF		$7.00

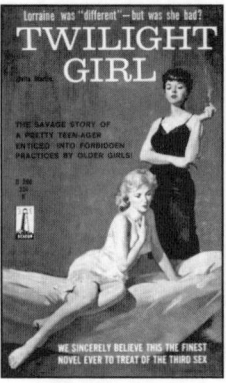

Beacon B357 VGF $30   Beacon B388 VG+ $7   Beacon B390 VG+ $15   Beacon B416 VG $16

PUBLISHER	PUB. #	TITLE	DATE	AUTHOR	COND.	TYPE	PRICE
BEACON	B 498	The Office Couch	1962	Gregory, P.	AF-		$7.00
BEACON	B 501	Woman Alone	1962	Vincent, G.	AF-		$8.00
BEACON	B 501	Woman Alone	1962	Vincent, G.	AF		$7.00
BEACON	B 502	Bedroom Beat	1962	Gold, R.C.	AF		$7.00
BEACON	B 503	She Devil	1962	Taylor, R.W.	VGF		$7.00
BEACON	B 504	Witch With Blue Eyes	1962	Donovan, C.	AF		$12.00
BEACON	B 504	Witch With Blue Eyes	1962	Donovan, C.	VG		$5.00
BEACON	B 506	The Skin Tight Sheath	1962	Brill, L.	VG-		$4.00
BEACON	B 508	High School Jungle	1962	Carter, A.	VGF+		$22.00 A
BEACON	B 508	High School Jungle	1962	Carter, A.	VG+		$12.00
BEACON	B 510	The Warden's Wife	1962	Trainer, R.	VG+		$6.00
BEACON	B 512	Suburban Affair	1962	Dorian, E.	AF		$7.00
BEACON	B 514	Lust In Orbit	1962	Layne, J.	AF		$7.00
BEACON	B 517	Like A Tigress At Bay	1962	Gregory, P.	VGF		$5.00
BEACON	B 518	Weekend Arrangements	1962	Winters, D.	AF-		$8.00
BEACON	B 521	The Deal Makers	1962	Savage, G.	AF		$7.00
BEACON	B 522	Sex Dancer	1962	Matthews, C.	AF		$12.00
BEACON	B 524	The Casting Couch	1962	Gregory, P.	AF		$7.00
BEACON	B 525	Bait	1962	Cassidy, G.	AF		$10.00
BEACON	B 525	Bait	1962	Cassidy, G.	VGF		$8.00
BEACON	B 526	Strange Sisters	1962	Turner, R.	AF		$24.00 A
BEACON	B 534	Rage To Rape	1962	Reeves, A.J.	AF		$8.00
BEACON	B 536	The Love Itch	1962	Barry, K.	AF		$8.00
BEACON	B 537	Girl In A Cage	1962	Gibbs, C.	F		$7.00
BEACON	B 539	Campus Scandal	1962	Joyce, C.	VGF		$7.00
BEACON	B 540	Love Hungry Women	1962	Roberts, H.	AF		$8.00
BEACON	B 541	The One Between	1962	Adlon, A.	VG		$8.00
BEACON	B 543	Yesterday's Virgin	1962	Furlough, J.	VG+		$7.00
BEACON	B 544	Her Mother's Lover	1962	Pruett, H.O.	AF		$8.00
BEACON	B 546	Strange Nurse	1962	Adlon, A.	VGF		$6.00
BEACON	B 550	No Empty Bed For Her	1962	McCoy, D.	AF		$8.00
BEACON	B 553	Woman's Doctor	1962	James, T.	VGF		$7.00
BEACON	B 557	The Price Was Perversity	1962	Gregory, P.	AF		$9.00 A
BEACON	B 560	The Country Club Set	1962	Dorian, E.	VGF		$7.00
BEACON	B 563	Anything To Win	1962	McCoy, D.	VGF+		$8.00
BEACON	B 564	Strange Seduction	1962	Adlon, A.	AF-		$16.00 A
BEACON	B 564	Strange Seduction	1962	Adlon, A.	VG+		$13.00 A
BEACON	B 564	Strange Seduction	1962	Adlon, A.	VG+		$10.00
BEACON	B 565	And Sex Is The Payoff	1962	Richard, L.	VGF		$6.00
BEACON	B 567	The Empty Bed	1963	Lorraine, L.	AF		$12.00
BEACON	B 568	Change Partners	1963	Carter, A.	AF		$9.00 A
BEACON	B 569	Bella Vista's Wives	1963	Hart, B.	VG+		$5.00
BEACON	B 571	The Party Game	1963	Layne, J.	VG+		$5.00
BEACON	B 574	Fever In The Sun	1963	Lord, S.*	VG+		$6.00
BEACON	B 577	Floating Bedroom	1963	Shubin, S.	F		$7.00
BEACON	B 577	Floating Bedroom	1963	Shubin, S.	AF		$7.00
BEACON	B 579	Summer Swap	1963	White, W.M.	AF		$10.00
BEACON	B 579	Summer Swap	1963	White, W.M.	VG+		$6.00

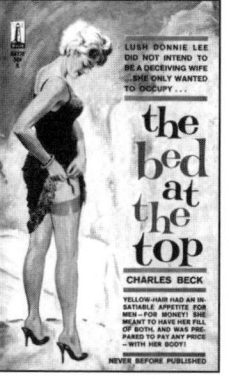

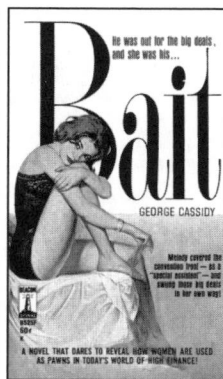

Beacon B460 AF $15	Beacon B465 F $13	Beacon B477 VGF $14	Beacon B525 AF $10

PUBLISHER	PUB. #	TITLE	DATE	AUTHOR	COND.	TYPE	PRICE
BEACON	B 582	The Saturday Night Party	1963	Geis, R.E.	VGF		$16.00 A
BEACON	B 582	The Saturday Night Party	1963	Geis, R.E.	VGF		$14.00 A
BEACON	B 587	Girl In The Motel	1963	Layne, J.	AF		$8.00
BEACON	B 588	Wellville, U.S.A.	1963	Shubin, S.	VG		$6.00
BEACON	B 593	Stranger In Her Bed	1963	Albert, J.	F		$7.00
BEACON	B 595	Lonesome Widow	1963	Trainer, R.	AF		$10.00
BEACON	B 595	Lonesome Widow	1963	Trainer, R.	VG+		$6.00
BEACON	B 596	Faithful For 8 Hours	1963	Blake, A.	VG+		$6.00
BEACON	B 597	The Bigamist	1963	Barry, K.	VGF		$7.00
BEACON	B 598	The Friendship Club	1963	McCoy, D.	VGF		$7.00
BEACON	B 600	Never Leave My Bed	1963	Rogers, J.T.	F		$8.00
BEACON	B 600	Never Leave My Bed	1963	Rogers, J.T.	VGF		$6.00
BEACON	B 601	The Dean's Wife	1963	Thomas, L.	VG+		$7.00
BEACON	B 602	She Who Strays	1963	Adlon, A.	AF		$10.00
BEACON	B 603	The Bedroom Route	1963	Lord, S.*	VGF		$8.00
BEACON	B 604	The Love Camp	1963	Furlough, J.	VGF		$5.00
BEACON	B 606	A Woman's Wants	1963	Thomas, L.	AF		$8.00
BEACON	B 608	7 Days To Love	1963	Johns, C.	F		$9.00
BEACON	B 612	The Wife Sharers	1963	Adlon, A.	AF		$8.00
BEACON	B 613	Paid Lover	1963	Dare, W.	VGF-		$6.00
BEACON	B 614	Season For Sin	1963	Lorraine, L.	VGF		$7.00
BEACON	B 618	Lost Virgin	1963	Pruett, H.O.	AF		$8.00
BEACON	B 619	The Other Kind	1963	Villanova, R.	F		$23.00 A
BEACON	B 623	Jeanne	1963	Black, B.	AF		$8.00
BEACON	B 625	Sex-Swinger	1963	Blake, A.	VGF		$7.00
BEACON	B 626	The Doctor's Wife	1963	Avallone, M.	VG+		$8.00
BEACON	B 628	The Eager Beavers	1963	Richards, L.	AF		$12.00
BEACON	B 629	The Free Lovers	1963	Carter, A.	VGF		$8.00
BEACON	B 630	The Wife Game	1963	Donovan, C.	AF		$7.00
BEACON	B 631	Her Shacktown Lover	1963	James, N.	F		$7.00
BEACON	B 632	The Love Seekers	1963	Carr, J.	AF		$8.00
BEACON	B 632	The Love Seekers	1963	Carr, J.	VG+		$7.00
BEACON	B 633	The Perfumed World	1963	Anders, B.	AF		$7.00
BEACON	B 633	The Perfumed World	1963	Anders, B.	VG+		$5.00
BEACON	B 634	The Night It Happened	1963	McCoy, D.	VGF		$5.00
BEACON	B 637	Cravings	1963	Woodford, J.	VG+		$5.00
BEACON	B 644	The Twisted Ones	1963	Foran, T.	G		$6.00
BEACON	B 646	A Bunch Of Women	1963	North, K.	VGF+		$7.00
BEACON	B 648	The Husband Hunters	1963	McCoy, D.	VGF		$5.00
BEACON	B 649	The Third Sex	1963	Smith, A.	VGF		$12.00
BEACON	B 654	The Middle Sex	1963	Clubb, S.	VG		$4.00
BEACON	B 655	Sin Doll	1963	Hitt, O.	AF		$14.00
BEACON	B 656	Web Of Women	1963	Dare, W.	AF		$6.00
BEACON	B 658	What Color Is Love?	1963	MacLeod, K.	VG		$7.00
BEACON	B 659	The Sisterhood	1963	Lord, S.*	VGF+		$22.00 A
BEACON	B 673	The Love Trap	1963	Hilton, H.	VGF		$9.00 A
BEACON	B 673	The Love Trap	1963	Hilton, H.	VG+		$6.00
BEACON	B 675	Vacation Girls	1963	Carr, J.	VGF		$5.00

Beacon B526 AF $24 Beacon B567 AF $12 Beacon B582 VGF $16 Beacon B603 VGF $8

PUBLISHER	PUB. #	TITLE	DATE	AUTHOR	COND.	TYPE	PRICE
BEACON	B 678	Artist's Woman	1963	Richard, L.	AF		$7.00
BEACON	B 681	The Night Lovers	1963	Gibbs, C.	AF		$6.00
BEACON	B 684	Mazie	1963	Thomas, L.	AF		$7.00
BEACON	B 691	A Room At Polly's Place	1964	McGuire, S.	VG+		$4.00
BEACON	B 698	His Brother's Wife	1964	Stuart, C.*	VG		$10.00
BEACON	B 706	The Punks	1964	Richards, L.	AF		$28.00 A
BEACON	B 708	Sherri	1964	Collier, M.	AF		$8.00
BEACON	B 714	The Tempted	1964	Holland, K.*	VG		$15.00
BEACON	B 727	Strange Lovers	1964	Bartell, D.	VGF		$7.00
BEACON	B 730	The Scuba Set	1964	Carver, J.	VG		$6.00
BEACON	B 731	Tutor From Lesbos	1964	Williams, A.P.	VG		$7.00
BEACON	B 734	The Bored Young Wives	1964	Morgan, J.	VG+		$6.00
BEACON	B 735	Summer Of Sin	1964	Hitt, O.	AF		$8.00
BEACON	B 737	Sexurbia County	1964	Hitt, O.	VG		$4.00
BEACON	B 739	Suzy	1964	Sherman, J.	VGF		$5.00
BEACON	B 740	Cheating Wives	1964	Devlin, B.	AF		$5.00
BEACON	B 741	Anatomy Of A Heel	1964	Edmund, M.	AF		$6.00
BEACON	B 745	Nina	1964	Black, B.	AF		$7.00
BEACON	B 749	The Hot Blood Of Youth	1964	Clubb, S.	VGF+		$7.00 A
BEACON	B 756	Party Going	1964	McEvilley, T.	VGF+		$7.00
BEACON	B 757	The Sex Shuffle	1964	Lord, S.*	G		$3.00
BEACON	B 758	Shayne	1964	Thompson, J.B.	VG+		$7.00
BEACON	B 764	Shopping Center Sex	1964	Lang, O.A.	VG		$6.00
BEACON	B 767	Resort Girls	1964	Wolffe, C.X.	VGF		$12.00
BEACON	B 769	Campus Nymph	1964	Carver, J.	VG+		$4.00
BEACON	B 773	Mother, Daughter And Lover	1964	Fickling, G.G.	VG+		$4.00
BEACON	B 774	House-Boy Lover	1964	McCoy, D.	AF-		$8.00
BEACON	B 775	Wives And Lovers	1964	Lorraine, L.	VG+		$6.00
BEACON	B 781	Women Who Cheat	1964	Burke, F.	AF-		$5.00
BEACON	B 782	That Motel Weekend	1964	Donner, J.	VGF		$6.00
BEACON	B 787	The Seduction Of Denby Martin	1964	Adlon, A.	VGF		$8.00
BEACON	B 789	Young Wife	1964	Burke, F.	VGF		$8.00
BEACON	B 791	Baby Face	1964	Salem, R.	VG		$20.00 A
BEACON	B 793	Neighbors And Lovers	1964	Gibbs, C.	VG		$3.00
BEACON	B 795	The Odd Kind (3rd)	1964	Adlon, A.	AF-		$7.00
BEACON	B 797	The Female Animal	1965	Adlon, A.	AF		$7.00
BEACON	B 798	Lust For Youth	1965	Preston, L.	AF		$5.00
BEACON	B 798	Lust For Youth	1965	Preston, L.	VG+		$5.00
BEACON	B 803	Free Loving Wives	1965	McCoy, D.	VGF+		$7.00
BEACON	B 804	Sex Off Limits	1965	Simon, C.	AF		$7.00
BEACON	B 816	Lend Me Your Wife	1965	Layne, J.	AF		$25.00 A
BEACON	B 816	Lend Me Your Wife	1965	Layne, J.	VG+		$7.00
BEACON	B 819	Sorority Sin	1965	Seeley, E.S.	VG+		$11.00 A
BEACON	B 824	Sex Pit	1965	Fickling, G.G.	VG+		$6.00
BEACON	B 828	Wrong Way Love	1965	Burke, F.	VGF		$7.00
BEACON	B 838	Abnormal Wife	1965	Hastings, M.	AF		$5.00
BEACON	B 841	A Night With Lana	1965	Cardinal, M.	VGF		$6.00
BEACON	B 853	The Oddballs	1965	Clubb, S.	VGF+		$23.00 A

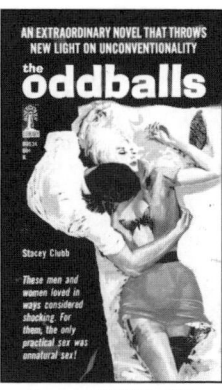

| Beacon B816 AF $25 | Beacon B819 VG+ $11 | Beacon B853 VGF+ $23 | Beagle 95042 VGF + $7 |

PUBLISHER	PUB. #	TITLE	DATE	AUTHOR	COND.	TYPE	PRICE
BEACON	B 854	The Secrets	1965	Black, B.	AF		$7.00
BEACON	B 857	Morgan's Girls	1965	Harding, M.	VGF+		$8.00
BEACON	B 867	Older Woman	1965	Lord, S.*	VG		$7.00
BEACON	B 872	The Sex Kitten Grows Up	1965	Naylor, A.	VG+		$6.00
BEACON	B 888	The Split Level Game	1965	Lorraine, L.	VGF		$7.00
BEACON	B 890	Suburbia After Dark	1965	Gibbs, C.	AF		$7.00
BEACON	B 892	The Weekend Group	1965	Balt, J.	VGF		$7.00
BEACON	B 893	The Skin Tight Sheath	1965	Brill, L.	VG		$5.00
BEACON	B 899	The Strange Ones	1965	Travis, B.	VG+		$4.00
BEACON	B 902	Behind Respectable Doors	1965	Gibbs, C.	VG+		$5.00
BEACON	B 905	Velvet Jackpot	1965	Carter, A.	AF		$8.00
BEACON	B 919	Boy-Lover	1966	Carter, A.	AF		$8.00
BEACON	B 929	Yesterday's Virgin	1966	Furlough, J.	AF		$6.00
BEACON	B 942	Woman Alone	1966	Vincent, G.	VG		$4.00
BEACON	B 945	The Place	1966	Adlon, A.	VGF		$6.00
BEACON	B 949	Weekday Widows	1966	Gibbs, C.	AF		$8.00
BEACON	B 964	The Awakening	1966	Blaine, J.	VG		$4.00
BEACON	B 983	The Punks	1966	Richards, L.	VGF		$15.00 A
BEACON	B 983	The Punks	1966	Richards, L.	VG		$10.00
BEACON	B 991	The Naked View	1966	Munroe, V.	VG+		$4.00
BEACON	B 1006	The College Crowd	1967	Woodford, J.	VG+		$4.00
BEACON	B 1018	Outcast	1967	Lord, S.*	VG+		$7.00
BEACON	B 1036	The Girl From Underground	1967	Maxwell, G.	VGF-		$8.00 A
BEACON	B 1038	Girl In A Go-Go Cage	1967	Orth, R.	VGF		$10.00 A
BEACON	B 1038	Girl In A Go-Go Cage	1967	Orth, R.	VG+		$8.00
BEACON	B 1051	Sex Web	1967	Agar, B.	VGF+		$7.00
BEACON	B 1055	The Wife And The Wanton	1967	Carver, J.	AF		$7.00
BEACON	B 1060	Pick Up	1967	Willeford, C.	VG		$27.00 A
BEACON	B 1065	Sex Is A Woman	1967	Lord, S.*	AF		$12.00
BEACON	B 1094	The Women He Used	1968	Pauley, J.H.	VG+		$4.00
BEACON	B 1102	Backwoods Virgin	1968	Abbott, D.W.	VG+		$4.00
BEACON	B 1106	Commuter County	1968	Roderick, J.	VGF		$5.00
BEACON	B 1108	Suburban Sin	1968	Hitt, O.	VGF		$7.00
BEACON	B 1112	Sexual Twilight	1968	Herbert, A.	VGF		$9.00 A
BEACON	B 1118	Cheat	1968	Hitt, O.	VG		$7.00
BEACON	B 1143	Summer Of Sin	1969	Hitt, O.	F	DBL	$12.00
		The Love Season		Hitt, O.			
BEACON	DB 112	The Empty Bed	1966	Lorraine, L.	VG	DBL	$5.00
		The Fair Young Wives		Carver, J.			
BEACON	S 75128	Dirt Farm	1969	Hitt, O.	VGF		$7.00
BEACON	S 75129	Sex Habits Of Single Women	1969	Preston, L.	VG+		$7.00
BEACON	S 75131	Sex Off Limits	1970	Simon, G.	AF-		$6.00
BEACON	S 75134	The Jebson Kids	1970	Burke, F.	VGF		$5.00
BEACON	S 75141	Virgins No More	1970	Hitt, O.	AF		$6.00
BEACON	S 75163	The Club	1970	Yardley, S.	AF		$6.00
BEACON	S 75168	The Sex Shuffle	1970	Lord, S.*	AF-		$15.00 A
BEACON	S 75177	Her Raging Needs	1970	Johnson, K.	AF		$6.00 A
BEACON	S 75179	After Office Hours	1970	Black, B.	VGF+		$5.00

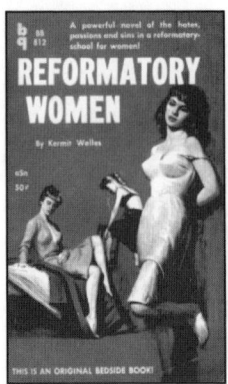
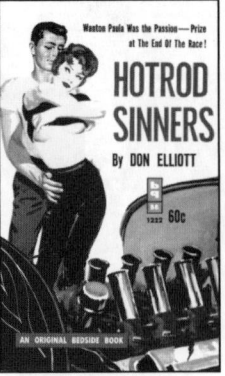

Bedside 812 VG $31   Bedside 1222 VG+ $23   Bedtime 951 VG $6   Bee-Line 126 VGF+ $13

PUBLISHER	PUB. #	TITLE	DATE	AUTHOR	COND.	TYPE	PRICE
BEACON	S 95159	Trap Of Lesbos	1970	Clubb, S.	AF		$22.00 A
BEACON	S 95183	The Shadowy Sex	1970	Hilton, H.	AF		$20.00 A
BEACON	S 95189	The Sisterhood	1970	Lord, S.*	AF-		$28.00 A
BEACON	S 95196	Abnormal Wife	1970	Hastings, M.	AF		$5.00
BEACON	S 95198	Ex-Virgin	1970	Hitt, O.	VGF		$7.00
BEACON	S 95201	Her High-School Lover	1970	Malaponte, M.*	AF		$36.00 A
BEACON	S 95201	Her High-School Lover	1970	Malaponte, M.*	F		$31.00 A
BEACON	S 95201	Her High-School Lover	1970	Malaponte, M.*	VGF+		$22.00 A
BEACON	S 95212	Cheat	n/d	Hitt, O.	VGF		$5.00
BEACON	S 95236	The Ecstasy Kick	n/d	Blake, A.	AF		$15.00 A
BEACON	S 95245	Rotten To The Core	n/d	Hitt, O.	G		$5.00
BEACON ENVOY	E 103	The League Of Gentlemen	n/d	Boland, J.	AF	MTI	$17.00 A
BEAGLE	95042	The Lurking Fear	1971	Lovecraft, H.P.	VGF+		$7.00
BEDSIDE	BB 805	Naked Sinner	1959	Frame, B.	VG		$6.00
BEDSIDE	BB 806	A Game Of Flesh	1959	Trinian, J.	VGF		$12.00
BEDSIDE	BB 811	Beatnik Party	1959	Schuyler, J.	VG+		$39.00 A
BEDSIDE	BB 812	Reformatory Women	1959	Welles, K.	VG		$31.00 A
BEDSIDE	BB 813	Streets Of Sin	1959	Ryan, M.	VG-		$24.00 A
BEDSIDE	BB 818	Wild Wanton	1959	Welles, K.	VG		$15.00 A
BEDSIDE	BB 820	French Sin Port	1959	Challon, D.*	VG+		$7.00
BEDSIDE	BB 821	Thirst For Love	1959	Challon, D.*	VG+		$8.00
BEDSIDE	BB 822	Passion In Paris	1959	Stone, H.	VGF-		$8.00
BEDSIDE	BB 824	Savage Delinquents	1959	Bennett, A.	VGF		$46.00 A
BEDSIDE	BB 826	Borrowed Lover	1959	Clark, D.	VG		$7.00
BEDSIDE	BB 958	Trailer Camp Woman	1959	Duperrault, D.	VGF		$12.00
BEDSIDE	BB 958	Trailer Camp Woman	1959	Duperrault, D.	VG+		$12.00
BEDSIDE	BB 1202	Off Limits	1961	Marshall, A.*	VG+		$15.00
BEDSIDE	BB 1202	Off Limits	1961	Marshall, A.*	G		$3.00
BEDSIDE	BB 1205	Showcase For Sin	1961	Hudson, D.	VG+		$7.00
BEDSIDE	BB 1211	The Warped Ones	1962	Marshall, A.*	VG		$12.00
BEDSIDE	BB 1216	Sex Escort	1962	Tasker, W.B.	VG+		$7.00
BEDSIDE	BB 1217	Web Of Flesh	1962	Allison, C.	VGF		$20.00
BEDSIDE	BB 1222	Hotrod Sinners	1962	Elliott, D.*	VG+		$23.00
BEDSIDE	BB 1222	Hotrod Sinners	1962	Elliott, D.*	AF		$20.00
BEDSIDE	BB 1224	Gutter Girl	1962	Shaw, A.*	VG+		$30.00
BEDSIDE	BB 1224	Gutter Girl	1962	Shaw, A.*	AF		$25.00 A
BEDTIME	951	Forbidden Thrills	1959	Dean, R.	VG		$6.00
BEDTIME	953	Exotic Sinner	1959	Sheppard, S.*	AF		$24.00 A
BEDTIME	955	Girl Crazy	1959	Conway, S.	AF-		$14.00 A
BEDTIME	961	Suburban Affair	1960	Challon, D.*	VG		$8.00
BEDTIME	961	Suburban Affair	1960	Challon, D.*	AF		$7.00
BEE-LINE	107	Ride A Hot Mile	1966	Seedy, I.	AF		$8.00
BEE-LINE	111	For Whom The Belles Toil	1966	Dodd, C.	AF		$15.00 A
BEE-LINE	114	Lotita	1966	Grahame, G.G.	VGF		$8.00
BEE-LINE	126	The Girl From A.U.N.T.Y.	1966	Seedy, I.	VGF+		$13.00 A
BEE-LINE	131	The Indiana Torture Slaying	1966	Dean, J.	VG		$20.00
BEE-LINE	137	The Girl In The Grey Flannel Suit	1966	Allen, C.	VGF		$8.00 A
BEE-LINE	141	From Here To Maternity	1966	Earle, R.	VG		$10.00

Belmont 216 AF $44   Belmont 239 VGF $30   Belmont 241 VG+ $6

PUBLISHER	PUB. #	TITLE	DATE	AUTHOR	COND.	TYPE	PRICE
BEE-LINE	186	All The Girls Together	1967	Reed, R.	VG+		$20.00 A
BEE-LINE	277	Confessions Of An Immoral Model	1967	Normann, E.	VGF+		$10.00 A
BEE-LINE	347	Lesbian Jungle	1968	Morgan, A.	VGF		$24.00 A
BEE-LINE	357	Only Girls Can Play	1969	Harmon, J.	AF		$8.00
BELL-RINGER	506	Passion Behind Bars	1964	Johns, D.	AF		$20.00 A
BELL-RINGER	508	Two-Way Woman	1964	Miles, R.	AF		$7.00
BELL-RINGER	509	Racket Babe	1965	Kane, K.	AF		$18.00 A
BELMONT	201	Temptress	1960	Maurois, A.	AF		$15.00
BELMONT	203	Payola Woman	1960	Bingham, C.	F		$5.00
BELMONT	204	Johnny Havoc	1960	Jakes, J.	VG		$8.00
BELMONT	205	Who Live In Shadow	1960	Harris, S.	AF		$18.00 A
BELMONT	206	Bloody Precinct	1960	Douglas, B.	VG+		$8.00
BELMONT	207	The Cruel City	1960	Mackey, J.	VG		$7.00
BELMONT	208	The Slave	1960	Maurel, M.	F		$10.00
BELMONT	209	Hong Kong Kill	1960	Peters, B.	F		$10.00
BELMONT	216	Concha	1960	Sollers, P.	AF		$44.00 A
BELMONT	218	Sex-Clusive	1960	Anthology	AF		$10.00
BELMONT	220	South Pacific Affair	1961	Lacy, E.	VG		$8.00
BELMONT	221	Vice-Cop	1961	Deming, R.	VGF		$10.00
BELMONT	221	Vice-Cop	1961	Deming, R.	VG		$7.00
BELMONT	224	Lonely Boy Blues	1961	Kapelner, A.	VGF		$6.00
BELMONT	228	The Ladies Man	1961	Winston, C.	VG+	MTI	$5.00
BELMONT	229	Ten Against The Third Reich	1961	Smith, S.	AF		$7.00
BELMONT	230	Creeps By Night	1961	Anthology	VGF+		$22.00 A
BELMONT	230	Creeps By Night	1961	Anthology	VG+		$19.00 A
BELMONT	230	Creeps By Night	1961	Anthology	VG+		$10.00 A
BELMONT	232	The Day The War Ends	1961	Shaw, I.	AF-		$6.00
BELMONT	233	Nightmares	1961	Bloch, R.	F		$37.00 A
BELMONT	233	Nightmares	1961	Bloch, R.	F		$32.00 A
BELMONT	233	Nightmares	1961	Bloch, R.	AF		$27.00 A
BELMONT	233	Nightmares	1961	Bloch, R.	VGF		$23.00
BELMONT	235	A Gun For Cantrell	1961	Drago, H.S.	VGF		$7.00
BELMONT	238	13 Against The Rising Sun	1961	Smith, S.	AF		$7.00
BELMONT	239	The Red Brain	1961	Anthology	VGF		$30.00 A
BELMONT	239	The Red Brain	1961	Anthology	VGF		$20.00
BELMONT	239	The Red Brain	1961	Anthology	VG		$10.00
BELMONT	241	The Trial Of Johnny Dice	1961	Drago, H.S.	VG+		$6.00
BELMONT	246	The Horror Expert	1961	Long, F.	VGF		$20.00 A
BELMONT	91 248	The Demise Of A Louse	1962	Shepherd, J.	AF		$9.00 A
BELMONT	91 251	Gun-Hunt For The Sundance Kid	1962	Nye, N.	AF		$7.00
BELMONT	91 253	Private Life Of A Strip-Tease Artist	1962	Cooper, M.	VGF		$8.00
BELMONT	91 260	Women Of The Evening	1962	Gaddis, P.	VG+		$7.00
BELMONT	90 261	Johnny Havoc Meets Zelda	1962	Jakes, J.	G		$5.00
BELMONT	90 262	Arena Of Love	1962	Eliat, H.	AF		$7.00
BELMONT	90 263	Doctors And Nurses	1963	McDonnell, V.	VG+		$6.00

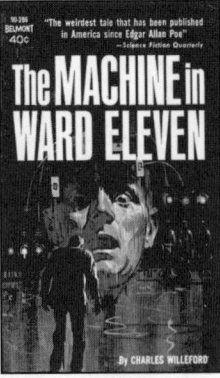
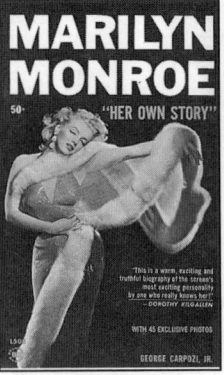
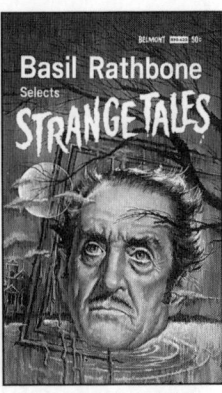

Belmont 90-265 VG+ $40   Belmont 90-286 VG $20   Belmont L508 AF- $34   Belmont B50-633 AF $20

PUBLISHER	PUB. #	TITLE	DATE	AUTHOR	COND.	TYPE	PRICE
BELMONT	90 265	Jailbait Jungle	1962	Brown, W.	VG+		$40.00 A
BELMONT	90 268	By-Line, Mona Knox	1962	Turner, J.	VG+		$27.00 A
BELMONT	90 278	Young Nurse Desmond	1963	Gaddis, P.	VG		$4.00
BELMONT	90 280	The Professor And The Co-Ed	1963	Hall, B.	VG+		$8.00 A
BELMONT	90 281	TCOT Radioactive Redhead	1963	Fickling, G.G.	VG+		$10.00
BELMONT	90 283	My Profession Is Sin	1963	Anonymous	VG+		$7.00
BELMONT	90 286	The Machine In Ward Eleven	1963	Willeford, C.	VG		$20.00
BELMONT	90 292	Episode With Erika	1963	Brossard, C.	VG		$6.00
BELMONT	90 296	There Was A Rustle . . .	1963	McAlmon, R.	AF		$17.00 A
BELMONT	90 297	Tales Of The Frightened	1963	Avallone, M.	VG		$6.00
BELMONT	90 298	The Return Of The Shadow (2nd)	1964	Gibson, W.B.	VG		$5.00
BELMONT	90 302	Nobody Loves A Loser	1963	Kane, H.	VGF		$7.00
BELMONT	90 309	Snake River Ambush	1964	Bennet, R.A.	AF		$6.00
BELMONT	L 505	The Cheat	1961	Jackson, C.	VG+		$6.00
BELMONT	L 508	Marilyn Monroe	1961	Carpozi, G.	AF-		$34.00 A
BELMONT	L 519	Khrushchev's Mein Kampf	1961	Salisbury, H.E.	AF		$5.00
BELMONT	L92 527	Yours Truly, Jack The Ripper	1962	Bloch, R.	G		$5.00
BELMONT	L92 528	Heroic Battles Of WWII	1962	Anthology	VGF		$7.00
BELMONT	L92 530	More Nightmares	1962	Bloch, R.	G		$7.00
BELMONT	L92 537	Terror	1962	Bloch, R.	AF		$20.00 A
BELMONT	L92 541	The Weird Ones	1962	Anthology	VG		$6.00
BELMONT	L92 546	My Friend, Henry Miller	1962	Perles, A.	AF		$6.00
BELMONT	L92 552	Normal & Abnormal Sex Ways	1962	Klein, L.	AF		$7.00
BELMONT	L92 556	Vince Edwards	1962	Carpozi, G.	AF-	TVTI	$6.00 A
BELMONT	L92 564	6 And The Silent Scream	1963	Anthology	AF		$8.00
BELMONT	L92 567	Novelets Of Science Fiction	1963	Anthology	VGF		$6.00
BELMONT	L92 570	Shock Corridor	1963	Avallone, M.	AF		$16.00 A
BELMONT	L92 581	Bed Of An Empress	1964	Masoch, L.S.	VGF		$8.00 A
BELMONT	L92 582	Things	1964	Anthology	AF		$6.00
BELMONT	L92 582	Things	1964	Anthology	VGF-		$6.00
BELMONT	L92 594	Mr. George & Other Odd Persons	1964	Derleth, A.	AF		$11.00 A
BELMONT	92 603	The Penultimate Truth	1964	Dick, P.K.	VG		$7.00
BELMONT	92 609	The Crazy Mixed-Up Nude	1964	Fickling, G.G.	VGF		$12.00
BELMONT	92 617	The Case Of Charles Dexter Ward	1965	Lovecraft, H.P.	VGF		$11.00
BELMONT	92 617	The Case Of Charles Dexter Ward	1965	Lovecraft, H.P.	VG+		$5.00
BELMONT	92 618	Time Out Of Joint	1965	Dick, P.K.	VGF		$12.00
BELMONT	92 618	Time Out Of Joint	1965	Dick, P.K.	VG+		$8.00
BELMONT	92 618	Time Out Of Joint	1965	Dick, P.K.	VG		$8.00
BELMONT	90 623	Dirty Gertie	1965	Kane, H.	G+		$5.00
BELMONT	B50 626	Dive, Dive!	1965	Smith, S.	AF		$6.00
BELMONT	B50 633	Basil Rathbone Strange Tales	1965	Anthology	AF		$20.00 A
BELMONT	B50 676	Get Off My World!	1966	Leinster, M.	VG		$5.00
BELMONT	B50 699	The Four Day Weekend	1966	Smith, G.H.	VG		$6.00
BELMONT	B50 704	The Miss From S.I.S.	1966	Tralins, B.	VG		$6.00
BELMONT	B50 707	What A Way To Go!	1966	O'Shea, S.	VG		$7.00
BELMONT	B50 718	The Chic Chick Spy	1966	Tralins, B.	VGF		$27.00 A
BELMONT	B50 733	The Reluctant Spy	1966	Laflin, J.	VG		$3.00
BELMONT	B50 737	The Shadow: Destination Moon	1967	Grant, M.*	VG+		$15.00

Belmont B50-718 VGF $27   Belmont B50-737 VG+ $15   Belmont B50-779 VG $8   Belmont B50-782 VGF $22

PUBLISHER	PUB. #	TITLE	DATE	AUTHOR	COND.	TYPE	PRICE
BELMONT	B50 738	Skuldoggery	1967	Flora, F.	VGF		$7.00
BELMONT	B50 741	Hawk	1966	Hardwick, R.	VGF	TVTI	$10.00
BELMONT	B50 745	The Ring-A-Ding UFOs	1967	Tralins, B.	VG+		$7.00
BELMONT	B50 771	Twisted	1967	Anthology	VGF-		$7.00
BELMONT	B50 774	The Wild Girls	1967	Gaddis, P.	VG		$7.00
BELMONT	B50 779	Doomsman	1967	Ellison, H.	VG	DBL	$8.00
		Telepower		Hoffman, L.			
BELMONT	B50 779	Doomsman	1967	Ellison, H.	G	DBL	$6.00
BELMONT	B50 782	The Nymph Island Affair	1967	O'Shea, S.	VGF		$22.00 A
BELMONT	B50 787	The Living Demons	1967	Bloch, R.	VG		$6.00
BELMONT	B50 839	Basil Rathbone Strange Tales	1968	Anthology	VG+		$7.00
BELMONT	B50 840	The Third Eye	1968	Cogswell, T.	F		$7.00
BELMONT	B50 846	Space Tug	1968	Leinster, M.	VGF		$5.00
BELMONT	B50 1039	There Oughta Be A Law	1969	Shorten, H.	AF		$4.00
BELMONT	B50 1060	Dragons And Nightmares	1969	Bloch, R.	G		$6.00
BELMONT	B45 901	Trouble At Moon Pass	1965	Arthur, B.	VGF		$5.00
BELMONT	B45 905	Town Tamer	1965	Gruber, F.	VG	MTI	$3.00
BELMONT	B60 69	From The Land Of Fear	1967	Ellison, H.	AF		$15.00 A
BELMONT	B60 77	A Lamp For Medusa	1968	Tenn, W.	VGF	DBL	$7.00
		The Players Of Hell		Van Arnam, D.			
BELMONT	B60 80	Ladies' Day	1968	Bloch, R.	AF	DBL	$43.00 A
		This Crowded Earth		Bloch, R.			
BELMONT	B60 80	Ladies' Day	1968	Bloch, R.	VG+	DBL	$9.00
BELMONT	B60 80	Ladies' Day	1968	Bloch, R.	VG	DBL	$7.00
BELMONT	B60 86	The Topless Kitties	1968	O'Shea, S.	AF		$18.00 A
BELMONT	B75 202	I Am A Nymphomaniac	1965	Woodward, L.T.*	VGF		$7.00
BELMONT	B75 203	This Side Of Love	1966	Christian, P.	VG+	DBL	$15.00 A
		Edge Of Twilight		Christian, P.			
BELMONT	B75 1044	The Stonehedge Slaves	1969	Fox, G.F.	VGF		$11.00 A
BELMONT	B75 1091	Over The Edge	1970	Ellison, H.	VG		$10.00
BELMONT	B75 2001	The Lemmings	1970	Blackstock, C.	VGF		$5.00
BELMONT	B75 2041	The Corpse Moved Upstairs	1970	Gruber, F.	AF		$6.00
BELMONT	BT 40119	Dragons And Nightmares	1972	Bloch, R.	AF		$14.00 A
BELMONT	BT 50244	Doomsman	1972	Ellison, H.	VGF	DBL	$8.00
		The Thief Of Toth		Carter, L.			
BELMONT	BT 50282	Over The Edge	1972	Ellison, H.	VGF		$27.00 A
BELMONT	BT 50529	From The Land Of Fear	1973	Ellison, H.	VGF		$7.00
BELMONT	BT 50529	From The Land Of Fear	1973	Ellison, H.	VG+		$5.00
BELMONT	BT 50529	From The Land Of Fear	1973	Ellison, H.	VG-		$4.00
BELMONT	BT 50536	A Place Of Demons	1973	Graat, H.	VGF		$5.00
BELMONT	BT 50566	5 Beds To Mecca	1973	Gray, R.	VGF+		$7.00
BELMONT	BT 50582	South Of The Bordello	1973	Gray, R.	VG+		$7.00
BELMONT	BT 50617	The Lady From L.U.S.T. #8	1973	Gray, R.	AF		$7.00
BELMONT	BT 50617	The Hot Mahatma (L.U.S.T. #8)	1973	Gray, R.	VG		$5.00
BELMONT	BT 50628	To Russia With L.U.S.T.	1973	Gray, R.	VGF+		$7.00 A
BELMONT	BT 50649	The Lady From L.U.S.T. #11	1974	Gray, R.	AF		$5.00
BELMONT	BT 50750	From The Land Of Fear	1974	Ellison, H.	AF-		$10.00
BELMONT	BT 50759	Ladies' Day/This Crowded Earth	1974	Bloch, R.	VGF	DBL	$7.00

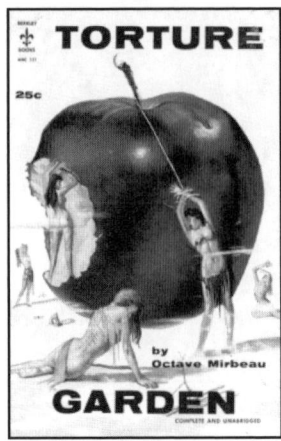

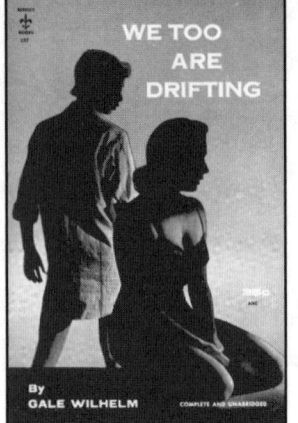

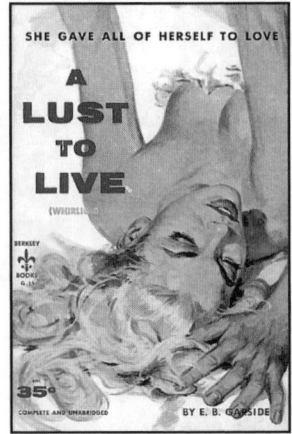

Berkley 111 F $25   Berkley 327 AF $40   Berkley G15 VGF $6

PUBLISHER	PUB. #	TITLE	DATE	AUTHOR	COND.	TYPE	PRICE
BELMONT	BT 50793	Mannix #1 - Faces Of Murder	1975	MacCargo, J.T.*	VG	TVTI	$7.00
BELMONT	BT 51143	Time Out Of Joint	n/d	Dick, P.K.	AF		$10.00
BELMONT	BT 51181	Thirty Seconds Over New York	1976	Buchard, R.	VGF		$6.00
BERKLEY	101	Pleasures Of The Jazz Age	1955	Anthology	AF		$8.00
BERKLEY	102	Loveliest Of Friends	1955	Donisthorpe, G.S.	VG+		$15.00
BERKLEY	103	S.S. San Pedro	1955	Cozzens, J.G.	VGF+		$7.00
BERKLEY	107	Border Raider	1955	Hopson, W.	VG		$5.00
BERKLEY	108	They Shoot Horses, Don't They?	1955	McCoy, H.	F		$22.00 A
BERKLEY	111	Torture Garden	1955	Mirbeau, O.	F		$25.00 A
BERKLEY	111	Torture Garden	1955	Mirbeau, O.	AF		$20.00 A
BERKLEY	315	Eleven Blue Men	1955	Roueche, B.	AF		$7.00
BERKLEY	319	Portrait Of A Woman	1955	Preston, J.H.	VG+		$7.00
BERKLEY	327	We Too Are Drifting	1955	Wilhelm, G.	AF		$40.00 A
BERKLEY	328	I Should Have Stayed Home	1955	McCoy, H.	AF		$52.00 A
BERKLEY	328	I Should Have Stayed Home	1955	McCoy, H.	F		$48.00 A
BERKLEY	328	I Should Have Stayed Home	1955	McCoy, H.	VG+		$10.00
BERKLEY	329	Who's In Charge Here?	1955	Price, G.	VG+		$5.00
BERKLEY	334	Manhunt	1955	Stern, P.	VGF		$5.00
BERKLEY	337	Only A Woman	1955	Carco, F.	VGF		$10.00 A
BERKLEY	337	Only A Woman	1955	Carco, F.	VG+		$8.00
BERKLEY	351	The Magician	1956	Simenon, G.	VG+		$5.00
BERKLEY	358	Bailey's Daughters	1956	De Meyer, J.	AF		$17.00 A
BERKLEY	359	Loveliest Of Friends	1956	Donisthorpe, G.S.	VGF-		$10.00
BERKLEY	361	Seven Men From Now	1956	Kennedy, B.	VG	MTI	$8.00
BERKLEY	362	Pattern For Panic	1956	Prather, R.S.	VG+		$7.00
BERKLEY	377	Twist Of The Knife	1957	Canning, V.	VG+		$8.00
BERKLEY	380	The Time Machine	1957	Wells, H.G.	VGF		$7.00
BERKLEY	386	Phyllis	1959	Key, T.	VGF		$5.00
BERKLEY	G 1	The Lost Weekend	1955	Jackson, C.	VGF+		$14.00
BERKLEY	G 2	Sexual Conduct Of The Teen-Ager	1955	Lawton, S.U.	VG		$7.00
BERKLEY	G 3	Possible Worlds Of Science Fiction	1955	Conklin, G.	VG-		$4.00
BERKLEY	G 5	Salambo	1955	Flaubert, G.	F		$25.00 A
BERKLEY	G 5	Salambo	1955	Flaubert, G.	AF		$20.00
BERKLEY	G 6	If He Hollers Let Him Go	1955	Himes, C.B.	AF		$41.00 A
BERKLEY	G 6	If He Hollers Let Him Go	1955	Himes, C.B.	F		$34.00 A
BERKLEY	G 6	If He Hollers Let Him Go	1955	Himes, C.B.	VG+		$12.00
BERKLEY	G 10	Lone Star Preacher	1955	Thomason, J.W.	VG+		$6.00
BERKLEY	G 12	Crazy Mixed-Up Kids	1955	Anthology	VGF		$15.00
BERKLEY	G 12	Crazy Mixed-Up Kids	1955	Anthology	VG+		$10.00
BERKLEY	G 13	The Sign Of Eros	1955	Bodin, P.	VGF		$7.00
BERKLEY	G 13	The Sign Of Eros	1955	Bodin, P.	VG+		$6.00
BERKLEY	G 14	Messalina	1955	Crockett, V.	AF		$13.00 A
BERKLEY	G 14	Messalina	1955	Crockett, V.	VG+		$8.00
BERKLEY	G 15	A Lust To Live	1956	Garside, E.B.	VGF		$6.00
BERKLEY	G 16	Jungle Fury	1956	White, R.	VGF		$13.00 A

Berkley G48 VGF $20

Berkley G72 AF $18

Berkley G74 AF $22

PUBLISHER	PUB. #	TITLE	DATE	AUTHOR	COND.	TYPE	PRICE
BERKLEY	BG 18	Modern Writing	1956	Anthology	VGF		$8.00
BERKLEY	G 20	Paris My Love	1956	Calet, H.	AF		$7.00 A
BERKLEY	G 20	Paris My Love	1956	Calet, H.	VG+		$7.00
BERKLEY	G 22	Renee	1956	Lenormand, H.R.	VG+		$8.00
BERKLEY	G 22	Renee	1956	Lenormand, H.R.	VGF		$7.00
BERKLEY	G 24	Adios O'Shaughnessy	1956	Tallman, R.	VGF		$12.00
BERKLEY	G 26	Love On The Rocks	1956	Chaze, E.	F		$25.00
BERKLEY	G 27	The Blaze Of Noon	1956	Heppenstall, R.	VG+		$6.00
BERKLEY	G 28	Young Man Of Paris	1956	Calet, H.	VGF		$9.00
BERKLEY	G 31	Science Fiction Omnibus	1956	Anthology	VG+		$5.00
BERKLEY	G 33	Perversity	1956	Carco, F.	AF		$20.00 A
BERKLEY	G 33	Perversity	1956	Carco, F.	VG+		$10.00
BERKLEY	G 33	Perversity	1956	Carco, F.	G+		$6.00
BERKLEY	BG 35	Night Rider	1956	Warren, R.P.	VG+		$6.00
BERKLEY	G 37	Virgie, Goodbye	1956	Rothman, N.	VGF		$7.00
BERKLEY	G 39	Torture Garden	1956	Mirbeau, O.	VG+		$12.00 A
BERKLEY	G 43	The Captain's Doll	1957	Lawrence, D.H.	VG+		$7.00
BERKLEY	G 44	My Sister, My Beloved	1957	Mark, E.	AF		$18.00 A
BERKLEY	G 46	Aphrodite	1957	Louys, P.	VGF+		$39.00 A
BERKLEY	G 48	The Eight Of Swords	1957	Carr, J.D.	VGF		$20.00 A
BERKLEY	G 49	A Dime A Throw	1957	Weidman, J.	VGF		$10.00
BERKLEY	G 50	Diana	1957	Fredericks, D.	VG		$5.00
BERKLEY	G 55	Love In A Hot Climate	1957	Schiddel, E.	AF		$17.00 A
BERKLEY	G 56	Jungle Fury	1957	White, R.	VGF-		$10.00
BERKLEY	G 58	How Cheap Can You Get?	1957	Abzug, M.	VGF		$10.00
BERKLEY	G 58	How Cheap Can You Get?	1957	Abzug, M.	VG+		$8.00
BERKLEY	G 60	TCOT Constant Suicides	1957	Carr, J.D.	VG		$5.00
BERKLEY	G 62	The Most Dangerous Game	1957	Anthology	VG		$8.00
BERKLEY	BG 66	Time Must Have A Stop	1957	Huxley, A.	VG		$5.00
BERKLEY	G 68	This Is My Body	1957	Anthology	AF		$15.00
BERKLEY	G 72	Poison In Jest	1957	Carr, J.D.	AF		$18.00 A
BERKLEY	BG 73	Salambo	1957	Flaubert, G.	VG		$6.00 A
BERKLEY	G 74	Olivia	1957	Olivia	AF		$22.00 A
BERKLEY	G 77	Beachheads In Space	1957	Anthology	VGF		$5.00
BERKLEY	G 78	Harlem Is My Heaven	1957	Gordon, I.	AF		$23.00 A
BERKLEY	G 78	Harlem Is My Heaven	1957	Gordon, I.	VGF		$15.00
BERKLEY	G 78	Harlem Is My Heaven	1957	Gordon, I.	VG		$9.00
BERKLEY	G 80	The Blind Barber	1957	Carr, J.D.	AF		$17.00 A
BERKLEY	G 81	Depravity	1957	Carco, F.	VG+		$14.00
BERKLEY	G 83	Martha Crane	1957	Gorham, C.	VGF		$11.00 A
BERKLEY	G 91	The Four False Weapons	1957	Carr, J.D.	AF		$24.00 A
BERKLEY	G 91	The Four False Weapons	1957	Carr, J.D.	VGF		$13.00
BERKLEY	G 91	The Four False Weapons	1957	Carr, J.D.	VG		$6.00
BERKLEY	G 92	Legend Of The Lost	1957	Golightly, B.	VG	MTI	$8.00
BERKLEY	G 93	All Women's Flesh	1957	Bodin, P.	VGF		$7.00

Berkley G78 AF $23

Berkley G83 VGF $11

Berkley G111 AF- $18

PUBLISHER	PUB. #	TITLE	DATE	AUTHOR	COND.	TYPE	PRICE
BERKLEY	G 93	All Women's Flesh	1957	Bodin, P.	VG+		$6.00
BERKLEY	BG 96	Rommel, The Desert Fox	1958	Young, D.	F		$4.00
BERKLEY	G 97	Nude Croquet	1958	Anthology	VG+		$7.00 A
BERKLEY	G 97	Nude Croquet	1958	Anthology	VG-		$6.00
BERKLEY	BG 100	Finnley Wren	1958	Wylie, P.	VG+		$6.00
BERKLEY	G 101	Death Watch	1958	Carr, J.D.	AF		$20.00 A
BERKLEY	BG 102	Stalingrad	1958	Pilevier, T.	VGF		$7.00
BERKLEY	G 104	Beyond Time And Space	1958	Anthology	AF		$8.00 A
BERKLEY	G 107	Escape From Colditz	1958	Reid, P.R.	AF	MTI	$4.00
BERKLEY	G 111	The Strange Path	1958	Wilhelm, G.	AF-		$18.00 A
BERKLEY	G 114	The End Of The Track	1958	Garve, A.	VGF		$7.00
BERKLEY	G 119	The Enormous Radio	1958	Cheever, J.	VG		$6.00
BERKLEY	G 125	So It Doesn't Whistle	1958	Smith, R.P.	VGF		$20.00 A
BERKLEY	G 125	So It Doesn't Whistle	1958	Smith, R.P.	VG+		$8.00
BERKLEY	G 126	Naomi Martin	1958	Crane, C.	AF-		$17.00 A
BERKLEY	BG 128	Sex In Our Changing World	1958	McPartland, J.	VGF+		$20.00 A
BERKLEY	G 129	Hag's Nook	1958	Carr, J.D.	VG-		$6.00
BERKLEY	G 130	Thieves Like Us	1958	Anderson, E.	VG-		$5.00
BERKLEY	G 132	Tormented	1958	Weston, C.	AF-		$14.00
BERKLEY	G 133	Tropic Moon	1958	Simenon, G.	AF		$13.00 A
BERKLEY	G 133	Tropic Moon	1958	Simenon, G.	AF		$8.00 A
BERKLEY	G 134	I Should Have Stayed Home	1958	McCoy, H.	AF		$17.00 A
BERKLEY	BG 135	The German Generals Talk	1958	Hart, B.H.L.	F		$4.00
BERKLEY	G 137	The 31st Of February	1958	Symons, J.	VGF		$14.00
BERKLEY	G 137	The 31st Of February	1958	Symons, J.	VGF		$11.00 A
BERKLEY	G 140	Infamy	1958	Carco, F.	VG+		$10.00 A
BERKLEY	G 141	My Sister, My Beloved	1958	Mark, E.	VG		$5.00
BERKLEY	G 146	The Man Within	1958	Greene, G.	AF		$10.00
BERKLEY	G 146	The Man Within	1958	Greene, G.	F		$9.00 A
BERKLEY	BG 149	Ah King	1958	Maugham, W.S.	AF		$22.00 A
BERKLEY	G 155	Perversity	1958	Carco, F.	VGF		$14.00
BERKLEY	G 153	The Last Of Mr. Norris	1958	Isherwood, C.	AF		$27.00 A
BERKLEY	G 156	Laughter In The Dark	1958	Nabokov, V.	VG+		$8.00
BERKLEY	G 159	Marcia - Private Secretary	1958	Macdonald, Z.K.	AF		$6.00
BERKLEY	G 162	The Evil That Men Do	1958	Martin, G.V.	AF		$13.00
BERKLEY	G 167	Adam And Evil	1958	Carlova, J.	AF-		$11.00 A
BERKLEY	G 168	Renee	1958	Lenormand, H.R.	AF		$12.00
BERKLEY	G 170	Devil's Holiday	1958	Malloy, F.	VGF+		$22.00 A
BERKLEY	G 171	Stag Stripper	1958	Hanley, J.	AF		$12.00 A
BERKLEY	G 172	Loveliest Of Friends	1958	Donisthorpe, G.S.	AF		$20.00 A
BERKLEY	BG 177	Pocket Battleship	1958	Krancke, T.	VG+		$5.00
BERKLEY	BG 178	The Hucksters	1958	Wakeman, F.	VGF		$7.00
BERKLEY	BG 178	The Hucksters	1958	Wakeman, F.	VG+		$7.00
BERKLEY	G 179	No Bed Of Her Own	1958	Schiller, C.	F		$13.00 A
BERKLEY	G 180	Boots And Saddles	1958	Bracco, E.J.	VGF		$7.00

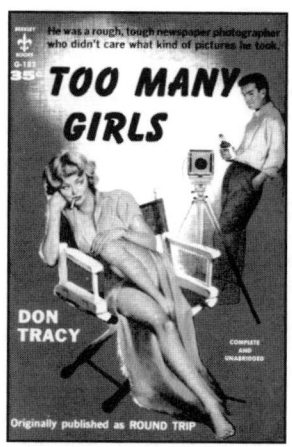

Berkley G182 VGF+ $20   Berkley G222 VGF $7   Berkley G228 VGF $16

PUBLISHER	PUB. #	TITLE	DATE	AUTHOR	COND.	TYPE	PRICE
BERKLEY	G 182	Too Many Girls	1958	Tracy, D.	VGF+		$20.00 A
BERKLEY	G 182	Too Many Girls	1958	Tracy, D.	VG		$7.00
BERKLEY	G 184	The Shameless Ones	1958	Quintavalle, U.	VGF		$10.00
BERKLEY	G 184	The Shameless Ones	1958	Quintavalle, U.	VGF		$7.00
BERKLEY	G 189	Time To Come	1958	Anthology	VGF		$7.00
BERKLEY	G 193	South Street	1958	Smith, W.G.	AF		$10.00
BERKLEY	G 195	Hot Money Girl	1958	Wayne, A.	VG+		$8.00
BERKLEY	BG 197	The Professional	1959	Heinz, W.C.	AF		$13.00 A
BERKLEY	G 199	Make Me An Offer	1959	Gorham, C.	VG		$7.00
BERKLEY	G 200	Sexual Conduct Of The Teen-Ager	1959	Lawton, S.U.	VGF-		$25.00 A
BERKLEY	G 203	Love Around The World	1959	Anthology	VGF		$10.00
BERKLEY	G 203	Love Around The World	1959	Anthology	VG+		$7.00
BERKLEY	G 205	Forbidden Pleasures	1959	Devlin, B.	VGF		$15.00
BERKLEY	G 205	Forbidden Pleasures	1959	Devlin, B.	VG		$7.00
BERKLEY	G 206	The Sinning Lens	1956	Tryon, M.	VG		$6.00
BERKLEY	G 208	Mystery In Blue	1958	Mallette, G.E.	VG		$5.00
BERKLEY	BG 213	First Person Singular	1959	Maugham, W.S.	VGF+		$37.00 A
BERKLEY	G 214	The Bowstring Murders	1959	Dickson, C.*	VG+		$14.00 A
BERKLEY	G 216	The Sign Of Eros	1959	Bodin, P.	VG		$5.00
BERKLEY	G 219	Sandy	1959	Thompson, J.B.	VG+		$10.00 A
BERKLEY	G 220	The Fire That Burns	1959	Tryon, M.	VGF		$14.00
BERKLEY	G 222	The Big Book Of Horse Stories	1959	Anthology	VGF		$7.00
BERKLEY	G 224	I Flew For The Fuhrer	1959	Knoke, H.	AF		$7.00
BERKLEY	G 225	What D'ya Know For Sure?	1959	Zinberg, L.	AF-		$24.00 A
BERKLEY	G 227	Blaze	1959	Stone, S.	VG+		$15.00 A
BERKLEY	G 228	Dreamboat	1959	Lucas, R.	VGF		$16.00 A
BERKLEY	G 229	Easy Living	1959	Ford, T.	VG+		$7.00 A
BERKLEY	G 232	Deadlier Than The Male	1959	Gunn, J.	AF		$14.00
BERKLEY	G 233	Imagination Unlimited	1959	Anthology	AF		$7.00
BERKLEY	G 234	Guns Of Horse Prarie	1959	Nye, N.C.	F		$7.00
BERKLEY	G 236	A Woman Called Desire	1959	Marshe, R.	VG+		$10.00
BERKLEY	G 240	House Of Fury	1959	Swados, F.	G+		$5.00
BERKLEY	G 241	Pattern For Panic	1959	Prather, R.S.	VG+		$5.00
BERKLEY	G 244	Vice Girl	1959	Albert, S.	F		$24.00 A
BERKLEY	G 244	Vice Girl	1959	Albert, S.	VGF		$17.00 A
BERKLEY	G 248	Three Of A Kind	1959	Wolfson, P.J.	F		$22.00
BERKLEY	G 252	Immoral Woman	1959	Hanley, J.	AF		$12.00
BERKLEY	G 256	The Incredible Truth	1959	Massie, C.	VG		$7.00
BERKLEY	G 257	Woman Of The Night	1959	Carse, R.	AF		$12.00 A
BERKLEY	BG 263	The Knights Of Bushido	1959	Russell, L.	VGF		$4.00
BERKLEY	G 272	The Edge Of Tomorrow	1959	Dooley, T.	AF		$6.00
BERKLEY	G 300	The Mystery Of The Stolen Plans	1960	Coles, M.	VG+		$6.00
BERKLEY	G 461	Men Into Space	1960	Leinster, M.	VG		$3.00
BERKLEY	G 467	Heroes Of The Army	1960	Jacobs, B.	VGF		$7.00
BERKLEY	G 474	Frenzy	1960	Carco, F.	AF		$7.00

Berkley Y658 F $67   Berkley Y705 VGF $90   Berkley X1372 AF $20   Berkley X2058 F $23

PUBLISHER	PUB. #	TITLE	DATE	AUTHOR	COND.	TYPE	PRICE
BERKLEY	G 480	I Can Lick Seven	1960	Richards, R.	VGF		$5.00
BERKLEY	G 497	Here's Beaver	1961	Cleary, B.	VG	TVTI	$4.00
BERKLEY	G 502	Kill Me In Yoshiwara	1961	Norman, E.	VG-		$5.00
BERKLEY	G 507	Titan's Daughter	1961	Blish, J.	AF		$10.00
BERKLEY	G 507	Titan's Daughter	1961	Blish, J.	AF		$10.00 A
BERKLEY	G 509	A Taste For Sin	1961	Brewer, G.	G		$6.00
BERKLEY	G 514	Gideon's Risk	1961	Marric, J.J.	AF		$5.00
BERKLEY	BG 517	The Road To Wigan Pier	1961	Orwell, G.	VG+		$7.00
BERKLEY	G 547	Hospital Zone	1961	Stolz, M.	AF		$6.00
BERKLEY	G 549	Creatures Of The Abyss	1961	Leinster, M.	AF		$6.00
BERKLEY	G 557	Beaver And Wally	1961	Cleary, B.	VG	TVTI	$7.00
BERKLEY	F 579	Paths Of Love	1961	Vercors	VGF		$7.00
BERKLEY	G 584	Outlaw Canyon	1961	Patten, L.B.	VGF		$7.00
BERKLEY	Y 603	Berkley Crossword Puzzles	1962	Luzzatto, J.	VG		$7.00
BERKLEY	X 614	Assault!	1962	Hanrahan, G.Z.	VGF		$5.00
BERKLEY	Y 615	Voyage To Eros	1962	Bollene, A.D.	VG+		$4.00
BERKLEY	G 618	Trouble Shooter	1962	MacDonald, W.C.	AF		$7.00
BERKLEY	F 621	Burn Witch Burn (Conjure Wife)	1962	Leiber, F.	AF	MTI	$30.00
BERKLEY	F 621	Burn Witch Burn (Conjure Wife)	1962	Leiber, F.	AF	MTI	$24.00
BERKLEY	Y 632	Forbid Me Not	1962	Fuller, B.	VGF		$7.00
BERKLEY	Y 641	Hell On Wheels	1962	Butterworth, W.E.	VGF		$8.00
BERKLEY	Y 650	Venus In Mink	1962	Massart, P.	VGF		$5.00
BERKLEY	Y 658	One For The Money	1962	Chaze, E.	F		$67.00 A
BERKLEY	Y 658	One For The Money	1962	Chaze, E.	G+		$8.00
BERKLEY	Y 661	Surgical Nurse	1962	Ives, R.	VGF		$5.00
BERKLEY	F 666	Ghosts And Things	1962	Anthology	VG		$6.00
BERKLEY	G 681	Classroom Capers	1962	Knowlton, B.	AF		$8.00
BERKLEY	Y 698	The Girl In The Black Bikini	1962	Butterworth, W.E.	VGF		$6.00
BERKLEY	Y 699	Visiting Nurse	1962	Brennan, A.	AF		$5.00
BERKLEY	Y 705	Have Nude, Will Travel	1962	Allison, C.	VGF		$90.00 A
BERKLEY	G 868	Tall Tales	1963	Jaffee, A.	VGF+		$7.00
BERKLEY	F 1000	Gently In The Sun	1964	Hunter, A.	F		$5.00
BERKLEY	F 1001	Gently Floating	1964	Hunter, A.	F		$5.00
BERKLEY	F 1021	Gently Go Man	1964	Hunter, A.	F		$5.00
BERKLEY	F 1040	Gently To The Summit	1965	Hunter, A.	VGF+		$5.00
BERKLEY	F 1261	The Crazy Kill	1966	Himes, C.	G+		$5.00
BERKLEY	F 1270	The Big Gold Dream	1966	Himes, C.	VG		$7.00
BERKLEY	N 1277	LSD: Consciousness Drug	1966	Anthology	VG+		$8.00
BERKLEY	H 1277	LSD: Consciousness Drug	1966	Anthology	VG		$6.00
BERKLEY	F 1293	Change Of Command	1966	Whitman, S.E.	VGF		$6.00
BERKLEY	X 1372	Counter-Clock World	1967	Dick, P.K.	AF		$20.00 A
BERKLEY	X 1372	Counter-Clock World	1967	Dick, P.K.	VGF		$17.00
BERKLEY	X 1380	The Crystal World	1967	Ballard, J.G.	AF		$5.00
BERKLEY	F 1410	The Floating Game (Avengers #1)	1967	Garforth, J.	VGF	TVTI	$7.00
BERKLEY	F 1411	The Laugh Was On Lazarus (Av.#2)	1967	Garforth, J.	AF-	TVTI	$7.00
BERKLEY	S 1625	The Pussycat Transplant	1968	Mark, T.	VG+		$5.00
BERKLEY	X 1637	The Avengers #8	1968	Daniels, N.	VGF	TVTI	$7.00
BERKLEY	S 1653	The Beatles - The Real Story	1968	Fast, J.	AF		$7.00

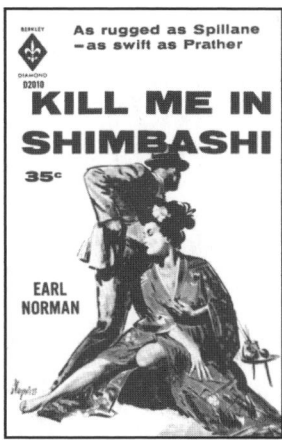

| Berkley D2010 VG+ $10 | Berkley D2020 AF $25 | Best Detective Selection 6 G+ $7 |

PUBLISHER	PUB. #	TITLE	DATE	AUTHOR	COND.	TYPE	PRICE
BERKLEY	S 1653	The Beatles - The Real Story	1968	Fast, J.	VGF		$7.00
BERKLEY	N 1704	Dangerous Visions #2	1969	Anthology	AF-		$12.00
BERKLEY	X 1705	Galactic Pot Healer	1969	Dick, P.K.	VGF		$10.00 A
BERKLEY	X 1713	Dark Ways To Death	1968	Saxon, P.	AF		$6.00
BERKLEY	X 1746	Purple Aces (G-8 #2)	1970	Hogan, R.J.	AF		$20.00
BERKLEY	X 1746	Purple Aces (G-8 #2)	1970	Hogan, R.J.	VG		$10.00 A
BERKLEY	S 1754	Back Home At O.R.G.Y. (3rd)	1969	Mark, T.	VGF		$6.00
BERKLEY	X 1782	Wings Of The Black Death	1969	Stockbridge, G.	VG+		$7.00
BERKLEY	X 1795	City Of Flaming Shadows	1970	Stockbridge, G.	VG+		$7.00
BERKLEY	Z 1818	I Am Curious (Thirty)	1970	Emerson, J.*	F		$27.00 A
BERKLEY	N 1923	20 Years Of Fantasy & Sci. Fi.	1970	Anthology	VGF		$8.00
BERKLEY	X 2004	Vultures Of The White Death	1971	Hogan, R.J.	F		$17.00 A
BERKLEY	X 2023	Flight From The Grave	1971	Hogan, R.J.	F		$10.00 A
BERKLEY	X 2023	Flight From The Grave	1971	Hogan, R.J.	VG		$7.00
BERKLEY	S 2041	The Omega Man (2nd)	1971	Matheson, R.	VGF+	MTI	$7.00
BERKLEY	X 2058	The Mark Of The Vulture	1971	Hogan, R.J.	F		$23.00 A
BERKLEY	S 2160	Steve McQueen	1972	Nolan, W.	VG		$5.00
BERKLEY	N 2239	Come Back Charleston Blue	1972	Himes, C.	VGF	MTI	$5.00
BERKLEY	2355	Slay-Ground	1973	Stark, R.*	VGF		$9.00
BERKLEY	2412	A Choice Of Gods	1973	Simak, C.D.	VGF		$6.00
BERKLEY	2457	Killtown	1973	Stark, R.*	VGF		$9.00
BERKLEY	2502	Deadly Edge	1974	Stark, R.*	VGF		$9.00
BERKLEY	2511	Kiai! (Jason Striker #1)	1974	Anthony, P.	VGF+		$6.00
BERKLEY	2543	The Man In The High Castle	1974	Dick, P.K.	VGF		$3.00
BERKLEY	2569	Galactic Pot-Healer	1974	Dick, P.K.	VGF		$6.00
BERKLEY	2623	Mistress Of Death (J. Striker #2)	1974	Anthony, P.	VGF		$6.00
BERKLEY	2656	Paradox Lost	1974	Brown, F.	AF		$7.00
BERKLEY	N 2716	Bamboo Bloodbath (J. Striker #3)	1974	Anthony, P.	VGF+		$6.00
BERKLEY	N 2821	Ninja's Revenge	1975	Anthony, P.	VGF-		$6.00
BERKLEY	N 2923	Nightmare Journey	1975	Koontz, D.R.	VGF		$33.00 A
BERKLEY	N 2923	Nightmare Journey	1975	Koontz, D.R.	VG		$8.00
BERKLEY	N 2923	Nightmare Journey	1975	Koontz, D.R.	G		$5.00
BERKLEY	Z 3082	Switch	1976	Jahn, M.	VGF	TVTI	$6.00
BERKLEY	4139	Battlestar Gallactica	1979		VGF	MTI	$6.00
BERKLEY	4209	Shock III	1979	Matheson, R.	VG+		$5.00
BERKLEY	425 6276	The Cosmic Puppets	1983	Dick, P.K.	AF		$7.00
BERKLEY	No#	The Spider #2 (free promo. ed.)	1969	Scott, R.T.M.	VGF		$6.00
BERKLEY DIAMOND	D 2009	Rifle Law	1959	Floren, L.	VG+		$5.00
BERKLEY DIAMOND	D 2010	Kill Me In Shimbashi	1959	Norman, E.	VG+		$10.00
BERKLEY DIAMOND	D 2010	Kill Me In Shimbashi	1959	Norman, E.	VG		$6.00
BERKLEY DIAMOND	D 2011	Vengeance Trail	1959	Martin, C.	VGF		$6.00
BERKLEY DIAMOND	D 2017	Guns Along The Pecos	1959	Floren, L.	VG+		$7.00
BERKLEY DIAMOND	D 2019	Married To Murder	1959	Whittington, H.	VG+		$20.00
BERKLEY DIAMOND	D 2020	Naked Fury	1959	Keene, D.	AF		$25.00
BERKLEY DIAMOND	D 2022	Martha Crane	1960	Gorham, C.	VG		$4.00

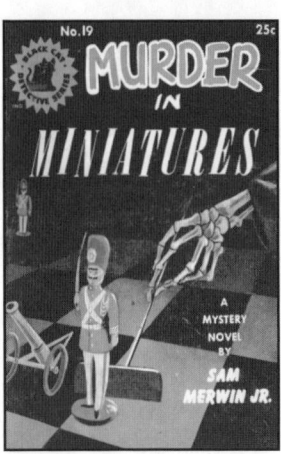

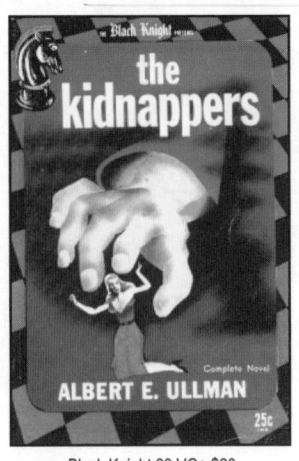

Black Cat Detective 19 VGF $18   Black Knight 28 VG+ $20   Bleak House 17 VGF+ $17

PUBLISHER	PUB. #	TITLE	DATE	AUTHOR	COND.	TYPE	PRICE
BERKLEY DIAMOND	D 2031	Street Of The Lost	1960	Carco, F.	VGF		$20.00 A
BERKLEY DIAMOND	D 2032	The Naked Hunter	1960	Woolfolk, W.	VGF		$8.00 A
BERKLEY DIAMOND	D 2034	Nude Croquet	1960	Anthology	VG		$14.00
BERKLEY DIAMOND	D 2036	Hell Cop	1960	Wolfson, P.J.	VG+		$11.00 A
BERKLEY DIAMOND	D 2037	You'll Get Yours	1960	Ard, W.	VG		$9.00
BEST DETECTIVE SELECTION	6	Wail For The Corpse	1943	Treat, L.	G+	Digest	$7.00
BEST DETECTIVE SELECTION	8	Modeled In Murder	1943	Long, M.	VG	Digest	$7.00
BEST DETECTIVE SELECTION	10	Murder R.F.D.	1943	Petersen, H.	VG+	Digest	$12.00
BEST SCIENCE FICTION	2	The Best Science Fiction	1964	Anthology	VG	Digest	$18.00 A
BEST WESTERN	2 2	Best Western 6/51	1951	Anthology	G-	Digest	$5.00
BESTSELLER MYSTERY	No# 3	More Adventures Of E. Queen	1940	Queen, E.	VG+	Digest	$8.00
BESTSELLER MYSTERY	B 6	24 Hours	1940	Bromfield, L.	VG+	Digest	$5.00
BESTSELLER MYSTERY	B 106	The Bleeding Scissors	1949	Fischer, B.	VG+	Digest	$7.00
BESTSELLER MYSTERY	B 137	He Didn't Mind Danger	1951	Gilbert, M.	VG	Digest	$7.00
BESTSELLER MYSTERY	B 173	Corpse With Too Many Friends	1954	Stone, H.	AF	Digest	$7.00
BESTSELLER MYSTERY	B 198	Black Alibi	1956	Woolrich, C.	VGF+	Digest	$38.00 A
BESTSELLER MYSTERY	B 198	Black Alibi	1956	Woolrich, C.	VG	Digest	$27.00 A
BESTSELLER MYSTERY	B 204	I Wake Up Screaming	1957	Fisher, S.	G+	Digest	$5.00
BESTSELLER MYST. MAG.	1 1	Bestseller Mystery Mag. 7/58	1958	Anthology	AF	Digest	$15.00 A
BESTSELLER MYST. MAG.	1 3	Bestseller Mystery Mag. 11/58	1958	Anthology	AF	Digest	$10.00 A
BESTSELLER MYST. MAG.	1 4	Bestseller Mystery Mag. 1/59	1959	Anthology	AF	Digest	$13.00 A
BESTSELLER MYST. MAG.	1 5	Bestseller Mystery Mag. 3/59	1959	Anthology	VG	Digest	$7.00
BEYOND FICTION	9	Beyond Fiction Vol 2-#3	1954	Anthology	F	Digest	$8.00
THE BIG STORY	1 1	The Big Story - 10/51	1951	Anthology	VG+	Digest	$9.00
THE BIG STORY	1 2	The Big Story - 11/51	1951	Anthology	VGF	Digest	$14.00
THE BIG STORY	1 3	The Big Story - 12/51	1951	Anthology	VGF	Digest	$19.00 A
BIZARRE!	1 1	Bizarre! Mystery Mag. 10/65	1965	Anthology	AF	Digest	$17.00 A
BIZARRE!	1 1	Bizarre! Mystery Mag. 10/65	1965	Anthology	AF	Digest	$11.00 A
BLACK CAT DETECTIVE	6	Death Thumbs A Ride	1943	Lilly, J.	VGF	Digest	$18.00 A
BLACK CAT DETECTIVE	7	The Beast Must Die	1943	Blake, N.	VGF	Digest	$7.00
BLACK CAT DETECTIVE	8	The Body In The Road	1944	Dalton, M.	VG-	Digest	$6.00
BLACK CAT DETECTIVE	14	Dark Power	1945	Holding, E.S.	G+	Digest	$6.00
BLACK CAT DETECTIVE	15	Headlong For Murder	1945	Mace, M.	VGF	Digest	$16.00 A
BLACK CAT DETECTIVE	15	Headlong For Murder	1945	Mace, M.	VG+	Digest	$8.00
BLACK CAT DETECTIVE	19	Murder In Miniatures	1945	Merwin, S.	VGF	Digest	$18.00 A
BLACK CAT DETECTIVE	26	Murder In Haste	1947	Fenwick, E.P.	G	Digest	$5.00
BLACK CAT WESTERN	31	Blue River Riders	1948	Joscelyn, A.	VG+	Digest	$7.00
BLACK CAT WESTERN	31	Blue River Riders	1948	Joscelyn, A.	VG	Digest	$6.00
BLACK CAT WESTERN	36	Trail Trouble	1949	Ermine, W.	VG-	Digest	$5.00
BLACK CAT WESTERN	46	Six Gun Pay-Off	n/d	Montana, Z.	VG+	Digest	$6.00
BLACK KNIGHT	16	Last Year's Snow	1946	Tracy, D.	VG+	Digest	$14.00
BLACK KNIGHT	27	The Psychiatric Murders	1947	Michel, M.S.	VGF		$25.00
BLACK KNIGHT	27	The Psychiatric Murders	1947	Michel, M.S.	VG+		$7.00 A
BLACK KNIGHT	28	The Kidnappers	1947	Ullman, A.E.	VG+		$20.00 A
BLACK KNIGHT	29	Green For A Grave	1947	Stokes, M.L.	VG+		$22.00 A

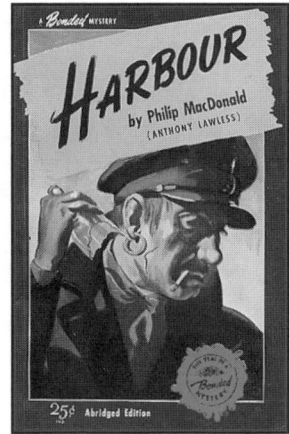

Bobley Books 4 VGF $22   Bonded No# VG+ $38   Bonded Mystery 13 VG $12

PUBLISHER	PUB. #	TITLE	DATE	AUTHOR	COND.	TYPE	PRICE
BLACK LIZARD	No#	A Swell Looking Babe	1986	Thompson, J.	VGF		$10.00
BLACK LIZARD	No#	Carny Kill	1986	Alter, R.E.	VGF		$5.00
BLACK LIZARD	No#	Cockfighter	1987	Willeford, C.	AF		$7.00
BLACK LIZARD	No#	His Name Was Death	1987	Brown, F.	VG+		$5.00
BLACK LIZARD	No#	Jealous Woman	1989	Cain, J.M.	F		$6.00
BLACK LIZARD	No#	Nightfall	1987	Goodis, D.	F		$7.00
BLACK LIZARD	No#	Pick-Up	1987	Willeford, C.	AF		$14.00
BLACK LIZARD	No#	Pop. 1280	1984	Thompson, J.	F		$16.00
BLACK LIZARD	No#	Pop. 1280	1984	Thompson, J.	VG+		$5.00
BLACK LIZARD	No#	Second Crime Anthology	1988	Anthology	VGF		$30.00
BLACK LIZARD	No#	Seven Slayers	1987	Cain, P.	VGF		$5.00
BLACK LIZARD	No#	Sinful Woman	1989	Cain, J.M.	F		$6.00
BLACK LIZARD	No#	The Criminal	1986	Thompson, J.	AF		$14.00
BLACK LIZARD	No#	The Truth Of The Matter	1988	Lutz, J.	F		$6.00
BLEAK HOUSE	14	TCOT Blood-Stained Dime	1947	Barton, M.	VGF		$38.00 A
BLEAK HOUSE	15	TCOT Missing Corpse	1947	Langer, J.	VGF+		$34.00 A
BLEAK HOUSE	15	TCOT Missing Corpse	1947	Langer, J.	VG		$10.00
BLEAK HOUSE	17	The Skyscraper Murder	1948	Spewack, S.	VGF+		$17.00 A
BLEAK HOUSE	22	White For A Shroud	1948	Cameron, D.	G		$7.00
BLUE MURDER	No#	Texas By The Tail	1990	Thompson, J.	F		$7.00
BLUE MURDER	No#	The Burglar	1988	Goodis, D.	F	MTI	$10.00 A
BLUE SEAL	2	Old Hell (dust jkt.)	1937	Gowen, E.	VG-		$7.00
BOARDMAN	44	Rumour Hath It	1947	Hale, C.	VG	Digest	$7.00
BOARDMAN	140	No Place Like Earth	1954	Anthology	VG		$26.00 A
BOBLEY BOOKS	B 4	Best Read Short Stories	1946	Anthology	VGF		$22.00
BONDED	No#	Lady On A Train	1945	Charteris, L.	VG+	MTI	$38.00 A
BONDED	2	Featuring The Saint	1945	Charteris, L.	VG+	Digest	$22.00 A
BONDED	4	The Saint's Choice - Vol.1	1945	Anthology	VGF	Digest	$20.00 A
BONDED	7	Paging The Saint	1945	Charteris, L.	G	Digest	$7.00
BONDED MYSTERY	4	Murder Strikes Thrice	1946	Booth, C.G.	VG+	Digest	$10.00 A
BONDED MYSTERY	5	I'll Eat You Last	1946	Branson, H.C.	VG		$6.00 A
BONDED MYSTERY	7	Death Blew Out The Match	1946	Knight, K.M.	VG		$5.00 A
BONDED MYSTERY	13	Harbour	1947	MacDonald, P.	VG		$12.00 A
BOOK CO. OF AMERICA	4	Kennedy And Big Business	1964	Gershenson, A.H.	VG		$5.00
BOOK CO. OF AMERICA	8	Whodunit? Hollywood Style	1965	Nuetzel, C.	VG		$8.00
BOOK CO. OF AMERICA	8	Whodunit? Hollywood Style	1965	Nuetzel, C.	VG+		$7.00
BOOK CO. OF AMERICA	9	Over My Dead Body	1965	Mayfair, F.	F		$7.00
BOOK CO. OF AMERICA	12	Telephone A-Go-Go	1965	Olivetti, W.	VG-		$5.00
BOOK CO. OF AMERICA	13	Club Tycoon	1965	Mendelsohn, F.	VG+		$6.00
BOOK CO. OF AMERICA	14	Planets For Sale	1965	Van Vogt, A.E.	VG		$6.00
BOOK CO. OF AMERICA	15	If This Goes On	1965	Nuetzel, C.	VGF		$7.00
BOOK CO. OF AMERICA	15	If This Goes On	1965	Nuetzel, C.	VG+		$7.00
BOOKS INC.	63	Kidnapped	n/d	Stevenson, R.L.	VG	Digest	$6.00
BOOKS INC.	64	Toby Tyler	n/d	Otis, J.	VGF	Digest	$7.00
BOOKS INC.	77	The Prince And The Pauper	n/d	Twain, M.	VG+	Digest	$7.00

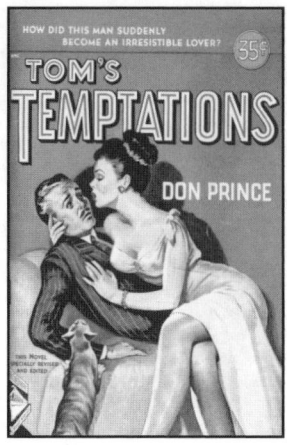

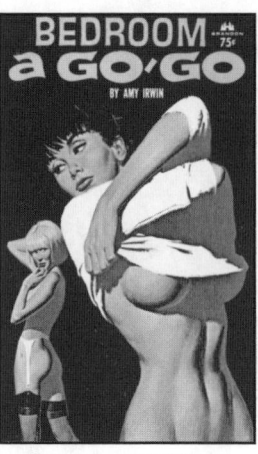

Broadway Novel 4 AF $67   Brandon House 732 VGF+ $24   Broadway Novel 8 VG+ $48

PUBLISHER	PUB. #	TITLE	DATE	AUTHOR	COND.	TYPE	PRICE
BOUDOIR	103	Girls Afire	1962	Hudson, J.*	VGF		$10.00
BOUDOIR	1005	Sexpot Senoritas	1962	Denton, J.	VGF		$8.00
BOUDOIR	1028	Hell's Wenches	1963	Norwood, V.G.C.	VG+		$7.00
BOUDOIR	1029	Headline Harlot	1963	Parrish, J.	VG		$7.00
BOYS' AND GIRLS' FICTION*		*See SAMUEL LOWE					
BRANDON HOUSE	609	Lesbian Sin Song	1963	Curson, S.	VGF		$13.00
BRANDON HOUSE	612	Passion Hill	1963	Curson, S.	VGF		$7.00
BRANDON HOUSE	615	Rawhide Killer	1963	Adams, G.D.	AF		$37.00 A
BRANDON HOUSE	617	L Is For Lesbian	1963	Ford, J.D.	VGF		$27.00 A
BRANDON HOUSE	619	Two Women In Love	1963	Curson, S.	VG+		$12.00
BRANDON HOUSE	703	Twisted Love	1963	Abel, E.	AF		$27.00 A
BRANDON HOUSE	706	Queer Beach	1964	Swenson, P.*	VGF+		$27.00 A
BRANDON HOUSE	707	The Girls At Wendy's	1964	Raymond, R.	VGF		$30.00 A
BRANDON HOUSE	710	The Three Way Apartment	1964	Swenson, P.*	AF		$23.00 A
BRANDON HOUSE	714	Mr. Sex	1964	Willard, B.	VGF		$14.00 A
BRANDON HOUSE	717	The Hard Sell Girls	1964	Britt, D.	F		$41.00 A
BRANDON HOUSE	718	Two Kinds Of Love	1966	Jay, V.	VGF		$30.00 A
BRANDON HOUSE	721	Candy	1965	Kenton, M.*	VG+		$7.00
BRANDON HOUSE	728	The Three Day Lover	1965	Marshall, S.	AF		$17.00 A
BRANDON HOUSE	729	Born To Be Made	1965	Jay, V.	F		$25.00
BRANDON HOUSE	732	Bedroom A Go-Go	1965	Irwin, A.	VGF+		$24.00 A
BRANDON HOUSE	732	Bedroom A Go-Go	1965	Irwin, A.	VG+		$10.00
BRANDON HOUSE	733	Executive Lesbian	1965	Curson, S.	AF		$48.00 A
BRANDON HOUSE	904	Suzy And Vera	1964	Swenson, P.*	VGF		$26.00 A
BRANDON HOUSE	907	The Lavender Girls	1964	O'Dair, S.	VGF		$20.00 A
BRANDON HOUSE	918	Sophisticated Sinner	1965	Trelos, T.	AF		$19.00 A
BRANDON HOUSE	921	Carnival Mistress	1965	O'Dair, S.	VG-		$5.00
BRANDON HOUSE	922	The 9 To 5 Mistresses (2nd)	1967	Stevens, G.	VG+		$14.00 A
BRANDON HOUSE	924	The Lavender House	1965	Weldon, R.	VGF		$84.00 A
BRANDON HOUSE	927	Amateur Night (2nd)	1966	Swenson, P.*	VG		$10.00
BRANDON HOUSE	928	The Bedroom Broker	1965	Stevens, G.	VG		$8.00
BRANDON HOUSE	930	A Man Called Sex	1966	Kanto, P.	VGF		$40.00 A
BRANDON HOUSE	945	Love Me Wild	1965	Weldon, R.	AF		$14.00 A
BRANDON HOUSE	945	Love Me Wild	1965	Weldon, R.	VGF		$12.00
BRANDON HOUSE	956	Bedroom Suburb	1966	Anthony, J.	VG+		$10.00
BRANDON HOUSE	956	Bedroom Suburb	1966	Anthony, J.	VGF		$9.00 A
BRANDON HOUSE	963	The Passion Thing	1966	Colson, F.	VGF+		$10.00
BRANDON HOUSE	971	So Violent My Love	1966	Hammond, C.	AF		$17.00 A
BRANDON HOUSE	972	The Pleasure Studio	1966	Newbury, W.	VG		$6.00
BRANDON HOUSE	1038	The Carnal Trap	1966	Owen, R.N.	VGF		$10.00
BRANDON HOUSE	1073	The Wilder Scene	1967	Wallace, W.	AF		$8.00
BRANDON HOUSE	1076	This Bed Is Warm	1967	Parks, C.	AF-		$8.00
BRANDON HOUSE	1081	Party Wife	1967	Weldon, R.	AF		$8.00
BRANDON HOUSE	1095	The Primal Urge	1967	Spatari, W.C.	VG+		$8.00
BRANDON HOUSE	1121	The Wayward Bride	1967	Genell, L.	G+		$5.00

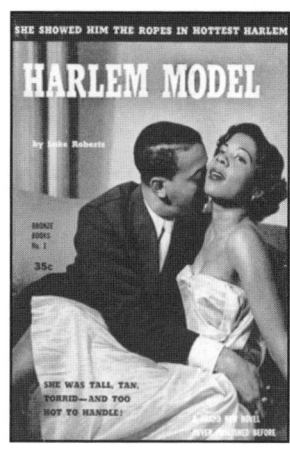

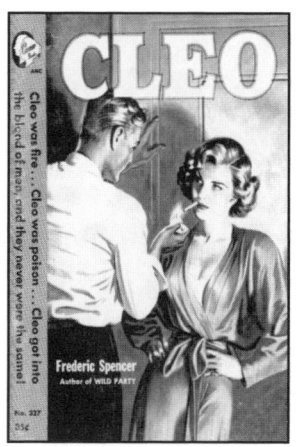

Bronze Books 1 G $22   Cameo 327 VG+ $23   Candid Love Novels 22 VG+ $15

PUBLISHER	PUB. #	TITLE	DATE	AUTHOR	COND.	TYPE	PRICE
BRANDON HOUSE	2046	Suddenly, Wonderfully Gay	1968	Kanto, P.	AF		$8.00
BRIDBOOKS	No#	Therefore I Killed Him	1968	Jobson, H.	VGF		$5.00
BROADWAY NOVEL	1	Infidelity	1949	Weigal, A.	VG+	Digest	$19.00 A
BROADWAY NOVEL	4	Tom's Temptation	1949	Prince, D.	AF	Digest	$67.00 A
BROADWAY NOVEL	8	Blonde Baby	1949	Collison, W.	VG+	Digest	$48.00 A
BROADWAY NOVEL	9	Dangerous Love	1950	Woodford, J.	AF	Digest	$73.00 A
BROADWAY NOVEL	9	Dangerous Love	1950	Woodford, J.	VG	Digest	$7.00
BRONZE BOOKS	1	Harlem Model	1952	Roberts, L.	G	Digest	$22.00 A
BULL'S-EYE	1	Silent Terror	1944	Jacobs, T.C.H.	VG	Digest	$12.00
CAMEO	310	Pleasure Bound	1952	Welles, K.	VG+	Digest	$25.00 A
CAMEO	313	Three-Time Sinner	1952	Bligh, N.	VG+	Digest	$36.00 A
CAMEO	314	The Big Tease	1952	Arnold, W.	VG+	Digest	$30.00 A
CAMEO	316	Soft Shoulders	1952	Bligh, N.	VG	Digest	$15.00
CAMEO	324	Young Nurse	1952	Erskine, S.	G	Digest	$8.00
CAMEO	326	At Ruby's Place	1952	Tucker, J.	AF	Digest	$22.00 A
CAMEO	327	Cleo	1953	Spencer, F.	VG+	Digest	$23.00 A
CAMEO	328	The Affairs Of A Country Girl	1953	Jordan, G.	VGF	Digest	$47.00 A
CAMEO	329	Backwoods Bride	1953	Reynolds, R.E.	VG+	Digest	$17.00 A
CAMEO	338	Shanty Boat Girl	1953	Welles, K.	VG+	Digest	$27.00 A
CAMEO	343	Slum Doctor	1954	Clay, M.	G	Digest	$6.00
CAMEO	355	Runaway Girl	1954	Arnold, W.	G-	Digest	$5.00
CAMEO	361	Shanty Boat Girl	1954	Westley, K.	G	Digest	$7.00
CAMEO	368	Blonde Hellcat	n/d	Marin, A.	G	Digest	$11.00
CANDID LOVE NOVELS	21	Wild Weekend	1949	Harvey, G.	VG	Digest	$12.00 A
CANDID LOVE NOVELS	22	Notorious Woman	1949	Harlow, J.	VG+	Digest	$15.00
CANDID READER	CA 901	The Sin Funnel	1967	Allison, C.	AF		$88.00 A
CANDID READER	CA 902	Wander-Lust	1967	Holliday, D.	AF		$23.00 A
CANDID READER	CA 908	Wanton Tripper	1967	Calvano, T.	VGF+		$55.00 A
CANDID READER	CA 908	Wanton Tripper	1967	Calvano, T.	VGF		$21.00 A
CANDID READER	CA 912	Lethal Lover	1967	Shaw, A.*	VG		$8.00
CANDID READER	CA 918	The Ravisher	1968	Bellmore, D.	AF		$40.00 A
CANDID READER	CA 922	Upper-Crust Lust	1968	Bellmore, D.	VGF		$15.00
CANDID READER	CA 927	Bed Of Vengeance	1968	Marshall, A.*	F		$32.00 A
CANDID READER	CA 928	Julie's Jollies	1968	Bellmore, D.	AF		$35.00 A
CANDID READER	CA 930	The Desert Damsels	1968	Allison, C.	VG+		$192.00 A
CANDID READER	CA 937	Lust For Kicks	1968	Dexter, J.	VG-		$8.00
CANDID READER	CA 940	Sin Seance	1968	Bellmore, D.	AF		$62.00 A
CANDID READER	CA 988	The Pink Box	1969	Dexter, J.	VGF		$50.00 A
CANDID READER	CA 1010	A Hard Man Is Good To Find	1970	Aldrich, C.	AF		$22.00 A
CANDID READER	CA 1032	Come In From The Cold	1970	Lee, W.	VGF		$9.00 A
CANDLELIGHT	CB 101	Lust Hangover	1964	Ward, T.	VG+		$7.00
CANDLELIGHT	CB 103	Roots Of Sex	1964	Corning, V.	VGF		$8.00
CANDLELIGHT	CB 105	Bawdy Setup	1964	Selmard, T.	VGF		$7.00
CANDLELIGHT	CB 106	Harlot's Bedlam	1964	Postman, D.	AF		$10.00
CANDLELIGHT	CB 111	Flesh Kick	1964	Burd, B.	VGF		$5.00

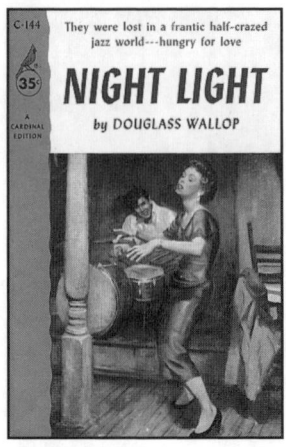

Cardinal C144 AF- $42   Cardinal C236 F $44   Carnival 918 VG- $49

PUBLISHER	PUB. #	TITLE	DATE	AUTHOR	COND.	TYPE	PRICE
CARDINAL	C 31	Man With The Golden Arm (2nd)	1956	Algren, N.	VG+	MTI	$7.00
CARDINAL	C 120	Giant (movie edition)	1956	Ferber, E.	AF	MTI	$12.00
CARDINAL	C 135	The Exploration Of Space	1954	Clarke, A.C.	AF		$6.00
CARDINAL	C 144	Night Light	1954	Wallop, D.	AF-		$42.00 A
CARDINAL	C 173	N.Y., N.Y.	1955	Oursler, W.	VGF		$6.00
CARDINAL	C 187	The Blackboard Jungle (7th)	1955	Hunter, E.	AF		$9.00
CARDINAL	C 209	The Virginian	1956	Wister, O.	AF		$6.00
CARDINAL	C 210	Somebody Up There Likes Me	1956	Graziano, R.	VGF		$7.00
CARDINAL	C 236	Quartet In "H"	1956	Hunter, E.	F		$44.00 A
CARDINAL	C 236	Quartet In "H"	1956	Hunter, E.	AF		$22.00 A
CARDINAL	C 236	Quartet In "H"	1956	Hunter, E.	VG+		$9.00 A
CARDINAL	C 248	Will Acting Spoil M. Monroe?	1957	Martin, P.	VG		$25.00
CARDINAL	C 296	Halfway Down The Stairs	1958	Thompson, C.	VGF		$8.00
CARDINAL	C 298	No Down Payment	1957	McPartland, J.	AF	MTI	$15.00
CARDINAL	C 309	TCOT Sulky Girl	1958	Gardner, E.S.	VG		$6.00
CARDINAL	C 315	Kings Go Forth (3rd)	1958	Brown, J.D.	VG	MTI	$6.00
CARDINAL	C 316	Odds Against Tomorrow	1958	McGivern, W.P.	VGF+		$8.00
CARDINAL	C 319	New Tales Of Space & Time	1958	Anthology	AF		$7.00
CARDINAL	C 320	TCOT One-Eyed Witness	1959	Gardner, E.S.	VG+		$6.00
CARDINAL	C 344	The Lady In The Lake	1959	Chandler, R.	VG		$7.00
CARDINAL	C 371	Gazella	1959	Cloete, S.	AF		$6.00
CARDINAL	C 375	Playback	1960	Chandler, R.	VGF		$17.00 A
CARDINAL	C 375	Playback	1960	Chandler, R.	VGF		$10.00
CARDINAL	C 401	The Rat Race	1960	Kanin, G.	VG+	MTI	$7.00
CARDINAL	C 412	Ocean's Eleven (5th)	1960	Johnson, G.C.	VG	MTI	$6.00
CARDINAL	C 437	Hatari!	1962	Milner, M.	F	MTI	$10.00
CARDINAL	GC 28	Youngblood	1955	Killens, J.O.	AF		$7.00
CARDINAL	GC 56	Strangers When We Meet (5th)	1960	Hunter, E.	VGF	MTI	$5.00
CARDINAL	GC 68	The Best Of Everything (4th)	1959	Jaffe, R.	VG+	MTI	$6.00
CARDINAL	GC 72	Parrish (5th)	1961	Savage, M.	VGF	MTI	$6.00
CARDINAL	GC 74	Compulsion	1959	Levin, M.	AF	MTI	$8.00
CARDINAL	GC 75	Ben Hur	1959	Wallace, L.	VGF	MTI	$10.00
CARDINAL	GC 94	The Young Savages (3rd)	1961	Hunter, E.	VGF	MTI	$15.00
CARDINAL	GC 122	West Side Story	1961	Shulman, I.	VGF	MTI	$5.00
CARDINAL	GC 128	The Light In The Plaza	1961	Spencer, E.	VG	MTI	$6.00
CARDINAL	GC 181	50 American Authors	1963	Maleska, E.T.	AF-		$7.00
CARDINAL	GC 210	Happy New Year, Herbie	1964	Hunter, E.	VGF		$12.00 A
CARDINAL	GC 210	Happy New Year, Herbie	1964	Hunter, E.	VG+		$6.00
CARDINAL	35011	Death Of A Pusher	1964	Deming, R.	VG+		$8.00
CARDINAL	35011	Death Of A Pusher	1964	Deming, R.	VG+		$7.00 A
CARDINAL	35012	Fear In A Desert Town	1964	Ruller, R.	VG+	TVTI	$6.00
CARDINAL	35027	The Pocket Puzzler #2	1964	Nichols, C.M.	AF		$9.00 A
CARDINAL	35036	Corpus Delectable	1964	Powell, T.	VGF		$8.00
CARNIVAL	903	Lovers Bewitched	1952	Gordon, W.E.	VGF	Digest	$17.00 A
CARNIVAL	905	Strangers In The Dark	1952	Gaddis, P.	VG-	Digest	$20.00 A

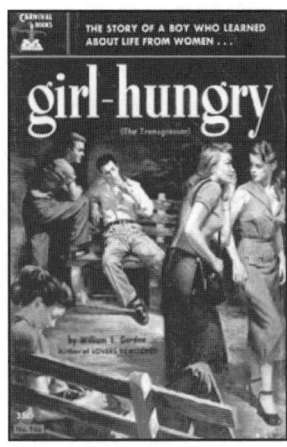

| Carnival 946 VG $46 | Century 37 VG $147 | Century 104 VG $40 |

PUBLISHER	PUB. #	TITLE	DATE	AUTHOR	COND.	TYPE	PRICE
CARNIVAL	910	Pick-Up!	1952	Quandt, A.L.	AF	Digest	$44.00 A
CARNIVAL	911	Affairs Of A Ward Nurse	1952	Coleman, M.	VGF+	Digest	$44.00 A
CARNIVAL	913	Affairs Of A Career Girl	1953	Coleman, M.	VGF	Digest	$21.00 A
CARNIVAL	918	Rapture Alley	1953	Harrison, W.*	VG-	Digest	$49.00 A
CARNIVAL	925	Reckless!	1954	Welles, K.	VGF	Digest	$94.00 A
CARNIVAL	930	Social Club	1954	Quandt, A.L.	VG	Digest	$37.00 A
CARNIVAL	932	Boy Madness	1954	Douglas, R.	VG	Digest	$5.00 A
CARNIVAL	946	Girl-Hungry	1954	Gordon, W.E.	VG	Digest	$46.00 A
CARNIVAL	947	Social Club	1954	Quandt, A.L.	VGF	Digest	$36.00 A
CAROUSEL	501	Sin Club	1962	Lee, R.H.	AF		$6.00
CAROUSEL	522	The Deadly Nude	1964	Channing, S.	AF-		$17.00 A
CAROUSEL	525	Sex Is A Deadly Weapon	1964	Arnold, J.	VGF		$10.00
CAVALCADE	No#	Madman On A Drum	1944	De Mexico, N.R.	G	Digest	$6.00
CAVALCADE	1	Men Are Molehills	1946	Livingston, R.	VG-	Digest	$6.00
CAVALCADE	2	Magic For Murder	1946	Livingston, A.	AF	Digest	$16.00 A
CAVALCADE	2	Magic For Murder	1946	Livingston, A.	VG+	Digest	$6.00
CENTURY	20	Gun Bulldogger	1945	Cunningham, E.	G+	Digest	$6.00
CENTURY	21	The Sulu Sea Murders	1945	Mason, V.W.	G	Digest	$4.00
CENTURY	22	Trigger Vengeance	1945	Trace, J.	VG	Digest	$6.00
CENTURY	23	Death Came Dancing	1945	Knight, K.M.	VG	Digest	$12.00
CENTURY	34	Red Gardinias	1946	Latimer, J.	VG	Digest	$14.00 A
CENTURY	37	Singapore	1947	Bogart, W.G.	VG	Digest	$147.00 A
CENTURY	37	Singapore	1947	Bogart, W.G.	G	Digest	$45.00
CENTURY	52	Danger On The Border	1946	Bechdolt, F.R.	VG+	Digest	$6.00
CENTURY	73	Saddles West!	1947	Hickey, H.B.	VG-		$5.00
CENTURY	80	Cue For Passion	1948	Semple, G.	VGF-		$16.00 A
CENTURY	82	Ranger Justice	1948	Grinstead, J.E.	VGF		$15.00 A
CENTURY	91	Scandalous	1948	Carter, R.	VG-		$7.00
CENTURY	93	Flesh Pots	1948	Branch, F.	VGF		$7.00 A
CENTURY	95	Teaser	1948	Shepard, C.	VG+		$12.00
CENTURY	104	The Green Man	1948	Sherman, H.M.	VG	Digest	$40.00
CENTURY	114	Passion's Program	1948	Branch, F.	AF		$17.00 A
CENTURY	123	Past Folly	1950	Branch, F.	AF		$17.00 A
CENTURY (Adult)	1	My Naughty, Naughty Life	1964	Doren, M.V.	VGF+		$21.00 A
CENTURY (Adult)	4	Dictionary Of Sexual Terms	1964	Blake, R.	VGF+		$7.00
CENTURY (Adult)	120	The Hippie Love Cults	1970	Mennen, E. Ph.D.	VG+		$8.00
CHARIOT	CB 101	Convention Girl	1959	Wright, D.M.	VG+		$7.00
CHARIOT	CB 101	Convention Girl	1959	Wright, D.M.	G+		$6.00
CHARIOT	CB 103	The Naked Lovers	1959	Little, C.	VG+		$7.00
CHARIOT	CB 105	Sex On Tap	1959	Noderheim, B.	VG		$6.00
CHARIOT	CB 108	The New Bathroom Reader	1959	Lawrence, D.H.	VG+		$10.00
CHARIOT	CB 111	Broadway Bait	1959	Damon, R.	VGF		$7.00
CHARIOT	CB 112	Queen Of Sheba	1959	Sardoux, V.	VG		$7.00
CHARIOT	CB 114	The Deadly Passion	1959	Bernard, R.	AF		$17.00 A
CHARIOT	CB 114	The Deadly Passion	1960	Bernard, R.	VG+		$17.00

Chariot 123 G+ $6　　　Chariot 150 AF $11　　　Checkerbooks 6 AF $35　　　Checkerbooks 8 VGF $49

PUBLISHER	PUB. #	TITLE	DATE	AUTHOR	COND.	TYPE	PRICE
CHARIOT	CB 119	A Time To Love	1960	O'Hara, N.	VG		$7.00
CHARIOT	CB 120	Bad Girl Abroad	1960	Adlon, A.	VG+		$7.00
CHARIOT	CB 123	Woman From Another Planet	1960	Long, F.	G+		$6.00
CHARIOT	CB 125	Lover Girl	1960	Devlin, R.	VG		$6.00
CHARIOT	CB 131	Backstage Girl	1960	Lindsey, H.	VG+		$7.00
CHARIOT	CB 138	Sex Behavior Of The Am. Secretary	1960	Sprague, W.H.	VGF		$7.00
CHARIOT	CB 139	Black Is A Man	1960	Roskolenko, H.	G+		$5.00
CHARIOT	CB 149	Passion Slave	1960	MacDonald, W.	VGF		$8.00
CHARIOT	CB 150	The Last 14	1960	Barr, T.C.	AF		$11.00 A
CHARIOT	CB 150	The Last 14	1960	Barr, T.C.	VG+		$10.00
CHARIOT	CB 151	Dungaree Sin	1960	Lorenz, F.	VG		$27.00 A
CHARIOT	CB 154	Driven Virgin	1960	Adlon, A.	VG		$6.00
CHARIOT	CB 170	Hot Bed Hotel	1961	Stemmer, A.	VG		$7.00
CHARIOT	CB 175	Company Girl (2nd)	1961	Clark, V.S.	VG		$5.00
CHARIOT	CB 177	Passion Club	1961	Seeley, E.S.	VG+		$7.00
CHARIOT	CB 179	Key Club Girl	1961	Adlon, A.	VG+		$7.00
CHARIOT	CB 182	The Private Life Of Eleanor	1961	Coss, R.	VG+		$7.00
CHARIOT	CB 186	Gay Wanton	1960	Thompson, J.B.	VG		$7.00
CHARIOT	CB 187	Man's Nurse	1961	Hitt, O.	VGF-		$16.00 A
CHARIOT	CB 187	Man's Nurse	1961	Hitt, O.	VG-		$6.00
CHARIOT	CB 193	Wild Flesh	1961	Calley, J.	VG+		$7.00
CHARIOT	CB 193	Wild Flesh	1961	Calley, J.	VG+		$7.00
CHARIOT	CB 195	Hot Blood	1961	Hitt, O.	AF		$11.00 A
CHARIOT	CB 195	Hot Blood	1961	Hitt, O.	VGF+		$10.00 A
CHARIOT	CB 195	Hot Blood	1961	Hitt, O.	VG		$7.00
CHARIOT	CB 196	Nylon Lovers	1961	Newland, N.M.	VGF		$13.00 A
CHARIOT	CB 197	Swamp Girl	1961	Craig, D.W.	AF		$30.00 A
CHARIOT	CB 198	Arlette	1961	Oliver, A.E.	VGF		$10.00 A
CHARIOT	CB 198	Arlette	1961	Oliver, A.E.	VGF		$7.00
CHARIOT	CB 202	Hotel Girl	1960	Hitt, O.	VGF		$8.00
CHARIOT	CB 203	Love Cult	1962	Thurman, W.	VG+		$6.00
CHARIOT	CB 204	Tramp Nurse	1962	Adlon, A.	VGF		$10.00
CHARIOT	CB 206	Virgin Nurse	1962	Adlon, A.	VGF+		$7.00
CHARIOT	CB 208	Love For Hire	1962	Anderson, B.	F		$11.00 A
CHARIOT	CB 209	Passion Hostess	1962	Hitt, O.	AF		$14.00 A
CHARIOT	CB 209	Passion Hostess	1962	Hitt, O.	VG		$8.00
CHARIOT	CB 211	Man Hunger	1962	Craig, D.W.	F		$7.00
CHARIOT	CB 212	Torrid Cheat	1962	Hitt, O.	VGF+		$10.00 A
CHARIOT	CB 213	Tonite	1962	Oliver, A.E.	VGF		$16.00 A
CHARIOT	CB 213	Tonite	1962	Oliver, A.E.	VG+		$7.00
CHARIOT	CB 217	Man Bait	1962	Roget, A.	VGF		$6.00
CHARIOT	CB 222	The Sheer Affair	1962	Simon, G.	VG+		$10.00
CHARIOT	CB 223	Open House	1963	Oliver, A.E.	VGF		$6.00
CHARIOT	CB 1601	Love For Sale	1961	Craig, D.W.	VGF		$8.00
CHARIOT	CB 1602	Cold Wife	1961	Adlon, A.	AF		$8.00
CHARIOT	CB 1602	Cold Wife	1961	Adlon, A.	VG+		$8.00
CHARIOT	CB 1606	Heat Wave	1961	Powers, J.	VGF		$7.00
CHARIOT	CB 1609	Sin Gym	1962	Simon, G.	VGF		$7.00

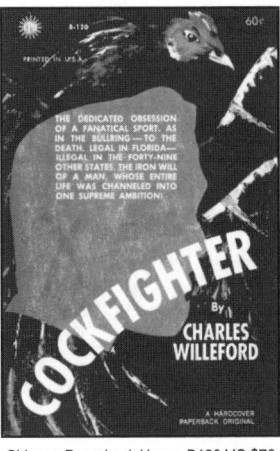

Chartered 18 VG $13   Chicago Paperback House A101 AF $7   Chicago Paperback House B120 VG $73

PUBLISHER	PUB. #	TITLE	DATE	AUTHOR	COND.	TYPE	PRICE
CHARIOT	CB 1610	Twin Beds	1962	Hitt, O.	VGF+		$12.00 A
CHARIOT	CB 1612	Lonely Wife	1962	Craig, D.W.	VG+		$8.00
CHARIOT	CB 1615	Body Bait	1962	Shepard, L.	VGF		$7.00
CHARIOT	CB 1617	Libby Sin	1962	Hitt, O.	VGF		$11.00 A
CHARIOT	CB 1617	Libby Sin	1962	Hitt, O.	VGF		$10.00 A
CHARIOT	CB 1622	I Am A Lesbian	1962	Laverne P.	VG+		$23.00 A
CHARIOT	CB 1626	Strange Longings	1963	Hitt, O.	VG+		$7.00
CHARIOT	CB 1626	Strange Longings	1963	Hitt, O.	G		$5.00
CHARIOT	6C 629	The Dike Twins	1963	Craig, D.W.	VGF		$22.00 A
CHARIOT	6C 630	Nylon Jungle	1963	Elgun, M.	VGF		$8.00 A
CHARLIE CHAN	1 1	Charlie Chan Mag. 11/73	1973	Anthology	VG-	Digest	$6.00
CHARTERED	18	Deadlier Than The Male	1946	Gunn, J.	VG	Digest	$13.00
CHECKERBOOKS	2	The Broadway Butterfly Murders	1949	Bliss, T.	VGF		$20.00
CHECKERBOOKS	5	Horror And Homicide	1949	Anthology	VG		$16.00 A
CHECKERBOOKS	6	Duke Herring	1949	Bodenheim, M.	AF		$35.00
CHECKERBOOKS	6	Duke Herring	1949	Bodenheim, M.	VG+		$27.00 A
CHECKERBOOKS	6	Duke Herring	1949	Bodenheim, M.	VG		$20.00 A
CHECKERBOOKS	8	Taxi	1949	Bernstein, A.	VGF		$49.00 A
CHECKERBOOKS	9	The Florentine Dagger	1949	Hecht, B.	VG-		$14.00
CHECKERBOOKS	10	Lady, Mind That Corpse	1949	Janson, H.	VG		$80.00 A
CHERRY TREE	404	The Last Space Ship	n/d	Leinster, M.	VG	Digest	$9.00 A
CHEVRON	109	Demon Mona	1967	Edwards, J.	AF		$31.00 A
CHEVRON	113	Love Bait	1967	King, D.	AF		$12.00
CHICAGO PB HOUSE	A 101	Murder, Absolutely Murder	1962	Cloutier, H.	AF		$7.00
CHICAGO PB HOUSE	A 106	Power's Pool	1962	Hansen, Z.	AF		$7.00
CHICAGO PB HOUSE	A 107	House Of The Hunter	1962	Taylor, F.	VG		$4.00
CHICAGO PB HOUSE	A 108	Another Man's Hell	1962	Kemper, W.E.	AF		$10.00
CHICAGO PB HOUSE	A 108	Another Man's Hell	1962	Kemper, W.E.	AF		$7.00
CHICAGO PB HOUSE	A 110	Nothing But Blood	1962	Smith, P.C.	AF		$7.00
CHICAGO PB HOUSE	A 111	Wail Of The Lonely Wench	1962	Collins, A.J.	VG		$12.00
CHICAGO PB HOUSE	B 100	Eyewitness To Exodus	1962	Levin, B.	AF		$7.00
CHICAGO PB HOUSE	B 110	The Paths Are Three	1962	Marino. V.	AF		$8.00
CHICAGO PB HOUSE	B 120	Cockfighter	1962	Willeford, C.	VG		$73.00 A
CHICAGO PB HOUSE	B 130	Home Away From Home	1962	Woodford, J.	F		$8.00
CHICAGO PB HOUSE	B 140	Postmark Of America	1962	Glenn, R.T.	AF		$7.00
COLLECTORS LIBRARY	No#	The Woman Thing	1967	Daimler, H.	VG+		$6.00
COLLECTORS LIBRARY	21260	Pinktoes	1968	Himes, C.	VG		$7.00
COLLIER	AS 392	The Supernatural Reader	1962	Anthology	VGF		$6.00
COLLIER	AS 606	The Bride Wore Black	1964	Woolrich, C.	VGF		$3.00
COMEDY	8 48	Comedy - July 1959	1959	Anthology	VG	Digest	$6.00
COMET	1	Wagons Westward	1948	Sperry, A.	VGF	Digest	$7.00
COMET	10	The Tattooed Man (2nd)	1948	Pease, H.	VG+	Digest	$6.00
COMET	13	The Green Turtle Mystery	1949	Queen, E., Jr.	VG+	Digest	$7.00
COMET	14	Silver	1948	Hinkle, T.C.	VGF	Digest	$7.00
COMET	31	Indian Paint	1949	Balch, G.	AF	Digest	$7.00

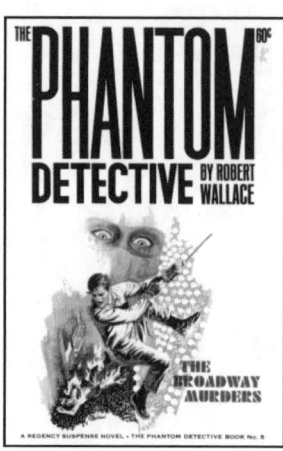

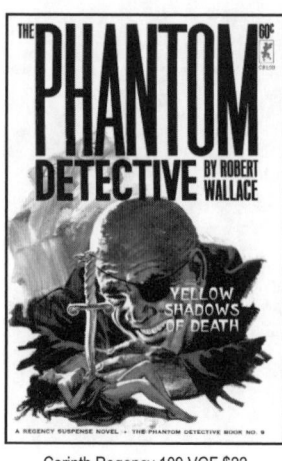

Comet 1 VGF $7   Corinth Regency 105 VGF+ $24   Corinth Regency 109 VGF $22

PUBLISHER	PUB. #	TITLE	DATE	AUTHOR	COND.	TYPE	PRICE
COMPANION	CB 501	The Snow Tigress	1967	Dexter, J.	AF		$9.00 A
COMPANION	CB 502	Passion By Proxy	1967	Williams, J.X.	AF		$33.00 A
COMPANION	CB 502	Passion By Proxy	1967	Williams, J.X.	AF		$24.00 A
COMPANION	CB 503	The Sin-Hop	1967	Bellmore, D.	VG+		$15.00 A
COMPANION	CB 511	Dusky Desire	1967	Marshall, A.*	AF		$14.00
COMPANION	CB 517	Tycoon's Tart	1967	Dexter, J.	VGF		$8.00
COMPANION	CB 518	Falling In Lust	1967	Shaw, A.*	AF		$8.00
COMPANION	CB 523	Acid Orgy	1967	Calvano, T.	AF		$82.00 A
COMPANION	CB 528	S.O.S. For Sin	1967	Miller, M.	F		$18.00 A
COMPANION	CB 531	Shame Dynasty	1967	Williams, J.X.	VG+		$8.00
COMPANION	CB 535	Billion-Dollar Boudoir	1967	Marshall, A.*	VGF		$10.00
COMPANION	CB 536	Lust For A Green Beret	1967	Bellmore, D.	VG+		$16.00 A
COMPANION	CB 540	Professor Of Passion	1967	Marshall, A.*	VG+		$7.00
COMPANION	CB 542	Tart Of The Town	1967	Dexter, J.	AF		$13.00 A
COMPANION	CB 567	Trip 'N' Trade	1968	Dexter, J.	G		$6.00
COMPANION	CB 586	For Lust's Sake	1968	Dexter, J.	AF		$14.00 A
COMPANION	CB 658	Northwest Passion	1970	Bellmore, D.	AF		$15.00
COMPASS LINE	CL 146	Untamed Passions	1966	Brook, S.	VG-		$5.00
COMPASS LINE	CL 156	Left Bank Lust	1967	Wilner, L.S.	VGF		$5.00
CONFLICT	1 1	Conflict - Fall 1953	1953	Anthology	VGF	Digest	$27.00 A
CONFLICT	1 1	Conflict - Fall 1953	1953	Anthology	VGF	Digest	$22.00 A
CONSUL	M 1041	Hide And Kill	1961	York, J.*	VG+		$16.00 A
CORGI	No#	Savage Night	1988	Thompson, J.	F		$33.00 A
CORGI	No#	Savage Night	1988	Thompson, J.	AF		$20.00
CORGI	No#	Wild Town	1989	Thompson, J.	F		$10.00
CORGI	P 35	The Secret Fear	1954	O'Farrell, W.	VG		$6.00
CORGI	SS 820	The Golden Apples Of The Sun	1960	Bradbury, R.	VG+		$10.00
CORINTH REGENCY	CR 101	The Phantom Detective #1	1965	Wallace, R.	AF		$14.00 A
CORINTH REGENCY	CR 101	The Phantom Detective #1	1965	Wallace, R.	VG+		$13.00
CORINTH REGENCY	CR 102	The Phantom Detective #2	1965	Wallace, R.	VG		$12.00
CORINTH REGENCY	CR 103	The Phantom Detective #3	1965	Wallace, R.	VGF+		$29.00 A
CORINTH REGENCY	CR 104	The Phantom Detective #4	1965	Wallace, R.	VGF+		$24.00 A
CORINTH REGENCY	CR 105	The Phantom Detective #5	1965	Wallace, R.	VGF+		$24.00 A
CORINTH REGENCY	CR 106	The Phantom Detective #6	1965	Wallace, R.	AF		$31.00 A
CORINTH REGENCY	CR 106	The Phantom Detective #6	1965	Wallace, R.	VGF		$15.00
CORINTH REGENCY	CR 106	The Phantom Detective #6	1965	Wallace, R.	G-		$3.00
CORINTH REGENCY	CR 107	The Phantom Detective #7	1965	Wallace, R.	AF		$25.00 A
CORINTH REGENCY	CR 107	The Phantom Detective #7	1965	Wallace, R.	VGF		$14.00
CORINTH REGENCY	CR 107	The Phantom Detective #7	1965	Wallace, R.	VG		$10.00
CORINTH REGENCY	CR 108	The Phantom Detective #8	1965	Wallace, R.	VGF		$24.00 A
CORINTH REGENCY	CR 108	The Phantom Detective #8	1965	Wallace, R.	AF-		$17.00 A
CORINTH REGENCY	CR 109	The Phantom Detective #9	1965	Wallace, R.	VGF		$22.00
CORINTH REGENCY	CR 109	The Phantom Detective #9	1965	Wallace, R.	VG		$10.00
CORINTH REGENCY	CR 110	The Phantom Detective #10	1965	Wallace, R.	VGF		$23.00
CORINTH REGENCY	CR 111	The Phantom Detective #11	1966	Wallace, R.	VGF		$24.00 A

Crest 151 AF $33   Crest 173 VGF $73   Crest 187 VG $10   Crest 234 F $13

PUBLISHER	PUB. #	TITLE	DATE	AUTHOR	COND.	TYPE	PRICE
CORINTH REGENCY	CR 111	The Phantom Detective #11	1966	Wallace, R.	G		$3.00
CORINTH REGENCY	CR 112	The Phantom Detective #12	1966	Wallace, R.	VGF		$22.00
CORINTH REGENCY	CR 112	The Phantom Detective #12	1966	Wallace, R.	VG+		$13.00
CORINTH REGENCY	CR 113	The Phantom Detective #13	1966	Wallace, R.	VGF+		$20.00 A
CORINTH REGENCY	CR 113	The Phantom Detective #13	1966	Wallace, R.	VGF		$13.00
CORINTH REGENCY	CR 114	The Phantom Detective #14	1966	Wallace, R.	VGF+		$29.00 A
CORINTH REGENCY	CR 115	The Phantom Detective #15	1966	Wallace, R.	VGF+		$24.00 A
CORINTH REGENCY	CR 115	The Phantom Detective #15	1966	Wallace, R.	VGF		$15.00
CORINTH REGENCY	CR 117	The Phantom Detective #16	1966	Wallace, R.	VGF+		$23.00 A
CORINTH REGENCY	CR 117	The Phantom Detective #16	1966	Wallace, R.	VG+		$20.00
CORINTH REGENCY	CR 119	The Phantom Detective #17	1966	Wallace, R.	VGF+		$23.00 A
CORINTH REGENCY	CR 120	Operator 5 #2	1966	Steele, C.	AF		$19.00 A
CORINTH REGENCY	CR 123	The Phantom Detective #18	1966	Wallace, R.	VG+		$13.00
CORINTH REGENCY	CR 124	Operator 5 #3	1966	Steele, C.	AF		$14.00 A
CORINTH REGENCY	CR 127	The Phantom Detective #19	1966	Wallace, R.	AF		$32.00
CORINTH REGENCY	CR 127	The Phantom Detective #19	1966	Wallace, R.	VGF		$14.00
CORINTH REGENCY	CR 128	Operator 5 #4	1966	Steele, C.	VGF		$20.00
CORINTH REGENCY	CR 130	Secret Agent X #3	1966	House, B.	VGF		$15.00
CORINTH REGENCY	CR 131	The Phantom Detective #20	1966	Wallace, R.	VGF+		$19.00 A
CORINTH REGENCY	CR 132	Operator 5 #5	1966	Steele, C.	VGF		$23.00 A
CORINTH REGENCY	CR 135	The Phantom Detective #21	1966	Wallace, R.	F		$18.00 A
CORINTH REGENCY	CR 135	The Phantom Detective #21	1966	Wallace, R.	VG		$12.00
CORINTH REGENCY	CR 141	Dusty Ayres #3	1966	Bowen, R.S.	VGF		$23.00
COSMOS	1	Cosmos SF & Fantasy - 9/53	1953	Anthology	VGF	Digest	$25.00
COSMOS	2	Cosmos SF & Fantasy - 11/53	1953	Anthology	VGF	Digest	$41.00 A
COSMOS	2	Cosmos SF & Fantasy - 11/53	1953	Anthology	VG+	Digest	$20.00 A
COSMOS	4	Cosmos SF & Fantasy - 7/54	1954	Anthology	VG+	Digest	$25.00 A
COSMOS	4	Cosmos SF & Fantasy - 7/54	1954	Anthology	VGF	Digest	$15.00 A
COUGAR	NT 829	Hippie Harlot	1967	O'Brien, T.	VG+		$11.00 A
COVEN 13	1 1	Coven 13	1969	Anthology	AF	Digest	$17.00
COVEN 13	1 3	Coven 13 - 1/70	1970	Anthology	VGF	Digest	$5.00 A
CREST	115	Run Thief Run	1955	Gruber, F.	VGF		$11.00 A
CREST	115	Run Thief Run	1955	Gruber, F.	VG+		$8.00
CREST	122	A Journey With Love	1956	Baker, D.V.	VGF-		$5.00
CREST	s 124	The Golden Hussy	1956	Cohen, O.R.	F		$18.00
CREST	126	Captive In The Night	1956	Stokes, D.	VG+		$8.00
CREST	127	Education Of A French Model	1956	Kiki	G		$3.00
CREST	132	Lie Down, Killer (2nd)	1957	Prather, R.S.	AF		$12.00
CREST	132	Lie Down, Killer (2nd)	1957	Prather, R.S.	VGF		$7.00
CREST	139	So Nude, So Dead	1956	Marsten, R.	VGF-		$8.00
CREST	141	Sex Without Tears	1956	Lockridge, N.	AF		$10.00
CREST	141	Sex Without Tears	1956	Lockridge, N.	VG+		$9.00 A
CREST	142	Dagger Of Flesh	1956	Prather, R.S.	AF		$24.00 A
CREST	142	Dagger Of Flesh	1956	Prather, R.S.	VGF+		$22.00 A
CREST	142	Dagger Of Flesh (2nd)	1957	Prather, R.S.	VGF-		$5.00
CREST	151	Saturday Night Town	1956	Whittington, H.	AF		$33.00 A
CREST	151	Saturday Night Town	1956	Whittington, H.	G-		$5.00
CREST	d 157	A Walk On The Wild Side	1957	Algren, N.	VG+		$15.00

Crest 238 F $22   Crest 248 F $38   Crest 254 VGF $11   Crest 260 AF $55

PUBLISHER	PUB. #	TITLE	DATE	AUTHOR	COND.	TYPE	PRICE
CREST	162	Seawife	1957	Scott, J.M.	VG+	MTI	$5.00
CREST	169	Evil In The Night	1957	Verissimo, E.	AF-		$8.00
CREST	172	TCOT Brunette Bombshell	1957	Waugh, H.	VG-		$2.00
CREST	173	Little Tramp	1957	Brewer, G.	VGF		$73.00 A
CREST	173	Little Tramp (2nd)	1958	Brewer, G.	AF		$15.00
CREST	173	Little Tramp (2nd)	1958	Brewer, G.	VG+		$7.00
CREST	s 178	The Spiked Heel	1957	Marsten, R.	VGF-		$12.00
CREST	187	Whisper Their Love	1957	Taylor, V.	VG		$10.00
CREST	187	Whisper Their Love (2nd)	1958	Taylor, V.	AF		$23.00 A
CREST	s 188	Beyond Defeat (2nd)	1958	Richter, H.W.	AF		$7.00
CREST	s 190	Sweepings	1957	Cohen, L.	VGF		$7.00
CREST	193	Rider From Thunder Mountain	1957	Huffaker, C.	VGF		$5.00
CREST	195	Meet Morrocco Jones	1957	Baynes, J.	F		$12.00 A
CREST	196	New Crossword Puzzle Book	1957	Freeman, J.	VGF+		$69.00 A
CREST	d 199	Eastern Love	1958	Mathers, E.P.	VGF		$4.00
CREST	205	High Hell	1958	Frazee, S.	VG+	MTI	$7.00
CREST	s 209	The 27th Day	1958	Mantley, J.	VGF		$7.00
CREST	s 212	Night Of Fire And Snow	1958	Coppel, A.	F		$7.00
CREST	s 212	Night Of Fire And Snow	1958	Coppel, A.	AF		$7.00
CREST	s 217	The Legion Of The Damned	1958	Hassel, S.	VGF		$7.00
CREST	222	Posse From Hell	1958	Huffaker, C.	VG+	MTI	$4.00
CREST	224	Hand Of The Mafia	1957	Baynes, J.	F		$12.00 A
CREST	224	Hand Of The Mafia	1957	Baynes, J.	AF		$10.00
CREST	225	Root Of Evil	1958	Cross, J.	AF		$6.00
CREST	s 226	Ralph 124C 41+	1958	Gernsback, H.	VGF		$12.00
CREST	s 226	Ralph 124C 41+	1958	Gernsback, H.	VG		$6.00
CREST	234	The Peeping Tom Murders	1958	Baynes, J.	F		$13.00 A
CREST	234	The Peeping Tom Murders	1958	Baynes, J.	VGF		$10.00
CREST	238	The Vengeful Virgin	1958	Brewer, G.	F		$22.00 A
CREST	239	Cartoon Laffs From True	1958	Anthology	VGF		$5.00
CREST	s 240	The Best Of Crunch And Des	1958	Wylie, P.	F		$20.00 A
CREST	s 240	The Best Of Crunch And Des	1958	Wylie, P.	AF		$12.00
CREST	s 243	The Dangerous Games	1958	Torres, T.	F		$22.00
CREST	s 245	Race To The Stars	1958	Anthology	VGF		$5.00
CREST	246	The Long Nightmare	1958	Roeburt, J.	AF		$16.00 A
CREST	248	End Of A Call Girl	1958	Gault, W.C.	F		$38.00 A
CREST	253	Murder Bait	1958	Yarnell, D.	AF		$23.00 A
CREST	s 254	Bad Girls	1958	Anthology	VGF		$11.00 A
CREST	d 256	A Treasury Of True	1958	Anthology	VGF		$7.00
CREST	s 257	Pappy's Women	1958	Gotshall, J.	VGF		$5.00
CREST	s 258	6 From Worlds Beyond	1958	Anthology	AF		$7.00
CREST	260	Night Lady	1958	Gault, W.C.	AF		$55.00 A
CREST	260	Night Lady	1958	Gault, W.C.	VG		$7.00
CREST	266	Clementine Cherie	1959	Bellus, J.	VGF+		$8.00 A
CREST	268	The Vanishing Vixen	1959	Sparkia, R.B.	VGF		$7.00
CREST	s 272	Young And Deadly	1959	Anthology	G		$5.00
CREST	s 273	The Caves Of Night	1959	Christopher, J.	VGF		$5.00
CREST	s 279	Enter Laughing	1959	Reiner, C.	VGF		$5.00

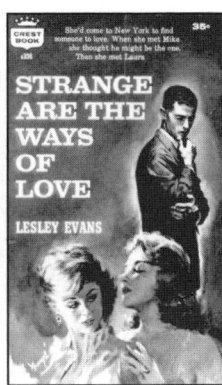

| Crest 272 G $5 | Crest 281 F $18 | Crest 286 VGF $33 | Crest 336 AF $82 |

PUBLISHER	PUB. #	TITLE	DATE	AUTHOR	COND.	TYPE	PRICE
CREST	281	The Wayward Widow	1959	Gault, W.C.	F		$18.00 A
CREST	281	The Wayward Widow	1959	Gault, W.C.	VGF-		$14.00 A
CREST	281	The Wayward Widow	1959	Gault, W.C.	VG		$7.00
CREST	286	Dead Dolls Don't Talk	1959	Keene, D.	VGF		$33.00 A
CREST	286	Dead Dolls Don't Talk	1959	Keene, D.	VG		$10.00
CREST	287	The Cautious Bachelor	1959	Eimerl, S.	AF		$7.00
CREST	294	Pardon My Blooper	1959	Schafer, K.	AF-		$5.00
CREST	s 295	The Executioners	1959	MacDonald, J.D.	VG		$8.00
CREST	297	Doctor's Temptation	1959	Lieferant, S.	F		$8.00
CREST	s 299	The Way We Live Now	1959	Miller, W.	F		$8.00
CREST	s 302	The Girl Cage	1959	Mergendahl, C.	AF		$5.00
CREST	304	Creole Woman	1959	Fox, G.F.	VG		$7.00
CREST	s 307	The Horn	1959	Holmes, J.C.	VG+		$9.00
CREST	s 308	A Stir Of Echoes	1959	Matheson, R.	G		$7.00
CREST	s 308	A Stir Of Echoes	1959	Matheson, R.	G		$6.00
CREST	309	Sweet Wild Wench	1959	Gault, W.C.	VGF		$36.00 A
CREST	309	Sweet Wild Wench	1959	Gault, W.C.	VG+		$9.00
CREST	310	The Red Scarf	1959	Brewer, G.	VGF		$100.00 A
CREST	310	The Red Scarf	1959	Brewer, G.	VG+		$16.00 A
CREST	310	The Red Scarf	1959	Brewer, G.	VG		$12.00
CREST	d 312	Showcase	1959	Dibner, M.	VGF		$7.00
CREST	316	Danger In My Blood	1959	Brackeen, S.	VGF		$10.00
CREST	s 321	The Shook-Up Generation	1959	Salisbury, H.E.	F		$10.00 A
CREST	s 321	The Shook-Up Generation	1959	Salisbury, H.E.	VGF		$8.00
CREST	325	Morocco Jones	1959	Baynes, J.	AF-		$6.00 A
CREST	s 327	Murder On The Mistral	1959	Malo, V.G.	F		$7.00
CREST	s 328	The Bystander	1959	Guerard, A.J.	F		$8.00
CREST	s 329	The Star Of Life	1959	Hamilton, E.	AF		$7.00
CREST	s 332	Someone From The Past	1959	Bennett, M.	F		$7.00
CREST	334	Kill My Love	1959	Hunt, K.	AF		$10.00
CREST	s 336	Strange Are The Ways Of Love	1959	Evans, L.*	AF		$82.00 A
CREST	339	Lyn Darling, M.D.	1959	Dorien, R.	AF		$5.00
CREST	340	Jimmy Hoffa's Hot	1959	Martin, J.B.	VGF		$6.00
CREST	s 341	The Badge	1959	Webb, J.	F	TVTI	$20.00
CREST	s 341	The Badge	1959	Webb, J.	VG+	TVTI	$7.00
CREST	s 342	No Place On Earth	1959	Charbonneau, L.	VG+		$6.00
CREST	s 343	The Ruling Passion	1959	De Mare, G.	F		$6.00
CREST	s 345	Young Love	1960	Allen, J.	VGF		$7.00
CREST	s 347	The Steel Cocoon	1960	Platzmann, B.	VGF+		$7.00
CREST	349	Devil In Dungarees	1960	Conroy, A.	VGF+		$13.00 A
CREST	349	Devil In Dungarees	1960	Conroy, A.	VG		$5.00
CREST	s 353	The Bright Young Things	1960	Vail, A.	VG		$5.00
CREST	357	Trouble Rides Tall	1960	Whittington, H.	AF		$18.00 A
CREST	s 359	Please Write For Details	1960	MacDonald, J.D.	VG+		$10.00
CREST	s 359	Please Write For Details	1960	MacDonald, J.D.	VG		$7.00
CREST	361	Million Dollar Tramp	1960	Gault, W.C.	AF		$27.00 A
CREST	s 380	The Notion Of Sin	1960	McLaughlin, R.	VGF		$7.00 A
CREST	s 381	The Con Man	1960	Cushman, D.	VGF		$7.00

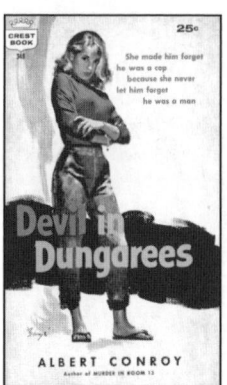
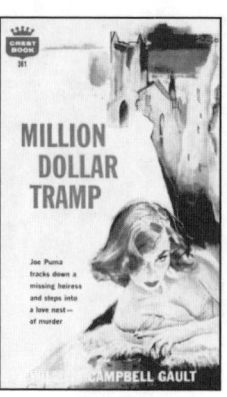

Crest 349 VGF+ $13   Crest 361 AF $27   Crest 421 VGF $16   Crest 479 AF $24

PUBLISHER	PUB. #	TITLE	DATE	AUTHOR	COND.	TYPE	PRICE
CREST	s 385	Psycho	1960	Bloch, R.	VG+	MTI	$10.00
CREST	s 385	Psycho (Signed)	1960	Bloch, R.	VG	MTI	$20.00
CREST	s 386	The Cool World	1960	Miller, W.	AF		$7.00
CREST	s 386	The Cool World	1960	Miller, W.	VG+		$6.00
CREST	s 392	Of Love Forbidden	1960	Weirauch, A.E.	VG+		$8.00
CREST	398	Seven Ways From Sundown	1960	Huffaker, C.	VG+	MTI	$7.00
CREST	s 400	The Crossroads	1960	MacDonald, J.D.	VGF		$16.00 A
CREST	403	Clash Of Shadows	1960	Rigsby, H.	VGF		$6.00
CREST	s 407	Warrior's Rest	1960	Rochefort, C.	AF		$6.00
CREST	d 411	The Longest Day	1960	Ryan, C.	AF		$6.00
CREST	d 412	Invitation To A Beheading	1960	Nabokov, V.	VG		$2.50
CREST	s 413	The Lion House	1960	Lee, M.	VG		$10.00
CREST	d 417	The Affair In Arcady	1960	Wellard, J.	AF		$7.00
CREST	s 419	Back Alley Jungle	1960	Anthology	AF		$18.00 A
CREST	s 419	Back Alley Jungle	1960	Anthology	VG+		$9.00 A
CREST	s 420	Back Of Sunset	1960	Cleary, J.	VGF		$5.00
CREST	s 421	Flaming Lance	1960	Huffaker, C.	VGF	MTI	$16.00 A
CREST	d 422	The Tattooed Rood (2nd)	1961	Onstott, K.	VGF		$5.00
CREST	d 427	The Ivy Trap	1961	Angus, D.	F		$8.00
CREST	d 428	Gemini	1961	Kelley, W.	VGF		$5.00
CREST	S 429	True Spy Stories	1961	Anthology	AF		$7.00
CREST	s 430	Welcome Honorable Visitors	1961	Raspail, J.	F		$6.00
CREST	s 431	The Looters	1961	Conroy, A.	AF		$6.00
CREST	d 434	Brood Of Fury	1961	Shelton, J.	AF		$12.00
CREST	s 436	The Great Escape	1961	Brickhill, P.	AF		$7.00
CREST	s 439	Auschwitz	1961	Nyiszle, M.	AF-		$6.00
CREST	d 440	The Deathmakers	1961	Sire, G.	AF		$7.00
CREST	d 441	The 13th Apostle	1961	Vale, E.	AF		$6.00
CREST	s 442	The Dangerous Games	1961	Torres, T.	VGF		$19.00 A
CREST	s 442	The Dangerous Games	1961	Torres, T.	AF		$12.00
CREST	s 442	The Dangerous Games (2nd)	1961	Torres, T.	VG		$6.00
CREST	d 445	The Happy Medium	1961	Charell, L.	AF		$7.00
CREST	s 447	Road Show	1961	Haase, J.	VGF		$10.00
CREST	s 448	Sail A Crooked Ship	1961	Benchley, N.	VGF		$5.00
CREST	s 451	Some Angry Angel	1961	Condon, R.	AF		$6.00
CREST	s 452	False Scent	1961	Marsh, N.	AF		$8.00
CREST	d 455	Zsa Zsa Gabor	1961	Frank, G.	VGF		$7.00
CREST	d 458	True Civil War Stories	1961	Anthology	AF		$7.00
CREST	d 461	All Quiet On Western Front (4th)	1961	Remarque, E.M.	VG+		$5.00
CREST	s 464	The End Of The Night	1961	MacDonald, J.D.	AF		$27.00 A
CREST	s 464	The End Of The Night	1961	MacDonald, J.D.	AF		$16.00 A
CREST	s 464	The End Of The Night	1961	MacDonald, J.D.	VG		$6.00
CREST	d 469	Young Man Willing	1961	Doliner, R.	VGF+		$9.00
CREST	d 469	Young Man Willing	1961	Doliner, R.	AF		$7.00
CREST	s 471	Aground	1961	Williams, C.	AF		$20.00
CREST	s 478	Hey! B.C.	1961	Hart, J.	VGF		$7.00
CREST	s 479	Vengeance Is The Spur	1961	Whittington, H.	AF		$24.00 A
CREST	s 479	Vengeance Is The Spur	1961	Whittington, H.	VGF+		$15.00 A

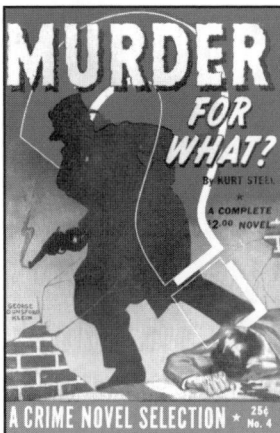

Crime Lab 1-1 AF- $16   Crime Novel Selection 4 VG $27   Croydon 60 VG+ $60

PUBLISHER	PUB. #	TITLE	DATE	AUTHOR	COND.	TYPE	PRICE
CREST	s 481	Handsome's Seven Women	1961	Pratt, T.	AF		$6.00
CREST	s 485	Daily Bread	1961	Maloney, R.	VG+		$7.00
CREST	s 491	Countdown To Murder	1961	Kastle, H.D.	VG+		$6.00
CREST	s 495	Edge Of Twilight	1961	Christian, P.	VGF		$10.00
CREST	s 498	True Album Of Cartoons	1962	Anthology	AF		$7.00
CREST	s 499	Seven Lies South	1962	McGivern, W.P.	VG+		$7.00
CREST	S 518	Nightmare	1962	Blaisdell, A.	AF		$7.00
CREST	s 520	Cape Fear	1962	MacDonald, J.D.	G+	MTI	$2.00
CREST	R 575	The Longest Day (4th)	1962	Ryan, C.	VG	MTI	$6.00
CREST	d 578	The Watchman	1962	Grubb, D.	VG+		$5.00
CREST	d 578	The Watchman	1962	Grubb, D.	VG		$3.00
CREST	d 579	True Tales Of Hitler's Reich	1962	Hanser, R.	VGF		$6.00
CREST	k 596	Warrior's Rest	1963	Rochefort, C.	VG	MTI	$6.00
CREST	k 646	Kids Sure Rite Funny	1963	Linkletter, A.	VG+		$3.00
CREST	R 647	Letters From The Earth	1963	Twain, M.	VGF		$5.00
CREST	s 663	Top Sacred	1963	Burnett, H.	VG+		$5.00
CREST	k 674	The Wizard Of Oz (2nd)	1963	Baum, L.F.	VG+		$7.00
CREST	k 700	The Cool World	1964	Miller, W.	VGF	MTI	$5.00
CREST	r 717	The Moonspinners	1964	Stewart, M.	AF	MTI	$5.00
CREST	d 773	A For Andromeda	1964	Hoyle, F.	AF		$6.00
CREST	d 775	The Shook-Up Generation	1964	Salisbury, H.E.	VGF		$5.00
CREST	d 814	12 Tales Of Suspense	1965	Grubb, D.	VGF		$12.00
CREST	d 814	12 Tales Of Suspense	1965	Grubb, D.	AF		$8.00
CREST	T 816	The Third Day	1965	Hayes, J.	VGF	MTI	$6.00
CREST	r 836	Owl's Watch	1965	Saul, G.B.	AF		$7.00
CREST	m 851	Little Big Man	1965	Berger, T.	VGF		$7.00
CREST	R 877	The Q Document	1965	Roberts, J.H.	AF		$5.00
CREST	R 899	Modesty Blaise	1968	O'Donnell, P.	VGF+		$16.00 A
CREST	R 920	The Man Who Wrote Dirty Books	1966	Dresner, H.	VG+		$8.00
CREST	T 968	Sex And The College Student	1966	Wheelright, J.B.	VGF		$5.00
CREST	R 1065	Sabre-Tooth	1967	O'Donnell, P.	VGF+		$14.00 A
CREST	t 1084	The Battle Of Britain	1968	Jullian, M.	VGF+		$6.00
CREST	T 1163	On The Yard	1968	Braly, M.	F		$10.00
CREST	R 1166	Strange Beasts And Monsters	1969	Anthology	VGF		$6.00
CREST	P 1231	Mandingo	1969	Onstott, K.	F		$12.00
CREST	T 1244	We Are The People . . .	1969	Hoffman, N.V.	VGF		$7.00
CREST	M 1603	Cruising	1971	Walker, G.	AF		$7.00
CREST	M 1845	Night World	1972	Bloch, R.	VGF		$4.00
CREST	P 1876	The Stepford Wives	1973	Levin, I.	AF		$6.00
CREST	M 2044	What Of Terry Conniston?	1974	Garfield, B.	AF	MTI	$7.00
CREST	P 2268	Death Wish	1974	Garfield, B.	F	MTI	$7.00
CREST	Q 2650	After The Last Race	1975	Koontz, D.R.	VG		$14.00
CREST	Q 2650	After The Last Race	1975	Koontz, D.R.	VG-		$9.00
CREST	X 2691	Jones - Portrait Of A Mugger	1976	Willwerth, J.	AF		$8.00
CREST	X 2691	Jones - Portrait Of A Mugger	1976	Willwerth, J.	VGF		$7.00

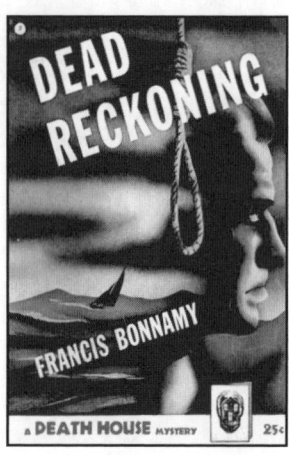

Croydon 94 VG $22   Curtis Warren No# VG $17   Death House 5 VG+ $14

PUBLISHER	PUB. #	TITLE	DATE	AUTHOR	COND.	TYPE	PRICE
CREST	X 2750	Two Much	1976	Westlake, D.E.	AF		$12.00
CREST	Q 2778	This Suitcase Is Going To Explode	1976	Ardies, T.	F		$20.00
CREST	Q 2778	This Suitcase Is Going To Explode	1976	Ardies, T.	VG		$8.00
CREST	2892	The City 2000 A.D.	1976	Anthology	VG-		$5.00
CREST	3056	King Of White Lady	1975	Hill, R.L.	VG		$7.00
CREST	3345	Prison Of Ice	1976	Axton, D.*	VG+		$34.00 A
CREST	3525	Condominium	n/d	MacDonald, J.D.	VGF		$8.00
CRIME AND JUSTICE	4	Crime And Justice 3/57	1957	Anthology	VG-	Digest	$10.00
CRIME CASE BOOK	1 1	Crime Case Book 1/54	1954	Anthology	VG+	Digest	$17.00 A
CRIME CASE BOOK	1 2	Crime Case Book 3/54	1954	Anthology	VG+	Digest	$23.00 A
CRIME LAB	1 1	Crime Lab Mystery Mag. 10/54	1954	Anthology	AF-	Digest	$16.00 A
CRIME LAB	1 1	Crime Lab Mystery Mag. 10/54	1954	Anthology	VG	Digest	$8.00
CRIME LAB	1 1	Crime Lab Mystery Mag. 10/54	1954	Anthology	VG-	Digest	$6.00
CRIME NOVEL SELECTION	2	The Traveling Corpses	1942	Steel, K.	VG+	Digest	$15.00
CRIME NOVEL SELECTION	4	Murder For What?	1943	Steel, K.	VG	Digest	$27.00 A
CROYDON	13	Reckless Virgin	1949	Watkins, G.	VG+		$11.00 A
CROYDON	16	Sinner	1950	Semple, G.	VGF+		$23.00 A
CROYDON	23	Sins Of A Private Secretary	1952	Jordan, G.	VGF+	Digest	$24.00 A
CROYDON	24	Love Hungry Doctor	1952	Stonebraker, F.	AF	Digest	$42.00 A
CROYDON	41	Secrets Of Paris Nights	1953	Marcelle, D.	VG	Digest	$12.00
CROYDON	41	Secrets Of Paris Nights	1953	Marcelle, D.	VG	Digest	$10.00
CROYDON	44	Confessions Of A B-Girl	1953	Albert, S.	G	Digest	$14.00 A
CROYDON	47	Read-Headed Sinners	1953	Craig, J.	VGF	Digest	$25.00 A
CROYDON	55	Shameless Play-Girl	1954	Stonebraker, F.	G	Digest	$8.00
CROYDON	59	Scandals At A Country Club	1954	Frame, B.	VG	Digest	$10.00
CROYDON	60	Forbidden Passions	1954	Williams, W.	VG+	Digest	$60.00 A
CROYDON	60	Forbidden Passions	1954	Williams, W.	VGF	Digest	$29.00 A
CROYDON	70	Conf. Of A Ladies' Chauffeur	1954	Stonebraker, F.	VGF	Digest	$16.00
CROYDON	71	Bad Girls' Club	1954	Davids, W.	G-	Digest	$5.00
CROYDON	77	French Sinner	1954	Albert, S.	VGF	Digest	$20.00 A
CROYDON	94	Tenement Girl	1955	Bennett, A.	VG	Digest	$22.00 A
CURTIS	1043	Shockproof Sydney Skate	n/d	Meaker, M.	VG+		$7.00
CURTIS	7215	Fever Heat	n/d	Felsen, H.G.	VGF		$6.00
CURTIS	7303	The Alarming Clock	1973	Avallone, M.	VGF+		$5.00
CURTIS	9253	Wine, Women . . . And Death	1974	Deptula, W.	AF		$7.00
CURTIS	9254	Naked Mistress	1974	Deptula, W.	AF		$7.00
CURTIS WARREN	No#	Hostile Worlds	1951	Hunt, G.	VG-	Digest	$7.00 A
CURTIS WARREN	No#	King Hunters	1951	Garron, M.	VG	Digest	$22.00 A
CURTIS WARREN	No#	Moon War	1951	Hughes, D.	VG	Digest	$7.00 A
CURTIS WARREN	No#	Planet X	1951	Hunt, G.	VG+	Digest	$22.00 A
CURTIS WARREN	No#	Space Line	1951	Lang, K.	VG	Digest	$17.00 A
CURTIS WARREN	No#	Tribal War	1951	Garron, M.	VG+	Digest	$33.00 A
DAGGER HOUSE	24	If A Body Kill A Body	1946	Mortimer, P.	VG	Digest	$7.00
DALE	62	Return Of The Living Dead	1978	Russo, J.	VGF	MTI	$18.00 A
DALE	565	The Plastic Nightmare	1978	Neely, R.	VG-		$4.00

Dell 1 VG+ $55   Dell 4 VG+ $41   Dell 8 VGF $48

PUBLISHER	PUB. #	TITLE	DATE	AUTHOR	COND.	TYPE	PRICE
DAVIS PUBLICATIONS	n/a	Science Fiction By Asimov	1986	Asimov, I.	VG+	Digest	$5.00 A
DAW	12	A Darkness In My Soul	1972	Koontz, D.R.	VG		$12.00
DAW	14	We Can Build You	1972	Dick, P.K.	VG+		$8.00
DAW	20	Ole Doc Methuselah	1972	Hubbard, L.R.	VGF		$12.00
DAW	44	The Book Of Philip K. Dick	1973	Dick, P.K.	VG+		$22.00 A
DAW	44	The Book Of Philip K. Dick	1973	Dick, P.K.	VG		$12.00
DAW	146	Flow My Tears, . . .	1975	Dick, P.K.	VGF+		$10.00
DAW	146	Flow My Tears, . . .	1975	Dick, P.K.	VG		$6.00
DAW	186	The Wrath Of Fu Manchu	1976	Rohmer, S.	VGF		$15.00
DAW	533	A Maze Of Death	1983	Dick, P.K.	VGF		$8.00
DAW	559	Deus Irae	1983	Dick, P.K.	AF		$8.00
DAW	1274	A Darkness In My Soul	n/d	Koontz, D.R.	VG+		$10.00
DAW	1793	We Can Build You	1987	Dick, P.K.	VGF		$6.00
DEATH HOUSE	4	TCOT Nameless Corpse	1944	Goldthwaite, E.K.	VG	Digest	$14.00
DEATH HOUSE	5	Dead Reckoning	1945	Bonnamy, F.	VG+	Digest	$14.00
DELL	No#	Dick Tracy & The Woo Woo Sisters	1947	Gould, C.	VG		$45.00 A
DELL	No#	Blondie And Dagwood	1947	Young, C.	VG		$41.00 A
DELL	1	Death In The Library	1943	Ketchum, P.	VG+		$55.00 A
DELL	4	The American Gun Mystery	1943	Queen, E.	VG+		$41.00 A
DELL	4	The American Gun Mystery	1943	Queen, E.	VG		$20.00
DELL	4	The American Gun Mystery	1943	Queen, E.	G		$5.00
DELL	4	The American Gun Mystery-2nd	1943	Queen, E.	VG+		$15.00
DELL	5	Four Frightened Women	1943	Coxe, G.H.	G		$6.00
DELL	6	Ill Met By Moonlight	1943	Ford, L.	VG+		$15.00
DELL	6	Ill Met By Moonlight	1943	Ford, L.	G+		$6.00
DELL	8	The Tuesday Club Murders	1943	Christie, A.	VGF		$48.00 A
DELL	9	Double For Death	1943	Stout, R.	VG+		$37.00 A
DELL	10	The Lone Wolf	1943	Vance, L.J.	VG+		$40.00 A
DELL	11	Hearses Don't Hurry	1943	Ransome, S.	VG		$17.00
DELL	12	Wife vs. Secretary	1943	Baldwin, F.	G		$7.00
DELL	13	Death Wears A White Gardenia	1943	Popkin, Z.	VG		$14.00
DELL	13	Death Wears A White Gardenia	1943	Popkin, Z.	G		$5.00
DELL	14	The Doctor Died At Dusk	1943	Homes, G.	VG		$20.00
DELL	14	The Doctor Died At Dusk	1943	Homes, G.	VG+		$16.00 A
DELL	15	The Golden Swan Murder	1943	Disney, D.C.	VG		$15.00
DELL	15	The Golden Swan Murder	1943	Disney, D.C.	VG-		$12.00
DELL	17	The Dead Can Tell	1943	Reilly, H.	VG		$39.00 A
DELL	17	The Dead Can Tell	1943	Reilly, H.	G		$5.00
DELL	18	The Puzzle Of The Silver Persian	1943	Palmer, S.	G+		$6.00
DELL	20	Tambray Gold	1943	Adams, S.H.	VG+		$15.00
DELL	21	I Was A Nazi Flier	1943	Leske, G.	VGF-		$22.00 A
DELL	21	I Was A Nazi Flier	1943	Leske, G.	VG		$17.00
DELL	21	I Was A Nazi Flier	1943	Leske, G.	G		$10.00
DELL	22	Holiday Homicide	1943	King, R.	VG+		$29.00 A
DELL	22	Holiday Homicide	1943	King, R.	VG		$24.00

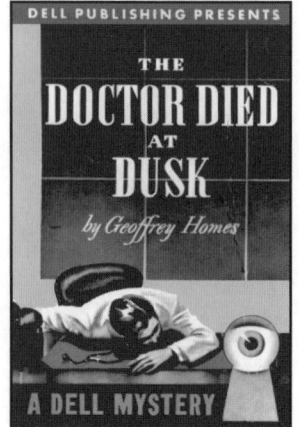
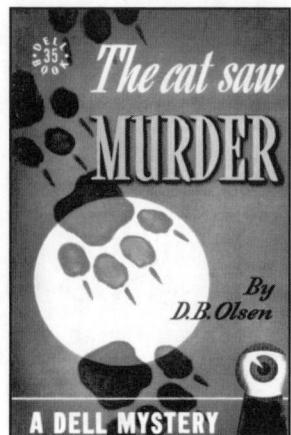

Dell 11 VG $17   Dell 14 VG $20   Dell 35 VG+ $38

PUBLISHER	PUB. #	TITLE	DATE	AUTHOR	COND.	TYPE	PRICE
DELL	22	Holiday Homicide	1943	King, R.	VG		$16.00
DELL	23	The Private Practice Of M. Shayne	1943	Halliday, B.	VGF		$15.00
DELL	24	Phantom Of The Opera	1943	Leroux, G.	VGF		$20.00 A
DELL	26	The Mountain Cat Murders	1944	Stout, R.	VG		$14.00
DELL	29	Curtains For The Copper	1944	Polsky, T.	VG		$8.00
DELL	31	The Fallen Sparrow	1944	Hughes, D.B.	G		$6.00
DELL	33	Dance Of Death	1944	McCloy, H.	VG		$14.00
DELL	35	The Cat Saw Murder	1944	Olsen, D.B.	VG+		$38.00 A
DELL	35	The Cat Saw Murder	1944	Olsen, D.B.	VG+		$17.00 A
DELL	35	The Cat Saw Murder	1944	Olsen, D.B.	G		$4.00
DELL	39	Murder Challenges Valcour	1944	King, R.	VG+		$20.00 A
DELL	39	Murder Challenges Valcour	1944	King, R.	VG-		$7.00
DELL	42	Murders At Scandal House	1944	Hunt, P.	VG		$11.00 A
DELL	42	Murders At Scandal House	1944	Hunt, P.	G		$4.00
DELL	43	Midnight Sailing	1944	Blochman, L.G.	G		$4.00
DELL	47	Keeper Of The Keys	1944	Biggers, E.D.	G		$7.00
DELL	53	Blood Money	1944	Hammett, D.	VG+		$50.00 A
DELL	53	Blood Money	1944	Hammett, D.	VG		$11.00 A
DELL	57	The Window At The White Cat	1944	Rinehart, M.R.	VG		$18.00 A
DELL	57	The Window At The White Cat	1944	Rinehart, M.R.	VG		$13.00 A
DELL	58	Murder For The Asking	1944	Coxe, G.H.	VG+		$15.00
DELL	58	Murder For The Asking	1944	Coxe, G.H.	G		$4.00
DELL	62	The Strawstack Murders	1944	Disney, D.C.	AF		$32.00 A
DELL	64	Blood On The Black Market	1944	Halliday, B.	VG+		$13.00 A
DELL	72	The Man In The Moonlight	1945	McCloy, H.	VG		$5.00 A
DELL	75	The Affair Of The Scarlet Crab	1945	Knight, C.	VG+		$88.00 A
DELL	86	The Man Who Murdered Goliath	1945	Homes, G.	VG+		$82.00 A
DELL	89	Dell Book Of Jokes	1945	Anthology	G		$12.00
DELL	90	A Man Called Spade	1945	Hammett, D.	VG-		$7.00
DELL	94	No Crime For A Lady	1945	Popkin, Z.	VG		$10.00
DELL	100	The So Blue Marble	1946	Hughes, D.B.	VG		$5.00
DELL	102	You Only Hang Once	1946	Roden, H.W.	VGF		$40.00 A
DELL	103	Murder Is A Kill-Joy	1946	Holding, E.S.	VGF		$31.00 A
DELL	103	Murder Is A Kill-Joy	1946	Holding, E.S.	VG		$8.00
DELL	104	The Crooking Finger	1946	Adams, C.F.	G		$4.00
DELL	105	Appointment With Death	1946	Christie, A.	AF		$20.00 A
DELL	105	Appointment With Death	1946	Christie, A.	VG		$7.00
DELL	107	The Deadly Truth	1946	McCloy, H.	VG+		$10.00
DELL	108	Death In Five Boxes	1946	Dickson, C.*	VGF		$10.00
DELL	109	Spill The Jackpot	1946	Fair, A.A.*	VGF		$36.00 A
DELL	109	Spill The Jackpot	1946	Fair, A.A.*	VGF		$20.00
DELL	109	Spill The Jackpot	1946	Fair, A.A.*	VG		$7.00
DELL	110	Wall Of Eyes	1946	Millar, M.	AF		$16.00
DELL	110	Wall Of Eyes	1946	Millar, M.	VG		$8.00
DELL	111	Greenmask	1946	Farjeon, J.	VGF		$24.00 A

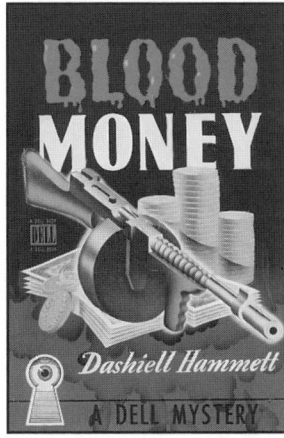

Dell 53 VG+ $50   Dell 75 VG+ $88   Dell 86 VG+ $82

PUBLISHER	PUB. #	TITLE	DATE	AUTHOR	COND.	TYPE	PRICE
DELL	113	The Whistling Hangman	1946	Kendrick, B.H.	VG		$8.00
DELL	116	Honor Bound	1946	Baldwin, F.	VG+		$7.00
DELL	117	Women Are Like That	1946	Lambert, A.E.	VG+		$5.00
DELL	119	Robin Hill	1946	Larrimore, L.	VGF		$10.00
DELL	120	Man In The Saddle	1946	Haycox, E.	VG		$7.00
DELL	121	Footprints On The Ceiling	1946	Rawson, C.	G+		$6.00
DELL	123	Too Many Bones	1946	Wallis, R.S.	VG+		$10.00
DELL	123	Too Many Bones	1946	Wallis, R.S.	VG		$7.00
DELL	125	Dreadful Hollow	1946	Karlova, I.	VG-		$6.00
DELL	126	Murderer's Choice	1946	Wells, A.M.	VGF		$15.00 A
DELL	127	Old Bones	1946	Petersen, H.	G		$6.00
DELL	128	Murder And The Married Virgin	1946	Halliday, B.	VG		$8.00
DELL	129	The Continental Op	1946	Hammett, D.	VGF		$23.00 A
DELL	129	The Continental Op	1946	Hammett, D.	VG		$16.00
DELL	129	The Continental Op	1946	Hammett, D.	G+		$8.00
DELL	133	Cobweb House	1946	Holloway, E.H.	VG+		$47.00 A
DELL	134	Wives To Burn	1946	Blochman, L.G.	VG+		$7.00
DELL	134	Wives To Burn	1946	Blochman, L.G.	G		$3.00
DELL	136	Wolf In Man's Clothing	1946	Eberhart, M.G.	VG+		$7.00
DELL	137	Crimson Friday	1946	Disney, D.C.	VG+		$10.00
DELL	137	Crimson Friday	1946	Disney, D.C.	VG+		$8.00
DELL	140	Footprint Of Cinderella	1946	Wylie, P.	VG+		$7.00
DELL	141	The Swift Hour	1946	Thurman, H.	VG+		$8.00
DELL	142	Cold Steal	1946	Tilton, A.	G+		$5.00
DELL	143	Bar The Doors!	1946	Anthology	VGF		$24.00 A
DELL	143	Bar The Doors!	1946	Anthology	G+		$7.00
DELL	144	The White Brigand	1947	Marshall, E.	VGF		$12.00
DELL	144	The White Brigand	1947	Marshall, E.	VG+		$8.00
DELL	145	Murder In Mesopotamia	1947	Christie, A.	VG		$8.00
DELL	147	The Lady Is Afraid	1947	Coxe, G.H.	VGF		$14.00
DELL	151	Who's Calling?	1947	McCloy, H.	VG+		$17.00 A
DELL	152	Jokes, Gags And Wisecracks	1947	Shane, T.	VG+		$22.00 A
DELL	154	Return Of The Continental Op	1947	Hammett, D.	VG+		$24.00
DELL	154	Return Of The Continental Op	1947	Hammett, D.	VG		$22.00
DELL	154	Return Of The Continental Op	1947	Hammett, D.	G		$10.00
DELL	154	Return Of The Continental Op	1947	Hammett, D.	G		$7.00
DELL	156	Blow Down	1947	Blochman, L.G.	VG+		$8.00
DELL	159	If A Body	1947	Yates, G.W.	VG		$5.00
DELL	168	The Corpse Came Calling	1947	Halliday, B.	VG		$7.00
DELL	171	Octagon House	1947	Taylor, P.A.	VG+		$23.00 A
DELL	172	Sad Cypress	1947	Christie, A.	VG+		$20.00 A
DELL	173	Rim Of The Pit	1947	Talbot, H.	VGF		$15.00
DELL	173	Rim Of The Pit	1947	Talbot, H.	VG+		$9.00
DELL	174	The Sheik	1947	Hull, E.M.	VG+		$8.00
DELL	175	And So To Murder	1947	Dickson, C.*	VG		$7.00

Dell 105 AF $20   Dell 129 VGF $23   Dell 143 VGF $24

PUBLISHER	PUB. #	TITLE	DATE	AUTHOR	COND.	TYPE	PRICE
DELL	182	No Time To Kill	1947	Coxe, G.H.	VG-		$6.00
DELL	184	Murder Is My Business	1947	Halliday, B.	VGF		$10.00
DELL	184	Murder Is My Business	1947	Halliday, B.	VG		$7.00
DELL	187	N Or M?	1947	Christie, A.	VG		$8.00
DELL	189	Kind Are Her Answers	1947	Renault, M.	VGF		$8.00
DELL	192	Tugboat Annie	1947	Raine, N.R.	VG		$10.00
DELL	196	Rich Girl, Poor Girl	1947	Baldwin, F.	VGF		$8.00
DELL	201	The First Men In The Moon	1947	Wells, H.G.	VG-		$6.00
DELL	202	Mrs. Murdock Takes A Case	1947	Coxe, G.H.	VGF		$27.00 A
DELL	203	The State vs. Elinor Norton	1947	Rinehart, M.R.	VG		$8.00
DELL	206	Hold Your Breath	1948	Anthology	VG		$15.00
DELL	208	The Black Curtain	1948	Woolrich, C.	VG+		$27.00 A
DELL	208	The Black Curtain	1948	Woolrich, C.	G		$10.00
DELL	209	The Iron Gates	1948	Millar, M.	VG-		$6.00
DELL	213	Unidentified Woman	1948	Eberhart, M.G.	VG		$6.00
DELL	215	Dr. Parrish Resident	1948	Thompson, S.	VG+		$7.00
DELL	217	Gun Smoke Yarns	1948	Anthology	VG		$8.00
DELL	220	Hospital Nocturne	1948	Lambert, A.E.	VG		$7.00
DELL	221	Dark Passage	1948	Goodis, D.	G+		$30.00
DELL	221	Dark Passage	1948	Goodis, D.	VG		$20.00
DELL	222	Marked For Murder	1948	Halliday, B.	VG+		$8.00 A
DELL	223	Hammett Homicides	1948	Hammett, D.	VG+		$34.00
DELL	223	Hammett Homicides	1948	Hammett, D.	VG		$17.00
DELL	225	Silent Are The Dead	1948	Coxe, G.H.	VG+		$10.00
DELL	227	Trail Town	1948	Haycox, E.	VG+		$7.00
DELL	231	A Halo For Nobody	1948	Kane, H.	VG+		$44.00 A
DELL	233	The Upstart	1948	Marshall, E.	VG		$7.00
DELL	236	Skyscraper	1948	Baldwin, F.	VG		$7.00
DELL	237	House Of Darkness	1948	MacKinnon, A.	VG+		$12.00 A
DELL	241	The Bat	1948	Rinehart, M.R.	VG		$8.00
DELL	242	The Unafraid	1948	Butler, G.	VGF	MTI	$22.00 A
DELL	244	Judas Incorporated	1948	Steel, K.	VG+		$8.00
DELL	251	Banbury Bog	1948	Taylor, P.A.	VG+		$6.00
DELL	252	Benefit Performance	1948	Sale, R.	VG-		$5.00
DELL	253	Treasure Of The Brasada	1948	Savage, L.	VG+		$7.00
DELL	254	Bats Fly At Dusk	1948	Fair, A.A.*	VGF		$10.00
DELL	255	Enchanted Oasis	1948	Baldwin, F.	VG		$7.00
DELL	257	Murder In Retrospect	1948	Christie, A.	G		$4.00
DELL	260	Chinese Red	1948	Burke, R.	VGF		$17.00
DELL	261	Do Not Disturb	1948	McCloy, H.	VG-		$7.00
DELL	262	Rope	1948	Hitchcock, A.	VGF	MTI	$23.00 A
DELL	262	Rope	1948	Hitchcock, A.	VG+	MTI	$17.00
DELL	263	The Panic Stricken	1948	Wilson, M.	VG+		$8.00
DELL	264	Fear And Trembling	1948	Hitchcock, A.	VG		$7.00
DELL	264	Fear And Trembling	1948	Hitchcock, A.	VG-		$6.00

Dell 192 VG $10   Dell 208 VG+ $20   Dell 222 VG+ $8

PUBLISHER	PUB. #	TITLE	DATE	AUTHOR	COND.	TYPE	PRICE
DELL	267	Not Quite Dead Enough	1948	Stout, R.	VG+		$10.00
DELL	270	It Ain't Hay	1949	Dodge, D.	VG+		$27.00 A
DELL	270	It Ain't Hay	1949	Dodge, D.	G		$6.00 A
DELL	272	The Velvet Fleece	1949	Eby, L.	VG+		$7.00
DELL	273	Death Knell	1949	Kendrick, B.	VG+		$12.00
DELL	275	Where There's Smoke	1949	Sterling, S.	VG		$7.00
DELL	276	Murder For Two	1949	Coxe, G.H.	VGF		$13.00 A
DELL	277	Ex-Wife	1949	Parrott, U.	VGF		$8.00
DELL	279	Sons Of The Sheik	1949	Hull, E.M.	VG+		$8.00
DELL	282	Western Stories	1949	Raine, W.M.	VG		$6.00
DELL	285	Anthony Adverse In America	1949	Allen, H.	VG		$6.00
DELL	286	Eisenhower Was My Boss	1949	Summersby, K.	VGF		$7.00
DELL	287	The Silver Leopard	1949	Reilly, H.	VG+		$39.00 A
DELL	288	The Heart Remembers	1949	Baldwin, F.	VG		$6.00
DELL	289	Bitter Ending	1949	Irving, A.	VG		$8.00
DELL	290	The Pioneers	1949	Cooper, C.R.	VG+		$8.00
DELL	291	So Dear To My Heart	1949	North, S.	VG+	MTI	$25.00 A
DELL	294	Jim The Conqueror	1949	Kyne, P.B.	VG+		$7.00
DELL	295	The Goblin Market	1949	McCloy, H.	VG		$8.00
DELL	296	Little Women	1949	Alcott, L.M.	VG+	MTI	$10.00
DELL	297	The Great Mistake	1949	Rinehart, M.R.	VGF		$12.00
DELL	297	The Great Mistake	1949	Rinehart, M.R.	VG		$7.00
DELL	304	Dr. Hudson's Secret Journal	1949	Douglas, L.C.	VG+		$7.00
DELL	305	Invasion From Mars	1949	Welles, O.	G+		$4.00
DELL	305	Invasion From Mars	1949	Welles, O.	G		$3.00
DELL	308	Dead Yellow Women	1949	Hammett, D.	VG		$17.00
DELL	308	Dead Yellow Women	1949	Hammett, D.	VG-		$15.00
DELL	309	Satin Straps	1949	Greig, M.	VGF		$8.00
DELL	311	Bengal Fire	1949	Blochman, L.G.	VG+		$10.00
DELL	311	Bengal Fire	1949	Blochman, L.G.	VG-		$7.00
DELL	312	The Gaunt Woman	1949	Gilligan, E.	VGF		$7.00
DELL	316	Armchair In Hell	1949	Kane, H.	VG+		$10.00
DELL	316	Armchair In Hell	1949	Kane, H.	VG		$8.00
DELL	317	Alder Gulch	1949	Haycox, E.	VG+		$7.00
DELL	318	Alimony	1949	Baldwin, F.	VGF		$8.00
DELL	322	Death Of A Tall Man	1949	Lockridge, F.	VG+		$7.00
DELL	323	Murder And The Married Virgin	1949	Halliday, B.	VG+		$6.00
DELL	325	Michael Shayne's Long Chance	1949	Halliday, B.	VGF		$12.00
DELL	326	Murder Is My Business	1949	Halliday, B.	VG		$8.00
DELL	326	Murder Is My Business	1949	Halliday, B.	VG		$7.00
DELL	327	Leave Cancelled	1949	Monsarrat, N.	VG+		$8.00
DELL	328	Can You Top This?	1949	Anthology	G		$3.00
DELL	330	Report For A Corpse	1949	Kane, H.	VG+		$7.00
DELL	331	Anna Lucasta	1949	Yordan, P.	VG+	MTI	$22.00 A
DELL	338	The Lady Regrets	1949	Fox, J.M.	VG		$6.00

Dell 237 VG+ $12   Dell 276 VGF $13   Dell 277 VGF $8

PUBLISHER	PUB. #	TITLE	DATE	AUTHOR	COND.	TYPE	PRICE
DELL	339	She	1949	Haggard, H.R.	G		$4.00
DELL	342	Sons Of The Sheik	1949	Hull, E.M.	VG+		$5.00
DELL	349	Too Busy To Die	1949	Roden, H.W.	VG+		$8.00
DELL	351	Showdown	1949	Flynn, E.	VGF		$9.00
DELL	353	Yankee Pasha	1949	Marshall, E.	VGF		$8.00
DELL	358	To A God Unknown	1949	Steinbeck, J.	VGF		$14.00
DELL	358	To A God Unknown	1949	Steinbeck, J.	VGF		$8.00
DELL	360	Don Lorenzo's Bride	1949	Savage, J.	VG+		$7.00
DELL	363	Blue City	1949	Millar, K.	VG+		$29.00 A
DELL	365	The Death Of A Worldly Woman	1949	Cunningham, A.B.	VGF		$27.00 A
DELL	367	Suspense Stories	1949	Anthology	VG-		$6.00
DELL	370	He Wouldn't Kill Patience	1950	Dickson, C.*	VG		$8.00
DELL	372	Buckaroo's Code	1950	Overholser, W.D.	VGF		$7.00
DELL	374	Night And The City	1950	Kersh, G.	AF	MTI	$34.00 A
DELL	374	Night And The City	1950	Kersh, G.	VGF	MTI	$16.00
DELL	374	Night And The City	1950	Kersh, G.	VG	MTI	$7.00
DELL	375	Date With Darkness	1950	Hamilton, D.	VG+		$10.00
DELL	376	Out of Control	1950	Kendrick, B.	VG+		$8.00
DELL	379	Nightmare Town	1950	Hammett, D.	VG		$15.00
DELL	379	Nightmare Town	1950	Hammett, D.	G+		$7.00
DELL	382	Celeste	1950	Marshall, R.	VG+		$8.00
DELL	385	Blood On The Stars	1950	Halliday, B.	VG		$6.00
DELL	392	Virgin With Butterflies	1950	Powers, T.	VG		$6.00
DELL	393	Code Of The Woosters	1950	Wodehouse, P.G.	VG		$6.00
DELL	400	New York: Confidential!	1950	Lait, J.	G		$3.00
DELL	402	The Captive Of The Sahara	1950	Hull, E.M.	VG		$6.00
DELL	404	The Case Of Jenny Brice	1950	Rinehart, M.R.	VG		$7.00
DELL	411	A Man Called Spade	1950	Hammett, D.	VG		$15.00
DELL	415	Ladies In Hades	1950	Kummer, F.A.	VG		$6.00
DELL	416	They Drive By Night	1950	Bezzerides, A.I.	VG		$6.00
DELL	427	Dead Man's Diary	1950	Halliday, B.	VG		$8.00
DELL	431	Benjamin Blake: Son Of Fury	1950	Marshall, E.	VG		$7.00
DELL	432	Stag Night	1950	Rogers, P.	VG		$7.00
DELL	433	King Solomon's Mines	1950	Haggard, H.R.	VG	MTI	$6.00
DELL	444	Tender Mercy	1950	Kaufman, L.	VG+		$7.00
DELL	446	Yours Ever	1950	Greig, M.	VGF		$7.00
DELL	452	A Man Called Spade	1950	Hammett, D.	VG		$12.00
DELL	452	A Man Called Spade	1950	Hammett, D.	G+		$12.00
DELL	458	A Taste For Violence	1950	Halliday, B.	VGF		$7.00
DELL	469	Uncle Dynamite	1950	Wodehouse, P.G.	VG		$6.00
DELL	470	Flight Of An Angel	1951	Chute, V.	VG+		$7.00
DELL	471	Vigilante	1951	Summers, R.	VG+		$7.00
DELL	478	Plunder Of The Sun	1951	Dodge, D.	VG+		$11.00 A
DELL	482	Women Must Weep	1951	Knight, R.A.	VG		$7.00
DELL	483	What A Body	1951	Green, A.	VG		$7.00

Dell 363 VG+ $29   Dell 525 VGF $44   Dell 538 VGF $41

PUBLISHER	PUB. #	TITLE	DATE	AUTHOR	COND.	TYPE	PRICE
DELL	483	What A Body	1951	Green, A.	G+		$6.00
DELL	485	The Queen And The Corpse	1951	Murray, M.	VG		$6.00
DELL	486	Blood Money	1951	Hammett, D.	G		$12.00
DELL	486	Blood Money	1951	Hammett, D.	VG		$10.00
DELL	487	Castle In The Swamp	1951	Marshall, E.	VG		$6.00
DELL	501	The Demon Caravan	1951	Surdez, G.	VGF		$8.00
DELL	507	Francis	1951	Stern, D.	VG		$6.00
DELL	510	You Play The Black, Red Comes Up	1951	Hallas, R.	VG		$7.00
DELL	511	Slippery Hitch	1951	Butler, G.	VG+		$7.00
DELL	512	The Robbed Heart	1951	Cuthbert, C.	VGF-		$7.00
DELL	516	No Highway	1951	Shute, N.	VGF	MTI	$12.00
DELL	516	No Highway	1951	Shute, N.	VG	MTI	$7.00
DELL	518	Shell Game	1951	Powell, R.	VG+		$7.00
DELL	524	Once In Vienna	1951	Baum, V.	VG+		$8.00
DELL	525	Diamond Lil	1951	West, M.	VGF		$44.00 A
DELL	526	The Gentle Hangman	1951	Fox, J.M.	VG		$8.00
DELL	531	Death In Four Colors	1951	Bird, B.	G+		$5.00
DELL	532	The Incredible Year	1951	Baldwin, F.	VG+		$6.00
DELL	533	This Is It, Michael Shayne	1951	Halliday, B.	VG		$7.00
DELL	535	Edge Of Panic	1951	Kane, H.	VG		$5.00
DELL	536	Tarzan And The Lost Empire	1951	Burroughs, E.R.	VGF		$18.00 A
DELL	538	The Creeping Siamese	1951	Hammett, D.	VGF		$41.00 A
DELL	538	The Creeping Siamese	1951	Hammett, D.	G+		$8.00
DELL	542	Fools Die On Friday (orig. cover)	1951	Fair, A.A.*	VG		$20.00 A
DELL	546	Hunt With The Hounds	1951	Eberhart, M.G.	VG+		$8.00
DELL	547	Date With Death	1951	Ford, L.	VG		$6.00
DELL	549	The Jade Venus	1951	Coxe, G.H.	VGF-		$5.00 A
DELL	553	The Mark Of Zorro	1951	McCulley, J.	VG		$10.00
DELL	553	The Mark Of Zorro	1951	McCulley, J.	VG		$7.00
DELL	555	Causeway To The Past	1951	O'Farrell, W.	VG-		$6.00
DELL	556	Draw Or Drag	1951	Overholser, W.D.	VG		$6.00
DELL	561	Crescent Carnival	1952	Keyes, F.P.	VG		$6.00
DELL	562	Raw Land	1952	Short, L.	VG+		$7.00
DELL	565	The Red Tassel	1952	Dodge, D.	VG+		$8.00
DELL	565	The Red Tassel	1952	Dodge, D.	VG		$7.00
DELL	567	The Harem	1952	Royer, L.C.	AF		$10.00
DELL	572	Dark Moon Of March	1952	Gowen, E.	VG+		$7.00
DELL	573	The Wheel Is Fixed	1952	Fox, J.M.	VG		$7.00
DELL	574	For Richer, For Poorer	1952	Baldwin, F.	VGF		$7.00
DELL	575	Montana, Here I Be	1952	Cushman, D.	VG+		$8.00
DELL	576	Murder At Arroways	1952	Reilly, H.	VG		$7.00
DELL	585	The Circular Staircase	1952	Rinehart, M.R.	VG-		$6.00
DELL	596	The Taste Of Murder	1952	Cannan, J.	VG+		$5.00
DELL	599	Heaven Ran Last	1952	McGivern, W.P.	VG		$6.00
DELL	602	Tequila	1952	Hood, M.P.	VGF		$8.00

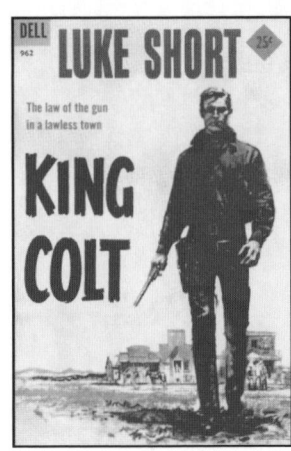

Dell 681 VGF $8   Dell 738 VG+ $33   Dell 962 AF $7

PUBLISHER	PUB. #	TITLE	DATE	AUTHOR	COND.	TYPE	PRICE
DELL	605	The Congo Venus	1952	Head, M.	VG+		$6.00
DELL	617	Dividend On Death	1952	Halliday, B.	VG+	A	$9.00
DELL	622	Age Of Consent	1952	Yore, C.	VGF		$7.00
DELL	624	Steel To The South	1952	Overholser, W.D.	VGF		$6.00
DELL	630	Untamed	1952	Moray, H.	VG+		$7.00
DELL	633	Three Blind Mice	1952	Christie, A.	VGF		$8.00
DELL	637	Indian Beef	1952	Wire, H.C.	VG		$7.00
DELL	652	The Bat	1953	Rinehart, M.R.	VG-		$6.00
DELL	658	To Catch A Thief	1953	Dodge, D.	VG+		$5.00
DELL	661	Stormy Present	1953	Field, H.	VGF		$7.00
DELL	661	Stormy Present	1953	Field, H.	VG		$6.00
DELL	664	The Boomerang Clue	1953	Christie, A.	VG+		$6.00
DELL	678	Fashioned For Murder	1953	Coxe, G.H.	AF	A	$17.00
DELL	679	Night Has 1000 Eyes	1953	Irish, W.*	VGF	A	$31.00
DELL	679	Night Has 1000 Eyes	1953	Irish, W.*	G+		$8.00
DELL	681	The Picture Of Dorian Gray	1953	Wilde, O.	VGF		$8.00
DELL	682	The Gallows In My Garden	1953	Deming, R.	AF	A	$8.00
DELL	683	An Overdose Of Death	1953	Christie, A.	VG+		$7.00
DELL	685	The Scarlet Slippers	1953	Fox, J.M.	VG+		$8.00
DELL	700	Curtains For The Copper	1953	Polsky, T.	G+		$5.00
DELL	703	The Stockade	1953	Lamott, K.	VG+		$7.00
DELL	728	Bowling Handbook	1953	Falcaro, J.	VG+		$5.00
DELL	730	Vanish In An Instant	1953	Millar, M.	VGF	A	$40.00
DELL	738	Nothing More Than Murder	1953	Thompson, J.	VG+	A	$33.00
DELL	738	Nothing More Than Murder	1953	Thompson, J.	VG+	A	$33.00
DELL	746	The Bloody Bokhara	1953	Gault, W.C.	VG+		$12.00
DELL	746	The Bloody Bokhara	1953	Gault, W.C.	VG+	A	$9.00
DELL	749	Bare Trap	1954	Kane, F.	VG+		$8.00
DELL	752	Spider Lily	1954	Fischer, B.	VG+		$9.00
DELL	768	What Really Happened	1954	Halliday, B.	VG+		$7.00
DELL	768	What Really Happened	1954	Halliday, B.	VG		$7.00
DELL	774	Natural Golf	1954	Snead, S.	VG		$5.00
DELL	781	Beyond Infinity	1954	Carr, R.S.	VG+		$6.00
DELL	786	Hold It, Florence	1954	Darrow, W.	VGF		$7.00
DELL	791	The Long Loud Silence	1954	Tucker, W.	VG		$7.00
DELL	809	Some Women Won't Wait	1954	Fair, A.A.*	VG+		$6.00
DELL	817	The Pigskin Bag	1954	Fischer, B.	G-		$5.00
DELL	829	Before I Wake	1955	Halliday, B.	AF	A	$11.00
DELL	835	Blood On The Boards	1955	Gault, W.C.	VG		$7.00
DELL	856	To Walk The Night	1955	Sloane, W.	VG		$6.00
DELL	862	My Favorite Football Stories	1955	Grange, R.	AF		$7.00
DELL	863	The Law At Randado	1955	Leonard, E.	VG		$8.00
DELL	867	She Woke To Darkness	1955	Halliday, B.	VGF		$7.00
DELL	868	Run, Killer, Run	1955	Gault, B.	VG+		$8.00
DELL	868	Run, Killer, Run	1955	Gault, B.	VG-		$7.00

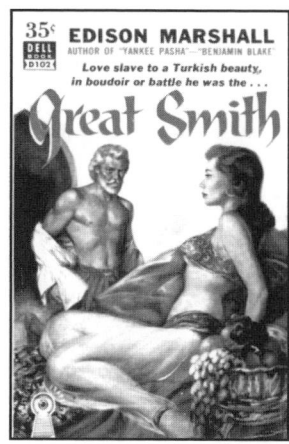

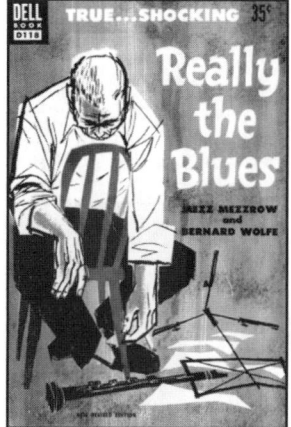

Dell D102 VGF $10   Dell D118 G $5   Dell D364 VG+ $10

PUBLISHER	PUB. #	TITLE	DATE	AUTHOR	COND.	TYPE	PRICE
DELL	870	The Danger Within	1955	Gilbert, M.	VG		$6.00
DELL	878	The Border Jumpers	1955	Brown, W.C.	VG+		$7.00
DELL	896	The Butcher's Wife	1956	Cameron, O.	AF		$7.00
DELL	898	Gulf Coast Girl	1956	Williams, C.	AF		$13.00 A
DELL	898	Gulf Coast Girl	1956	Williams, C.	VG		$10.00
DELL	910	The Restless Hands	1956	Fischer, B.	VG		$7.00
DELL	926	Murder In The Raw	1956	Gault, B.	VG		$8.00
DELL	926	Murder In The Raw	1956	Gault, B.	G+		$5.00
DELL	935	Border Guns	1957	Cunningham, E.	AF		$6.00
DELL	943	Man Who Had Too Much To Lose	1957	Stone, H.	VGF+		$8.00 A
DELL	962	King Colt	1957	Short, L.	AF		$7.00
DELL	968	The Blonde Died Dancing	1958	Roos, K.	VGF		$6.00
DELL	974	Stampede At Blue Springs	1958	Olson, G.	VGF		$5.00
DELL	975	Return Of A Fighter	1958	Haycox, E.	VG+		$6.00
DELL	986	Man Of The West	1958	Brown, W.C.	VG+	MTI	$7.00
DELL	991	Deadly Beloved	1958	Ard, W.	VG		$6.00
DELL	1003	Once A Widow	1959	Roberts, L.	VG		$7.00
DELL	1012	Death Out Of Focus	1960	Gault, B.	VG+		$12.00
DELL	1012	Death Out Of Focus	1960	Gault, B.	VG-		$6.00
DELL	1013	The Man Who Disappeared	1960	Bohle, E.	VG		$7.00
DELL	1174	The Sheik	1951	Hull, E.M.	VG+	MTI	$8.00
DELL	1174	The Sheik	1951	Hull, E.M.	VG	MTI	$7.00
DELL	1367	Suspense Stories	1950	Anthology	G+		$5.00
DELL	D 101	Chicago Confidential	1952	Lait, J.	VGF		$8.00
DELL	D 102	Great Smith	1952	Marshall, E.	VGF		$10.00
DELL	D 111	Gold For My Fair Lady	1952	Courtier, S.H.	VGF		$8.00
DELL	D 118	Really The Blues	1952	Mezzrow, M.	G		$5.00
DELL	D 123	The Legacy	1953	Shute, N.	VG+		$7.00
DELL	D 127	Diamond Head	1953	Branch, H.	VG+		$7.00
DELL	D 137	The Bold Saboteurs	1954	Brossard, C.	VG-		$9.00
DELL	D 204	The Mark Of Zorro	1958	McCulley, J.	VG+	TVTI	$6.00
DELL	D 207	Phantom Lady	1957	Irish, W.*	AF		$6.00
DELL	D 244	Falling Through Space	1958	Hillary, R.	VGF		$7.00
DELL	D 283	Murder And The Wanton Bride	1959	Halliday, B.	AF		$8.00
DELL	D 293	Dividend On Death	1959	Halliday, B.	F		$7.00
DELL	D 293	Dividend On Death	1959	Halliday, B.	VG		$7.00
DELL	D 294	The Sensualists	1959	Hecht, B.	VGF		$7.00
DELL	D 303	Only Akiko	1959	Thorp, D.	F		$7.00
DELL	D 304	Angel's Ransom	1959	Dodge, D.	AF		$12.00
DELL	D 306	The April Robin Murders	1959	Rice, C.	VGF		$8.00
DELL	D 309	Top Of The Heap	1959	Fair, A.A.*	VGF		$10.00
DELL	D 328	Moment Of Danger	1959	MacKenzie, D.	VGF		$7.00
DELL	D 331	Murder In Miami	1959	Anthology	F		$10.00
DELL	D 334	Poisons Unknown	1960	Kane, F.	AF		$6.00
DELL	D 338	The Girl Who Cried Wolf	1960	Waugh, H.	VG+		$8.00

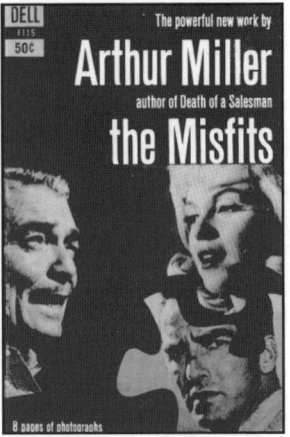

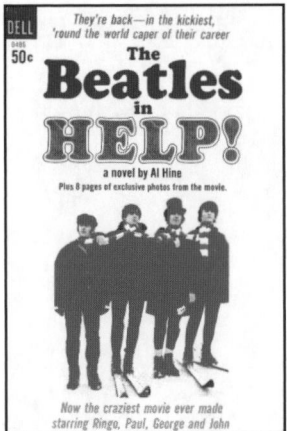

Dell D424 VG+ $7   Dell F115 VG $8   Dell 0 486 VG $7

PUBLISHER	PUB. #	TITLE	DATE	AUTHOR	COND.	TYPE	PRICE
DELL	D 341	A Terrible Beauty	1960	Roth, A.J.	AF	MTI	$12.00
DELL	D 346	One Minute Past Eight	1960	Coxe, G.H.	VG		$7.00
DELL	D 359	When Dorinda Dances	1960	Halliday, B.	VG+		$7.00
DELL	D 362	Dead, Man, Dead	1960	Alexander, D.	AF		$7.00
DELL	D 364	Wanted: Danny Fontaine	1960	Ard, W.	VG+		$10.00
DELL	D 364	Wanted: Danny Fontaine	1960	Ard, W.	VG		$7.00
DELL	D 364	Wanted: Danny Fontaine	1960	Ard, W.	VG-		$5.00
DELL	D 381	What Really Happened	1960	Halliday, B.	VGF		$5.00
DELL	D 410	The Sailcloth Shroud	1961	Williams, C.	VG		$8.00
DELL	D 410	The Sailcloth Shroud	1961	Williams, C.	VG-		$5.00
DELL	D 424	Dolls Are Deadly	1961	Halliday, B.	VG+	TVTI	$7.00
DELL	D 425	Stranger In Town	1961	Halliday, B.	VGF		$5.00
DELL	D 446	She Woke To Darkness	1962	Halliday, B.	F		$8.00
DELL	F 67	The Viking	1958	Marshall, E.	AF	MTI	$8.00
DELL	F 76	The Horse Soldiers	1959	Sinclair, J.	VG	MTI	$7.00
DELL	F 81	The Raw Edge	1959	Appel, B.	VGF		$5.00
DELL	F 84	The Beat Generation	1959	Anthology	AF		$26.00 A
DELL	F 84	The Beat Generation	1959	Anthology	VG		$8.00
DELL	F 91	Return To Peyton Place	1960	Metalious, G.	VG+	MTI	$5.00
DELL	F 106	The Trapp Family Singers	1960	Trapp, M.	VG-	MTI	$3.00
DELL	F 115	The Misfits	1961	Miller, A.	VG	MTI	$8.00
DELL	F 115	The Misfits	1961	Miller, A.	VG	MTI	$6.00
DELL	F 158	The Nightmare	1961	Forester, C.S.	VGF		$4.00
DELL	F 164	Town Without Pity	1961	Gregor, M.	VGF	MTI	$7.00
DELL	F 180	The Bad Seed	1961	March, W.	VG+		$5.00
DELL	F 182	The Man With Miraculous Hands	1962	Kessel, J.	AF		$4.00
DELL	R 123	Calling Dr. Kildare	1961	Brand, M.	AF		$5.00
DELL	0 19	Acapulco G.P.O.	1967	Keene, D.	VG-		$4.00
DELL	0 180	Afro-6	1969	Lopez, H.	VG		$3.00
DELL	0 486	The Beatles In Help	1965	Hine, A.	VG	MTI	$7.00
DELL	0 489	The Beatles In A Hard Day's Night	1964	Burke, J.	VG+	MTI	$7.00
DELL	0 575	Black Thursday	1962	Caidin, M.	VG+		$6.00
DELL	0 579	The Blackboard Jungle	1966	Hunter, E.	VGF		$6.00
DELL	0 615	The Beatles Lyrics Illustrated	1975	Brautigan, R.	VGF		$4.00
DELL	0 628	The Big Knockover	1967	Hammett, D.	VG		$6.00
DELL	0 689	The Butterfly	1964	Cain, J.M.	VGF		$5.00
DELL	0 773	The Boys In The Band	1970	Crowley, M.	F	MTI	$6.00
DELL	1114	Cassidy's Girl	1967	Goodis, D.	VGF		$13.00 A
DELL	1114	Cassidy's Girl	1967	Goodis, D.	VG		$9.00
DELL	1114	Cassidy's Girl	1967	Goodis, D.	G		$6.00
DELL	1198	Chicago 11	1966	Keene, D.	G		$3.00
DELL	1513	Cotton Comes To Harlem	1966	Himes, C.	VGF		$8.00
DELL	1513	Cotton Comes To Harlem	1970	Himes, C.	VG	MTI	$6.00
DELL	1739	Deadly Honeymoon	1973	Block, L.	AF	MTI	$5.00
DELL	1780	Different Strokes	1974	Wells, J.W.*	VG+		$25.00 A

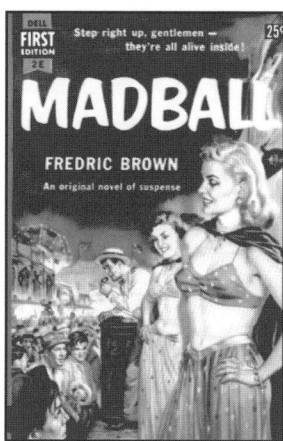

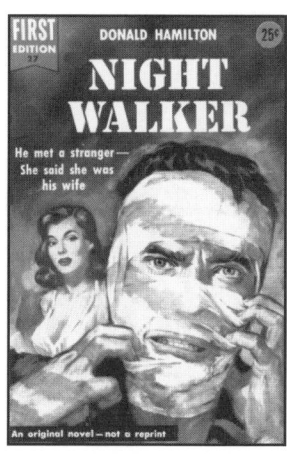

Dell First Edition 2E VG+ $66   Dell First Edition 13 VG+ $14   Dell First Edition 27 VGF $10

PUBLISHER	PUB. #	TITLE	DATE	AUTHOR	COND.	TYPE	PRICE
DELL	2131	Don't Rely On Gemini	1970	Packer, V.*	AF		$5.00
DELL	2156	Drive, He Said	1966	Larner, J.	AF		$6.00
DELL	2338	Evergreen Review - Spring 1973	1973	Anthology	VGF		$7.00
DELL	2626	The Fly On The Wall	1973	Hillerman, T.	VGF		$8.00
DELL	2672	For Bond Lovers Only	1965	Anthology	VG+		$5.00
DELL	2863	The Gestapo	1965	Delarue, J.	VGF		$4.00
DELL	2919	Glide Path	1965	Clarke, A.C.	AF		$7.00
DELL	3231	Green Hornet-The Infernal Light	1966	Friend, E.	VG+	TVTI	$7.00
DELL	3546	The Heat's On	1967	Himes, C.	G		$5.00
DELL	3589	Here Goes Kitten	1965	Gover, R.	VGF		$5.00
DELL	4331	The Jungle Kids	1967	Hunter, E.	VG+		$7.00
DELL	4449	Kids, Crime And Chaos	1964	Tunley, R.	VGF		$6.00
DELL	4503	Beauty And The Bug	1975	Mark, T.	VGF		$5.00
DELL	4604	The Airport Affair (Toma #2)	1975	Toma, D.	AF		$7.00
DELL	4606	L.A. 46	1964	Keene, D.	VG+		$7.00
DELL	5284	The Unhappy Hooker (Toma #3)	1976	Toma, D.	AF		$7.00
DELL	5437	Hanging On	1973	Koontz, D.R.	VGF		$16.00
DELL	5437	Hanging On	1976	Koontz, D.R.	VG		$10.00
DELL	5437	Hanging On	1976	Koontz, D.R.	G		$7.00
DELL	5598	Miami 59	1965	Keene, D.	VG		$5.00
DELL	5611	Midnight Cowboy	1969	Herlihy, J.L.	AF	MTI	$6.00
DELL	5642	Mink Is For A Minx	1964	Anthology	VGF		$7.00
DELL	6813	Palm Springs Weekend	1963	Albert, M.H.	VG+	MTI	$4.00
DELL	6918	Pinktoes	1966	Himes, C.	VGF		$5.00
DELL	7397	Room At The Topless	1973	Mark, T.	VG+		$6.00
DELL	7536	Run Man Run	1969	Himes, C.	VG		$3.00
DELL	7733	Seed Of Doubt	1962	Keene, D.	VGF		$5.00
DELL	7829	Shock II	1964	Matheson, R.	VG+		$14.00 A
DELL	7830	Shock III	1966	Matheson, R.	VGF		$14.00
DELL	7830	Shock III	1966	Matheson, R.	VGF		$10.00
DELL	8794	This Is It, Michael Shayne	1962	Halliday, B.	VGF		$8.00
DELL	9200	UBIK	1970	Dick, P.K.	VGF		$16.50 A
DELL	11489	Dr. Bloodmoney	1980	Dick, P.K.	VGF		$4.00
DELL FIRST EDITION	2E	Madball	1953	Brown, F.	VG+		$66.00 A
DELL FIRST EDITION	2E	Madball	1953	Brown, F.	G+		$14.00 A
DELL FIRST EDITION	4	Girl On The Beach	1953	Albee, G.S.	VG		$5.00
DELL FIRST EDITION	5	The Bloody Spur	1953	Einstein, C.	VG+		$10.00
DELL FIRST EDITION	6	Next Time Is For Life	1953	Warren, P.	G		$5.00
DELL FIRST EDITION	8	Back Country	1954	Fuller, W.	VG		$7.00
DELL FIRST EDITION	12	Area Of Suspicion	1954	MacDonald, J.D.	VG+		$40.00 A
DELL FIRST EDITION	12	Area Of Suspicion	1954	MacDonald, J.D.	VG+		$20.00
DELL FIRST EDITION	12	Area Of Suspicion	1954	MacDonald, J.D.	VG		$15.00
DELL FIRST EDITION	12	Area Of Suspicion	1954	MacDonald, J.D.	G+		$8.00
DELL FIRST EDITION	13	Fever Heat	1954	Vicker, A.	VG+		$14.00
DELL FIRST EDITION	13	Fever Heat	1954	Vicker, A.	VG-		$8.00

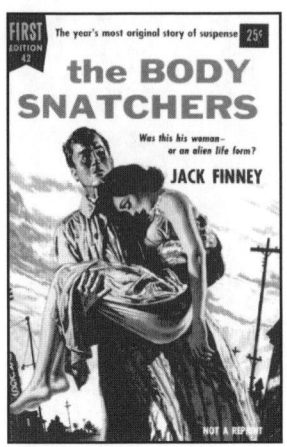

Dell First Edition 42 G- $6

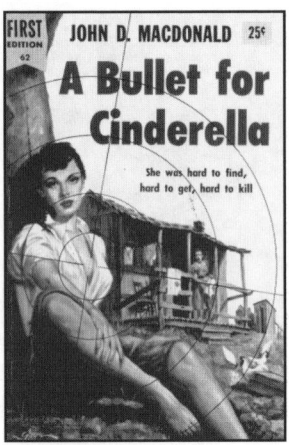

Dell First Edition 62 VG $17

Dell First Edition 77 AF- $10

PUBLISHER	PUB. #	TITLE	DATE	AUTHOR	COND.	TYPE	PRICE
DELL FIRST EDITION	17	The Crooked City	1954	Kyle, R.	VG+		$7.00
DELL FIRST EDITION	24	The Joys She Chose	1954	Peters, M.	VG+		$5.00
DELL FIRST EDITION	27	Night Walker	1954	Hamilton, D.	VGF		$10.00
DELL FIRST EDITION	27	Night Walker (Signed)	1954	Hamilton, D.	VG		$28.00 A
DELL FIRST EDITION	28	Goat Island	1954	Fuller, W.	VG+		$7.00
DELL FIRST EDITION	29	Sole Survivor	1954	Falstein, L.	AF		$8.00
DELL FIRST EDITION	30	Plain Murder	1954	Forester, C.S.	VG+		$7.00
DELL FIRST EDITION	32	Year Of Consent	1954	Crossen, K.F.	VG		$8.00
DELL FIRST EDITION	37	Last Of The Breed	1954	Savage, L.	AF		$10.00
DELL FIRST EDITION	37	Last Of The Breed	1954	Savage, L.	VGF		$7.00
DELL FIRST EDITION	41	Dakota Rifle	1955	O'Rourke, F.	VG		$7.00
DELL FIRST EDITION	42	The Body Snatchers	1955	Finney, J.	G-		$6.00
DELL FIRST EDITION	47	The Only Game In Town	1955	Einstein, C.	AF		$19.00 A
DELL FIRST EDITION	47	The Only Game In Town	1955	Einstein, C.	VG		$8.00
DELL FIRST EDITION	49	A Gun For Billy Reo	1955	Thompson, C.H.	VG+		$5.00
DELL FIRST EDITION	62	A Bullet For Cinderella	1955	MacDonald, J.D.	VG		$17.00
DELL FIRST EDITION	63	Hunger Mountain	1955	Scott, W.R.	VG		$7.00
DELL FIRST EDITION	70	Marauders' Moon	1955	Short, L.	VGF		$10.00
DELL FIRST EDITION	70	Marauders' Moon	1955	Short, L.	VG+		$6.00
DELL FIRST EDITION	D 72	How To Build A Model Railroad	1955	McClintock, M.	VG		$5.00
DELL FIRST EDITION	73	In His Blood	1955	Daniels, H.R.	VG+		$6.00
DELL FIRST EDITION	76	Wiretap!	1955	Einstein, C.	VG		$7.00
DELL FIRST EDITION	77	Dangerous Dames	1955	Anthology	AF-		$10.00
DELL FIRST EDITION	78	Little Iodine	1955	Hatlo, J.	VGF		$6.00 A
DELL FIRST EDITION	79	The $64,000 Question	1956	Anonymous	VGF	TVTI	$6.00
DELL FIRST EDITION	85	April Evil	1956	MacDonald, J.D.	VG		$15.00 A
DELL FIRST EDITION	D 90	The Last Enemy	1956	Roueche, B.	VGF		$8.00
DELL FIRST EDITION	91	Mad River	1956	Hamilton, D.	VGF		$12.00
DELL FIRST EDITION	91	Mad River	1956	Hamilton, D.	VGF+		$8.00
DELL FIRST EDITION	93	Forever Funny	1956	Yates, B.	VG+		$5.00
DELL FIRST EDITION	94	Atlantic Avenue	1956	Halper, A.	VG+		$5.00
DELL FIRST EDITION	95	The Devil's Spawn	1956	Carse, R.	VG		$5.00
DELL FIRST EDITION	96	The Great Locomotive Chase	1956	Roberts, M.	VG+	MTI	$7.00
DELL FIRST EDITION	105	The Pace That Kills	1956	Fuller, W.	G+		$5.00
DELL FIRST EDITION	106	Be My Victim	1956	Dietrich, R.*	VGF		$9.00
DELL FIRST EDITION	107	Singapore Passage	1956	Chidsey, D.B.	VGF		$9.00
DELL FIRST EDITION	109	Cry Passion	1956	Jessup, R.	VGF		$8.00
DELL FIRST EDITION	A 113	Murder In The Wind	1956	MacDonald, J.D.	VG+		$15.00 A
DELL FIRST EDITION	A 114	The Big Bite	1956	Williams, C.	VG+		$27.00 A
DELL FIRST EDITION	A 120	Wetback	1956	O'Farrell, W.	VGF+		$10.00
DELL FIRST EDITION	A 120	Wetback	1956	O'Farrell, W.	VG		$4.00
DELL FIRST EDITION	A 121	The Last Laugh	1956	Einstein, C.	VGF+		$8.00
DELL FIRST EDITION	A 128	The King And Four Queens	1956	Sturgeon, T.	AF	MTI	$24.00
DELL FIRST EDITION	A 128	The King And Four Queens	1956	Sturgeon, T.	G+	MTI	$7.00
DELL FIRST EDITION	A 130	Death Trap	1957	MacDonald, J.D.	VG+		$15.00

Dell First Edition A113 VG+ $15

Dell First Edition B145 VGF $45

Dell First Edition B163 AF $10

PUBLISHER	PUB. #	TITLE	DATE	AUTHOR	COND.	TYPE	PRICE
DELL FIRST EDITION	A 135	Desert Guns	1957	Frazee, S.	AF		$12.00
DELL FIRST EDITION	A 140	Tall Wyoming	1957	Cushman, D.	VG		$7.00
DELL FIRST EDITION	A 151	The Man On The Blue	1957	Short, L.	VGF		$8.00
DELL FIRST EDITION	A 155	Blackmail, Inc.	1958	Kyle, R.	VGF		$10.00
DELL FIRST EDITION	A 156	The Body Looks Familiar	1958	Wormser, R.	AF		$10.00
DELL FIRST EDITION	A 158	Miami Manhunt	1958	Fuller, W.	G+		$5.00
DELL FIRST EDITION	A 160	A Bullet For A Blonde	1958	Kruger, P.	VG		$5.00
DELL FIRST EDITION	A 161	Come Back For More	1958	Fray, A.	VG+		$8.00
DELL FIRST EDITION	A 165	All The Way	1958	Williams, C.	VG		$7.00
DELL FIRST EDITION	A 168	Revenge	1958	Ehrlich, J.	VG		$4.00
DELL FIRST EDITION	A 175	The House On Q Street	1959	Dietrich, R.*	VG		$7.00
DELL FIRST EDITION	A 176	77 Sunset Strip	1959	Huggins, R.	VG+	TVTI	$6.00
DELL FIRST EDITION	A 178	The Other Woman	1959	Yates, B.	VGF		$5.00
DELL FIRST EDITION	A 180	The Naked City	1959	Silliphant, S.	VG+	TVTI	$5.00
DELL FIRST EDITION	A 184	Last Stand At Saber Ridge	1959	Leonard, E.	VG+		$20.00
DELL FIRST EDITION	A 184	Last Stand At Saber Ridge	1959	Leonard, E.	VG+		$15.00
DELL FIRST EDITION	A 184	Last Stand At Saber Ridge	1959	Leonard, E.	G		$7.00
DELL FIRST EDITION	A 188	Corruption City	1959	McCoy, H.	VGF		$31.00 A
DELL FIRST EDITION	A 194	The Deadly Duo	1959	Jessup, R.	VG		$4.00
DELL FIRST EDITION	A 197	End Of A Stripper	1960	Dietrich, R.*	VGF		$8.00
DELL FIRST EDITION	A 202	The Half Caste	1960	Cushman, D.	AF		$10.00
DELL FIRST EDITION	A 209	Nellie's Bedfellows	1960	Kaz	VGF+		$5.00
DELL FIRST EDITION	B 105	Moses & The 10 Commandments	1956	Ilton, P.	VG+		$7.00
DELL FIRST EDITION	B 107	Stories For The Dead Of Night	1957	Anthology	VGF		$12.00
DELL FIRST EDITION	B 107	Stories For The Dead Of Night	1957	Anthology	VG		$8.00
DELL FIRST EDITION	B 107	Stories For The Dead Of Night	1957	Anthology	VG		$7.00
DELL FIRST EDITION	B 110	The Year's Greatest Sci-Fi	1957	Anthology	AF		$12.00
DELL FIRST EDITION	B 112	A Man Of Affairs	1957	MacDonald, J.D.	VG		$10.00
DELL FIRST EDITION	B 114	Girl Out Back	1958	Williams, C.	AF		$28.00 A
DELL FIRST EDITION	B 115	The Big Country	1958	Hamilton, D.	AF	MTI	$12.00
DELL FIRST EDITION	B 117	The Deceivers	1958	MacDonald, J.D.	VG+		$13.00 A
DELL FIRST EDITION	B 117	The Deceivers	1958	MacDonald, J.D.	G+		$8.00
DELL FIRST EDITION	B 119	The Year's Greatest Sci-Fi	1958	Anthology	AF	MTI	$10.00
DELL FIRST EDITION	B 120	The Cosmic Rape	1958	Sturgeon, T.	VG+		$32.00 A
DELL FIRST EDITION	B 121	Soft Touch	1958	MacDonald, J.D.	VGF+		$37.00 A
DELL FIRST EDITION	B 122	Untamed	1958	Hall, W.	AF		$8.00
DELL FIRST EDITION	B 127	Deadly Welcome	1959	MacDonald, J.D.	VG		$8.00
DELL FIRST EDITION	B 129	Year's Greatest Sci-Fi & Fantasy	1959	Anthology	AF		$8.00
DELL FIRST EDITION	B 134	On The Make	1960	MacDonald, J.D.	VG+		$17.00 A
DELL FIRST EDITION	B 134	On The Make	1960	MacDonald, J.D.	VG		$8.00
DELL FIRST EDITION	B 138	The Sirens Of Titan	1959	Vonnegut, K.	VG+		$16.00
DELL FIRST EDITION	B 139	Sin Street	1959	Bristow, B.	VG+		$10.00
DELL FIRST EDITION	B 141	The Lethal Sex	1959	Anthology	VGF		$15.00
DELL FIRST EDITION	B 141	The Lethal Sex	1959	Anthology	VG		$8.00
DELL FIRST EDITION	B 142	Poker According To Maverick	1959		AF-	TVTI	$17.00

Dell Ten Cent 27 VGF+ $22   Dell Ten Cent 33 VG $73   Dell Ten Cent 35 VG $81

PUBLISHER	PUB. #	TITLE	DATE	AUTHOR	COND.	TYPE	PRICE
DELL FIRST EDITION	B 142	Poker According To Maverick	1959		VGF+	TVTI	$11.00 A
DELL FIRST EDITION	B 142	Poker According To Maverick	1959		VG	TVTI	$7.00
DELL FIRST EDITION	B 145	When She Was Bad	1960	Ard, W.	VGF		$45.00 A
DELL FIRST EDITION	B 146	April Evil	1960	MacDonald, J.D.	VG		$13.00
DELL FIRST EDITION	B 146	April Evil	1960	MacDonald, J.D.	VG		$9.00
DELL FIRST EDITION	B 146	April Evil	1960	MacDonald, J.D.	VG-		$8.00
DELL FIRST EDITION	B 155	Peter Gunn	1960	Kane, H.	VGF	TVTI	$8.00
DELL FIRST EDITION	B 156	Have Gun Will Travel	1960	Loomis, N.	VG+	TVTI	$8.00
DELL FIRST EDITION	B 159	Time To Prey	1960	Kane, F.	VG		$5.00
DELL FIRST EDITION	B 160	Crack In The Mirror	1960	Haedrich, M.	F	MTI	$10.00
DELL FIRST EDITION	B 162	Mistress To Murder	1960	Dietrich, R.*	VG+		$8.00
DELL FIRST EDITION	B 163	Murder On Her Mind	1960	Dietrich, R.*	AF		$10.00
DELL FIRST EDITION	B 165	Mr. Lucky	1960	Conroy, A.	VGF		$8.00
DELL FIRST EDITION	B 174	Due Or Die	1961	Kane, F.	VGF		$6.00
DELL FIRST EDITION	B 190	Calling Nurse Nellie!	1961	Kaz	VGF		$6.00
DELL FIRST EDITION	B 195	Shock!	1961	Matheson, R.	AF		$15.00
DELL FIRST EDITION	B 195	Shock!	1961	Matheson, R.	VGF		$15.00
DELL FIRST EDITION	B 195	Shock!	1961	Matheson, R.	VG		$6.00
DELL FIRST EDITION	B 198	My Darlin' Evangeline	1961	Kane, H.	VG+		$9.00
DELL FIRST EDITION	B 203	Angel Eyes	1961	Dietrich, R.*	VGF		$9.00
DELL FIRST EDITION	B 206	Never Take Candy From A Stranger	1961	Garis, R.	VG+	MTI	$6.00
DELL FIRST EDITION	B 209	Riding High	1961	Flynn, T.T.	VGF		$5.00
DELL FIRST EDITION	B 213	Nellie's New Frontier	1961	Kaz	VGF+		$5.00
DELL FIRST EDITION	B 215	Go, Honeylou	1962	Dewey, T.B.	VGF+		$15.00
DELL FIRST EDITION	B 227	Cry, Baby	1962	Ehrlich, J.	VG+		$8.00
DELL FIRST EDITION	C 108	Combat, Pacific Theatre	1958	Anthology	VGF		$5.00
DELL FIRST EDITION	C 111	6 Great Sci-Fi Novels	1960	Anthology	VG+		$6.00
DELL FIRST EDITION	C 117	By Appointment Only	1961	Boltar, R.	VGF		$6.00
DELL FIRST EDITION	K 103	Night School	1961	Cassill, R.V.	AF		$11.00 A
DELL FIRST EDITION	K 109	Mike Shayne's Torrid Twelve	1961	Anthology	VGF		$13.00 A
DELL FIRST EDITION	K 116	Soft Touch	1962	MacDonald, J.D.	VG-		$6.00
DELL FIRST EDITION	1382	Combat, War With Japan	1962	Anthology	AF		$7.00
DELL FIRST EDITION	3577	Hemingway: The Wild Years	1962	Hemingway, E.	VG+		$8.00
DELL MYSTERY NOVELS	1	Dell Mystery Novels	1955	Anthology	G+	Digest	$10.00
DELL TEN CENT	1	Trumpets West!	1951	Short, L.	VGF		$30.00 A
DELL TEN CENT	2	Rain	1951	Maugham, W.S.	AF		$36.00 A
DELL TEN CENT	3	Night Bus	1951	Adams, S.H.	VGF-		$14.00 A
DELL TEN CENT	3	Night Bus	1951	Adams, S.H.	VG		$10.00
DELL TEN CENT	4	Locked Doors	1951	Rinehart, M.R.	VG+		$24.00 A
DELL TEN CENT	5	Bride From Broadway	1951	Baldwin, F.	VG		$34.00 A
DELL TEN CENT	5	Bride From Broadway	1951	Baldwin, F.	VGF		$20.00 A
DELL TEN CENT	7	Deadly Is The Diamond	1951	Eberhart, M.G.	VG+		$27.00 A
DELL TEN CENT	7	Deadly Is The Diamond	1951	Eberhart, M.G.	VGF		$25.00 A
DELL TEN CENT	8	Journey For Life	1951	Buck, P.S.	VG+		$27.00 A
DELL TEN CENT	9	Strangers In Love	1951	Delmar, V.	VGF		$48.00 A

Detective Novel Classic 22 VGF $6   Diversey Prize 6 VG+ $60   Dollar Double 955 VGF $25

PUBLISHER	PUB. #	TITLE	DATE	AUTHOR	COND.	TYPE	PRICE
DELL TEN CENT	9	Strangers In Love	1951	Delmar, V.	VGF		$34.00 A
DELL TEN CENT	10	Trees Die At The Top	1951	Ferber, E.	VGF		$20.00 A
DELL TEN CENT	11	Marijuana	1951	Irish, W.*	VG		$65.00
DELL TEN CENT	12	The Longhorn Legion	1951	Fox, N.A.	VGF		$33.00 A
DELL TEN CENT	12	The Longhorn Legion	1951	Fox, N.A.	VG+		$15.00 A
DELL TEN CENT	13	Sun, Sea And Sand	1951	Marquand, J.P.	VGF		$24.00 A
DELL TEN CENT	14	The Name Is Mary	1951	Hurst, F.	VGF		$43.00 A
DELL TEN CENT	14	The Name Is Mary	1951	Hurst, F.	VG+		$10.00
DELL TEN CENT	15	A Taste For Cognac	1951	Halliday, B.	VGF		$53.00 A
DELL TEN CENT	15	A Taste For Cognac	1951	Halliday, B.	VGF		$44.00 A
DELL TEN CENT	15	A Taste For Cognac	1951	Halliday, B.	VG+		$12.00 A
DELL TEN CENT	17	Remembering Laughter	1951	Stegner, W.	VGF		$27.00 A
DELL TEN CENT	17	Remembering Laughter	1951	Stegner, W.	VG-		$10.00
DELL TEN CENT	18	Free Woman	1951	Brush, K.	VGF+		$22.00 A
DELL TEN CENT	18	Free Woman	1951	Brush, K.	VG+		$11.00 A
DELL TEN CENT	19	Death Walks In Marble Halls	1951	Blochman, L.G.	VGF		$51.00 A
DELL TEN CENT	20	Broken Arrow Range	1951	Blackburn, T.W.	VGF		$22.00 A
DELL TEN CENT	21	Door To Death	1951	Stout, R.	VGF		$28.00 A
DELL TEN CENT	21	Door To Death	1951	Stout, R.	VG+		$16.00 A
DELL TEN CENT	22	Alibi For Isabel	1951	Rinehart, M.R.	VGF		$44.00 A
DELL TEN CENT	23	The Lamp Of God	1951	Queen, E.	VGF		$24.00 A
DELL TEN CENT	25	South Of Cancer	1951	Hersey, J.	VGF		$30.00 A
DELL TEN CENT	25	South Of Cancer	1951	Hersey, J.	VG		$7.00
DELL TEN CENT	27	Thief Is An Ugly Word	1951	Gallico, P.	VGF+		$22.00 A
DELL TEN CENT	28	Beauty Marks The Spot	1951	Roos, K.	VGF+		$84.00 A
DELL TEN CENT	29	Delilah Of The Back Stairs	1951	Household, G.	VGF+		$73.00 A
DELL TEN CENT	31	Chinese Nightmare	1951	Pentecost, H.	VG		$20.00
DELL TEN CENT	32	The Murderer Who Wanted More	1951	Kendrick, B.	VGF		$39.00 A
DELL TEN CENT	32	The Murderer Who Wanted More	1951	Kendrick, B.	VG+		$18.00 A
DELL TEN CENT	33	TCOT Dancing Sandwiches	1951	Brown, F.	VG		$73.00 A
DELL TEN CENT	33	TCOT Dancing Sandwiches	1951	Brown, F.	VG		$65.00
DELL TEN CENT	33	TCOT Dancing Sandwiches	1951	Brown, F.	G+		$55.00 A
DELL TEN CENT	34	Better Off Dead	1951	McCloy, H.	VG+		$40.00 A
DELL TEN CENT	35	Superstition Farm	1951	Stowe, P.	VG		$81.00 A
DENNIS MCMILLAN	No#	Kiss Your Ass Goodbye	1987	Willeford, C.	VGF		$18.00 A
DERBY	6	The Long Night	1949	Lederer, J.	VG		$11.00
DETECTIVE NOVEL CLASSIC	22	Murder For A Wanton	1943	Chambers, W.	VGF	Digest	$6.00
DETECTIVE NOVEL CLASSIC	29	Death Over Hollywood	1944	Saxby, C.	VG+	Digest	$7.00
DETECTIVE NOVEL CLASSIC	31	Bodies Are Where You Find Them	1944	Halliday, B.	VG	Digest	$7.00
DETECTIVE TRUE CRIME	1 1	Detective True Crime - Winter 1951	1951	Anthology	VG	Digest	$10.00
DETECTIVE FILES	103	The Craig Rice Casebook	1956	Rice, C.	AF	Digest	$27.00 A
DETECTIVE STORY	171 5	Detective Story - 3/46	1946	Anthology	VG	Digest	$7.00
DETECTIVE STORY	176 4	Detective Story - 9/48	1948	Anthology	VG+	Digest	$12.00
DIGIT	R 335	Journey To Center Of The Earth	n/d	Verne, J.	G	MTI	$6.00
DIGIT	R 338	Cry Scandal	n/d	Ard, W.	VG		$14.00 A

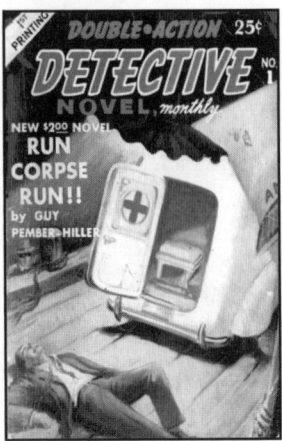

Double-Action Det. Novel 1 VG $14

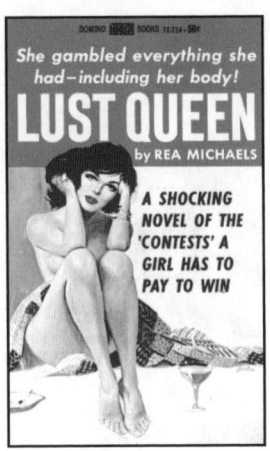

Domino 72-714 AF- $35

Eagle 1 VGF $12

PUBLISHER	PUB. #	TITLE	DATE	AUTHOR	COND.	TYPE	PRICE
DIGIT	R 771	The Uninhibited	1963	Morgan, D.	VG+		$7.00
DIMEDIA	89300	The Prince Of Evil	1985	Stockbridge, G.	VG+		$8.00
DIVERSEY LOVE BOOK	1	Bedroom Eyes	1948	Dekobra, M.	VG	Digest	$18.00
DIVERSEY NOVELS	1	Broadway Virgin	1949	Bull, L.	VG	Digest	$20.00 A
DIVERSEY PRIZE	3	Passions Of Linda Lane	1949	Marion, F.	VG	Digest	$12.00
DIVERSEY PRIZE	6	The Amorous Interne	1949	Reltid, E.	VG+	Digest	$60.00 A
DIVERSEY PRIZE	6	The Amorous Interne	1949	Reltid, E.	AF	Digest	$51.00 A
DOC SAVAGE	26 2	Doc Savage - 10/45	1945	Anthology	G	Digest	$5.00 A
DOC SAVAGE	27 6	Doc Savage - 8/46	1946	Anthology	VG	Digest	$25.00 A
DOC SAVAGE	29 3	Doc Savage - 7/47	1947	Anthology	VGF	Digest	$56.00
DOC SAVAGE	29 6	Doc Savage - Jan.-Feb. 1948	1948	Anthology	VG+	Digest	$25.00 A
DOLLAR DOUBLE	952	Platinum Blonde	1962	Glaser, A.B.	VGF	DBL	$10.00
		The Sporting Parlor		*Lane, W.*			
DOLLAR DOUBLE	954	The Third Sex Syndrome	1962	Hastings, M.	AF	DBL	$13.00 A
		Honey At Her Lips		*Bell, S.*			
DOLLAR DOUBLE	955	The Beatniks	1962	Geis, R.E.	VGF	DBL	$25.00 A
		Every Bed Is Narrow		*Laird, A.*			
DOMINO	72 700	Too Many Men	1963	Gordon, I.	VG+		$5.00
DOMINO	72 703	Passion Pool	1964	Hitt, O.	AF		$10.00 A
DOMINO	72 708	Embassy Girls	1964	Gordon, I.	AF-		$18.00 A
DOMINO	72 712	The Passion Hunters	1964	Hitt, O.	VGF		$25.00 A
DOMINO	72 714	Lust Queen	1964	Michaels, R.	AF-		$35.00 A
DOMINO	72 719	Weekend Wanton	1964	Gordon, I.	VG		$5.00
DOMINO	72 735	How Dark, My Love	1964	Michaels, R.	AF		$14.00
DOMINO	72 741	Two-Way Street	1964	Michaels, R.	AF		$24.00 A
DOMINO	72 741	Two-Way Street	1964	Michaels, R.	AF		$18.00 A
DOMINO	72 743	Teen Temptress	1964	Michaels, B.	VG+		$15.00 A
DOMINO	72 744	Where The Sin Is	1964	Roget, A.L.	VG+		$6.00
DOMINO	72 765	Deliver Her To Evil	1964	Sharon, S.	AF		$10.00
DOMINO	74 848	The Golden Nymph	1965	Whitmore, L.	AF		$7.00
DOMINO	72 914	To Drown Our Lusts	1965	Spain, V.	AF		$5.00
DOMINO	72 915	Women Like Me	1965	Richards, D.	VG		$4.00
DOMINO	72 930	In Love's Dark Corners	1965	Behan, L.	AF		$10.00
DOMINO	72 931	Rapture For Three	1965	Sharon, S.	AF		$6.00
DOMINO	72 948	The Sins Of Tonia	1965	Sharon, S.	AF		$10.00
DOMINO	82 103	Naked In The Night	1965	Michaels, R.	AF		$10.00
DOMINO	82 105	The Constant Urge	1966	Richards, D.	AF		$15.00 A
DOMINO	82 107	This Wild Desire	1966	Hitt, O.	AF		$7.00
DOMINO	82 108	The Hours Of Rapture	1966	Lord, S.*	VGF		$10.00
DOMINO MYSTERY	1	The "Q" Squad	1944	Verner, G.	VG	Digest	$5.00 A
DOUBLE-ACTION DETECTIVE	1	Double-Action Detective	1954	Anthology	AF-	Digest	$18.00 A
DOUBLE-ACTION DETECTIVE	4	Double-Action Detective	1956	Anthology	VG	Digest	$10.00
DOUBLE-ACTION DETECTIVE	5	Double-Action Detective	1956	Anthology	AF	Digest	$15.00 A
DOUBLE-ACTION DETECTIVE	12	Double-Action Det. 9/58	1958	Anthology	F	Digest	$15.00 A
DOUBLE-ACTION DETECTIVE	15	Double-Action Det. 3/59	1959	Anthology	AF	Digest	$33.00 A

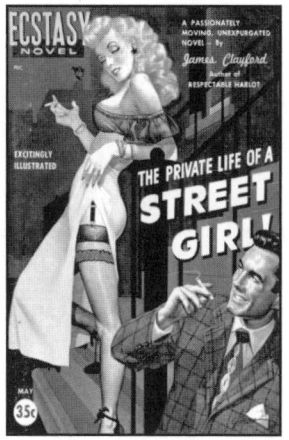

Ecstasy Novel 4 VGF $82	Ecstasy Novel 6 VGF $60	Epic 101 VGF $25

PUBLISHER	PUB. #	TITLE	DATE	AUTHOR	COND.	TYPE	PRICE
DOUBLE-ACTION DETECTIVE	17	Double Action Det. 7/59	1959	Anthology	AF	Digest	$15.00 A
DOUBLE-ACTION DETECTIVE	19	Double-Action Det. 11/59	1959	Anthology	AF	Digest	$47.00 A
DOUBLE-ACTION DET. NOVEL	1	Double-Action Det. Novel	1943	Hiller, G.P.	VG	Digest	$14.00
DOVE	DB 109	Any Bed, Any Time	n/d	Anonymous	VG+		$6.00
DRAGON EDITION	DE 128	Wanton Lust	1966	Delman, R.	VG		$6.00
DRAGON EDITION	DE 132	Game Of Sin	1966	Crawley, R.	AF		$7.00
DRAGON EDITION	DE 141	Carny Vice	1966	Stoner, R.	F		$13.00 A
DRAGON EDITION	DE 143	Erotic Interlude	1966	Elmer, B.	AF		$30.00 A
DREAM WORLD	1 1	Dream World - 2/57	1957	Anthology	VGF-	Digest	$30.00 A
DREAM WORLD	1 1	Dream World - 2/57	1957	Anthology	VGF	Digest	$15.00
EAGLE	1	Dear Sir	1944	Lowell, J.	VGF	Digest	$12.00 A
EAGLE	No# 2	Kitty	1945	Marshall, R.	VGF		$25.00 A
ECSTASY NOVEL	1	A Body To Own	1949	Hamilton, T.	VGF	Digest	$34.00 A
ECSTASY NOVEL	2	Paula Has A Price	1949	Lindsay, P.	VGF	Digest	$61.00 A
ECSTASY NOVEL	3	Harlot In Her Heart	1950	Bligh, N.	VGF+	Digest	$41.00 A
ECSTASY NOVEL	4	Private Life Of A Street Girl!	1950	Clayford, J.	VGF	Digest	$82.00 A
ECSTASY NOVEL	6	Reno Tramp	1950	Stonebraker, F.	VGF	Digest	$60.00 A
ECSTASY NOVEL	8	Virgin Or Harlot	1950	Gaddis, P.	VG+	Digest	$67.00 A
ECSTASY NOVEL	9	Bed-Time Angel	1951	Bligh, N.	VG	Digest	$55.00 A
ECSTASY NOVEL	10	Never Say "No"	1951	Gordon, L.	G-	Digest	$5.00
EDGAR WALLACE	1 1	Edgar Wallace Mystery Mag. - 3/66	1966	Anthology	AF	Digest	$15.00
EDGAR WALLACE	1 1	Edgar Wallace Mystery Mag. - 3/66	1966	Anthology	VGF	Digest	$12.00
EDMORE	No#	The Rock Revolution	1967	Dean, M.	VGF		$6.00
EERIE	6	The Pleasure Primer	1944	Anthology	VG	Digest	$20.00
EERIE	9	Haunted Harbor	1945	Douglas, D.	VG+	Digest	$10.00 A
ELLERY QUEEN'S ANTH.	8	Ellery Queen's Anthology #8	1965	Anthology	AF	Digest	$7.00
ELLERY QUEEN'S ANTH.	10	Ellery Queen's Anthology #10	1966	Anthology	AF	Digest	$7.00
ELLERY QUEEN'S ANTH.	11	Ellery Queen's Anthology #11	1966	Anthology	AF	Digest	$6.00
ELLERY QUEEN'S ANTH.	13	Ellery Queen's Anthology #13	1967	Anthology	AF	Digest	$7.00
ELLERY QUEEN'S ANTH.	14	Ellery Queen's Anthology #14	1968	Anthology	AF	Digest	$8.00
ELLERY QUEEN'S ANTH.	16	Ellery Queen's Anthology #16	1969	Anthology	VGF	Digest	$7.00
ELLERY QUEEN'S ANTH.	31	Ellery Queen's Anthology #31	1976	Anthology	VG+	Digest	$6.00
ELLERY QUEEN'S MYSTERY	79	Ellery Queen's Myst. Mag. 6/50	1950	Anthology	AF	Digest	$6.00
ELLERY QUEEN'S MYSTERY	82	Ellery Queen's Myst. Mag. 9/50	1950	Anthology	VGF	Digest	$6.00 A
ELLERY QUEEN'S MYSTERY	93	Ellery Queen's Myst. Mag. 8/51	1951	Anthology	VG+	Digest	$6.00
ELLERY QUEEN'S MYSTERY	118	Ellery Queen's Myst. Mag. 9/53	1953	Anthology	VGF	Digest	$15.00
ELLERY QUEEN'S MYSTERY	118	Ellery Queen's Myst. Mag. 9/53	1953	Anthology	VGF	Digest	$14.00
ELLERY QUEEN'S MYSTERY	131	Ellery Queen's Myst. Mag. 10/54	1954	Anthology	VG+	Digest	$5.00
ELLERY QUEEN'S MYSTERY	135	Ellery Queen's Myst. Mag. 2/55	1955	Anthology	VG	Digest	$6.00
ELLERY QUEEN'S MYSTERY	136	Ellery Queen's Myst. Mag. 3/55	1955	Anthology	VGF	Digest	$7.00
ELLERY QUEEN'S MYSTERY	139	Ellery Queen's Myst. Mag. 6/55	1955	Anthology	VGF	Digest	$5.00
ELLERY QUEEN'S MYSTERY	140	Ellery Queen's Myst. Mag. 7/55	1955	Anthology	VGF	Digest	$9.00 A
ELLERY QUEEN'S MYSTERY	152	Ellery Queen's Myst. Mag. 7/56	1956	Anthology	VG+	Digest	$59.00 A
ELLERY QUEEN'S MYSTERY	156	Ellery Queen's Myst. Mag. 11/56	1956	Anthology	VGF	Digest	$6.00
ELLERY QUEEN'S MYSTERY	158	Ellery Queen's Myst. Mag. 1/57	1957	Anthology	VG+	Digest	$5.00

Eton 116 VG $45   Eton 123 VGF $41   Fabian 121 VG+ $8   Fabian 141 VG+ $12

PUBLISHER	PUB. #	TITLE	DATE	AUTHOR	COND.	TYPE	PRICE
ELLERY QUEEN'S MYST.	167	Ellery Queen's Myst. Mag. 10/57	1957	Anthology	VG+	Digest	$6.00
ELLERY QUEEN'S MYST.	168	Ellery Queen's Myst. Mag. 11/57	1957	Anthology	VG+	Digest	$6.00
ELLERY QUEEN'S MYST.	175	Ellery Queen's Myst. Mag. 6/58	1958	Anthology	VGF	Digest	$7.00
ELLERY QUEEN'S MYST.	183	Ellery Queen's Myst. Mag. 2/59	1959	Anthology	VGF	Digest	$8.00
ELLERY QUEEN'S MYST.	191	Ellery Queen's Myst. Mag. 10/59	1959	Anthology	VG	Digest	$4.00
ELLERY QUEEN'S MYST.	192	Ellery Queen's Myst. Mag. 11/59	1959	Anthology	VG+	Digest	$8.00
ELLERY QUEEN'S MYST.	208	Ellery Queen's Myst. Mag. 3/61	1961	Anthology	AF	Digest	$9.00 A
ELLERY QUEEN'S MYST.	218	Ellery Queen's Myst. Mag. 1/62	1962	Anthology	VG	Digest	$6.00
ELLERY QUEEN'S MYST.	252	Ellery Queen's Myst. Mag. 11/64	1964	Anthology	VGF	Digest	$7.00
ELLERY QUEEN'S MYST.	262	Ellery Queen's Myst. Mag. 9/65	1965	Anthology	AF	Digest	$6.00
ELLERY QUEEN'S MYST.	272	Ellery Queen's Myst. Mag. 7/66	1966	Anthology	AF	Digest	$7.00
EMBER BOOK	EB 901	Flesh Act	1963	Wellman, D.	VGF		$8.00
EMBER BOOK	EB 902	Dial O-R-G-Y	1963	Eliot, D.	AF		$8.00
EMBER BOOK	EB 903	Strumpet	1963	King, W.	VGF-		$6.00
EMBER BOOK	EB 905	Nympho	1963	Eliot, D.	VGF		$7.00
EMBER BOOK	EB 908	Sin Merchant	1963	Anderson, C.*	AF		$17.00
EMBER BOOK	EB 921	Shame Cult	n/d	Dexter, J.	VGF		$7.00
EMBER BOOK	EB 924	Lust Mob	n/d	Calvano, T.	VGF		$7.00
EMBER BOOK	EB 926	Lust Lease	n/d	Williams, J.X.	AF		$15.00
EMBER BOOK	EB 927	The Flesh Game	n/d	Allison, C.	AF		$16.00 A
EMBER BOOK	EB 930	Sin Made	n/d	Elliott, D.*	AF		$10.00
EMBER BOOK	EB 934	The Lust Ladder	1964	Shaw, A.*	VGF+		$15.00
EMBER BOOK	EB 935	West End Wanton	1964	Hudson, D.	VGF		$7.00
EMBER BOOK	EB 938	Sin Hidden	1964	Marshall, A.*	AF		$8.00
EMBER BOOK	EB 943	Shame Agent	1964	Bellmore, D.	VGF		$6.00
EMBER BOOK	EB 945	Passion Ph.D.	1964	Williams, J.X.	VGF		$7.00
EMBER BOOK	EB 948	The Satin Vise	1964	Calvano, T.	VGF		$7.00
EMBER LIBRARY	EL 305	Our Girl From Mephisto	1965	Allison, C.	VG		$75.00
EMBER LIBRARY	EL 306	The Sins Of Seena	1965	Elliott, D.*	VG+		$10.00
EMBER LIBRARY	EL 309	Nautipuss	1965	Allison, C.	VG		$48.00 A
EMBER LIBRARY	EL 311	The Tragic Temptress	1965	Dexter, J.	VG+		$16.00 A
EMBER LIBRARY	EL 312	Sinner Come Home	1965	Hudson, D.	VG		$11.00 A
EMBER LIBRARY	EL 313	Go-Go Sadisto	1966	Allison, C.	VG+		$67.00 A
EMBER LIBRARY	EL 316	Sintown Setup	1966	Shaw, A.*	VG-		$5.00
EMBER LIBRARY	EL 318	Queen Of Tramps	1966	Calvano, T.	AF		$24.00 A
EMBER LIBRARY	EL 322	The Sin Collector	1966	Williams, J.X.	VG+		$20.00 A
EMBER LIBRARY	EL 330	Drifters Delight	1966	Holliday, D.	VG		$9.00
EMBER LIBRARY	EL 344	Odd Girl Out	1966	Williams, J.X.	AF		$22.00 A
EMBER LIBRARY	EL 347	The Bikini Bride	1966	Aldrich, C.	AF		$17.00 A
EMBER LIBRARY	EL 349	Randy	1966	Hudson, D.	VGF		$30.00 A
EMBER LIBRARY	EL 351	In Warm Desire	1966	Kane, W.	AF		$36.00 A
EMBER LIBRARY	EL 353	Widow's Delight	1966	Williams, J.X.	AF		$16.00 A
EMBER LIBRARY	EL 354	Playboy's Lament	1966	Dexter, J.	AF		$15.00 A
EMBER LIBRARY	EL 355	Travelin' Tramp	1966	Marshall, A.*	F		$18.00 A
EMBER LIBRARY	EL 358	Sweet Holly	1966	Miller, M.	AF		$30.00 A
EMBER LIBRARY	EL 375	Hot Rod Rogues	1967	Shaw, A.*	VGF		$33.00 A
EMBER LIBRARY	EL 375	Hot Rod Rogues	1967	Shaw, A.*	VG		$30.00 A
EMBER LIBRARY	EL 378	Flesh Tryst	1967	Elliott, D.*	F		$31.00 A

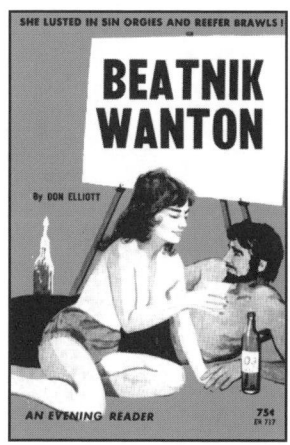

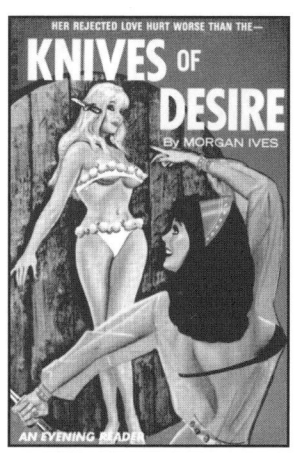

Evening Reader 717 VGF $44   Evening Reader 1240 F $122   Exotic Novel 3 VGF+ $55

PUBLISHER	PUB. #	TITLE	DATE	AUTHOR	COND.	TYPE	PRICE
EMBER LIBRARY	EL 389	The Passion Pretenders	1967	Dexter, J.	VGF		$22.00 A
EMBER LIBRARY	EL 395	Hypno-Sin	1967	Williams, J.X.	VG+		$41.00 A
EMBER LIBRARY	EL 396	The Passionate Pioneer	1967	Lynn, D.	VG		$10.00
EMERALD READER	ER 104	Pit Of Shame	1964	Fay, C.	VGF		$7.00
EPIC	101	Hot Cargo	1961	Davidson, J.*	VGF		$25.00 A
EPIC	102	Passion's Web	1961	Hudson, J.*	VG		$9.00
EPIC	103	1976 Year Of Terror	1961	Smith, G.H.	VGF		$9.00 A
EPIC	104	Vixen Hollow	1961	Harmon, J.	AF		$11.00
EPIC	104	Vixen Hollow	1961	Harmon, J.	VGF		$8.00
EPIC	105	Love Me To Death	1961	Blake, A.	VGF		$10.00
EPIC	113	Satan's Daughter	1961	Hudson, J.*	VG+		$20.00
EPIC	113	Satan's Daughter	1961	Hudson, J.*	VG+		$16.00 A
EPIC	114	The Lusty Hillbilly	1961	Brandon, R.	VGF		$8.00
EPIC	117	Lust On Wheels	1961	Koby, D.	AF		$15.00
EPIC	119	Wanton Witch	1961	Grey, J.	VGF		$10.00
EPIC	127	Red Hot Berlin Blonde	1962	Kuenne, W.	AF		$7.00
EPIC	132	Airborne Passions	1962	Koby, D.	AF		$11.00
EPIC	142	Tropic Of Passion	1962	Davidson, J.*	AF		$10.00
EPIC	707	Rock Me Baby!	1962	Randolph, G.	VG+		$8.00 A
ERNEST BENN	n/a	Psyche	1961	De Lisser, H.G.	VG		$15.00 A
ESPIONAGE	1 2	Espionage Magazine 2/85	1985	Anthology	F	Digest	$8.00
ESSEX HOUSE	107	How Many Blocks In The Pile?	1968	Meltzer, D.	AF		$31.00 A
ESSEX HOUSE	112	Season Of The Witch	1968	Stine, H.	VG		$26.00 A
ETON	E 106	The Show Of Violence	1951	Wertham, F.	VG+		$5.00
ETON	E 111	Sin In their Blood	1952	Lacy, E.	AF		$20.00
ETON	E 111	Sin In Their Blood (2nd)	1952	Lacy, E.	VG		$5.00
ETON	E 115	I'll Bring Her Back	1952	Cheyney, P.	VG		$5.00
ETON	E 116	The Marijuana Mob	1952	Chase, J.H.	VG		$45.00 A
ETON	E 116	The Marijuana Mob	1952	Chase, J.H.	VG		$27.00 A
ETON	E 117	Invitation To Dishonor	1952	Arthur, E.	VG		$7.00
ETON	E 120	Mark It With A Stone	1952	Martin, G.V.	VG		$5.00 A
ETON	E 122	Paris Escort	1953	Harper, D.	VGF		$8.00
ETON	E 122	Paris Escort	1953	Harper, D.	VG		$6.00
ETON	E 123	Strip For Violence	1953	Lacy, E.	VGF		$41.00 A
ETON	E 123	Strip For Violence	1953	Lacy, E.	AF		$21.00 A
ETON	E 125	Gunfighter	1953	Craig, P.	AF		$14.00 A
ETON	E 129	Wit From Overseas	1953	Anthology	AF		$10.00 A
ETON	E 129	Wit From Overseas	1953	Anthology	VGF		$7.00
ETON	E 129	Wit From Overseas	1953	Anthology	G+		$4.00
ETON	E 132	Hide-Out	1953	Holden, L.	VG+		$17.00 A
EUGENICS	K 101	The Torch Of Life	1952	Rossiter, F.M.	VGF		$8.00
EUROPA	1104	Satan's Daughters	1963	Leech, J.	AF		$27.00 A
EVENING READER	ER 702	Sin Doll	1963	Eliot, D.	AF		$8.00
EVENING READER	ER 703	Flesh Den	1963	Marsh, A.	AF		$12.00 A
EVENING READER	ER 708	Sin Prowl	1964	Marshall, A.*	F		$10.00

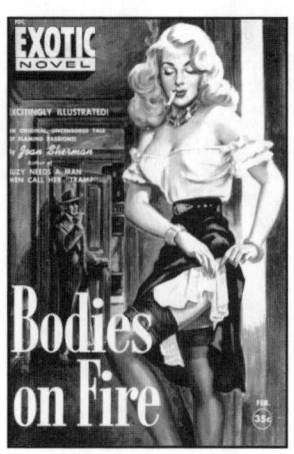

Exotic Novel 9 AF $165   Exotic Novel 12 AF $84   Exotic Novel 19 VGF+ $181

PUBLISHER	PUB. #	TITLE	DATE	AUTHOR	COND.	TYPE	PRICE
EVENING READER	ER 708	Sin Prowl	1964	Marshall, A.*	VG		$10.00
EVENING READER	ER 709	Shame Club	n/d	Shaw, A.*	AF		$8.00
EVENING READER	ER 711	Flesh Baron	n/d	Dexter, J.	VGF		$9.00
EVENING READER	ER 712	Sin Sold	n/d	Elliott, D.*	VGF		$9.00
EVENING READER	ER 714	Lust League	1965	Elliott, D.*	VG-		$6.00
EVENING READER	ER 715	Leftover Lust	n/d	Dexter, J.	VGF		$7.00
EVENING READER	ER 717	Beatnik Wanton	1964	Elliott, D.*	VGF		$44.00 A
EVENING READER	ER 719	Shame Mates	1964	Shaw, A.*	VGF		$8.00
EVENING READER	ER 720	The Lust Sleepers	1964	Dexter, J.	VG+		$6.00
EVENING READER	ER 721	Lust Chained	1964	Williams, J.X.	VG+		$7.00
EVENING READER	ER 736	Lust Linc	1964	Dexter, J.	VG+		$6.00
EVENING READER	ER 737	Sinners' Seance	1964	Dexter, J.	VG+		$5.00
EVENING READER	ER 747	Flesh Hunt	1964	Williams, J.X.	VGF		$7.00
EVENING READER	ER 751	Passion Adonis	1964	Hudson, D.	VGF		$7.00
EVENING READER	ER 759	The Sin Testers	1964	Holliday, D.	VGF		$7.00
EVENING READER	ER 764	Sin Partners	1964	Elliott, D.*	AF		$8.00
EVENING READER	ER 766	Passion Hideout	1965	Dexter, J.	VGF		$6.00
EVENING READER	ER 767	Woodland Wanton	1965	Shay, A.	VGF		$8.00
EVENING READER	ER 768	Sin Whisper	1965	Marshall, A.*	VGF		$8.00
EVENING READER	ER 769	Sinkeeper	1965	Hudson, D.	VGF		$8.00
EVENING READER	ER 770	Passion Carnival	1965	Calvano, T.	VG+		$5.00
EVENING READER	ER 776	Flesh Man	1965	Elliott, D.*	AF		$8.00
EVENING READER	ER 777	Flesh Bigamist	1965	Elliott, D.*	AF		$9.00
EVENING READER	ER 783	Sexcess	1965	Hudson, D.	AF		$7.00
EVENING READER	ER 785	Key Club Sinners	1965	Allison, C.	F		$12.00
EVENING READER	ER 787	The Golden Tramps	1965	Dexter, J.	VGF		$8.00
EVENING READER	ER 790	Sin Shill	1965	Bellmore, D.	VGF		$6.00
EVENING READER	ER 791	The Erotics	1965	Williams, J.X.	AF		$9.00 A
EVENING READER	ER 794	Sex Trek	1965	Williams, J.X.	AF		$9.00
EVENING READER	ER 795	Siesta Sin	1965	Aldrich, C.	AF		$12.00 A
EVENING READER	ER 1203	Passion Mask	1965	Calvano, T.	AF		$7.00
EVENING READER	ER 1206	Tokyo Tramp	1965	Marshall, A.*	AF		$10.00
EVENING READER	ER 1215	Would-Be Sinner	1965	Elliott, D.*	AF		$12.00
EVENING READER	ER 1216	The Lust Years	1965	Marshall, A.*	F		$10.00
EVENING READER	ER 1221	Passion Profiteer	1966	Shaw, A.*	AF-		$7.00
EVENING READER	ER 1222	Lust Holiday	1966	Calvano, T.	VGF		$7.00
EVENING READER	ER 1227	Flesh Pact	1966	Dexter, J.	VGF		$7.00
EVENING READER	ER 1228	Sin Heist	1966	Marshall, A.*	F		$8.00
EVENING READER	ER 1229	Strong Man	1966	Marshall, A.*	AF		$10.00
EVENING READER	ER 1233	Miss Understanding	1966	Shaw, A.*	VGF		$8.00
EVENING READER	ER 1236	When Sinners Meet	1966	Marshall, A.*	AF		$10.00
EVENING READER	ER 1238	On Call	1966	Dexter, J.	VGF		$7.00
EVENING READER	ER 1240	Knives Of Desire	1966	Ives, M.*	F		$122.00 A
EVENING READER	ER 1241	No Adam For Eve	1966	Dexter, J.	F		$66.00 A
EVENING READER	ER 1242	Ladies Choice	1966	Williams, J.X.	AF-		$10.00 A

Falcon 21 AF $67

Falcon 30 VG $60

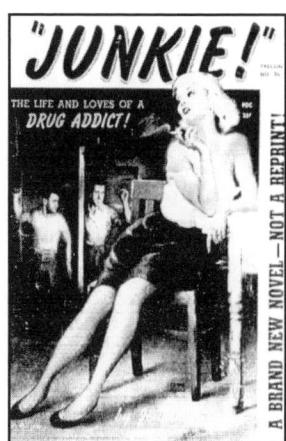

Falcon 36 VG+ $532

PUBLISHER	PUB. #	TITLE	DATE	AUTHOR	COND.	TYPE	PRICE
EVENING READER	ER 1246	Daughters Of Sappho	1966	Williams, J.X.	F		$28.00 A
EVENING READER	ER 1247	The Girl's Place	1966	Craig, S.	AF		$33.00 A
EVENING READER	ER 1248	The Gay Girls	1966	Elliott, D.*	AF		$39.00 A
EVENING READER	ER 1252	The French Way	1966	Williams, J.X.	AF		$10.00
EVENING READER	ER 1255	The Scandal Man	1966	Marshall, A.*	F		$8.00
EVENING READER	ER 1261	Waylin's Wantons	1966	Dexter, J.	AF		$6.00
EVERGREEN REV.	11	Evergreen Review - 1/60	1960	Anthology	VGF+	Digest	$33.00 A
EVERGREEN REV.	18	Evergreen Review - 5/61	1961	Anthology	VGF+	Digest	$8.00 A
EVERGREEN REV.	31	Evergreen Review - 7/63	1963	Anthology	VGF	Digest	$16.00
EXECUTIONER	1 7	The Executioner Mystery Mag.	1975	Anthology	VGF	Digest	$7.00
EXOTIC NOVEL	3	Divorce Bait!	1949	Clayford, J.	VGF+	Digest	$55.00 A
EXOTIC NOVEL	3	Divorce Bait!	1949	Clayford, J.	VG	Digest	$36.00 A
EXOTIC NOVEL	5	Buy My Love!	1949	Lindsay, P.	VG	Digest	$35.00
EXOTIC NOVEL	6	Passion's Slave	1950	Harvey, G.	VGF-	Digest	$29.00 A
EXOTIC NOVEL	9	Suzy Needs A Man!	1950	Sherman, J.	AF	Digest	$165.00 A
EXOTIC NOVEL	12	Bodies On Fire	1951	Sherman, J.	AF	Digest	$84.00 A
EXOTIC NOVEL	17	Ten Toes Up	1951	Scott, A.	VG	Digest	$15.00
EXOTIC NOVEL	19	Fever Hot!	1951	Balmer, J.	VGF+	Digest	$181.00 A
EXOTIC NOVEL	20	Lovers Don't Sleep	1951	Hale, L.	VG	Digest	$22.00 A
EXOTIK	W 19	Nightmare In Leather	1965	Woods, J.	AF		$19.00 A
EXOTIK	W 22	Sex A Go Go!	1966	Trainer, R.	VG		$36.00 A
EXOTIK	W 22	Sex A Go Go!	1966	Trainer, R.	AF		$30.00
EXOTIK	W 23	Night Lust	1966	Gardner, K.	VGF		$18.00 A
EXPLORING THE UNKNOWN	1 1	Exploring The Unknown 1/60	1960	Anthology	AF	Digest	$14.00
FABIAN	Z 101	Each Won Two	1959	Bates, M.	AF		$10.00
FABIAN	Z 112	The Black Night (3rd)	1957	Short, B.	VG+		$6.00
FABIAN	Z 114	Stairways To Sin	1958	Madigan, K.	VG		$7.00
FABIAN	Z 115	Long December (4th)	1958	Hayes, R.	VG+		$7.00
FABIAN	Z 116	The Rambling Maids (4th)	1958	Short, B.	VG		$7.00
FABIAN	Z 118	Tainted Wife	1957	Peters, W.	VG+		$7.00
FABIAN	Z 119	Violent Surrender	1957	Southern, C.	VG		$7.00
FABIAN	Z 120	Taxi Dancers (3rd)	1959	Linkletter, E.	VGF		$6.00
FABIAN	Z 121	Push-Over	1958	Sela, L.	VG+		$8.00
FABIAN	Z 123	Beach Maverick	1958	Haynes, F.	VGF		$7.00
FABIAN	Z 124	The Gay Ones	1958	Linkletter, E.	VGF		$10.00
FABIAN	Z 124	The Gay Ones	1958	Linkletter, E.	VG+		$7.00
FABIAN	Z 126	Nor Feats Of Hell	1959	Bennett, W.	VG		$6.00
FABIAN	Z 127	Imposed Rebellion	1959	Williams, J.	VG+		$7.00
FABIAN	Z 128	Our Flesh Was Cheap	1959	Linkletter, E.	VG+		$10.00
FABIAN	Z 129	One Violent Year	1959	Brandon, R.	VGF		$7.00
FABIAN	Z 132	Naked Return	1960	McIntosh, G.	VG+		$7.00
FABIAN	Z 133	Rose Of Sharon	1960	Bradley, L.	VG+		$6.00
FABIAN	Z 134	Witch Finder	1960	Brandon, R.	VGF		$22.00 A
FABIAN	Z 135	Never To Belong	1960	Williams, J.	VGF		$7.00
FABIAN	Z 136	The Third Bedroom	1960	Baker, B.	AF		$12.00

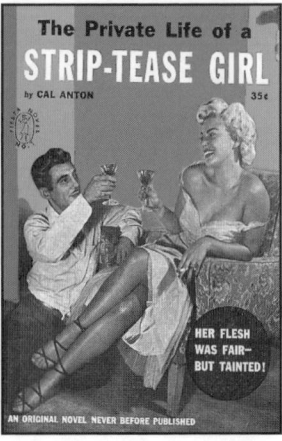

Famous Mystery 1 G $7　　　Fast Action Detective 6-1 VG- $15　　　Fiesta Novel 1 VG+ $46

PUBLISHER	PUB. #	TITLE	DATE	AUTHOR	COND.	TYPE	PRICE
FABIAN	Z 136	The Third Bedroom	1960	Baker, B.	VG+		$6.00
FABIAN	Z 137	Between The Two	1960	Freeman, A.	AF		$11.00 A
FABIAN	Z 141	Beyond The Realm	1960	Turni, M.	VG+		$12.00
FABIAN	Z 142	Age Of Insolence	1960	Rowell, D.	VGF		$7.00
FABIAN	Z 143	Emotional Jungle	1961	Freeman, A.	VGF		$8.00
FABIAN	Z 145	The Violent And The Fair	1961	Beeley, J.H.	AF		$7.00
FABIAN	Z 155	Girl In The Middle	1962	Blake, R.	AF-		$8.00
FABIAN	Z 157	Love Queen	1966	Blake, R.	G+		$6.00
FABIAN	Z 165	Her Unholy Flame	1967	Brian, G.	VG+		$8.00
FALCON	21	Season For Sin	1952	Scott, A.	AF	Digest	$67.00 A
FALCON	27	Lida Lynn	1952	Dann, N.	VG-	Digest	$14.00
FALCON	30	Dagger Of Flesh	1952	Prather, R.S.	VG	Digest	$60.00 A
FALCON	31	Slave Girl	1952	Roan, T.	G	Digest	$35.00 A
FALCON	33	Yellow-Head	1952	Evens, H.	VGF	Digest	$55.00
FALCON	36	Junkie!	1952	Craig, J.	VG+	Digest	$532.00 A
FALCON	37	Woman Hunter	1952	Hale, L.	VG+	Digest	$50.00 A
FALCON (Adult)	1003	Black Silk Harem	1964	Samarov, S.	VGF		$9.00
FAMOUS MYSTERY	1	Murder Takes A Honeymoon	1944	Fleming, E.	G	Digest	$7.00
FAMOUS MYSTERY	2	The Pay-Off	1944	Barry, J.	G	Digest	$6.00
FANTASTIC UNIVERSE	2 5	Fantastic Universe - 12/54	1954	Anthology	VGF	Digest	$10.00 A
FANTASTIC UNIVERSE	8 1	Fantastic Universe - 7/57	1957	Anthology	VG	Digest	$5.00
FANTASTIC UNIVERSE	8 2	Fantastic Universe - 8/57	1957	Anthology	G+	Digest	$4.00
FANTASTIC	1 1	Fantastic - Summer, 1952	1952	Anthology	AF	Digest	$14.00 A
FANTASTIC	1 2	Fantastic - Fall, 1952	1952	Anthology	AF	Digest	$27.00 A
FANTASTIC	1 3	Fantastic - Dec. 1952	1952	Anthology	VGF	Digest	$25.00 A
FANTASTIC	2 1	Fantastic - Jan.- Feb. 1953	1953	Anthology	AF-	Digest	$22.00
FANTASTIC	2 2	Fantastic - Mar-April 1953	1953	Anthology	AF	Digest	$27.00 A
FANTASTIC	2 3	Fantastic - May-June 1953	1953	Anthology	AF-	Digest	$22.00
FANTASTIC	2 5	Fantastic - Sept-Oct 1953	1953	Anthology	VGF+	Digest	$7.00
FANTASTIC	2 6	Fantastic - Dec. 1953	1953	Anthology	F	Digest	$7.00
FANTASTIC	3 2	Fantastic - April 1954	1954	Anthology	AF	Digest	$7.00
FANTASTIC	3 4	Fantastic - Aug. 1954	1954	Anthology	VGF	Digest	$7.00
FANTASTIC	5 5	Fantastic - Oct. 1956	1956	Anthology	VG+	Digest	$6.00
FANTASTIC	7 11	Fantastic - Nov. 1958	1958	Anthology	VG+	Digest	$7.00
FANTASTIC	9 1	Fantastic - Jan. 1960	1960	Anthology	VGF	Digest	$7.00
FANTASTIC	13 6	Fantastic - June 1964	1964	Anthology	VG	Digest	$7.00
FANTASY	1 1	Magazine Of Fantasy-Fall '49	1949	Anthology	AF	Digest	$24.00 A
FANTASY & SCI-FI	60	Fantasy & Sci-Fi - 5/56	1956	Anthology	VG+	Digest	$6.00
FANTASY & SCI-FI	314	Fantasy & Sci-Fi - 7/77	1977	Anthology	AF	Digest	$10.00
FANTASY FICTION	1 1	Fantasy Fiction - May 1950	1950	Anthology	VGF	Digest	$12.00
FANTASY FICTION	1 2	Fantasy Fiction - 6/53	1953	Anthology	AF	Digest	$33.00 A
FANTASY FICTION	1 3	Fantasy Fiction - 8/53	1953	Anthology	VGF	Digest	$13.00 A
FANTASY MAGAZINE	1 1	Fantasy Magazine - 3/53	1953	Anthology	AF	Digest	$33.00
FANTASY MAGAZINE	1 1	Fantasy Magazine - 3/53	1953	Anthology	VG+	Digest	$7.00
FAR-OUT	4	Is That You Simon?	1961	Piombo, A.D.	VG+		$8.00

Five Star 46 VG $32   Flagship 735 VG+ $20   Galaxy 2 AF $13

PUBLISHER	PUB. #	TITLE	DATE	AUTHOR	COND.	TYPE	PRICE
FAST ACTION DETECTIVE	6 1	Fast Action Detective - 8/57	1957	Anthology	VG-	Digest	$15.00
FAST ACTION DETECTIVE	6 3	Fast Action Detective - 2/58	1958	Anthology	VG	Digest	$13.00
FATE	4 4	Fate - 5/51	1951	Anthology	VGF	Digest	$10.00
FATE	10 12	Fate - 12/57	1957	Anthology	AF	Digest	$6.00
FAWCETT	No#	Prize Stories From Life	1941	Anthology	VG+	Digest	$7.00
FAWCETT PREMIER	R 274	The Addict (2nd)	1966	Anthology	VG+		$5.00
FAWCETT PREMIER	R 365	Teen Age Tyranny	1967	Hechinger, G.	VG+		$3.00
FAWCETT PREMIER	T 424	The Siege Of Harlem (2nd)	1969	Miller, W.	VG		$4.00
FEAR!	1 1	Fear! - 5/60	1960	Anthology	F	Digest	$22.00
FEAR!	1 2	Fear! - 7/60	1960	Anthology	VGF	Digest	$13.00 A
FIESTA NOVEL	1	Private Life Of A Strip-Tease Girl	1952	Anton, C.	VG+	Digest	$46.00 A
FIGHTING WESTERN NOVEL	23	The Bar D Boss	1949	Lee, R.	VG	Digest	$5.00
FINGERPRINTS DETECTIVE	1	Fingerprints Detective #1	n/d	Anthology	VG+	Digest	$16.00 A
FIRST NITER	102	Running Wild	1963	Kosloff, M.	VGF		$34.00 A
FIRST NITER	226	Mask Of Evil	1966	White, C.	VGF+		$57.00 A
FIRST NITER	239	Captured	1966	Braun, L.	AF		$83.00 A
FIRST NITER	250	Wild And Winsome	1967	Delon, R.	VGF		$8.00
FIRST NITER	251	Half-Stoned	1967	Patterson, O.	AF-		$24.00 A
FITZ	FB 1010	Double Trouble	1964	Wassam, R.	VGF		$8.00
FIVE STAR	4	Death Comes To Dinner	1945	Yates, P.	VG	Digest	$8.00
FIVE STAR	6	Murder Seeks An Agent	1945	Brown, W.	G+	Digest	$19.00 A
FIVE STAR	6	Murder Seeks An Agent	1945	Brown, W.	VG+	Digest	$17.00 A
FIVE STAR	41	Death's Long Shadow	1946	Wolffe, K.	VG	Digest	$7.00
FIVE STAR	46	Kill To Fit	1946	Fischer, B.	VG	Digest	$32.00
FIVE STAR	46	Kill To Fit	1946	Fischer, B.	VG+	Digest	$24.00 A
FLAGSHIP	702	Pink Dolphin	1967	Olemy, P.T.	AF		$7.00
FLAGSHIP	715	Moonspin	1967	Carpenter, E.J.	AF		$8.00
FLAGSHIP	715	Moonspin	1967	Carpenter, E.J.	VGF		$7.00
FLAGSHIP	717	Bawdy Songs	1967	Brand, O.	VG+		$5.00
FLAGSHIP	727	The Early Days Of August	1967	Kovalsky, J.R.	VG+		$6.00
FLAGSHIP	728	Malachi Breen Times 2	1967	Pope, L.	VG		$5.00
FLAGSHIP	735	The Man From M.O.D.	1968	Day, W.B.	VG+		$20.00 A
FLAGSHIP	840	The Clones	1968	Olemy, P.T.	VG+		$5.00
FLAGSHIP	846	Lay-Over Town	1968	Brennan, D.	VG		$7.00
FLAGSHIP	852	The Duke	1968	Manson, W.	VGF		$5.00
FLAGSHIP	864	Exile And Other Tales Of Fantasy	1968	Cummings, M.A.	VGF		$7.00
FOR MEN ONLY!	1 8	For Men Only! - 11/37	1937	Anthology	VG	Digest	$6.00
FOTONOVEL	5	Hair	1979	Ragni, G.	F	MTI	$25.00 A
FOUR SQUARE	185	Tarzan The Untamed	1960	Burroughs, E.R.	VG-		$5.00
FOUR SQUARE	339	Tarzan Triumphant	1961	Burroughs, E.R.	VG		$6.00
FOUR SQUARE	1216	The Master Mind Of Mars	1964	Burroughs, E.R.	VGF		$7.00
FOUR SQUARE	1692	Batman vs. The Penguin	1966	Kane, B.	VG		$6.00
FOUR SQUARE	1758	John Carter Of Mars	1968	Burroughs, E.R.	VGF		$7.00
FRANCE	F 3	Ring-A-Ding Lover	1962	Ahriman, S.	VGF		$7.00
FRANCE	F 4	Time Out For Sex	1962	Novak, D.	VGF		$7.00

Galaxy 4 AF $15   Galaxy 23 VG+ $10   Galaxy 32 AF $13

PUBLISHER	PUB. #	TITLE	DATE	AUTHOR	COND.	TYPE	PRICE
FRANCE	F 5	The Fare Sex	1962	Meline, F.	AF		$6.00
FRANCE	F 8	Bedroom City	1962	Geis, R.E.	VG+		$8.00
FRANCE	F 24	Strange Harem	1962	Hudson, J.*	VG+		$7.00
FRANCE	F 35	Girlsville	1963	Geis, R.E.	VG		$8.00
FRANCE	F 37	Prisoners Of Lesbos	1963	Richards, D.	VG+		$8.00
FRANCE	F 53	Virgin No More	1963	Swenson, P.*	VG		$7.00
FRANCE	F 55	Greeks Had A Sex For It	1963	Novak, S.	VGF		$34.00 A
FREEWAY PRESS	FP 2056	The Yellow Scourge	1974	Steele, C.	AF		$15.00
FUTURA	7214	French Connection II	1975	Moore, R.	AF	MTI	$6.00
FUTURE SCI-FI	41	Future Science Fiction 2/59	1959	Anthology	VGF+	Digest	$12.00 A
GALAXY	1	Sinister Barrier	1950	Russell, E.F.	VG+	Digest	$14.00
GALAXY	2	The Legion Of Space	1950	Williamson, J.	AF	Digest	$13.00
GALAXY	4	The Amphibians	1950	Wright, S.F.	AF	Digest	$15.00
GALAXY	4	The Amphibians	1950	Wright, S.F.	AF	Digest	$14.00
GALAXY	5	The World Below	1951	Wright, S.F.	AF	Digest	$15.00
GALAXY	5	The World Below	1951	Wright, S.F.	VGF	Digest	$13.00
GALAXY	6	The Alien	1951	Jones, R.E.	F	Digest	$18.00
GALAXY	7	Empire	1951	Simak, C.D.	AF	Digest	$23.00
GALAXY	7	Empire	1951	Simak, C.D.	AF	Digest	$16.00 A
GALAXY	7	Empire	1951	Simak, C.D.	VGF+	Digest	$15.00
GALAXY	9	Four Sided Triangle	1951	Temple, W.F.	VG-	Digest	$6.00
GALAXY	10	Rat Race	1952	Franklin, J.	VG	Digest	$6.00
GALAXY	11	The City In The Sea	1952	Tucker, W.	AF	Digest	$11.00
GALAXY	11	The City In The Sea	1952	Tucker, W.	VG+	Digest	$7.00
GALAXY	12	The House Of Many Worlds	1952	Merwin, S.	VG	Digest	$6.00
GALAXY	13	Seeds Of Life	1952	Taine, J.	VG	Digest	$6.00
GALAXY	14	Pebble In The Sky	1953	Asimov, I.	VG+	Digest	$11.00
GALAXY	15	Three Go Back	1953	Mitchell, J.L.	VGF	Digest	$16.00
GALAXY	15	Three Go Back	1953	Mitchell, J.L.	VGF	Digest	$12.00
GALAXY	16	The Warriors Of Day	1953	Blish, J.	VGF	Digest	$12.00
GALAXY	17	Well Of The Worlds	1953	Padgett, L.	VG+	Digest	$12.00
GALAXY	17	Well Of The Worlds	1953	Padgett, L.	VG-	Digest	$6.00
GALAXY	18	City At World's End	1953	Hamilton, E.	VGF	Digest	$8.00
GALAXY	18	City At World's End	1953	Hamilton, E.	VG-	Digest	$6.00
GALAXY	19	Jack Of Eagles	1953	Blish, J.	VGF	Digest	$15.00
GALAXY	20	The Black Galaxy	1954	Leinster, M.	AF	Digest	$15.00
GALAXY	20	The Black Galaxy	1954	Leinster, M.	AF	Digest	$14.00
GALAXY	21	The Humanoids	1954	Williamson, J.	VGF	Digest	$15.00
GALAXY	21	The Humanoids	1954	Williamson, J.	VG	Digest	$10.00
GALAXY	22	Killer To Come	1954	Merwin, S.	AF	Digest	$16.00
GALAXY	23	Murder In Space	1954	Reed, D.V.	VG+	Digest	$10.00
GALAXY	24	Lest Darkness Fall	1956	De Camp, L.S.	VGF	Digest	$12.00
GALAXY	26	Chessboard Planet	1956	Padgett, L.	VGF	Digest	$15.00
GALAXY	27	Tarnished Utopia	1956	Jameson, M.	VG+	Digest	$10.00
GALAXY	28	Destiny Times Three	1957	Leiber, F.	VG	Digest	$6.00

| Galaxy 35 AF $15 | Gaslight 124 VGF $30 | Girl From UNCLE 1-1 VG $7 |

PUBLISHER	PUB. #	TITLE	DATE	AUTHOR	COND.	TYPE	PRICE
GALAXY	28	Destiny Times Three	1957	Leiber, F.	VG-	Digest	$6.00
GALAXY	30	Double Jeopardy	1957	Pratt, F.	AF	Digest	$15.00
GALAXY	31	Shambleau	1957	Moore, C.L.	VG+	Digest	$17.00
GALAXY	32	Address: Centauri	1958	Wallace, F.L.	AF		$13.00
GALAXY	32	Address: Centauri	1958	Wallace, F.L.	VG-		$6.00
GALAXY	33	Mission Of Gravity	1958	Clement, H.	VG+		$10.00
GALAXY	34	Twice In Time	1958	Wellman, M.W.	VG+		$14.00
GALAXY	34	Twice In Time	1958	Wellman, M.W.	VG		$7.00
GALAXY	35	The Forever Machine	1958	Clifton, M.	AF		$15.00
GALAXY	35	The Forever Machine	1958	Clifton, M.	VGF		$14.00
GALAXY	35	The Forever Machine	1958	Clifton, M.	VGF-		$9.00
GALAXY (Adult)	806	Madam Murder	1967	Gregory, S.	G		$6.00
GALAXY (Adult)	819	Weekend For Two	1968	Weston, J.	VGF+		$5.00
GALAXY MAGABOOK	2	Magabook #2	1963	Williamson, J.	VGF	Digest	$6.00
GALAXY MAGAZINE	1 4	Galaxy Science Fiction 1/51	1951	Anthology	AF	Digest	$20.00 A
GALAXY MAGAZINE	10 6	Galaxy Science Fiction 9/55	1955	Anthology	VG+	Digest	$5.00
GALAXY/BARMARY	No#	25 Short Stories From Colliers	1953	Anthology	VG	Digest	$67.00 A
GAMMA	2 1	Gamma	1964	Anthology	VGF	Digest	$5.00
GASLIGHT	107	Payoff For Passion	1964	North, K.	VG+		$6.00
GASLIGHT	121	Play With Passion	1964	Donalds, R.	AF		$6.00
GASLIGHT	124	Hot-Rod Babe	1964	Haunt, T.	VGF		$30.00 A
GASLIGHT	137	Vice In Vegas	1964	Haunt, T.	VGF		$7.00
GASLIGHT	138	Sex At Sea	1965	Johns, D.	AF		$17.00 A
GAYWOOD PRESS	No#	Dames Are Dynamite	n/d	Capelli, A.	VG+	Digest	$68.00 A
GAYWOOD PRESS	No#	The Trembling World	n/d	Del Martia, A.	VG	Digest	$23.00 A
GIANT MANHUNT	1	Giant Manhunt #1	1951	Anthology	VGF	Digest	$50.00
GIANT MANHUNT	4	Giant Manhunt #4	1953	Anthology	VGF	Digest	$47.00
GIANT MANHUNT	5	Giant Manhunt #5	1953	Anthology	VG+	Digest	$45.00
GIANT MANHUNT	6	Giant Manhunt #6	1956	Anthology	VGF	Digest	$45.00
GIANT MANHUNT	6	Giant Manhunt #6	1956	Anthology	G	Digest	$10.00
GIANT MANHUNT	7	Giant Manhunt #7	1956	Anthology	VGF	Digest	$45.00
GIANT MANHUNT	8	Giant Manhunt #8	1956	Anthology	VGF	Digest	$45.00
GIANT MANHUNT	9	Giant Manhunt #9	1956	Anthology	VGF	Digest	$45.00
GIRL FROM UNCLE	1 1	Girl From UNCLE Mag. 12/66	1966	Anthology	VG	Digest	$7.00
GIRL FROM UNCLE	1 2	Girl From UNCLE Mag. 2/67	1967	Anthology	VG-	Digest	$6.00
GIRL FROM UNCLE	1 6	Girl From UNCLE Mag. 10/67	1967	Anthology	VGF	Digest	$10.00
GIRL FROM UNCLE	1 6	Girl From UNCLE Mag. 10/67	1967	Anthology	VG+	Digest	$7.00
GOLD MEDAL	No# 99	The Best From True	1949	Anthology	VG		$14.00
GOLD MEDAL	No# 100	Marriage And Sex	1949	Today's Woman	VG		$14.00
GOLD MEDAL	101	We Are The Public Enemies	1949	Hynd, A.	VG		$10.00
GOLD MEDAL	102	Man Story	1950	Anthology	VGF		$20.00
GOLD MEDAL	103	The Persian Cat	1950	Flagg, J.	AF		$62.00 A
GOLD MEDAL	103	The Persian Cat	1950	Flagg, J.	VG+		$10.00
GOLD MEDAL	105	Nude In Mink	1950	Rohmer, S.	VGF		$27.00 A
GOLD MEDAL	105	Nude In Mink	1950	Rohmer, S.	VG+		$26.00

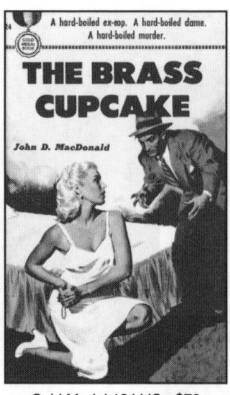

Gold Medal 103 AF $62   Gold Medal 107 VG+ $8   Gold Medal 124 VG+ $73   Gold Medal 126 VG- $7

PUBLISHER	PUB. #	TITLE	DATE	AUTHOR	COND.	TYPE	PRICE
GOLD MEDAL	105	Nude In Mink	1950	Rohmer, S.	VG		$24.00
GOLD MEDAL	106	Stretch Dawson	1950	Burnett, W.R.	VGF	MTI	$10.00
GOLD MEDAL	107	The Flying Saucers Are Real	1950	Keyhoe, D.	VG+		$8.00
GOLD MEDAL	107	The Flying Saucers Are Real	1950	Keyhoe, D.	VG		$7.00
GOLD MEDAL	108	Devil May Care	1950	Miller, W.	VG+		$8.00
GOLD MEDAL	108	Devil May Care	1950	Miller, W.	VG-		$6.00
GOLD MEDAL	108	Devil May Care (3rd)	1950	Miller, W.	VG+		$7.00
GOLD MEDAL	109	Awakening Of Jenny	1950	Colter, L.	AF		$15.00
GOLD MEDAL	112	Your Child And You	1950	Gruenberg, S.	VGF		$6.00
GOLD MEDAL	113	The Violent Ones	1950	Hunt, H.	VG+		$10.00
GOLD MEDAL	114	No Business For A Lady	1950	Rubel, J.L.	VG+		$12.00
GOLD MEDAL	115	Help Wanted - For Murder	1950	Rohde, W.L.	VG		$8.00
GOLD MEDAL	116	The Slaughtered Lovelies	1950	Stanford, D.	AF		$24.00 A
GOLD MEDAL	117	State Department Murders	1950	Ronns, E.*	VG+		$12.00
GOLD MEDAL	117	State Department Murders	1950	Ronns, E.*	VG		$8.00
GOLD MEDAL	118	The Goldfish Murders	1950	Mitchell, W.	VG+		$8.00
GOLD MEDAL	120	The Man Who Said No	1950	Grove, W.	VGF+		$23.00 A
GOLD MEDAL	120	The Man Who Said No (2nd)	1951	Grove, W.	VGF		$9.00
GOLD MEDAL	123	House Of Flesh	1950	Fischer, B.	AF		$23.00 A
GOLD MEDAL	123	House Of Flesh	1950	Fischer, B.	VGF		$17.00
GOLD MEDAL	123	House Of Flesh	1950	Fischer, B.	VG		$7.00
GOLD MEDAL	123	House Of Flesh (2nd)	1951	Fischer, B.	VGF		$16.00
GOLD MEDAL	124	The Brass Cupcake	1950	MacDonald, J.D.	VG+		$73.00 A
GOLD MEDAL	125	The Obsessed	1950	Schweitzer, G.	VGF		$8.00
GOLD MEDAL	125	The Obsessed	1950	Schweitzer, G.	VG+		$8.00
GOLD MEDAL	126	Dallas	1950	Jenkins, W.F.	VG-	MTI	$7.00
GOLD MEDAL	127	Case Of The Vanishing Beauty	1950	Prather, R.S.	AF		$25.00 A
GOLD MEDAL	127	Case Of The Vanishing Beauty	1950	Prather, R.S.	VGF		$18.00
GOLD MEDAL	127	Case Of The Vanishing Beauty	1950	Prather, R.S.	VG		$8.00
GOLD MEDAL	128	Three Secrets	1950	Runbeck, M.L.	AF-	MTI	$15.00
GOLD MEDAL	129	Mansion Of Evil	1950	Millard, J.	VG+		$78.00 A
GOLD MEDAL	130	A Man Of Parts	1950	Connell, V.	VGF		$12.00
GOLD MEDAL	130	A Man Of Parts	1950	Connell, V.	VGF		$10.00
GOLD MEDAL	131	Guns At Broken Bow	1950	Heuman, W.	VGF		$7.00
GOLD MEDAL	132	Women's Barracks	1950	Torres, T.	VGF		$11.00 A
GOLD MEDAL	132	Women's Barracks (2nd)	1951	Torres, T.	VGF		$14.00
GOLD MEDAL	132	Women's Barracks (2nd)	1951	Torres, T.	VG+		$7.00
GOLD MEDAL	133	Catspaw Ordeal	1950	Ronns, E.*	VGF		$47.00 A
GOLD MEDAL	133	Catspaw Ordeal	1950	Ronns, E.*	VG+		$12.00
GOLD MEDAL	134	Hell-Bent For Danger	1950	Grove, W.	VGF		$12.00
GOLD MEDAL	135	Bar Guide	1950	Shane, T.	VG		$5.00
GOLD MEDAL	136	Savage Bride	1950	Woolrich, C.	AF-		$45.00 A
GOLD MEDAL	137	War Bonnet Pass	1950	Stewart, L.	VGF		$8.00
GOLD MEDAL	138	The Corpse That Walked	1951	Cohen, O.R.	VG+		$10.00
GOLD MEDAL	138	The Corpse That Walked	1951	Cohen, O.R.	VGF		$8.00
GOLD MEDAL	139	Stolen Woman	1950	Miller, W.	F		$15.00 A
GOLD MEDAL	141	Hill Girl	1951	Williams, C.	VG		$17.00
GOLD MEDAL	141	Hill Girl (3rd)	1951	Williams, C.	VG+		$6.00

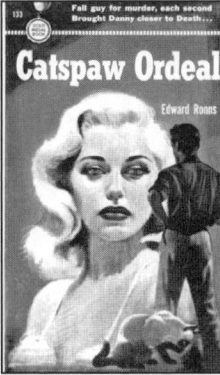

Gold Medal 131 VGF $7   Gold Medal 133 VGF $47   Gold Medal 163 VG+ $27   Gold Medal 169 VG- $24

PUBLISHER	PUB. #	TITLE	DATE	AUTHOR	COND.	TYPE	PRICE
GOLD MEDAL	141	Hill Girl (6th)	1951	Williams, C.	VG+		$6.00
GOLD MEDAL	142	Jewel Of The Java Sea	1951	Cushman, D.	AF		$17.00 A
GOLD MEDAL	142	Jewel Of The Java Sea	1951	Cushman, D.	VGF+		$12.00
GOLD MEDAL	142	Jewel Of The Java Sea	1951	Cushman, D.	VGF		$10.00
GOLD MEDAL	143	The Chinese Keyhole	1951	Himmel, R.	AF		$54.00 A
GOLD MEDAL	143	The Chinese Keyhole	1951	Himmel, R.	VG+		$7.00
GOLD MEDAL	144	Winchester Cut	1951	Sabin, M.	G		$2.00
GOLD MEDAL	145	High Red For Dead	1951	Rohde, W.L.	G+		$3.00
GOLD MEDAL	146	Roll The Wagons	1951	Heuman, W.	AF		$8.00
GOLD MEDAL	146	Roll The Wagons	1951	Heuman, W.	VG+		$7.00
GOLD MEDAL	147	Bodies In Bedlam	1951	Prather, R.S.	VG+		$12.00
GOLD MEDAL	148	The Lady Kills	1951	Fischer, B.	VGF		$22.00
GOLD MEDAL	148	The Lady Kills (2nd)	1951	Fischer, B.	G+		$5.00
GOLD MEDAL	149	Gunsmoke Reckoning	1951	Chadwick, J.	AF		$8.00
GOLD MEDAL	150	Come Murder Me	1951	Kieran, J.	VGF		$20.00 A
GOLD MEDAL	150	Come Murder Me	1951	Kieran, J.	VG+		$7.00
GOLD MEDAL	151	Death And The Naked Lady	1951	Flagg, J.	VG+		$10.00
GOLD MEDAL	151	Death And The Naked Lady	1951	Flagg, J.	G+		$3.00
GOLD MEDAL	152	The Killer (2nd)	1951	Miller, W.	VGF		$6.00
GOLD MEDAL	153	Cocotte	1951	Pratt, T.	VGF+		$11.00
GOLD MEDAL	153	Cocotte	1951	Pratt, T.	VG+		$8.00
GOLD MEDAL	153	Cocotte (2nd)	1951	Pratt, T.	VGF		$7.00
GOLD MEDAL	154	A Gun In His Hand	1951	Rosen, V.	VGF		$14.00
GOLD MEDAL	155	The Apache	1951	Bellah, J.W.	AF		$16.00
GOLD MEDAL	155	The Apache	1951	Bellah, J.W.	G		$3.00
GOLD MEDAL	157	Westport Landing	1951	Hatten, H.	VGF		$15.00
GOLD MEDAL	158	Naked Ebony (3rd)	1951	Cushman, D.	VGF		$7.00
GOLD MEDAL	162	Bargain In Blood	1951	Stanford, D.	VG+		$7.00
GOLD MEDAL	163	Big City Girl	1951	Williams, C.	VG+		$27.00 A
GOLD MEDAL	163	Big City Girl	1951	Williams, C.	VG		$10.00
GOLD MEDAL	163	Big City Girl	1951	Williams, C.	G+		$5.00
GOLD MEDAL	163	Big City Girl (3rd)	1951	Williams, C.	VG+		$7.00
GOLD MEDAL	164	Murder For The Bride	1951	MacDonald, J.D.	VG		$24.00
GOLD MEDAL	164	Murder For The Bride	1951	MacDonald, J.D.	VG-		$15.00
GOLD MEDAL	165	Everybody Had A Gun	1951	Prather, R.S.	VGF		$12.00
GOLD MEDAL	165	Everybody Had A Gun	1951	Prather, R.S.	VG+		$10.00
GOLD MEDAL	166	I Can't Stop Running	1951	Ronns, E.*	VGF		$10.00
GOLD MEDAL	166	I Can't Stop Running	1951	Ronns, E.*	VG+		$7.00
GOLD MEDAL	166	I Can't Stop Running	1951	Ronns, E.*	VG		$5.00
GOLD MEDAL	167	The Judas Hour	1951	Hunt, H.	AF		$16.00 A
GOLD MEDAL	167	The Judas Hour	1951	Hunt, H.	VG		$8.00
GOLD MEDAL	167	The Judas Hour	1951	Hunt, H.	VG		$6.00
GOLD MEDAL	169	Satan Is A Woman	1951	Brewer, G.	VG-		$24.00 A
GOLD MEDAL	169	Satan Is A Woman	1951	Brewer, G.	VG+		$20.00
GOLD MEDAL	169	Satan Is A Woman	1951	Brewer, G.	VG-		$10.00
GOLD MEDAL	170	Death On A Ferris Wheel	1951	Martin, A.L.	VGF+		$12.00
GOLD MEDAL	170	Death On A Ferris Wheel	1951	Martin, A.L.	VG		$4.00
GOLD MEDAL	172	Lost Lady	1951	Cohen, O.R.	VGF		$10.00

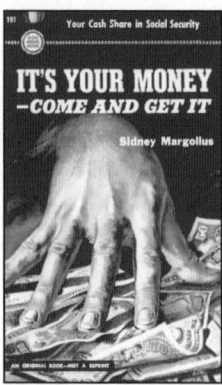
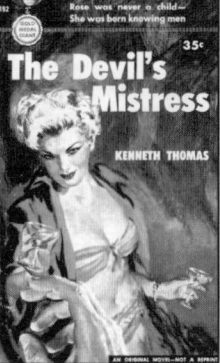

Gold Medal 191 VGF $10　　Gold Medal 192 AF $39　　Gold Medal 196 VG+ $70　　Gold Medal 206 VGF $60

PUBLISHER	PUB. #	TITLE	DATE	AUTHOR	COND.	TYPE	PRICE
GOLD MEDAL	172	Lost Lady	1951	Cohen, O.R.	VG+		$7.00
GOLD MEDAL	173	The Tiger's Wife	1951	Miller, W.	VG		$8.00
GOLD MEDAL	174	Rider From Nowhere	1951	Chadwick, J.	VGF		$7.00
GOLD MEDAL	175	Gay Ghastly Holiday	1951	Blayne, S.	VGF+		$14.00
GOLD MEDAL	176	Crockett's Woman	1951	Hatch, E.	AF-		$15.00
GOLD MEDAL	177	This Is Costello	1951	Prall, R.H.	VGF		$12.00
GOLD MEDAL	177	This Is Costello	1951	Prall, R.H.	VG		$6.00
GOLD MEDAL	178	Cabin Road (3rd)	1951	Faulkner, J.	AF		$8.00
GOLD MEDAL	178	Cabin Road (3rd)	1951	Faulkner, J.	VGF		$7.00
GOLD MEDAL	181	Shanghai Flame	1951	Fleischman, A.S.	VGF		$24.00 A
GOLD MEDAL	181	Shanghai Flame	1951	Fleischman, A.S.	VG+		$10.00
GOLD MEDAL	181	Shanghai Flame (2nd)	1951	Fleischman, A.S.	VG+		$6.00
GOLD MEDAL	182	They Died Healthy	1951	Stewart, L.	VGF		$8.00
GOLD MEDAL	183	. . . And Be My Love	1951	Baker, L.	VG		$7.00
GOLD MEDAL	184	Thunderclap	1951	Sheridan, J.	AF		$14.00
GOLD MEDAL	184	Thunderclap	1951	Sheridan, J.	VG+		$7.00
GOLD MEDAL	185	We Never Called Him Henry	1951	Bennett, H.	AF		$18.00 A
GOLD MEDAL	185	We Never Called Him Henry	1951	Bennett, H.	VG+		$10.00
GOLD MEDAL	186	Judge Me Not	1951	MacDonald, J.D.	VG+		$41.00 A
GOLD MEDAL	186	Judge Me Not	1951	MacDonald, J.D.	VG		$9.00
GOLD MEDAL	189	Cassidy's Girl	1951	Goodis, D.	G+		$16.00
GOLD MEDAL	189	Cassidy's Girl	1951	Goodis, D.	G		$15.00
GOLD MEDAL	190	Fires That Destroy	1951	Whittington, H.	G		$7.00
GOLD MEDAL	191	It's Your Money - Come & Get It	1951	Margolius, S.	VGF		$10.00
GOLD MEDAL	192	The Devil's Mistress	1951	Thomas, K.	AF		$39.00 A
GOLD MEDAL	192	The Devil's Mistress	1951	Thomas, K.	VGF		$10.00
GOLD MEDAL	193	The Trail	1951	Stewart, L.	VGF		$11.00 A
GOLD MEDAL	196	So Rich, So Dead	1951	Brewer, G.	VG+		$70.00 A
GOLD MEDAL	196	So Rich, So Dead	1951	Brewer, G.	VG+		$50.00 A
GOLD MEDAL	197	The Lady And The Cheetah	1951	Flagg, J.	AF		$16.00
GOLD MEDAL	199	Sumuru	1951	Rohmer, S.	VG+		$16.00
GOLD MEDAL	199	Sumuru	1951	Rohmer, S.	VG-		$5.00
GOLD MEDAL	200	Weep For Me	1951	MacDonald, J.D.	VG		$35.00
GOLD MEDAL	203	Find This Woman	1951	Prather, R.S.	VGF		$10.00
GOLD MEDAL	204	Death For Mr. Big	1951	Gonzales, J.	VG+		$33.00 A
GOLD MEDAL	G 205	Handsome	1951	Pratt, T.	VGF		$18.00
GOLD MEDAL	206	To Kiss Or Kill	1951	Keene, D.	VGF		$60.00 A
GOLD MEDAL	206	To Kiss Or Kill	1951	Keene, D.	VG+		$20.00
GOLD MEDAL	G 207	River Girl	1951	Williams, C.	AF		$49.00 A
GOLD MEDAL	G 207	River Girl	1951	Williams, C.	AF		$45.00
GOLD MEDAL	G 207	River Girl	1951	Williams, C.	G		$5.00
GOLD MEDAL	208	Wild Blood	1951	Abbott, A.C.	VG+		$9.00
GOLD MEDAL	209	Fools Walk In	1951	Fischer, B.	AF		$18.00 A
GOLD MEDAL	211	13 French Street	1951	Brewer, G.	VGF		$83.00 A
GOLD MEDAL	211	13 French Street	1951	Brewer, G.	AF		$66.00 A
GOLD MEDAL	211	13 French Street	1951	Brewer, G.	VG+		$16.00
GOLD MEDAL	211	13 French Street (2nd)	1951	Brewer, G.	VGF		$20.00
GOLD MEDAL	G 212	Deep Is The Pit	1952	Dixon, H.V.	AF		$30.00 A

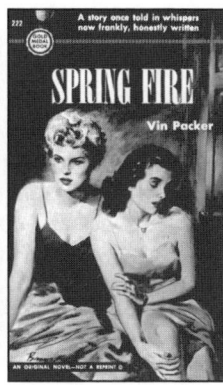

Gold Medal 207 AF $49   Gold Medal 212 AF $30   Gold Medal 219 VG+ $30   Gold Medal 222 VGF $74

PUBLISHER	PUB. #	TITLE	DATE	AUTHOR	COND.	TYPE	PRICE
GOLD MEDAL	G 212	Deep Is The Pit	1952	Dixon, H.V.	VG+		$14.00
GOLD MEDAL	213	The Golden Woman	1952	Hatch, E.	VG+		$10.00
GOLD MEDAL	214	Fear Comes Calling	1952	Martin, A.L.	AF		$20.00 A
GOLD MEDAL	216	Red Runs The River	1952	Heuman, W.	AF		$30.00 A
GOLD MEDAL	216	Red Runs The River	1952	Heuman, W.	VG+		$9.00
GOLD MEDAL	217	Passage To Terror	1952	Ronns, E.*	AF		$33.00 A
GOLD MEDAL	217	Passage To Terror	1952	Ronns, E.*	VG+		$8.00
GOLD MEDAL	218	Here Is My Body	1952	Mooney, B.	VG+		$7.00
GOLD MEDAL	219	The Sheltering Night	1952	Fisher, S.	VG+		$30.00 A
GOLD MEDAL	220	Give A Man A Gun	1952	Ernenwein, L.	AF		$15.00
GOLD MEDAL	220	Give A Man A Gun	1952	Ernenwein, L.	VG+		$10.00
GOLD MEDAL	221	The Forbidden Room	1952	Steele, J.	VG+		$8.00
GOLD MEDAL	221	The Forbidden Room	1952	Steele, J.	VG+		$6.00
GOLD MEDAL	222	Spring Fire	1952	Packer, V.*	VGF		$74.00 A
GOLD MEDAL	222	Spring Fire	1952	Packer, V.*	AF		$36.00 A
GOLD MEDAL	222	Spring Fire	1952	Packer, V.*	VGF		$25.00
GOLD MEDAL	223	Look Behind You Lady	1952	Fleischman, A.S.	VGF		$10.00
GOLD MEDAL	225	Home Is The Sailor	1952	Keene, D.	AF		$33.00 A
GOLD MEDAL	225	Home Is The Sailor	1952	Keene, D.	G+		$6.00
GOLD MEDAL	225	Home Is The Sailor	1952	Keene, D.	G		$5.00
GOLD MEDAL	226	Of Tender Sin	1952	Goodis, D.	VGF-		$200.00 A
GOLD MEDAL	226	Of Tender Sin	1952	Goodis, D.	VGF		$83.00 A
GOLD MEDAL	227	The Creeping Shadow	1952	Merwin, S.	AF-		$16.00 A
GOLD MEDAL	227	The Creeping Shadow	1952	Merwin, S.	VGF+		$15.00
GOLD MEDAL	228	Appointment In Paris	1952	Adams, F.	AF		$30.00 A
GOLD MEDAL	228	Appointment In Paris	1952	Adams, F.	VG+		$5.00
GOLD MEDAL	229	Little Sister	1952	Roberts, L.	VG+		$7.00
GOLD MEDAL	229	Little Sister	1952	Roberts, L.	G		$5.00
GOLD MEDAL	231	The Road's End	1952	Conroy, A.	AF		$22.00 A
GOLD MEDAL	231	The Road's End	1952	Conroy, A.	VG		$5.00
GOLD MEDAL	232	Woman Soldier	1952	Rodin, A.	AF		$16.00
GOLD MEDAL	233	Way Of A Wanton	1952	Prather, R.S.	VGF		$12.00
GOLD MEDAL	234	The Sharp Edge	1952	Himmel, R.	VGF		$12.00
GOLD MEDAL	235	The Avenger	1952	Blood, M.	AF		$15.00 A
GOLD MEDAL	235	The Avenger	1952	Blood, M.	VG+		$12.00
GOLD MEDAL	235	The Avenger	1952	Blood, M.	VG+		$10.00
GOLD MEDAL	236	Lone Star	1952	Chase, B.	VG+		$6.00
GOLD MEDAL	237	Terror In The Sun	1952	Glendinning, R.	VG+		$8.00
GOLD MEDAL	238	Uncle Good's Girls	1952	Faulkner, J.	VGF		$14.00
GOLD MEDAL	238	Uncle Good's Girls	1952	Faulkner, J.	VGF		$12.00
GOLD MEDAL	240	The Damned (3rd)	1952	MacDonald, J.D.	VG+		$5.00
GOLD MEDAL	242	Trapped	1952	Hayward, R.	AF-		$20.00 A
GOLD MEDAL	244	The Cheaters	1952	Baker, L.	VG+		$7.00
GOLD MEDAL	245	Double Cross	1952	Chadwick, J.	VG+		$12.00
GOLD MEDAL	246	The Scarlet Venus	1952	Green, C.	VGF		$14.00
GOLD MEDAL	246	The Scarlet Venus	1952	Green, C.	VG+		$10.00
GOLD MEDAL	246	The Scarlet Venus	1952	Green, C.	G		$3.00
GOLD MEDAL	248	Blackmailer	1952	Axelrod, G.	AF		$18.00 A

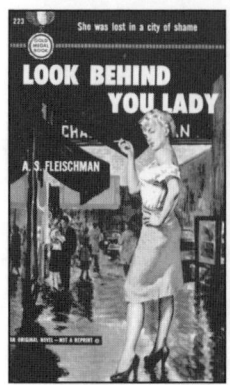
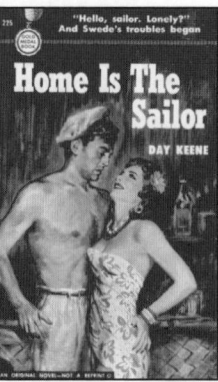

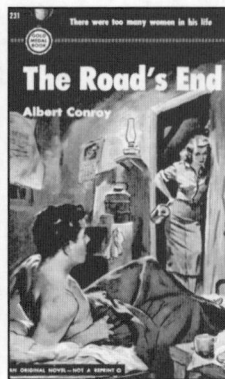

Gold Medal 223 VGF $10   Gold Medal 225 AF $33   Gold Medal 226 VGF- $200   Gold Medal 231 AF $22

PUBLISHER	PUB. #	TITLE	DATE	AUTHOR	COND.	TYPE	PRICE
GOLD MEDAL	248	Blackmailer	1952	Axelrod, G.	VG		$6.00
GOLD MEDAL	250	Dark Intruder	1952	Packer, V.*	VGF		$20.00 A
GOLD MEDAL	250	Dark Intruder	1952	Packer, V.*	VG		$14.00
GOLD MEDAL	250	Dark Intruder	1952	Packer, V.*	VG-		$8.00
GOLD MEDAL	251	The Caged	1952	Nichols, F.	VGF		$17.00 A
GOLD MEDAL	252	Satan Takes The Helm	1952	Clements, C.	AF		$11.00 A
GOLD MEDAL	253	The Crimson Frame	1952	Martin, A.L.	AF		$10.00 A
GOLD MEDAL	256	Street Of The Lost	1952	Goodis, D.	VGF-		$67.00 A
GOLD MEDAL	256	Street Of The Lost	1952	Goodis, D.	G		$16.00
GOLD MEDAL	259	Walk In Fear	1952	Ballard, W.T.	VG+		$13.00 A
GOLD MEDAL	260	Men Into Beasts	1952	Viereck, G.S.	VG+		$12.00
GOLD MEDAL	262	Who Evil Thinks	1952	Glendinning, R.	VG+		$7.00
GOLD MEDAL	263	Love Me Now	1952	McPartland, J.	AF-		$26.00
GOLD MEDAL	263	Love Me Now	1952	McPartland, J.	G		$5.00
GOLD MEDAL	264	Brenda	1952	Zane, L.	AF-		$22.00
GOLD MEDAL	264	Brenda	1952	Zane, L.	VGF		$15.00
GOLD MEDAL	265	Darling, It's Death	1952	Prather, R.S.	VG+		$10.00
GOLD MEDAL	265	Darling, It's Death	1952	Prather, R.S.	VG		$10.00
GOLD MEDAL	266	Plunder	1952	Appel, B.	VG+		$7.00
GOLD MEDAL	266	Plunder	1952	Appel, B.	VG		$5.00
GOLD MEDAL	269	The Devil Drives	1952	Ames, R.	VGF-		$70.00 A
GOLD MEDAL	270	The Fast Buck	1952	Fischer, B.	VGF		$33.00 A
GOLD MEDAL	270	The Fast Buck	1952	Fischer, B.	VG+		$17.00 A
GOLD MEDAL	270	The Fast Buck	1952	Fischer, B.	VG		$10.00
GOLD MEDAL	271	Blood On The Sun	1952	Merriman, C.	VGF		$12.00
GOLD MEDAL	272	Take Me As I Am	1952	Fielding, W.H.	VG+		$9.00
GOLD MEDAL	273	Unholy Flame	1952	Rosamanith, O.	AF-		$21.00 A
GOLD MEDAL	273	Unholy Flame	1952	Rosamanith, O.	VG+		$10.00
GOLD MEDAL	275	Move Along Stranger	1952	Castle, F.	G+		$3.00
GOLD MEDAL	276	Mountain Girl	1952	Wainer, C.	VGF		$14.00
GOLD MEDAL	276	Mountain Girl	1952	Wainer, C.	VGF		$12.00 A
GOLD MEDAL	277	Flight To Darkness	1952	Brewer, G.	VG+		$23.00
GOLD MEDAL	278	That French Girl	1952	Hilton, J.	VGF		$10.00
GOLD MEDAL	279	The Big Guy	1953	Miller, W.	VGF		$26.00 A
GOLD MEDAL	282	Woman Of Cairo	1953	Flagg, J.	AF-		$15.00
GOLD MEDAL	282	Woman Of Cairo	1953	Flagg, J.	VGF		$13.00
GOLD MEDAL	282	Woman Of Cairo	1953	Flagg, J.	VG		$8.00
GOLD MEDAL	283	The Fire Goddess	1952	Rohmer, S.	VG		$17.00
GOLD MEDAL	283	The Fire Goddess	1952	Rohmer, S.	VG		$10.00
GOLD MEDAL	284	Whip Hand	1953	Chadwick, J.	AF		$16.00
GOLD MEDAL	287	On To Santa Fe	1953	Heuman, W.	AF		$17.00 A
GOLD MEDAL	287	On To Santa Fe	1953	Heuman, W.	VG+		$12.00
GOLD MEDAL	288	Maggie – Her Marriage	1953	Caldwell, T.	VGF		$15.00
GOLD MEDAL	289	The Chiselers	1953	Conroy, A.	VGF		$7.00
GOLD MEDAL	290	Jungle She	1953	Cushman, D.	AF		$40.00 A
GOLD MEDAL	290	Jungle She	1953	Cushman, D.	VG		$18.00 A
GOLD MEDAL	291	Whom Gods Destroy	1953	Adams, C.	AF		$12.00 A
GOLD MEDAL	291	Whom Gods Destroy	1953	Adams, C.	VG		$9.00

Gold Medal 245 VG+ $12   Gold Medal 251 VGF $17   Gold Medal 256 VGF- $67   Gold Medal 265 VG+ $10

PUBLISHER	PUB. #	TITLE	DATE	AUTHOR	COND.	TYPE	PRICE
GOLD MEDAL	292	Run, Chico, Run	1953	Brown, W.	AF		$44.00 A
GOLD MEDAL	294	The Girl In The Red Velvet Swing	1953	Samuels, C.	VGF		$14.00
GOLD MEDAL	294	The Girl In The Red Velvet Swing	1953	Samuels, C.	VGF		$10.00
GOLD MEDAL	296	Black Wings Has My Angel	1953	Chaze, E.	G		$8.00
GOLD MEDAL	298	Dead Low Tide	1953	MacDonald, J.D.	VG		$15.00
GOLD MEDAL	298	Dead Low Tide	1953	MacDonald, J.D.	G+		$14.00
GOLD MEDAL	302	Masquerade Into Madness	1952	Meservey, R.	VGF		$13.00
GOLD MEDAL	306	The Girl In The Death Cell	1953	Cook, F.J.	VGF		$43.00 A
GOLD MEDAL	307	Witch Of Salem	1953	Siegel, B.	VGF		$16.00
GOLD MEDAL	307	Witch Of Salem	1953	Siegel, B.	VG+		$10.00
GOLD MEDAL	309	Sword In His Hand	1953	Vail, J.	AF		$33.00 A
GOLD MEDAL	309	Sword In His Hand	1953	Vail, J.	VG+		$8.00
GOLD MEDAL	310	Keelboats North	1953	Heuman, W.	VG+		$10.00
GOLD MEDAL	311	Thieves Fall Out	1953	Kay, C.*	AF		$39.00 A
GOLD MEDAL	311	Thieves Fall Out	1953	Kay, C.*	VG		$6.00
GOLD MEDAL	S 312	Treasury Of American Verse	1953	Anthology	AF		$10.00
GOLD MEDAL	S 312	Treasury Of American Verse	1953	Anthology	VG		$3.00
GOLD MEDAL	314	Gunsmoke Reckoning	1953	Chadwick, J.	VG+		$7.00
GOLD MEDAL	316	Up A Winding Stair	1953	Dixon, H.V.	F		$38.00 A
GOLD MEDAL	316	Up A Winding Stair	1953	Dixon, H.V.	VG		$4.00
GOLD MEDAL	319	The Crooked Mile	1953	Fagan, N.	VGF		$12.00
GOLD MEDAL	319	The Crooked Mile	1953	Fagan, N.	VG+		$7.00
GOLD MEDAL	320	Escape From Morales	1953	Myers, V.	VG+		$7.00
GOLD MEDAL	322	Guns At Broken Bow	1953	Heuman, W.	AF		$13.00
GOLD MEDAL	322	Guns At Broken Bow	1953	Heuman, W.	VGF		$7.00
GOLD MEDAL	323	The Neon Jungle	1953	MacDonald, J.D.	G+		$16.00
GOLD MEDAL	323	The Neon Jungle	1953	MacDonald, J.D.	VG		$12.00 A
GOLD MEDAL	323	The Neon Jungle	1953	MacDonald, J.D.	G		$12.00
GOLD MEDAL	324	Look Back To Love	1953	Packer, V.*	VG		$8.00
GOLD MEDAL	324	Look Back To Love	1953	Packer, V.*	G+		$7.00
GOLD MEDAL	329	Gunfighter's Return	1953	Ernenwein, L.	VG		$4.00
GOLD MEDAL	331	South Of The Sun	1953	Miller, W.	VGF		$26.00 A
GOLD MEDAL	331	South Of The Sun	1953	Miller, W.	G+		$7.00
GOLD MEDAL	331	South Of The Sun	1953	Miller, W.	VG		$6.00
GOLD MEDAL	332	Timberjack	1953	Cushman, D.	VG+		$9.00
GOLD MEDAL	333	To Love, To Hate	1953	Adams, F.	AF		$20.00 A
GOLD MEDAL	334	The Girl In Lover's Lane	1953	Boswell, C.	VGF		$7.00
GOLD MEDAL	336	Tokyo Doll	1953	McPartland, J.	VG+		$53.00 A
GOLD MEDAL	336	Tokyo Doll	1953	McPartland, J.	VG		$14.00
GOLD MEDAL	s 339	Escape To Eden	1953	Pratt, T.	AF		$17.00
GOLD MEDAL	341	Ride A High Horse	1953	Prather, R.S.	VG+		$8.00
GOLD MEDAL	343	Run For Your Life	1953	Fischer, B.	VG+		$16.00 A
GOLD MEDAL	344	Wagon Train Woman	1953	Henry, A.	VGF		$8.00
GOLD MEDAL	345	Hell's Our Destination	1953	Brewer, G.	VG		$20.00
GOLD MEDAL	347	Hondo	1953	L'Amour, L.	VG	MTI	$35.00
GOLD MEDAL	347	Hondo	1953	L'Amour, L.	VG-	MTI	$23.00
GOLD MEDAL	347	Hondo	1953	L'Amour, L.	G	MTI	$10.00
GOLD MEDAL	348	The Moon In The Gutter	1953	Goodis, D.	VGF+		$126.00 A

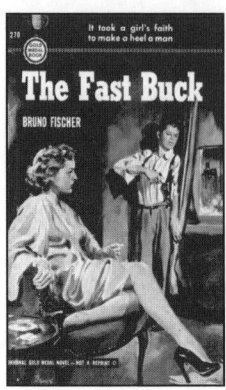

Gold Medal 270 VGF $33   Gold Medal 279 VGF $26   Gold Medal 287 AF $17   Gold Medal 290 AF $40

PUBLISHER	PUB. #	TITLE	DATE	AUTHOR	COND.	TYPE	PRICE
GOLD MEDAL	348	The Moon In The Gutter	1953	Goodis, D.	VG+		$92.00 A
GOLD MEDAL	348	The Moon In The Gutter	1953	Goodis, D.	VG-		$55.00
GOLD MEDAL	349	I Came To Kill	1953	Davis, G.	VGF+		$16.00 A
GOLD MEDAL	350	Rage In Texas	1953	Rigsby, H.	VGF		$12.00
GOLD MEDAL	350	Rage In Texas	1953	Rigsby, H.	VG+		$7.00
GOLD MEDAL	351	The Girl In The Poison Cottage	1953	Hoffmann, R.H.	AF		$16.00
GOLD MEDAL	351	The Girl In The Poison Cottage	1953	Hoffmann, R.H.	AF-		$12.00
GOLD MEDAL	351	The Girl In The Poison Cottage	1953	Hoffmann, R.H.	VGF		$10.00
GOLD MEDAL	354	Big Red's Daughter	1953	McPartland, J.	VGF		$8.00 A
GOLD MEDAL	355	Big Stan	1953	Monahan, J.	VG		$10.00
GOLD MEDAL	356	Paradise Motel	1953	Sheridan, J.	AF		$15.00
GOLD MEDAL	357	Guns Along The Wickiup	1953	Newton, D.B.	VG+		$6.00
GOLD MEDAL	359	The Girl In The House Of Hate	1953	Samuels, C.	AF		$40.00 A
GOLD MEDAL	359	The Girl In The House Of Hate	1953	Samuels, C.	G		$3.00
GOLD MEDAL	360	One Sword For Love	1953	Fox, G.F.	VGF		$15.00
GOLD MEDAL	361	Rampage	1953	Ernenwein, L.	AF		$16.00
GOLD MEDAL	362	Come Back, My Love	1953	Aarons, E.S.	VGF		$18.00 A
GOLD MEDAL	362	Come Back, My Love	1953	Aarons, E.S.	VGF		$15.00
GOLD MEDAL	363	Come Destroy Me	1954	Packer, V.*	VG		$6.00
GOLD MEDAL	365	Monte Carlo Mission	1954	Connell, V.	VG		$5.00
GOLD MEDAL	366	The Woman Is Mine	1954	Whittington, H.	VG		$12.00
GOLD MEDAL	367	Rails West	1954	Stewart, L.	VGF		$10.00 A
GOLD MEDAL	369	Seminole	1954	Pratt, T.	AF-		$25.00 A
GOLD MEDAL	369	Seminole	1954	Pratt, T.	VG		$7.00
GOLD MEDAL	371	Go Home, Stranger	1954	Williams, C.	VG		$22.00
GOLD MEDAL	372	Notorious	1954	Keene, D.	G-		$3.00
GOLD MEDAL	373	Two Deaths Must Die	1954	Himmel, R.	AF		$24.00 A
GOLD MEDAL	373	Two Deaths Must Die	1954	Himmel, R.	VGF		$13.00 A
GOLD MEDAL	375	As A Man Falls	1954	Rigsby, H.	AF		$66.00 A
GOLD MEDAL	375	As A Man Falls	1954	Rigsby, H.	VG+		$7.00
GOLD MEDAL	377	The Range Grabbers	1954	Stewart, S.	VG+		$10.00
GOLD MEDAL	378	Let Them Eat Bullets	1954	Schoenfeld, H.	VG+		$10.00
GOLD MEDAL	379	Women's Barracks	1954	Torres, T.	VG+		$14.00
GOLD MEDAL	380	A Killer Is Loose	1954	Brewer, G.	VGF-		$27.00 A
GOLD MEDAL	380	A Killer Is Loose	1954	Brewer, G.	VG		$12.00
GOLD MEDAL	381	Fury On The Plains	1954	Merriman, C.	VGF		$12.00
GOLD MEDAL	382	One Against The Odds	1954	Fagan, N.	VGF+		$15.00
GOLD MEDAL	382	One Against The Odds	1954	Fagan, N.	G		$3.00
GOLD MEDAL	383	Cartoon Fun	1954	Anthology	VG		$5.00
GOLD MEDAL	384	The Girl With The Scarlet Band	1954	Boswell, C.	AF-		$12.00
GOLD MEDAL	D 387	Driven	1954	Gehman, R.	AF		$32.00
GOLD MEDAL	D 387	Driven	1954	Gehman, R.	VGF		$20.00
GOLD MEDAL	D 387	Driven	1954	Gehman, R.	VG		$8.00
GOLD MEDAL	388	I'll Take What's Mine	1954	Jones, N.	VG		$6.00
GOLD MEDAL	393	The Face Of Evil	1954	McPartland, J.	VGF-		$27.00 A
GOLD MEDAL	393	The Face Of Evil	1954	McPartland, J.	VG+		$22.00
GOLD MEDAL	394	The Gentleman Rogue	1954	Fox, G.F.	VG+		$12.00
GOLD MEDAL	394	The Gentleman Rogue	1954	Fox, G.F.	VG		$8.00

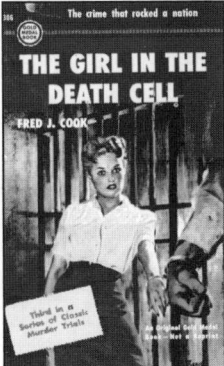

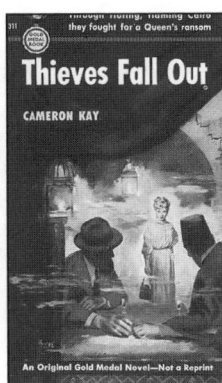

Gold Medal 292 AF $44   Gold Medal 306 VGF $43   Gold Medal 309 AF $33   Gold Medal 311 AF $39

PUBLISHER	PUB. #	TITLE	DATE	AUTHOR	COND.	TYPE	PRICE
GOLD MEDAL	394	The Gentleman Rogue	1954	Fox, G.F.	VG		$5.00
GOLD MEDAL	397	The Girl On The Gallows	1954	Patrick, Q.	VGF		$15.00
GOLD MEDAL	398	Spring Fire	1956	Packer, V.*	VG-		$5.00
GOLD MEDAL	400	Lucinda	1954	Rigsby, H.	AF-		$10.00
GOLD MEDAL	401	Saddle The Storm	1954	Whittington, H.	VG		$18.00 A
GOLD MEDAL	401	Saddle The Storm	1954	Whittington, H.	VG		$12.00
GOLD MEDAL	402	French For Murder	1954	Mara, B.*	VGF+		$137.00 A
GOLD MEDAL	402	French For Murder	1954	Mara, B.*	VG-		$14.00 A
GOLD MEDAL	402	French For Murder	1954	Mara, B.*	G+		$7.00
GOLD MEDAL	s 403	Portrait Of Lisa	1954	Brothers, W.P.	VG		$6.00
GOLD MEDAL	405	There Was A Crooked Man	1954	Keene, D.	F		$49.00 A
GOLD MEDAL	406	Affair In Tokyo	1954	McPartland, J.	VG-		$12.00
GOLD MEDAL	406	Affair In Tokyo	1954	McPartland, J.	VG+		$11.00 A
GOLD MEDAL	408	Return Of Sumuru	1954	Rohmer, S.	AF		$30.00 A
GOLD MEDAL	408	Return Of Sumuru	1954	Rohmer, S.	VG-		$4.00
GOLD MEDAL	409	Some Must Die	1954	Brewer, G.	G		$8.00
GOLD MEDAL	411	Black Horse Canyon	1954	Savage, L.	VG+	MTI	$13.00
GOLD MEDAL	411	Black Horse Canyon	1954	Savage, L.	VG	MTI	$8.00
GOLD MEDAL	413	Always Leave 'Em Dying	1954	Prather, R.S.	AF		$12.00
GOLD MEDAL	413	Always Leave 'Em Dying (2nd)	1955	Prather, R.S.	VG+		$9.00
GOLD MEDAL	414	Ride For Texas	1954	Heuman, W.	AF		$8.00
GOLD MEDAL	414	Ride For Texas	1954	Heuman, W.	VG		$5.00
GOLD MEDAL	415	Runaway Black	1954	Marsten, R.	G		$4.00
GOLD MEDAL	416	Jezebel In Crinoline	1954	Hatten, H.	G+		$3.00
GOLD MEDAL	418	13 French Street	1954	Brewer, G.	VGF		$10.00
GOLD MEDAL	418	13 French Street	1954	Brewer, G.	G		$3.00
GOLD MEDAL	419	Come Murder Me	1954	Kieran, J.	VG		$8.00
GOLD MEDAL	420	All These Condemned	1954	MacDonald, J.D.	VG		$24.00
GOLD MEDAL	421	Smash-Up	1954	Pratt, T.	VG+		$8.00
GOLD MEDAL	423	Blood Is A Lovely Dame	1954	Blood, M.	VGF+		$16.00 A
GOLD MEDAL	425	TCOT Vanishing Beauty (3rd)	1956	Prather, R.S.	VG+		$7.00
GOLD MEDAL	429	The Range Buster	1954	Heuman, W.	AF		$14.00
GOLD MEDAL	429	The Range Buster	1954	Heuman, W.	AF		$8.00
GOLD MEDAL	431	The Girl On The Lonely Beach	1954	Cook, F.J.	AF		$14.00
GOLD MEDAL	431	The Girl On The Lonely Beach	1954	Cook, F.J.	VGF+		$14.00
GOLD MEDAL	S 433	Somebody Loves Me	1954	Morgan, N.	AF		$27.00 A
GOLD MEDAL	434	A Touch Of Death	1954	Williams, C.	AF		$75.00 A
GOLD MEDAL	434	A Touch Of Death	1954	Williams, C.	VG		$17.00
GOLD MEDAL	434	A Touch Of Death	1954	Williams, C.	G-		$3.00
GOLD MEDAL	435	The Dangerous One	1954	Ames, R.	VG+		$8.00 A
GOLD MEDAL	436	The Man From Riondo	1954	Dean, D.	F		$12.00
GOLD MEDAL	437	So Wicked My Love	1954	Fischer, B.	VGF+		$30.00 A
GOLD MEDAL	437	So Wicked My Love	1954	Fischer, B.	VG		$6.00
GOLD MEDAL	438	Woman Of Kali	1954	Fox, G.F.	VGF+		$82.00 A
GOLD MEDAL	438	Woman Of Kali	1954	Fox, G.F.	VGF		$17.00
GOLD MEDAL	438	Woman Of Kali	1954	Fox, G.F.	VGF		$16.00
GOLD MEDAL	S 440	The Cunning And The Haunted	1954	Jessup, R.	VGF+		$41.00 A
GOLD MEDAL	442	Rebel Raider	1954	Chadwick, J.	F		$10.00

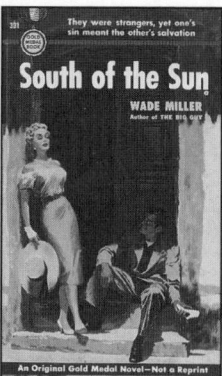
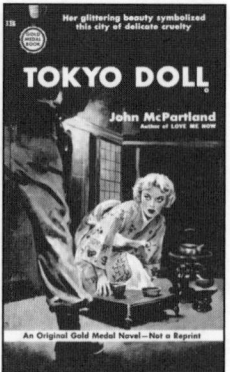

| Gold Medal 323 G+ $16 | Gold Medal 331 VGF $26 | Gold Medal 336 VG+ $53 | Gold Medal 347 VG $35 |

PUBLISHER	PUB. #	TITLE	DATE	AUTHOR	COND.	TYPE	PRICE
GOLD MEDAL	443	Wild Breed	1954	Stratton, T.	VG+		$7.00
GOLD MEDAL	444	Mission To Murder	1954	Glendinning, R.	VG+		$7.00
GOLD MEDAL	444	Mission To Murder	1954	Glendinning, R.	G+		$4.00
GOLD MEDAL	445	Funny Cartoons	1954	Partch, V.	VG+		$5.00
GOLD MEDAL	447	Make My Coffin Strong	1954	Cox, W.R.	VG		$8.00
GOLD MEDAL	447	Make My Coffin Strong	1954	Cox, W.R.	VG		$6.00
GOLD MEDAL	448	77 Rue Paradis	1954	Brewer, G.	VGF		$63.00 A
GOLD MEDAL	448	77 Rue Paradis	1954	Brewer, G.	AF		$34.00 A
GOLD MEDAL	448	77 Rue Paradis	1954	Brewer, G.	G		$6.00
GOLD MEDAL	450	Strange But True	1954	Anthology	VG		$5.00
GOLD MEDAL	451	Bad Day At Black Rock	1954	Niall, M.	AF	MTI	$15.00 A
GOLD MEDAL	455	The Sin Shouter Of Cabin Road	1955	Faulkner, J.	F		$10.00
GOLD MEDAL	455	The Sin Shouter Of Cabin Road	1955	Faulkner, J.	VG+		$7.00
GOLD MEDAL	456	Shanghai Incident	1955	Dodge, S.	VGF		$18.00 A
GOLD MEDAL	456	Shanghai Incident	1955	Dodge, S.	VG		$10.00
GOLD MEDAL	457	Many Rivers To Cross	1955	Frazee, S.	VG+	MTI	$33.00 A
GOLD MEDAL	458	The Girl In Murder Flat	1955	Heimer, M.	VG+		$7.00
GOLD MEDAL	463	Strangers In My Bed	1955	O'Quinn, A.	AF		$16.00 A
GOLD MEDAL	463	Strangers In My Bed	1955	O'Quinn, A.	VGF		$13.00 A
GOLD MEDAL	464	Bullet Barricade	1955	Ernenwein, L.	VG+		$7.00
GOLD MEDAL	466	Death Was The Bridegroom	1955	Samuels, C.	AF		$14.00 A
GOLD MEDAL	466	Death Was The Bridegroom	1955	Samuels, C.	VG		$7.00
GOLD MEDAL	468	Forever Is Today	1955	Mason, R.	AF		$10.00
GOLD MEDAL	469	Mad Baxter	1955	Miller, W.	VG		$7.00
GOLD MEDAL	470	The Big Caper	1955	White, L.	VG		$8.00
GOLD MEDAL	472	A Bullet For My Lady	1955	Mara, B.*	AF		$165.00 A
GOLD MEDAL	473	Violence In The Night	1955	Hynd, A.	VGF		$22.00 A
GOLD MEDAL	473	Violence In The Night	1955	Hynd, A.	VG+		$6.00
GOLD MEDAL	475	Angels In The Gutter	1955	Hilton, J.	G		$7.00
GOLD MEDAL	476	Blond Savage	1955	Vail, J.	AF		$10.00
GOLD MEDAL	478	Heller With A Gun	1955	L'Amour, L.	VGF		$110.00 A
GOLD MEDAL	480	The Girls In Nightmare House	1955	Boswell, C.	VGF		$17.00
GOLD MEDAL	480	The Girls In Nightmare House	1955	Boswell, C.	VGF		$15.00 A
GOLD MEDAL	485	West To The Sun	1955	Loomis, N.	AF		$7.00
GOLD MEDAL	486	Dark Heritage	1955	Foster, J.	VGF		$10.00
GOLD MEDAL	487	The Truth About Belle Gunness	1955	De la Torre, L.	AF-		$8.00 A
GOLD MEDAL	488	Cry Of The Flesh	1955	Himmel, R.	AF		$15.00
GOLD MEDAL	489	Blood Alley	1955	Fleischman, A.S.	VG+	MTI	$33.00 A
GOLD MEDAL	490	Mine To Avenge	1955	Wills, T.	VGF		$22.00 A
GOLD MEDAL	491	Assignment To Disaster	1955	Aarons, E.S.	AF		$11.00 A
GOLD MEDAL	492	Plunder Range	1955	Hatten, H.	VGF		$10.00
GOLD MEDAL	492	Plunder Range	1955	Hatten, H.	VG+		$6.00
GOLD MEDAL	493	The Golden Frame	1955	Chadwick, J.	VG		$6.00
GOLD MEDAL	494	Who Has Wilma Lathrop?	1955	Keene, D.	VGF		$22.00 A
GOLD MEDAL	494	Who Has Wilma Lathrop?	1955	Keene, D.	VG+		$10.00
GOLD MEDAL	495	Hell Strip	1955	Richards, L.	AF-		$15.00 A
GOLD MEDAL	495	Hell Strip	1955	Richards, L.	VGF+		$12.00 A
GOLD MEDAL	496	Bodies In Bedlam (4th)	1956	Prather, R.S.	VGF		$8.00

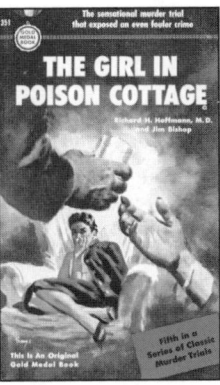

| Gold Medal 348 VGF+ $126 | Gold Medal 351 AF $16 | Gold Medal 375 AF $66 | Gold Medal 434 AF $75 |

PUBLISHER	PUB. #	TITLE	DATE	AUTHOR	COND.	TYPE	PRICE
GOLD MEDAL	496	Bodies In Bedlam (4th)	1956	Prather, R.S.	VG		$4.00
GOLD MEDAL	497	Way Of A Wanton (4th)	1957	Prather, R.S.	VG+		$7.00
GOLD MEDAL	498	One Of Our H Bombs Is Missing	1955	Brennan, F.H.	VG+		$7.00
GOLD MEDAL	498	One Of Our H Bombs Is Missing	1955	Brennan, F.H.	G+		$4.00
GOLD MEDAL	499	Blood Alley	1955	Fleischman, A.S.	VG+	MTI	$13.00
GOLD MEDAL	499	Blood Alley	1955	Fleischman, A.S.	VG	MTI	$10.00
GOLD MEDAL	500	So Fair, So Evil	1955	Connolly, P.	AF		$12.00 A
GOLD MEDAL	500	So Fair, So Evil	1955	Connolly, P.	VG+		$7.00
GOLD MEDAL	504	Everybody Had A Gun	1955	Prather, R.S.	VGF		$8.00
GOLD MEDAL	504	Everybody Had A Gun	1955	Prather, R.S.	VGF		$7.00
GOLD MEDAL	504	Everybody Had A Gun (4th)	1957	Prather, R.S.	VGF		$5.00
GOLD MEDAL	505	Darling, It's Death	1955	Prather, R.S.	VGF		$7.00
GOLD MEDAL	506	Stop This Man!	1955	Rabe, P.	VGF		$14.00 A
GOLD MEDAL	506	Stop This Man!	1955	Rabe, P.	G		$5.00
GOLD MEDAL	507	Murder In The Navy	1955	Marsten, R.	AF		$20.00
GOLD MEDAL	508	Strip For Murder	1955	Prather, R.S.	VGF		$8.00
GOLD MEDAL	509	We Walk Alone	1955	Aldrich, A.*	VG+		$15.00
GOLD MEDAL	509	We Walk Alone	1955	Aldrich, A.*	VG		$10.00
GOLD MEDAL	509	We Walk Alone	1955	Aldrich, A.*	G		$4.00
GOLD MEDAL	509	We Walk Alone (2nd)	1956	Aldrich, A.*	VGF		$15.00
GOLD MEDAL	514	Shanghai Flame	1955	Fieischman, A.D.	VG+		$7.00
GOLD MEDAL	516	To Tame A Land	1955	L'Amour, L.	VGF		$95.00 A
GOLD MEDAL	519	Lie Down With Lions	1955	Albert, M.H.	VG+		$8.00
GOLD MEDAL	521	The Killer	1955	Miller, W.	AF		$7.00
GOLD MEDAL	521	The Killer	1955	Miller, W.	VG+		$7.00
GOLD MEDAL	526	Gunsmoke Empire	1955	Patten, L.B.	AF		$6.00
GOLD MEDAL	529	The Decoy	1955	Ronns, E.*	VGF+		$15.00 A
GOLD MEDAL	530	The Wounded And The Slain	1955	Goodis, D.	VG		$200.00 A
GOLD MEDAL	530	The Wounded And The Slain	1955	Goodis, D.	VG-		$28.00 A
GOLD MEDAL	531	The Dead Darling	1955	Craig, J.	VGF		$18.00 A
GOLD MEDAL	535	Port Orient	1955	Cushman, D.	VGF		$67.00 A
GOLD MEDAL	537	House Of Flesh	1955	Fischer, B.	VGF+		$17.00 A
GOLD MEDAL	538	The Flesh And Mr. Rawlie	1955	Cooper, M.	AF		$14.00
GOLD MEDAL	538	The Flesh And Mr. Rawlie	1955	Cooper, M.	VG+		$7.00
GOLD MEDAL	539	Rain Of Terror	1955	Douglas, M.	AF		$15.00 A
GOLD MEDAL	539	Rain Of Terror	1955	Douglas, M.	VG+		$7.00
GOLD MEDAL	540	Zowie! Girl Meets Boy	1955	Anthology	AF		$13.00 A
GOLD MEDAL	543	The Chinese Keyhole	1955	Himmel, R.	VGF		$20.00 A
GOLD MEDAL	544	Cassidy's Girl	1955	Goodis, D.	G-		$8.00
GOLD MEDAL	546	Killer In White	1956	Thomey, T.	VG+		$15.00 A
GOLD MEDAL	546	Killer In White	1956	Thomey, T.	G		$3.00
GOLD MEDAL	547	A House In Naples	1956	Rabe, P.	VG+		$14.00
GOLD MEDAL	s 549	Queen Of Sheba	1956	Fox, G.F.	VGF		$15.00
GOLD MEDAL	s 549	Queen Of Sheba	1956	Fox, G.F.	VG+		$7.00
GOLD MEDAL	s 549	Queen Of Sheba	1956	Fox, G.F.	VG		$7.00
GOLD MEDAL	s 550	Down To Eternity	1956	O'Connor, R.	VGF	MTI	$14.00
GOLD MEDAL	s 550	Down To Eternity	1956	O'Connor, R.	VGF-	MTI	$11.00 A
GOLD MEDAL	551	Too Many Crooks	1956	Prather, R.S.	VG+		$8.00

Gold Medal 435 VG+ $8   Gold Medal 437 VGF+ $30   Gold Medal 438 VGF+ $82   Gold Medal 440 VGF+ $41

PUBLISHER	PUB. #	TITLE	DATE	AUTHOR	COND.	TYPE	PRICE
GOLD MEDAL	552	Men Into Beasts	1956	Viereck, G.S.	VGF+		$12.00
GOLD MEDAL	553	The Law And Jake Wade	1956	Albert, M.H.	VG+		$8.00
GOLD MEDAL	555	Sinister Madonna	1956	Rohmer, S.	VGF		$81.00 A
GOLD MEDAL	555	Sinister Madonna	1956	Rohmer, S.	G		$6.00
GOLD MEDAL	556	Hold Back The Sun	1956	Vail, J.	VGF		$7.00
GOLD MEDAL	557	Hot, Sweet And Blue	1956	Baird, J.	G		$5.00
GOLD MEDAL	563	Build My Gallows High	1956	Sparkia, R.B.	VGF		$10.00
GOLD MEDAL	563	Build My Gallows High	1956	Sparkia, R.B.	VG		$7.00
GOLD MEDAL	s 564	Cry Blood	1956	Dixon, H.V.	AF		$22.00 A
GOLD MEDAL	s 564	Cry Blood	1956	Dixon, H.V.	VG		$5.00
GOLD MEDAL	570	My Mistress, Death	1956	Spafford, R.	VG		$7.00
GOLD MEDAL	571	I'll See You In Hell	1956	McPartland, J.	AF		$18.00 A
GOLD MEDAL	571	I'll See You In Hell	1956	McPartland, J.	VG+		$9.00
GOLD MEDAL	571	I'll See You In Hell	1956	McPartland, J.	G		$6.00
GOLD MEDAL	573	Rope Law	1956	Patten, L.B.	F		$8.00
GOLD MEDAL	574	Danger For Breakfast	1956	McPartland, J.	G		$5.00
GOLD MEDAL	575	Mecca For Murder	1956	Marlowe, S.	G		$4.00
GOLD MEDAL	576	Catch A Falling Star	1956	Marr, R.	VG+		$5.00
GOLD MEDAL	s 577	The Shrinking Man	1956	Matheson, R.	VG+		$24.00 A
GOLD MEDAL	s 577	The Shrinking Man	1956	Matheson, R.	G		$14.00
GOLD MEDAL	579	The Road's End	1956	Conroy, A.	AF-		$8.00
GOLD MEDAL	581	The Young And Violent	1956	Packer, V.*	VG		$10.00
GOLD MEDAL	s 583	Hypnosis And You	1956	Tawney, H.D.	VG+		$7.00
GOLD MEDAL	s 583	Hypnosis And You	1956	Tawney, H.D.	VG		$4.00
GOLD MEDAL	s 587	Johnny Concho (2nd)	1957	Loomis, N.	VG-	MTI	$3.00
GOLD MEDAL	594	Kill The Boss Goodbye	1956	Rabe, P.	VG		$20.00
GOLD MEDAL	595	Brute In Brass	1956	Whittington, H.	G		$7.00
GOLD MEDAL	596	The Wild Party	1956	McPartland, J.	VGF	MTI	$67.00 A
GOLD MEDAL	596	The Wild Party	1956	McPartland, J.	VG	MTI	$36.00 A
GOLD MEDAL	600	Fools Walk In	1956	Fischer, B.	VG		$5.00
GOLD MEDAL	606	Operation Murder	1956	White, L.	VGF		$16.00 A
GOLD MEDAL	s 607	The Diamond Bikini	1956	Williams, C.	VGF		$68.00 A
GOLD MEDAL	611	Desire In The Dust	1956	Whittington, H.	VG+		$32.00 A
GOLD MEDAL	611	Desire In The Dust	1956	Whittington, H.	G+		$8.00
GOLD MEDAL	612	Dig My Grave Deep	1956	Rabe, P.	VG		$22.00
GOLD MEDAL	615	Three Violent People	1956	Praskins, L.	VG+	MTI	$7.00
GOLD MEDAL	s 616	Killer In Silk	1956	Dixon, H.V.	VGF		$8.00
GOLD MEDAL	617	About Doctor Ferrel	1956	Keene, D.	VG+		$12.00
GOLD MEDAL	617	About Doctor Ferrel	1956	Keene, D.	VG		$6.00
GOLD MEDAL	619	Prarie Reckoning	1956	Durst, P.	VG+		$7.00
GOLD MEDAL	622	Murder On The Side	1956	Keene, D.	VG		$20.00
GOLD MEDAL	622	Murder On The Side	1956	Keene, D.	VG+		$16.00
GOLD MEDAL	623	Down There	1956	Goodis, D.	VG		$80.00 A
GOLD MEDAL	s 624	Dark Don't Catch Me	1956	Packer, V.*	VG		$16.00
GOLD MEDAL	s 624	Dark Don't Catch Me	1956	Packer, V.*	VG		$14.00
GOLD MEDAL	625	Go Home, Stranger	1956	Williams, C.	VGF		$24.00 A
GOLD MEDAL	625	Go Home, Stranger	1956	Williams, C.	VG+		$14.00
GOLD MEDAL	625	Go Home, Stranger	1956	Williams, C.	G		$3.00

Gold Medal 448 VGF $63   Gold Medal 451 AF $15   Gold Medal 457 VG+ $33   Gold Medal 472 AF $165

PUBLISHER	PUB. #	TITLE	DATE	AUTHOR	COND.	TYPE	PRICE
GOLD MEDAL	626	Of Tender Sin	1957	Goodis, D.	AF		$45.00
GOLD MEDAL	629	The Deadly Chase	1957	Cullen, C.	AF		$17.00 A
GOLD MEDAL	s 632	Search For Surrender	1957	Deal, B.	AF		$14.00
GOLD MEDAL	633	The Sin Shouter Of Cabin Rd.	1957	Faulkner, J.	VGF		$6.00
GOLD MEDAL	634	State Department Murders	1957	Ronns, E.*	AF		$8.00
GOLD MEDAL	635	Seminole	1957	Pratt, T.	G+		$5.00
GOLD MEDAL	637	Running Target	1957	Frazee, S.	VG		$5.00
GOLD MEDAL	637	Running Target	1957	Frazee, S.	G+		$4.00
GOLD MEDAL	638	Women Without Men	1957	Marr, R.	AF		$15.00 A
GOLD MEDAL	638	Women Without Men	1957	Marr, R.	VG+		$15.00
GOLD MEDAL	640	The Wicked Streets	1957	Brown, W.	VG		$16.00
GOLD MEDAL	640	The Wicked Streets	1957	Brown, W.	VG		$15.00
GOLD MEDAL	s 641	The Golden Sorrow	1957	Pratt, T.	AF		$8.00
GOLD MEDAL	s 642	Sweet Money Girl	1957	Appel, B.	AF		$18.00 A
GOLD MEDAL	643	I Am Legend	1957	Matheson, R.	AF		$42.00 A
GOLD MEDAL	643	I Am Legend	1957	Matheson, R.	G		$6.00
GOLD MEDAL	644	Ride The Gold Mare	1957	Demaris, O.	AF		$54.00 A
GOLD MEDAL	644	Ride The Gold Mare	1957	Demaris, O.	G+		$6.00
GOLD MEDAL	648	Terror Over London	1957	Fox, G.F.	AF		$27.00 A
GOLD MEDAL	648	Terror Over London	1957	Fox, G.F.	VG		$8.00
GOLD MEDAL	s 649	The Wings Of Eagles	1957	Grove, W.	VG	MTI	$7.00
GOLD MEDAL	650	The Corpse That Walked	1957	Cohen, O.R.	VGF		$10.00
GOLD MEDAL	650	The Corpse That Walked	1957	Cohen, O.R.	VG		$3.00
GOLD MEDAL	652	Street Of The Lost	1957	Goodis, D.	AF		$37.00 A
GOLD MEDAL	652	Street Of The Lost	1957	Goodis, D.	VG		$20.00
GOLD MEDAL	s 653	Odd Girl Out	1957	Bannon, A.	VGF		$28.00 A
GOLD MEDAL	s 653	Odd Girl Out	1957	Bannon, A.	VGF		$27.00 A
GOLD MEDAL	s 653	Odd Girl Out	1957	Bannon, A.	G-		$3.00
GOLD MEDAL	654	Pure Sweet Hell	1957	Douglas, M.	AF		$100.00 A
GOLD MEDAL	657	The Out Is Death	1957	Rabe, P.	G-		$2.00
GOLD MEDAL	658	Murder Is My Dish	1957	Marlowe, S.	VG		$5.00
GOLD MEDAL	s 661	The Maricopa Trail	1957	Loomis, N.	VG+		$8.00
GOLD MEDAL	663	Death Takes The Bus	1957	White, L.	VG		$10.00
GOLD MEDAL	664	So I'm A Heel	1957	Heller, M.	VGF		$10.00
GOLD MEDAL	664	So I'm A Heel	1957	Heller, M.	VG		$7.00
GOLD MEDAL	664	So I'm A Heel	1957	Heller, M.	VG		$6.00
GOLD MEDAL	668	Don't Let Her Die	1957	Scott, T.	AF		$22.00 A
GOLD MEDAL	668	Don't Let Her Die	1957	Scott, T.	VG+		$10.00
GOLD MEDAL	669	So Young, So Wicked	1957	Craig, J.	VG		$6.00
GOLD MEDAL	670	Agreement To Kill	1957	Rabe, P.	AF-		$25.00
GOLD MEDAL	s 673	Women's Barracks	1957	Torres, T.	VGF		$14.00
GOLD MEDAL	s 673	Women's Barracks (11th)	1958	Torres, T.	VGF+		$10.00
GOLD MEDAL	675	One Wild Oat	1957	Kantor, M.	AF		$12.00
GOLD MEDAL	676	Nice Guys Finish Dead	1957	Conroy, A.	AF		$13.00
GOLD MEDAL	678	It's My Funeral	1957	Rabe, P.	AF		$24.00 A
GOLD MEDAL	680	The Hoods Take Over	1957	Demaris, O.	VGF+		$25.00 A
GOLD MEDAL	680	The Hoods Take Over	1957	Demaris, O.	VG		$7.00
GOLD MEDAL	s 684	Re-Enter Fu Manchu	1957	Rohmer, S.	VG+		$12.00

Gold Medal 475 G $7   Gold Medal 499 VG+ $13   Gold Medal 535 VGF $67   Gold Medal 546 VG+ $15

PUBLISHER	PUB. #	TITLE	DATE	AUTHOR	COND.	TYPE	PRICE
GOLD MEDAL	s 684	Re-Enter Fu Manchu	1957	Rohmer, S.	VG		$7.00
GOLD MEDAL	s 684	Re-Enter Fu Manchu	1957	Rohmer, S.	VG		$5.00
GOLD MEDAL	687	Hostage For A Hood	1957	White, L.	AF		$110.00 A
GOLD MEDAL	687	Hostage For A Hood	1957	White, L.	VG		$7.00
GOLD MEDAL	s 688	The Girl In The Belfry	1957	Jackson, J.H.	AF		$10.00
GOLD MEDAL	s 688	The Girl In The Belfry	1957	Jackson, J.H.	G+		$5.00
GOLD MEDAL	689	Three-Day Terror	1957	Packer, V.*	VGF		$29.00 A
GOLD MEDAL	689	Three-Day Terror	1957	Packer, V.*	G+		$5.00
GOLD MEDAL	689	Three-Day Terror	1957	Packer, V.*	G		$3.00
GOLD MEDAL	690	Crockett's Woman	1957	Hatch, E.	VG+		$7.00
GOLD MEDAL	691	Fire In The Flesh	1957	Goodis, D.	VGF-		$50.00
GOLD MEDAL	691	Fire In The Flesh	1957	Goodis, D.	VG		$36.00 A
GOLD MEDAL	693	Killers Are My Meat	1957	Marlowe, S.	F		$18.00 A
GOLD MEDAL	693	Killers Are My Meat	1957	Marlowe, S.	VGF		$8.00
GOLD MEDAL	694	Murder In The Raw	1957	Fischer, B.	F		$40.00 A
GOLD MEDAL	694	Murder In The Raw	1957	Fischer, B.	VG		$6.00
GOLD MEDAL	695	Lovely And Lethal	1957	Castle, F.	AF-		$14.00
GOLD MEDAL	695	Lovely And Lethal (2nd)	1958	Castle, F.	VG+		$7.00
GOLD MEDAL	700	The Tall Stranger	1957	L'Amour, L.	VG	MTI	$14.00 A
GOLD MEDAL	700	The Tall Stranger	1957	L'Amour, L.	G+	MTI	$12.00
GOLD MEDAL	700	The Tall Stranger	1957	L'Amour, L.	G-	MTI	$3.00
GOLD MEDAL	702	TCOT Beautiful Body	1957	Craig, J.	F		$14.00
GOLD MEDAL	702	TCOT Beautiful Body	1957	Craig, J.	VG+		$11.00 A
GOLD MEDAL	703	The Voodoo Murders	1957	Avallone, M.	VG+		$14.00
GOLD MEDAL	s 704	This Is Costello	1957	Prall, R.H.	F		$15.00
GOLD MEDAL	705	Stagecoach West	1957	Heuman, W.	VGF		$8.00
GOLD MEDAL	708	The Brat	1957	Brewer, G.	AF-		$47.00 A
GOLD MEDAL	708	The Brat	1957	Brewer, G.	AF		$23.00 A
GOLD MEDAL	708	The Brat	1957	Brewer, G.	G+		$7.00
GOLD MEDAL	708	The Brat (2nd)	1958	Brewer, G.	VGF		$15.00
GOLD MEDAL	708	The Brat (2nd)	1958	Brewer, G.	VG+		$5.00
GOLD MEDAL	709	Murder In Red	1957	Castle, F.	VG		$5.00
GOLD MEDAL	710	Journey Into Terror	1957	Rabe, P.	AF		$24.00 A
GOLD MEDAL	711	A Man Of Parts	1957	Connell, V.	VGF		$12.00
GOLD MEDAL	713	Summons To Silverhorn	1957	Fowler, K.	VG		$6.00
GOLD MEDAL	715	Case Of The Deadly Kiss	1957	Ozaki, M.K.	F		$48.00 A
GOLD MEDAL	715	Case Of The Deadly Kiss	1957	Ozaki, M.K.	VGF		$8.00
GOLD MEDAL	716	Come Night, Come Evil	1957	Craig, J.	F		$14.00
GOLD MEDAL	716	Come Night, Come Evil	1957	Craig, J.	VG+		$6.00
GOLD MEDAL	717	For Love Of Imabelle	1957	Himes, C.	G+		$6.00
GOLD MEDAL	718	The Crazy Mixed-Up Corpse	1957	Avallone, M.	F		$14.00
GOLD MEDAL	718	The Crazy Mixed-Up Corpse	1957	Avallone, M.	VG		$7.00
GOLD MEDAL	719	Savage Bride	1957	Woolrich, C.	VGF		$23.00 A
GOLD MEDAL	719	Savage Bride	1957	Woolrich, C.	AF		$20.00
GOLD MEDAL	720	Barren Land Showdown	1957	Short, L.	VGF		$7.00
GOLD MEDAL	721	Murder On The Line	1957	Rohde, W.L.	AF-		$10.00
GOLD MEDAL	721	Murder On The Line	1957	Rohde, W.L.	VG+		$5.00
GOLD MEDAL	722	A Town To Tame	1958	Chadwick, J.	VGF		$8.00

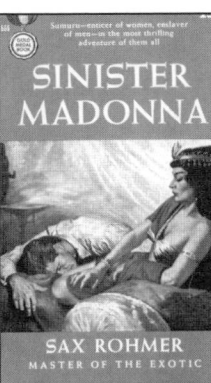
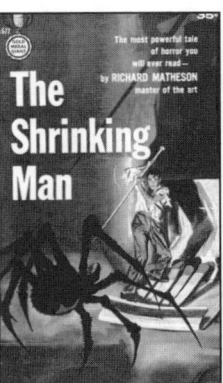

Gold Medal 550 VGF $14   Gold Medal 555 VGF $81   Gold Medal 577 VG+ $24   Gold Medal 596 VGF $67

PUBLISHER	PUB. #	TITLE	DATE	AUTHOR	COND.	TYPE	PRICE
GOLD MEDAL	723	Five Rode West	1958	Patten, L.B.	AF		$12.00
GOLD MEDAL	s 727	We, Too, Must Love	1958	Aldrich, A.*	VGF+		$30.00 A
GOLD MEDAL	s 727	We, Too, Must Love	1958	Aldrich, A.*	AF		$24.00
GOLD MEDAL	s 727	We, Too, Must Love	1958	Aldrich, A.*	VG		$10.00
GOLD MEDAL	s 727	We, Too, Must Love	1958	Aldrich, A.*	VG		$6.00
GOLD MEDAL	728	Heller With A Gun	1958	L'Amour, L.	VG		$12.00
GOLD MEDAL	728	Heller With A Gun	1958	L'Amour, L.	VG		$8.00
GOLD MEDAL	728	Heller With A Gun	1958	L'Amour, L.	G		$3.00
GOLD MEDAL	729	Uncle Good's Girls	1958	Faulkner, J.	F		$12.00
GOLD MEDAL	s 731	5:45 To Suburbia	1958	Packer, V.*	F		$34.00 A
GOLD MEDAL	s 731	5:45 To Suburbia	1958	Packer, V.*	AF		$16.00 A
GOLD MEDAL	s 731	5:45 To Suburbia	1958	Packer, V.*	VGF+		$12.00
GOLD MEDAL	732	Ripe Fruit	1958	McPartland, J.	AF		$27.00 A
GOLD MEDAL	732	Ripe Fruit	1958	McPartland, J.	F		$24.00
GOLD MEDAL	s 734	Teen-Age Terror	1958	Brown, W.	AF		$32.00 A
GOLD MEDAL	s 734	Teen-Age Terror	1958	Brown, W.	VGF		$28.00 A
GOLD MEDAL	s 735	The Rich And The Damned	1958	Himmel, R.	F		$12.00
GOLD MEDAL	737	Dead Low Tide	1958	MacDonald, J.D.	G		$5.00
GOLD MEDAL	740	Web Of Murder	1958	Whittington, H.	VG+		$50.00 A
GOLD MEDAL	740	Web Of Murder	1958	Whittington, H.	VGF-		$42.00 A
GOLD MEDAL	743	I Like 'Em Tough	1958	Cannon, C.*	F		$27.00 A
GOLD MEDAL	743	I Like 'Em Tough	1958	Cannon, C.*	VG+		$5.00
GOLD MEDAL	744	The Secret Of Sylvia	1958	Borden, L.	AF		$14.00
GOLD MEDAL	745	Take A Murder, Darling	1958	Prather, R.S.	VGF		$12.00
GOLD MEDAL	745	Take A Murder, Darling	1958	Prather, R.S.	VG+		$5.00
GOLD MEDAL	745	Take A Murder, Darling (2nd)	1959	Prather, R.S.	AF		$12.00
GOLD MEDAL	750	The Lusting Drive	1958	Demaris, O.	F		$15.00
GOLD MEDAL	750	The Lusting Drive	1958	Demaris, O.	VG+		$8.00
GOLD MEDAL	752	Dakota Boomtown	1958	Castle, F.	VGF		$7.00
GOLD MEDAL	753	So Wicked My Love	1958	Fischer, B.	AF		$15.00
GOLD MEDAL	753	So Wicked My Love	1958	Fischer, B.	F		$11.00 A
GOLD MEDAL	753	So Wicked My Love	1958	Fischer, B.	VGF		$9.00
GOLD MEDAL	754	The Obsessed (2nd)	1958	Schweitzer, G.	VG		$3.00
GOLD MEDAL	755	The Lady Kills	1958	Fischer, B.	AF		$40.00 A
GOLD MEDAL	755	The Lady Kills	1958	Fischer, B.	VG+		$14.00
GOLD MEDAL	755	The Lady Kills	1958	Fischer, B.	VG		$7.00
GOLD MEDAL	756	The Law And Jake Wade	1958	Albert, M.H.	AF	MTI	$12.00
GOLD MEDAL	758	Devil May Care	1958	Miller, W,	F		$15.00
GOLD MEDAL	759	Wyoming Jones	1958	Telfair, R.	AF		$10.00
GOLD MEDAL	759	Wyoming Jones	1958	Telfair, R.	VG+		$6.00
GOLD MEDAL	760	The Bounty Killer	1958	Albert, M.H.	VGF		$8.00
GOLD MEDAL	761	Park Avenue Tramp	1958	Flora, F.	VG+		$10.00
GOLD MEDAL	s 762	The Tycoon And The Tigress	1958	Cox, W.	AF		$10.00
GOLD MEDAL	763	Stop This Man!	1958	Rabe, P.	F		$44.00 A
GOLD MEDAL	763	Stop This Man!	1958	Rabe, P.	AF		$22.00 A
GOLD MEDAL	s 764	The Rise & Fall Of Dr. Carey	1958	Osborne, O.O.	VGF		$7.00
GOLD MEDAL	765	No Business For A Lady	1958	Rubel, J.L.	VG+		$8.00
GOLD MEDAL	766	Catspaw Ordeal	1958	Ronns, E.*	AF		$10.00

Gold Medal 623 VG $80	Gold Medal 642 AF $18	Gold Medal 644 AF $54	Gold Medal 653 VGF $28

PUBLISHER	PUB. #	TITLE	DATE	AUTHOR	COND.	TYPE	PRICE
GOLD MEDAL	d 768	The Lost Years Of Jesus	1958	Potter, C.F.	VGF		$5.00
GOLD MEDAL	769	Violence Is My Business	1958	Marlowe, S.	AF		$12.00
GOLD MEDAL	770	The Scrambled Yeggs	1958	Prather, R.S.	AF		$12.00
GOLD MEDAL	770	The Scrambled Yeggs	1958	Prather, R.S.	VGF		$12.00
GOLD MEDAL	771	Texas Outlaw	1958	Jessup, R.	F		$8.00
GOLD MEDAL	772	Feud At Forked River	1958	Ketchum, P.	VGF		$12.00
GOLD MEDAL	s 773	Mission For Vengeance	1958	Rabe, P.	AF		$20.00
GOLD MEDAL	774	We Walk Alone	1958	Aldrich, A.*	VGF		$25.00 A
GOLD MEDAL	774	We Walk Alone	1958	Aldrich, A.*	AF		$22.00
GOLD MEDAL	775	Coffin For A Hood	1958	White, L.	VG+		$54.00 A
GOLD MEDAL	776	Murder Comes Calling	1958	Douglas, M.	F		$13.00 A
GOLD MEDAL	776	Murder Comes Calling	1958	Douglas, M.	VG+		$10.00
GOLD MEDAL	s 777	Clemmie (2nd)	1959	MacDonald, J.D.	VG		$5.00
GOLD MEDAL	779	Tucson	1958	Peil, P.L.	VGF	MTI	$8.00
GOLD MEDAL	780	The Mob Says Murder	1958	Conroy, A.	AF		$15.00 A
GOLD MEDAL	781	Here Is My Body	1958	Mooney, B.	AF		$12.00
GOLD MEDAL	782	Judge Me Not	1958	MacDonald, J.D.	VG+		$10.00
GOLD MEDAL	s 783	The Fast Buck	1958	Fischer, B.	VGF		$15.00
GOLD MEDAL	s 783	The Fast Buck	1958	Fischer, B.	VGF		$12.00
GOLD MEDAL	s 783	The Fast Buck	1958	Fischer, B.	VG		$7.00
GOLD MEDAL	784	TCOT Petticoat Murder	1958	Craig, J.	F		$10.00
GOLD MEDAL	785	The Forbidden Land	1958	Cushman, D.	F		$14.00
GOLD MEDAL	786	Too Young To Die	1958	White, L.	AF		$17.00 A
GOLD MEDAL	786	Too Young To Die	1958	White, L.	VG		$10.00
GOLD MEDAL	787	Death's Lovely Mask	1958	Flagg, J.	F		$33.00 A
GOLD MEDAL	789	Tall In The West	1958	Howard, V.	AF		$7.00
GOLD MEDAL	s 790	The Neon Jungle	1958	MacDonald, J.D.	VGF		$8.00
GOLD MEDAL	s 791	Branded Woman	1958	Miller, W.	AF		$10.00
GOLD MEDAL	s 791	Branded Woman	1958	Miller, W.	VG+		$7.00
GOLD MEDAL	792	The Brass Cupcake	1958	MacDonald, J.D.	AF		$27.00 A
GOLD MEDAL	792	The Brass Cupcake	1958	MacDonald, J.D.	VG		$7.00
GOLD MEDAL	s 793	Spring Fire	1958	Packer, V.*	F		$23.00 A
GOLD MEDAL	s 793	Spring Fire	1958	Packer, V.*	AF		$20.00
GOLD MEDAL	794	Trouble At Borrasca Rim	1958	Owen, M.	VG+		$8.00
GOLD MEDAL	795	Case Of The Cop's Wife	1958	Ozaki, M.K.	F		$13.00 A
GOLD MEDAL	795	Case Of The Cop's Wife	1958	Ozaki, M.K.	VG+		$7.00
GOLD MEDAL	s 796	Self-Made Widow	1958	Race, P.	F		$34.00 A
GOLD MEDAL	s 797	The Evil Friendship	1958	Packer, V.*	AF		$50.00 A
GOLD MEDAL	s 797	The Evil Friendship	1958	Packer, V.*	AF		$22.00 A
GOLD MEDAL	799	Assignment Madeline	1958	Aarons, E.S.	F		$12.00
GOLD MEDAL	800	Two Deaths Must Die	1958	Himmel, R.	AF		$44.00 A
GOLD MEDAL	s 801	The Man Who Said No	1958	Grove, W.	F		$13.00
GOLD MEDAL	803	Buchanan Gets Mad	1958	Ward, J.	VG+		$7.00
GOLD MEDAL	804	Relentless Gun	1958	Lutz, G.A.	VGF		$8.00
GOLD MEDAL	806	Murder In Room 13	1958	Conroy, A.	F		$25.00 A
GOLD MEDAL	806	Murder In Room 13	1958	Conroy, A.	VGF		$14.00
GOLD MEDAL	808	Party Girl	1958	Albert, M.H.	AF	MTI	$13.00
GOLD MEDAL	808	Party Girl	1958	Albert, M.H.	F	MTI	$12.00

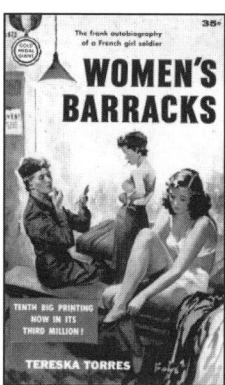

Gold Medal 673 VGF $14	Gold Medal 680 VGF+ $25	Gold Medal 687 AF $110	Gold Medal 691 VGF- $50

PUBLISHER	PUB. #	TITLE	DATE	AUTHOR	COND.	TYPE	PRICE
GOLD MEDAL	808	Party Girl	1958	Albert, M.H.	VG+	MTI	$5.00
GOLD MEDAL	s 809	Plunder	1958	Appel, B.	AF		$14.00
GOLD MEDAL	811	Take Your Last Look	1958	Brady, M.	AF		$14.00
GOLD MEDAL	811	Take Your Last Look	1958	Brady, M.	AF		$10.00
GOLD MEDAL	s 812	The Ungilded Lily	1958	Cooper, M.	AF		$8.00
GOLD MEDAL	813	Terror Is My Trade	1958	Marlowe, S.	VG+		$7.00
GOLD MEDAL	814	I'm Cannon For Hire	1958	Cannon, C.*	F		$28.00 A
GOLD MEDAL	814	I'm Cannon For Hire	1958	Cannon, C.*	G+		$5.00
GOLD MEDAL	814	I'm Cannon For Hire	1958	Cannon, C.*	G		$2.50
GOLD MEDAL	816	Fort Desperation	1958	Castle, F.	VGF		$7.00
GOLD MEDAL	s 817	Slab Happy	1958	Prather, R.S.	F		$12.00
GOLD MEDAL	s 817	Slab Happy	1958	Prather, R.S.	AF		$8.00
GOLD MEDAL	819	Bodies In Bedlam	1960	Prather, R.S.	AF		$7.00
GOLD MEDAL	820	TCOT Vanishing Beauty (6th)	1960	Prather, R.S.	F		$10.00
GOLD MEDAL	821	Find This Woman (5th)	1958	Prather, R.S.	VG+		$6.00
GOLD MEDAL	822	Man On The Run	1958	Williams, C.	AF		$24.00 A
GOLD MEDAL	823	Passage To Samoa	1958	Keene, D.	VG+		$12.00
GOLD MEDAL	823	Passage To Samoa	1958	Keene, D.	VG		$8.00
GOLD MEDAL	824	Trail Of A Tramp	1958	Quarry, N.	VG		$5.00
GOLD MEDAL	s 825	Blood On The Desert	1958	Rabe, P.	VGF		$24.00 A
GOLD MEDAL	826	Renegade Posse	1958	Albert, M.H.	VGF+		$8.00
GOLD MEDAL	827	Day Of The Gun	1958	Telfair, R.	AF		$8.00
GOLD MEDAL	827	Day Of The Gun	1958	Telfair, R.	VGF		$7.00
GOLD MEDAL	s 828	Naked Ebony	1958	Cushman, D.	AF		$7.00 A
GOLD MEDAL	s 829	Awakening Of Jenny	1958	Colter, L.	AF		$8.00
GOLD MEDAL	831	Fires That Destroy	1958	Whittington, H.	VGF-		$17.00 A
GOLD MEDAL	831	Fires That Destroy	1958	Whittington, H.	G		$5.00
GOLD MEDAL	s 832	The Monster From Earth's End	1959	Leinster, M.	F		$14.00
GOLD MEDAL	d 833	I Am A Woman	1959	Bannon, A.	AF		$84.00 A
GOLD MEDAL	834	Assignment - Carlotta Cortez	1959	Aarons, E.S.	VG+		$7.00
GOLD MEDAL	s 836	Smoke In The Valley	1959	Frazee, S.	AF		$12.00
GOLD MEDAL	838	Darling It's Death	1959	Prather, R.S.	F		$8.00
GOLD MEDAL	838	Darling It's Death	1959	Prather, R.S.	AF		$6.00
GOLD MEDAL	s 840	Jewel Of The Java Sea	1959	Cushman, D.	F		$9.00 A
GOLD MEDAL	s 840	Jewel Of The Java Sea	1959	Cushman, D.	VG		$3.00
GOLD MEDAL	841	. . . And Be My Love	1959	Baker, L.	AF		$15.00
GOLD MEDAL	s 844	Third On A Seesaw	1959	MacNeil, N.	VG+		$5.00
GOLD MEDAL	s 845	Kitten With A Whip	1959	Miller, W.	F		$15.00 A
GOLD MEDAL	s 845	Kitten With A Whip	1959	Miller, W.	VG+		$8.00
GOLD MEDAL	846	That Jane From Maine	1959	Albert, M.H.	VG	MTI	$6.00
GOLD MEDAL	847	The Bloody Medallion	1959	Telfair, R.	AF		$12.00
GOLD MEDAL	847	The Bloody Medallion	1959	Telfair, R.	VGF		$8.00
GOLD MEDAL	848	Strip For Murder	1959	Prather, R.S.	F		$7.00
GOLD MEDAL	849	Always Leave 'Em Dying	1959	Prather, R.S.	VGF		$6.00
GOLD MEDAL	850	Too Many Crooks	1959	Prather, R.S.	F		$10.00
GOLD MEDAL	d 852	The Tempest	1959	Cassill, R.V.	VGF	MTI	$8.00
GOLD MEDAL	s 853	The Rest Must Die	1959	Foster, R.	AF		$10.00
GOLD MEDAL	854	Murder With Love	1959	Howard, V.	F		$25.00 A

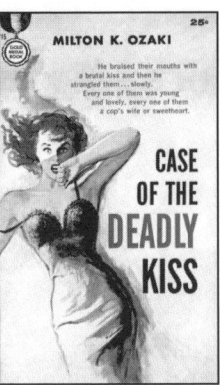

Gold Medal 705 VGF $8   Gold Medal 708 AF- $47   Gold Medal 710 AF $24   Gold Medal 715 F $48

PUBLISHER	PUB. #	TITLE	DATE	AUTHOR	COND.	TYPE	PRICE
GOLD MEDAL	855	Secret Of The Second Door	1959	Colby, R.	VG+		$8.00
GOLD MEDAL	855	Secret Of The Second Door	1959	Colby, R.	G		$3.00
GOLD MEDAL	856	The Reformed Gun	1959	Albert, M.H.	VGF		$7.00
GOLD MEDAL	857	Savage Breed	1959	Chadwick, J.	VG+		$7.00
GOLD MEDAL	857	Savage Breed	1959	Chadwick, J.	VG		$5.00
GOLD MEDAL	s 859	Beyond Desire	1959	Himmel, R.	AF		$12.00
GOLD MEDAL	s 861	The Twisted Ones	1959	Packer, V.*	AF		$28.00 A
GOLD MEDAL	s 861	The Twisted Ones	1959	Packer, V.*	VG		$8.00
GOLD MEDAL	s 861	The Twisted Ones	1959	Packer, V.*	G-		$3.00
GOLD MEDAL	862	A Ticket To Hell	1959	Whittington, H.	VG-		$8.00
GOLD MEDAL	864	Bring Me Another Corpse	1959	Rabe, P.	VG		$10.00
GOLD MEDAL	866	The Ruthless Men	1959	Patten, L.B.	VG+		$7.00
GOLD MEDAL	867	Smash-Up	1959	Pratt, T.	F		$10.00
GOLD MEDAL	868	Return Of Sumuru	1959	Rohmer, S.	AF		$43.00 A
GOLD MEDAL	868	Return Of Sumuru	1959	Rohmer, S.	VGF		$30.00 A
GOLD MEDAL	s 869	The Judas Hour	1959	Hunt, H.	VG		$4.00
GOLD MEDAL	870	Let Them Eat Bullets	1959	Schoenfeld, H.	VGF		$8.00
GOLD MEDAL	872	Case Of The Nervous Nude	1959	Craig, J.	F		$16.00
GOLD MEDAL	872	Case Of The Nervous Nude	1959	Craig, J.	VG		$5.00
GOLD MEDAL	873	Prowler In The Night	1959	Matcha, J.	AF		$7.00 A
GOLD MEDAL	874	Take A Step To Murder	1959	Keene, D.	VGF		$44.00 A
GOLD MEDAL	874	Take A Step To Murder	1959	Keene, D.	VG+		$10.00
GOLD MEDAL	875	Armande	1959	May, D.	F		$10.00
GOLD MEDAL	876	The Brave Rifles	1959	Shirreffs, G.D.	VGF		$8.00
GOLD MEDAL	878	Murder On Her Mind	1959	Howard, V.	AF		$14.00
GOLD MEDAL	879	Wake Up And Scream	1959	Ozaki, M.K.	AF		$65.00 A
GOLD MEDAL	879	Wake Up And Scream	1959	Ozaki, M.K.	VG		$8.00
GOLD MEDAL	879	Wake Up And Scream	1959	Ozaki, M.K.	G-		$2.50
GOLD MEDAL	880	Homicide Is My Game	1959	Marlowe, S.	F		$10.00
GOLD MEDAL	880	Homicide Is My Game	1959	Marlowe, S.	VGF		$8.00
GOLD MEDAL	881	The Kingdom Of Johnny Cool	1959	McPartland, J.	AF		$36.00 A
GOLD MEDAL	881	The Kingdom Of Johnny Cool	1959	McPartland, J.	VGF		$24.00 A
GOLD MEDAL	881	The Kingdom Of Johnny Cool	1959	McPartland, J.	VG		$13.00
GOLD MEDAL	881	The Kingdom Of Johnny Cool	1959	McPartland, J.	VG+		$10.00
GOLD MEDAL	883	Wyoming Jones For Hire	1959	Telfair, R.	AF		$13.00
GOLD MEDAL	885	The Mating Cry	1959	Daniels, F.	AF		$12.00
GOLD MEDAL	886	House Of Flesh	1959	Fischer, B.	AF		$20.00
GOLD MEDAL	888	Killer Take All	1959	Race, P.	F		$12.00
GOLD MEDAL	888	Killer Take All	1959	Race, P.	VGF		$8.00
GOLD MEDAL	888	Killer Take All	1959	Race, P.	VGF-		$7.00
GOLD MEDAL	889	Backwoods Tramp	1959	Whittington, H.	VG+		$33.00 A
GOLD MEDAL	889	Backwoods Tramp	1959	Whittington, H.	VGF		$32.00 A
GOLD MEDAL	889	Backwoods Tramp	1959	Whittington, H.	VG		$17.00 A
GOLD MEDAL	889	Backwoods Tramp	1959	Whittington, H.	VG		$16.00
GOLD MEDAL	890	The Corpse That Talked	1959	Telfair, R.	VG+		$7.00
GOLD MEDAL	890	The Corpse That Talked	1959	Telfair, R.	VG		$4.00
GOLD MEDAL	891	A Hole In The Head	1959	Schulman, A.	F	MTI	$16.00 A
GOLD MEDAL	891	A Hole In The Head	1959	Schulman, A.	VGF	MTI	$14.00

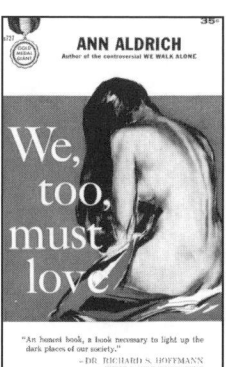

Gold Medal 727 VGF+ $30   Gold Medal 729 F $12   Gold Medal 734 AF $32   Gold Medal 740 VG+ $50

PUBLISHER	PUB. #	TITLE	DATE	AUTHOR	COND.	TYPE	PRICE
GOLD MEDAL	891	A Hole In The Head	1959	Schulman, A.	VG+	MTI	$12.00
GOLD MEDAL	892	Marshall Without A Badge	1959	Hogan, R.	AF		$8.00
GOLD MEDAL	893	To Tame A Land	1959	L'Amour, L.	VG-		$10.00
GOLD MEDAL	895	Assignment To Disaster	1959	Aarons, E.S.	VGF		$8.00
GOLD MEDAL	s 897	Cry Kill	1959	Brown, W.	VGF		$20.00 A
GOLD MEDAL	s 898	2 Guns For Hire	1959	MacNeil, N.	AF		$14.00
GOLD MEDAL	900	Return To Vicki	1959	Tomerlin, J.	VG+		$6.00
GOLD MEDAL	901	The Lustful Ape	1959	Fischer, B.	VG		$10.00
GOLD MEDAL	s 903	The Thrill Kids	1959	Packer, V.*	VG		$8.00
GOLD MEDAL	s 903	The Thrill Kids	1959	Packer, V.*	VG		$6.00
GOLD MEDAL	906	Assignment Stella Marni	1959	Aarons, E.S.	VG+		$7.00
GOLD MEDAL	s 908	Uncle Sagamore And His Girls	1959	Williams, C.	VGF		$33.00 A
GOLD MEDAL	s 910	The Slasher	1959	Demaris, O.	AF		$16.00
GOLD MEDAL	s 910	The Slasher	1959	Demaris, O.	VG		$6.00
GOLD MEDAL	s 911	Assignment - Lili Lamaris	1959	Aarons, E.S.	AF		$8.00
GOLD MEDAL	912	Gun Shy	1959	Savage, L.	VG+		$4.00
GOLD MEDAL	s 913	Angels In The Gutter	1959	Hilton, J.	F		$17.00 A
GOLD MEDAL	s 913	Angels In The Gutter	1959	Hilton, J.	VG		$15.00
GOLD MEDAL	915	It's My Funeral	1959	Rabe, P.	VGF		$12.00
GOLD MEDAL	915	It's My Funeral	1959	Rabe, P.	VG+		$8.00
GOLD MEDAL	916	Bullet Barricade	1959	Ernenwein, L.	VGF		$8.00
GOLD MEDAL	s 917	Teen-Age Mafia	1959	Brown, W.	VG+		$16.00 A
GOLD MEDAL	918	Pillow Talk	1959	Albert, M.H.	VG+	MTI	$7.00
GOLD MEDAL	s 919	Women In The Shadows	1959	Bannon, A.	AF-		$34.00
GOLD MEDAL	920	Top Man With A Gun	1959	Patten, L.B.	AF		$7.00
GOLD MEDAL	921	The Wife Next Door	1959	Cassill, R.V.	VGF		$10.00
GOLD MEDAL	921	The Wife Next Door	1959	Cassill, R.V.	AF		$8.00
GOLD MEDAL	s 922	To Hell Together	1959	Dixon, H.V.	AF		$12.00
GOLD MEDAL	s 922	To Hell Together	1959	Dixon, H.V.	F		$10.00
GOLD MEDAL	923	Assignment Suicide	1959	Aarons, E.S.	VG+		$8.00
GOLD MEDAL	d 926	Double In Trouble	1959	Prather, S.	AF		$24.00
GOLD MEDAL	d 926	Double In Trouble	1959	Prather, S.	VG+		$7.00
GOLD MEDAL	928	Second-Hand Nude	1959	Fischer, B.	AF		$28.00 A
GOLD MEDAL	928	Second-Hand Nude	1959	Fischer, B.	VG		$15.00
GOLD MEDAL	928	Second-Hand Nude	1959	Fischer, B.	VG		$8.00
GOLD MEDAL	s 929	Emporer Fu Manchu	1959	Rohmer, S.	VG		$7.00
GOLD MEDAL	s 929	Emporer Fu Manchu	1959	Rohmer, S.	G+		$5.00
GOLD MEDAL	930	Case Of The Village Tramp	1959	Craig, J.	VGF		$49.00 A
GOLD MEDAL	931	Too Hot To Hold	1959	Keene, D.	VGF+		$22.00 A
GOLD MEDAL	931	Too Hot To Hold	1959	Keene, D.	G+		$5.00
GOLD MEDAL	s 936	The Big Guy	1959	Miller, W.	AF		$14.00
GOLD MEDAL	s 936	The Big Guy	1959	Miller, W.	VGF		$7.00
GOLD MEDAL	s 936	The Big Guy	1959	Miller, W.	G		$2.00
GOLD MEDAL	938	The Girl With No Place To Hide	1959	Quarry, N.	AF		$13.00
GOLD MEDAL	938	The Girl With No Place To Hide	1959	Quarry, N.	VG+		$8.00
GOLD MEDAL	939	Time Enough To Die	1959	Rabe, P.	AF		$45.00
GOLD MEDAL	940	The Deadly Desire	1959	Colby, R.	VG+		$10.00
GOLD MEDAL	s 941	The Young And Violent	1959	Packer, V.*	VG		$12.00

Gold Medal 763 F $44   Gold Medal 774 VGF $25   Gold Medal 775 VG+ $54   Gold Medal 783 VGF $15

PUBLISHER	PUB. #	TITLE	DATE	AUTHOR	COND.	TYPE	PRICE
GOLD MEDAL	s 941	The Young And Violent	1959	Packer, V.*	VG		$8.00
GOLD MEDAL	942	Witness This Woman	1959	Fox, G.F.	F		$16.00
GOLD MEDAL	943	Stage To Painted Creek	1959	Howard, V.	VG+		$7.00
GOLD MEDAL	944	The Range Buster	1959	Heuman, W.	VGF		$8.00
GOLD MEDAL	944	The Range Buster	1959	Heuman, W.	VGF		$6.00
GOLD MEDAL	s 946	Thunderclap	1959	Sheridan, J.	VGF		$8.00
GOLD MEDAL	s 946	Thunderclap (3rd)	1959	Sheridan, J.	AF		$8.00
GOLD MEDAL	948	Kiss Off The Dead	1960	Garrity	AF		$10.00
GOLD MEDAL	s 949	Lament For A Virgin	1960	White, L.	AF		$83.00 A
GOLD MEDAL	s 949	Lament For A Virgin	1960	White, L.	VG+		$30.00
GOLD MEDAL	s 949	Lament For A Virgin	1960	White, L.	VG+		$16.00 A
GOLD MEDAL	s 949	Lament For A Virgin	1960	White, L.	VG		$8.00
GOLD MEDAL	950	Backwoods Teaser	1960	Brewer, G.	VG+		$24.00
GOLD MEDAL	954	So Young, So Wicked	1960	Craig, J.	VG		$5.00
GOLD MEDAL	954	So Young, So Wicked	1960	Craig, J.	G+		$5.00
GOLD MEDAL	955	Heller With A Gun	1960	L'Amour, L.	G	MTI	$7.00
GOLD MEDAL	d 956	Teen-Age Terror	1960	Brown, W.	VG+		$16.00
GOLD MEDAL	d 956	Teen-Age Terror	1960	Brown, W.	VG		$7.00
GOLD MEDAL	957	Death Of A Citizen	1960	Hamilton, D.	F		$12.00
GOLD MEDAL	959	Heat Of Night	1960	Whittington, H.	VG+		$33.00 A
GOLD MEDAL	959	Heat Of Night	1960	Whittington, H.	G+		$7.00
GOLD MEDAL	s 961	Slam The Big Door	1960	MacDonald, J.D.	VG		$10.00
GOLD MEDAL	s 965	Odd Girl Out	1960	Bannon, A.	F		$22.00
GOLD MEDAL	s 965	Odd Girl Out	1960	Bannon, A.	VG-		$5.00
GOLD MEDAL	s 966	5:45 To Suburbia	1960	Packer, V.*	VG+		$7.00
GOLD MEDAL	967	My Lovely Executioner	1960	Rabe, P.	VG+		$11.00 A
GOLD MEDAL	967	My Lovely Executioner	1960	Rabe, P.	VG		$10.00
GOLD MEDAL	969	Thimk	1960	Anthology	VGF		$8.00 A
GOLD MEDAL	972	Pure Sweet Hell	1960	Douglas, M.	VG		$5.00
GOLD MEDAL	d 973	Driven	1960	Gehman, R.	AF		$12.00
GOLD MEDAL	974	Outcast Of Murder Mesa	1960	Fowler, K.	VG+		$7.00
GOLD MEDAL	s 975	World Without Women	1960	Keene, D.	F		$14.00
GOLD MEDAL	s 975	World Without Women	1960	Keene, D.	VG		$5.00
GOLD MEDAL	s 976	The Girl On The Best Seller List	1960	Packer, V.*	VG		$8.00
GOLD MEDAL	s 976	The Girl On The Best Seller List	1960	Packer, V.*	VG		$6.00
GOLD MEDAL	s 977	Journey To A Woman	1960	Bannon, A.	F		$45.00
GOLD MEDAL	s 977	Journey To A Woman	1960	Bannon, A.	VG+		$8.00
GOLD MEDAL	s 977	Journey To A Woman	1960	Bannon, A.	VG		$5.00
GOLD MEDAL	980	Johnny Stacatto	1960	Boyd, F.	VGF	TVTI	$11.00 A
GOLD MEDAL	s 982	The Beats	1960	Anthology	VG		$13.00
GOLD MEDAL	s 982	The Beats	1960	Anthology	VG+		$12.00
GOLD MEDAL	s 982	The Beats	1960	Anthology	VG		$10.00
GOLD MEDAL	993	Funny Cartoons By VIP	1960	Anthology	VGF		$8.00
GOLD MEDAL	994	Shanghai Incident	1960	Becker, S.	VGF		$5.00
GOLD MEDAL	995	Too Late For Mourning	1960	Foster, R.	AF		$10.00
GOLD MEDAL	995	Too Late For Mourning	1960	Foster, R.	VGF		$10.00
GOLD MEDAL	996	Murder Me For Nickles	1960	Rabe, P.	VG		$7.00
GOLD MEDAL	s 997	13 Great Stories Of Sci-Fi	1960	Anthology	AF		$8.00

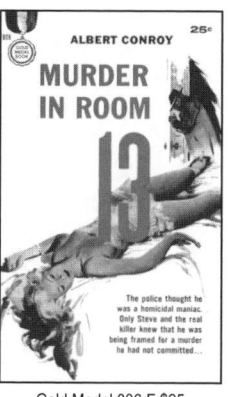

Gold Medal 792 AF $27   Gold Medal 796 F $34   Gold Medal 806 F $25   Gold Medal 823 VG+ $12

PUBLISHER	PUB. #	TITLE	DATE	AUTHOR	COND.	TYPE	PRICE
GOLD MEDAL	s 997	13 Great Stories Of Sci-Fi	1960	Anthology	VGF		$6.00
GOLD MEDAL	998	Steal Big	1960	White, L.	VGF		$51.00 A
GOLD MEDAL	s 1000	North Beach Girl	1960	Trinian, J.	VG+		$8.00
GOLD MEDAL	1001	South Of The Sun	1960	Miller, W.	VG		$6.00
GOLD MEDAL	s 1002	The Kid Was A Killer	1960	Chessman, C.	AF		$15.00
GOLD MEDAL	s 1002	The Kid Was A Killer	1960	Chessman, C.	VGF		$14.00
GOLD MEDAL	1003	The Second Longest Night	1960	Marlowe, S.	AF		$7.00
GOLD MEDAL	1003	The Second Longest Night	1960	Marlowe, S.	VG+		$7.00
GOLD MEDAL	1004	Funny Business	1960	Anthology	AF		$8.00
GOLD MEDAL	1006	Scream Bloody Murder	1960	Telfair, R.	VGF		$8.00
GOLD MEDAL	1006	Scream Bloody Murder	1960	Telfair, R.	VG		$6.00
GOLD MEDAL	1007	The Enforcer	1960	Demaris, O.	VG+		$10.00
GOLD MEDAL	s 1008	Pieces Of The Game	1960	Gifford, L.	F		$10.00
GOLD MEDAL	d 1009	Carol In A Thousand Cities	1960	Anthology	AF		$50.00 A
GOLD MEDAL	d 1009	Carol In A Thousand Cities	1960	Anthology	VGF		$50.00 A
GOLD MEDAL	d 1009	Carol In A Thousand Cities	1960	Anthology	VGF		$35.00
GOLD MEDAL	d 1009	Carol In A Thousand Cities	1960	Anthology	VG-		$6.00
GOLD MEDAL	1011	Murder In The Raw	1960	Fischer, B.	VG+		$8.00
GOLD MEDAL	s 1012	Hell Hath No Fury	1960	Williams, C.	VG+		$12.00
GOLD MEDAL	s 1012	Hell Hath No Fury	1960	Williams, C.	VG		$7.00
GOLD MEDAL	s 1013	The Murder Kick	1960	Brown, W.	VG+		$15.00
GOLD MEDAL	s 1015	The Only Girl In The Game	1960	MacDonald, J.D.	VG+		$8.00
GOLD MEDAL	1016	High Lawless	1960	Olsen, T.V.	AF		$7.00
GOLD MEDAL	1017	It Started In Naples	1960	Cooper, S.	VGF	MTI	$8.00
GOLD MEDAL	1017	It Started In Naples	1960	Cooper, S.	VGF	MTI	$7.00
GOLD MEDAL	1018	Peril Is My Pay	1960	Marlowe, S.	VGF		$8.00
GOLD MEDAL	1020	Hostage For A Hood	1960	White, L.	VG+		$12.00
GOLD MEDAL	1020	Hostage For A Hood	1960	White, L.	VG+		$8.00
GOLD MEDAL	1023	Hell To Eternity	1960	Aarons, E.S.	F	MTI	$10.00
GOLD MEDAL	1023	Hell To Eternity	1960	Aarons, E.S.	VGF	MTI	$7.00
GOLD MEDAL	1024	Meanwhile Back At The Morgue	1960	Avallone, M.	VGF-		$17.00 A
GOLD MEDAL	1024	Meanwhile Back At The Morgue	1960	Avallone, M.	VG+		$10.00
GOLD MEDAL	1024	Meanwhile Back At The Morgue	1960	Avallone, M.	G		$2.00
GOLD MEDAL	1025	The Wrecking Crew	1960	Hamilton, D.	AF		$10.00
GOLD MEDAL	1025	The Wrecking Crew	1960	Hamilton, D.	VGF		$8.00
GOLD MEDAL	1027	Sinner Take All	1960	Miller, W.	AF		$10.00
GOLD MEDAL	s 1028	Seminole	1960	Pratt, T.	VGF+		$10.00
GOLD MEDAL	1030	He Rode Alone	1960	Frazee, S.	VG+		$8.00
GOLD MEDAL	1031	Uncle Good's Week-End Party	1960	Faulkner, J.	VGF		$5.00
GOLD MEDAL	1033	No Chance In Hell	1960	Quarry, N.	AF		$20.00 A
GOLD MEDAL	1033	No Chance In Hell	1960	Quarry, N.	AF		$10.00 A
GOLD MEDAL	s 1036	Assignment - Mara Tirana	1960	Aarons, E.S.	AF		$8.00
GOLD MEDAL	1037	The Trouble With Love	1960	Heatter, B.	VGF		$10.00
GOLD MEDAL	s 1038	VIP's All New Bar Guide	1960	Armstong, J.	AF		$8.00
GOLD MEDAL	s 1040	Always Leave 'Em Dying (7th)	1963	Prather, R.S.	VGF		$5.00
GOLD MEDAL	1041	The Tall Stranger	1960	L'Amour, L.	VG		$15.00
GOLD MEDAL	1041	The Tall Stranger	1960	L'Amour, L.	VG		$8.00
GOLD MEDAL	s 1042	Run, Chico, Run	1960	Brown, W.	VGF+		$22.00 A

Gold Medal 825 VGF $24	Gold Medal 833 AF $84	Gold Medal 847 AF $12	Gold Medal 864 VG $10

PUBLISHER	PUB. #	TITLE	DATE	AUTHOR	COND.	TYPE	PRICE
GOLD MEDAL	s 1042	Run, Chico, Run	1960	Brown, W.	VG+		$12.00
GOLD MEDAL	1043	The Star Trap	1960	Colby, R.	AF		$22.00 A
GOLD MEDAL	1043	The Star Trap	1960	Colby, R.	VG-		$7.00
GOLD MEDAL	1044	Hell Can Wait	1960	Whittington, H.	VGF		$38.00 A
GOLD MEDAL	1044	Hell Can Wait	1960	Whittington, H.	VG		$14.00
GOLD MEDAL	s 1049	Have Gat - Will Travel (4th)	1962	Prather, R.S.	VGF		$7.00
GOLD MEDAL	1050	Desire In The Dust	1960	Whittington, H.	VG-	MTI	$13.00
GOLD MEDAL	s 1051	The Wailing Frail (5th)	1962	Prather, R.S.	VGF		$7.00
GOLD MEDAL	1054	The Girl Between	1960	Fischer, B.	VGF+		$23.00 A
GOLD MEDAL	1054	The Girl Between	1960	Fischer, B.	VGF+		$19.00 A
GOLD MEDAL	1054	The Girl Between	1960	Fischer, B.	VG		$5.00
GOLD MEDAL	1055	The Death Ride	1960	MacNeil, N.	VGF		$8.00
GOLD MEDAL	1055	The Death Ride	1960	MacNeil, N.	VG+		$7.00
GOLD MEDAL	s 1057	Rogue Moon	1960	Budrys, A.	VG+		$8.00
GOLD MEDAL	1058	Connolly's Woman	1960	Whittington, H.	AF		$30.00 A
GOLD MEDAL	s 1060	Three's A Shroud (5th)	1962	Prather, R.S.	VGF		$6.00
GOLD MEDAL	1062	Run From The Hunter	1960	Grantland, K.*	AF		$20.00
GOLD MEDAL	1062	Run From The Hunter	1960	Grantland, K.*	VG		$6.00
GOLD MEDAL	1063	The Late Mrs. Five	1960	Wormser, R.	VGF+		$9.00
GOLD MEDAL	s 1064	End Of A J.D.	1960	Gonzales, J.	VG+		$10.00
GOLD MEDAL	s 1065	Case Of The Laughing Virgin	1960	Craig, J.	VGF		$7.00
GOLD MEDAL	s 1066	The Marriage	1960	Bannon, A.	VG+		$6.00
GOLD MEDAL	s 1066	The Marriage	1960	Bannon, A.	VG		$5.00
GOLD MEDAL	s 1068	Wild Harvest	1960	Longstreet, S.	F		$15.00
GOLD MEDAL	s 1068	Wild Harvest	1960	Longstreet, S.	VG+		$5.00
GOLD MEDAL	s 1069	Judge Me Not	1960	MacDonald, J.D.	AF		$14.00
GOLD MEDAL	s 1069	Judge Me Not	1960	MacDonald, J.D.	VGF		$10.00
GOLD MEDAL	s 1074	The Damnation Of Adam Blessing	1961	Packer, V.*	VGF		$16.00
GOLD MEDAL	s 1074	The Damnation Of Adam Blessing	1961	Packer, V.*	AF		$15.00
GOLD MEDAL	s 1075	Felony Tank	1961	Braly, M.	VG+		$37.00 A
GOLD MEDAL	s 1076	Where Is Janice Gantry?	1961	MacDonald, J.D.	AF		$27.00 A
GOLD MEDAL	s 1076	Where Is Janice Gantry?	1961	MacDonald, J.D.	AF		$22.00
GOLD MEDAL	s 1077	The Slavers	1961	Telfair, R.	AF		$7.00
GOLD MEDAL	s 1078	Murder Is My Dish	1961	Marlowe, S.	AF		$12.00
GOLD MEDAL	s 1081	High Gun	1961	Ernenwein, L.	AF		$8.00
GOLD MEDAL	s 1082	The Removers	1961	Hamilton, D.	VG		$7.00
GOLD MEDAL	s 1083	Night Squad	1961	Goodis, D.	VG-		$24.00
GOLD MEDAL	s 1083	Night Squad	1961	Goodis, D.	VG		$20.00
GOLD MEDAL	s 1083	Night Squad	1961	Goodis, D.	G		$10.00
GOLD MEDAL	s 1085	Mona	1961	Block, L.	VG		$15.00
GOLD MEDAL	s 1085	Mona	1961	Block, L.	VG		$11.00
GOLD MEDAL	s 1085	Mona	1961	Block, L.	VG-		$8.00
GOLD MEDAL	s 1087	Whip Hand	1961	Sanders, W.F.*	AF		$180.00 A
GOLD MEDAL	s 1087	Whip Hand	1961	Sanders, W.F.*	VGF+		$132.00 A
GOLD MEDAL	s 1087	Whip Hand	1961	Sanders, W.F.*	VG		$96.00 A
GOLD MEDAL	s 1092	Pattern For Panic	1961	Prather, R.S.	F		$8.00
GOLD MEDAL	s 1093	Season Of Assassins	1961	Wagner, G.	F		$10.00
GOLD MEDAL	s 1093	Season Of Assassins	1961	Wagner, G.	VGF		$7.00

Gold Medal 868 AF $43	Gold Medal 889 VG+ $33	Gold Medal 941 VG $12	Gold Medal 976 VG $8

PUBLISHER	PUB. #	TITLE	DATE	AUTHOR	COND.	TYPE	PRICE
GOLD MEDAL	s 1094	Good Luck, Sucker	1961	Telfair, R.	AF		$10.00
GOLD MEDAL	s 1094	Good Luck, Sucker	1961	Telfair, R.	VG+		$7.00
GOLD MEDAL	s 1095	Swamp Sister	1961	Alter, R.E.	AF		$39.00 A
GOLD MEDAL	s 1096	The Deadly Companions	1961	Fleischman, A.S.	AF	MTI	$14.00
GOLD MEDAL	s 1096	The Deadly Companions	1961	Fleischman, A.S.	AF	MTI	$13.00
GOLD MEDAL	s 1098	Killers Are My Meat	1961	Marlowe, S.	AF		$8.00
GOLD MEDAL	s 1099	The Great Debauch	1961	Forrest, W.	AF		$8.00
GOLD MEDAL	s 1099	The Great Debauch	1961	Forrest, W.	AF		$7.00
GOLD MEDAL	s 1100	Death For Mr. Big	1961	Gonzales, J.	F		$40.00 A
GOLD MEDAL	s 1100	Death For Mr. Big	1961	Gonzales, J.	VGF		$7.00
GOLD MEDAL	s 1101	The Big Gamble	1961	Krepps, R.W.	F	MTI	$30.00 A
GOLD MEDAL	s 1101	The Big Gamble	1961	Krepps, R.W.	AF	MTI	$10.00 A
GOLD MEDAL	s 1102	Nurses' Quarters	1961	Cassill, R.V.	F		$54.00 A
GOLD MEDAL	s 1102	Nurses' Quarters	1961	Cassill, R.V.	VGF+		$52.00 A
GOLD MEDAL	s 1102	Nurses' Quarters	1961	Cassill, R.V.	AF		$43.00 A
GOLD MEDAL	s 1102	Nurses' Quarters	1961	Cassill, R.V.	VG+		$7.00
GOLD MEDAL	s 1104	The Savage Breast	1961	Trinian, J.	VGF		$13.00 A
GOLD MEDAL	s 1104	The Savage Breast	1961	Trinian, J.	VG		$4.00
GOLD MEDAL	s 1105	Chuka	1961	Jessup, R.	VGF		$8.00
GOLD MEDAL	s 1106	The Snow Leopard	1961	Miller, S.	AF		$12.00
GOLD MEDAL	s 1107	Short Ribs	1961	O'Neal, F.	AF		$7.00
GOLD MEDAL	s 1107	Short Ribs	1961	O'Neal, F.	VGF		$6.00
GOLD MEDAL	s 1108	Street Of No Return	1961	Goodis, D.	VGF		$44.00 A
GOLD MEDAL	s 1108	Street Of No Return	1961	Goodis, D.	F		$38.00 A
GOLD MEDAL	s 1108	Street Of No Return	1961	Goodis, D.	VG		$17.00
GOLD MEDAL	s 1109	Park Avenue Tramp	1961	Flora, F.	AF		$10.00
GOLD MEDAL	s 1109	Park Avenue Tramp	1961	Flora, F.	VGF		$8.00
GOLD MEDAL	s 1110	So Wicked My Love	1961	Fischer, B.	AF		$14.00
GOLD MEDAL	s 1110	So Wicked My Love	1961	Fischer, B.	F		$13.00
GOLD MEDAL	s 1113	Suddenly By Shotgun	1961	Daniels, N.	AF		$9.00
GOLD MEDAL	s 1113	Suddenly By Shotgun	1961	Daniels, N.	VGF+		$7.00
GOLD MEDAL	s 1114	The Big Red Ball	1961	Cameron, L.	F		$10.00
GOLD MEDAL	s 1114	The Big Red Ball	1961	Cameron, L.	AF		$10.00
GOLD MEDAL	s 1115	Isolation Booth	1961	Kaufman, B.	F		$10.00
GOLD MEDAL	s 1115	Isolation Booth	1961	Kaufman, B.	AF		$8.00
GOLD MEDAL	s 1116	Manhunt Is My Mission	1961	Marlowe, S.	AF		$12.00
GOLD MEDAL	s 1116	Manhunt Is My Mission	1961	Marlowe, S.	AF		$8.00
GOLD MEDAL	s 1116	Manhunt Is My Mission	1961	Marlowe, S.	VG+		$5.00
GOLD MEDAL	s 1120	I Like 'Em Tough	1961	Cannon, C.*	VG		$4.00
GOLD MEDAL	s 1121	The Last Sunset	1961	Howard, V.	F	MTI	$15.00
GOLD MEDAL	s 1121	The Last Sunset	1961	Howard, V.	VG+	MTI	$6.00
GOLD MEDAL	s 1123	Desert Stake-Out	1961	Whittington, H.	AF		$27.00 A
GOLD MEDAL	s 1124	Shadow Of A Doubt?	1961	Judd, H.	AF		$10.00
GOLD MEDAL	d 1125	Make My Bed In Hell	1961	Bishop, L.	VGF		$7.00
GOLD MEDAL	s 1132	Madball	1961	Brown, F.	VGF+		$72.00 A
GOLD MEDAL	s 1132	Madball	1961	Brown, F.	VGF		$66.00 A
GOLD MEDAL	s 1132	Madball	1961	Brown, F.	AF		$62.00 A
GOLD MEDAL	s 1132	Madball	1961	Brown, F.	VG		$20.00

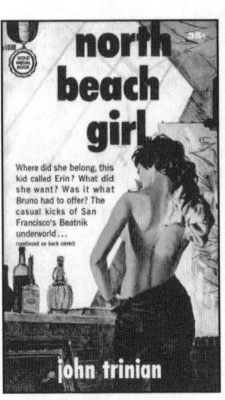

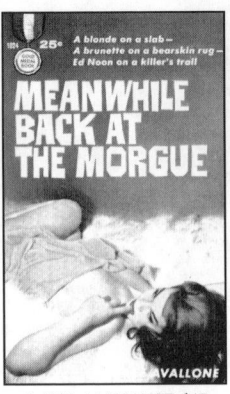
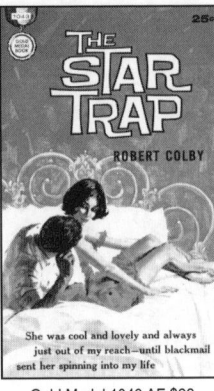

Gold Medal 1000 VG+ $8   Gold Medal 1009 AF $50   Gold Medal 1024 VGF- $17   Gold Medal 1043 AF $22

PUBLISHER	PUB. #	TITLE	DATE	AUTHOR	COND.	TYPE	PRICE
GOLD MEDAL	s 1133	Drive East On 66	1961	Wormser, R.	VG		$8.00
GOLD MEDAL	s 1134	God's Back Was Turned	1961	Whittington, H.	F		$55.00 A
GOLD MEDAL	s 1135	The Paradise Gun	1961	Flagg, J.	VG		$7.00
GOLD MEDAL	s 1136	Candyleg	1961	Demaris, O.	F		$33.00 A
GOLD MEDAL	s 1136	Candyleg	1961	Demaris, O.	AF		$18.00 A
GOLD MEDAL	s 1138	Hill Girl	1961	Williams, C.	AF		$16.00
GOLD MEDAL	s 1138	Hill Girl	1961	Williams, C.	AF		$12.00
GOLD MEDAL	d 1141	Inside The John Birch Society	1961	Grove, G.	AF		$12.00
GOLD MEDAL	s 1142	Angel With Dirty Wings	1961	Hasty, J.E.	F		$12.00
GOLD MEDAL	s 1145	Round The Clock At Volari's	1961	Burnett, W.R.	AF		$87.00 A
GOLD MEDAL	s 1145	Round The Clock At Volari's	1961	Burnett, W.R.	VG		$17.00
GOLD MEDAL	s 1145	Round The Clock At Volari's	1961	Burnett, W.R.	VG+		$16.00
GOLD MEDAL	s 1146	Something In The Shadows	1961	Packer, V.*	F		$47.00 A
GOLD MEDAL	s 1146	Something In The Shadows	1961	Packer, V.*	VGF		$25.00 A
GOLD MEDAL	s 1146	Something In The Shadows	1961	Packer, V.*	G		$5.00
GOLD MEDAL	s 1149	The Magnolia Murder	1961	Bell, W.	VGF+		$8.00
GOLD MEDAL	s 1149	The Magnolia Murder	1961	Bell, W.	VGF		$7.00
GOLD MEDAL	s 1151	Frantic	1961	Calef, N.	VGF	MTI	$7.00
GOLD MEDAL	s 1153	Canary In A Cat House	1961	Vonnegut, K.	VG		$40.00
GOLD MEDAL	s 1155	Devil May Care (6th)	1961	Miller, W.	VGF		$7.00
GOLD MEDAL	d 1158	The Grave Of Heroes	1961	Cross, J.	AF		$7.00
GOLD MEDAL	d 1158	The Grave Of Heroes	1961	Cross, J.	AF		$7.00
GOLD MEDAL	s 1159	Port Angelique	1961	Jessup, R.	AF		$12.00
GOLD MEDAL	s 1159	Port Angelique	1961	Jessup, R.	AF		$10.00
GOLD MEDAL	s 1159	Port Angelique	1961	Jessup, R.	VGF		$7.00
GOLD MEDAL	s 1160	Girls On The Rampage	1961	Brown, W.	AF		$43.00 A
GOLD MEDAL	s 1160	Girls On The Rampage	1961	Brown, W.	AF		$36.00 A
GOLD MEDAL	s 1160	Girls On The Rampage	1961	Brown, W.	VG		$8.00
GOLD MEDAL	s 1161	Rockabilly	1961	Ellison, H.	F		$225.00 A
GOLD MEDAL	s 1161	Rockabilly	1961	Ellison, H.	AF		$225.00 A
GOLD MEDAL	s 1161	Rockabilly	1961	Ellison, H.	VGF+		$74.00 A
GOLD MEDAL	s 1162	Death Pulls A Doublecross	1961	Block, L.	AF-		$25.00 A
GOLD MEDAL	s 1162	Death Pulls A Doublecross	1961	Block, L.	G		$3.00
GOLD MEDAL	s 1164	The Defenders	1961	Aarons, E.S.	VGF	TVTI	$10.00
GOLD MEDAL	s 1164	The Defenders	1961	Aarons, E.S.	G+	TVTI	$3.00
GOLD MEDAL	s 1165	Clemmie	1961	MacDonald, J.D.	AF		$15.00
GOLD MEDAL	s 1165	Clemmie	1961	MacDonald, J.D.	VG		$7.00
GOLD MEDAL	s 1166	Lie Down, Killer	1962	Prather, R.S.	VG		$3.00
GOLD MEDAL	d 1169	El Cid	1961	Bronston, S.	AF	MTI	$10.00
GOLD MEDAL	d 1169	El Cid	1961	Bronston, S.	VG+	MTI	$7.00
GOLD MEDAL	s 1170	Cry Me A Killer	1961	Garrity	AF		$14.00
GOLD MEDAL	s 1170	Cry Me A Killer	1961	Garrity	AF		$10.00
GOLD MEDAL	s 1170	Cry Me A Killer	1961	Garrity	VG+		$7.00
GOLD MEDAL	s 1171	Women's Barracks	1961	Torres, T.	VGF		$5.00
GOLD MEDAL	s 1172	Wolf Cop	1961	Jessup, R.	AF		$7.00 A
GOLD MEDAL	s 1172	Wolf Cop	1961	Jessup, R.	VG+		$7.00
GOLD MEDAL	s 1173	Carla	1961	Marshall, J.R.	VGF		$8.00
GOLD MEDAL	s 1173	Carla	1961	Marshall, J.R.	VGF		$7.00

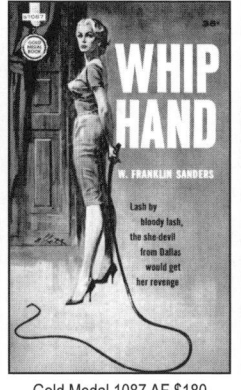

Gold Medal 1050 VG- $13   Gold Medal 1076 AF $27   Gold Medal 1087 AF $180   Gold Medal 1095 AF $39

PUBLISHER	PUB. #	TITLE	DATE	AUTHOR	COND.	TYPE	PRICE
GOLD MEDAL	s 1175	Gypsy, Go Home	1961	O'Farrell, W.	VGF		$8.00
GOLD MEDAL	d 1176	Wheels Of Terror	1961	Hassel, S.	AF		$7.00
GOLD MEDAL	s 1177	One Monday We Killed Them All	1961	MacDonald, J.D.	VG+		$13.00
GOLD MEDAL	s 1177	One Monday We Killed Them All	1961	MacDonald, J.D.	VGF		$12.00
GOLD MEDAL	s 1177	One Monday We Killed Them All	1961	MacDonald, J.D.	VG-		$10.00
GOLD MEDAL	s 1178	The Skin Game	1961	Bonham, F.	VGF		$10.00
GOLD MEDAL	s 1181	One Wild Oat	1961	Kantor, M.	AF-		$5.00
GOLD MEDAL	s 1182	Mexican Slay Ride	1962	MacNeil, N.	VGF		$7.00
GOLD MEDAL	s 1183	The Sky Divers	1962	Cameron, L.	VGF		$8.00
GOLD MEDAL	s 1183	The Sky Divers	1962	Cameron, L.	AF		$5.00
GOLD MEDAL	s 1184	The Name Of The Game Is Death	1962	Marlowe, D.J.	AF		$17.00 A
GOLD MEDAL	s 1184	The Name Of The Game Is Death	1962	Marlowe, D.J.	VGF		$12.00
GOLD MEDAL	s 1184	The Name Of The Game Is Death	1962	Marlowe, D.J.	VG+		$10.00
GOLD MEDAL	s 1190	A Haven For The Damned	1962	Whittington, H.	VG+		$15.00
GOLD MEDAL	s 1192	The Couch	1962	Bloch, R.	VG+	MTI	$14.00 A
GOLD MEDAL	s 1192	The Couch	1962	Bloch, R.	G	MTI	$5.00
GOLD MEDAL	s 1193	Lover Come Back	1962	Albert, M.H.	VG	MTI	$5.00
GOLD MEDAL	d 1196	We Walk Alone	1962	Aldrich, A.*	VG+		$8.00
GOLD MEDAL	s 1198	A Key To The Suite	1962	MacDonald, J.D.	G+		$2.50
GOLD MEDAL	s 1200	The Long Saturday Night	1962	Williams, C.	VGF+		$17.00 A
GOLD MEDAL	s 1200	The Long Saturday Night	1962	Williams, C.	VG		$7.00
GOLD MEDAL	s 1200	The Long Saturday Night	1962	Williams, C.	G		$3.00
GOLD MEDAL	s 1201	Perfect Pigeon	1962	Wormser, R.	AF		$14.00 A
GOLD MEDAL	d 1203	The Shrinking Man	1962	Matheson, R.	VGF		$20.00 A
GOLD MEDAL	d 1203	The Shrinking Man	1962	Matheson, R.	VG+		$15.00
GOLD MEDAL	s 1212	No French Leave	1962	Beech, W.	VGF		$7.00
GOLD MEDAL	s 1214	Jeopardy Is My Job	1962	Marlowe, S.	AF		$8.00
GOLD MEDAL	s 1221	The Girl From Midnight	1962	Miller, W.	AF		$10.00
GOLD MEDAL	d 1224	Beebo Brinker	1962	Bannon, A.	AF		$77.00 A
GOLD MEDAL	d 1224	Beebo Brinker	1962	Bannon, A.	G		$6.00
GOLD MEDAL	s 1225	Second Help!-ing	1962	Kurtzman, H.	VGF		$10.00 A
GOLD MEDAL	s 1226	For The Asking	1962	Daniels, H.R.	VG		$6.00
GOLD MEDAL	s 1228	Someone's Sleeping In My Bed	1962	Gonzales, J.	AF		$16.00 A
GOLD MEDAL	s 1231	Atoms And Evil	1962	Bloch, R.	VGF		$12.00
GOLD MEDAL	s 1231	Atoms And Evil	1962	Bloch, R.	VG+		$7.00
GOLD MEDAL	d 1234	Two Souls, One Body	1962	Marks, J.	VG+		$6.00
GOLD MEDAL	s 1241	Intimate Victims	1962	Packer, V.*	AF		$22.00 A
GOLD MEDAL	s 1241	Intimate Victims	1962	Packer, V.*	VGF		$10.00
GOLD MEDAL	k 1245	Last Days Of Sodom & Gomorrah	1962	Wormser, R.	VG	MTI	$6.00
GOLD MEDAL	s 1246	Murderer's Row	1962	Hamilton, D.	VGF+		$5.00
GOLD MEDAL	k 1247	The Desire Years	1962	Bishop, L.	VGF		$13.00 A
GOLD MEDAL	k 1251	Dance With The Dead	1962	Prather, R.S.	AF		$6.00
GOLD MEDAL	s 1253	Taras Bulba	1962	Krepps, R.W.	VGF	MTI	$8.00
GOLD MEDAL	s 1254	You Damn Men Are All Alike	1962	Anthology	VGF+		$8.00
GOLD MEDAL	s 1254	You Damn Men Are All Alike	1962	Anthology	VGF+		$7.00
GOLD MEDAL	s 1256	The Empty Quarter	1962	Cameron, L.	VGF		$5.00
GOLD MEDAL	s 1257	The Obsessed	1962	Schweitzer, G.	VGF		$5.00
GOLD MEDAL	s 1259	The Girl, The Gold Watch . . .	1962	MacDonald, J.D.	VGF		$12.00

Gold Medal 1096 AF $14   Gold Medal 1102 F $54   Gold Medal 1104 VGF $13   Gold Medal 1108 VGF $44

PUBLISHER	PUB. #	TITLE	DATE	AUTHOR	COND.	TYPE	PRICE
GOLD MEDAL	s 1260	One Wife's Ways	1962	Fox, G.F.	VGF		$12.00
GOLD MEDAL	s 1260	One Wife's Ways	1962	Fox, G.F.	VG		$6.00
GOLD MEDAL	s 1262	The Box	1962	Rabe, P.	VG+		$34.00 A
GOLD MEDAL	s 1262	The Box	1962	Rabe, P.	G+		$7.00
GOLD MEDAL	s 1266	We, Too, Must Love	1963	Aldrich, A.*	VG+		$6.00
GOLD MEDAL	s 1268	The Death Cycle	1963	Runyon, C.	VGF		$16.00 A
GOLD MEDAL	k 1276	The Man Who Fell To Earth	1963	Tevis, W.	VGF		$10.00
GOLD MEDAL	k 1276	The Man Who Fell To Earth	1963	Tevis, W.	VG+		$8.00
GOLD MEDAL	k 1277	The Peddler	1963	Prather, R.S.	AF		$8.00
GOLD MEDAL	k 1282	Too Many Crooks	1963	Prather, R.S.	VGF		$5.00
GOLD MEDAL	k 1284	Another Time, Another Woman	1963	Kaylin, W.	VGF		$6.00
GOLD MEDAL	k 1285	Francesca	1963	Marlowe, S.	VGF+		$7.00
GOLD MEDAL	k 1287	Shell Scott's 7 Slaughters	1963	Prather, R.S.	AF		$6.00
GOLD MEDAL	k 1289	Nothing In Her Way	1963	Williams, C.	G		$5.00
GOLD MEDAL	k 1291	I Could Go On Singing	1963	MacDonald, J.D.	VG+	MTI	$30.00 A
GOLD MEDAL	k 1292	On The Run	1963	MacDonald, J.D.	VGF		$16.00
GOLD MEDAL	k 1292	On The Run	1963	MacDonald, J.D.	VG+		$7.00
GOLD MEDAL	k 1294	Alone At Night	1963	Packer, V.*	VG-		$5.00
GOLD MEDAL	k 1294	Alone At Night	1963	Packer, V.*	G+		$5.00
GOLD MEDAL	k 1299	Whisper Their Love (3rd)	1963	Taylor, V.	VG		$5.00
GOLD MEDAL	k 1301	Island Of Love	1963	Edwards, H.	VG+	MTI	$7.00
GOLD MEDAL	k 1303	Don't Speak To Strange Girls	1963	Whittington, H.	VG		$14.00
GOLD MEDAL	k 1311	Shake Him Till He Rattles	1963	Braly, M.	VG+		$27.00 A
GOLD MEDAL	k 1320	Color Him Dead	1963	Runyon, C.	AF		$15.00 A
GOLD MEDAL	K 1321	The Green Wound	1963	Atlee, P.	VG+		$7.00
GOLD MEDAL	d 1324	Three Times Infinity	1963	Margulies, L.	AF		$6.00
GOLD MEDAL	d 1328	The Beats	1963	Anthology	AF		$29.00 A
GOLD MEDAL	d 1328	The Beats	1963	Anthology	VGF-		$20.00 A
GOLD MEDAL	d 1328	The Beats	1963	Anthology	VG+		$12.00
GOLD MEDAL	s 1330	The Appaloosa	1963	MacLeod, R.	VGF		$7.00
GOLD MEDAL	s 1331	Super Bloopers (2nd)	1963	Schafer, K.	VG+		$5.00
GOLD MEDAL	d 1332	The Addict	1963	Anthology	G+		$7.00
GOLD MEDAL	k 1334	Death Of A Citizen	1963	Hamilton, D.	AF		$5.00
GOLD MEDAL	k 1335	The Wrecking Crew	1963	Hamilton, D.	F		$5.00
GOLD MEDAL	k 1336	The Removers	1963	Hamilton, D.	F		$5.00
GOLD MEDAL	k 1337	A House In Naples	1963	Rabe, P.	AF		$10.00
GOLD MEDAL	k 1337	A House In Naples	1963	Rabe, P.	VG+		$7.00
GOLD MEDAL	k 1338	The Golden Urge	1963	Kyle, R.	VG+		$7.00
GOLD MEDAL	k 1340	Strongarm	1963	Marlowe, D.J.	AF		$22.00 A
GOLD MEDAL	k 1341	For Love Or Money	1963	Tessitore, J.	VG+	MTI	$7.00
GOLD MEDAL	k 1343	The Kingdom Of Johnny Cool	1963	McPartland, J.	VG-	MTI	$4.00
GOLD MEDAL	k 1344	Go Home, Stranger (3rd)	1963	Williams, C.	G		$3.00
GOLD MEDAL	k 1346	The Evil Friendship	1963	Packer, V.*	VGF+		$7.00
GOLD MEDAL	k 1346	The Evil Friendship	1963	Packer, V.*	VG		$5.00
GOLD MEDAL	k 1350	McLintock	1963	Wormser, R.	AF	MTI	$8.00
GOLD MEDAL	k 1350	McLintock	1963	Wormser, R.	VG	MTI	$5.00
GOLD MEDAL	d 1352	Age Of The Junkman	1963	Ballard, P.D.	VGF		$5.00
GOLD MEDAL	k 1353	A Touch Of Death	1963	Williams, C.	AF		$100.00 A

Gold Medal 1123 AF $27   Gold Medal 1132 VGF+ $72   Gold Medal 1134 F $55   Gold Medal 1138 AF $16

PUBLISHER	PUB. #	TITLE	DATE	AUTHOR	COND.	TYPE	PRICE
GOLD MEDAL	k 1353	A Touch Of Death	1963	Williams, C.	VG+		$12.00
GOLD MEDAL	k 1353	A Touch Of Death	1963	Williams, C.	VG		$7.00
GOLD MEDAL	s 1354	Slam The Big Door	1963	MacDonald, J.D.	G		$2.50
GOLD MEDAL	k 1358	Charade	1963	Stone, P.	VG	MTI	$6.00
GOLD MEDAL	k 1361	Adam Clayton Powell	1963	Lewis, C.	VGF		$7.00
GOLD MEDAL	k 1364	Look Behind You Lady	1963	Fleischman, A.S.	AF		$5.00
GOLD MEDAL	s 1365	Hang The Men High	1963	Loomis, N.	AF		$6.00
GOLD MEDAL	d 1366	12 Great Classics Of Sci-Fi	1963	Anthology	AF		$5.00
GOLD MEDAL	k 1367	The Venetian Blonde	1963	Fleischman, A.S.	VGF		$7.00
GOLD MEDAL	s 1369	The Lone Gun	1963	Rigsby, H.	VGF		$8.00
GOLD MEDAL	k 1370	Assignment-Helene	1963	Aarons, E.S.	AF		$5.00
GOLD MEDAL	k 1376	Joker In The Deck	1964	Prather, R.S.	VGF		$8.00
GOLD MEDAL	k 1376	Joker In The Deck	1964	Prather, R.S.	AF		$7.00
GOLD MEDAL	k 1380	Ring Around Rosy	1964	Davis, G.	VGF		$18.00 A
GOLD MEDAL	d 1385	The Fall Of The Roman Empire	1964	Whittington, H.	VG+	MTI	$8.00
GOLD MEDAL	d 1385	The Fall Of The Roman Empire	1964	Whittington, H.	VG	MTI	$5.00
GOLD MEDAL	K 1386	The Shadowers	1964	Hamilton, D.	F		$7.00
GOLD MEDAL	k 1388	Mail Order Bride	1964	Cort, V.	VG-	MTI	$5.00
GOLD MEDAL	s 1390	The Hell Fire Kid	1964	Shannon, S.	AF		$7.00
GOLD MEDAL	k 1391	Murderer's Row	1964	Hamilton, D.	VGF		$5.00
GOLD MEDAL	k 1391	Murderer's Row	1964	Hamilton, D.	F		$4.00
GOLD MEDAL	k 1392	The Silencers	1964	Hamilton, D.	F		$5.00
GOLD MEDAL	k 1396	Case Of The Silent Stranger	1964	Craig, J.	VG-		$3.00
GOLD MEDAL	k 1397	Four From Planet 5	1964	Leinster, M.	AF		$5.00
GOLD MEDAL	k 1401	Gun Talk At Yuma	1964	Castle, F.	VG+		$6.00
GOLD MEDAL	k 1403	Stop This Man!	1964	Rabe, P.	VG		$5.00
GOLD MEDAL	k 1403	Stop This Man!	1964	Rabe, P.	VG		$4.00
GOLD MEDAL	k 1405	The Deep Blue Good-By	1964	MacDonald, J.D.	VGF-		$20.00 A
GOLD MEDAL	k 1410	Pillow Talk	1964	Albert, M.H.	VGF	MTI	$5.00
GOLD MEDAL	d 1411	Odd Girl Out	1964	Bannon, A.	VG+		$5.00
GOLD MEDAL	k 1420	Drum Beat - Berlin	1964	Marlowe, S.	AF		$8.00
GOLD MEDAL	k 1426	Journey Into Terror	1964	Rabe, P.	VGF		$12.00
GOLD MEDAL	k 1438	Pop. 1280	1964	Thompson, J.	VG		$20.00
GOLD MEDAL	k 1438	Pop. 1280	1964	Thompson, J.	G+		$12.00
GOLD MEDAL	k 1439	Kill The Clown	1964	Prather, R.S.	AF		$5.00
GOLD MEDAL	s 1440	Last Command	1964	Cook, W.	VGF		$6.00
GOLD MEDAL	k 1446	The Day New York Went Dry	1964	Einstein, C.	AF		$10.00
GOLD MEDAL	k 1450	Women's Barracks	1964	Torres, T.	VG		$3.00
GOLD MEDAL	k 1452	The Ravagers	1964	Hamilton, D.	F		$5.00
GOLD MEDAL	r 1454	1964 Pro Football Almanac	1964	Wise, B.	AF		$12.00
GOLD MEDAL	k 1458	Re-Enter Fu Manchu	1964	Rohmer, S.	VGF		$8.00
GOLD MEDAL	k 1458	Re-Enter Fu Manchu	1964	Rohmer, S.	VG		$7.00
GOLD MEDAL	k 1461	The Damned	1964	MacDonald, J.D.	VGF		$5.00
GOLD MEDAL	k 1462	The Cockeyed Corpse	1964	Prather, R.S.	AF		$7.00
GOLD MEDAL	k 1462	The Cockeyed Corpse	1964	Prather, R.S.	VG+		$6.00
GOLD MEDAL	K 1464	The Quick Red Fox	1964	MacDonald, J.D.	VGF		$15.00
GOLD MEDAL	k 1466	Wild	1964	Brewer, G.	VG+		$7.00
GOLD MEDAL	k 1466	Wild	1964	Brewer, G.	G-		$2.00

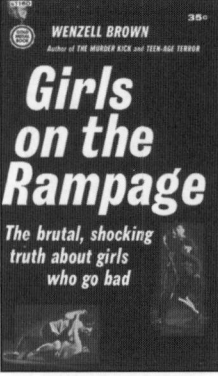

Gold Medal 1145 AF $87　　Gold Medal 1153 VG $40　　Gold Medal 1160 AF $43　　Gold Medal 1161 F $225

PUBLISHER	PUB. #	TITLE	DATE	AUTHOR	COND.	TYPE	PRICE
GOLD MEDAL	k 1472	Night Walker	1964	Hamilton, D.	AF		$6.00
GOLD MEDAL	d 1479	This Woman	1964	Idell, A.	VGF-		$6.00
GOLD MEDAL	k 1487	Mission For Vengeance	1964	Rabe, P.	G		$3.00
GOLD MEDAL	k 1488	Sunburst	1964	Gotlieb, P.	AF		$7.00
GOLD MEDAL	k 1488	Sunburst	1964	Gotlieb, P.	AF-		$7.00
GOLD MEDAL	k 1490	Kitten With A Whip	1964	Miller, W.	VG+	MTI	$8.00
GOLD MEDAL	L 1494	The Reassembled Man	1964	Kastle, H.D.	AF		$8.00
GOLD MEDAL	d 1499	A Deadly Shade Of Gold	1965	MacDonald, J.D.	VGF+		$14.00 A
GOLD MEDAL	k 1501	To Tame A Land	1964	L'Amour, L.	VG		$5.00
GOLD MEDAL	k 1503	The Company Girls	1965	Williams, M.	AF		$44.00 A
GOLD MEDAL	L 1504	World Without Women	1965	Keene, D.	AF		$10.00
GOLD MEDAL	k 1505	Assignment-Karachi	1965	Aarons, E.S.	F		$7.00
GOLD MEDAL	d 1506	Harvey Kurtzman's Fun And Games	1965	Kurtzman, H.	AF-		$28.00 A
GOLD MEDAL	k 1507	The Prettiest Girl I Ever Killed	1965	Runyon, C.	AF		$5.00
GOLD MEDAL	k 1508	Drum Beat - Dominique	1965	Marlowe, S.	VG+		$6.00
GOLD MEDAL	k 1511	None But The Brave	1965	Cameron, L.	VG+	MTI	$4.00
GOLD MEDAL	d 1514	The Humor Of JFK	1964	Herndon, B.	VG		$3.00
GOLD MEDAL	R 1516	1965 Baseball Almanac	1965	Wise, B.	VGF		$8.00
GOLD MEDAL	k 1519	Major Dundee	1965	Fink, H.J.	VG+	MTI	$7.00
GOLD MEDAL	k 1522	The Killer Inside Me	1965	Thompson, J.	VG		$27.00 A
GOLD MEDAL	k 1524	Death Deep Down	1965	Marlowe, D.J.	AF		$11.00 A
GOLD MEDAL	D 1528	Area Of Suspicion	1965	MacDonald, J.D.	VGF		$5.00
GOLD MEDAL	k 1535	Assignment - Angelina	1965	Aarons, E.S.	F		$7.00
GOLD MEDAL	k 1540	Girl In A Big Brass Bed	1965	Rabe, P.	VG		$10.00
GOLD MEDAL	k 1540	Girl In A Big Brass Bed	1965	Rabe, P.	VG-		$5.00
GOLD MEDAL	d 1544	Monsters Galore	1965	Hurwood, B.J.	VG+		$7.00
GOLD MEDAL	k 1547	All These Condemned	1965	MacDonald, J.D.	VG+		$4.00
GOLD MEDAL	R 1550	My Years With Churchill	1965	MacGowan, N.	VGF		$5.00
GOLD MEDAL	d 1552	A Man Of Affairs	1965	MacDonald, J.D.	VGF		$7.00
GOLD MEDAL	k 1555	The Girl With The Long Green Heart	1965	Block, L.	VGF		$20.00 A
GOLD MEDAL	d 1559	Assignment - Manchurian Doll	1965	Aarons, E.S.	AF		$7.00
GOLD MEDAL	d 1561	Night Slaves	1965	Sohl, J.	VGF+		$7.00
GOLD MEDAL	d 1561	Night Slaves	1965	Sohl, J.	VGF		$7.00
GOLD MEDAL	R 1565	WWII: A Photographic Record	1965	Martin, R.G.	VGF		$5.00
GOLD MEDAL	k 1569	Once A Thief	1965	Marko, Z.	AF	MTI	$7.00
GOLD MEDAL	k 1569	Once A Thief	1965	Marko, Z.	VG	MTI	$4.00
GOLD MEDAL	d 1572	Bogart	1965	Gehman, R.	AF		$6.00
GOLD MEDAL	d 1582	Generation X	1965	Hamblett, C.	VG+		$10.00
GOLD MEDAL	d 1582	Generation X	1965	Hamblett, C.	VG		$7.00
GOLD MEDAL	d 1583	Assignment - Cairo Dancers	1965	Aarons, E.S.	F		$7.00
GOLD MEDAL	d 1584	Poor H. Allen Smith's Almanac	1965	Anthology	VGF		$10.00
GOLD MEDAL	d 1586	The Magic Man	1965	Beaumont, C.	VG		$8.00
GOLD MEDAL	d 1586	The Magic Man	1965	Beaumont, C.	VG+		$7.00
GOLD MEDAL	d 1591	Hot Prowl	1965	Kastle, H.D.	VG		$7.00
GOLD MEDAL	d 1599	The Drowner	1965	MacDonald, J.D.	VG+		$10.00
GOLD MEDAL	k 1603	Desert Stake-Out	1965	Whittington, H.	AF		$18.00 A
GOLD MEDAL	k 1603	Desert Stake-Out	1965	Whittington, H.	VG		$5.00
GOLD MEDAL	d 1608	The Devastators	1965	Hamilton, D.	F		$5.00

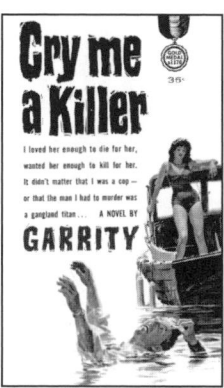
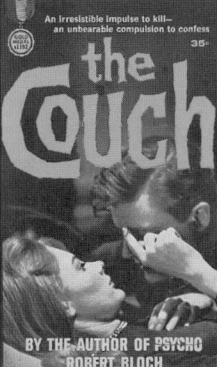

Gold Medal 1170 AF $14   Gold Medal 1192 VG+ $14   Gold Medal 1200 VGF+ $17   Gold Medal 1203 VGF $20

PUBLISHER	PUB. #	TITLE	DATE	AUTHOR	COND.	TYPE	PRICE
GOLD MEDAL	d 1611	Carny Kill	1966	Alter, R.E.	VG		$8.00
GOLD MEDAL	d 1611	Carny Kill	1966	Alter, R.E.	G		$2.00
GOLD MEDAL	d 1612	Assignment - Burma Girl	1966	Aarons, E.S.	AF		$7.00
GOLD MEDAL	d 1613	Assignment - Madeline	1966	Aarons, E.S.	F		$5.00
GOLD MEDAL	d 1616	Moment To Moment	1966	Coppel, A.	AF	MTI	$8.00 A
GOLD MEDAL	d 1617	The Steel Mirror	1966	Hamilton, D.	F		$5.00
GOLD MEDAL	d 1623	Murder Twice Told	1966	Hamilton, D.	F		$5.00
GOLD MEDAL	d 1626	The Rare Breed	1966	Sturgeon, T.	VGF	MTI	$15.00
GOLD MEDAL	d 1628	Another Part Of The Galaxy	1966	Anthology	AF		$6.00
GOLD MEDAL	d 1630	Assignment-Ankara	1966	Aarons, E.S.	F		$5.00
GOLD MEDAL	k 1631	Assignment-Zoraya	1966	Aarons, E.S.	F		$5.00
GOLD MEDAL	d 1634	The Paper Pistol Contract	1966	Atlee, P.	F		$7.00
GOLD MEDAL	d 1639	The Girl From Midnight	1966	Miller, W.	VG-		$2.50
GOLD MEDAL	d 1640	Assignment-School For Spies	1966	Aarons, E.S.	F		$5.00
GOLD MEDAL	d 1647	The Hungry One	1966	Brewer, G.	AF		$48.00 A
GOLD MEDAL	d 1647	The Hungry One	1966	Brewer, G.	VG-		$5.00
GOLD MEDAL	d 1654	Assignment - Sulu Sea	1966	Aarons, E.S.	AF		$6.00
GOLD MEDAL	d 1656	Assignment - Treason	1966	Aarons, E.S.	AF		$7.00
GOLD MEDAL	d 1661	Assignment - Girl In The Gondola	1966	Aarons, E.S.	F		$5.00
GOLD MEDAL	d 1664	The Dirty War Of Sgt. Slade	1966	Cameron, L.	AF		$7.00
GOLD MEDAL	d 1673	The Ravagers	1966	Hamilton, D.	AF		$5.00
GOLD MEDAL	d 1683	It's Cold Out There	1966	Braly, M.	VG+		$5.00
GOLD MEDAL	d 1685	The Comfortable Coffin	1966	Anthology	VG-		$7.00
GOLD MEDAL	d 1691	The Map On The Ceiling	1966	Pierce, J.	VGF		$5.00
GOLD MEDAL	d 1692	Assignment - Carlotta Cortez	1966	Aarons, E.S.	F		$5.00
GOLD MEDAL	d 1694	The Irish Beauty Contract	1966	Atlee, P.	F		$7.00
GOLD MEDAL	d 1701	A Party To Murder	1966	White, L.	VGF		$11.00 A
GOLD MEDAL	d 1703	Assignment To Disaster	1966	Aarons, E.S.	F		$5.00
GOLD MEDAL	d 1707	Assignment-Lili Lamaris	1966	Aarons, E.S.	F		$5.00
GOLD MEDAL	d 1714	The Spy Who Was 3 Feet Tall	1966	Rabe, P.	AF-		$19.00 A
GOLD MEDAL	d 1714	The Spy Who Was 3 Feet Tall	1966	Rabe, P.	VGF		$15.00 A
GOLD MEDAL	d 1714	The Spy Who Was 3 Feet Tall	1966	Rabe, P.	VG+		$10.00
GOLD MEDAL	d 1714	The Spy Who Was 3 Feet Tall	1966	Rabe, P.	VG-		$4.00
GOLD MEDAL	d 1719	The Fickle Finger Of Fate	1966	Keel, J.A.	F		$24.00 A
GOLD MEDAL	d 1719	The Fickle Finger Of Fate	1966	Keel, J.A.	AF		$15.00 A
GOLD MEDAL	m 1724	The Black Sun	1966	Horner, L.	VGF+		$6.00
GOLD MEDAL	m 1724	The Black Sun	1966	Horner, L.	G+		$3.00
GOLD MEDAL	d 1726	Assignment Lowlands	1966	Aarons, E.S.	F		$5.00
GOLD MEDAL	d 1727	The Scarf	1966	Bloch, R.	VGF		$18.00
GOLD MEDAL	d 1727	The Scarf	1966	Bloch, R.	VGF+		$11.00 A
GOLD MEDAL	d 1727	The Scarf	1966	Bloch, R.	VG		$7.00
GOLD MEDAL	d 1728	Catspaw Ordeal	1966	Aarons, E.S.	F		$6.00
GOLD MEDAL	d 1729	Assignment Stella Marni	1966	Aarons, E.S.	F		$5.00
GOLD MEDAL	d 1736	The Betrayers	1966	Hamilton, D.	AF		$5.00
GOLD MEDAL	d 1737	Passage To Terror	1966	Aarons, E.S.	F		$6.00
GOLD MEDAL	d 1740	Assignment Sorrento Siren	1966	Aarons, E.S.	F		$5.00
GOLD MEDAL	d 1743	Escape To Love	1966	Aarons, E.S.	F		$6.00
GOLD MEDAL	d 1747	The Cancelled Czech	1966	Block, L.	VGF-		$9.00

| Gold Medal 1224 AF $77 | Gold Medal 1337 AF $10 | Gold Medal 1458 VGF $8 | Gold Medal 1503 AF $44 |

PUBLISHER	PUB. #	TITLE	DATE	AUTHOR	COND.	TYPE	PRICE
GOLD MEDAL	d 1752	Seven Come Infinity	1966	Anthology	VGF		$5.00
GOLD MEDAL	d 1753	Assignment - Palermo	1966	Aarons, E.S.	F		$7.00
GOLD MEDAL	d 1755	The Decoy	1966	Aarons, E.S.	F		$6.00
GOLD MEDAL	d 1756	Come Back, My Love	1966	Aarons, E.S.	F		$6.00
GOLD MEDAL	d 1762	Don't Cry, Beloved	1966	Aarons, E.S.	F		$6.00
GOLD MEDAL	d 1770	The Star Ruby Contract	1967	Atlee, P.	AF		$7.00
GOLD MEDAL	d 1771	The Sinners	1966	Aarons, E.S.	F		$9.00
GOLD MEDAL	d 1772	Girl On The Run	1966	Aarons, E.S.	F		$6.00
GOLD MEDAL	d 1777	Hondo	1967	L'Amour, L.	VGF		$10.00
GOLD MEDAL	d 1780	The Green Wound Contract	1967	Atlee, P.	AF		$5.00
GOLD MEDAL	d 1781	Wonder Wart-Hog & Capt. Crud	1967	Anthology	VGF+		$15.00 A
GOLD MEDAL	d 1791	Route Of The Red Gold	1967	Marlowe, D.J.	VG+		$8.00
GOLD MEDAL	d 1792	The Girl, The Gold Watch . . .	1967	MacDonald, J.D.	VG		$4.00
GOLD MEDAL	d 1803	The Rare Coin Score	1967	Stark, R.*	AF-		$33.00 A
GOLD MEDAL	d 1803	The Rare Coin Score	1967	Stark, R.*	VGF		$15.00 A
GOLD MEDAL	R 1805	The Bobby Kennedy Nobody Knows	1967	Nicholas, W.	VG+		$3.00
GOLD MEDAL	d 1810	The Widowmaster	1967	Bergson, L.	F		$7.00
GOLD MEDAL	d 1823	Assignment - Black Viking	1967	Aarons, E.S.	F		$7.00
GOLD MEDAL	d 1830	Code Name Gadget	1967	Rabe, P.	AF		$20.00 A
GOLD MEDAL	d 1843	A Girl Called Fathom	1967	Forrester, L.	VG+	MTI	$7.00
GOLD MEDAL	d 1843	A Girl Called Fathom	1967	Forrester, L.	VG	MTI	$5.00
GOLD MEDAL	d 1849	Assignment - Moon Girl	1967	Aarons, E.S.	AF		$7.00
GOLD MEDAL	d 1854	Hour Of The Gun	1967	Krepps, R.	VGF	MTI	$6.00
GOLD MEDAL	d 1854	Hour Of The Gun	1967	Krepps, R.	VG+	MTI	$4.00
GOLD MEDAL	d 1856	Point Blank!	1967	Stark, R.*	VG	MTI	$4.00
GOLD MEDAL	D 1856	Point Blank!	1967	Stark, R.*	G+	MTI	$3.00
GOLD MEDAL	d 1858	Cool Hand Luke	1967	Pearce, D.	VGF	MTI	$8.00
GOLD MEDAL	d 1858	Cool Hand Luke	1967	Pearce, D.	AF	MTI	$5.00
GOLD MEDAL	d 1861	The Green Eagle Score	1967	Stark, R.*	AF		$37.00 A
GOLD MEDAL	d 1861	The Green Eagle Score	1967	Stark, R.*	VGF		$20.00
GOLD MEDAL	d 1861	The Green Eagle Score	1967	Stark, R.*	VG+		$14.00
GOLD MEDAL	d 1861	The Green Eagle Score	1967	Stark, R.*	G+		$3.00
GOLD MEDAL	D 1873	The Black Moth	1967	Runyon, C.	VGF		$8.00
GOLD MEDAL	d 1874	The Raven Is A Blood Red Bird	1967	Marlowe, D.J.	VG+		$5.00
GOLD MEDAL	d 1877	A Great Day For Dying	1968	Dillon, J.	AF		$4.00
GOLD MEDAL	d 1884	The Menacers	1968	Hamilton, D.	F		$5.00
GOLD MEDAL	d 1886	The Death Bird Contract	1968	Atlee, P.	AF		$5.00
GOLD MEDAL	d 1890	The Cool Man	1968	Burnett, W.R.	VG+		$7.00
GOLD MEDAL	R 1891	Double In Trouble	1968	Prather, R.S.	AF		$12.00
GOLD MEDAL	d 1894	Soft Touch	1968	MacDonald, J.D.	AF		$12.00
GOLD MEDAL	d 1896	Two For Tanner	1968	Block, L.	VGF+		$12.00 A
GOLD MEDAL	d 1896	Two For Tanner	1968	Block, L.	VG		$8.00
GOLD MEDAL	d 1911	The Scalp Hunters	1968	Friend, E.	VGF	MTI	$10.00
GOLD MEDAL	d 1911	The Scalp Hunters	1968	Friend, E.	VG+	MTI	$8.00
GOLD MEDAL	R 1918	Survival Margin	1968	Maine, C.E.	AF		$7.00
GOLD MEDAL	R 1924	7 Trips Through Time And Space	1968	Anthology	F		$7.00
GOLD MEDAL	D 1933	Knockover	1967	Thornburg, N.	AF		$8.00
GOLD MEDAL	d 1949	The Black Ice Score	1968	Stark, R.*	AF		$16.00 A

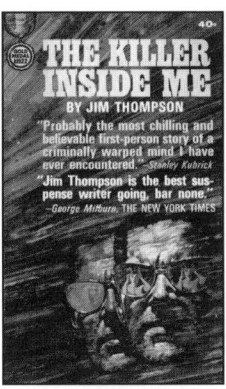

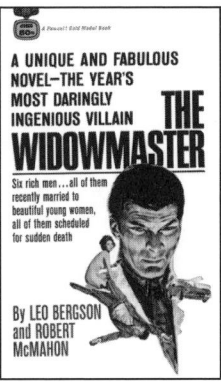

| Gold Medal 1522 VG $27 | Gold Medal 1719 F $24 | Gold Medal 1810 F $7 | Gold Medal 1830 AF $20 |

PUBLISHER	PUB. #	TITLE	DATE	AUTHOR	COND.	TYPE	PRICE
GOLD MEDAL	D 1956	A Thrill A Minute	1968	Godey, J.	VG+		$7.00
GOLD MEDAL	D 1971	Murder At Shirttail Flats	1968	Franklin, K.	F		$6.00
GOLD MEDAL	D 1987	The Body Trade	1968	Taylor, T.	VGF		$7.00
GOLD MEDAL	T 1992	A Flash Of Green	1968	MacDonald, J.D.	VGF		$5.00
GOLD MEDAL	D 1997	The Split	1968	Stark, R.*	F	MTI	$16.00
GOLD MEDAL	R 2000	Assignment Nuclear Nude	1968	Aarons, E.S.	VGF		$6.00
GOLD MEDAL	R 2008	Here Comes A Hero	1968	Block, L.	VGF		$13.00 A
GOLD MEDAL	R 2008	Here Comes A Hero	1968	Block, L.	VG-		$6.00
GOLD MEDAL	R 2037	The Sour Lemmon Score	1969	Stark, R.*	VG		$8.00
GOLD MEDAL	R 2044	The Others	1969	Anthology	AF		$8.00
GOLD MEDAL	R 2044	The Others	1969	Anthology	VGF		$7.00
GOLD MEDAL	R 2050	One Endless Hour	1969	Marlowe, D.J.	VG		$3.00
GOLD MEDAL	r 2063	Charro!	1969	Whittington, H.	VG	MTI	$4.00
GOLD MEDAL	R 2071	Assignment - Zoraya	1969	Aarons, E.S.	VGF		$6.00
GOLD MEDAL	T 2073	The Interlopers	1969	Hamilton, D.	AF		$5.00
GOLD MEDAL	R 2079	The Big Bounce	1969	Leonard, E.	VGF	MTI	$33.00 A
GOLD MEDAL	R 2079	The Big Bounce	1969	Leonard, E.	VGF	MTI	$20.00
GOLD MEDAL	R 2082	The Messenger	1969	Wright, C.	VG		$6.00
GOLD MEDAL	R 2087	The Ill Wind Contract	1969	Atlee, P.	F		$7.00
GOLD MEDAL	T 2092	Black Champion	1969	Farar, F.	VGF		$12.00
GOLD MEDAL	r 2095	To Tame A Land	1969	L'Amour, L.	VG+		$4.00
GOLD MEDAL	r 2106	End Of The Tiger	1969	MacDonald, J.D.	VG+		$8.00
GOLD MEDAL	R 2108	Silken Baroness Contract	1969	Atlee, P.	VGF		$5.00
GOLD MEDAL	R 2114	Tales For A Rainy Night	1969	Anthology	F		$7.00
GOLD MEDAL	R 2145	Assignment Peking	1969	Aarons, E.S.	F		$5.00
GOLD MEDAL	D 2156	Graffiti	1969	Leary, B.	VGF+		$7.00
GOLD MEDAL	R 2157	The Dragon's Eye	1969	Stone, S.C.S.	VGF+		$7.00
GOLD MEDAL	R 2161	The Gypsy Moths	1969	Drought, J.	AF	MTI	$5.00
GOLD MEDAL	R 2162	Million Dollar Murder	1969	Aarons, E.S.	F		$6.00
GOLD MEDAL	R 2168	The Molly Maguires	1969	O'Neill, J.	VGF	MTI	$7.00
GOLD MEDAL	D 2178	Meet Fred Basset	1969	Graham	VGF+		$7.00
GOLD MEDAL	R 2180	A Funny Thing Happened . . .	1969	Ward, B.	F		$14.00 A
GOLD MEDAL	D 2194	Signs Of Laughter	1970	Anthology	AF-		$7.00
GOLD MEDAL	D 2195	The Easy Gun	1970	Parsons, E.M.	AF		$6.00
GOLD MEDAL	R 2197	Before It's Too Late	1970	Cameron, M.	VG+		$5.00
GOLD MEDAL	R 2202	Assignment White Rajah	1970	Aarons, E.S.	AF		$7.00
GOLD MEDAL	R 2207	The High Side	1970	Ehrlich, M.	VG		$7.00
GOLD MEDAL	T 2248	Sudden Endings	1970	Packer, V.*	G+		$7.00
GOLD MEDAL	T 2271	Worlds To Come	1970	Anthology	AF		$5.00
GOLD MEDAL	T 2281	Assignment Star Stealers	1970	Aarons, E.S.	F		$7.00
GOLD MEDAL	T 2285	No Score	1970	Harrison, C.*	VG+		$10.00
GOLD MEDAL	R 2317	Hondo	1970	L'Amour, L.	VGF		$5.00
GOLD MEDAL	R 2328	Valdez Is Coming	1970	Leonard, E.	VG+	MTI	$35.00 A
GOLD MEDAL	R 2328	Valdez Is Coming	1970	Leonard, E.	VG+	MTI	$30.00 A
GOLD MEDAL	R 2363	True Cartoon Treasury	1971	Anthology	AF		$7.00
GOLD MEDAL	r 2381	Last Stand At Papago Wells	1971	L'Amour, L.	VGF		$5.00
GOLD MEDAL	T 2392	The Poisoners	1971	Hamilton, D.	F		$5.00
GOLD MEDAL	T 2412	Seven	1971	MacDonald, J.D.	VG+		$7.00

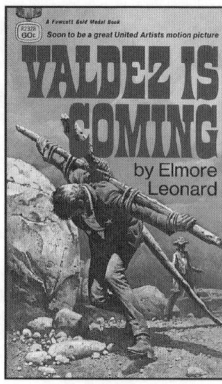

Gold Medal 1861 AF $37   Gold Medal 2008 VGF $13   Gold Medal 2079 VGF $33   Gold Medal 2328 VG+ $35

PUBLISHER	PUB. #	TITLE	DATE	AUTHOR	COND.	TYPE	PRICE
GOLD MEDAL	T 2421	Chip Harrison Scores Again	1971	Harrison, C.*	VG		$8.00
GOLD MEDAL	T 2421	Chip Harrison Scores Again	1971	Harrison, C.*	G-		$5.00
GOLD MEDAL	T 2438	Numerology Dreambook	1971	Zolar	VGF		$9.00
GOLD MEDAL	T 2450	The Canadian Bomber Contract	1971	Atlee, P.	F		$6.00
GOLD MEDAL	T 2471	Assignment Golden Girl	1971	Aarons, E.S.	AF		$7.00
GOLD MEDAL	T 2486	Operation Breakthrough	1971	Marlowe, D.J.	VGF		$7.00
GOLD MEDAL	t 2493	Behind The Scarlet Door	1971	Cameron, L.	VGF		$10.00
GOLD MEDAL	T 2508	The White Wolverine Contract	1971	Atlee, P.	F		$7.00
GOLD MEDAL	M 2513	A Tan And Sandy Silence	1971	MacDonald, J.D.	AF		$7.00 A
GOLD MEDAL	T 2524	The Invader	1972	Wormser, R.	AF		$5.00
GOLD MEDAL	T 2530	The Kiwi Contract	1972	Atlee, P.	F		$6.00
GOLD MEDAL	T 2541	Operation Drumfire	1972	Marlowe, D.J.	VGF		$5.00
GOLD MEDAL	T 2581	Not Dead Yet	1972	Banko, D.	VG+		$8.00
GOLD MEDAL	M 2592	War Of The Dons	1972	Rabe, P.	VGF		$8.00
GOLD MEDAL	M 2592	War Of The Dons	1972	Rabe, P.	G+		$3.00
GOLD MEDAL	P 2623	Child Of The Sun	1972	Onstott, K.	VGF		$7.00
GOLD MEDAL	T 2624	Eight Strange Tales	1972	Anthology	AF		$6.00
GOLD MEDAL	T 2624	Eight Strange Tales	1972	Anthology	VGF		$5.00
GOLD MEDAL	T 2643	The Price Of Murder	n/d	MacDonald, J.D.	VGF		$5.00
GOLD MEDAL	T 2656	Buchanan's Gamble	1973	Ward, J.	AF		$7.00
GOLD MEDAL	T 2658	Double Kill	1973	Da Cruz, D.	VGF+		$7.00
GOLD MEDAL	M 2659	The Intriguers	1973	Hamilton, D.	F		$5.00
GOLD MEDAL	T 2662	One Endless Hour	1973	Marlowe, D.J.	AF		$7.00
GOLD MEDAL	T 2697	The Spice Route Contract	1973	Atlee, P.	AF		$7.00
GOLD MEDAL	T 2704	The Trembling Earth Contract	1973	Atlee, P.	VGF		$6.00
GOLD MEDAL	M 2723	Operation Stranglehold	1973	Marlowe, D.J.	VGF		$6.00
GOLD MEDAL	T 2736	The Scarred Man	1973	Heatter, B.	VGF		$7.00
GOLD MEDAL	M 2851	A Bullet For Cinderella	1973	MacDonald, J.D.	VGF		$4.00
GOLD MEDAL	P 2853	Rogue Roman	1973	Horner, L.	VGF+		$7.00
GOLD MEDAL	M 2877	Operation Breakthrough	1973	Marlowe, D.J.	VGF		$4.00
GOLD MEDAL	M 2888	Assignment Ceylon	1973	Aarons, E.S.	AF		$7.00
GOLD MEDAL	M 2904	Assignment Amazon Queen	1974	Aarons, E.S.	F		$5.00
GOLD MEDAL	T 2918	Valdez Is Coming	1974	Leonard, E.	VGF		$8.00
GOLD MEDAL	M 2925	The Underground Cities Contract	1974	Atlee, P.	AF		$7.00
GOLD MEDAL	P 2938	The Intimidators	1974	Hamilton, D.	F		$5.00
GOLD MEDAL	M 2944	The Seven-Ups	1973	Posner, R.	VGF+	MTI	$6.00
GOLD MEDAL	M 2974	Operation Hammerlock	1974	Marlowe, D.J.	VGF		$7.00
GOLD MEDAL	M 3029	Make Out With Murder	1974	Harrison, C.*	G+		$8.00
GOLD MEDAL	M 3029	Make Out With Murder (Signed)	1974	Harrison, C.*	VG+		$20.00
GOLD MEDAL	M 3057	Heller With A Gun	1974	L'Amour, L.	VGF		$4.00
GOLD MEDAL	T 3087	Dennis The Menace	1974	Ketcham, H.	VGF		$5.00
GOLD MEDAL	M 3152	The Mexico Run	1974	White, L.	VG		$7.00
GOLD MEDAL	M 3171	Operation Deathmaker	1975	Marlowe, D.J.	VGF		$4.00
GOLD MEDAL	P 3224	Assignment Quayle Question	1975	Aarons, E.S.	F		$5.00
GOLD MEDAL	P 3274	The Topless Tulip Caper	1975	Harrison, C.*	VG+		$15.00
GOLD MEDAL	P 3382	Utah Blaine	1975	L'Amour, L.	VGF		$4.00
GOLD MEDAL	X 3441	Thin Ice	1976	Cartwright, G.	AF		$8.00
GOLD MEDAL	P 3442	The Dogfighter	1976	Betuel, J.	VG+		$6.00

| Gold Medal U.K. 635 VG- $7 | Gold Star 14 F $17 | Gold Star 26 AF $30 | Gold Star 42 VG+ $10 |

PUBLISHER	PUB. #	TITLE	DATE	AUTHOR	COND.	TYPE	PRICE
GOLD MEDAL	P 3454	Operation Counterpunch	1976	Marlowe, D.J.	VGF		$7.00
GOLD MEDAL	P 3459	Mrs. Pruneface	1976	Gould, C.	VG+		$6.00
GOLD MEDAL	P 3460	The Invisible Man	1975	Jahn, M.	F	TVTI	$10.00
GOLD MEDAL	P 3460	The Invisible Man	1975	Jahn, M.	VGF	TVTI	$7.00
GOLD MEDAL	P 3527	Assignment Afghan Dragon	1976	Aarons, E.S.	AF		$7.00
GOLD MEDAL	3567	The Retaliators	1976	Hamilton, D.	F		$5.00
GOLD MEDAL	3585	Master Of Blackoaks (4th)	1976	Carter, A.*	VG		$5.00
GOLD MEDAL	3585	Master Of Blackoaks (5th)	1976	Carter, A.*	VG		$5.00
GOLD MEDAL	3865	The Terrorizers	1977	Hamilton, D.	F		$5.00
GOLD MEDAL	4025	Panama	1978	Carter, A.*	VG		$7.00
GOLD MEDAL	4074	Rampage	1978	Whittington, H.	VG		$7.00
GOLD MEDAL	4090	Taproots Of Falconhurst	1978	Carter, A.*	G-		$5.00
GOLD MEDAL	4286	Sicilian Woman	1979	Whittington, H.	VG		$15.00
GOLD MEDAL	4334	Scandal Of Falconhurst	1980	Carter, A.*	VG+		$10.00
GOLD MEDAL	4424	Heritage Of Blackoaks	1981	Carter, A.*	G+		$6.00
GOLD MEDAL	12767	Miz Lucretia Of Falconhurst	1986	Carter, A.*	G+		$6.00
GOLD MEDAL	12918	Get Off At Babylon	1987	Albert, M.	AF		$4.00
GOLD MEDAL	13406	Falconhurst Fugitive	1988	Carter, A.*	VGF		$14.00
GOLD MEDAL (U.K.)	627	Four-Time Loser	1963	Lynch, D.	VG+		$7.00
GOLD MEDAL (U.K.)	635	Dead Dolls Don't Talk	1963	Keene, D.	VG-		$7.00
GOLD MEDAL (U.K.)	637	Delfina	1963	Bracken, S.	VG		$5.00
GOLD MEDAL (U.K.)	688	The Beach Girls	1964	MacDonald, J.D.	VG		$7.00
GOLD MEDAL (U.K.)	693	The Damned	1964	MacDonald, J.D.	G+		$5.00
GOLD MEDAL (U.K.)	694	The Girl, The Gold Watch . . .	1964	MacDonald, J.D.	VG		$7.00
GOLD MEDAL (U.K.)	697	Judge Me Not	1964	MacDonald, J.D.	G+		$5.00
GOLD MEDAL (U.K.)	714	Age Of The Junkman	1964	Ballard, P.D.	VG		$5.00
GOLD MEDAL BOOKS	No#	Five Sisters	n/d	Kazarine, V.	G	Digest	$7.00
GOLD MEDAL BOOKS	No#	Georgie May	n/d	Bodenheim, M.	G	Digest	$7.00
GOLD MEDAL BOOKS	No#	Private Secretary	n/d	Schultz, A.B.	G	Digest	$7.00
GOLD MEDAL BOOKS	No#	Show Girl	n/d	McEvoy, J.P.	G	Digest	$7.00
GOLD MEDAL BOOKS	No#	The Desert Of Love	n/d	Mauriac, F.	G	Digest	$7.00
GOLD STAR	IL7 12	Lover	1963	Janson, H.	AF		$15.00 A
GOLD STAR	IL7 14	A Nice Way To Die	1963	Janson, H.	F		$17.00 A
GOLD STAR	IL7 14	A Nice Way To Die	1963	Janson, H.	VG-		$6.00
GOLD STAR	IL7 15	It's Bedtime Baby!	1964	Janson, H.	VG+		$12.00
GOLD STAR	IL7 19	Demented	1964	Young, D.J.	VG		$6.00
GOLD STAR	IL7 21	Sanitarium Of Tears	1964	Thurman, S.	AF		$12.00
GOLD STAR	IL7 24	Lay Down Dead	1964	Bradley, M.	VGF		$12.00 A
GOLD STAR	IL7 24	Lay Down Dead	1964	Bradley, M.	VG		$7.00
GOLD STAR	IL7 25	Shocking Tales Of Perversion	1964	Anthology	VG		$7.00
GOLD STAR	IL7 26	All The Gay Girls	1964	Frame, M.	AF		$30.00
GOLD STAR	IL7 26	All The Gay Girls	1964	Frame, M.	VGF		$28.00 A
GOLD STAR	IL7 28	Fanny	1964	Janson, H.	AF		$12.00
GOLD STAR	IL7 30	The Hackamore Feud	1964	Stuart, M.	VGF		$5.00
GOLD STAR	IL7 31	Whiplash	1964	Taylor, R.W.	VGF		$5.00 A
GOLD STAR	IL7 34	Buffalo Bill's Spy Shadower	1964	LeBlanc, E.T., ed.	VG+		$7.00
GOLD STAR	IL7 35	Campus Call Girl	1964	O'Neill, S.	VGF		$14.00 A
GOLD STAR	IL7 37	Running The Gauntlet	1964	LeBlanc, E.T., ed.	VGF		$7.00

Golden Willow 53 VG+ $17

Graphic 46 VG+ $46

Graphic 60 VGF $49

PUBLISHER	PUB. #	TITLE	DATE	AUTHOR	COND.	TYPE	PRICE
GOLD STAR	IL7 39	Love Is For Everybody	1964	Gilbert, A.	AF		$53.00 A
GOLD STAR	IL7 41	Girl Possessed	1964	Owen, D.	AF		$20.00 A
GOLD STAR	IL7 42	Tarzan And The Silver Globe	1964	Werper, B.	VG+		$10.00 A
GOLD STAR	IL7 44	Buffalo Bill's Feather-Weight	1964	LeBlanc, E.T., ed.	VGF		$7.00
GOLD STAR	IL7 44	Buffalo Bill's Feather-Weight	1964	LeBlanc, E.T., ed.	VG		$4.00
GOLD STAR	IL7 46	Prarie Pioneers	1964	LeBlanc, E.T., ed.	AF		$7.00
GOLD STAR	IL7 46	Prarie Pioneers	1964	LeBlanc, E.T., ed.	VGF		$7.00
GOLD STAR	IL7 47	The Renegade Rustlers	1964	LeBlanc, E.T., ed.	AF		$7.00
GOLD STAR	IL7 49	Tarzan And The Cave City	1964	Werper, B.	VG+		$10.00
GOLD STAR	IL7 55	Sex And The Jet Set	1964	O'Neill, S.	AF		$8.00
GOLD STAR	IL7 56	What Makes You Tick?	1964	Mason, M.	VG		$4.00
GOLD STAR	IL7 57	The Sexy Vixen	1964	Janson, H.	VGF-		$12.00
GOLD STAR	IL7 58	Wild West And The Salted Mines	1965	LeBlanc, E.T., ed.	VGF		$7.00
GOLD STAR	IL7 59	Whirlwind Riders	1965	LeBlanc, E.T., ed.	VGF		$7.00
GOLD STAR	IL7 61	Sex And The Divorcee	1965	O'Neill, S.	VGF		$6.00
GOLD STAR	IL7 63	The Affairs Of Paula	1965	Janson, H.	VG+		$10.00
GOLD STAR	IL7 64	Part-Time Call Girl	1965	Anonymous	AF		$11.00 A
GOLD STAR	IL7 70	Becky	1965	Janson, H.	VG		$6.00
GOLD STAR	IL7 74	Buffalo Bill's Square Deal	1965	LeBlanc, E.T., ed.	VGF		$7.00
GOLDEN WILLOW	53	Try To Forget Me	1946	Nielsen, V.	VG+	Digest	$17.00
GOLLANCZ	4686	Kiss Your Ass Goodbye	1990	Willeford, C.	AF		$16.00 A
GRAFTON	No#	A Maze Of Death (2nd)	1986	Dick, P.K.	F		$7.00
GRAPHIC	12	If I Live To Dine	1949	Waugh, H.	VGF		$16.00 A
GRAPHIC	14	Death Commits Bigamy	1949	Fox, J.M.	VG		$6.00
GRAPHIC	15	Tex	1949	Mulford, C.E.	VG		$7.00
GRAPHIC	16	Deadline At Dawn	1949	Irish, W.*	VG		$8.00
GRAPHIC	16	Deadline At Dawn	1949	Irish, W.*	G+		$7.00
GRAPHIC	19	Lures Of Death	1950	Whelton, P.	G+		$6.00
GRAPHIC	20	Dilemma Of The Dead Lady	1950	Irish, W.*	G+		$8.00
GRAPHIC	22	Tough Cop	1950	Roeburt, J.	VGF+		$14.00 A
GRAPHIC	24	Uninvited Corpse	1950	Whelton, P.	VG+		$9.00 A
GRAPHIC	24	Uninvited Corpse	1950	Whelton, P.	VG+		$7.00
GRAPHIC	26	Murder Can't Stop	1950	Ballard, W.T.	VG+		$7.00
GRAPHIC	26	Murder Can't Stop	1950	Ballard, W.T.	VG		$7.00
GRAPHIC	27	Corpse On The Town	1950	Roeburt, J.	VG+		$8.00
GRAPHIC	29	Memo For Murder	1951	Wilmer, D.*	VGF+		$17.00 A
GRAPHIC	29	Memo For Murder	1951	Wilmer, D.*	VGF		$10.00
GRAPHIC	29	Memo For Murder	1951	Wilmer, D.*	VG+		$7.00
GRAPHIC	29	Memo For Murder	1951	Wilmer, D.*	G+		$3.00
GRAPHIC	31	Deadly Night Call	1951	Irish, W.*	VGF		$44.00 A
GRAPHIC	32	Hangover House	1951	Rohmer, S.	G		$7.00
GRAPHIC	33	The Dummy Murder Case	1951	Ozaki, M.K.	VG+		$9.00
GRAPHIC	33	The Dummy Murder Case	1951	Ozaki, M.K.	VG		$8.00
GRAPHIC	36	Call Me Killer	1951	Whittington, H.	G		$7.00
GRAPHIC	37	Pardon My Blood	1951	Whelton, P.	VG		$7.00

Graphic 76 VGF $28　　　　Graphic 84 VGF $11　　　　Graphic 87 VG+ $22

PUBLISHER	PUB. #	TITLE	DATE	AUTHOR	COND.	TYPE	PRICE
GRAPHIC	38	Tough Cop	1951	Roeburt, J.	VG		$5.00
GRAPHIC	40	The Crooked Circle	1951	Stokes, M.L.	VG+		$9.00
GRAPHIC	41	Murder Is My Mistress	1951	Whittington, H.	VG		$24.00 A
GRAPHIC	41	Murder Is My Mistress	1951	Whittington, H.	VG		$22.00
GRAPHIC	41	Murder Is My Mistress	1951	Whittington, H.	G+		$7.00
GRAPHIC	42	Dead Men In Manhatten	1951	Roeburt, J.	VG		$5.00
GRAPHIC	43	If The Coffin Fits	1952	Keene, D.	VG		$12.00
GRAPHIC	43	If The Coffin Fits	1952	Keene, D.	G		$8.00
GRAPHIC	45	Death For A Hussy	1952	Martin, A.L.	VGF		$13.00 A
GRAPHIC	45	Death For A Hussy	1952	Martin, A.L.	VGF		$10.00 A
GRAPHIC	45	Death For A Hussy	1952	Martin, A.L.	VG+		$8.00
GRAPHIC	46	Mourn The Hangman	1952	Whittington, H.	VG+		$46.00 A
GRAPHIC	46	Mourn The Hangman	1952	Whittington, H.	VG		$35.00
GRAPHIC	46	Mourn The Hangman	1952	Whittington, H.	VG-		$12.00
GRAPHIC	48	Pattern For Murder	1952	Knight, D.*	VG+		$12.00
GRAPHIC	48	Pattern For Murder	1952	Knight, D.*	VG		$7.00
GRAPHIC	49	In Comes Death	1952	Whelton, P.	AF		$16.00 A
GRAPHIC	51	Framed In Guilt	1952	Keene, D.	G+		$8.00
GRAPHIC	54	Murder - Queen High	1952	Miller, W.	AF		$18.00 A
GRAPHIC	54	Murder - Queen High	1952	Miller, W.	VG+		$7.00
GRAPHIC	54	Murder - Queen High	1952	Miller, W.	G-		$2.50
GRAPHIC	57	The Deadly Pick-Up	1952	Ozaki, M.K.	G		$3.00
GRAPHIC	58	Strange Witness	1953	Keene, D.	VG+		$12.00
GRAPHIC	58	Strange Witness	1953	Keene, D.	VG		$10.00
GRAPHIC	58	Strange Witness	1953	Keene, D.	G-		$6.00
GRAPHIC	60	Dead Man's Tide	1953	Richards, W.*	VGF		$49.00 A
GRAPHIC	60	Dead Man's Tide	1953	Richards, W.*	VGF+		$17.00 A
GRAPHIC	60	Dead Man's Tide	1953	Richards, W.*	VG+		$15.00
GRAPHIC	61	There Oughta Be A Law	1953	Fagaly, A.	VGF		$8.00
GRAPHIC	62	Gun Hawk	1953	Ernenwein, L.	VG+		$7.00
GRAPHIC	63	Tough Cop	1953	Roeburt, J.	VG+		$7.00
GRAPHIC	64	Walk The Bloody Boulevard	1953	Marcus, A.A.	VG+		$7.00
GRAPHIC	67	Post-Mark Homicide	1953	Marcus, A.A.	VG		$6.00
GRAPHIC	67	Post-Mark Homicide	1953	Marcus, A.A.	G		$3.00
GRAPHIC	68	The Net	1953	Ronns, E.*	VG+		$17.00
GRAPHIC	68	The Net	1953	Ronns, E.*	G+		$3.00
GRAPHIC	69	Runyon First & Last	1953	Runyon, D.	VGF		$8.00
GRAPHIC	73	Handle With Fear	1954	Dewey, T.B.	VGF		$10.00
GRAPHIC	73	Handle With Fear	1954	Dewey, T.B.	VG		$7.00
GRAPHIC	75	The Big Kiss-Off	1954	Keene, D.	VG		$10.00
GRAPHIC	75	The Big Kiss-Off	1954	Keene, D.	VG-		$9.00
GRAPHIC	76	Say It With Murder	1954	Ronns, E.*	VGF		$28.00 A
GRAPHIC	76	Say It With Murder	1954	Ronns, E.*	VG-		$3.00
GRAPHIC	78	Hangover House	1954	Rohmer, S.	AF-		$20.00 A
GRAPHIC	78	Hangover House	1954	Rohmer, S.	VGF		$12.00

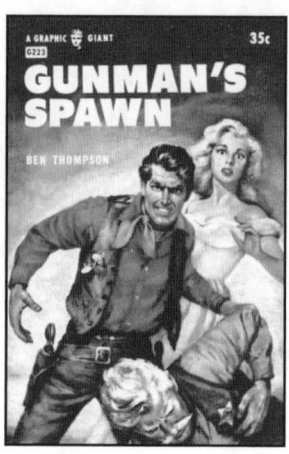

Graphic 93 AF $22   Graphic 108 VGF $16   Graphic G223 VGF $8

PUBLISHER	PUB. #	TITLE	DATE	AUTHOR	COND.	TYPE	PRICE
GRAPHIC	78	Hangover House	1954	Rohmer, S.	VG+		$10.00
GRAPHIC	79	Dressed To Kill	1954	Ozaki, M.	VG+		$7.00
GRAPHIC	81	Deadly Night Call	1954	Irish, W.*	VG+		$12.00
GRAPHIC	84	Your Shot, Darling!	1954	Bergquist, L.	VGF		$11.00 A
GRAPHIC	84	Your Shot, Darling!	1954	Bergquist, L.	VG+		$8.00
GRAPHIC	86	Texas Pride	1954	Martin, C.	VG		$7.00
GRAPHIC	87	Homicidal Lady	1954	Keene, D.	VG		$22.00 A
GRAPHIC	89	The Scarab Murder Case	1954	Van Dine, S.S.	VGF		$12.00
GRAPHIC	93	Say It With Bullets	1954	Powell, R.	AF		$22.00 A
GRAPHIC	93	Say It With Bullets	1954	Powell, R.	VG		$8.00
GRAPHIC	94	Model For Murder	1955	Marlowe, S.	VGF		$30.00 A
GRAPHIC	94	Model For Murder	1955	Marlowe, S.	AF		$22.00 A
GRAPHIC	94	Model For Murder	1955	Marlowe, S.	VGF+		$17.00
GRAPHIC	97	One Touch Of Blood	1955	Baker, S.S.	VG+		$8.00
GRAPHIC	97	One Touch Of Blood	1955	Baker, S.S.	VG		$5.00
GRAPHIC	101	Cry Torment	1955	Johnson, V.H.	VG+		$6.00
GRAPHIC	104	Mugs, Molls And Dr. Harvey	1955	Malcolm-Smith, G.	VGF		$10.00
GRAPHIC	106	Trap	1955	Jones, G.E.	VG		$5.00
GRAPHIC	108	The Phantom Lady	1955	Irish, W.*	VGF		$16.00
GRAPHIC	108	The Phantom Lady	1955	Irish, W.*	VG		$10.00
GRAPHIC	108	The Phantom Lady	1955	Irish, W.*	G+		$8.00
GRAPHIC	110	The Hollow Man	1955	Roeburt, J.	F		$20.00 A
GRAPHIC	110	The Hollow Man	1955	Roeburt, J.	VGF		$12.00 A
GRAPHIC	111	A Dame Called Murder	1955	Saber, R.O.	G		$7.00
GRAPHIC	113	Unfinished Crime	1955	McCloy, H.	VG		$5.00
GRAPHIC	114	They All Ran Away	1955	Ronns, E.*	VG		$8.00
GRAPHIC	115	Make Way For Murder	1955	Marcus, A.A.	G		$2.00
GRAPHIC	117	Murder Can't Wait	1955	Stokes, M.	VG+		$7.00
GRAPHIC	118	And Kill Once More	1955	Fray, A.	VG		$7.00
GRAPHIC	120	Texas Guns	1956	Ernenwein, L.	VGF		$6.00
GRAPHIC	123	A Time For Murder	1956	Saber, R.O.	G+		$5.00
GRAPHIC	124	Gunpoint!	1956	Shelley, J.L.	VGF		$6.00
GRAPHIC	125	The Intruder	1956	Cohen, O.R.	VG		$6.00
GRAPHIC	125	The Intruder	1956	Cohen, O.R.	VG-		$3.00
GRAPHIC	126	Murder's End	1956	Kelston, R.	VG		$6.00
GRAPHIC	128	Two Gun Fury	1956	Martin, C.	VG+		$6.00
GRAPHIC	130	Late Last Night	1956	Reach, J.	VG		$5.00
GRAPHIC	131	This Kill Is Mine	1956	Evans, D.	VGF		$12.00
GRAPHIC	132	I Prefer Murder	1956	Landolf, C.A.	VG+		$7.00
GRAPHIC	135	Murder - Very Dry	1956	Baker, S.S.	VG+		$7.00
GRAPHIC	137	Blood On The Range	1956	Colter, E.	VGF		$7.00
GRAPHIC	138	The Corpse Next Door	1956	Farris, J.	AF		$22.00
GRAPHIC	141	Dressed To Kill	1956	Ozaki, M.	VGF		$8.00
GRAPHIC	141	Dressed To Kill	1956	Ozaki, M.	VG+		$8.00
GRAPHIC	142	Fair Prey	1956	Duke, W.*	G+		$3.00

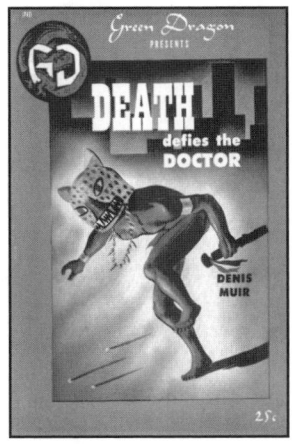

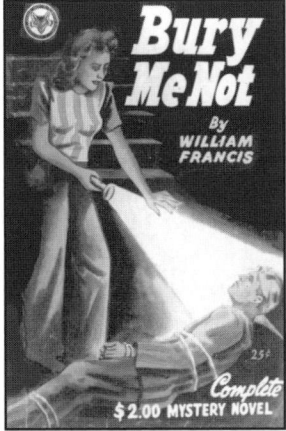

Green Dragon 19 VG $10   Green Publishing 4 VG $38   Griffin No# AF $35

PUBLISHER	PUB. #	TITLE	DATE	AUTHOR	COND.	TYPE	PRICE
GRAPHIC	143	Three Must Die!	1956	Gregory, D.	VGF		$8.00
GRAPHIC	144	Gunman's Greed	1957	Holmes, L.P.	VGF		$7.00
GRAPHIC	145	While Murder Waits	1957	Cassiday, B.	VG		$5.00
GRAPHIC	147	Killer Take All!	1957	Causey, J.O.	VGF		$16.00 A
GRAPHIC	147	Killer Take All!	1957	Causey, J.O.	VG+		$8.00
GRAPHIC	147	Killer Take All!	1957	Causey, J.O.	VG		$7.00
GRAPHIC	148	Say It With Bullets	1957	Powell, R.	VG+		$8.00
GRAPHIC	149	Murder Without Tears	1957	Lupton, L.	VGF		$12.00
GRAPHIC	150	Too Young To Die	1957	Saber, R.O.	F		$19.00 A
GRAPHIC	150	Too Young To Die	1957	Saber, R.O.	AF		$16.00 A
GRAPHIC	150	Too Young To Die	1957	Saber, R.O.	VGF+		$14.00
GRAPHIC	151	Gun Proud	1957	Patten, L.B.	AF		$10.00
GRAPHIC	151	Gun Proud	1957	Patten, L.B.	VGF		$7.00
GRAPHIC	152	Call Me Deadly	1957	Braham, H.	AF		$39.00 A
GRAPHIC	152	Call Me Deadly	1957	Braham, H.	VG+		$10.00
GRAPHIC	152	Call Me Deadly	1957	Braham, H.	VG		$3.00
GRAPHIC	154	Outlaw Justice	1957	Pendleton, F.	VGF		$6.00
GRAPHIC	155	Gun Chance	1957	Pendleton, F.	VGF		$7.00
GRAPHIC	156	Sucker Bait	1957	Saber, R.O.	AF		$15.00
GRAPHIC	157	Hell Rider	1957	Pendleton, F.	VGF		$6.00
GRAPHIC	G 101	Captain For Elizabeth	1952	Westcott, J.	VGF		$7.00
GRAPHIC	G 203	45 Murderers	1954	Rice, C.	VGF		$16.00 A
GRAPHIC	G 208	Swords For Charlemagne	1955	Pei, M.	VGF		$8.00
GRAPHIC	G 213	The Gladiators	1956	Koestler, A.	VG		$3.00
GRAPHIC	G 214	Captain Bashful	1956	Chidsey, D.B.	VGF		$7.00
GRAPHIC	G 215	Call Me Duke	1956	Grey, H.	AF		$11.00 A
GRAPHIC	G 215	Call Me Duke	1957	Grey, H.	VG		$7.00
GRAPHIC	G 215	Call Me Duke	1957	Grey, H.	VG-		$4.00
GRAPHIC	G 217	Eve's Daughters	1957	Anthology	AF		$6.00
GRAPHIC	G 218	Guns Of Hell Valley	1957	Prescott, J.	VGF		$8.00
GRAPHIC	G 222	The Fair And The Bold	1957	O'Hara, D.	VGF		$7.00
GRAPHIC	G 223	Gunman's Spawn	1957	Thompson, B.	VGF		$8.00
GRAPHIC (Canada)	503	Dealing Out Death	1955	Ballard, W.T.	VG		$7.00
GREEN DRAGON	3	Johnny On The Spot	1944	Dell, A.	VG	Digest	$7.00
GREEN DRAGON	5	Moscow Mystery	1944	Litvinoff, I.	VG+	Digest	$18.00 A
GREEN DRAGON	5	Moscow Mystery	1944	Litvinoff, I.	VG	Digest	$8.00
GREEN DRAGON	9	Murder Moves On	1944	Dall, J.	VG	Digest	$7.00
GREEN DRAGON	14	Talent For Murder	1945	Benton, J.L.	VGF	Digest	$12.00
GREEN DRAGON	14	Talent For Murder	1945	Benton, J.L.	VG	Digest	$7.00
GREEN DRAGON	17	And Death Drove On	1945	Fleming, R.	VG	Digest	$7.00
GREEN DRAGON	19	Death Defies The Doctor	1945	Muir, D.	VG	Digest	$10.00
GREEN DRAGON	25	She Screamed Blue Murder	1945	Secrist, K.	VG+		$14.00
GREEN DRAGON	28	Headsman's Holiday	1946	Hawkins, D.	VG-		$7.00
GREEN DRAGON	32	The Men In Her Death	1947	Blizard, M.	VG		$15.00
GREEN PUBLISHING	3	Murder On Shark Island	1944	DeWitt, J.	G+	Digest	$6.00

Guilty 5-3 VGF $27

Gunfire Western 29 VG $6

Handi-Book 14 VG+ $90

PUBLISHER	PUB. #	TITLE	DATE	AUTHOR	COND.	TYPE	PRICE
GREEN PUBLISHING	4	Bury Me Not	1944	Francis, W.	VG	Digest	$38.00 A
GREEN PUBLISHING	5	The Little Dog Barked	1944	Rowe, A.	VG	Digest	$9.00
GREEN PUBLISHING	6	Some Like It Hot	1945	Marshall, S.	VGF	Digest	$12.00
GREEN PUBLISHING	6	Some Like It Hot	1945	Marshall, S.	VG+	Digest	$10.00
GREEN PUBLISHING	10	Death In The Sun	1945	Saxby, C.	VGF	Digest	$10.00
GREEN PUBLISHING	13	Murder Stalks The Mayor	n/d	Scott, R.	VG	Digest	$17.00 A
GREEN PUBLISHING	14	The Backstage Mystery	n/d	Cohen, O.R.	VG	Digest	$11.00 A
GREEN PUBLISHING	14	The Backstage Mystery	n/d	Cohen, O.R.	G	Digest	$6.00
GREENLEAF	GC 218	The Love Box	1967	Kalnen, R.	VGF+		$11.00 A
GREENLEAF	GC 218	The Love Box	1967	Kalnen, R.	VG		$6.00
GREENLEAF	GC 225	Morfie	1967	Du Breuil, L.	AF		$34.00 A
GRIFFIN	No#	Love Siren	n/d	Branch, F.	AF	Digest	$85.00 A
GRIFFIN	No#	Stolen Love	n/d	Stone, T.	AF	Digest	$35.00 A
GROVE	P 7	The Stars	1960	Morin, E.	VGF		$49.00 A
GROVE	BA 35	Shoot The Piano Player	1962	Goodis, D.	VG	MTI	$5.00
GROVE	BC 53	Maybe I'll Pitch Forever	1963	Paige, S.	VG-		$5.00
GROVE	ERS 2	The Devil In Miss Jones	1973	Danziger, D.	VG+	MTI	$7.00
GUILTY	1 5	Guilty - 3/57	1957	Anthology	VG	Digest	$27.00 A
GUILTY	2 4	Guilty - 1/58	1958	Anthology	VG	Digest	$12.00
GUILTY	3 3	Guilty - 11/58	1958	Anthology	VG+	Digest	$30.00 A
GUILTY	3 4	Guilty - 1/59	1959	Anthology	VG	Digest	$9.00 A
GUILTY	3 5	Guilty - 3/59	1959	Anthology	VG+	Digest	$31.00 A
GUILTY	3 5	Guilty - 3/59	1959	Anthology	VG+	Digest	$22.00
GUILTY	4 6	Guilty - 6/60	1960	Anthology	AF	Digest	$21.00 A
GUILTY	5 1	Guilty - 9/60	1960	Anthology	AF	Digest	$22.00 A
GUILTY	5 2	Guilty - 12/60	1960	Anthology	AF	Digest	$20.00 A
GUILTY	5 2	Guilty - 12/60	1960	Anthology	G+	Digest	$5.00
GUILTY	5 3	Guilty - 3/61	1961	Anthology	VGF	Digest	$27.00 A
GUILTY	5 4	Guilty - 6/61	1961	Anthology	AF	Digest	$23.00 A
GUILTY	6 1	Guilty - 9/61	1961	Anthology	VGF	Digest	$27.00 A
GUILTY	6 2	Guilty - 12/61	1961	Anthology	AF	Digest	$22.00 A
GUNFIRE WESTERN	29	The Horseshoe Kid	1948	Clay, W.	VG	Digest	$6.00
GUNFIRE WESTERN	35	Botched Brand	1949	West, T.	VG+	Digest	$6.00
GUNFIRE WESTERN	40	Wind River Outlaw	1949	Ermine, W.	VG+	Digest	$6.00
GUNSMOKE	1 2	Gunsmoke - 8/53	1953	Anthology	VGF	Digest	$18.00 A
HACHETTE (French)	No#	L'Univers En Folie	1953	Brown, F.	VG+		$22.00 A
HAMILTON	No#	Man, Woman - And Android	1951	Hay, G.	G+	Digest	$7.00
HAMILTON	No#	Moment Out Of Time	1952	Sheldon, R.	VG	Digest	$15.00 A
HAMILTON	No#	Sci-Fi Monthly #11	1951	Campbell, H.J.	VG	Digest	$5.00 A
HANDI-BOOK	1	Odds On The Hot Seat	1941	Philips, J.	VG+	Digest	$28.00 A
HANDI-BOOK	13	Lazarus #7	1943	Sale, R.	VG+	Digest	$40.00
HANDI-BOOK	14	Black Alibi	1943	Woolrich, C.	VG+	Digest	$90.00 A
HANDI-BOOK	14	Black Alibi	1943	Woolrich, C.	G	Digest	$24.00
HANDI-BOOK	15	TCOT Walking Corpse	1943	Halliday, B.	VG+	Digest	$28.00 A
HANDI-BOOK	17	Footsteps Behind Her	1943	Wilson, M.	VG	Digest	$12.00

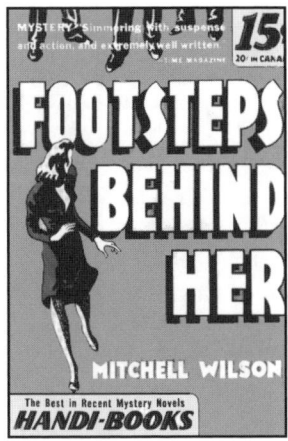

Handi-Book 17 VG $12

Handi-Book 120 VG+ $50

Harborough No# VGF $18

PUBLISHER	PUB. #	TITLE	DATE	AUTHOR	COND.	TYPE	PRICE
HANDI-BOOK	20	To A Blindfold Lady	1943	Purtell, J.	VG+	Digest	$14.00 A
HANDI-BOOK	21	TCOT Shivering Chorus Girls	1943	Phillips, J.A.	G	Digest	$5.00
HANDI-BOOK	24	Murder In Marble	1944	Philips, J.	VGF	Digest	$44.00 A
HANDI-BOOK	24	Murder In Marble	1944	Philips, J.	VG+	Digest	$24.00 A
HANDI-BOOK	25	The Court Of Shadows	1944	Jackson, G.	VGF	Digest	$16.00 A
HANDI-BOOK	26	To Catch A Thief	1944	Sanders, D.	VGF	Digest	$30.00 A
HANDI-BOOK	27	I Wake Up Screaming	1944	Fisher, S.	VGF	Digest	$77.00 A
HANDI-BOOK	28	The Frightened Man	1944	Chambers, D.	VG+	Digest	$17.00
HANDI-BOOK	29	The Woman In Red	1944	Gilbert, A.	AF	Digest	$22.00 A
HANDI-BOOK	32	No Good From A Corpse	1944	Brackett, L.	VGF	Digest	$33.00 A
HANDI-BOOK	32	No Good From A Corpse	1944	Brackett, L.	VG	Digest	$14.00 A
HANDI-BOOK	33	Up Jumped The Devil	1944	Adams, C.F.	VG+	Digest	$22.00 A
HANDI-BOOK	38	The Man With The Lumpy Nose	1945	Lariar, L.	VG+	Digest	$14.00
HANDI-BOOK	38	The Man With The Lumpy Nose	1945	Lariar, L.	VG-	Digest	$5.00
HANDI-BOOK	44	Knife In My Back	1945	Merwin, S.	VG	Digest	$12.00
HANDI-BOOK	45	The Blonde Is Dead	1945	Dow, J.	VG	Digest	$6.00
HANDI-BOOK	46	TCOT Tearless Widow	1946	Roeburt, J.	G+	Digest	$5.00
HANDI-BOOK	48	The Body Next Door	1946	Goldthwaite, E.K.	VG+	Digest	$15.00 A
HANDI-BOOK	48	The Body Next Door	1946	Goldthwaite, E.K.	VG	Digest	$7.00
HANDI-BOOK	50	The Dangerous Dead	1946	Brandon, W.	VG+	Digest	$12.00
HANDI-BOOK	52	The Triple Cross	1946	Barry, J.	VG-	Digest	$7.00
HANDI-BOOK	52	The Triple Cross	1946	Barry, J.	G	Digest	$5.00
HANDI-BOOK	62	The Murder Of The U.S.A.	1947	Jenkins, W.F.	VG	Digest	$8.00
HANDI-BOOK	68	Killers Play Rough	1947	Ring, A.	VG	Digest	$8.00
HANDI-BOOK	72	Death About Face	1948	Kane, F.	VG-	Digest	$8.00
HANDI-BOOK	82	Witch's Moon	1949	Jackson, G.	G	Digest	$7.00
HANDI-BOOK	83	The Faro Kid	1949	Ernenwein, L.	VG+	Digest	$7.00
HANDI-BOOK	83	The Faro Kid	1949	Ernenwein, L.	VG	Digest	$7.00
HANDI-BOOK	84	Yaller Gal	1949	Lee, C.	VG	Digest	$7.00
HANDI-BOOK	86	Dig Another Grave	1949	Cameron, D.	VG-	Digest	$5.00
HANDI-BOOK	88	Hope To Die	1949	Waugh, H.	VG+	Digest	$8.00
HANDI-BOOK	89	The King Of Thunder Valley	1949	Joscelyn, A.	VG	Digest	$7.00
HANDI-BOOK	90	Love To Burn	1949	Gaddis, P.	VG+	Digest	$7.00
HANDI-BOOK	93	Rebel Yell	1949	Ernenwein, L.	VGF	Digest	$9.00
HANDI-BOOK	93	Rebel Yell	1949	Ernenwein, L.	VG+	Digest	$8.00
HANDI-BOOK	100	Too Many Women	1950	Ozaki, M.K.	VG	Digest	$8.00
HANDI-BOOK	106	Three For The Money	1950	Barry, J.	VG	Digest	$12.00
HANDI-BOOK	110	The Glass Ladder	1950	Fairman, P.W.	G	Digest	$5.00
HANDI-BOOK	110	The Glass Ladder	1950	Fairman, P.W.	G	Digest	$4.00
HANDI-BOOK	114	False Face	1950	Edgley, L.	VG+	Digest	$10.00
HANDI-BOOK	120	Slay Ride For A Lady	1950	Whittington, H.	VG+	Digest	$50.00 A
HANDI-BOOK	121	Rawhide Summons	1950	Austin, B.	G+	Digest	$5.00
HANDI-BOOK	123	When Texans Ride	1950	Grinstead, J.E.	VG+	Digest	$5.00 A
HANDI-BOOK	126	Yaller Gal	1951	Lee, C.	VG		$8.00
HANDI-BOOK	130	The Dove	1951	Saber, R.O.	VG+		$37.00 A

Harlequin 40 VG $27   Harlequin 160 AF $143   Harlequin 187 VGF- $39   Harlequin 359 VG $10

PUBLISHER	PUB. #	TITLE	DATE	AUTHOR	COND.	TYPE	PRICE
HANDI-BOOK	138	The Brass Monkey	1951	Whittington, H.	VG		$22.00 A
HANDI-BOOK	138	The Brass Monkey	1951	Whittington, H.	G+		$20.00 A
HANDI-BOOK WESTERN	2	Rio Renegade	1946	Ernenwein, L.	VGF-		$25.00 A
HANDI-BOOK WESTERN	4	West Of The Wolverine	1947	Lehman, P.E.	VG-	Digest	$11.00 A
HANGMAN'S HOUSE	2	Puzzle In Paint	1946	Kootz	VG+	Digest	$18.00 A
HANGMAN'S HOUSE	4	The Man Who Feared	1946	Jenkins, W.F.	VG+	Digest	$18.00
HANGMAN'S HOUSE	8	Death Like Thunder	1946	Holman, H.	VG	Digest	$6.00
HANGMAN'S HOUSE	11	Murder Wore Green	1946	Koehler, R.P.	VG	Digest	$8.00
HARBOROUGH	No#	Love	n/d	Renin, P.	VGF	Digest	$24.00 A
HARBOROUGH	No#	Men Women Love	n/d	Renin, P.	VGF	Digest	$18.00 A
HARBOROUGH	No#	Men Women Love	n/d	Renin, P.	VGF	Digest	$15.00
HARBOROUGH	No#	When Passion Rules	n/d	Renin, P.	VG+	Digest	$20.00
HARLEQUIN	7	The House On Craig Street	1949	Cooke, R.J.	VG		$7.00
HARLEQUIN	16	No Nice Girl	1949	Lindsay, P.	VG-		$10.00
HARLEQUIN	17	The D.A.'s Daughter	1949	Petersen, H.	G		$7.00
HARLEQUIN	24	Painted Outlaws	1949	Gunn, T.	G		$7.00
HARLEQUIN	28	One Year With Grace	1950	Mooney, M.	VGF		$21.00 A
HARLEQUIN	40	Pass Key To Murder	1950	Reed, B.	VG		$27.00 A
HARLEQUIN	51	The Pocket Purity Cook Book	1950		G		$12.00
HARLEQUIN	57	Murder Man	1950	Bogart, W.	VG		$20.00 A
HARLEQUIN	100	Black Rider	1951	Cole, J.	VG-		$7.00
HARLEQUIN	148	Wagon Train Westward	1952	Westland, L.	VG+		$5.00 A
HARLEQUIN	160	Twelve Chinks And A Woman	1952	Chase, J.H.	AF		$143.00 A
HARLEQUIN	164	Captain For Elizabeth (2nd)	1952	Westcott, J.	VG-		$7.00
HARLEQUIN	169	Lady Of Cleves	1952	Barnes, M.C.	VG+		$5.00 A
HARLEQUIN	171	Savage Justice	1952	Ernenwein, L.	G		$6.00
HARLEQUIN	177	The House That Stood Still	1952	Van Vogt, A.E.	VGF		$90.00 A
HARLEQUIN	181	The Wicked Lady Skelton	1952	King-Hall, M.	VG		$22.00 A
HARLEQUIN	187	Shanghai Jezebel	1955	Corrigan, M.	VGF-		$39.00 A
HARLEQUIN	191	Prison Doctor	1952	Berg, L.	VGF		$18.00 A
HARLEQUIN	215	Turn Back The River	1953	Hardy, W.G.	VG		$7.00
HARLEQUIN	218	The Golden Amazon	1953	Fearn, J.R.	VGF+		$100.00 A
HARLEQUIN	218	The Golden Amazon	1953	Fearn, J.R.	VG+		$42.00 A
HARLEQUIN	228	Drums Of Dambala	1953	Jones, H.B.	VG+		$30.00 A
HARLEQUIN	257	One Man Front	1953	Rennie, G.M.	VG		$7.00
HARLEQUIN	262	The Body On Mount Royal	1953	Montrose, D.	G+		$7.00
HARLEQUIN	286	Colonel Blood	1954	Peacock, M.	VG		$5.00 A
HARLEQUIN	289	The Black Donnellys (6th)	1961	Kelley, T.P.	VGF-		$12.00
HARLEQUIN	290	The Violent Years	1954	Timms, E.V.	VG+		$8.00
HARLEQUIN	291	Heart Of Asia	1954	Andrews, R.C.	VG+		$15.00 A
HARLEQUIN	301	Mary Read, Buccaneer	1954	Rush, P.	VG		$20.00 A
HARLEQUIN	337	The Man In The Brown Suit	1955	Christie, A.	VGF		$6.00 A
HARLEQUIN	352	The India-Rubber Men	1956	Wallace, E.	VG		$19.00 A
HARLEQUIN	358	Redrock Gold	1956	Lehman, P.E.	G+		$6.00
HARLEQUIN	359	The Secret Adversary	1956	Christie, A.	VG		$10.00
HARLEQUIN	361	Clue Of The Silver Key	1956	Wallace, E.	VGF		$18.00 A
HARLEQUIN	387	White Face	1957	Wallace, E.	VGF		$18.00 A
HARLEQUIN	395	The Angel Of Terror	1957	Wallace, E.	AF		$33.00 A

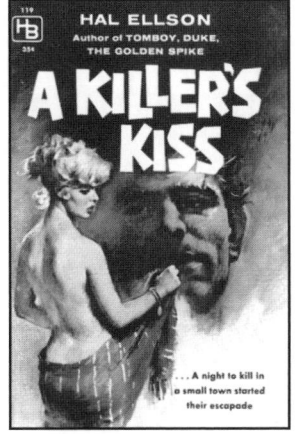

Hercules No# VG+ $22　　　　　Hillman 119 VGF + $25　　　　　Hillman 138 F $20

PUBLISHER	PUB. #	TITLE	DATE	AUTHOR	COND.	TYPE	PRICE
HARLEQUIN	411	Range King	1958	Grinstead, J.E.	VG-		$7.00
HARLEQUIN	420	The Squeaker	1958	Wallace, E.	VGF+		$25.00 A
HARLEQUIN	426	World's Greatest Spy Stories	1958	Anthology	VGF		$12.00
HARLEQUIN	50001	Harlequin's 30th Aniversary	1979		VGF		$27.00 A
HC	152	Black Magic - Satanism - Vodoo	1972	Martello, L.T.	VGF		$8.00
HEADLINE	106	Six In Hell!	1960	Winski, N.	VGF		$5.00 A
HEADLINE	108	Blood Money	1960	Lewis, J.	AF-		$15.00
HERALD READER	HR 101	The Couch Game	1964	Patton, G.	AF		$7.00
HERCULES	No#	D - As In Dead	1943	Treat, L.	VG+	Digest	$22.00 A
HILLMAN	1	Let's Make Mary (4th)	1952	Hanley, J.	VG		$6.00
HILLMAN	2	Tumbling River Range	1948	Tuttle, W.C.	VG		$5.00
HILLMAN	3	Casanova's Memoirs	1948	Casanova, J.	VGF		$6.00
HILLMAN	7	Sex And Marriage Problems-2nd	1948	Taylor, E.B.	VGF		$7.00
HILLMAN	10	Murder Under Construction	1949	MacVeigh, S.	VG+		$7.00
HILLMAN	12	Ten Droll Tales	1949	Balzac, H.D.	VG+		$7.00
HILLMAN	15	Hanging Judge	1949	Hamilton, B.	VG+		$5.00
HILLMAN	15	Hanging Judge	1949	Hamilton, B.	G		$5.00
HILLMAN	20	Dark Hazard	1949	Burnett, W.R.	VG		$6.00
HILLMAN	40	Trouble At The JHC	1949	Tuttle, W.C.	VG+		$6.00
HILLMAN	43	Arizona Nights	1950	White, S.E.	VGF		$7.00
HILLMAN	48	Father Of The Bride	1950	Streeter, E.	VGF	MTI	$27.00 A
HILLMAN	100	The Witnesses	1957	Simenon, G.	VG		$7.00
HILLMAN	103	The Short Night	1957	Turner, R.	VGF		$7.00
HILLMAN	106	Sex Without Guilt	1959	Ellis, A.	VGF		$5.00
HILLMAN	107	The Tormenters	1959	Payne, R.	AF		$20.00 A
HILLMAN	109	Horses, Women And Guns	1959	Nye, N.C.	VG+		$5.00
HILLMAN	110	Greatest Lover In The World	1959	Austin, A.	VG		$5.00
HILLMAN	112	The Sins Of Skid Row	1959	White, J.	F		$10.00
HILLMAN	113	Soldier's Women	1959	Smith, S.	F		$10.00
HILLMAN	114	Temptation In A Southern Town	1959	Heath, W.L.	F		$20.00
HILLMAN	114	Temptation In A Southern Town	1959	Heath, W.L.	F		$16.00 A
HILLMAN	119	A Killer's Kiss	1959	Ellson, H.	VGF+		$25.00 A
HILLMAN	120	Let's Make Mary	1959	Hanley, J.	F		$16.00 A
HILLMAN	121	The Sinful One	1959	Mark, E.	VGF		$6.00 A
HILLMAN	127	Maverick Gun	1959	Cord, B.	VGF		$6.00
HILLMAN	128	Elisa	1959	Goncourt, E.D.	VGF		$7.00
HILLMAN	130	The Elvis Presley Story	1960	Gregory, J.	VGF		$65.00 A
HILLMAN	131	An Acre Of Love	1959	Brennan, A.	VGF		$7.00
HILLMAN	134	Warrior's Mistress	1960	Anthony, E.	VGF		$7.00
HILLMAN	135	The Intimate Ones	1960	Golightly, B.	VGF		$7.00
HILLMAN	138	The Whispered Sex	1960	Martin, K.	F		$20.00
HILLMAN	138	The Whispered Sex	1960	Martin, K.	VG		$7.00
HILLMAN	140	The Devil Sword	1960	Matthews, K.*	VGF		$10.00
HILLMAN	140	The Devil Sword	1960	Matthews, K.*	VG-		$7.00
HILLMAN	141	Sextasy	1960	Lowe, L.	VGF		$5.00

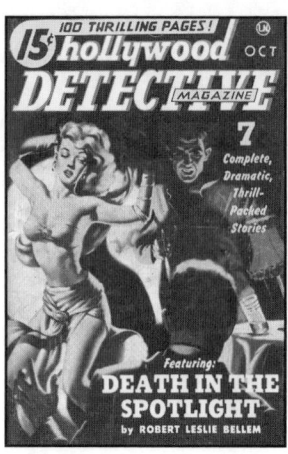
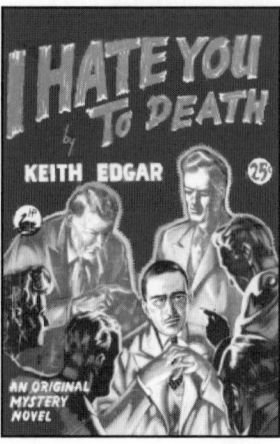

Hillman Detective Novel 1 G+ $8   Hollywood Detective 10-5 VG+ $169   Howard Publications No# G $6

PUBLISHER	PUB. #	TITLE	DATE	AUTHOR	COND.	TYPE	PRICE
HILLMAN	143	You Killed Elizabeth	1960	Halliday, B.	VG		$5.00
HILLMAN	143	You Killed Elizabeth	1960	Halliday, B.	G		$4.00
HILLMAN	145	A Lover's Blade	1960	Fox, J.M.	VG+		$7.00
HILLMAN	147	Shield For A Killer	1960	Cody, A.	AF		$6.00
HILLMAN	152	Sex Marks The Spot	1960	Scott, T.	VG		$6.00
HILLMAN	154	Scandal In Suburbia	1960	Fox, G.F.	VGF		$12.00
HILLMAN	162	The Shades Of Evil	1960	Golightly, B.	AF-		$17.00 A
HILLMAN	162	The Shades Of Evil	1960	Golightly, B.	F		$12.00
HILLMAN	164	Gunfight At The O.K. Corral	1960	Nye, N.C.	VG+	MTI	$10.00
HILLMAN	165	Kriegie	1960	Simmons, K.W.	AF		$5.00
HILLMAN	174	The Return	1960	Mitgang, H.	AF		$5.00
HILLMAN	175	Bedeviled	1960	Mason, R.	F		$12.00
HILLMAN	184	City Of Vice	1961	Gosling, J.	AF		$7.00
HILLMAN	190	Payment In Sin	1961	Martin, K.	AF		$10.00 A
HILLMAN	190	Payment In Sin	1961	Martin, K.	VGF		$8.00
HILLMAN	190	Payment In Sin	1961	Martin, K.	VG		$4.00
HILLMAN	192	More Sextasy	1961	Anthology	VGF		$6.00
HILLMAN	193	Murder, Murder, Murder	1961	Anthology	AF		$8.00 A
HILLMAN	193	Murder, Murder, Murder	1961	Anthology	VGF		$7.00
HILLMAN	194	The Taste Of Ashes	1961	Stern, B.	VGF		$6.00
HILLMAN	205	Cardboard Lover	1961	Matthews, K.*	VGF		$8.00
HILLMAN	50 109	The Wasted Years	1961	Stearn, J.	VGF		$12.00 A
HILLMAN	50 109	The Wasted Years	1961	Stearn, J.	VG+		$6.00
HILLMAN DET. NOVEL	1	The Arabian Nights Murder	1943	Carr, J.D.	G+		$8.00
HOLLOWAY HOUSE	HH 102	Hemmingway - Life And Death	1961	Singer, K.	AF		$7.00
HOLLOWAY HOUSE	HH 103 –104	Loves Of Casanova (2 vol. set)	1961	Casanova, J.	AF		$27.00 A
HOLLOWAY HOUSE	HH 105	Hollywood Screwballs	1962	Guild, L.	VG+		$15.00 A
HOLLOWAY HOUSE	HH 106	The Best Of Adam	1962	Anthology	VG+		$7.00
HOLLOWAY HOUSE	HH 120	Inside The Dodgers	1966	Thompson, F.	VG+		$7.00
HOLLOWAY HOUSE	HH 139	Pimp - The Story Of My Life	1967	Iceberg Slim	VG		$24.00 A
HOLLOWAY HOUSE	HH 154	The Hellcats	1968	Slatzer, R.F.	VG	MTI	$15.00 A
HOLLOWAY HOUSE	HH 158	Honeyman	1968	Panos, M.	AF		$15.00 A
HOLLOWAY HOUSE	HH 168	The Studio	1969	Guild, L.	VGF+		$7.00
HOLLOWAY HOUSE	BH 451	Never Die Alone	1974	Goines, D.	VG+		$7.00
HOLLOWAY HOUSE	BH 452	The Iceman #3	1974	Nazel, J.	VGF		$4.00
HOLLOWAY HOUSE	BH 465	Doomsday Squad	1975	Gober, D.	VG+		$4.00
HOLLOWAY HOUSE	BH 609	Death Wish	1977	Beck, R.	VG+		$7.00
HOLLOWAY HOUSE	BH 622	White Man's Justice . . .	n/d	Goines, D.	VG+		$7.00
HOLLOWAY HOUSE	BH 814	Hell Has No Exit	n/d	Gilmer, J.L.	VG+		$5.00
HOLLYWOOD DETECTIVE	10 5	Hollywood Detective - 10/50	1950	Anthology	VG+	Digest	$169.00 A
HOMICIDE	1 1	Homicide Det. Story 9/56	1956	Anthology	AF	Digest	$37.00 A
HORROR	11	Magazine Of Horror - 11/65	1965	Anthology	AF	Digest	$8.00
HORROR	16	Magazine Of Horror - Summer 1967	1967	Anthology	AF	Digest	$7.00
HORROR	17	Magazine Of Horror - Fall 1967	1967	Anthology	AF	Digest	$7.00
HORROR	17	Magazine Of Horror - Fall 1967	1967	Anthology	VGF	Digest	$7.00

Infantry Journal No# VG+ $7   Intimate Edition 705 VGF $10   Intimate Novels 11 VGF $24

PUBLISHER	PUB. #	TITLE	DATE	AUTHOR	COND.	TYPE	PRICE
HOURGLASS LIBRARY	1006	Psychedelia Sexualis	1969	Giles, J.H.	VGF		$8.00
HOWARD PUBLICATIONS	No#	I Hate You To Death	1944	Edgar, K.	G	Digest	$6.00
HUNTED	11	Hunted Det. Story 8/56	1956	Anthology	VGF	Digest	$22.00 A
HUNTED	11	Hunted Det. Story 8/56	1956	Anthology	G	Digest	$7.00
IDLE HOUR	IH 403	Fleshpot	1964	Hudson, D.	VGF		$8.00
IDLE HOUR	IH 417	The Sun Sinners	1964	Holliday, D.	VG+		$6.00
IDLE HOUR	IH 422	Roadhouse Wanton	1964	Hudson, D.	VG+		$6.00
IDLE HOUR	IH 433	Wanton Bait	1965	Dexter, J.	VGF		$7.00
IDLE HOUR	IH 451	Passion Pusher	1965	Elliott, D.*	AF		$9.00
IDLE HOUR	IH 459	Sin Cats	1965	Hudson, D.	VGF		$8.00
IDLE HOUR	IH 460	Man Hater	1965	Williams, J.X.	AF		$30.00 A
IDLE HOUR	IH 461	Members Of The Club	1965	Marshall, A.*	AF		$12.00
IDLE HOUR	IH 470	Alternate Wife	1965	Elliott, D.*	AF		$12.00
IDLE HOUR	IH 475	Sin Spin	1965	Elliott, D.*	AF		$8.00
IDLE HOUR	IH 480	The Lust Bosses	1966	Dexter, J.	AF		$7.00
IDLE HOUR	IH 488	The Panderer	1966	Dexter, J.	VGF		$7.00
IDLE HOUR	IH 490	The Playboy And The Prostitute	1966	Dexter, J.	AF		$7.00
IDLE HOUR	IH 495	Shame Chateau	1966	Dexter, J.	AF		$12.00 A
IDLE HOUR	IH 501	Campus Traders	1966	Elliott, D.*	F		$7.00
IDLE HOUR	IH 503	The Swingers	1966	Marshall, A.*	VGF		$8.00
IDLE HOUR	IH 506	The Virtous Ones	1966	Elliott, D.*	AF		$8.00
IDLE HOUR	IH 511	Sinsurance	1966	Colman, C.	AF		$7.00
IDLE HOUR	IH 513	Designing Dame	1966	Williams, J.X.	AF		$10.00 A
IDLE HOUR	IH 516	Dream Lover	1966	Hudson, D.	AF		$18.00 A
IDLE HOUR	IH 517	Fugitive Lover	1966	Shaw, A.*	AF		$9.00
IDLE HOUR	IH 519	The Nylon Jungle	1966	Calvano, T.	VG		$4.00
IDLE HOUR	IH 521	A Shower Of Sins	1966	Dexter, J.	VGF		$6.00
IF	1 5	If - 11/52	1952	Anthology	VG+	Digest	$6.00 A
IMAGINATION	5 7	Imagination - 7/54	1954	Anthology	VG+	Digest	$14.00 A
IMAGINATION	6 1	Imagination - 1/55	1955	Anthology	VG+	Digest	$8.00
IMAGINATIVE TALES	1 1	Imaginative Tales 9/54	1954	Anthology	AF	Digest	$12.00 A
IMAGINATIVE TALES	1 5	Imaginative Tales 5/55	1955	Anthology	AF	Digest	$12.00 A
IMAGINATIVE TALES	1 6	Imaginative Tales 7/55	1955	Anthology	VGF	Digest	$14.00
IMPACT LIBRARY	IL 348	The Gadget Lovers	1969	Romer, W.T.	AF		$6.00
IMPERIAL	710	Secret Lesbian Society	1965	Hanson, D.	AF		$10.00
IMPERIAL	716	Wanton Women	1965	Miles, R.	VG		$6.00
IMPERIAL	757	Party Girl Market	1966	Frank, W.F.	AF		$8.00
IMPERIAL	758	Sin Teacher	1966	Haunt, T.	F		$8.00
IMPERIAL	764	The Bronze Sinner	1966	Ryan, S.	F		$12.00
IMPERIAL	774	Sex Betrayal	1966	Haunt, T.	F		$10.00
IN BOOKS	218	All Woman	1967	Ellis, V.	VGF		$10.00
INFANTRY JOURNAL	No#	Our Enemy Japan	1944	Fleisher, W.	VG+		$7.00
INFANTRY JOURNAL	No#	Report On The Army	1943	Marshall, G.C.	VGF		$6.00
INFANTRY JOURNAL	No#	Sgt. T. Bull: Ideas On War	1943	Bull, T.	VG+		$7.00
INFANTRY JOURNAL	No#	The Fight At Pearl Harbor	1943	Clark, B.	VG+		$7.00

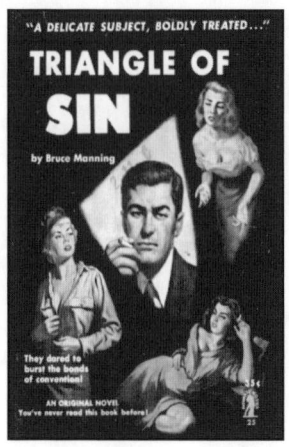

Intimate Novels 25 VGF $50   John Spencer No# VG $11   Justice 1-2 VGF- $44

PUBLISHER	PUB. #	TITLE	DATE	AUTHOR	COND.	TYPE	PRICE
INFANTRY JOURNAL	No#	The Lost Battalion	1943	Pratt, F.	VG+		$7.00
INFANTRY JOURNAL	No#	We Cannot Escape History	1944	Whitaker, J.T.	VG+		$6.00
INFANTRY JOURNAL	F 21	So You're Going Overseas!	1944	Barker, S.H.	AF		$10.00
INFANTRY JOURNAL	J 101	Boomerang	1945	Chambliss, W.C.	VGF		$8.00
INFANTRY JOURNAL	J 102	U.S. Marines On Iwo Jima	1945	Henri, R.	AF		$10.00
INFINITY	2 2	Infinity - 4/57	1957	Anthology	AF	Digest	$10.00
INFINITY	3 4	Infinity - 4/58	1958	Anthology	VG+	Digest	$7.00
INFINITY	3 6	Infinity - 8/58	1958	Anthology	AF	Digest	$5.00
INTERNATIONAL SCI-FI	1 1	International Sci-Fi 11/67	1967	Anthology	VGF	Digest	$9.00 A
INTIMATE EDITION	701	Sweet Smell Of Lust	1962	Marmor, A.	VG		$7.00
INTIMATE EDITION	705	Sunset Strip Sex Agent	1962	Bolin, G.	VGF		$10.00 A
INTIMATE EDITION	708	I Was A Chain Gang Love Slave	1962	Denton, J.	AF		$17.00 A
INTIMATE EDITION	710	Call Me Casanova	1962	Jans, J.	AF		$5.00
INTIMATE EDITION	717	Strip Wench	1963	Cross, G.	VG		$5.00
INTIMATE NOVELS	1	Wayward Bride	1950	Gaillard, P.	AF	Digest	$27.00 A
INTIMATE NOVELS	3	Cheap Hotel	1950	Foster, G.	G	Digest	$3.00
INTIMATE NOVELS	8	Gin Wedding	1951	Lawrence, A.	VG+	Digest	$31.00 A
INTIMATE NOVELS	8	Gin Wedding	1951	Lawrence, A.	VGF	Digest	$22.00 A
INTIMATE NOVELS	8	Gin Wedding	1951	Lawrence, A.	VG+	Digest	$20.00 A
INTIMATE NOVELS	9	Temptress	1951	Brewster, E.	VG+	Digest	$10.00
INTIMATE NOVELS	11	Swamp Girl	1951	Lindsay, P.	VGF	Digest	$24.00 A
INTIMATE NOVELS	18	Hot Lips	1952	Hanley, J.	G	Digest	$4.00
INTIMATE NOVELS	20	Pleasure Alley	1952	Carter, R.	VG	Digest	$12.00
INTIMATE NOVELS	20	Pleasure Alley	1952	Carter, R.	G	Digest	$3.00
INTIMATE NOVELS	21	Doctor Randolph's Women	1952	Stone, T.	VG	Digest	$5.00 A
INTIMATE NOVELS	22	Office Wife	1952	Grant, R.	VG	Digest	$15.00
INTIMATE NOVELS	24	The Whipping Room	1952	Branch, F.	G+	Digest	$15.00
INTIMATE NOVELS	24	The Whipping Room	1952	Branch, F.	VG	Digest	$14.00
INTIMATE NOVELS	25	Triangle Of Sin	1952	Manning, B.	VGF	Digest	$50.00 A
INTIMATE NOVELS	26	Very Private Secretary	1952	Hanley, J.	VG	Digest	$10.00
INTIMATE NOVELS	30	Tent-Show Bride	1953	Hanley, J.	VG	Digest	$12.00
INTIMATE NOVELS	30	Tent-Show Bride	1953	Hanley, J.	G	Digest	$3.00
INTIMATE NOVELS	31	Naked Desire	1953	Nixon, H.L.	VG	Digest	$7.00
INTIMATE NOVELS	36	Waterfront Blonde	1953	Semple, G.	VG	Digest	$8.00
INTIMATE NOVELS	49	Strange Circle	1953	Sydney, G.	G	Digest	$4.00
INTIMATE NOVELS	56	Odd Girl	1954	Moore, H.R.	VG+	Digest	$15.00
INTRIGUE	1 1	Intrigue - 10/65	1965	Anthology	VGF-	Digest	$8.00
JACK LONDON'S	1 1	Jack London's Adventure 10/58	1958	Anthology	AF	Digest	$38.00
JADE	203	House Of Evil	1963	Corbin, G.	VG		$8.00
JEST	6 40	Jest - 9/58	1958	Anthology	VG	Digest	$7.00
JOHN SPENCER	No#	Worlds Of Fantasy #3	1950	Anthology	VG	Digest	$14.00 A
JOHN SPENCER	No#	Worlds Of Fantasy #8	1953	Anthology	VG-	Digest	$16.00 A
JOHN SPENCER	No#	Tales Of Tomorrow #3	1950	Anthology	VG	Digest	$12.00 A
JOHN SPENCER	No#	Futuristic Science Stories #3	1950	Anthology	VG+	Digest	$15.00 A
JOHN SPENCER	No#	Futuristic Science Stories #4	1951	Anthology	VG	Digest	$15.00 A

Keyhole Detective 2-1 AF $23   Killers Mystery 4 VG+ $47   Knickerbocker No# VG+ $10

PUBLISHER	PUB. #	TITLE	DATE	AUTHOR	COND.	TYPE	PRICE
JOHN SPENCER	No#	Wonders Of The Spaceways #1	1951	Anthology	VG	Digest	$11.00 A
JOHN SPENCER	WF 101	The Unpossessed	1978	Muller, J.E.	VGF		$7.00
JONATHAN PRESS	J 4	The Bowstring Murders	1943	Dickson, C.*	VG+	Digest	$4.00
JONATHAN PRESS	J 5	The French Powder Mystery	1943	Queen, E.	VG	Digest	$3.00
JONATHAN PRESS	J 6	Over My Dead Body	1943	Stout, R.	VG+	Digest	$4.00
JONATHAN PRESS	J 8	Maigret Sits It Out	1944	Simenon, G.	VG+	Digest	$6.00
JONATHAN PRESS	J 9	The Broken Vase	1944	Stout, R.	VGF	Digest	$7.00
JONATHAN PRESS	J 59	Woman In The Dark	1952	Hammett, D.	VG+	Digest	$35.00
JOVE	A 4036	Doc Phoenix (Weird Heroes #5)	1977	Wolfman, M.	VGF+		$6.00
JOVE	M 4257	Weird Heroes #8	1977	Anthology	VG+		$4.00
JOVE	V 4279	Fingers Of Death (Shadow #17)	1977	Grant, M.*	VG+		$8.00
JOVE	V 4280	Murder Trail (The Shadow #18)	1977	Grant, M.*	AF		$12.00
JOVE	V 4280	Murder Trail (The Shadow #18)	1977	Grant, M.*	VGF		$10.00
JOVE	V 4281	The Silent Death (The Shadow #19)	1978	Grant, M.*	AF		$20.00 A
JOVE	V 4284	Charg, Monster (The Shadow #20)	1977	Grant, M.*	AF		$10.00
JOVE	K 4861	The Outlanders	1979	Stevens, B.*	VG		$8.00
JOVE	M 4879	Lies	1979	Neely, R.	VG+		$6.00
JOVE	S 5433	The Bastard - Photostory	1980	Jakes, J.	VG+	TVTI	$6.00
JOVE	T 5584	Longarm #28	1981	Evans, T.*	AF		$7.00
JOVE	T 5592	Longarm #35	1981	Evans, T.*	AF		$10.00
JOVE	T 5592	Longarm #35	1981	Evans, T.*	VG		$6.00
JOVE	5600	Longarm #44	1982	Evans, T.*	VGF		$7.00
JOVE	5604	Longarm #48	1982	Evans, T.*	VGF		$7.00
JOVE	5621	Embrace The Wind	1982	Stevens, B.*	VG		$7.00
JOVE	5726	The Funhouse	1980	West, O.*	VGF		$7.00
JOVE	5726	The Funhouse (advance ed.)	1980	West, O.*	VGF		$145.00
JOVE	7413	Longarm #40 (3rd)	1983	Evans, T.*	VG		$5.00
JOVE	8039	Cambodian Hellhole	1985	Buchanan, J.*	VGF		$5.00
JOVE	8228	Hanoi Deathgrip	1985	Buchanan, J.*	VGF		$6.00
JOVE	8363	Mountain Massacre	1985	Buchanan, J.*	VG		$5.00
JOVE	9107	Saigon Slaughter	1987	Buchanan, J.*	VG+		$6.00
JOVE	10032	Desert Death Raid	1989	Buchanan, J.*	VGF		$5.00
JUSTICE	1 2	Justice - 7/55	1955	Anthology	VGF-	Digest	$44.00 A
JUSTICE	1 2	Justice - 7/55	1955	Anthology	VG	Digest	$20.00 A
JUSTICE	1 3	Justice - 10/55	1955	Anthology	G	Digest	$37.00 A
JUSTICE	2 1	Justice - 1/56	1956	Anthology	VG-	Digest	$15.00 A
KEEP WORTHY	4	12 World Famous Love Novels	1946	Anthology	G		$5.00
KEYHOLE	1 1	Keyhole Mystery - 4/60	1960	Anthology	AF	Digest	$34.00 A
KEYHOLE	1 2	Keyhole Mystery - 6/60	1960	Anthology	VGF	Digest	$26.00 A
KEYHOLE	1 3	Keyhole Mystery - 8/60	1960	Anthology	VGF+	Digest	$20.00 A
KEYHOLE	2 1	Keyhole Detective - 1/62	1962	Anthology	AF	Digest	$23.00 A
KEYHOLE	2 2	Keyhole Detective - 4/62	1962	Anthology	AF	Digest	$33.00 A
KEYHOLE	2 3	Keyhole Detective - 6/62	1962	Anthology	VGF	Digest	$33.00 A
KEYHOLE	2 4	Keyhole Detective - 9/62	1962	Anthology	AF	Digest	$27.00 A
KILLERS MYSTERY	2	Killers Mystery Story - 11/56	1956	Anthology	VG-	Digest	$17.00

Jove 4281 AF $20	Jove 5726 (adv.) VGF $145	Kozy 111 AF $17	Kozy 173 AF $8

PUBLISHER	PUB. #	TITLE	DATE	AUTHOR	COND.	TYPE	PRICE
KILLERS MYSTERY	4	Killers Mystery Story - 3/57	1957	Anthology	VG+	Digest	$47.00 A
KILLERS MYSTERY	4	Killers Mystery Story - 3/57	1957	Anthology	G	Digest	$7.00
KNICKERBOCKER	No#	A Little Sin	n/d	Carter, R.	F	Digest	$10.00
KNICKERBOCKER	No#	Army Widow	n/d	Saxon, J.	VGF	Digest	$15.00
KNICKERBOCKER	No#	Beautiful Body	1948	Williams, W.	VGF	Digest	$15.00
KNICKERBOCKER	No#	Blonde Peril	1947	Bennett, H.	VG+	Digest	$16.00
KNICKERBOCKER	No#	Blonde Peril	1947	Bennett, H.	VG	Digest	$6.00
KNICKERBOCKER	No#	Born to Sin	n/d	Gates, H.L.	VG+	Digest	$8.00
KNICKERBOCKER	No#	Born To Sin	n/d	Gates, H.L.	VG+	Digest	$8.00
KNICKERBOCKER	No#	Dangerous Loves	n/d	James, G.	VG+	Digest	$10.00 A
KNICKERBOCKER	No#	Her Day Of Sin	n/d	Keller, H.A.	VGF	Digest	$22.00 A
KNICKERBOCKER	No#	Illicit Passion	n/d	Gay, C.	VG+	Digest	$8.00
KNICKERBOCKER	No#	Immoral Woman	n/d	Strong, C.S.	AF	Digest	$8.00 A
KNICKERBOCKER	No#	Love At A Price	n/d	Norcross, R.	G	Digest	$7.00
KNICKERBOCKER	No#	Made For Love	n/d	Jordan, G.	VGF	Digest	$12.00 A
KNICKERBOCKER	No#	Pick-Up Girl	n/d	Branch, F.	VG+	Digest	$8.00
KNICKERBOCKER	No#	The Playboy's Handbook	1946	Anthology	VG	Digest	$24.00 A
KNICKERBOCKER	No#	Pleasure Girl	n/d	Saxon, J.	VG+	Digest	$8.00
KNICKERBOCKER	No#	Pleasure Girl	n/d	Saxon, J.	VG	Digest	$7.00
KNICKERBOCKER	No#	Shameless Woman	n/d	Lindsay, P.	G	Digest	$4.00
KNICKERBOCKER	No#	Studio Lovers	n/d	Jacquin, L.	AF	Digest	$24.00
KNICKERBOCKER	No#	Unfaithful	n/d	Branch, F.	AF-	Digest	$12.00 A
KNICKERBOCKER	No#	Wayward Girl	n/d	Baker, C.	VG+	Digest	$7.00
KNICKERBOCKER	No#	The Wife And The Wolf	n/d	Jacquin, L.	VG+	Digest	$8.00
KOZY	K 90	Burlesque Jungle	1957	Boyer, P.	VG+		$17.00 A
KOZY	K 93	Fallen Virtues	1959	Brown, M.	AF		$17.00 A
KOZY	K 105	Too Many Loves	1960	Thomas, E.	AF		$7.00
KOZY	K 111	Split-Level Love	1960	Snavely, A.	AF		$17.00 A
KOZY	K 116	Temptress	1960	St. John, M.	VGF		$12.00
KOZY	K 124	Bait	1961	Snavely, A.	VGF		$11.00 A
KOZY	K 134	Twisted Lovers	1961	Hitt, O.	VG+		$8.00
KOZY	K 142	Pleasure Ground	1961	Hitt, O.	F		$17.00 A
KOZY	K 145	Wild Lovers	1961	Hitt, O.	AF		$11.00 A
KOZY	K 146	Man For Hire	1962	Harley, M.	VG+		$5.00
KOZY	K 148	The Girl With The Golden G-String	1962	Berkey, B.	VG+		$15.00 A
KOZY	K 151	Bold Affair	1962	Hitt, O.	VGF+		$14.00 A
KOZY	K 152	Campus Tramp	1962	Hitt, O.	VGF		$14.00 A
KOZY	K 154	Water Witch	1962	Morton, B.	AF		$16.00 A
KOZY	K 155	The Trouble With Redheads	1962	Mayo, D.	VGF		$7.00
KOZY	K 156	No Hope Of Heaven	1962	Evans, G.	VGF		$7.00
KOZY	K 157	I Was A $100 A Night Call Girl	1962	Carter, A.	AF		$16.00 A
KOZY	K 158	Kiss Or Kill	1962	Thompson, J.B.	VGF		$13.00 A
KOZY	K 160	Wine, Women And Love	1962	Snavely, A.	VGF		$8.00
KOZY	K 161	Madame	1962	Berkey, B.	AF		$16.00 A
KOZY	K 168	Virgins Of Veldt	1962	Thompson, B.	AF		$8.00
KOZY	K 170	Moments Of Passion	1962	Anderton, B.	VGF		$8.00
KOZY	K 172	Bed And Board	1962	Ward, J.	VGF		$18.00 A
KOZY	K 173	Casting Couch	1962	Thompson, J.B.	AF		$8.00

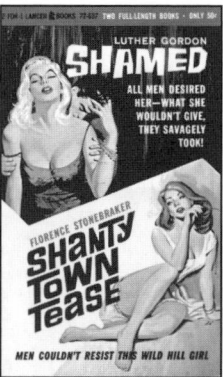

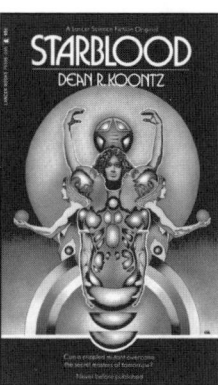

Lancer 70-052 VG- $7	Lancer 72-637 VG+ $10	Lancer 75-294 VG $12	Lancer 75-306 AF $20

PUBLISHER	PUB. #	TITLE	DATE	AUTHOR	COND.	TYPE	PRICE
KOZY	K 179	Blondes Don't Give A Damn	1963	Skinner, M.	VG+		$6.00
KOZY	K 181	Love Drive	1963	Snavely, A.	AF		$12.00 A
KOZY	K 182	Nude Doll	1963	Hitt, O.	F		$21.00 A
KOZY	K 182	Nude Doll	1963	Hitt, O.	F		$18.00
KOZY	K 183	The Girl Who Invented Sex	1963	Bell, A.	F		$16.00 A
KOZY	K 185	Love, Blood And Tears	1963	Weaver, N.*	F		$27.00 A
KOZY	K 185	Love, Blood And Tears	1963	Weaver, N.*	AF		$24.00 A
KOZY	K 186	Love On The Rocks	1963	Tod, N.	AF		$18.00 A
KOZY	K 187	Wild Cat	1963	Burke, J.	AF		$8.00
KOZY	K 188	Love Or Kill Them All	1963	Weaver, N.*	F		$26.00 A
KOZY	K 188	Love Or Kill Them All	1963	Weaver, N.*	AF		$20.00
KOZY	K 189	Name Your Vice	1963	Spain, N.	AF		$22.00 A
LANCER	70 6	Ben Casey	1962	Johnston, W.	VG+	TVTI	$7.00
LANCER	70 7	Dr. Kildare's Secret Romance	1962	Daniels, N.	VG	TVTI	$7.00
LANCER	70 10	My Body	1962	Dietrich, R.*	VG		$6.00
LANCER	70 11	Ben Casey	1962	Daniels, N.	VG	TVTI	$7.00
LANCER	70 13	Frenzy	1962	Craig, J.	AF		$30.00
LANCER	70 34	The Raven	1963	Sudak, E.	VG	MTI	$5.00
LANCER	70 37	The Strength Of His Hands	1963	Elkin, S.	VG+	TVTI	$6.00
LANCER	70 43	Dr. Kildare -The Heart Has Wings	1963	Johnston, W.	VG+	TVTI	$7.00
LANCER	70 49	Dr. Kildare	1963	Johnston, W.	G+	TVTI	$5.00
LANCER	70 51	High Saddle	1963	Hopson, W.	VGF		$5.00
LANCER	70 52	X	1963	Sudak, E.	VG-	MTI	$7.00
LANCER	70 56	Ramrod	1963	Coburn, W.	VGF	DBL	$3.00
		Sons Of Gunfighters		Coburn, W.			
LANCER	70 63	Gun Grudge	1963	Coburn, W.	AF		$4.00
LANCER	71 313	Premature Burial	1962	Danne, M.H.	VGF	MTI	$27.00 A
LANCER	71 313	Premature Burial	1962	Danne, M.H.	G+	MTI	$7.00
LANCER	71 319	Hitler	1962	Sheridan, M.	AF	MTI	$7.00
LANCER	71 325	Poe's Tales Of Terror	1962	Matheson, R.	G	MTI	$6.00
LANCER	72 120	The Navy At Guadalcanal	1966	Smith, S.	VGF		$3.00
LANCER	72 128	The House Next Door	1966	White, L.	AF		$8.00
LANCER	72 155	The Secret People	1967	Harris, J.B.	VGF		$6.00
LANCER	72 167	To London With Love	1967	Lawrence, S.	VG		$5.00
LANCER	72 171	The Mods	1967	Lawrence, S.	VG		$6.00
LANCER	72 173	The Man Who Tamed Dodge	1967	Ketchum, P.	VGF		$4.00
LANCER	607	The Big Love	1961	Thomey, T.	AF		$24.00 A
LANCER	607	The Big Love	1961	Thomey, T.	AF		$20.00
LANCER	72 615	Diary Of A Nymph	1961	Shiff, N.A.	VGF		$6.00
LANCER	72 629	Naked Canvas	1962	Arnold, W.	VGF	DBL	$12.00
		French Maid		Cooper, M.			
LANCER	72 631	Backwoods Shack	1962	Whittington, H.	G-	DBL	$7.00
		Spotlight On Sin		Duperrault, D.			
LANCER	72 633	Who Has Wilma Lathrop?	1962	Keene, D.	VG+	DBL	$24.00 A
		Murder On The Side		Keene, D.			
LANCER	72 633	Who Has Wilma Lathrop?	1962	Keene, D.	VG+	DBL	$11.00 A
LANCER	72 633	Who Has Wilma Lathrop?	1962	Keene, D.	VG	DBL	$10.00
LANCER	72 633	Who Has Wilma Lathrop?	1962	Keene, D.	G	DBL	$4.00

Lancer 75-365 VG $88   Lancer 75-386 VGF+ $49   Lancer 75-393 AF- $65   Lancer 75-445 VG+ $15

PUBLISHER	PUB. #	TITLE	DATE	AUTHOR	COND.	TYPE	PRICE
LANCER	72 637	Shamed	1962	Gordon, L.	VG+	DBL	$10.00
		Shanty Town Tease		*Stonebraker, F.*			
LANCER	72 639	Hollywood Tragedy	1962	Carr, W.A.	VGF		$9.00
LANCER	72 656	Terror By Night	1963	Hurwood, B.J.	VGF+		$7.00
LANCER	72 725	The Masque Of The Red Death	1964	Poe, E.A.	VG-	MTI	$7.00
LANCER	72 732	The Beatle Book	1964	Anonymous	VG+		$5.00
LANCER	72 740	Golden Blood	1964	Williamson, J.	AF		$6.00
LANCER	72 745	Sex And The Secretary	1964	Sprague, W.D.	VG		$7.00
LANCER	72 769	The Kept Man	1964	Brown, W.	VGF		$6.00
LANCER	72 918	The Man From O.R.G.Y.	1965	Mark, T.	AF		$11.00 A
LANCER	72 935	Experiment In Crime	1965	Wylie, P.	AF		$6.00
LANCER	72 959	Last Of The Conquerors	1965	Smith, W.G.	VGF		$5.00
LANCER	73 409	Nelson Algren's Book Of Monsters	1962	Anthology	VGF		$8.00
LANCER	73 409	Nelson Algren's Book Of Monsters	1962	Anthology	VG+		$6.00
LANCER	73 425	The Colour Out Of Space	1964	Lovecraft, H.P.	AF		$14.00
LANCER	73 440	Sexual Rebellion In The 60s	1965	Sprague, W.D.	VGF		$11.00 A
LANCER	73 446	The Girl From Pussycat	1965	Mark, T.	VG+		$10.00
LANCER	73 461	Pussycat, Pussycat! (2nd)	1966	Mark, T.	VG+		$7.00
LANCER	73 485	My Son, The Double Agent	1966	Mark, T.	AF		$7.00
LANCER	73 490	The Real Gone Girls	1968	Mark, T.	VGF		$5.00
LANCER	73 500	Ian Fleming: The Fantastic 007 Man	1966	Gant, R.	VG+		$9.00
LANCER	73 500	Ian Fleming: The Fantastic 007 Man	1966	Gant, R.	VG		$6.00
LANCER	73 510	The Bold Saboteurs	1966	Brossard, C.	F		$12.00 A
LANCER	73 544	But The Doctor Died	1967	Rice, C.	AF		$7.00
LANCER	73 550	The Girls From Planet 5	1967	Wilson, R.	VG+		$6.00
LANCER	73 573	Slaves Of Sleep	1967	Hubbard, L.R.	VGF+		$14.00
LANCER	73 583	The Gaunt Woman	1967	Blackburn, J.	F		$5.00
LANCER	73 607	Gorgonzola, Please Come Home	1967	Ames, C.*	VG+		$8.00
LANCER	73 607	Gorgonzola, Please Come Home	1967	Ames, C.*	VG		$7.00
LANCER	73 620	Circle Of Sin	1967	Mark, T.	VG+		$6.00
LANCER	73 627	Death Of A Pornographer	1967	Lejeune, A.	G+		$5.00
LANCER	73 629	In Black And Whitey	1967	Lacy, E.	VGF		$9.00 A
LANCER	73 684	Bonnie And Clyde	1968	Hirschfeld, B.	VGF	MTI	$7.00
LANCER	73 759	Sock It To Me Zombie	1968	Paul, F.W.	VGF		$5.00
LANCER	73 826	Bang The Doll Slowly	1969	Ames, C.*	VG		$8.00
LANCER	73 876	Nanny And The Professor	1970	Johnston, W.	VG+	TVTI	$6.00
LANCER	74 531	The Planned Parenthood Caper	1969	Paul, F.W.	VGF		$5.00
LANCER	74 600	The Long Loud Silence	1969	Tucker, W.	F		$5.00
LANCER	74 621	The Dark Symphony	1970	Koontz, D.R.	VG+		$16.00
LANCER	74 656	Hell's Gate	1970	Koontz, D.R.	VG+		$18.00 A
LANCER	74 656	Hell's Gate	1970	Koontz, D.R.	G+		$8.00
LANCER	74 813	The Sexual Deviate	1963	Morse, B.*	VG+		$14.00 A
LANCER	74 831	From Torment To Rapture	1964	Sharon, S.	AF		$11.00 A
LANCER	74 839	Lady Sings The Blues	1965	Holiday, B.	AF-		$5.00
LANCER	74 887	Upbeat	1967	Shulman, I.	VGF		$5.00
LANCER	74 897	The Kept Woman	1967	Brown, W.	VGF		$7.00
LANCER	75 108	Infinity One	1970	Anthology	VG		$14.00
LANCER	75 156	Up Your Banners	1970	Westlake, D.E.	VGF		$8.00

| Laser 9 VGF $15 | Laser 57 VG $20 | Leisure Book 1179 AF $53 | Leisure Books 3 VG $8 |

PUBLISHER	PUB. #	TITLE	DATE	AUTHOR	COND.	TYPE	PRICE
LANCER	75 173	Moving Through Here	1970	McNeill, D.	VGF		$7.00
LANCER	75 177	Alcindor And The Big O	1971	Devaney, J.	VG		$6.00
LANCER	75 247	The Dunwich Horror	1971	Lovecraft, H.P.	VGF		$6.00
LANCER	75 248	The Colour Out Of Space	1971	Lovecraft, H.P.	F		$8.00
LANCER	75 294	A Darker Heritage	1972	Cerra, G.A.	VG		$12.00
LANCER	75 294	A Darker Heritage	1972	Cerra, G.A.	G		$8.00
LANCER	75 298	Vida	1972	Deming, R.	VG+		$7.00
LANCER	75 306	Starblood	1972	Koontz, D.R.	AF		$20.00 A
LANCER	75 320	Infinity Three	1972	Anthology	VGF		$8.00
LANCER	75 365	Children Of The Storm	1972	Dwyer, D.*	VG		$88.00 A
LANCER	75 365	Children Of The Storm	1972	Dwyer, D.*	G		$66.00 A
LANCER	75 386	Warlock	1972	Koontz, D.R.	VGF+		$49.00 A
LANCER	75 386	Warlock	1972	Koontz, D.R.	VGF		$20.00
LANCER	75 393	The Dark Of Summer	1972	Dwyer, D.*	AF-		$65.00
LANCER	75 393	The Dark Of Summer	1972	Dwyer, D.*	G+		$12.00
LANCER	75 419	Shamus	1973	Beckerman, B.	VGF	MTI	$6.00
LANCER	75 445	The Haunted Earth	1973	Koontz, D.R.	VG+		$15.00
LANCER	75 445	The Haunted Earth	1973	Koontz, D.R.	VG		$15.00
LANCER	75 465	The Devil's Generation	1973	Anthology	AF		$7.00
LANCER	75 465	The Devil's Generation	1973	Anthology	VG		$7.00
LANCER	75 477	Infinity Five	1973	Anthology	VGF		$10.00
LANCER	78 704	The Fall Of New York	1971	Donis, M.	AF		$13.00 A
LANCER	78 704	The Fall Of New York	1971	Donis, M.	AF		$12.00
LANCER	78 746	Conan The Warrior	1971	Howard, R.E.	AF		$7.00
LANCER	33021	Case Histories From Communes	1972	Sprague, W.D.	VG		$4.00
LASER	3	Crash Landing On Iduna	1975	Tofte, A.	AF		$6.00
LASER	6	Serving In Time	1975	Eklund, G.	F		$6.00
LASER	7	Seeklight	1975	Jeter, K.W.	VG+		$5.00
LASER	8	Caravan	1975	Goldin, S.	F		$6.00
LASER	9	Invasion	1975	Wolfe, A.*	VGF		$15.00
LASER	9	Invasion	1975	Wolfe, A.*	VG		$8.00
LASER	11	Unto The Last Generation	1975	Coulson, J.	AF		$6.00
LASER	12	The King Of Eolim	1975	Jones, R.F.	F		$6.00
LASER	14	Birthright	1975	Sky, K.	AF		$6.00
LASER	19	The Unknown Shore	1976	Malcolm, D.	F		$6.00
LASER	28	The Skies Discrowned	1976	Powers, T.	VG		$6.00
LASER	29	The Iron Rain	1976	Malcolm, D.	F		$6.00
LASER	30	The Seeker	1976	Bischoff, D.	VGF		$4.00
LASER	36	Jeremy Case	1976	DeWeese, G.	F		$6.00
LASER	38	Ice Prison	1976	Sky, K.	AF		$6.00
LASER	45	Finish Line	1976	Goldin, S.	F		$4.00
LASER	47	Epitaph In Rust	1976	Powers, T.	VGF		$7.00
LASER	51	Mindwipe!	1976	Hahn, S.	VGF		$5.00
LASER	52	The Extraterritorial	1977	Morressy, J.	AF		$6.00
LASER	53	The Ecolog	1977	Nelson, R.F.	VGF		$7.00
LASER	54	The River And The Dream	1977	Jones, R.F.	AF		$8.00
LASER	55	Shepard	1977	Holly, J.H.	VG		$20.00
LASER	56	Gift Of The Manti	1977	Bone, J.F.	VG		$20.00

Leisure Book 613 AF $17   Leisure Library 2 VGF $40   Leisure Library 10 VGF $21

PUBLISHER	PUB. #	TITLE	DATE	AUTHOR	COND.	TYPE	PRICE
LASER	56	Gift Of The Manti	1977	Bone, J.F.	VG+		$17.00
LASER	57	Shadow On The Stars	1977	Marcus, R.B.	VG		$20.00
LATE HOUR	LL 703	Teach Me To Love	1967	Williams, J.X.	AF		$7.00
LATE HOUR	LL 712	Fishers Of Flesh	1967	Shaw, A.*	AF		$10.00
LATE HOUR	LL 714	Passion Bash	1967	Holliday, D.	AF		$8.00
LATE HOUR	LL 724	Lusty Lane	1967	Dexter, J.	AF		$9.00
LATE HOUR	LL 725	Sin-Town South	1967	Dexter, J.	AF		$8.00
LATE HOUR	LL 754	Sin Ship Skipper	1968	Marshall, A.*	VG+		$7.00 A
LATE HOUR	LL 842	Holly's Harem	1969	Carlin, G.	VGF		$27.00 A
LATE LATE BOOK	LL 202	The Professor's Wife	1966	Harding, M.	F		$7.00 A
LAUGH BOOK	6 7	Laugh Book - 2/51	1951	Anthology	VGF	Digest	$6.00
LAUGH DIGEST	56	Laugh Digest - 6/60	1960	Anthology	VG	Digest	$6.00
LAUGH DIGEST	62	Laugh Digest - 6/64	1964	Anthology	VGF	Digest	$4.00
LEISURE BOOK	LB 603	Passion Madman	1963	Shole, A.	VGF		$7.00
LEISURE BOOK	LB 611	Lust Bums	1963	Elliott, D.*	VGF		$9.00
LEISURE BOOK	LB 613	Sin Alley	1963	Shaw, A.*	AF		$17.00 A
LEISURE BOOK	LB 619	Sin Ring	1963	Dexter, J.	VG+		$7.00
LEISURE BOOK	LB 621	The Sinner	1964	Shaw, A.*	VGF+		$9.00 A
LEISURE BOOK	LB 622	Lust Tramp	1964	Dexter, J.	VGF		$7.00
LEISURE BOOK	LB 623	Passion Pair	1964	Elliott, D.*	VG+		$7.00
LEISURE BOOK	LB 631	The Flesh Seekers	1964	Elliott, D.*	AF		$9.00
LEISURE BOOK	LB 633	Sin Service	1964	Elliott, D.*	VG+		$7.00
LEISURE BOOK	LB 637	By Lust Repossessed	1964	Holliday, D.	VG+		$5.00
LEISURE BOOK	LB 638	Prowl Girls	1964	Dexter, J.	VG		$5.00
LEISURE BOOK	LB 643	Wanton D.O.A.	1964	Shay, A.	VGF		$8.00
LEISURE BOOK	LB 657	Sin Warped	1964	Elliott, D.*	VGF		$8.00
LEISURE BOOK	LB 664	Passion Poison	1964	Dexter, J.	VGF		$7.00
LEISURE BOOK	LB 665	Sin Gun	1964	Williams, J.X.	VGF		$7.00
LEISURE BOOK	LB 667	Sex Charter	1964	Dexter, J.	VGF		$6.00
LEISURE BOOK	LB 681	The Romans	1965	Holliday, D.	VG+		$10.00
LEISURE BOOK	LB 682	The Thrill Seekers	1965	Marshall, A.*	AF		$24.00
LEISURE BOOK	LB 684	Sing A Song Of Sin	1965	Aldrich, C.	AF		$12.00
LEISURE BOOK	LB 687	Quest For Ecstasy	1965	Hudson, D.	AF		$12.00
LEISURE BOOK	LB 688	Penthouse Players	1965	Shaw, A.*	VGF		$13.00 A
LEISURE BOOK	LB 1102	Nude In A Mink Raincoat	1965	Williams, J.X.	AF		$14.00 A
LEISURE BOOK	LB 1103	The Wedding Affair	1965	Dexter, J.	VGF		$15.00 A
LEISURE BOOK	LB 1105	Passion Hangover	1965	Williams, J.X.	VGF		$8.00
LEISURE BOOK	LB 1107	Hasbeen	1965	Hudson, D.	AF		$8.00
LEISURE BOOK	LB 1109	Million Dollar Minx	1965	Belimore, D.	F		$33.00 A
LEISURE BOOK	LB 1112	Bedtime Standin	1965	Aldrich, C.	AF		$13.00 A
LEISURE BOOK	LB 1126	Every Bed Her Own	1966	Elliott, D.*	AF		$30.00 A
LEISURE BOOK	LB 1131	Boudoir Decoy	1966	Dexter, J.	VG+		$14.00 A
LEISURE BOOK	LB 1132	Sinners Shroud	1966	Hudson, D.	VGF		$28.00 A
LEISURE BOOK	LB 1133	Six Months To Love	1966	Allison, C.	VGF		$35.00
LEISURE BOOK	LB 1133	Six Months To Love	1966	Allison, C.	AF		$27.00 A

Lev Gleason 103 AF $21   Lev Gleason 106 AF $27   Lion 23 VG $33

PUBLISHER	PUB. #	TITLE	DATE	AUTHOR	COND.	TYPE	PRICE
LEISURE BOOK	LB 1133	Six Months To Love	1966	Allison, C.	VGF		$20.00 A
LEISURE BOOK	LB 1134	Fraternity Of Shame	1966	Shaw, A.*	VG+		$45.00 A
LEISURE BOOK	LB 1141	The Trysting Place	1966	Kane, W.	VGF		$8.00
LEISURE BOOK	LB 1159	The Merciless Mermaid	1966	Allison, C.	G		$25.00
LEISURE BOOK	LB 1163	The Taste Of Desire	1966	Colman, C.	VGF		$8.00
LEISURE BOOK	LB 1170	Busy Bodies	1966	Hudson, D.	VGF		$41.00 A
LEISURE BOOK	LB 1170	Busy Bodies	1966	Hudson, D.	VG-		$13.00
LEISURE BOOK	LB 1176	Roburta The Conqueress	1966	Allison, C.	VG		$35.00 A
LEISURE BOOK	LB 1178	Anytime Amy	1966	Dexter, J.	F		$55.00 A
LEISURE BOOK	LB 1179	Sinners After Six	1966	Colman, C.	AF		$53.00 A
LEISURE BOOK	LB 1180	From Rapture With Love	1966	Allison, C.	VG		$77.00 A
LEISURE BOOK	LB 1185	The Lust Shop	1967	Aldrich, C.	AF		$21.00 A
LEISURE BOOK	LB 1188	The Flesh Adjuster	1967	Holliday, D.	F		$25.00 A
LEISURE BOOK	LB 1189	Turnabout Tarts	1967	Dexter, J.	AF		$18.00 A
LEISURE BOOK	LB 1189	Turnabout Tarts	1967	Dexter, J.	VG+		$12.00
LEISURE BOOK	LB 1190	The Wheel Of Sin	1967	Williams, J.X.	AF		$15.00 A
LEISURE BOOK	LB 1192	Sextus	1967	Hudson, D.	AF		$16.00 A
LEISURE BOOK	LB 1193	Eyes Of Lust	1967	Calvano, T.	AF		$14.00 A
LEISURE BOOK	LB 1210	A Blaze Of Passion	1967	Williams, J.X.	VG		$15.00
LEISURE BOOKS	LB 3	Final Blackout	1970	Hubbard, L.R.	VG		$8.00
LEISURE BOOKS	LB 40	Angela	1971	Professor, The	VGF		$8.00
LEISURE BOOKS	LB 112	Tong In Cheek	1972	Chase, G.	AF		$7.00
LEISURE BOOKS	LB 119	Up Your Ante	1973	Chase, G.	VG		$4.00
LEISURE BOOKS	LB 138	Chuck You, Farley!	1973	Chase, G.	VGF		$7.00
LEISURE BOOKS	LB 149	The Sky's The Limit	1973	Keel, C.	VGF		$6.00
LEISURE BOOKS	LB 165	Broad Jump	1974	Chase, G.	VG+		$7.00
LEISURE BOOKS	LB 167	Silverfinger	1973	Chase, G.	VGF		$10.00
LEISURE BOOKS	LB 203	Shannon #1	1974	Quinn, J.	AF		$6.00
LEISURE BOOKS	LB 214	Busted	1974	Chase, G.	VG+		$7.00
LEISURE BOOKS	LB 265	The Big Bankroll	1975	Chase, G.	VGF		$7.00
LEISURE BOOKS	LB 284	Kyrik Fights The Demon World	1975	Fox, G.F.	AF		$6.00
LEISURE BOOKS	LB 285	The Penultimate Truth	1975	Dick, P.K.	VGF		$7.00
LEISURE BOOKS	LB 293	Roman Candle	1975	Chase, G.	VGF		$7.00
LEISURE BOOKS	LB 333	Kyrik And The Wizard's Sword	1976	Fox, G.F.	AF		$6.00
LEISURE BOOKS	LB 398	The Bold Ones	1976	Fox, G.F.	VG		$7.00
LEISURE BOOKS	LB 462	Greek Fire	1977	Chase, G.	VGF		$7.00
LEISURE BOOKS	LB 473	The Devil To Pay	1977	Chase, G.	VG		$7.00
LEISURE BOOKS	LB 476	Return Of Jack The Ripper	1977	Andrews, M.	VG+		$4.00
LEISURE BOOKS	LB 489	The Moorland Monster	1977	Chase, G.	VGF		$5.00
LEISURE LIBRARY	1	My Life Is My Own	1952	Morac, J.	VGF-	Digest	$17.00 A
LEISURE LIBRARY	2	Death For A Doll	1952	Morelli, S.	VGF	Digest	$40.00 A
LEISURE LIBRARY	4	Make Mine A Shroud	1952	Storme, M.	VGF	Digest	$11.00 A
LEISURE LIBRARY	5	Hot Dames On Cold Slabs	1952	Storme, M.	VGF-	Digest	$47.00 A
LEISURE LIBRARY	7	This Way For Hell	1952	Morelli, S.	VG+	Digest	$10.00
LEISURE LIBRARY	7	This Way For Hell	1952	Morelli, S.	VG-	Digest	$8.00

Lion 68 VGF $100   Lion 99 G- $99   Lion 120 G $35

PUBLISHER	PUB. #	TITLE	DATE	AUTHOR	COND.	TYPE	PRICE
LEISURE LIBRARY	8	White Slave Racket	1952	Vane, R.	VGF-	Digest	$15.00 A
LEISURE LIBRARY	10	Midnight Sinner	1952	Renin, P.	VGF	Digest	$21.00 A
LEISURE LIBRARY	12	Bertrand And The Blondes	1952	Morac, J.	VG	Digest	$15.00
LEISURE LIBRARY	16	Amourous Adventuress	1952	Vane, R.	VG	Digest	$10.00
LEISURE LIBRARY	19	A Corpse Spells Danger	1953	Storme, M.	VG	Digest	$15.00
LEISURE LIBRARY	22	Thou Shalt Not	1953	Renin, P.	G	Digest	$6.00
LEISURE LIFE	PL 511	The Killer From Queer Street	1966	Brullete, J.	VGF+		$7.00
LEISURE LIFE	PL 514	The Sex Rebels	1966	Nolan, J.	VGF		$5.00
LEV GLEASON	103	The Wench Is Willing	1949	James, G.	AF	Digest	$21.00 A
LEV GLEASON	106	Dishonorable Lady	1950	Lee, R.	AF	Digest	$27.00 A
LIBRARY OF CONGRESS	No#	Reading For Survival (Book Club)	1987	MacDonald, J.D.	AF		$17.00
LION	8	Hungry Men	1949	Anderson, E.	VG		$12.00
LION	8	Hungry Men	1949	Anderson, E.	G		$7.00
LION	9	Anniversary	1949	Lewisohn, L.	VG-		$6.00
LION	15	Soft Shoulders	1949	Shelley, P.	VG		$10.00
LION	16	The Devil's Daughter	1949	Marsh, P.	VG		$8.00
LION	16	The Devil's Daughter	1949	Marsh, P.	VG		$6.00
LION	18	Christ In Concrete	1950	Di Donato, P.	VG	MTI	$7.00
LION	19	He Ran All The Way	1950	Ross, S.	VG+		$12.00
LION	19	He Ran All The Way	1950	Ross, S.	VG		$7.00
LION	21	To Keep Or Kill	1950	Tucker, W.	G+		$6.00
LION	22	The French Touch	1950	Iams, J.	VGF		$8.00
LION	23	Baseball Stars Of 1950	1950	Anthology	VG		$33.00 A
LION	25	The Intimate Stranger	1950	Lynch, W.	VG+		$8.00
LION	29	Walk Hard - Talk Loud	1950	Zinberg, L.	VG		$10.00
LION	30	Indiscreet Confessions Of Nice Girl	1950	Anonymous	VG+		$10.00
LION	33	The Continental Touch	1950	Wechsberg, J.	VG		$6.00
LION	35	Man Tracks	1950	Foster, B.	G		$3.00
LION	36	The Road Through The Wall	1950	Jackson, S.	VG		$10.00
LION	36	The Road Through The Wall	1950	Jackson, S.	G		$5.00
LION	37	Guns On The Sante Fe	1950	Dawson, P.	G+		$4.00
LION	38	The Lustful Ape	1950	Gray, R.	G+		$5.00
LION	39	Brain Guy	1950	Appel, B.	VG		$7.00
LION	40	All Thy Conquests	1950	Hayes, A.	VG		$8.00
LION	41	The Big Night	1950	Ellin, S.	VG		$10.00
LION	42	Spring Riot	1950	Presson, J.	VG		$8.00
LION	43	Massacre	1950	Bellah, J.W.	G+		$6.00
LION	44	His Dead Wife	1950	Eastman, E.	VG		$10.00
LION	45	How Sleeps The Beast	1950	Tracy, D.	VG		$25.00 A
LION	46	A Slight Case Of Scandal	1950	Iams, J.	VG+		$8.00
LION	47	Trouble Follows Me	1950	Millar, K.	VG		$12.00
LION	47	Trouble Follows Me	1950	Millar, K.	G		$7.00
LION	49	All Quiet On Western Front	1950	Remarque, E.M.	G		$2.50
LION	52	No Letters For The Dead	1951	Wilhelm, G.	VG		$10.00
LION	53	Arena Of Love	1951	Eliat, H.	VG+		$18.00 A

Lion 133 VG- $38   Lion 149 VG+ $150   Lion 184 VG $82

PUBLISHER	PUB. #	TITLE	DATE	AUTHOR	COND.	TYPE	PRICE
LION	58	Art Colony	1951	Cuthbert, C.	VGF-		$16.00 A
LION	58	Art Colony	1951	Cuthbert, C.	VG+		$15.00
LION	59	Border Woman	1951	Mason, G.	VGF		$12.00
LION	59	Border Woman	1951	Mason, G.	VG+		$9.00
LION	59	Border Woman	1951	Mason, G.	VG		$8.00
LION	60	Murders In Silk	1951	Teagle, M.	VGF		$17.00
LION	60	Murders In Silk	1951	Teagle, M.	VG		$8.00
LION	61	Wolf Dog Range	1951	Watson, W.	VGF		$12.00
LION	62	Blondes Are Skin Deep	1951	Trimble, L.	VG+		$24.00 A
LION	62	Blondes Are Skin Deep	1951	Trimble, L.	VG		$10.00
LION	63	Cage Me A Peacock	1951	Langley, N.	VGF		$18.00 A
LION	63	Cage Me A Peacock	1951	Langley, N.	VG+		$8.00
LION	63	Cage Me A Peacock	1951	Langley, N.	VG+		$7.00
LION	64	The Savage	1951	Artzybasheff, M.	VG+		$6.00
LION	65	Killers Five	1951	Hopson, W.	VG+		$8.00
LION	66	The Ranch Cat	1951	Hopson, W.	VG		$12.00
LION	68	My Flesh Is Sweet	1951	Keene, D.	VGF		$100.00 A
LION	69	The Cheat	1951	Tracy, D.	VG		$8.00
LION	70	We Too Are Drifting	1951	Wilhelm, G.	VG		$25.00 A
LION	71	America's Cities Of Sin	1951	Sarlat, N.	VG		$10.00
LION	72	The Tigress	1951	Bogar, J.	VGF		$24.00 A
LION	73	Innocent Madame	1951	Browne, E.	VGF		$13.00 A
LION	74	Either Is Love	1952	Craigin, E.	VG		$14.00
LION	74	Either Is Love	1952	Craigin, E.	VG-		$12.00 A
LION	76	A Walk In The Sun	1952	Brown, H.	G+		$5.00
LION	77	The Lust Of Private Cooper	1952	Gordon, J.	VG-		$5.00
LION	79	My Gun, Her Body	1952	Bogar, J.	VG-		$8.00
LION	80	Third Ward, Newark	1952	Lucas, C.	VG		$14.00
LION	83	Bodies Are Dust	1952	Wolfson, P.J.	VG		$15.00
LION	84	Earth Woman	1952	Becker, E.J.	VG		$7.00
LION	85	Lie Down, Killer	1952	Prather, R.S.	G		$6.00
LION	88	The Missouri Maiden	1952	Harrison, C.W.	VG+		$8.00
LION	92	South Sea Tales	1952	London, J.	VG		$10.00
LION	93	The Big Feeling	1952	Karp, D.	VG		$12.00
LION	94	Lona	1952	Evans, J.*	G		$10.00
LION	95	Hell's Kitchen	1952	Appel, B.	G+		$8.00
LION	97	America's Cities Of Sin	1952	Anthology	VG		$8.00
LION	98	Prelude To A Certain Midnight	1952	Kersh, G.	VG+		$18.00
LION	99	The Killer Inside Me	1952	Thompson, J.	G-		$99.00 A
LION	101	Joy Street	1952	Cuthbert, C.	VG+		$8.00
LION	102	Bailey's Daughters	1952	De Meyer, J.	VGF		$73.00 A
LION	102	Bailey's Daughters	1952	De Meyer, J.	VG+		$18.00 A
LION	102	Bailey's Daughters	1952	De Meyer, J.	VG+		$10.00
LION	102	Bailey's Daughters	1952	De Meyer, J.	VG		$6.00
LION	104	Little Killer	1952	Paul, G.	VGF		$27.00 A

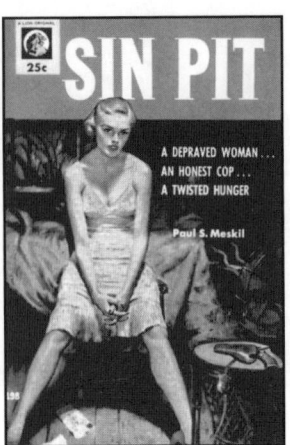
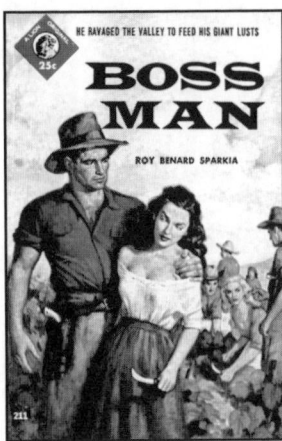

Lion 192 G $25   Lion 198 VGF $55   Lion 211 VG+ $9

PUBLISHER	PUB. #	TITLE	DATE	AUTHOR	COND.	TYPE	PRICE
LION	104	Little Killer	1952	Paul, G.	VG		$8.00
LION	104	Little Killer	1952	Paul, G.	VG-		$5.00
LION	105	The Brotherhood Of Velvet	1952	Karp, D.	VGF		$47.00 A
LION	105	The Brotherhood Of Velvet	1952	Karp, D.	VG		$23.00
LION	107	Candide	1952	Voltaire	VGF		$12.00
LION	111	Company K	1952	March, W.	VG+		$7.00
LION	112	The Man I Killed	1952	Walker, S.	VG+		$11.00 A
LION	112	The Man I Killed	1952	Walker, S.	VG		$10.00
LION	114	Luther	1952	Flannagan, R.	VG+		$18.00 A
LION	114	Luther	1952	Flannagan, R.	VG		$6.00
LION	115	Cora Potts	1952	Greene, W.	VG		$7.00
LION	118	The Haploids	1953	Sohl, J.	VG-		$10.00
LION	120	Recoil	1953	Thompson, J.	G		$35.00
LION	120	Recoil	1953	Thompson, J.	G		$24.00 A
LION	121	The Strange Path	1953	Wilhelm, G.	VG		$18.00
LION	122	Life, Death In Soviet Russia	1953	El Campesino	VGF		$8.00
LION	123	Don't Dig Deeper	1953	Francis, W.	VG		$8.00
LION	124	The Burglar	1953	Goodis, D.	G		$65.00
LION	125	Baseball Stars Of 1953	1953	Jacobs, B.	G		$10.00
LION	130	Sharp The Bugle Calls	1953	Frazee, S.	VG		$4.00
LION	131	Bourbon Street	1953	Otis, G.H.	VG		$10.00
LION	132	Cry, Flesh	1953	Karp, D.	VGF		$15.00 A
LION	132	Cry, Flesh	1953	Karp, D.	VG-		$10.00
LION	132	Cry, Flesh	1953	Karp, D.	VG-		$6.00
LION	133	The Dark Chase	1953	Goodis, D.	VG-		$38.00 A
LION	134	Colorado Creek	1953	Halleran, E.E.	VGF		$14.00
LION	139	Gunman's Grudge	1953	Appell, G.C.	VG+		$8.00
LION	140	Cockpit	1953	Scott, W.	VGF-		$12.00
LION	141	Rooming House	1953	Roueche, B.	VGF		$20.00 A
LION	144	A Tent On Corsica	1953	Quigley, M.	VG		$5.00
LION	147	The Wench And The Flame	1953	Trimnell, R.L.	VG+		$12.00
LION	148	Doomsday	1953	Scott, W.	VG		$15.00
LION	148	Doomsday	1953	Scott, W.	VG		$12.00
LION	149	Bad Boy	1953	Thompson, J.	VG+		$150.00 A
LION	149	Bad Boy	1953	Thompson, J.	VG+		$146.00 A
LION	149	Bad Boy	1953	Thompson, J.	G+		$44.00 A
LION	150	Lawman's Feud	1953	Frazee, S.	VG-		$5.00
LION	151	Slaughter Street	1953	Falstein, L.	VG+		$13.00 A
LION	151	Slaughter Street	1953	Falstein, L.	VG		$10.00
LION	152	A Rage At Sea	1953	Lorenz, F.	VG+		$12.00
LION	152	A Rage At Sea	1953	Lorenz, F.	VG		$6.00
LION	153	Tough Guy	1953	Bezzerides, A.I.	VG		$12.00
LION	154	Naked In The Dark	1953	Paul, G.	VGF+		$16.00 A
LION	154	Naked In The Dark	1953	Paul, G.	G+		$7.00
LION	155	Savage Night	1953	Thompson, J.	VG		$133.00 A

Lion 218 VGF+ $176   Lion 225 VG+ $22   Lion 231 VGF+ $33

PUBLISHER	PUB. #	TITLE	DATE	AUTHOR	COND.	TYPE	PRICE
LION	156	Hero's Lust	1953	Jaediker, K.	VG		$22.00 A
LION	159	Sin People	1953	Milburn, G.	VG		$10.00
LION	161	The Hoodlum	1953	Lipsky, E.	VG+		$22.00 A
LION	162	Angel	1953	Lucas, C.	VG		$10.00
LION	163	Gunsight	1953	Gruber, F.	VG+		$8.00
LION	165	The Big Lure	1953	Manners, W.	VG+		$12.00
LION	166	Dock Walloper	1953	Appel, B.	VG		$15.00
LION	166	Dock Walloper	1953	Appel, B.	VG		$12.00
LION	166	Dock Walloper	1953	Appel, B.	G+		$5.00
LION	169	The Gunslammer	1953	Floren, L.	VG+		$8.00
LION	170	Sailor's Luck	1953	Heatter, B.	VG		$8.00
LION	171	Hot Cargo	1953	Otis, G.H.	VG		$16.00
LION	172	Korea's Heroes	1953	Jacobs, B.	VG		$7.00
LION	173	The Dream And The Flesh	1953	Connell, V.	VG+		$8.00
LION	174	The Corrupters	1953	Francis, W.	VG		$8.00
LION	177	Men And Women	1953	Anthology	VG+		$8.00
LION	179	Conjure Wife	1953	Leiber, F.	VGF		$52.00 A
LION	179	Conjure Wife	1953	Leiber, F.	G		$7.00
LION	180	Fury On Sunday	1953	Matheson, R.	VGF		$440.00 A
LION	182	O'Mara	1953	Greene, L.	VGF		$13.00
LION	184	The Criminal	1953	Thompson, J.	VG		$82.00 A
LION	184	The Criminal	1953	Thompson, J.	VG		$50.00
LION	186	Blonde On The Street Corner	1954	Goodis, D.	G		$32.00
LION	188	The Naked Year	1954	Atlee, P.	VG+		$15.00
LION	189	Two Gun Texan	1954	Arthur, B.	VGF-		$5.00
LION	190	The Joy Wheel	1954	Fairman, P.W.	VG		$12.00
LION	191	Strange Desires	1954	Anthology	AF		$40.00 A
LION	191	Strange Desires	1954	Anthology	VGF		$14.00
LION	191	Strange Desires	1954	Anthology	VG+		$8.00
LION	192	The Golden Gizmo	1954	Thompson, J.	G		$25.00
LION	192	The Golden Gizmo	1954	Thompson, J.	G		$20.00
LION	193	Night Never Ends	1954	Lorenz, F.	AF		$25.00 A
LION	196	A Dog's Head	1954	Dutourd, J.	VG		$8.00
LION	197	The Naked Night	1954	Brennan, D.	VG+		$10.00
LION	198	Sin Pit	1954	Meskil, P.S.	VGF		$55.00 A
LION	198	Sin Pit	1954	Meskil, P.S.	G+		$8.00
LION	199	Ambush Hell	1954	Appell, G.C.	VG-		$4.00
LION	200	The Long Thrill	1954	Rosmanith, O.	VG+		$12.00
LION	200	The Long Thrill	1954	Rosmanith, O.	VG		$7.00
LION	202	Hoboes And Harlots	1954	Milburn, G.	VG+		$8.00
LION	202	Hoboes And Harlots	1954	Milburn, G.	G		$2.50
LION	205	Human?	1954	Anthology	VG+		$17.00
LION	205	Human?	1954	Anthology	VG		$12.00 A
LION	206	Alley Girl	1954	Craig, J.	VG		$8.00
LION	207	Tiger Street	1954	Trevor, E.	VG		$7.00

Lion Library 6 VGF $12   Lion Library 8 VGF $9   Lion Library 10 AF $15   Lion Library 97 VG+ $55

PUBLISHER	PUB. #	TITLE	DATE	AUTHOR	COND.	TYPE	PRICE
LION	209	A Way With Women	1954	Gwinn, W.	VG+		$12.00
LION	209	A Way With Women	1954	Gwinn, W.	VG		$8.00
LION	210	Joy House	1954	Keene, D.	G		$7.00
LION	211	Boss Man	1954	Sparkia, R.B.	VG+		$9.00 A
LION	214	Fully Dressed, In Right Mind	1954	Fessier, M.	VG+		$15.00
LION	215	Strange Sisters	1954	Flora, F.	VGF		$28.00
LION	217	The Gun-Throwers	1954	Frazee, S.	VGF		$12.00
LION	217	The Gun-Throwers	1954	Frazee, S.	VG		$8.00
LION	218	A Hell Of A Woman	1954	Thompson, J.	VGF+		$176.00 A
LION	221	The Naked & The Lost	1954	Davis, F.M.	VG+		$8.00
LION	222	Evil Roots	1954	Untermeyer, L.	G+		$6.00
LION	222	Evil Roots	1954	Untermeyer, L.	G		$6.00
LION	223	The Savage Chase	1954	Lorenz, F.	VG+		$6.00 A
LION	225	Jazz Bum	1954	Gwinn, W.	VG+		$22.00 A
LION	225	Jazz Bum	1954	Gwinn, W.	G+		$10.00
LION	226	Tina	1954	Bruce, R.	VG		$6.00
LION	228	Act Of Violence	1954	Heatter, B.	VGF		$20.00 A
LION	228	Act Of Violence	1954	Heatter, B.	VG		$6.00
LION	229	Champs And Bums	1954	Anthology	VGF		$13.00
LION	229	Champs And Bums	1954	Anthology	VGF		$10.00 A
LION	230	False Night	1954	Budrys, A.	AF		$41.00 A
LION	231	House Of Evil	1954	Lipman, C.	VGF+		$33.00 A
LION	231	House Of Evil	1954	Lipman, C.	VG		$8.00
LION	233	The Deluge	1954	Da Vinci, L.	VG		$8.00
LION	233	The Deluge	1955	Da Vinci, L.	VG-		$7.00
LION LIBRARY	LL 2	A Woman's Life	1954	De Maupassant, G.	VG+		$8.00
LION LIBRARY	LL 4	The Flesh Baron	1954	Wolfson, P.J.	AF-		$7.00
LION LIBRARY	LL 5	The Sin And The Flesh	1954	Thompson, L.S.	VGF		$9.00
LION LIBRARY	LL 6	The Damned (2nd)	1956	Anthology	VGF		$12.00
LION LIBRARY	LL 8	Gods And Demons	1954	Komroff, M.	VGF		$9.00
LION LIBRARY	LL 10	Escape To Nowhere	1955	Karp, D.	AF		$15.00 A
LION LIBRARY	LL 11	Dark Plunder	1955	Rosen, V.	VG		$7.00
LION LIBRARY	LL 13	Hell's Pavement	1955	Knight, D.	F		$24.00 A
LION LIBRARY	LL 13	Hell's Pavement	1955	Knight, D.	VG		$9.00
LION LIBRARY	LL 13	Hell's Pavement	1955	Knight, D.	VG		$6.00
LION LIBRARY	LL 15	The Unleashed Will	1955	Clark, C.	AF		$14.00
LION LIBRARY	LL 21	How I Made A Million	1955	Anthology	VG+		$7.00
LION LIBRARY	LL 24	For Stags Only	1955	Anthology	VGF+		$20.00
LION LIBRARY	LL 25	Galaxy Of Ghouls	1955	Anthology	AF		$25.00 A
LION LIBRARY	LL 31	Nineteen Stories	1955	Greene, G.	VGF		$10.00
LION LIBRARY	LL 33	The Storm And The Silence	1955	Walker, D.	VG+		$8.00
LION LIBRARY	LL 33	The Storm And The Silence	1955	Walker, D.	VG+		$7.00
LION LIBRARY	LL 35	The Fall Of Valor	1955	Jackson, C.	VG		$5.00
LION LIBRARY	LL 44	Desperate Asylum	1955	Flora, F.	VG-		$20.00 A
LION LIBRARY	LL 53	Great Tales Of City Dwellers	1955	Anthology	VG+		$7.00
LION LIBRARY	LL 53	Great Tales Of City Dwellers	1955	Anthology	VG+		$6.00
LION LIBRARY	LL 60	The Sins Of Joy Munson	1955	Lewisohn, L.	VG		$7.00
LION LIBRARY	LB 62	Company K	1955	March, W.	VG+		$7.00

Lion Books 131 AF $42   Lion Library 151 VGF $8   MacFadden 50-366 VG+ $6   MacFadden 60-371 F $27

PUBLISHER	PUB. #	TITLE	DATE	AUTHOR	COND.	TYPE	PRICE
LION LIBRARY	LL 64	Kill The Beloved	1956	Kauffmann, L.	VGF		$8.00
LION LIBRARY	LL 64	Kill The Beloved	1956	Kauffmann, L.	VG		$6.00
LION LIBRARY	LL 71	Cage Me A Peacock	1956	Langley, N.	AF		$22.00
LION LIBRARY	LL 73	A Handfull Of Hell	1956	Anthology	VGF		$8.00
LION LIBRARY	LB 78	Pistolman	1956	Frazee, S.	VG+		$8.00
LION LIBRARY	LL 83	Rogues And Lovers	1956	Anthology	AF		$12.00
LION LIBRARY	LL 87	The Brass Bed	1956	Flora, F.	F		$27.00 A
LION LIBRARY	LL 87	The Brass Bed	1956	Flora, F.	VG		$7.00
LION LIBRARY	LL 88	Great Tales Of The Far West	1956	Anthology	VG+		$5.00
LION LIBRARY	LL 89	The Gunslingers	1956	Anthology	AF		$15.00
LION LIBRARY	LL 89	The Gunslingers	1956	Anthology	AF		$12.00
LION LIBRARY	LL 96	Kiss Her Goodbye	1956	Miller, W.	G-		$2.50
LION LIBRARY	LL 97	Sorority House	1956	Park, J.*	VG+		$55.00 A
LION LIBRARY	LB 101	The Utah Kid	1956	Richmond, R.	VG+		$5.00
LION LIBRARY	LL 104	Ruby	1956	Lorenz, F.	VG+		$6.00
LION LIBRARY	LB 108	Lawman's Feud	1956	Frazee, S.	VG+		$7.00
LION LIBRARY	LL 111	Wives And Lovers	1956	Anthology	AF		$10.00
LION LIBRARY	LL 113	World So Wide	1956	Lewis, S.	AF		$8.00
LION LIBRARY	LB 117	The Lone Gunhawk	1956	Gruber, F.	AF		$10.00
LION LIBRARY	LB 117	The Lone Gunhawk	1956	Gruber, F.	AF		$8.00
LION LIBRARY	LB 129	You'll Get Yours	1956	Wills, T.	G+		$5.00
LION LIBRARY	LB 131	Nightfall	1956	Goodis, D.	AF	MTI	$42.00
LION LIBRARY	LB 131	Nightfall	1956	Goodis, D.	VG+	MTI	$24.00
LION LIBRARY	LB 131	Nightfall	1956	Goodis, D.	VG+	MTI	$20.00
LION LIBRARY	LB 131	Nightfall	1956	Goodis, D.	VG	MTI	$17.00 A
LION LIBRARY	LB 131	Nightfall	1956	Goodis, D.	G+	MTI	$15.00
LION LIBRARY	LL 134	Raft Of Despair	1956	Tiira, E.	VG+		$7.00
LION LIBRARY	LB 137	Killer's Game	1956	Hudiburg, E.	VG		$5.00
LION LIBRARY	LB 138	A Hell Of A Woman	1956	Thompson, J.	VG		$24.00
LION LIBRARY	LL 141	Women Without Men	1957	Anthology	VG-		$2.50
LION LIBRARY	LL 143	Thread Of Evil	1957	Jackson, C.	VGF		$8.00
LION LIBRARY	LB 144	Hot	1956	Lorenz, F.	VG		$8.00 A
LION LIBRARY	LB 145	.44	1956	DeRosso, H.A.	VG		$5.00
LION LIBRARY	LL 148	The Bedside Corpse	1957	Fiedman, S.	AF		$8.00
LION LIBRARY	LL 151	Brain Guy	1957	Appel, B.	VGF		$8.00 A
LION LIBRARY	LL 151	Brain Guy	1957	Appel, B.	VG+		$8.00
LION LIBRARY	LB 152	Dolls Are Murder	1957	Masur, H.Q.	VGF		$10.00
LION LIBRARY	LB 152	Dolls Are Murder	1957	Masur, H.Q.	VG+		$10.00
LION LIBRARY	LB 153	Valerie	1957	Park, J.*	VG		$5.00
LION LIBRARY	LL 160	Hoboes And Harlots	1957	Milburn, G.	AF		$8.00
LION LIBRARY	LL 161	Gunman's Grudge	1957	Appell, G.C.	AF		$8.00
LION LIBRARY	LB 165	A Rage At Sea	1957	Lorenz, F.	VG+		$6.00
LION LIBRARY	LL 168	The Bedside Bachelor	1957	Steiner, P.	VG		$7.00
LION LIBRARY	LL 170	The Red Lily	1957	France, A.	F		$8.00 A
LION LIBRARY	LB 172	Slaughter Street	1957	Falstein, L.	AF		$44.00 A
LITTLE BLUE BOOK	No#	Catalogue of 1092 titles	n/d		VG+		$6.00
LITTLE BLUE BOOK	No#	Catalogue of 500 titles	n/d		VG+		$7.00
LITTLE BLUE BOOK	No#	KKK	1924	Anthology	VG+		$6.00

Magazine Village 6 VGF $47   Magazine Village 7 VGF $20   Malcolm's 1-3 AF $13

PUBLISHER	PUB. #	TITLE	DATE	AUTHOR	COND.	TYPE	PRICE
LITTLE BLUE BOOK	143	In The Time Of Terror	n/d	Balzac, H.D.	VG+		$5.00
LITTLE BLUE BOOK	943	Masterpieces Of Mystery	n/d	Poe, E.A.	VG+		$6.00
LOVE BOOK MONTHLY*		* See Diversey Love Book					
LYNX	55802	Island Of Kings	1989	Stevens, B.*	G		$8.00
MACFADDEN	No#	New Unpublished True Stories	1954	Anthology	VGF	Digest	$8.00
MACFADDEN	50 127	Carnival Of Angels	1962	De Maria, R.	AF		$7.00
MACFADDEN	50 183	The Day Krushchev Panicked	1963	Mair, G.B.	VG		$6.00
MACFADDEN	50 200	Undercover Agent - Narcotics	1964	Agnew, D.	VGF		$7.00
MACFADDEN	50 203	Dead Man Control	1964	Reilly, H.	AF		$7.00
MACFADDEN	50 213	The Dead Don't Care	1964	Latimer, J.	AF		$10.00
MACFADDEN	50 213	The Dead Don't Care	1964	Latimer, J.	VGF		$8.00
MACFADDEN	50 219	All Concerned Notified	1964	Reilly, H.	AF		$5.00
MACFADDEN	50 271	Mrs Homicide	1966	Keene, D.	VG		$3.00
MACFADDEN	50 275	Departure Deferred	1966	Baker, W.H.	VG+	TVTI	$7.00
MACFADDEN	50 280	Hell For Tomorrow	1966	Leslie, P.	VG	TVTI	$7.00
MACFADDEN	50 328	Tokyo After Dark	1966	Fitzpatrick, W.	VGF		$5.00
MACFADDEN	50 330	I, The Hangman	1967	Ballinger, W.A.	AF		$8.00
MACFADDEN	50 350	The Witches Of Notting Hill	1967	Ballinger, W.A.	AF		$5.00
MACFADDEN	50 366	The Black Satin Jungle	1967	Frame, B.	VG+		$6.00
MACFADDEN	60 160	Women A-Z	1964	Romanaet, J.J.	AF		$6.00
MACFADDEN	60 191	A Man Called Paladin	1964	Robertson, F.G.	VG	TVTI	$6.00
MACFADDEN	60 235	Hong Kong After Dark (2nd)	1966	Fitzpatrick, W.	AF		$5.00
MACFADDEN	60 240	The 3 Stigmata Of P. Eldrich	1966	Dick, P.K.	VG		$10.00
MACFADDEN	60 246	The Saint Goes West	1966	Charteris, L.	AF		$7.00
MACFADDEN	60 259	London After Dark	1966	Nash, N.	VGF		$6.00
MACFADDEN	60 262	The Saint Intervenes	1966	Charteris, L.	VG+		$6.00
MACFADDEN	60 277	The Ant Men	1967	North, E.	VG		$7.00
MACFADDEN	60 284	Death Demands An Audience	1967	Reilly, H.	AF		$5.00
MACFADDEN	60 345	Visa To Death	1968	Lacy, E.	VGF		$7.00
MACFADDEN	60 353	Frenzy In The Flesh	1968	Reid, R.	AF		$5.00
MACFADDEN	60 365	Thanks To The Saint	1968	Charteris, L.	VGF		$6.00
MACFADDEN	60 368	The Brimstone Bed	1968	Keene, D.	VG		$3.00
MACFADDEN	60 371	Naked Lust	1969	Shepard, S.*	F		$27.00
MACFADDEN	60 375	Death Is My Shadow	1969	Aarons, E.S.	AF		$6.00
MACFADDEN	60 381	Star Crossed	1969	Mead, M.	VGF		$6.00
MACFADDEN	60 416	The Changeling	1969	Van Vogt, A.E.	VGF+		$6.00
MACFADDEN	60 424	The Big Kiss-Off	1969	Keene, D.	VGF		$7.00
MACFADDEN	75 141	Sex On Celluloid	1964	Milner, M.	AF		$7.00
MACFADDEN	75 193	The Train Ride	1968	Loughran, P.	F		$5.00
MACFADDEN	75 252	The Hypocritical American	1969	Collier, J.	VG		$6.00
MACFADDEN	75 254	The Story Of Mia	1969	Piccone, J.	VG+		$7.00
MACFADDEN	75 299	The Evil Friendship	1970	Packer, V.*	VG		$3.00
MACFADDEN	75 315	Cute And Deadly Surf Twins	1970	Morgan, P.	AF		$7.00
MACFADDEN	75 328	The Love Kick	1970	Nichols, F.	VG+		$7.00
MACFADDEN	75 369	Strange Witness	1970	Keene, D.	VG+		$4.00

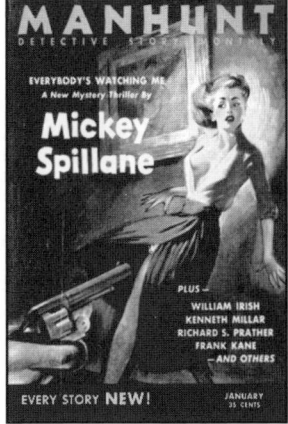

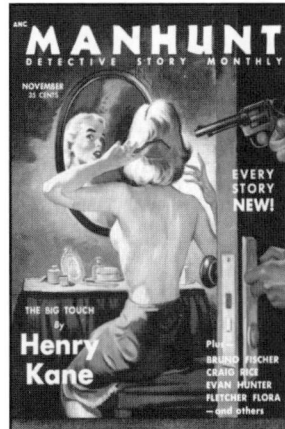

Man From UNCLE 2-2 VGF $10   Manhunt 1-1 VG+ $45   Manhunt 1-11 VG+ $34

PUBLISHER	PUB. #	TITLE	DATE	AUTHOR	COND.	TYPE	PRICE
MACFADDEN	75 399	3 Stigmata of P. Eldritch	1971	Dick, P.K.	VGF		$11.00
MACFADDEN	95 123	Sex On Celluloid	1969	Milner, M.	VG+		$5.00
MACKILL'S	2 4	MacKill's 7/53	1953	Anthology	VGF	Digest	$8.00 A
MACKILL'S	2 5	MacKill's 9/53	1953	Anthology	VG+	Digest	$26.00 A
MACKILL'S	3 4	MacKill's 2/54	1954	Anthology	VGF	Digest	$7.00
MACKILL'S	3 6	MacKill's 4/54	1954	Anthology	VGF	Digest	$8.00
MACKILL'S	4 1	MacKill's 5/54	1954	Anthology	AF	Digest	$7.00
MACKILL'S	4 1	MacKill's 5/54	1954	Anthology	VG+	Digest	$5.00
MAGAZINE VILLAGE	6	Illicit Honeymoon	1948	Bull, L.	VGF	Digest	$47.00 A
MAGAZINE VILLAGE	7	Hard Boiled Mistress	1948	Keating, E.T.	VGF	Digest	$20.00 A
MAGENTA	M 116	Silk Sheets	1965	North, K.	VG+		$7.00
MAGENTA	M 122	Party Girls	1966	Miller, R.	AF		$17.00 A
MAGNET	MB 301	Forbidden Magic	1959	Clark, D.	VG		$5.00
MAGNET	MB 302	Love-Starved Hellcat	1959	Ryan, M.	VG		$7.00 A
MAGNET	MB 305	Wild French Nurse	1959	Stonebraker, F.	VG+		$7.00
MAGNET	MB 311	The Golden Strip	1960	Andrews, P.	VG		$7.00
MAGNET	MB 314	The Hot Beat	1960	Vincent, S.	AF		$16.00 A
MAGNET	MB 315	Wild Cargo	1960	Barton, S.	AF		$9.00 A
MAGNUM	73 516	Hell's Brigade	1975	Anthology	VG+		$6.00
MAGNUM	75 309	Dance With the Devil	1975	Dwyer, D.*	VG+		$15.00
MAGNUM	74 783	Cannon	1975	Gallagher, R.	AF	TVTI	$6.00
MAJOR	3018	Seven Steps To The Arbiter	1975	Hubbard, L.R.	VGF		$10.00
MAJOR	3018	Seven Steps To The Arbiter	1975	Hubbard, L.R.	VG		$7.00
MALCOLM'S	1 1	Malcolm's 1/54	1954	Anthology	AF	Digest	$33.00
MALCOLM'S	1 3	Malcolm's 5/54	1954	Anthology	AF	Digest	$13.00 A
MALCOLM'S	1 3	Malcolm's 5/54	1954	Anthology	VG+	Digest	$7.00 A
MAN FROM UNCLE	1 3	Man From UNCLE Mag. 4/66	1966	Anthology	VGF+	Digest	$7.00
MAN FROM UNCLE	1 5	Man From UNCLE Mag. 6/66	1966	Anthology	VGF	Digest	$11.00 A
MAN FROM UNCLE	2 2	Man From UNCLE Mag. 9/66	1966	Anthology	VGF	Digest	$10.00
MAN FROM UNCLE	2 2	Man From UNCLE Mag. 9/66	1966	Anthology	VG	Digest	$7.00
MAN FROM UNCLE	3 3	Man From UNCLE Mag. 4/67	1967	Anthology	VGF	Digest	$7.00
MAN FROM UNCLE	3 4	Man From UNCLE Mag. 5/67	1967	Anthology	VGF	Digest	$8.00
MAN FROM UNCLE	4 2	Man From UNCLE Mag. 9/67	1967	Anthology	VG+	Digest	$7.00
MANHUNT	1 1	Manhunt 1/53	1953	Anthology	VG+	Digest	$45.00 A
MANHUNT	1 1	Manhunt 1/53	1953	Anthology	G	Digest	$8.00
MANHUNT	1 2	Manhunt 2/53	1953	Anthology	VG-	Digest	$8.00
MANHUNT	1 2	Manhunt 2/53	1953	Anthology	G-	Digest	$5.00
MANHUNT	1 3	Manhunt 3/53	1953	Anthology	G	Digest	$8.00
MANHUNT	1 4	Manhunt 4/53	1953	Anthology	VG+	Digest	$24.00 A
MANHUNT	1 5	Manhunt 5/53	1953	Anthology	VG	Digest	$41.00 A
MANHUNT	1 6	Manhunt 6/53	1953	Anthology	VG-	Digest	$8.00
MANHUNT	1 10	Manhunt 10/53	1953	Anthology	VG+	Digest	$55.00 A
MANHUNT	1 10	Manhunt 10/53	1953	Anthology	VG-	Digest	$14.00
MANHUNT	1 11	Manhunt 11/53	1953	Anthology	VG+	Digest	$34.00 A
MANHUNT	1 12	Manhunt 12/53	1953	Anthology	G	Digest	$8.00

| Manhunt 4-7 VGF- $100 | Manhunt 6-4 VGF+ $33 | Ed McBain's Mystery Book 1 VG $42 |

PUBLISHER	PUB. #	TITLE	DATE	AUTHOR	COND.	TYPE	PRICE
MANHUNT	2 2	Manhunt 2/54	1954	Anthology	G+	Digest	$5.00
MANHUNT	2 4	Manhunt 6/54	1954	Anthology	VG	Digest	$16.00
MANHUNT	2 5	Manhunt 7/54	1954	Anthology	VG-	Digest	$14.00
MANHUNT	2 7	Manhunt 9/54	1954	Anthology	VGF	Digest	$19.00 A
MANHUNT	2 7	Manhunt 9/54	1954	Anthology	G	Digest	$5.00
MANHUNT	2 8	Manhunt 10/54	1954	Anthology	G+	Digest	$12.00
MANHUNT	2 9	Manhunt 11/54	1954	Anthology	VG	Digest	$15.00
MANHUNT	2 10	Manhunt 12/54	1954	Anthology	G	Digest	$5.00
MANHUNT	2 11	Manhunt 12/25/54	1954	Anthology	VG+	Digest	$35.00 A
MANHUNT	3 3	Manhunt 3/55	1955	Anthology	VG	Digest	$25.00 A
MANHUNT	3 4	Manhunt 4/55	1955	Anthology	VG+	Digest	$14.00
MANHUNT	3 11	Manhunt 11/55	1955	Anthology	VG-	Digest	$17.00
MANHUNT	3 12	Manhunt 12/55	1955	Anthology	VG-	Digest	$15.00
MANHUNT	4 1	Manhunt 1/56	1956	Anthology	VG	Digest	$12.00
MANHUNT	4 2	Manhunt 2/56	1956	Anthology	VG+	Digest	$30.00 A
MANHUNT	4 2	Manhunt 2/56	1956	Anthology	G-	Digest	$5.00
MANHUNT	4 3	Manhunt 3/56	1956	Anthology	VG+	Digest	$15.00
MANHUNT	4 4	Manhunt 4/56	1956	Anthology	VG+	Digest	$33.00 A
MANHUNT	4 6	Manhunt 6/56	1956	Anthology	VG	Digest	$15.00
MANHUNT	4 7	Manhunt 7/56	1956	Anthology	VGF-	Digest	$100.00 A
MANHUNT	4 8	Manhunt 8/56	1956	Anthology	VGF	Digest	$16.00 A
MANHUNT	4 8	Manhunt 8/56	1956	Anthology	VG	Digest	$10.00
MANHUNT	4 9	Manhunt 9/56	1956	Anthology	VG	Digest	$7.00
MANHUNT	4 9	Manhunt 9/56	1956	Anthology	G	Digest	$5.00
MANHUNT	5 1	Manhunt 1/57	1957	Anthology	G+	Digest	$8.00
MANHUNT	5 6	Manhunt 6/57	1957	Anthology	G	Digest	$8.00
MANHUNT	6 4	Manhunt 6/58	1958	Anthology	VGF+	Digest	$33.00 A
MANHUNT	6 5	Manhunt 8/58	1958	Anthology	AF	Digest	$24.00 A
MANHUNT	6 5	Manhunt 8/58	1958	Anthology	VG	Digest	$11.00
MANHUNT	6 6	Manhunt 10/58	1958	Anthology	VGF+	Digest	$38.00 A
MANHUNT	6 6	Manhunt 10/58	1958	Anthology	VG	Digest	$10.00
MANHUNT	6 7	Manhunt 12/58	1958	Anthology	AF	Digest	$42.00 A
MANHUNT	7 1	Manhunt 2/59	1959	Anthology	AF-	Digest	$24.00 A
MANHUNT	7 1	Manhunt 2/59	1959	Anthology	VG	Digest	$10.00
MANHUNT	7 2	Manhunt 4/59	1959	Anthology	VGF+	Digest	$44.00 A
MANHUNT	7 3	Manhunt 6/59	1959	Anthology	AF	Digest	$15.00 A
MANHUNT	7 4	Manhunt 8/59	1959	Anthology	AF	Digest	$25.00 A
MANHUNT	7 4	Manhunt 8/59	1959	Anthology	VG	Digest	$7.00
MANHUNT	7 5	Manhunt 10/59	1959	Anthology	AF	Digest	$25.00 A
MANHUNT	7 6	Manhunt 12/59	1959	Anthology	AF	Digest	$20.00 A
MANHUNT	7 6	Manhunt 12/59	1959	Anthology	G	Digest	$5.00
MANHUNT	8 1	Manhunt 2/60	1960	Anthology	VG	Digest	$28.00 A
MANHUNT	8 1	Manhunt 2/60	1960	Anthology	VG-	Digest	$10.00
MANHUNT	8 2	Manhunt 4/60	1960	Anthology	VG	Digest	$10.00
MANHUNT	8 3	Manhunt 6/60	1960	Anthology	AF	Digest	$18.00 A

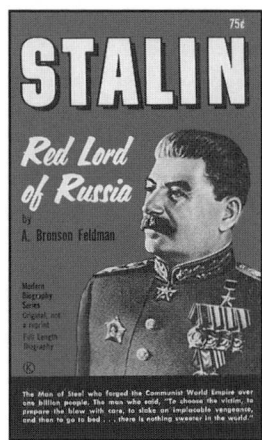

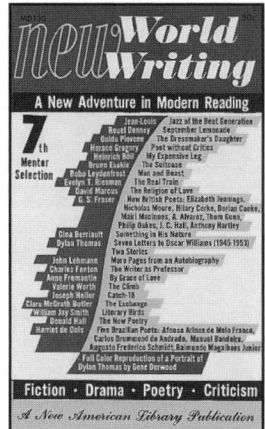

Mercury Books Inc. 102 VGF $30   Mercury Book 28 VG+ $6   Mentor MD 130 VGF $30

PUBLISHER	PUB. #	TITLE	DATE	AUTHOR	COND.	TYPE	PRICE
MANHUNT	8 5	Manhunt 10/60	1960	Anthology	VG	Digest	$12.00
MANHUNT	8 6	Manhunt 12/60	1960	Anthology	VG	Digest	$7.00
MANHUNT	12 6	Manhunt 11/64	1964	Anthology	AF	Digest	$10.00
MANHUNT	14 3	Manhunt - June-July 1966	1966	Anthology	AF	Digest	$10.00
MANHUNT	15 1	Manhunt - Feb-Mar. 1967	1967	Anthology	VG+	Digest	$12.00
MANHUNT	15 1	Manhunt - Feb-Mar. 1967	1967	Anthology	G	Digest	$5.00
MANHUNT	15 2	Manhunt - April-May 1967	1967	Anthology	VGF	Digest	$12.00
MANHUNT	15 2	Manhunt - April-May 1967	1967	Anthology	G-	Digest	$5.00
MANOR	95 260	The Surrogate Womb	1973	Cassiday, B.	AF	TVTI	$7.00
MANOR	95 296	A Quality Of Fear	1973	Cassiday, B.	AF	TVTI	$7.00
MANOR	12215	To Get Along With Girls	1974	Cassiday, B.	AF	TVTI	$7.00
MANOR	12235	The Year Of The Dragon	1974	Chang, L.	AF		$7.00
MANOR	12296	The 3 Stigmata Of P. Eldrich	1975	Dick, P.K.	VGF+		$6.00
MANOR	12410	Now Wait For Last Year	1976	Dick, P.K.	AF		$10.00
MANOR	12410	Now Wait For Last Year	1976	Dick, P.K.	VGF+		$10.00 A
MANOR	12527	Deep Freeze	1977	Whyte, H.W.	VG-		$5.00
MANOR	15114	Groucho And Me	1976	Marx, G.	VGF+		$3.00
MANOR	15194	The Unhatched Egghead	1976	Mark, T.	VGF		$6.00
MANOR	19162	The King Is Dead: Elvis	1977	Grove, M.A.	VG+		$8.00
MANOR	23189	Alien Atlas	1979	Alexander, C.M.	VG		$8.00
MARK GOULDEN	9	Carson Of Venus	n/d	Burroughs, E.R.	VGF	Digest	$14.00 A
MARVEL SCIENCE	3 3	Marvel Science Stories 5/51	1951	Anthology	G+	Digest	$5.00
MARVEL SCIENCE	3 5	Marvel Science Fiction 11/51	1951	Anthology	VG+	Digest	$7.00
MASK READER	MR 104	Potion Of Sin	1964	Brand, N.	VG+		$5.00
MAX BRAND'S	3 4	Max Brand's Western - 2/51	1951	Anthology	G	Digest	$15.00
MAYFLOWER	11717	Last Summer	1970	Hunter, E.	VG	MTI	$7.00
MCBAIN'S MYSTERY BOOK	1	Ed McBain's Mystery Book #1	1960	Anthology	VG	Digest	$42.00 A
MCBAIN'S MYSTERY BOOK	1	Ed McBain's Mystery Book #1	1960	Anthology	G+	Digest	$7.00
MCBAIN'S MYSTERY BOOK	2	Ed McBain's Mystery Book #2	1960	Anthology	VG+	Digest	$30.00 A
MCBAIN'S MYSTERY BOOK	2	Ed McBain's Mystery Book #2	1960	Anthology	VG+	Digest	$20.00
MCBAIN'S MYSTERY BOOK	2	Ed McBain's Mystery Book #2	1960	Anthology	VG	Digest	$7.00
MCBAIN'S MYSTERY BOOK	3	Ed McBain's Mystery Book #3	1960	Anthology	VG+	Digest	$28.00 A
MEDICAL FICTION	201	Two Loves Has Nurse Powell	1963	Johnston, W.	AF		$10.00 A
MEDICAL FICTION	202	Young Doctor In Town	1963	Ackworth, R.	VGF		$10.00 A
MELLIFONT	16	Dangerous Corner (dust jkt.)	n/d	Priestley, J.B.	VG+		$22.00 A
MENACE	1 1	Menace Mystery Fiction 11/54	1954	Anthology	AF	Digest	$17.00 A
MEN'S DIGEST	25	The Men's Digest 4/61	1961	Anthology	VGF	Digest	$17.00 A
MEN'S DIGEST	30	The Men's Digest 9/61	1961	Anthology	VGF	Digest	$8.00
MEN'S DIGEST	32	The Men's Digest 11/61	1961	Anthology	AF	Digest	$14.00 A
MEN'S DIGEST	54	The Men's Digest 10/64	1964	Anthology	VGF	Digest	$16.00 A
MENTOR	M 82	The Wonderful World Of Books	1953	Anthology	VGF+		$5.00
MENTOR	Ms 90	The Golden Treasury	1953	Anthology	VG		$3.00
MENTOR	Ms 96	New World Writing #4	1953	Anthology	AF		$5.00
MENTOR	M 104	Highlights Of Modern Lit.	1954	Anthology	VGF		$5.00
MENTOR	M 129	The Way Of Life	1955	Tzu, L.	VG+		$5.00

Mercury Mystery 214 AF $8

Merit 557 VG+ $7

Merit Books B10 VG+ $21

PUBLISHER	PUB. #	TITLE	DATE	AUTHOR	COND.	TYPE	PRICE
MENTOR	MD 130	New World Writing #7	1955	Anthology	VGF		$30.00 A
MENTOR	MD 130	New World Writing #7	1955	Anthology	VGF		$23.00
MENTOR	MD 240	The Story Of Jazz	1958	Stearns, M.	VGF+		$7.00
MERCURY (Adult)	8	Bedroom Road	1966	Preston, L.	AF		$12.00
MERCURY (Adult)	8	Bedroom Road	1966	Preston, L.	VGF-		$7.00
MERCURY (Adult)	102	Tennis Anyone?	n/d	Latham, M.	F		$12.00
MERCURY BOOKS INC.	MB 101	The Life Of Adolf Hitler	1961	Gerber, A.B.	VGF		$8.00
MERCURY BOOKS INC.	MB 102	Stalin Red Lord Of Russia	1962	Feldman, A.B.	VGF		$30.00 A
MERCURY BOOKS INC.	MB 104	Cleopatra Queen Of Egypt	1962	Weigall, A.	VG+	MTI	$8.00 A
MERCURY BOOK	11	Mantrap	1938	Lewis, S.	VG+	Digest	$5.00
MERCURY BOOK	14	Death In The Deep South	1939	Greene, W.	VG+	Digest	$7.00
MERCURY BOOK	20	Cup Of Gold	1939	Steinbeck, J.	VG	Digest	$6.00
MERCURY BOOK	21	The Missing Miniature	1939	Kastner, E.	VG	Digest	$6.00
MERCURY BOOK	22	Country Court	1939	Flannagan, R.	VG+	Digest	$5.00
MERCURY BOOK	24	Divide By Two	1940	Gilman, M.	VG	Digest	$6.00
MERCURY BOOK	28	Jamaica Inn	1940	Du Maurier, D.	VG+	Digest	$6.00
MERCURY BOOK	29	Class Reunion	1940	Werfel, F.	VG+	Digest	$6.00
MERCURY BOOK	31	The Death Of Monsieur Gallet	1940	Simenon, G.	VG+	Digest	$6.00
MERCURY BOOK	34	Strawstack	1940	Disney, D.C.	VG+	Digest	$5.00
MERCURY MYSTERY	36	The Siamese Twin Mystery	1941	Queen, E.	VG+	Digest	$6.00
MERCURY MYSTERY	61	The Singing Clock	1943	Perdue, V.	VG+	Digest	$6.00
MERCURY MYSTERY	65	Verdict Of Twelve	1943	Postgate, R.	VGF	Digest	$6.00
MERCURY MYSTERY	67	Mystery In The Woodshed	1943	Gilbert, A.	VGF	Digest	$6.00
MERCURY MYSTERY	82	I Wouldn't Be In Your Shoes	1944	Irish, W.*	AF	Digest	$27.00 A
MERCURY MYSTERY	83	Tinsley's Bones	1944	Wilde, P.	VG+	Digest	$5.00
MERCURY MYSTERY	84	The Moving Finger	1945	Christie, A.	VG+	Digest	$6.00
MERCURY MYSTERY	123	The Whitebird Murders	1948	Black, T.B.	VG	Digest	$6.00
MERCURY MYSTERY	163	Give Up The Ghost	1951	Erskine, M.	VG+	Digest	$5.00
MERCURY MYSTERY	182	The Dead Don't Care	1953	Latimer, J.	G+	Digest	$7.00
MERCURY MYSTERY	186	Clues To Burn	1953	Offord, L.G.	VGF	Digest	$5.00
MERCURY MYSTERY	188	Death Is A Lover	1953	Tyre, N.	VG	Digest	$5.00
MERCURY MYSTERY	198	Murder Of A Mistress	1954	Sherwood, J.	VGF	Digest	$5.00
MERCURY MYSTERY	201	The Deadly Chase	1954	Eshleman, J.M.	VG+	Digest	$5.00
MERCURY MYSTERY	204	They Buried A Man	1955	Davis, M.	VG+	Digest	$5.00
MERCURY MYSTERY	205	You Die Today	1955	Kendrick, B.	VG+	Digest	$5.00
MERCURY MYSTERY	210	Shoot A Sitting Duck	1955	Alexander, D.	AF	Digest	$15.00
MERCURY MYSTERY	212	The Red Scarf	1955	Brewer, G.	VG	Digest	$15.00
MERCURY MYSTERY	214	The Virgin Victim	1956	Trimble, L.	AF	Digest	$8.00
MERCURY MYSTERY	214	The Virgin Victim	1956	Trimble, L.	AF	Digest	$7.00
MERCURY MYSTERY	216	Mercury Mystery - 3/56	1956	Thompson, J.	VG	Digest	$66.00 A
MERCURY MYSTERY	232	Mercury Mystery - 4/59	1959	Anthology	AF	Digest	$8.00
MERIT	353	The 13 Sinners	1960	Marmor, A.	VGF		$8.00
MERIT	518	Wild Pursuit	1961	Lauren, B.	VGF+		$8.00
MERIT	523	Valley Of Lust	1961	Coulter, A.	AF-		$10.00
MERIT	525	The Devil's Mistress	1961	Jade, G.	AF		$8.00

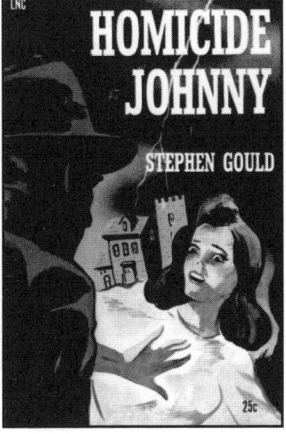

Merit Books B13 VGF- $24   Metro 7 VG $15   Midwood No# 5 VG $68

PUBLISHER	PUB. #	TITLE	DATE	AUTHOR	COND.	TYPE	PRICE
MERIT	528	Rebel Mistress	1961	Jade, G.	AF		$7.00
MERIT	536	Love Cheat	1961	Drake, D.	AF		$8.00
MERIT	544	Abnormal Passion	1962	Nemec, J.	AF		$8.00
MERIT	554	Torrid Love Nest	1962	Lauren, B.	AF		$10.00 A
MERIT	557	Modern Harem	1962	Vail, T.	VG+		$7.00
MERIT	605	Wicked Wench!	1962	Connor, C.	F		$7.00
MERIT	606	Exchange Lovers	1962	Goff, J.M.	VGF		$8.00 A
MERIT	611	Love Me Now!	1962	Goff, J.M.	AF		$7.00
MERIT	613	Loretta	1962	Montgomery, H.	VGF		$9.00 A
MERIT	624	Sadistic Wench	1962	North, K.	AF		$8.00
MERIT	630	Torrid Teaser	1962	Connor, C.	AF		$12.00
MERIT	639	Torrid Wenches	1962	Marmor, A.	AF		$8.00
MERIT	639	Torrid Wenches	1962	Marmor, A.	VGF		$7.00
MERIT	642	Abnormal Desire	1962	Marmor, A.	AF		$7.00
MERIT	654	3 Man-Hungry Women	1963	Cross, G.	VGF		$8.00
MERIT	6M 413	Urgent Desire!	1963	Montgomery, H.	VGF		$12.00 A
MERIT	6M 443	Fun Girl	n/d	Lauren, B.	VG+		$7.00
MERIT	6M 447	Shameless	1964	Goff, J.M.	G+		$4.00
MERIT	6M 453	Violent Passions	1964	Walker, A.	VGF		$8.00
MERIT	6M 458	Thrill-Crazy Tina	1964	Powers, T.	AF		$7.00 A
MERIT	6M 461	And Some Were Evil	1964	Willie, E.	G		$20.00
MERIT	6M 463	Modern Mistress	1964	Jade, G.	VGF+		$8.00
MERIT	6M 466	The Ultimate Urge	1964	Daniels, M.	AF		$12.00
MERIT	6M 469	Utterly Wanton	n/d	Lauren, B.	AF		$8.00
MERIT	6M 477	Expert Seductress	n/d	Royce, L.	VGF		$8.00
MERIT	6M 478	The Sensualites	n/d	Willie, E.	AF-		$6.00
MERIT	6M 490	Hollywood Film Monsters	1965	Steiger, B.	VG	MTI	$10.00 A
MERIT	6M 492	Code Of Vengeance	1965	Willie, E.	G-		$15.00
MERIT	7M 812	Sensual Imposter	1964	Goff, J.M.	VG+		$6.00
MERIT	7M 818	Garbo	1964	Steiger, B.	VGF		$18.00 A
MERIT BOOKS	B 10	Operation Interstellar	1950	Smith, G.O.	VG+	Digest	$21.00 A
MERIT BOOKS	B 10	Operation Interstellar	1950	Smith, G.O.	VGF	Digest	$14.00
MERIT BOOKS	B 10	Operation Interstellar	1950	Smith, G.O.	VG+	Digest	$13.00 A
MERIT BOOKS	B 13	World Of If	1951	Phillips, R.	VGF-	Digest	$24.00 A
METRO	7	Homicide Johnny	n/d	Gould, S.	VG	Digest	$15.00
MICHAEL SHAYNE MYST. MAG.*		*See MIKE SHAYNE MYSTERY					
MIDNIGHT READER	MR 405	Lust Damned	1961	Shaw, A.*	VGF		$11.00
MIDNIGHT READER	MR 405	Lust Damned	1961	Shaw, A.*	VG+		$10.00 A
MIDNIGHT READER	MR 427	Crossroads Of Lust	1962	Shaw, A.*	VGF		$10.00
MIDNIGHT READER	MR 433	Surfside Sex	1962	Marshall, A.*	F		$10.00
MIDNIGHT READER	MR 433	Surfside Sex	1962	Marshall, A.*	VGF		$7.00
MIDNIGHT READER	MR 438	Fast Talk Sinner	1962	Allison, C.	VGF+		$10.00 A
MIDNIGHT READER	MR 442	Passion Floor	1962	Hudson, D.	VGF		$8.00
MIDNIGHT READER	MR 459	China Tramp	1962	Marshall, A.*	VGF		$10.00 A
MIDNIGHT READER	MR 459	China Tramp	1962	Marshall, A.*	VGF		$8.00

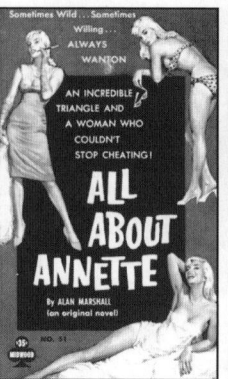
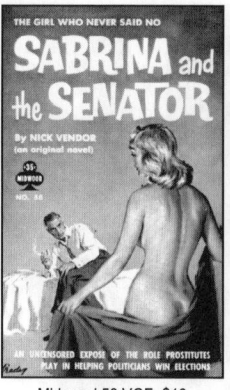

Midwood 28 VGF $28   Midwood 51 VGF $34   Midwood 58 VGF- $13   Midwood 61 AF $17

PUBLISHER	PUB. #	TITLE	DATE	AUTHOR	COND.	TYPE	PRICE
MIDNIGHT READER	MR 464	The Glass Mistress	1962	Hudson, D.	VGF		$9.00
MIDNIGHT READER	MR 465	Lust Pro	1962	Dexter, J.	G+		$3.00
MIDNIGHT READER	MR 467	Gutter Gang	1962	Calvano, T.	AF		$12.00
MIDNIGHT READER	MR 485	Sin Dealer	1963	Bellmore, D.	VG+		$5.00
MIDNIGHT READER	MR 487	Sin Hipster	1963	Holliday, D.	AF		$12.00
MIDNIGHT READER	MR 491	Sin Hostess	1963	Shaw, A.*	VGF		$8.00
MIDNIGHT READER	MR 7455	Bewitched And Shameful	1974	Craig, D.	VG		$6.00
MIDWOOD	No# 5	I Take What I Want	1958	Ellson, H.	VG		$68.00 A
MIDWOOD	No# 5	I Take What I Want	1958	Ellson, H.	G		$15.00
MIDWOOD	No# 6	Call Me Mistress	1958	Rede, T.	AF-		$40.00 A
MIDWOOD	8	Carla	1958	Lord, S.*	VG		$8.00
MIDWOOD	10	Affair With Lucy	1959	Hitt, O.	VG+		$18.00 A
MIDWOOD	11	Immoral Wife	1959	Mitchell, G.	VG		$7.00
MIDWOOD	12	Girl Of The Streets	1959	Hitt, O.	VG		$6.00
MIDWOOD	14	Born To Be Bad	1959	Lord, S.*	AF		$27.00 A
MIDWOOD	15	All My Lovers	1959	Marshall, A.*	VGF		$18.00 A
MIDWOOD	17	Backstage Love	1959	Marshall, A.*	AF		$25.00
MIDWOOD	18	Connie	1959	Beauchamp, L.*	VG+		$17.00 A
MIDWOOD	20	Man Hungry	1959	Marshall, A.*	VGF		$18.00
MIDWOOD	21	Unwilling Sinner	1959	Beauchamp, L.*	AF		$13.00 A
MIDWOOD	23	As Bad As They Come	1959	Hitt, O.	AF		$22.00 A
MIDWOOD	26	Just Ask For Margaret	1959	Tasker, W.B.	VGF		$23.00 A
MIDWOOD	26	Just Ask For Margaret	1959	Tasker, W.B.	VG+		$15.00
MIDWOOD	28	All The Girls Were Willing	1960	Marshall, A.*	VGF		$28.00 A
MIDWOOD	29	Another Night, Another Love	1959	Beauchamp, L.*	AF		$40.00 A
MIDWOOD	31	The Wife Next Door	1960	Marshall, A.*	VG+		$8.00 A
MIDWOOD	32	Woman Hater	1960	Carson, D.	VGF		$18.00 A
MIDWOOD	37	Anybody's Girl	1960	Hastings, M.	VGF+		$13.00 A
MIDWOOD	37	Anybody's Girl	1960	Hastings, M.	VG		$10.00
MIDWOOD	39	The Sins Of Martha Leslie	1960	Holliday, D.	VGF		$22.00
MIDWOOD	39	The Sins Of Martha Leslie	1960	Holliday, D.	AF		$18.00 A
MIDWOOD	40	Candy	1960	Lord, S.*	AF		$39.00 A
MIDWOOD	41	A Girl Called Honey	1960	Lord* & Marshall*	VG+		$40.00 A
MIDWOOD	46	Glad To Be Bad	1960	Roberts, A.	VGF-		$13.00 A
MIDWOOD	48	So Willing	1960	Lord*& Marshall*	G-		$5.00
MIDWOOD	51	All About Annette	1960	Marshall, A.*	VGF		$34.00 A
MIDWOOD	51	All About Annette	1960	Marshall, A.*	VGF		$22.00
MIDWOOD	51	All About Annette	1960	Marshall, A.*	VG		$15.00
MIDWOOD	52	Meet Marilyn	1960	Britain, S.	VGF+		$15.00 A
MIDWOOD	52	Meet Marilyn	1960	Britain, S.	VG+		$10.00
MIDWOOD	52	Meet Marilyn	1960	Britain, S.	VG-		$8.00
MIDWOOD	54	Lana	1960	Ellis, J.	AF		$50.00 A
MIDWOOD	58	Sabrina And The Senator	1960	Vendor, N.	VGF-		$13.00 A
MIDWOOD	59	A Twilight Affair	1960	Harvey, J.	AF		$17.00 A
MIDWOOD	61	Flame	1960	Ellis, J.	AF		$17.00 A
MIDWOOD	63	The Unfortunate Flesh	1960	Salem, R.	AF		$72.00 A
MIDWOOD	65	Nurse Carolyn	1960	Beauchamp, L.*	VGF		$44.00 A
MIDWOOD	67	A Touch Of Depravity	1960	Russo, P.V.	VG+		$15.00

Midwood 65 VGF $44 | Midwood 101 VGF $45 | Midwood 110 VGF $15 | Midwood 135 VGF+ $38

PUBLISHER	PUB. #	TITLE	DATE	AUTHOR	COND.	TYPE	PRICE
MIDWOOD	67	A Touch Of Depravity	1960	Russo, P.V.	VGF+		$14.00
MIDWOOD	69	Liza's Apartment	1961	Ellis, J.	AF		$18.00 A
MIDWOOD	70	Sin On Wheels	1961	Beauchamp, L.*	G		$5.00
MIDWOOD	71	A Woman	1961	Elliott, B.	AF		$29.00 A
MIDWOOD	72	The Path Between	1961	Warren, J.	VG+		$22.00
MIDWOOD	73	The Sex Peddlers	1961	Allison, C.	VG		$15.00
MIDWOOD	74	Connie	1961	Beauchamp, L.*	VGF-		$12.00
MIDWOOD	76	Pleasure Girl	1961	Ellis, J.	VGF		$15.00 A
MIDWOOD	F 78	Restless Virgin	1961	Russo, P.V.	VG		$8.00
MIDWOOD	79	Your Sins And Mine	1961	Parksmith, G.	VGF		$7.00
MIDWOOD	80	The Jealous And The Free	1961	Hastings, M.	VGF+		$15.00 A
MIDWOOD	80	The Jealous And The Free	1961	Hastings, M.	VG+		$8.00
MIDWOOD	F 82	These Curious Pleasures	1961	Britain, S.	VGF+		$23.00 A
MIDWOOD	85	Silky	1961	Mayo, D.	VGF		$12.00
MIDWOOD	89	Middle Of Time	1961	Wyckoff, J.	VG+		$8.00
MIDWOOD	F 101	Morals Charge	1961	Hunter, P.	VGF		$45.00
MIDWOOD	F 101	Morals Charge	1961	Hunter, P.	VG		$16.00
MIDWOOD	104	Judge Not My Sins	1961	James, S.	VGF		$7.00
MIDWOOD	106	Child Bride	1961	James, A.	AF		$18.00 A
MIDWOOD	F 107	The Hunger And The Hate	1961	Ellis, J.	VG-		$5.00
MIDWOOD	F 110	The Unloved	1961	Swenson, P.*	VGF		$15.00 A
MIDWOOD	112	A Girl Like That	1961	Plunkett, J.	AF		$12.00
MIDWOOD	115	Married Mistress	1961	Hitt, O.	VG		$7.00
MIDWOOD	116	So Wild	1961	Skinner, M.	VGF+		$33.00 A
MIDWOOD	122	House Of Sin	1961	Mayo, D.	VG		$7.00
MIDWOOD	124	Motel Hostess	1961	Richards, R.	VG+		$10.00
MIDWOOD	F 125	The Lowest Sins	1961	Castro, J.	VG		$7.00
MIDWOOD	126	Pound Of Flesh	1961	Hytes, J.	AF		$12.00
MIDWOOD	Y 127	Weak And Wicked	1961	James, A.	AF		$16.00
MIDWOOD	Y 127	Weak And Wicked	1961	James, A.	AF		$12.00
MIDWOOD	129	All My Lovers	1961	Marshall, A.*	VGF		$17.00 A
MIDWOOD	129	All My Lovers	1961	Marshall, A.*	VG		$7.00
MIDWOOD	F 130	Norma	1961	Glennon, G.	AF		$12.00
MIDWOOD	132	Stag Stripper	1961	Avallone, M.	VGF		$18.00 A
MIDWOOD	133	The Halfbreed	1961	James, A.	AF		$16.00 A
MIDWOOD	F 134	The Outcasts	1961	Hastings, M.	VGF		$12.00
MIDWOOD	Y 135	The Little Black Book	1961	Avallone, M.	VGF+		$38.00 A
MIDWOOD	Y 135	The Little Black Book	1961	Avallone, M.	VG-		$13.00 A
MIDWOOD	F 139	In The Shadows	1962	Ellis, J.	VG+		$10.00
MIDWOOD	F 140	August Heat	1962	Allen, R.	F		$12.00
MIDWOOD	F 141	Love Like A Shadow	1962	Kemp, K.	F		$37.00
MIDWOOD	F 141	Love Like A Shadow	1962	Kemp, K.	AF		$20.00 A
MIDWOOD	F 141	Love Like A Shadow	1962	Kemp, K.	VGF		$17.00 A
MIDWOOD	F 142	Woman Doctor	1962	Britain, S.	VGF		$20.00 A
MIDWOOD	143	Con Girl	1962	Anonymous	AF		$14.00
MIDWOOD	Y 144	I Know The Score	1962	Louis, O.	AF		$10.00
MIDWOOD	F 146	Sinners In White	1962	Avallone, M.	AF		$38.00 A
MIDWOOD	147	Man Hungry	1962	Marshall, A.*	AF		$24.00 A

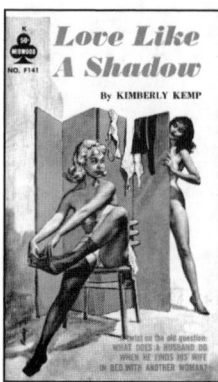
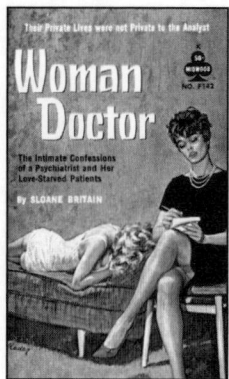

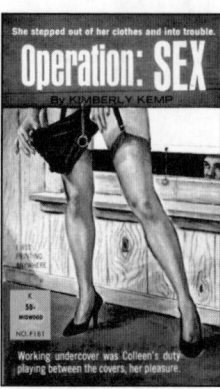

Midwood 141 F $37   Midwood 142 VGF $20   Midwood 176 VG $10   Midwood 181 VGF+ $52

PUBLISHER	PUB. #	TITLE	DATE	AUTHOR	COND.	TYPE	PRICE
MIDWOOD	148	Sin A La Carte	1962	Beauchamp, L.*	AF		$20.00
MIDWOOD	149	Apprentice Virgin	1962	Marshall, A.*	AF		$20.00 A
MIDWOOD	151	Jill Harvey	1962	Russo, P.V.	AF		$15.00
MIDWOOD	F 152	Office Tramp	1962	Porcelain, S.	AF		$11.00 A
MIDWOOD	F 152	Office Tramp	1962	Porcelain, S.	VG+		$8.00
MIDWOOD	Y 153	Skin Deep	1962	Dyer, W.	VGF+		$12.00 A
MIDWOOD	Y 153	Skin Deep	1962	Dyer, W.	VG		$7.00
MIDWOOD	F 154	The Lesbian In Our Society	1962	Sprague, W.D.	VG+		$24.00 A
MIDWOOD	F 154	The Lesbian In Our Society	1962	Sprague, W.D.	VG		$12.00
MIDWOOD	Y 155	Rita	1962	Hytes, J.	VGF		$8.00
MIDWOOD	Y 160	The Blonde	1962	Swenson, P.*	F		$14.00 A
MIDWOOD	Y 160	The Blonde	1962	Swenson, P.*	VG		$8.00
MIDWOOD	F 162	Perfume And Pain	1962	Kemp, K.	AF		$40.00 A
MIDWOOD	F 163	The Drifter	1962	Hastings, M.	VGF		$17.00
MIDWOOD	F 163	The Drifter	1962	Hastings, M.	VG+		$15.00
MIDWOOD	F 164	Ripe	1962	Richards, R.	AF		$8.00
MIDWOOD	165	Puta	1962	Lord, S.*	AF		$24.00 A
MIDWOOD	167	Sex Before Six	1962	Hytes, J.	F		$10.00
MIDWOOD	167	Sex Before Six	1962	Hytes, J.	VG		$6.00
MIDWOOD	F 170	The Passer	1962	Merwin, S.	VGF		$10.00
MIDWOOD	171	The Undoing Of Jenny	1962	Skinner, M.	AF		$10.00
MIDWOOD	Y 173	Sex With A Twist	1962	Ellis, J.	VGF		$14.00
MIDWOOD	Y 173	Sex With A Twist	1962	Ellis, J.	VG		$8.00
MIDWOOD	Y 175	Forever Amy	1962	Harris, A.	AF		$20.00
MIDWOOD	Y 176	The Doctor And The Dike	1962	Hytes, J.	VG		$10.00
MIDWOOD	Y 179	Chico's Women	1962	Hastings, M.	AF		$15.00 A
MIDWOOD	F 180	Prisoner Of My Past	1962	Fisher, E.	VGF		$10.00
MIDWOOD	F 181	Operation: Sex	1962	Kemp, K.	VGF+		$52.00 A
MIDWOOD	F 181	Operation: Sex	1962	Kemp, K.	VGF		$25.00 A
MIDWOOD	182	Campus Jungle	1962	Ellis, J.	VGF		$7.00
MIDWOOD	Y 184	All The Way	1962	Avallone, M.	AF		$16.00
MIDWOOD	Y 186	TV Tramps	1962	Dyer, W.	AF		$32.00
MIDWOOD	F 188	Twice With Julie	1962	Hytes, J.	F		$22.00 A
MIDWOOD	F 189	Sex Kitten	1962	Avallone, M.	VGF		$44.00 A
MIDWOOD	F 190	The Craving	1962	Mayo, D.	VGF		$8.00
MIDWOOD	F 191	Unnatural	1962	Britton, S.	VGF		$29.00 A
MIDWOOD	F 191	Unnatural	1962	Britton, S.	VG+		$22.00 A
MIDWOOD	F 193	Lady Wrestler	1962	Harvey, J.	VGF		$27.00 A
MIDWOOD	F 194	Daughter Of Shame	1962	Ellis, J.	AF		$29.00 A
MIDWOOD	F 194	Daughter Of Shame	1962	Ellis, J.	VG-		$5.00
MIDWOOD	F 195	One Way Ticket	1962	Hytes, J.	VG+		$7.00
MIDWOOD	F 196	The Soft Sin	1962	Salem, R.	AF		$30.00 A
MIDWOOD	F 198	Voluptuous Voyage	1962	Mayo, D.	VGF		$15.00
MIDWOOD	F 198	Voluptuous Voyage	1962	Mayo, D.	VGF		$12.00 A
MIDWOOD	F 200	Easy	1962	Swensen, P.*	AF		$8.00
MIDWOOD	F 202	The Platinum Trap	1962	Avallone, M.	AF		$40.00 A
MIDWOOD	F 205	Never Love A Call Girl	1962	Avallone, M.	AF		$27.00 A
MIDWOOD	F 205	Never Love A Call Girl	1962	Avallone, M.	VGF		$18.00 A

   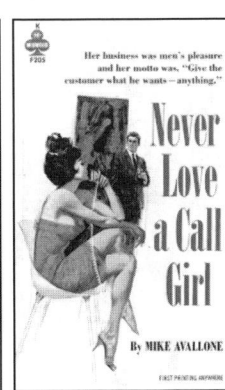

Midwood 191 VGF $29   Midwood 193 VGF $27   Midwood 202 AF $40   Midwood 205 AF $27

PUBLISHER	PUB. #	TITLE	DATE	AUTHOR	COND.	TYPE	PRICE
MIDWOOD	F 205	Never Love A Call Girl	1962	Avallone, M.	G+		$6.00
MIDWOOD	F 207	Over-Exposed	1962	Hytes, J.	AF		$33.00 A
MIDWOOD	F 207	Over-Exposed	1962	Hytes, J.	VGF		$22.00 A
MIDWOOD	F 208	By Flesh Alone	1962	Hastings, M.	F		$41.00 A
MIDWOOD	F 209	Carrie Corrupted	1962	Logano, R.	VGF+		$10.00
MIDWOOD	F 210	Intimate Nurse	1962	Kemp, K.	F		$22.00
MIDWOOD	F 212	Touch Me Gently	1962	Harris, A.	AF-		$10.00
MIDWOOD	F 212	Touch Me Gently	1962	Harris, A.	VG		$8.00
MIDWOOD	F 213	Sleep-In Maid	1962	Michaels, L.	VG		$7.00
MIDWOOD	F 214	Lap Of Luxury	1962	Kemp, K.	VGF		$10.00
MIDWOOD	F 216	Wait Your Turn	1962	Hytes, J.	VGF+		$14.00
MIDWOOD	F 217	Appointment For Sin	1962	Russo, P.V.	VGF		$15.00
MIDWOOD	F 220	Flight Into Sin	1962	Skinner, M.	VG+		$10.00
MIDWOOD	F 221	Yesterday's Virgin	1962	Hytes, J.	AF		$25.00 A
MIDWOOD	F 224	Whip Of Desire	1962	Hastings, M.	VGF		$12.00
MIDWOOD	F 224	Whip Of Desire	1962	Hastings, M.	VGF		$12.00 A
MIDWOOD	F 225	Unnatural Urge	1962	Hitt, O.	VGF		$27.00 A
MIDWOOD	F 225	Unnatural Urge	1962	Hitt, O.	AF		$18.00 A
MIDWOOD	F 225	Unnatural Urge	1962	Hitt, O.	VG		$17.00 A
MIDWOOD	F 226	Wayward Widow	1962	Beauchamp, L.*	VG+		$10.00
MIDWOOD	F 227	Resort Secretary	1962	English, A.	F		$10.00
MIDWOOD	F 228	The Girl Downstairs	1962	Anthony, R.	F		$12.00
MIDWOOD	F 228	The Girl Downstairs	1962	Anthony, R.	VG-		$6.00
MIDWOOD	F 229	This Is Elaine	1963	Hytes, J.	VG+		$6.00
MIDWOOD	D 231	The Wild Week	1963	Hytes, J.	AF	DBL	$85.00 A
		Imitation Lovers		Hastings, M.			
MIDWOOD	F 232	The Payoff	1963	Collier, M.	VG+		$14.00
MIDWOOD	F 233	Immoral Lady	1963	Gage, R.	AF		$14.00
MIDWOOD	F 234	Forbidden Sex	1963	Ellis, J.	AF		$24.00 A
MIDWOOD	F 235	The Passionate Virgin	1963	Skinner, M.	VGF+		$8.00
MIDWOOD	F 235	The Passionate Virgin	1963	Skinner, M.	VG+		$7.00
MIDWOOD	F 236	Wild Honey	1963	Karl, D.	VGF		$12.00
MIDWOOD	F 237	Never Enough	1963	Hytes, J.	VGF		$8.00
MIDWOOD	F 239	Sudden Hunger	1963	Dodge, P.	F		$54.00 A
MIDWOOD	F 239	Sudden Hunger	1963	Dodge, P.	AF		$44.00 A
MIDWOOD	F 239	Sudden Hunger	1963	Dodge, P.	AF		$33.00 A
MIDWOOD	F 240	The Soft Way	1963	Hastings, M.	AF		$8.00
MIDWOOD	F 241	The Pleasure And The Pain	1963	Louis, O.	VGF		$12.00
MIDWOOD	F 242	Don't Bet On Blondes	1963	Dyer, W.	AF		$8.00
MIDWOOD	F 243	Illicit Interlude	1963	Kemp, K.	F		$14.00
MIDWOOD	F 244	By Her Body Betrayed	1963	Anthony, R.	VGF		$33.00 A
MIDWOOD	F 244	By Her Body Betrayed	1963	Anthony, R.	VG+		$16.00
MIDWOOD	F 245	The Sex Plan	1963	Elder, P.	VGF+		$13.00
MIDWOOD	F 246	Swing Low Sweet Sinner	1963	Hytes, J.	VG+		$7.00
MIDWOOD	F 247	Sea Nymph	1963	Swenson, P.*	VG+		$7.00
MIDWOOD	F 248	Horizontal Secretary	1963	Harris, A.	VGF		$25.00 A
MIDWOOD	F 248	Horizontal Secretary	1963	Harris, A.	VGF		$22.00 A
MIDWOOD	F 248	Horizontal Secretary	1963	Harris, A.	VG		$20.00

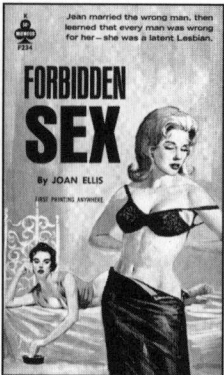

Midwood 231 AF $85   Midwood 234 AF $24   Midwood 248 VGF $25   Midwood 270 AF $15

PUBLISHER	PUB. #	TITLE	DATE	AUTHOR	COND.	TYPE	PRICE
MIDWOOD	F 249	None But The Wicked	1963	Craig, D.W.	AF-		$8.00
MIDWOOD	F 250	A Rage Within	1963	Hastings, M.	VG+		$12.00
MIDWOOD	F 251	Pagan	1963	Russo, P.V.	VG+		$10.00
MIDWOOD	F 253	Camera Club Model	1963	Harvey, J.	AF		$8.00
MIDWOOD	F 254	Without Shame	1963	Hytes, J.	VGF+		$8.00
MIDWOOD	F 254	Without Shame	1963	Hytes, J.	AF		$7.00
MIDWOOD	F 255	Again And Again	1963	Hastings, M.	VGF		$8.00
MIDWOOD	F 256	A Bit Of Fluff	1963	Kemp, K.	AF		$41.00 A
MIDWOOD	F 257	Once Too Often	1963	Ellis, J.	VGF		$7.00
MIDWOOD	F 258	Something Special	1963	Donalds, R.	VG+		$7.00
MIDWOOD	F 259	The Cruel Touch	1963	Marshall, A.*	VGF		$22.00
MIDWOOD	F 259	The Cruel Touch	1963	Marshall, A.*	F		$20.00 A
MIDWOOD	F 259	The Cruel Touch	1963	Marshall, A.*	VGF		$20.00
MIDWOOD	F 261	One Step More	1963	Draper, J.	VGF		$12.00
MIDWOOD	F 262	Girl In The Middle	1963	Thompson, J.B.	AF		$8.00
MIDWOOD	F 263	The Mark Of A Man	1963	Collier, M.	VGF		$7.00
MIDWOOD	F 264	Erica	1963	Harvey, J.	VGF		$7.00
MIDWOOD	F 265	All Of Me	1963	Harris, A.	AF		$35.00 A
MIDWOOD	F 265	All Of Me	1963	Harris, A.	F		$26.00 A
MIDWOOD	F 265	All Of Me	1963	Harris, A.	VG+		$10.00
MIDWOOD	F 266	Restless	1963	Hamilton, G.	AF		$38.00 A
MIDWOOD	F 266	Restless	1963	Hamilton, G.	VG+		$10.00
MIDWOOD	F 267	Everybody Welcome	1963	Mayo, D.	VGF		$14.00
MIDWOOD	F 267	Everybody Welcome	1963	Mayo, D.	AF		$12.00
MIDWOOD	F 268	The Unashamed	1963	Hastings, M.	VG-		$6.00
MIDWOOD	F 269	The Teaser	1963	Hytes, J.	VGF		$7.00
MIDWOOD	F 270	Sign Here For Sin	1963	Donalds, R.	AF		$15.00 A
MIDWOOD	F 270	Sign Here For Sin	1963	Donalds, R.	VG-		$4.00
MIDWOOD	F 271	Her Private Hell	1963	Hastings, M.	VGF		$133.00 A
MIDWOOD	F 271	Her Private Hell	1963	Hastings, M.	VG+		$70.00
MIDWOOD	F 272	Rusty	1963	Draper, J.	VGF		$10.00
MIDWOOD	F 273	Any Man Will Do	1963	Hamilton, G.	AF		$15.00
MIDWOOD	F 273	Any Man Will Do	1963	Hamilton, G.	VGF		$8.00
MIDWOOD	F 273	Any Man Will Do	1963	Hamilton, G.	VG		$6.00
MIDWOOD	F 274	Pajama Party	1963	Swenson, P.*	VGF		$54.00 A
MIDWOOD	F 275	Irma La Douce	1963	Wilder, B.	VGF+	MTI	$25.00
MIDWOOD	F 276	Sin On Wheels	1963	Beauchamp, L.*	AF		$15.00
MIDWOOD	F 276	Sin On Wheels	1963	Beauchamp, L.*	VGF		$15.00
MIDWOOD	S 277	Perfumed	1963	Hytes, J.	VG	DBL	$22.00
		Pampered		*Kemp, K.*			
MIDWOOD	F 278	Fringe Benefits	1963	Anthony, R.	VG		$8.00
MIDWOOD	F 279	Hold Me Tight	1963	Ellis, J.	VGF		$5.00
MIDWOOD	F 280	Take Care Of Me	1963	Turner, J.	AF		$14.00
MIDWOOD	F 280	Take Care Of Me	1963	Turner, J.	VGF		$14.00
MIDWOOD	F 281	Say When	1963	Collier, M.	AF		$8.00
MIDWOOD	F 282	Party Girls	1963	Russo, P.V.	F		$25.00
MIDWOOD	F 283	Honeysuckle	1963	Salem, R.	VG		$4.00
MIDWOOD	F 284	Meet Marilyn	1963	Britain, S.	AF		$16.00

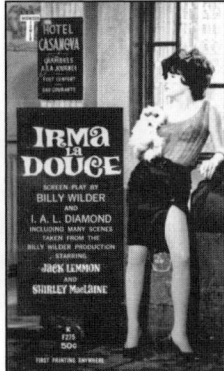

Midwood 271 VGF $133   Midwood 275 VGF+ $25   Midwood 276 AF $15   Midwood 277 VG $22

PUBLISHER	PUB. #	TITLE	DATE	AUTHOR	COND.	TYPE	PRICE
MIDWOOD	F 285	Whatever She Wanted	1963	Draper, J.	AF		$8.00
MIDWOOD	F 286	One Of The Girls	1963	Mezatesta. R.	VGF-		$20.00 A
MIDWOOD	F 287	Soft In The Shadows	1963	Turner, J.	AF		$13.00
MIDWOOD	F 287	Soft In The Shadows	1963	Turner, J.	VG+		$5.00
MIDWOOD	F 288	Night After Night	1963	Saxon, W.	AF		$6.00
MIDWOOD	F 289	Nine To Five	1963	Commings, J.	AF		$7.00
MIDWOOD	F 289	Nine To Five	1963	Commings, J.	VG+		$7.00
MIDWOOD	F 290	The Intruder	1963	Powell, J.	VGF-		$6.00
MIDWOOD	F 291	Lesbianism Around The World	1963	Hasselrodt, R.L.	AF		$44.00 A
MIDWOOD	F 291	Lesbianism Around The World	1963	Hasselrodt, R.L.	AF		$32.00 A
MIDWOOD	F 292	Nurse Carolyn	1963	Beauchamp, L.*	AF		$17.00 A
MIDWOOD	F 292	Nurse Carolyn	1963	Beauchamp, L.*	VG+		$15.00
MIDWOOD	F 293	Too Young To Marry	1963	Ellis, J.	VG+		$7.00
MIDWOOD	F 297	The Captive	1963	Turner, J.	F		$12.00
MIDWOOD	F 298	Made To Order	1963	Hamilton, G.	VGF		$12.00
MIDWOOD	F 299	Nothing To Lose	1963	Kemp, K.	VGF		$15.00
MIDWOOD	F 299	Nothing To Lose	1963	Kemp, K.	VGF		$10.00
MIDWOOD	F 301	Devil's Workshop	1963	James, S.	VG+		$7.00
MIDWOOD	F 301	Devil's Workshop	1963	James, S.	VG+		$6.00
MIDWOOD	F 305	The Come On	1963	Fields, V.	VGF		$7.00
MIDWOOD	F 306	Man Handled	1963	Scobie, E.L.	VG+		$6.00
MIDWOOD	F 307	No Way Back	1963	Trainer, R.	VGF		$18.00 A
MIDWOOD	F 308	Carole Came Back	1963	Turner, J.	AF		$13.00 A
MIDWOOD	F 308	Carole Came Back	1963	Turner, J.	VGF		$8.00
MIDWOOD	F 310	The Delicate Vice	1963	Britton, S.	F		$14.00 A
MIDWOOD	X 312	Tear Gas And Hungry Dogs	1963	Sloan, W.	VG		$8.00
MIDWOOD	X 312	Tear Gas And Hungry Dogs	1963	Sloan, W.	G+		$7.00
MIDWOOD	F 313	Man Trap	1963	Curtis, B.	AF		$13.00
MIDWOOD	F 315	When Lights Are Low	1963	Mayo, D.	VGF		$49.00 A
MIDWOOD	F 318	Stronger Than Love	1963	Draper, J.	AF		$13.00
MIDWOOD	F 319	Diane	1963	Collier, M.	VGF		$7.00
MIDWOOD	S 321	Lady Love	1963	Hytes, J.	AF	DBL	$15.00
		Harlot In Heels		Hamilton, G.			
MIDWOOD	F 324	So Eager To Please	1963	Hamilton, G.	F		$8.00
MIDWOOD	F 326	The Honeymoon Habit	1963	Corgan, G.	VGF		$14.00
MIDWOOD	F 327	Spring Fever	1963	Hughes, L.	AF		$30.00 A
MIDWOOD	F 327	Spring Fever	1963	Hughes, L.	VG		$6.00
MIDWOOD	F 328	Image Of Evil	1963	Russo, P.V.	AF-		$8.00
MIDWOOD	F 333	Teacher's Pet	1963	Clements, M.	G+		$4.00
MIDWOOD	F 334	The Vice Dolls	1963	Stark, J.	AF		$7.00
MIDWOOD	F 336	Nude In A Red Chair	1963	Moore, A.	AF		$40.00 A
MIDWOOD	F 337	Have Heels, Will Travel	1964	Wynne, A.	VGF		$8.00
MIDWOOD	F 340	Nikki	1963	Rico, D.	VGF		$12.00 A
MIDWOOD	F 342	The Baby Sitter	1964	Fields, V.	F		$24.00 A
MIDWOOD	F 344	Switch Partners	1963	Faye, S.	VGF		$6.00
MIDWOOD	F 350	The Spice Of Life	1964	Corgan, G.	F		$17.00 A
MIDWOOD	F 350	The Spice Of Life	1964	Corgan, G.	VGF		$8.00
MIDWOOD	F 352	A World All Their Own	1964	Kemp, K.	AF		$13.00 A

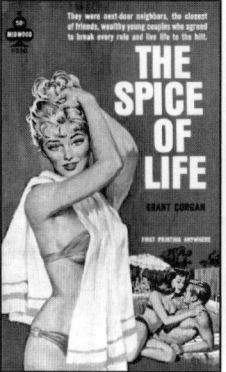

Midwood 327 AF $30	Midwood 350 F $17	Midwood 356 AF $17	Midwood 437 VGF $15

PUBLISHER	PUB. #	TITLE	DATE	AUTHOR	COND.	TYPE	PRICE
MIDWOOD	F 354	Love Or Lust	1964	Clements, M.	AF		$5.00
MIDWOOD	F 355	Anything Under The Sun	1964	Spaulding, M.	VGF		$7.00
MIDWOOD	F 356	For Services Rendered	1964	Curtis, B.	AF		$17.00 A
MIDWOOD	F 357	Where There's Smoke	1964	Burgess, M.	AF		$8.00
MIDWOOD	F 359	Duet	1964	Duchamp, L.	AF		$12.00 A
MIDWOOD	F 359	Duet	1964	Duchamp, L.	VGF		$8.00 A
MIDWOOD	F 360	After Class	1964	Ellis, J.	VGF		$7.00
MIDWOOD	F 361	Love Starved	1964	Trainer, R.	AF		$7.00
MIDWOOD	F 364	Early To Bed	1964	Clements, M.	VGF		$7.00
MIDWOOD	F 365	The Yes Girl	1964	Moore, A.	VGF		$11.00 A
MIDWOOD	F 374	Impatient	1964	Lawrence, D.	AF		$8.00
MIDWOOD	F 375	The Street Walker	1964	Hytes, J.	F		$10.00
MIDWOOD	F 376	Only In Secret	1964	Craig, D.W.	VG+		$36.00 A
MIDWOOD	F 377	The Teenage Trap	1964	Gold, R.C.	VG+		$7.00
MIDWOOD	F 380	Love Toy	1964	Harris, F.G.	VG		$6.00
MIDWOOD	F 384	Swing Shift	1964	Corgan, G.	VG+		$6.00
MIDWOOD	F 385	Man-Tamer	1964	Curtis, B.	AF		$11.00 A
MIDWOOD	F 386	The Third Street	1964	Ellis, J.	G		$2.00
MIDWOOD	F 391	Goodbye, Darling	1964	Duchamp, L.	AF		$10.00
MIDWOOD	F 392	Chains Of Silk	1964	Balmer, J.	VGF		$12.00
MIDWOOD	F 392	Chains Of Silk	1964	Balmer, J.	VG+		$12.00
MIDWOOD	F 393	The Adultress	1964	Harvey, J.	AF		$7.00
MIDWOOD	32 396	Talk Of The Town	1964	Ellis, J.	F		$7.00
MIDWOOD	32 397	Joy	1964	Lawrence, D.	AF		$7.00
MIDWOOD	32 401	Divorcee	1964	Vincent, J.	AF		$13.00 A
MIDWOOD	32 401	Divorcee	1964	Vincent, J.	AF-		$9.00
MIDWOOD	32 402	Warm And Willing	1964	Emerson, J.*	VG		$27.00 A
MIDWOOD	32 402	Warm And Willing	1964	Emerson, J.*	AF		$23.00 A
MIDWOOD	32 410	Hellcat	1964	Brooks, B.	AF		$9.00
MIDWOOD	32 411	A Labor Of Love	1964	Kemp, K.	VG		$8.00
MIDWOOD	32 413	Thank You, Call Again	1964	Duchamp, L.	AF		$8.00
MIDWOOD	32 414	The Roommates	1964	Clements, M.	VGF		$9.00
MIDWOOD	32 415	One After Another	1964	Fields, V.	VGF		$7.00
MIDWOOD	32 416	His To Command	1964	Collier, M.	AF		$15.00 A
MIDWOOD	32 420	Just This Once	1964	Burgess, M.	AF		$7.00
MIDWOOD	32 422	Pleasure Island	1964	York, A.	F		$8.00
MIDWOOD	32 423	Follow The Leader	1964	Hamilton, G.	VGF		$6.00
MIDWOOD	32 425	Private Property	1964	Curtis, B.	AF		$8.00
MIDWOOD	32 435	Into The Fire	1965	Russo, P.V.	AF		$18.00
MIDWOOD	32 437	Miss Dream Girl	1965	Hart, J.	VGF		$15.00 A
MIDWOOD	32 440	For Want Of Love	1965	Moore, A.	AF		$7.00
MIDWOOD	32 441	Night Shift	1965	Curtis, B.	VGF		$7.00
MIDWOOD	32 442	The Drifter	1965	Hastings, M.	AF		$10.00
MIDWOOD	32 442	The Drifter	1965	Hastings, M.	VG+		$7.00
MIDWOOD	32 448	Coming Out Party	1965	Kemp, K.	AF		$55.00 A
MIDWOOD	32 450	Daytime In Suburbia	1965	West, S.	VGF+		$8.00
MIDWOOD	32 452	Out Of Control	1965	Clements, M.	AF		$7.00
MIDWOOD	32 453	Tourist Trap	1965	Newbury, W.	VG+		$5.00

| Midwood 455 F $15 | Midwood 614 VG $7 | Midwood 780 VG+ $7 | Midwood 899 VGF $14 |

PUBLISHER	PUB. #	TITLE	DATE	AUTHOR	COND.	TYPE	PRICE
MIDWOOD	32 454	Master Pieces	1965	Kandel, H.	VGF		$8.00
MIDWOOD	32 454	Master Pieces	1965	Kandel, H.	VG+		$7.00
MIDWOOD	32 455	The Love Pirate	1965	York, A.	F		$15.00 A
MIDWOOD	34 457	Executive Sweet	1965	Ellis, J.	F	DBL	$11.00 A
		The Soft Sell		Nelson, C.			
MIDWOOD	32 464	Open House	1965	Ellis, J.	VGF		$10.00
MIDWOOD	32 465	Pagan Summer	1965	Mayo, D.	VGF-		$51.00 A
MIDWOOD	32 468	The Highest Bidder	1965	Fields, V.	VGF		$10.00
MIDWOOD	32 470	Punish Lesson	1965	Moore, A.	AF		$11.00 A
MIDWOOD	32 470	Punish Lesson	1965	Moore, A.	VG-		$2.50
MIDWOOD	34 476	Two-Timer	1965	Nelson, C.	AF	DBL	$14.00
		The Mate Exchange		Harris, F.			
MIDWOOD	32 478	The Swap Set	1965	Collier, M.	AF		$8.00
MIDWOOD	32 480	Trouble-Maker	1965	Trainer, R.	AF		$12.00
MIDWOOD	32 480	Trouble-Maker	1965	Trainer, R.	VGF+		$9.00 A
MIDWOOD	34 490	Problem Child	1965	Fields, V.	VG+	DBL	$12.00
		The Switch		Ellis, J.			
MIDWOOD	32 495	Down And Out	1965	Masters, L.	VGF		$10.00
MIDWOOD	32 497	The Sleek And Sensual	1965	Collier, M.	VGF+		$7.00
MIDWOOD	32 497	The Sleek And Sensual	1965	Collier, M.	VGF		$7.00
MIDWOOD	34 505	The Voluptuary	1965	Nelson, C.	AF	DBL	$30.00 A
		One For All		Woods, M.			
MIDWOOD	34 505	The Voluptuary	1965	Nelson, C.	G	DBL	$4.00
MIDWOOD	32 510	Obsession	1965	Paine, E.	F		$17.00 A
MIDWOOD	32 512	The Lady Awaits	1965	Hamilton, G.	VGF-		$6.00
MIDWOOD	34 519	None The Wiser	1965	Haney, C.	VGF	DBL	$18.00 A
		Change Partners		Corgan, G.			
MIDWOOD	34 519	None The Wiser	1965	Haney, C.	VG+	DBL	$10.00
MIDWOOD	32 520	Sooner Or Later	1965	Ellis, J.	VGF		$15.00 A
MIDWOOD	32 521	The Rebel	1965	Paine, E.	G		$4.00
MIDWOOD	32 527	Secret Session	1965	Hytes, J.	AF		$15.00 A
MIDWOOD	34 533	Runaway	1965	Nelson, C.	VG	DBL	$10.00
		Now Or Never		Haney, C.			
MIDWOOD	32 537	Mock Marriage	1965	Shaw, K.	AF		$7.00
MIDWOOD	32 538	Model Mistress	1965	Duchamp, L.	AF		$19.00 A
MIDWOOD	32 541	Twice With Julie	1965	Hytes, J.	AF		$10.00
MIDWOOD	34 547	Only In Shadows	1965	Woods, M.	AF	DBL	$20.00 A
		The Velvet Trap		Stevens, T.			
MIDWOOD	34 561	Lady Of Leisure	1965	Nelson, C.	VGF	DBL	$15.00
		Never Let Go		Stevens, T.			
MIDWOOD	34 561	Lady Of Leisure	1965	Nelson, C.	VG	DBL	$9.00
MIDWOOD	32 563	Boss Lady	1965	Grant, U.	F		$8.00
MIDWOOD	32 563	Boss Lady	1965	Grant, U.	F		$7.00
MIDWOOD	34 576	Girl About Town	1965	Grant, U.	VG	DBL	$10.00
		Do Unto Others		Stevens, T.			
MIDWOOD	32 578	All Together Now	1965	Mayo, D.	VG-		$5.00
MIDWOOD	32 579	Country Girl	1965	Ellis, J.	AF		$9.00
MIDWOOD	32 579	Country Girl	1965	Ellis, J.	F		$8.00

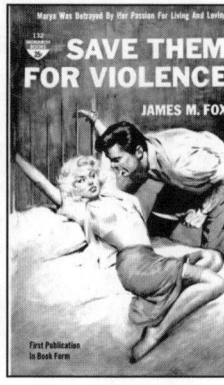

Monarch 101 F $20   Monarch 111 VG $8   Monarch 121 VGF- $60   Monarch 132 VG+ $20

PUBLISHER	PUB. #	TITLE	DATE	AUTHOR	COND.	TYPE	PRICE
MIDWOOD	32 584	The Last Resort	1966	Kemp, K.	AF		$20.00
MIDWOOD	34 595	Party, Party	1966	West, C.P.	AF	DBL	$16.00
		Dutch Treat		Williams, J.			
MIDWOOD	34 595	Party, Party	1966	West, C.P.	VG	DBL	$10.00
MIDWOOD	34 596	Wanton Widow	1966	Nelson, C.	AF	DBL	$12.00 A
		Two Times Two		Brooks, B.			
MIDWOOD	34 597	Pretty Playmate	1966	Newbury, W.	VG+	DBL	$16.00
		Every So Often		Stevens, T.			
MIDWOOD	32 599	Free And Easy	1966	Hamilton, G.	VGF		$10.00
MIDWOOD	32 602	No Last Names	1966	Ellis, J.	AF		$10.00
MIDWOOD	32 613	Man Hunt	1966	Clements, M.	VGF		$5.00
MIDWOOD	32 614	Girl On The Run	1966	Holbrook, J.	VG		$7.00
MIDWOOD	32 615	Sweet But Sinful	1966	Paine, E.	AF		$7.00
MIDWOOD	32 617	Hide And Seek	1966	King, N.A.	VGF		$5.00
MIDWOOD	32 618	Snow Bunnies	1966	Ellis, J.	AF		$9.00
MIDWOOD	34 624	Bold And Brazen	1966	Roote, L.	VGF	DBL	$8.00
		Private Secretary		Woods, M.			
MIDWOOD	32 628	Norma	1966	Glennon, G.	AF		$7.00
MIDWOOD	32 629	The Face Of Evil	1966	Bruce, R.	AF		$8.00
MIDWOOD	32 632	Label Her Shameless	1966	Thompson, J.B.	AF-		$10.00
MIDWOOD	32 632	Label Her Shameless	1966	Thompson, J.B.	AF		$9.00
MIDWOOD	32 694	Brandy Jones	1966	Thompson, J.B.	AF		$15.00 A
MIDWOOD	34 698	Pleasant Company	1966	Kemp, K.	VG		$5.00
MIDWOOD	33 715	Next Stop Shame	1966	Matty, B.	VGF		$7.00
MIDWOOD	34 725	Test In Temptation	1966	Duchamp, L.	VG	DBL	$7.00
		Cool And Collected		Randall, B.			
MIDWOOD	32 742	Apartment Party	1966	Kramer, G.	F		$10.00
MIDWOOD	33 742	Apartment Party	1966	Kramer, G.	AF		$7.00 A
MIDWOOD	33 751	Office Favorite	1966	Malloy, D.	F		$23.00
MIDWOOD	33 752	Earning Her Keep	1966	Comstock, J.C.	AF		$7.00
MIDWOOD	33 769	Professional Favors	1967	Harmon, J.	VGF		$12.00
MIDWOOD	33 780	This Is Elaine	1966	Hytes, J.	VG+		$7.00
MIDWOOD	34 781	Fascination	1967	Duchamp, L.	F	DBL	$7.00
MIDWOOD	33 786	Night School	1967	August, J.	VG+		$7.00
MIDWOOD	33 796	Adult Education	1967	Fields, V.	VG		$6.00
MIDWOOD	F 804	The Lady From L.U.S.T.	1967	Gray, R.	VG		$7.00
MIDWOOD	34 869	Love Like A Shadow	1967	Kemp, K.	G-		$2.00
MIDWOOD	34 896	Sleep-In Girl	1968	Kamp, D.	AF		$5.00
MIDWOOD	34 898	The Sex Tests	1968	Moore, A.	AF		$6.00
MIDWOOD	34 899	Stag Show	1968	Mayo, D.	VGF		$14.00 A
MIDWOOD	34 927	Pagan	1968	Russo, P.V.	F		$10.00
MIDWOOD	34 943	I, Lesbian	1968	Johnson, M.L.	F		$14.00
MIDWOOD	35 953	The Marriage Wrecker	1968	Shaffer, T.	AF	DBL	$6.00
MIDWOOD	34 965	Sex Ranch	1968	Harrison, C.	VGF+		$6.00
MIDWOOD	34 108	Pleasure Machine	1968	Lord, S.*	F		$12.00 A
MIDWOOD	34 118	Fun Girl	1968	Corgan, G.	AF		$13.00 A
MIDWOOD	35 146	I Want A Man	1968	Balmer, J.	VGF+	DBL	$8.00
MIDWOOD	34 147	Candy	1968	Lord, S.*	F		$12.00

Monarch 141 VG+ $7   Monarch 188 VGF $18   Monarch 189 VG+ $16   Monarch 225 VGF $10

PUBLISHER	PUB. #	TITLE	DATE	AUTHOR	COND.	TYPE	PRICE
MIDWOOD	35 194	Strange	1969	Mayo, D.	AF	DBL	$17.00
MIDWOOD	35 195	Running Wild	1969	Swenson, P.*	F	DBL	$7.00
MIDWOOD	37 224	Come One, Come All	1969	Hamilton, G.	AF	Triple	$7.00
MIDWOOD	35 229	The Sweetest Vice	1969	Hamilton, G.	AF	DBL	$16.00 A
MIDWOOD	37 231	Breaking Loose	1969	Ellis, J.	AF	Triple	$7.00
MIDWOOD	34 234	The Whispered Love	1969	Mayo, D.	AF		$12.00
MIDWOOD	35 239	Strange Worlds	1969	Hamilton, G.	AF	DBL	$18.00
MIDWOOD	34 252	Nymph	1969	Swenson, P.*	F		$8.00
MIDWOOD	35 253	Twisted	1969	Wilde, D.	F	DBL	$25.00 A
MIDWOOD	37 255	Season For Sin	1969	O'Mara. J.	AF	Triple	$7.00
MIDWOOD	37 292	Initiation	1969	Halden, P.	F	DBL	$20.00
MIDWOOD	37 310	Sweet Sin	1969	Ellis, J.	F	DBL	$7.00
MIDWOOD	125 20	The Perfect Oh	1969	Rider, S.	AF		$7.00
MIDWOOD	125 51	Busted	1970	Ramport, D.	AF		$10.00
MIDWOOD TOWER*		*See TOWER					
MICHAEL SHAYNE	1 2	Michael Shayne Mystery 10/56	1956	Anthology	G+	Digest	$7.00
MICHAEL SHAYNE	1 3	Michael Shayne Mystery 11/56	1956	Anthology	VG-	Digest	$6.00
MIKE SHAYNE	2 5	Mike Shayne Mystery 12/57	1957	Anthology	VG	Digest	$6.00
MIKE SHAYNE	3 3	Mike Shayne Mystery 8/58	1958	Anthology	VGF	Digest	$7.00
MIKE SHAYNE	3 5	Mike Shayne Mystery 10/58	1958	Anthology	VG	Digest	$42.00 A
MIKE SHAYNE	4 1	Mike Shayne Mystery 12/58	1958	Anthology	AF	Digest	$8.00
MIKE SHAYNE	4 2	Mike Shayne Mystery 1/59	1959	Anthology	AF	Digest	$7.00
MIKE SHAYNE	4 4	Mike Shayne Mystery 3/59	1959	Anthology	AF	Digest	$12.00
MIKE SHAYNE	5 5	Mike Shayne Mystery 10/59	1959	Anthology	VG+	Digest	$5.00
MIKE SHAYNE	7 5	Mike Shayne Mystery 10/60	1960	Anthology	VG	Digest	$5.00
MIKE SHAYNE	8 4	Mike Shayne Mystery 3/61	1961	Anthology	VGF+	Digest	$8.00
MIKE SHAYNE	9 4	Mike Shayne Mystery 9/61	1961	Anthology	VGF	Digest	$8.00
MIKE SHAYNE	15 4	Mike Shayne Mystery 9/64	1964	Anthology	VG	Digest	$7.00
MIKE SHAYNE	16 6	Mike Shayne Mystery 5/65	1965	Anthology	VG	Digest	$5.00
MIKE SHAYNE	36 2	Mike Shayne Mystery 2/75	1975	Anthology	VGF	Digest	$7.00
MIKE SHAYNE	38 1	Mike Shayne Mystery 1/76	1976	Anthology	AF	Digest	$6.00
MONARCH	101	Dark Hunger	1958	James, D.	F		$20.00 A
MONARCH	101	Dark Hunger	1958	James, D.	AF		$20.00 A
MONARCH	101	Dark Hunger	1958	James, D.	VG+		$8.00
MONARCH	102	Winter Range	1958	LeMay, A.	VG+		$7.00
MONARCH	103	Love Me Now	1958	Nichols, F.	AF		$16.00 A
MONARCH	103	Love Me Now	1958	Nichols, F.	VG+		$8.00
MONARCH	107	Wild To Possess	1959	Brewer, G.	VG+		$35.00 A
MONARCH	107	Wild To Possess	1959	Brewer, G.	VGF		$25.00 A
MONARCH	110	Touch Me Not	1959	Harwin, B.	VG		$6.00
MONARCH	111	Sword Of Casanova	1959	Kendricks, J.*	VG		$8.00
MONARCH	111	Sword Of Casanova	1959	Kendricks, J.*	VG-		$6.00
MONARCH	115	Madigan's Women	1959	Conway, J.	VG+		$8.00
MONARCH	117	Stronger Than Passion	1959	Byram, G.	VG+		$8.00
MONARCH	118	Way Of The Wicked	1959	Woolfolk, W.	VG+		$10.00 A
MONARCH	119	Occasion Of Sin	1959	Taylor, R.W.	VG+		$8.00
MONARCH	121	Kiss Me Quick	1959	Kramer, K.	VGF-		$60.00 A
MONARCH	123	Beyond Our Pleasure	1959	Kendricks, J.*	VGF		$8.00

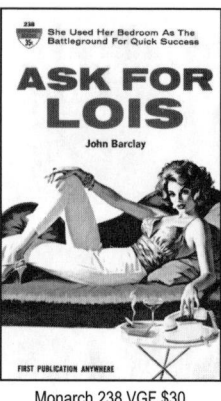
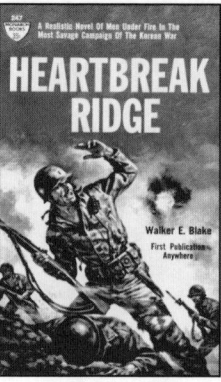
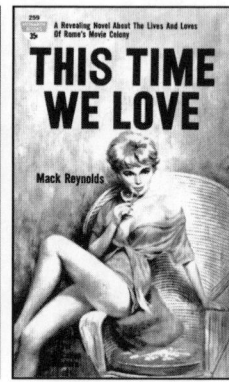

| Monarch 227 AF $16 | Monarch 238 VGF $30 | Monarch 247 VGF $8 | Monarch 259 F $16 |

PUBLISHER	PUB. #	TITLE	DATE	AUTHOR	COND.	TYPE	PRICE
MONARCH	125	Nikki (3rd)	1961	Friedman, S.	AF		$10.00 A
MONARCH	132	Save Them For Violence	1959	Fox, J.M.	VG+		$20.00 A
MONARCH	132	Save Them For Violence	1959	Fox, J.M.	VG		$12.00
MONARCH	133	The Flesh Peddlers	1959	Boyd, F.	VGF		$8.00
MONARCH	133	The Flesh Peddlers	1959	Boyd, F.	VG-		$3.00
MONARCH	138	Stephana	1959	Foster, J.	VGF+	MTI	$12.00 A
MONARCH	139	In Savage Surrender	1959	Chambers, W.	VG+		$5.00 A
MONARCH	140	The Glory Jumpers	1959	Stagg, D.	VG+		$8.00
MONARCH	141	Falcons Of France	1959	Nordhoff, C.	VG+		$7.00
MONARCH	141	Falcons Of France	1959	Nordhoff, C.	G		$3.00
MONARCH	143	Jack The Ripper	1960	James, S.	VGF	MTI	$18.00 A
MONARCH	143	Jack The Ripper	1960	James, S.	VG-	MTI	$15.00
MONARCH	150	Most Likely To Love	1960	Flora, F.	VG		$7.00
MONARCH	153	Frisco Flat	1960	James, S.	VG		$4.00
MONARCH	156	Manhandled	1960	Chambers, W.	VG		$7.00
MONARCH	157	Yield To The Night	1960	Karney, J.	G		$6.00
MONARCH	160	The Cage Of Love	1960	Carse, R.	VG		$8.00
MONARCH	161	Naked Before My Captors	1960	Newell, B.F.	VG+		$7.00
MONARCH	164	A Rage Of Desire	1960	Matthews, C.	VGF		$5.00
MONARCH	165	Young And Innocent	1960	West, E.*	VG+		$11.00 A
MONARCH	167	One Touch Of Ecstasy	1960	Wimberly, G.	VG		$8.00
MONARCH	168	Play It Hard	1960	Brewer, G.	G+		$6.00
MONARCH	171	Marilyn K.	1960	White, L.	VG		$5.00
MONARCH	173	The Satyr	1960	McKimmey, J.	VG		$5.00
MONARCH	174	Love In Suburbia	1960	Conway, J.	VGF+		$10.00 A
MONARCH	175	Arnhem	1960	Urquhart, R.E.	AF		$8.00
MONARCH	179	Run Naked In The Night	1960	Olive, H.	VGF		$11.00 A
MONARCH	182	This Bed We Made	1961	Smith, A.	VGF		$17.00 A
MONARCH	183	$50 A Night	1961	James, D.	VGF		$14.00 A
MONARCH	184	The Lovers Of Pompeii	1961	Pratt, T.	AF		$8.00
MONARCH	186	The Klaxon Girls	1961	Rowland, T.	VG-		$6.00
MONARCH	187	Appointment In Hell	1961	Brewer, G.	VGF		$27.00
MONARCH	188	The Girl From Big Pine	1961	Powell, T.	VGF		$18.00 A
MONARCH	189	Campus Doll	1961	West, E.*	VG+		$16.00
MONARCH	191	And Love So Wild	1961	Little, C.	VG+		$10.00
MONARCH	192	The Damned And The Innocent	1961	Canary, G.	AF		$13.00 A
MONARCH	194	Run Tough, Run Hard	1961	Bingham, C.	VGF		$20.00 A
MONARCH	197	Day Of Blood	1961	Vance, W.	VG		$7.00
MONARCH	202	Debbie	1961	Daniels, P.	VGF		$10.00
MONARCH	206	By Passion Obsessed	1961	Coberly, V.J.	VGF		$11.00 A
MONARCH	209	The Reckless Lovers	1961	Locke, R.D.	VG+		$9.00
MONARCH	210	Bloody Beaches	1961	Stagg, D.	AF		$10.00
MONARCH	212	Beyond All Desire	1961	Phillips, T.	VG		$7.00
MONARCH	213	The Green Planet	1961	Holly, J.H.	VG		$2.50
MONARCH	214	A Kiss Before Loving	1961	Reynolds, M.	AF		$13.00 A
MONARCH	216	Flight To Takla-Ma	1961	Thomey, T.	AF		$14.00
MONARCH	219	Make Every Kiss Count	1961	Simpson, R.	VG+		$12.00
MONARCH	221	My Father's Wife	1961	Carr, J.	VGF		$9.00 A

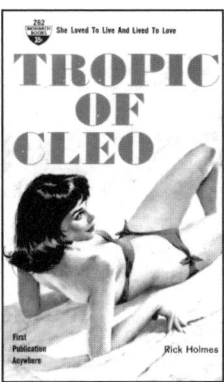
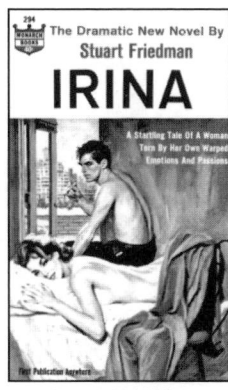

| Monarch 260 VG $7 | Monarch 262 AF $11 | Monarch 294 AF $12 | Monarch 303 VG- $8 |

PUBLISHER	PUB. #	TITLE	DATE	AUTHOR	COND.	TYPE	PRICE
MONARCH	224	Ladies Of The Dark	1961	Bolton, A.	VG		$7.00
MONARCH	225	Tropic Fury	1961	Gale, C.	VGF		$10.00
MONARCH	225	Tropic Fury	1961	Gale, C.	VG+		$7.00
MONARCH	226	Call Boy	1961	Newbury, W.	VGF		$16.00
MONARCH	227	It Happened In Hawaii	1961	Bingham, C.	AF		$16.00 A
MONARCH	233	Playboy	1962	Daniels, P.	VG+		$5.00 A
MONARCH	236	Bamboo Camp #10	1962	Davis, F.M.	F		$22.00 A
MONARCH	238	Ask For Lois	1962	Barclay, J.	VGF		$30.00 A
MONARCH	240	Encounter	1962	Holly, J.H.	AF		$8.00
MONARCH	240	Encounter	1962	Holly, J.H.	VGF		$5.00
MONARCH	241	Rasputin: The Mad Monk	1962	Friedman, S.	AF+		$15.00 A
MONARCH	241	Rasputin: The Mad Monk	1962	Friedman, S.	VGF		$11.00 A
MONARCH	242	Easy Come, Easy Love	1962	Tremont, P.	F		$16.00 A
MONARCH	243	Teen-Age Tramp	1962	Johnston, W.	G		$3.00
MONARCH	244	Kim	1962	Colby, R.	F		$18.00 A
MONARCH	244	Kim	1962	Colby, R.	VGF		$14.00
MONARCH	244	Kim	1962	Colby, R.	VG+		$9.00 A
MONARCH	245	Cancel These Vows	1962	Webster, S.	AF		$12.00
MONARCH	245	Cancel These Vows	1962	Webster, S.	AF		$11.00 A
MONARCH	247	Heartbreak Ridge	1962	Blake, W.E.	VGF		$8.00
MONARCH	250	The Lolita Lovers	1962	Clarke, J.	AF		$22.00 A
MONARCH	250	The Lolita Lovers	1962	Clarke, J.	VG+		$15.00
MONARCH	250	The Lolita Lovers	1962	Clarke, J.	VG		$9.00 A
MONARCH	252	The Space Egg	1962	Winterbotham, R.	VGF		$6.00
MONARCH	254	The Cover Girls	1962	Daniels, P.	AF		$11.00 A
MONARCH	254	The Cover Girls	1962	Daniels, P.	VG		$3.00
MONARCH	255	Frenzied	1962	Taylor, R.V.	VG+		$8.00
MONARCH	257	Ravaged	1962	Friedman, S.	VGF		$10.00
MONARCH	259	This Time We Love	1962	Reynolds, M.	F		$16.00 A
MONARCH	260	The Flying Eyes	1962	Holly, J.H.	VG		$7.00
MONARCH	261	That Girl Marian	1962	Dixon, H.V.	AF		$18.00 A
MONARCH	262	Tropic Of Cleo	1962	Holmes, R.	AF		$11.00 A
MONARCH	263	Tormented Lovers	1962	Winston, D.	AF-		$12.00 A
MONARCH	263	Tormented Lovers	1962	Winston, D.	VG		$3.00
MONARCH	268	The Wives Of Friends	1962	Webster, S.	F		$11.00 A
MONARCH	268	The Wives Of Friends	1962	Webster, S.	VGF		$9.00 A
MONARCH	270	The Red Planet	1962	Winterbotham, R.	VGF+		$8.00
MONARCH	270	The Red Planet	1962	Winterbotham, R.	VG+		$6.00
MONARCH	270	The Red Planet	1962	Winterbotham, R.	VG		$5.00
MONARCH	272	The Surgeons	1962	Friedman, S.	VGF		$5.00
MONARCH	275	Save Her For Loving	1962	Johnston, W.	VG+		$8.00
MONARCH	278	The Party Lovers	1962	Hadrian, P.	AF		$17.00 A
MONARCH	278	The Party Lovers	1962	Hadrian, P.	VGF		$11.00 A
MONARCH	280	The Sadist	1962	Canary, G.	VG+		$11.00 A
MONARCH	283	The Loves Of Dr. Devere	1962	Bingham, C.	VG		$6.00
MONARCH	285	The Pleasure In Women	1962	Lee, T.	AF		$8.00
MONARCH	286	Her Cheating Heart	1962	Kevin, L.	AF		$14.00 A
MONARCH	288	Suburban Lovers	1962	Carr, J.	F		$14.00 A

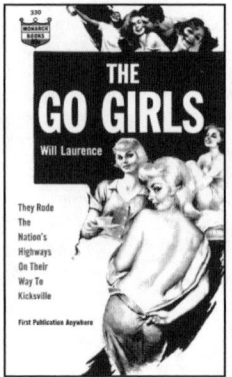

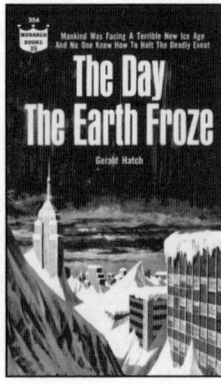

Monarch 308 VGF $8   Monarch 330 AF $22   Monarch 347 VG+ $10   Monarch 354 VG+ $7

PUBLISHER	PUB. #	TITLE	DATE	AUTHOR	COND.	TYPE	PRICE
MONARCH	288	Suburban Lovers	1962	Carr, J.	VGF		$8.00
MONARCH	289	Faithless	1962	Matthews, C.	F		$11.00 A
MONARCH	291	The Show Girls	1962	Daniels, P.	VG+		$8.00
MONARCH	292	Seven Brave Men	1962	Garland, B.	VGF		$7.00 A
MONARCH	294	Irina	1963	Friedman, S.	AF		$12.00 A
MONARCH	297	Ten From Infinity	1963	Jorgensen, I.	AF		$7.00
MONARCH	298	The Pleasure Seekers	1963	Dixon, H.V.	AF		$25.00 A
MONARCH	298	The Pleasure Seekers	1963	Dixon, H.V.	VG		$7.00
MONARCH	299	Ruby	1963	Daniels, P.	VG		$4.00
MONARCH	MA 300	King Of The Harem Heaven	1960	Sterling, A.	VG		$25.00
MONARCH	MA 300	King Of The Harem Heaven	1960	Sterling, A.	VG		$12.00
MONARCH	MA 303	Outlaw Queen	1960	Shirley, G.	VG-		$8.00
MONARCH	MA 303	Outlaw Queen	1960	Shirley, G.	VG		$7.00
MONARCH	MA 305	Blood & Guts Patton	1961	Pearl, J.	VGF		$7.00
MONARCH	MA 306	Break-Through	1961	Davis, F.M.	VGF		$7.00
MONARCH	MA 308	The Sam Houston Story	1961	Owen, D.	VGF		$8.00
MONARCH	MA 308	The Sam Houston Story	1961	Owen, D.	VGF		$8.00 A
MONARCH	MA 310	Harem Island	1961	Sterling, A.	VGF		$22.00 A
MONARCH	MA 310	Harem Island	1961	Sterling, A.	AF		$14.00 A
MONARCH	MA 311	The Dillinger Story	1961	Demaris, O.	VG		$4.00
MONARCH	MA 314	America's War Heroes	1961	Scott, J.	F		$7.00
MONARCH	MA 321	Tarawa	1962	Bailey, T.	AF-		$7.00
MONARCH	MA 323	The "Dutch" Schultz Story	1962	Addy, T.	VG+		$7.00
MONARCH	MA 324	The Sioux Indian Wars	1962	Conway, J.	VG+		$22.00 A
MONARCH	MA 325	King Of The Free Lovers	1962	Hunter, A.	AF		$29.00 A
MONARCH	MA 326	The Frank Costello Story	1962	Brennan, B.	VGF		$7.00
MONARCH	330	The Go Girls	1963	Laurence, W.	AF		$22.00 A
MONARCH	MA 333	The Texas Rangers	1963	Conway, J.	VG+		$7.00
MONARCH	335	Spare Her Heaven	1963	Ives, M.*	G+		$10.00
MONARCH	336	Emergency For Dr. Starr	1963	Johnston, W.	AF		$7.00
MONARCH	341	Naked When We Die	1963	Martin, T.	VGF		$11.00 A
MONARCH	342	The Running Man	1963	Holly, J.H.	VG+		$4.00
MONARCH	347	The Cruise Ship Girls	1963	Newbury, W.	VG+		$10.00
MONARCH	347	The Cruise Ship Girls	1963	Newbury, W.	VG		$9.00
MONARCH	MA 350	The U.S. Navy In Action	1963	Clagett, J.	VG+		$4.00
MONARCH	351	Fathers And Daughters	1963	Friedman, S.	VGF+		$27.00 A
MONARCH	351	Fathers And Daughters	1963	Friedman, S.	G		$3.00
MONARCH	352	My Sister, My Love	1963	Gardner, M.*	G		$8.00
MONARCH	354	The Day The Earth Froze	1963	Hatch, G.	VG+		$7.00
MONARCH	358	The Pitchmen	1963	James, D.	VG+		$5.00
MONARCH	360	The Kept Woman	1963	Reynolds, M.	VGF+		$12.00 A
MONARCH	362	Rest In Agony	1963	Jorgensen, I.	VGF+		$10.00 A
MONARCH	365	She'll Hate Me Tomorrow	1963	Deming, R.	VGF		$8.00
MONARCH	368	The Colors Of Space	1963	Bradley, M.Z.	VG+		$6.00
MONARCH	371	Wild Weekend	1963	Ellsworth, H.	VG+		$7.00
MONARCH	374	Hot Rod Fury	1963	Bowen, R.S.	VGF		$14.00
MONARCH	377	Nikki Revisited	1963	Friedman, S.	AF		$12.00
MONARCH	377	Nikki Revisited	1963	Friedman, S.	VG+		$5.00

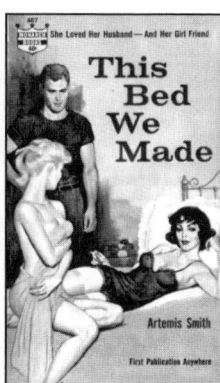

Monarch 371 VG+ $7   Monarch 453 AF $7   Monarch 464 VG+ $5   Monarch 467 VG $55

PUBLISHER	PUB. #	TITLE	DATE	AUTHOR	COND.	TYPE	PRICE
MONARCH	380	Season For Love	1963	Chambers, W.	G		$4.00
MONARCH	MA 384	The Violent Americans	1963	Porges, I.	VG+		$3.00
MONARCH	386	Obsession	1963	White, L.	AF		$16.00
MONARCH	389	Occasion Of Sin	1963	Taylor, R.W.	AF+		$10.00 A
MONARCH	390	The Hamelin Plague	1963	Chandler, A.B.	VGF		$7.00
MONARCH	397	21 Sunset Drive	1963	Ellsworth, H.	VG		$6.00
MONARCH	399	Jailbait Street	1963	Ellson, H.	AF		$21.00 A
MONARCH	399	Jailbait Street	1963	Ellson, H.	G		$3.00
MONARCH	405	The Jet Set	1964	Reynolds, M.	VGF		$7.00
MONARCH	408	Mary Adams, Student Nurse	1964	Brennan, A.	VG		$3.00
MONARCH	410	Young And Innocent	1964	West, E.*	F		$60.00 A
MONARCH	410	Young And Innocent	1964	West, E.*	AF		$30.00 A
MONARCH	412	November Reef	1964	Maugham, R.	VG		$3.00
MONARCH	414	The Gods Hate Kansas	1964	Millard, J.	AF		$7.00
MONARCH	414	The Gods Hate Kansas	1964	Millard, J.	VGF		$6.00
MONARCH	418	Twilight Lovers	1964	Gardner, M.*	AF		$57.00
MONARCH	418	Twilight Lovers	1964	Gardner, M.*	VG		$27.00 A
MONARCH	420	Louisa	1964	Allen, E.	AF		$15.00 A
MONARCH	422	Jealous	1964	Daniels, P.	AF		$38.00 A
MONARCH	422	Jealous	1964	Daniels, P.	VG+		$13.00
MONARCH	425	The Adulterers	1964	Kendricks, J.*	VGF		$16.00
MONARCH	426	Most Likely To Love	1964	Flora, F.	AF		$22.00 A
MONARCH	430	Silent Wings	1964	Bowen, R.S.	VG+		$8.00
MONARCH	431	Planet Big Zero	1964	Hadley, F.	VGF		$6.00
MONARCH	431	Planet Big Zero	1964	Hadley, F.	VG+		$4.00
MONARCH	433	Kiss Me Quick	1964	Kramer, K.	VG+		$6.00
MONARCH	434	Manhandled	1964	Chambers, W.	VGF-		$10.00
MONARCH	434	Manhandled	1964	Chambers, W.	VG+		$5.00 A
MONARCH	435	For Every Young Heart	1964	Francis, C.	VGF		$5.00
MONARCH	436	Adolescent Sexual Behavior	1964	Morse, B.*	VG+		$7.00 A
MONARCH	439	This Game Of Murder	1964	Deming, R.	VG+		$10.00
MONARCH	439	This Game Of Murder	1964	Deming, R.	VG+		$8.00
MONARCH	443	The Day The Oceans Overflowed	1964	Fontenay, C.	VGF		$8.00
MONARCH	444	Play It Hard	1964	Brewer, G.	VG+		$10.00
MONARCH	444	Play It Hard	1964	Brewer, G.	VG		$8.00
MONARCH	453	Invasion From 2500	1964	Edwards, N.	AF		$7.00
MONARCH	454	New Doctor At Tower General	1964	Miller, J.J.	AF		$7.00
MONARCH	455	Love In Suburbia	1964	Conway, J.	VG		$6.00
MONARCH	459	The Fantastic Lodge	1964	Hughes, H.M., ed.	VG		$7.00
MONARCH	460	The Golden Witch	1964	Brown, W.	VG		$7.00
MONARCH	464	The Unending Night	1964	Smith, G.H.	VG+		$5.00
MONARCH	467	This Bed We Made	1964	Smith, A.	VG		$55.00 A
MONARCH	471	The World Grabbers	1964	Fairman, P.W.	VGF	TVTI	$7.00
MONARCH	472	The Law And The Marriage Bed	1965	Gordon, G.	VGF-		$5.00
MONARCH	473	The Nez Perce Indian Wars	1964	Mathieson, T.	AF		$6.00
MONARCH	477	The Money Trap	1964	White, L.	VG		$8.00
MONARCH	479	World's Great Events: 1964	1965	Halacy, D.S.	VG		$4.00
MONARCH	483	The Girl From Big Pine	1964	Powell, T.	VG		$7.00

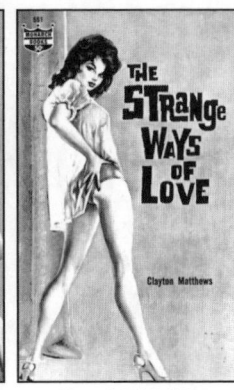

Monarch 487 AF $33   Monarch 510 VGF+ $60   Monarch 526 AF $67   Monarch 551 AF $22

PUBLISHER	PUB. #	TITLE	DATE	AUTHOR	COND.	TYPE	PRICE
MONARCH	486	The Damned And The Innocent	1964	Canary, G.	F		$10.00 A
MONARCH	486	The Damned And The Innocent	1964	Canary, G.	VG+		$6.00
MONARCH	487	Run Tough, Run Hard	1964	Bingham, C.	AF		$33.00 A
MONARCH	487	Run Tough, Run Hard	1964	Bingham, C.	VG+		$19.00 A
MONARCH	497	Brother And Sister	1965	West, E.*	VGF+		$30.00 A
MONARCH	497	Brother And Sister	1965	West, E.*	VG-		$5.00
MONARCH	498	She'll Get Hers	1965	Plunkett, J.	VGF		$12.00
MONARCH	MB 501	Women In Trouble	1959	Donner, J.	VGF		$36.00 A
MONARCH	MB 503	Tormented Women	1959	McGoldrick, E.J.	VG+		$18.00 A
MONARCH	MB 505	Crime And Passion	1960	Mozes, E.B.	AF		$16.00 A
MONARCH	MB 505	Crime And Passion	1960	Mozes, E.B.	VG		$7.00
MONARCH	MB 509	The Book Of Miracles	1961	Aradi, Z.	VG+		$8.00
MONARCH	MB 510	Bedeviled	1961	Brown, W.	VGF+		$60.00 A
MONARCH	MB 511	Sex Fiend	1961	Woodward, L.T.*	VGF+		$27.00 A
MONARCH	MB 514	It's Cheaper To Die	1961	Michelfelder, W.	AF		$8.00
MONARCH	MB 518	Sexual Surrender In Women	1962	Morse, B.*	AF		$38.00 A
MONARCH	MB 518	Sexual Surrender In Women	1962	Morse, B.*	VG		$12.00
MONARCH	MB 519	The Divorcee	1962	O'Hara, R.C.	VG+		$16.00 A
MONARCH	MB 521	Sex In Our Schools	1962	Woodward, L.T.*	VG+		$5.00 A
MONARCH	MB 522	Crack-Up In Suburbia	1962	Carr, J.	AF		$5.00
MONARCH	MB 524	Unwed Mothers	1962	Galus, H.S.	F		$35.00 A
MONARCH	MB 524	Unwed Mothers	1962	Galus, H.S.	VGF		$11.00 A
MONARCH	MB 526	I Am A Teen-Age Dope Addict	1962	Jordan, V.	AF		$67.00 A
MONARCH	MB 526	I Am A Teen-Age Dope Addict	1962	Jordan, V.	AF		$40.00 A
MONARCH	MB 526	I Am A Teen-Age Dope Addict	1962	Jordan, V.	AF-		$30.00 A
MONARCH	MB 531	The Sexual Revolution	1962	Morse, B.*	VG+		$42.00 A
MONARCH	MB 533	The Impotent Male	1963	Glover, L.E.	VG		$4.00
MONARCH	MB 534	Girls And Gangs	1963	James, D.	VGF		$21.00 A
MONARCH	MB 534	Girls And Gangs	1963	James, D.	VG+		$13.00 A
MONARCH	MB 535	The Sexually Promiscuous Female	1963	Morse, B.*	F		$30.00 A
MONARCH	MB 541	Sex And The Armed Services	1963	Woodward, L.T.*	VGF		$8.00 A
MONARCH	MB 546	Men, Women And Marriage	1963	Havemann, E.	VG		$4.00
MONARCH	551	The Strange Ways Of Love	1964	Matthews, C.	AF		$22.00 A
MONARCH	557	Riverfront Girl	1965	Holmes, R.	AF		$10.00
MONARCH	557	Riverfront Girl	1965	Holmes, R.	VG+		$7.00
MONARCH	558	The Despoiler	1965	Laurence, W.	AF		$12.00
MONARCH	563	The Child-Woman	1965	Holmes, R.	VGF		$10.00
MONARCH	MM 603	Gorgo	1960	Bingham, C.	VG+	MTI	$40.00 A
MONARCH	MM 603	Gorgo	1960	Bingham, C.	G+	MTI	$8.00
MONARCH	MM 604	Konga	1960	Owen, D.	VGF+	MTI	$55.00 A
MONARCH	MM 604	Konga	1960	Owen, D.	VG	MTI	$12.00
MONARCH	MM 605	Reptilicus	1961	Owen, D.	VG	MTI	$6.00
MONARCH	MM 606	The Street Is My Beat	1961	Bingham, C.	VGF+	MTI	$44.00 A
MONARCH	MM 606	The Street Is My Beat	1961	Bingham, C.	VG	MTI	$10.00
MONARCH	MM 606	The Street Is My Beat	1961	Bingham, C.	G+	MTI	$5.00
MONARCH	MM 607	"Mad Dog" Coll	1961	Thurman, S.	VG+	MTI	$10.00
MONARCH	SP 1	First American Into Space	1961	Silverberg, R.	VGF+		$8.00
MONARCH	SP 1	First American Into Space	1961	Silverberg, R.	VG+		$7.00

Moonlight Reader 103 AF $37   Murder 1-1 AF $29   Mystery Novel Classic 97 VG+ $8

PUBLISHER	PUB. #	TITLE	DATE	AUTHOR	COND.	TYPE	PRICE
MONARCH	MS 5	Planned Parenthood	1962	De Forrest, H.	VG		$4.00
MONARCH	MS 14	The Real Story On Cuba	1963	Bayard, J.	VG+		$3.00
MONARCH	MS 16	The Crisis In Cuba	1963	Freeman, T.	G		$3.00
MONARCH	MS 19	They Fought Under The Sea	1963	Navy Times	VG-		$6.00
MONARCH	MS 20	The Washington Waste-Makers	1963	Johnson, G.	VGF		$3.00
MONARCH	MS 21	The Cool Book	1963	Unger, A.	AF		$5.00
MONARCH	MS 23	Jaqueline Kennedy (3rd)	1963	Heller, D.	VG+		$3.00
MONARCH	MS 24	Battleground WWI	1964	Pearl, J.	VG		$2.00
MONARCH	K 50	Congo Song	1958	Cloete, S.	AF		$16.00 A
MONARCH	K 53	The Angry Time	1960	Bishop, L.	VG+		$17.00 A
MONARCH	K 58	The Loves Of Errol Flynn	1962	Thomey, T.	VGF+		$36.00 A
MONARCH	K 60	Princess Grace Kelly	1962	Newman, R.	VGF		$7.00
MONARCH	K 62	Shirley Temple	1962	Eby, L.	VG+		$7.00
MONARCH	K 62	Shirley Temple	1962	Eby, L.	G+		$3.00
MONARCH	K 63	Kim Novak: Goddess Of Love	1962	Fritch, C.E.	VG		$7.00
MONARCH	K 64	Eisenhower	1962	Johnson, G.	VGF		$3.00
MONARCH	K 66	R. F. Kennedy: Assistant President	1962	Gordon, G.	VG+		$3.00
MONARCH	K 67	Doris Day	1962	Thomey, T.	VGF		$6.00
MONARCH	K 68	The Fabulous Rockefellers	1963	Silverberg, R.	VG-		$2.00
MONARCH	K 71	Pope Paul VI	1963	Fabert, A.	VGF		$4.00
MONARCH	K 73	Great Events: 1932	1964	Halacy, D.S.	VGF		$3.00
MONOLITH	M 1001	The Fifth Sex	1969	Dylan, B., Ph.D.	VGF		$13.00 A
MOONLIGHT READER	MR 103	The Year For Love	n/d	Smith, G.H.	AF		$37.00 A
MOONLIGHT READER	MR 106	Lust Storm	1961	Anonymous	AF		$11.00 A
MOONLIGHT READER	MR 110	Love Cult	1961	Anonymous	AF		$16.00 A
MOONLIGHT READER	MR 112	Naked Diver	n/d	Anonymous	VGF		$17.00 A
MOONLIGHT READER	MR 123	Two Timing Tart	n/d	Anonymous	VG+		$12.00 A
MOST THRILLING SF	1	The Most Thrilling Sci-Fi	1966	Anthology	VG	Digest	$9.00
MURDER!	1 1	Murder! - 9/56	1956	Anthology	AF	Digest	$29.00 A
MURDER!	1 1	Murder! - 9/56	1956	Anthology	AF	Digest	$22.00 A
MURDER!	1 1	Murder! - 9/56	1956	Anthology	VGF-	Digest	$15.00 A
MURDER!	2 1	Murder! - 3/57	1957	Anthology	AF	Digest	$24.00 A
MURDER!	2 1	Murder! - 3/57	1957	Anthology	VGF	Digest	$16.00 A
MYSTERIOUS PRESS	40827	Fireworks	1989	Thompson, J.	VGF		$5.00
MYSTERIOUS TRAVELER	2	The Mysterious Traveller #2	1952	Anthology	VG	Digest	$21.00 A
MYSTERIOUS TRAVELER	5	The Mysterious Traveller #5	1952	Anthology	VG+	Digest	$18.00 A
MYSTERY BOOK	15	Mystery Book Magazine 10/46	1946	Anthology	VG	Digest	$8.00 A
MYSTERY DIGEST	1 1	Mystery Digest - 5/57	1957	Anthology	AF	Digest	$15.00
MYSTERY DIGEST	1 4	Mystery Digest - 11/57	1957	Anthology	VGF+	Digest	$7.00
MYSTERY DIGEST	2 5	Mystery Digest - 9/58	1958	Anthology	AF	Digest	$8.00
MYSTERY DIGEST	2 5	Mystery Digest - 9/58	1958	Anthology	G+	Digest	$6.00
MYSTERY DIGEST	2 7	Mystery Digest - 12/58	1958	Anthology	AF	Digest	$15.00 A
MYSTERY DIGEST	3 7	Mystery Digest July-Aug 1959	1959	Anthology	VG+	Digest	$6.00
MYSTERY MONTHLY	1 1	Mystery Monthly - 6/76	1976	Anthology	VGF	Digest	$10.00
MYSTERY MONTHLY	1 4	Mystery Monthly - 9/76	1976	Anthology	VG+	Digest	$7.00

Mystery Tales 1-1 AF $42   News Stand Library 7A VG+ $8   Newsstand Library U131 AF $56

PUBLISHER	PUB. #	TITLE	DATE	AUTHOR	COND.	TYPE	PRICE
MYSTERY MONTHLY	1 7	Mystery Monthly - 12/76	1976	Anthology	VGF	Digest	$7.00
MYSTERY NOVEL CLASSIC	56	The Glass Slipper	1944	Eberhart, M.G.	VGF	Digest	$8.00
MYSTERY NOVEL CLASSIC	61	Bring Me Another Murder	1944	Chambers, W.	G+	Digest	$4.00
MYSTERY NOVEL CLASSIC	79	Clue Of The Frightening Coin	1946	Ryan, J.	VG-	Digest	$5.00
MYSTERY NOVEL CLASSIC	97	The Butler Died In Brooklyn	1947	Fenisong, R.	VG+	Digest	$8.00
MYSTERY TALES	1 1	Mystery Tales 12/58	1958	Anthology	AF	Digest	$42.00 A
MYSTERY TALES	1 2	Mystery Tales 2/59	1959	Anthology	VG+	Digest	$15.00 A
MYSTERY TALES	1 3	Mystery Tales 4/59	1959	Anthology	VGF	Digest	$27.00 A
MYSTERY TALES	1 3	Mystery Tales 4/59	1959	Anthology	VG	Digest	$18.00 A
MYSTERY TALES	1 4	Mystery Tales 6/59	1959	Anthology	AF-	Digest	$46.00 A
MYSTERY TALES	1 5	Mystery Tales 8/59	1959	Anthology	AF	Digest	$33.00 A
MYSTERY TALES	1 6	Mystery Tales 10/59	1959	Anthology	VG+	Digest	$38.00 A
MYSTERY TALES	1 6	Mystery Tales 10/59	1959	Anthology	VG+	Digest	$33.00 A
N.P. INC.	4032	Pleasure Palace	1969	Leros, R.	VGF		$7.00
NATIONAL LIBRARY	NLB 106	Abnormals Anonymous	1964	Gray, S.	VG+		$10.00 A
NATIONAL LIBRARY	NLB 109	Want-Ad Wantons	1967	Palmer, D.	AF		$14.00
NATIONAL LIBRARY	NLB 112	Diary of Dr. Ramund	1968	Farrel, C.	VG+		$22.00 A
NERO WOLFE	1 3	Nero Wolfe Mystery Mag. 6/54	1954	Anthology	VG+	Digest	$7.00
NEW ENGLISH LIBRARY	9327	Llana Of Gathol	1971	Burroughs, E.R.	VGF		$8.00 A
NEW ENGLISH LIBRARY	25144	The Living Shadow	1976	Grant, M.*	VGF		$20.00 A
NEWS STAND LIBRARY	46	Listen To Their Lust	1949	Eldridge, P.	VG-		$5.00
NEWS STAND LIBRARY	100	Tomcat In Tights	1950	Hanley, J.	VG+		$15.00
NEWS STAND LIBRARY	103	Sin And Shackles	1950	Jordan, G.	VG		$8.00
NEWS STAND LIBRARY	134	Montreal Confidential	1950	Palmer, A.	VG		$5.00
NEWS STAND LIBRARY	1A	Negligee	1949	Sloan, G.	VG		$7.00
NEWS STAND LIBRARY	2A	The Long November	1949	Nablo, J.B.	VG-		$5.00
NEWS STAND LIBRARY	3A	Pay For Her Passion	1949	Wolfson, P.J.	VG+		$7.00
NEWS STAND LIBRARY	6A	Sin For Your Supper	1949	Douglas, M.	VG		$7.00
NEWS STAND LIBRARY	6A	Sin For Your Supper	1949	Douglas, M.	G+		$5.00
NEWS STAND LIBRARY	7A	The Pagans	1949	Benedict, J.	VG+		$8.00
NEWS STAND LIBRARY	9A	Torch Of Violence	1949	Forrest, D.	VG+		$14.00
NEWS STAND LIBRARY	9A	Torch Of Violence	1949	Forrest, D.	VG		$8.00
NEWS STAND LIBRARY	14A	Death Be My Destiny	1949	Perrin, N.H.	AF		$11.00 A
NEWS STAND LIBRARY	15A	Jesse James	1950	Kelley, T.P.	VGF		$11.00
NEWS STAND LIBRARY	16A	Daughters Of Desire	1950	Knight, F.	VG+		$12.00
NEWS STAND LIBRARY	17A	The Penthouse Killings	1950	Brown, H.	VGF-		$14.00
NEWS STAND LIBRARY	18A	Let Out The Beast	1950	Fischer, L.	VG+		$15.00 A
NEWS STAND LIBRARY	20A	Sugar Puss On Dorchester St.	1950	Palmer, A.	VG+		$7.00
NEWS STAND LIBRARY	20A	Sugar Puss On Dorchester St.	1950	Palmer, A.	VG		$7.00
NEWS STAND LIBRARY	23A	Pick-Up	1950	Scott, L.	VG		$7.00
NEWS STAND LIBRARY	25A	Strange Desires	1950	Malston, A.	VG+		$9.00
NEWS STAND LIBRARY	25A	Strange Desires	1950	Malston, A.	VG+		$8.00
NEWS STAND LIBRARY	26A	He Learned About Women	1950	Greenshade, T.	VG		$7.00
NEWSSTAND LIBRARY	U 101	Streets Paved With Gold	1958	Locke, F.	F		$10.00
NEWSSTAND LIBRARY	U 102	Fraudulent Broad (Bonfils cvr.)	1958	Rubel, J.L.	AF		$9.00

Newsstand Library U137 F $110   Newsstand Library U144 AF $44   Newsstand Library U182 F $161

PUBLISHER	PUB. #	TITLE	DATE	AUTHOR	COND.	TYPE	PRICE
NEWSSTAND LIBRARY	U 102	Fraudulent Broad (Stake cvr.)	1958	Rubel, J.L.	AF		$8.00
NEWSSTAND LIBRARY	U 106	The Demands Of The Flesh	1959	Hastings, M.	AF		$12.00
NEWSSTAND LIBRARY	U 106	The Demands Of The Flesh	1959	Hastings, M.	VGF+		$8.00 A
NEWSSTAND LIBRARY	U 110	Rip Tide	1959	Harsh, J.	F		$10.00
NEWSSTAND LIBRARY	U 111	20 Years Behind Red Curtains	1959	Dean, N.	AF		$15.00 A
NEWSSTAND LIBRARY	U 113	Six For Flight 13	1959	Nixon, H.L.	F		$7.00
NEWSSTAND LIBRARY	U 120	Private World	1959	Sellers, C.	AF		$20.00 A
NEWSSTAND LIBRARY	U 122	The Tenement Kid	1959	Edd, K.	F		$32.00 A
NEWSSTAND LIBRARY	U 122	The Tenement Kid	1959	Edd, K.	AF		$19.00 A
NEWSSTAND LIBRARY	U 122	The Tenement Kid	1959	Edd, K.	VG+		$16.00 A
NEWSSTAND LIBRARY	U 123	The Wife Traders	1959	Graeme, G.A.	AF-		$7.00
NEWSSTAND LIBRARY	U 129	Black Desire	1960	Hayes, R.	AF		$15.00 A
NEWSSTAND LIBRARY	U 131	Swamp Bred	1960	Smith, G.H.	AF		$56.00 A
NEWSSTAND LIBRARY	U 131	Swamp Bred	1960	Smith, G.H.	F		$26.00 A
NEWSSTAND LIBRARY	U 131	Swamp Bred	1960	Smith, G.H.	VG+		$20.00
NEWSSTAND LIBRARY	U 132	Arrividerci, Ava	1960	Marcus, C.	AF		$10.00
NEWSSTAND LIBRARY	U 133	The Wanton One	1960	Rubel, J.	AF		$34.00 A
NEWSSTAND LIBRARY	U 135	Shanty Girl	1960	Moore, H.R.	AF		$20.00 A
NEWSSTAND LIBRARY	U 137	The Woman Chaser	1960	Willeford, C.	F		$110.00 A
NEWSSTAND LIBRARY	U 137	The Woman Chaser	1960	Willeford, C.	VG+		$54.00 A
NEWSSTAND LIBRARY	U 144	Like Crazy, Man	1960	Geis, R.E.	AF		$44.00 A
NEWSSTAND LIBRARY	U 156	A Matter Of Adultery	1961	Lee, D.	AF		$10.00
NEWSSTAND LIBRARY	U 157	The 3rd Theme	1961	Hastings, M.	VG+		$25.00 A
NEWSSTAND LIBRARY	U 159	So Strange Our Love	1961	Heron, J.	AF		$8.00
NEWSSTAND LIBRARY	U 160	A Family Affair	1961	Vinning, K.	AF-		$8.00
NEWSSTAND LIBRARY	U 162	You Can't Escape Me	1961	Tyler, J.	AF		$11.00 A
NEWSSTAND LIBRARY	U 165	Commit The Sins	1961	Austin, W.A.	F		$10.00 A
NEWSSTAND LIBRARY	U 168	Make It On Temple Street	1961	Berryman, O.L.	AF		$8.00 A
NEWSSTAND LIBRARY	U 174	Whirlpool Of Thunder	1961	Caryl, W.	AF		$12.00
NEWSSTAND LIBRARY	U 176	Venus of Lesbos	1961	Bell, S.	AF		$14.00 A
NEWSSTAND LIBRARY	U 182	No Experience Necessary	1962	Willeford, C.	F		$161.00 A
NEWSSTAND LIBRARY	U 183	Sexy Psycho	1962	Dowling, L.	VGF+		$8.00
NEWSSTAND LIBRARY	501	The Lewd Angel	1959	Marcus, C.	AF		$20.00 A
NEWSSTAND LIBRARY	U 502	Honey Babe	1959	Bell, S.	VGF		$7.00
NEWSSTAND LIBRARY	503	The Gorgeous Devil	1959	Smith, G.H.	AF		$11.00 A
NEWSSTAND LIBRARY	U 504	Curiosities Of Medicine	1959	Di Giacomo Dee, R.	AF		$7.00
NEWSSTAND LIBRARY	U 504	Curiosities Of Medicine	1959	Di Giacomo Dee, R.	VG+		$7.00
NEWSSTAND LIBRARY	U 505	Savage Breed	1959	Douglas, W.K.	VGF		$14.00 A
NEWSSTAND LIBRARY	509	The Beckoning Flame	1960	Michaud, D.	AF		$7.00
NEWSSTAND LIBRARY	509	The Beckoning Flame	1960	Michaud, D.	VG+		$4.00
NEWSSTAND LIBRARY	510	Playhouse Of Passion	1960	Culver, E.	VG+		$5.00 A
NEWSSTAND LIBRARY	511	Office Playgirl	1960	Gillan, B.J.	VGF		$8.00
NEWSSTAND LIBRARY	513	The Syndicate	1960	Chestnut, R.	AF		$8.00
NEWSSTAND LIBRARY	515	Daughter Of Joy	1960	Harvey, J.	AF		$35.00 A
NEWSSTAND LIBRARY	516	Bobby Sox Sinners	1960	Mertes, J.	VG+		$11.00 A

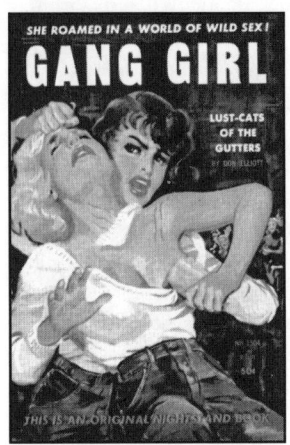

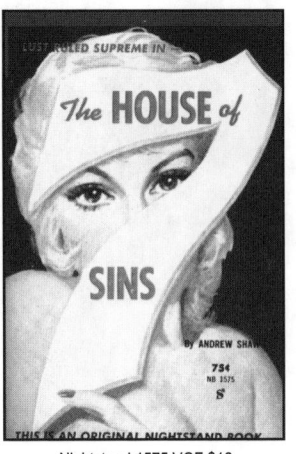

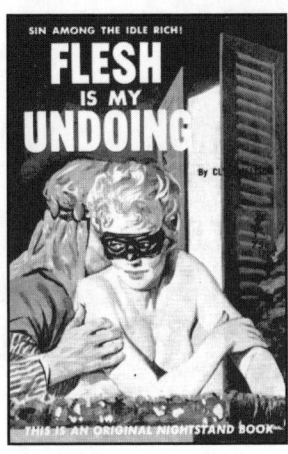

Nightstand 1504 VG+ $66   Nightstand 1575 VGF $12   Nightstand 1708 AF $30

PUBLISHER	PUB. #	TITLE	DATE	AUTHOR	COND.	TYPE	PRICE
NEWSSTAND LIBRARY	523	Have Wife Will Trade	1960	Robinson, G.D.	AF		$20.00 A
NEWSSTAND LIBRARY	U 524	Too Hot For Hell	1960	Laird, A.	AF		$8.00
NIGHT CRY	2 1	Night Cry - Fall 1986	1986	Anthology	VGF	Digest	$7.00
NIGHTSTAND	NB 1501	Love Addict	1959	Elliott, D.*	AF		$66.00 A
NIGHTSTAND	NB 1501R	Love Addict (2nd)	1959	Elliott, D.*	VG+		$18.00 A
NIGHTSTAND	NB 1504	Gang Girl	1959	Elliott, D.*	VG+		$66.00 A
NIGHTSTAND	NB 1504	Gang Girl	1959	Elliott, D.*	VGF		$30.00 A
NIGHTSTAND	NB 1504R	Gang Girl (2nd)	1959	Elliott, D.*	VGF		$33.00 A
NIGHTSTAND	NB 1505	Campus Tramp	1959	Shaw, A.*	VGF		$27.00 A
NIGHTSTAND	NB 1510	Born For Sin	1960	James, A.	VGF		$8.00
NIGHTSTAND	NB 1511	The Adulterers	1960	Shaw, A.*	VG+		$11.00 A
NIGHTSTAND	NB 1514	Sin Girls	1960	Longman, M.*	G		$5.00
NIGHTSTAND	NB 1516	Sin On Wheels	1960	Elliott, D.*	VGF		$14.00 A
NIGHTSTAND	NB 1516	Sin On Wheels	1960	Elliott, D.*	VGF		$12.00
NIGHTSTAND	NB 1520	The Sin-Damned	1960	Shaw, A.*	VGF		$8.00
NIGHTSTAND	NB 1525	The Lustful Ones	1960	Allison, C.	VG+		$12.00
NIGHTSTAND	NB 1526	The Wife-Swappers	1960	Shaw, A.*	VG+		$7.00
NIGHTSTAND	NB 1526R	The Wife-Swappers (2nd)	1960	Shaw, A.*	AF		$12.00
NIGHTSTAND	NB 1530	Stripper	1960	Williams, J.X.	AF		$15.00 A
NIGHTSTAND	NB 1533	Passion Shack	1960	Holliday, D.	VG+		$8.00
NIGHTSTAND	NB 1537	Mistress Of Sin	1960	Elliott, D.*	VG+		$10.00
NIGHTSTAND	NB 1541	Tramp	1961	Shaw, A.*	VGF		$11.00 A
NIGHTSTAND	NB 1546	$20 Lust	1961	Shaw, A.*	VGF		$8.00 A
NIGHTSTAND	NB 1549	Isle Of Sin	1961	Dexter, J.	VG+		$7.00
NIGHTSTAND	NB 1551	Lover	1961	Shaw, A.*	VG+		$22.00 A
NIGHTSTAND	NB 1555	Flesh Is My Undoing	1961	Allison, C.	VGF-		$8.00 A
NIGHTSTAND	NB 1558	Expense Account Sinners	1961	Elliott, D.*	VG		$8.00
NIGHTSTAND	NB 1561	The Sinning Season	1961	Calvano, T.	VG+		$5.00
NIGHTSTAND	NB 1575	The House Of 7 Sins	1961	Shaw, A.*	VGF		$12.00
NIGHTSTAND	NB 1580	Sin Resort	1961	Marshall, A.*	G		$8.00
NIGHTSTAND	NB 1582	Flesh For Hire	1961	Allison, C.	VGF		$12.00 A
NIGHTSTAND	NB 1589	The Pages Of Sin	1962	Marshall, A.*	AF		$10.00
NIGHTSTAND	NB 1601	The Lust Game	1962	Allison, C.	AF		$13.00 A
NIGHTSTAND	NB 1610	Sin Bait	1962	Elliott, D.*	AF-		$7.00 A
NIGHTSTAND	NB 1611	Passion Alley	1962	Shaw, A.*	VGF-		$9.00
NIGHTSTAND	NB 1619	Harlem Harlot	1962	Holliday, D.	VGF		$14.00 A
NIGHTSTAND	NB 1623	Reform School Girls	1962	Shaw, A.*	VGF		$16.00 A
NIGHTSTAND	NB 1626	Passion Gang	1962	Dexter, J.	AF		$18.00 A
NIGHTSTAND	NB 1632	Passion Prize	1962	Allison, C.	AF		$10.00
NIGHTSTAND	NB 1644	Sex, Inc.	1963	Allison, C.	VGF		$18.00 A
NIGHTSTAND	NB 1703	Trailer Trollop	n/d	Shaw, A.*	G		$5.00
NIGHTSTAND	NB 1705	$20 Lust	n/d	Shaw, A.*	VGF+		$15.00
NIGHTSTAND	NB 1705	$20 Lust	n/d	Shaw, A.*	VGF		$14.00
NIGHTSTAND	NB 1706	Isle Of Sin	n/d	Dexter, J.	VGF		$5.00
NIGHTSTAND	NB 1708	Flesh Is My Undoing	n/d	Allison, C.	AF		$30.00 A

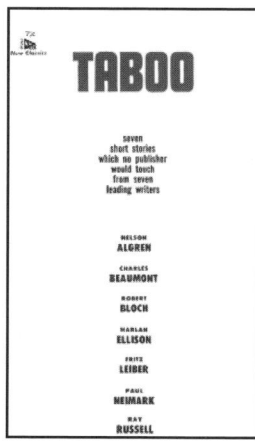

Novel Book 7N-730 VG+ $75	Novel Library 8 VGF+ $50	Novel Library 16 VGF $16

PUBLISHER	PUB. #	TITLE	DATE	AUTHOR	COND.	TYPE	PRICE
NIGHTSTAND	NB 1710	Malay Mistress	n/d	Allison, C.	VG		$5.00
NIGHTSTAND	NB 1722	Any Bed For Myra	1965	Holliday, D.	VG+		$7.00
NIGHTSTAND	NB 1723	Sinning Sam	1965	Williams, J.X.	VG+		$6.00
NIGHTSTAND	NB 1725	Sin Grifter	1965	Hudson, D.	VGF		$9.00
NIGHTSTAND	NB 1729	Shame Scheme	1965	Elliott, D.*	AF		$7.00
NIGHTSTAND	NB 1732	Passion Pool	1965	Allison, C.	AF		$17.00
NIGHTSTAND	NB 1733	The Art Sinner	1965	Hudson, D.	VGF		$9.00
NIGHTSTAND	NB 1740	Lust Parlor	1965	Marshall, A.*	AF		$12.00
NIGHTSTAND	NB 1741	Of Shame Reborn	1965	Elliott, D.*	VGF		$8.00
NIGHTSTAND	NB 1745	The House In Joy Court	1965	Shaw, A.*	VG		$5.00
NIGHTSTAND	NB 1746	Flesh Fiesta	1965	Hudson, D.	VGF		$8.00
NIGHTSTAND	NB 1748	Passion Hunt	1965	Marshall, A.*	VG+		$7.00
NIGHTSTAND	NB 1748	Passion Hunt	1965	Marshall, A.*	VG		$5.00
NIGHTSTAND	NB 1751	Good Girl Bad Girl	1965	Elliott, D.*	AF		$15.00 A
NIGHTSTAND	NB 1752	Skid Row Sinner	1965	Dexter, J.	AF		$7.00
NIGHTSTAND	NB 1757	Harlot Hater	1965	Holliday, D.	VGF		$7.00
NIGHTSTAND	NB 1768	The Sins Of Josh Young	1965	Marshall, A.*	F		$10.00
NIGHTSTAND	NB 1770	Falsie	1966	Marshall, A.*	AF		$9.00
NIGHTSTAND	NB 1773	Peeper	1966	Holliday, D.	AF		$7.00
NIGHTSTAND	NB 1776	The Sinning Room	1966	Dexter, J.	G		$4.00
NIGHTSTAND	NB 1777	Passion Lash	1966	Shaw, A.*	F		$10.00 A
NIGHTSTAND	NB 1779	Lez Lust	1966	Williams, J.X.	AF		$16.00
NIGHTSTAND	NB 1781	The Stolen One	1966	Holliday, D.	AF		$8.00
NIGHTSTAND	NB 1782	Dream Test	1966	Dexter, J.	VGF		$8.00
NIGHTSTAND	NB 1793	The Sensualists	1966	Calvano, T.	VGF		$10.00
NIGHTSTAND	NB 1794	Mariella's Sins	1966	Holliday, D.	AF		$7.00
NIGHTSTAND	NB 1795	The Love Seeker	1966	Dexter, J.	VG		$5.00
NIGHTSTAND	NB 1796	Door-To-Door Lover	1966	Williams, J.X.	VGF		$6.00
NIGHTSTAND	NB 1802	Scandal Street	1966	Marshall, A.*	VG+		$8.00
NIGHTSTAND	NB 1803	Passion's Prey	1966	Shaw, A.*	VGF+		$8.00
NIGHTSTAND	NB 1803	Passion's Prey	1966	Shaw, A.*	VG+		$7.00
NIGHTSTAND	NB 1804	Paid In Shame	1966	Williams, J.X.	VG+		$5.00
NIGHTSTAND	NB 1807	Squeeze-Play Girl	1966	Dexter, J.	AF		$7.00
NIGHTSTAND	NB 1809	The Sin Shark	1966	Marshall, A.*	VGF		$9.00
NIGHTSTAND	NB 1809	The Sin Shark	1966	Marshall, A.*	VGF		$7.00
NIGHTSTAND	NB 1811	Video Vixen	1966	Dexter, J.	VGF+		$7.00
NIGHTSTAND	NB 1813	The Pillow Trade	1966	Calvano, T.	VGF		$7.00
NIGHTSTAND	NB 1815	Wanton Wanted	1966	Williams, J.X.	VGF		$6.00
NIGHTSTAND	NB 1816	Sinning Simon	1966	Kane, W.	AF		$7.00
NIGHTSTAND	NB 1820	Studio For Shame	1967	Miller, M.	AF		$11.00 A
NIGHTSTAND	NB 1821	Carnal Counselor	1967	Elliott, D.*	AF		$8.00
NIGHTSTAND	NB 1823	Dante's Sinferno	1967	Calvano, T.	VGF+		$8.00
NIGHTSTAND	NB 1824	LSD Lusters	1967	Dexter, J.	AF		$30.00
NIGHTSTAND	NB 1828	Back-Seat Sinners	1967	Shaw, A.*	AF		$12.00
NIGHTSTAND	NB 1829	All The Best Beds	1967	Elliott, D.*	AF		$10.00

Novel Library 37 VG+ $42   Novel Library 46 VG+ $64   Novels Inc. 10 VGF $24

PUBLISHER	PUB. #	TITLE	DATE	AUTHOR	COND.	TYPE	PRICE
NIGHTSTAND	NB 1839	Flesh Therapist	1967	Dexter, J.	AF		$25.00 A
NIGHTSTAND	NB 1841	Savage Sex	1967	Dexter, J.	VGF		$20.00 A
NIGHTSTAND	NB 1843	Lust Is A Lady	1967	Williams, J.X.	AF		$47.00 A
NIGHTSTAND	NB 1843	Lust Is A Lady	1967	Williams, J.X.	VG+		$12.00
NIGHTSTAND	NB 1853	Charity Vice	1967	Craig, S.	VGF		$8.00 A
NIGHTSTAND	NB 1861	Belle Of The Bedroom	1967	Scott, M.	AF		$12.00 A
NIGHTSTAND	NB 1869	The Sex Quest	1968	Marshall, A.*	VGF		$10.00 A
NIGHTSTAND	NB 1871	The Lust Recruit	1968	James, J.	VG+		$15.00 A
NIGHTSTAND	NB 1898	The Bawdyguard	1968	Dexter, J.	AF		$15.00 A
NIGHTSTAND	NB 1901	Every Sin In The Book	1968	Aldrich, C.	AF		$12.00
NITE TIME	NT 93	Canary's Combo	1964	Nemec, J.	VG+		$8.00
NITE TIME	NT 98	Cosa Nostra Circus	1964	Corbin, G.	VGF	MTI	$7.00
NITE TIME	NT 121	Flamer	1964	Kahler, J.	VG+		$11.00 A
NITELIGHT READER	128	Sin Studio	1963	Anonymous	AF		$9.00 A
NITE-LITE	202	Strange Bedfellows	1963	Spencer, G.	G+		$8.00
NO EXIT PRESS	No#	Red Gardinias	1989	Latimer, J.	F		$6.00
NOVA	N 132	Hot-Rod Reporter	1965	Johnson, A.L.	VGF		$4.00
NOVEL BOOK	3503	Virgin Bounty	1959	Low, G.	VGF+		$7.00
NOVEL BOOK	3506	Chartered Love	1960	Dawn, C.	VG		$7.00
NOVEL BOOK	5001	Brute Passion	1960	Whelan, R.	AF-		$14.00
NOVEL BOOK	5002	Torrid Twins	1960	Lynn, J.	AF		$8.00
NOVEL BOOK	5005	Swamp Lust	1960	Smith, G.H.	G+		$6.00
NOVEL BOOK	5007	Loverboy!	1960	Lynn, J.	F		$12.00 A
NOVEL BOOK	5010	Bayou Babe	1960	Smith, G.O.	VGF		$10.00
NOVEL BOOK	5015	Any Time - Any Place	1960	Dawn, C.	VGF		$7.00
NOVEL BOOK	5030	Mad For Kicks	1961	Lynn, J.	AF		$12.00
NOVEL BOOK	5033	Brute Madness	1961	Baker, L.	AF		$14.00
NOVEL BOOK	5038	Women On The Loose	1961	Lynn, J.	VGF		$8.00
NOVEL BOOK	5039	Vagabond Lover	1961	Sellers, C.	VG		$6.00
NOVEL BOOK	5044	The Cheaters	1961	Hayes, B.	VG		$6.00
NOVEL BOOK	5045	Big Man	1961	Sellers, C.	VG+		$7.00
NOVEL BOOK	5046	Torrid Island	1961	Tralins, B.	VG+		$10.00
NOVEL BOOK	5048	Potent Stuff	1961	James, A.	AF-		$8.00
NOVEL BOOK	5058	Shocking Adultery	1961	Marshall, F.	AF		$5.00 A
NOVEL BOOK	5070	Passion Potion	1961	Tralins, B.	VG		$6.00
NOVEL BOOK	5077	Hired Nympho	1962	Tralins, B.	AF-		$12.00
NOVEL BOOK	5087	Any Time, Any Place	1962	Dawn, C.	AF		$12.00
NOVEL BOOK	5088	Loose Women	1962	Anthony, B.	AF		$15.00 A
NOVEL BOOK	5088	Loose Women	1962	Anthony, B.	VGF		$10.00
NOVEL BOOK	5092	Sadist On The Loose	1962	Smith, G.H.	VGF		$12.00
NOVEL BOOK	6014	Bed Crazy	1962	Hitt, O.	AF		$12.00
NOVEL BOOK	6017	Gigantic Passions	1962	Lark, J.	VG+		$9.00
NOVEL BOOK	6020	The Golden Hussy	1962	Smith, G.H.	AF		$8.00
NOVEL BOOK	6030	Mad For Kicks	1962	Lynn, J.	VGF		$15.00
NOVEL BOOK	6032	The Free Lovers	1962	Jordan, J.J.	AF		$8.00

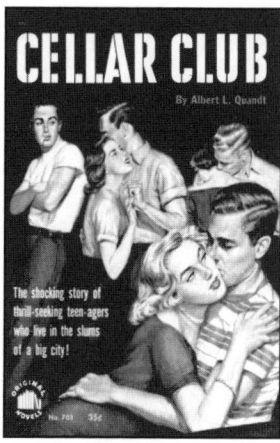

Off Beat Detective 5-1 VGF $25   Omnibus No# G- $7   Original Novels 703 AF $66

PUBLISHER	PUB. #	TITLE	DATE	AUTHOR	COND.	TYPE	PRICE
NOVEL BOOK	6036	Brute Passion	1962	Whelan, R.	VG-		$6.00
NOVEL BOOK	6040	Fever Hot Woman	1962	Smith, G.H.	AF		$9.00
NOVEL BOOK	6041	4 Nude Queens	1962	Tralins, B.	VGF		$10.00 A
NOVEL BOOK	6042	Overpassionate	1962	Oliver, R.	F		$9.00 A
NOVEL BOOK	6048	House Of Pleasure	1962	Sellers, C.	AF		$12.00
NOVEL BOOK	6056	Julie's Irresistible Body	1961	Brennan, D.	VGF		$15.00 A
NOVEL BOOK	6078	Bed-Crazy Blondes!	1963	Weldon, R.	VGF		$9.00
NOVEL BOOK	6082	White Hot Woman!	1963	Lynn, J.	AF		$13.00
NOVEL BOOK	6088	My Two Strangest Lovers	1963	Hitt, O.	G		$6.00
NOVEL BOOK	6090	Passion Parlor	1963	Tralins, B.	VG+		$8.00
NOVEL BOOK	60 112	Unique Urge	1964	Jordan, J.J.	AF		$8.00
NOVEL BOOK	6N 244	Escape To Eroticism	1964	Legget, E.	AF		$8.00
NOVEL BOOK	6N 274	One Hot Summer Night	1964	Brown, R.S.	VG+		$7.00
NOVEL BOOK	6N 284	Race To Passion	1964	Cannon, F.	VGF		$6.00
NOVEL BOOK	6N 290	The Superlative Woman	1964	Nemec, J.	VGF+		$8.00
NOVEL BOOK	6N 292	A Vision Of Ecstasy	1964	Macres, T.	VG+		$6.00
NOVEL BOOK	7N 730	Taboo	1964	Anthology	VG+		$75.00 A
NOVEL BOOK	7N 760	Taboo 2	1964	Anthology	VGF		$30.00 A
NOVEL LIBRARY	2	Ecstasy Girl	1948	Woodford, J.	VG+		$10.00
NOVEL LIBRARY	3	Free Lovers	1948	Woodford, J.	VG+		$10.00
NOVEL LIBRARY	4	The Passionate Princess	1948	Woodford, J.	VG-		$8.00
NOVEL LIBRARY	5	Wanton Venus	1948	LeBlanc, M.	VG+		$20.00
NOVEL LIBRARY	5	Wanton Venus	1948	LeBlanc, M.	G		$5.00
NOVEL LIBRARY	6	Peeping Tom	1948	Woodford, J.	VG		$11.00 A
NOVEL LIBRARY	6	Peeping Tom	1948	Woodford, J.	VG		$10.00 A
NOVEL LIBRARY	8	The Regenerate Lover	1948	Clarke, D.H.	VGF+		$50.00 A
NOVEL LIBRARY	9	The Street Of Painted Lips	1949	Dekobra, M.	VGF		$30.00
NOVEL LIBRARY	11	The Villain And The Virgin	1949	Chase, J.H.	VG-		$8.00
NOVEL LIBRARY	12	Uneasy Virtue	1949	Wilson, D.	VG		$8.00
NOVEL LIBRARY	13	A Good Time Man	1949	Keating, E.P.	VG+		$8.00
NOVEL LIBRARY	14	Gold Diggers	1949	Bull, L.	VG+		$7.00
NOVEL LIBRARY	15	Playthings Of Desire	1949	Putnam, J.W.	VGF		$10.00 A
NOVEL LIBRARY	15	Playthings Of Desire	1949	Putnam, J.W.	G		$4.00
NOVEL LIBRARY	16	Women To Love	1949	Drago, S.	VGF		$16.00 A
NOVEL LIBRARY	16	Women To Love	1949	Drago, S.	VG+		$8.00
NOVEL LIBRARY	18	Bedroom Eyes	1949	Dekobra, M.	VG+		$12.00 A
NOVEL LIBRARY	18	Bedroom Eyes	1949	Dekobra, M.	VG		$11.00
NOVEL LIBRARY	21	The Love Toy	1949	Anonymous	VG+		$7.00
NOVEL LIBRARY	22	Mirabelle: Woman Of Passion!	1949	Caren, E.	VG+		$8.00
NOVEL LIBRARY	24	Infidelity	1949	Weigal, A.	VG-		$8.00
NOVEL LIBRARY	25	Venus On Wheels	1949	Dekobra, M.	VGF		$8.00 A
NOVEL LIBRARY	26	The Immodest Maidens	1949	Browne, E.	VGF		$17.00 A
NOVEL LIBRARY	28	The Love Clinic	1949	Dekobra, M.	VG+		$12.00
NOVEL LIBRARY	29	All Dames Are Dynamite	1949	Trent, T.	VG		$10.00
NOVEL LIBRARY	32	Dishonorable Darling	1949	Collison, W.	AF		$14.00 A

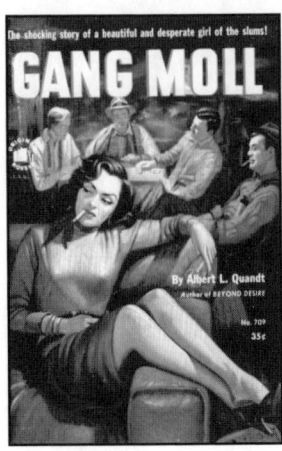

Original Novels 709 VG $60

Original Novels 712 G $24

Original Novels 723 VGF- $55

PUBLISHER	PUB. #	TITLE	DATE	AUTHOR	COND.	TYPE	PRICE
NOVEL LIBRARY	34	The Crystal Girl	1949	Longstreet, S.	VG+		$10.00
NOVEL LIBRARY	36	Male And Female	1950	Woodford, J.	VG		$5.00
NOVEL LIBRARY	37	12 Chinamen And A Woman	1950	Chase, J.H.	VG+		$42.00 A
NOVEL LIBRARY	37	12 Chinamen And A Woman	1950	Chase, J.H.	VGF		$40.00 A
NOVEL LIBRARY	38	60 Seconds	1950	Bodenheim, M.	VG+		$11.00 A
NOVEL LIBRARY	39	No Bed Of Her Own	1950	Lewton, V.	VGF		$18.00 A
NOVEL LIBRARY	40	Wild Parties	1950	Lief, M.	AF		$40.00 A
NOVEL LIBRARY	42	Lady For Love	1950	Schultz, A.	VGF		$40.00 A
NOVEL LIBRARY	43	How To Play Canasta	1949	Culbertson, E.	AF-		$7.00
NOVEL LIBRARY	46	Naked On Roller Skates	1950	Bodenheim, M.	VG+		$64.00
NOVEL SELECTIONS	51	The Bastard	1953	Caldwell, E.	VGF		$12.00
NOVEL SELECTIONS	52	Poor Fool	1953	Caldwell, E.	AF		$15.00 A
NOVEL SELECTIONS	52	Poor Fool	1953	Caldwell, E.	AF		$11.00 A
NOVELS INC.	No#	Come Sin With Me	n/d	Jordan, G.	G	Digest	$12.00 A
NOVELS INC.	10	The Tigress	n/d	Saxon, J.	VGF	Digest	$24.00 A
OFF BEAT	2 4	Off Beat Det. Stories 9/58	1958	Anthology	AF	Digest	$29.00 A
OFF BEAT	2 5	Off Beat Det. Stories 11/58	1958	Anthology	AF-	Digest	$22.00 A
OFF BEAT	2 5	Off Beat Det. Stories 11/58	1958	Anthology	VGF	Digest	$20.00 A
OFF BEAT	3 1	Off Beat Det. Stories 3/59	1959	Anthology	AF	Digest	$57.00 A
OFF BEAT	3 2	Off Beat Det. Stories 5/59	1959	Anthology	VG+	Digest	$33.00 A
OFF BEAT	3 6	Off Beat Det. Stories 1/60	1960	Anthology	AF	Digest	$65.00 A
OFF BEAT	4 4	Off Beat Det. Stories 9/60	1960	Anthology	VGF	Digest	$30.00 A
OFF BEAT	4 5	Off Beat Det. Stories 11/60	1960	Anthology	VGF	Digest	$38.00 A
OFF BEAT	5 1	Off Beat Det. Stories 3/61	1961	Anthology	VGF	Digest	$25.00 A
OFF BEAT	5 6	Off Beat Det. Stories 5/62	1962	Anthology	VGF+	Digest	$20.00 A
OFF BEAT	6 2	Off Beat Det. Stories 9/62	1962	Anthology	VGF	Digest	$28.00 A
OFF BEAT	6 2	Off Beat Det. Stories 9/62	1962	Anthology	VG-	Digest	$7.00
OFF BEAT	8 2	Off Beat Det. Stories 5/63	1963	Anthology	AF	Digest	$95.00 A
OMNIBUS	No#	Night Of Crime	1944	Armstrong, L.	G-	Digest	$7.00
ORBIT SCI-FI	3	Orbit Science Fiction #3	1954	Anthology	AF	Digest	$8.00
ORBIT SCI-FI	5	Orbit Science Fiction #5	1954	Anthology	VG	Digest	$5.00
ORIGINAL NOVELS	703	Cellar Club	1951	Quandt, A.L.	AF	Digest	$66.00 A
ORIGINAL NOVELS	704	Gambler's Girl	1951	Welles, K.	VG+	Digest	$46.00 A
ORIGINAL NOVELS	709	Gang Moll	1952	Quandt, A.L.	VG	Digest	$60.00 A
ORIGINAL NOVELS	709	Gang Moll	1952	Quandt, A.L.	VGF	Digest	$53.00 A
ORIGINAL NOVELS	712	Farewell To Passion	1952	Keene, D.	G	Digest	$24.00 A
ORIGINAL NOVELS	719	Harlem Woman	1952	Arnold, W.	G+	Digest	$18.00
ORIGINAL NOVELS	723	Backwoods Hussy	1952	Whitney, H.*	VGF-	Digest	$55.00 A
ORIGINAL NOVELS	725	Ringside Jezebel	1953	Nickerson, K.	VG+	Digest	$28.00 A
ORIGINAL NOVELS	725	Ringside Jezebel	1953	Nickerson, K.	VG	Digest	$13.00
ORIGINAL NOVELS	726	Dream Club	1953	Quandt, A.L.	AF-	Digest	$100.00 A
ORIGINAL NOVELS	727	Visiting Nurse	1953	Bligh, N.	G	Digest	$6.00
ORIGINAL NOVELS	733	Backwoods Hussy	1953	Whitney, H.*	G	Digest	$6.00
ORIGINAL NOVELS	736	Baby Sitter	1953	Quandt, A.L.	VG+	Digest	$45.00
ORIGINAL NOVELS	736	Baby Sitter	1953	Quandt, A.L.	G+	Digest	$14.00

Panther No# VG+ $28　　　　　Pan GP58 VGF $13　　　　　Panther 192 VG $15

PUBLISHER	PUB. #	TITLE	DATE	AUTHOR	COND.	TYPE	PRICE
ORIGINAL NOVELS	738	Cellar Club	1954	Quandt, A.L.	VG	Digest	$21.00 A
ORIGINAL NOVELS	738	Cellar Club	1954	Quandt, A.L.	VG	Digest	$20.00
ORIGINAL NOVELS	738	Cellar Club	1954	Quandt, A.L.	VG-	Digest	$8.00
ORIGINAL NOVELS	744	City Streets	1954	Harvey, G.	VG	Digest	$17.00 A
ORIGINAL NOVELS	746	French Alley	1954	Clay, M.	VG+	Digest	$17.00
ORIGINAL NOVELS	748	Streets Of Paris	1954	Reynolds, R.E.	VG+	Digest	$17.00
ORIGINAL NOVELS	749	City Girl	1954	Whitney, H.*	G	Digest	$18.00
ORIGINAL NOVELS	749	City Girl	1954	Whitney, H.*	G	Digest	$14.00
ORIGINAL SCI-FI	6 3	The Original Sci-Fi 11/55	1955	Anthology	VG	Digest	$7.00
ORIGINAL SCI-FI	9 1	Original Sci-Fi Stories 7/58	1958	Anthology	VG+	Digest	$6.00
OTHER WORLDS	4 1	Other Worlds 9/51	1951	Anthology	VGF	Digest	$8.00
P.E.C.	N 110	Call Girl	1965	Reyes, J.	AF		$10.00
P.E.C.	N 117	Telephone Lover	1965	Coulter, A.	AF		$12.00 A
P.E.C.	N 123	Odds-On Sex	1966	Hart, J.	AF		$14.00 A
P.E.C.	N 143	The Hypnotist	1966	Kahler, J.	AF		$24.00 A
P.E.C.	N 146	Neon Jungle	1966	Blake, J.D.	VG+		$8.00
P.E.C.	N 148	Dark Passion	1966	Adams, C.	AF		$10.00 A
P.E.C.	N 154	I've Got A Thing For Him	1967	Wilde, R.	VG		$7.00
P.E.C.	G 1112	Tormented Generation	1966	Commings, J.	VG+		$7.00
P.E.C.	G 1128	Confessions Of A Ski Instructor	1967	Blanchot, P.	AF		$18.00 A
P.E.C.	FL 4	Lesbian Jungle	1966	Evans, V.	VG+		$55.00 A
P.E.C.	FL 5	Whisper Of Silk	1966	Saxon, V.	G		$4.00
P.E.C.	AN 1	Cable Adress: Roma	1966	Marcus, C.	VG		$5.00
P.E.C.	AN 2	Valley Of The Doles	1967	Davis, G.	G+		$6.00
P.E.C.	AN 5	Mark Castle-Cable:Vienna	n/d	Marcus, C.	VG-		$6.00
P.E.C.	HU 2	How To Fly A Female	1969	Foor, L.	VG+		$39.00 A
P.E.C. SPECIAL	SP 1	Freedom On Trial	1966	Reitman, B.	VGF		$9.00 A
P.E.C. SPECIAL	SP 5	Was Oswald Alone?	1967	Chapman, G.	VGF		$18.00 A
P.E.C. SPECIAL	SP 8	Who's Listening Now?	1967	Chapman, G.	VG+		$12.00 A
P.E.C. SPECIAL	SP 10	Adam Clayton Powell	1967	Chapman, G.	VG+		$12.00
P.E.C. SPECIAL	SP 13	Devil Sex	1967	Breedlove, B.	AF		$22.00 A
P.E.C. SPECIAL	SP 14	The Love Generation	1967	Davis, J.P.	VG+		$41.00 A
P.E.C. SPECIAL	SP 15	Why Not Legalize Narcotics?	1967	Gale, W.C.	VG+		$27.00 A
PAD LIBRARY	PL 513	Lilly	1966	Kantor, H.	AF		$8.00 A
PAD LIBRARY	PL 517	The Nymph And The Virgin	1966	Kantor, H.	VGF		$6.00
PAD LIBRARY	PL 520	Mame's Girls	1966	Moren, L.	AF		$8.00 A
PAD LIBRARY	PL 524	A Chosen World	1966	Corley, C.	F		$8.00
PAD LIBRARY	PL 528	Wedding Night	1966	Kantor, H.	VGF		$8.00
PAD LIBRARY	PL 576	Flesh Or Fantasy	1967	Hall, K.	VG+		$4.00
PAD LIBRARY	761	The Wages Of Sin	1966	Kantor, H.	AF		$12.00
PAN	GP 58	Trial	1957	Mankiewicz, D.M.	VG	MTI	$13.00 A
PAN	GP 79	Venetian Bird	1957	Canning, V.	VG+	MTI	$6.00
PAN	GP 92	Sweet Thursday (2nd)	1958	Steinbeck, J.	VG		$4.00
PAN	G 335	Dr. No	1962	Fleming, I.	VG+	MTI	$5.00
PAN	X 32	Ben-Hur	1959	Wallace, L.	VGF	MTI	$7.00

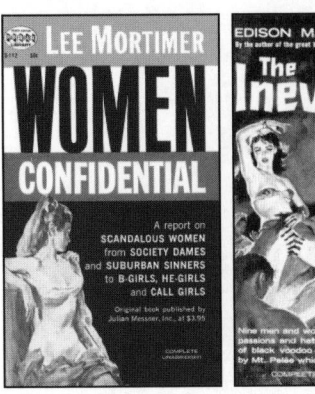

Paperback Lib. S-112 AF $11   Paperback Lib. 52-115 VGF $8   Paperback Lib. 52-123 VGF $6   Paperback Lib. 52-816 VG $29

PUBLISHER	PUB. #	TITLE	DATE	AUTHOR	COND.	TYPE	PRICE
PAN	X 527	The Man With The Golden Gun	1966	Fleming, I.	VG+		$3.00
PANTHER	No#	Cybernetic Controller	1952	Bulmer, H.K.	VG	Digest	$16.00 A
PANTHER	No#	The Dwellers	1954	Wright, S.F.	VG+	Digest	$28.00 A
PANTHER	No#	The Dwellers	1954	Wright, S.F.	VG	Digest	$17.00 A
PANTHER	48	The Stars Are Ours	1953	Bulmer, H.K.	VG+	Digest	$23.00 A
PANTHER	67	Another Space - Another Time	1953	Campbell, H.J.	VG	Digest	$15.00 A
PANTHER	68	Resurgent Dust	1953	Garner, R.	VG	Digest	$15.00 A
PANTHER	77	The Red Planet	1953	Campbell, H.J.	VG-	Digest	$12.00
PANTHER	85	Corridors Of Time	1953	Deegan, J.J.	VG	Digest	$12.00
PANTHER	95	Dark Andromeda	1954	Merak, A.J.	VG+	Digest	$16.00 A
PANTHER	118	Twilight Of Reason	1954	Burke, J.	VG-	Digest	$12.00
PANTHER	160	Once Upon A Space	1954	Campbell, H.J.	VG	Digest	$18.00 A
PANTHER	192	Revolt Of The Humans	1955	Burke, J.	VG	Digest	$15.00 A
PANTHER	587	The Happy Island	1956	Danielsson, B.	VG		$8.00
PANTHER	1041	Circus Of Horrors	1960	Owen, T.	AF		$19.00 A
PANTHER	586 4112	The Zap Gun	1975	Dick, P.K.	VGF		$8.00
PANTHER	586 4159	Clans Of The Alphane Moon	1975	Dick, P.K.	VGF		$8.00
PANTHER	586 4160	Doc Savage His Apocalyptic Life	1975	Farmer, P.J.	VG		$6.00
PANTHER	586 5034	James Bond And Moonraker	1979	Wood, C.	VGF	MTI	$5.00
PANTHER	25677	The Crazy Kill	1968	Himes, C.	VGF		$12.00
PAPERBACK LIBRARY	S 112	Women Confidential	1961	Mortimer, L.	AF		$11.00 A
PAPERBACK LIBRARY	52 115	The Inevitable Hour	1961	Marshall, E.	VGF		$8.00 A
PAPERBACK LIBRARY	52 123	Shoe The Wild Mare	1961	Fowler, G.	VGF		$6.00 A
PAPERBACK LIBRARY	52 127	Men Without Bones	1962	Kersh, G.	VGF		$8.00
PAPERBACK LIBRARY	52 127	Men Without Bones	1962	Kersh, G.	VG		$5.00
PAPERBACK LIBRARY	52 142	Dwellers In The Mirage	1962	Merritt, A.	VGF		$7.00
PAPERBACK LIBRARY	52 149	Ellison Wonderland	1962	Ellison, H.	VGF		$18.00 A
PAPERBACK LIBRARY	52 149	Ellison Wonderland	1962	Ellison, H.	VG+		$16.00 A
PAPERBACK LIBRARY	52 165	Delilah	1962	Cooper, J.*	VG		$8.00
PAPERBACK LIBRARY	51 173	Army Girl	1962	Harrison, W.*	G		$6.00
PAPERBACK LIBRARY	52 195	The G-String Murders	1963	Lee, G.R.	AF		$7.00
PAPERBACK LIBRARY	52 200	The Courtship Of Eddie's Father	1963	Toby, M.	VGF-	MTI	$5.00
PAPERBACK LIBRARY	52 205	The Answer	1963	Wylie, P.	F		$7.00
PAPERBACK LIBRARY	52 212	Mother Finds A Body	1963	Lee, G.R.	AF		$7.00
PAPERBACK LIBRARY	53 261	What's Happening?	1964	Ianuzzi, J.N.	VG+		$3.00
PAPERBACK LIBRARY	52 272	How Did A Nice Girl Like You	1964	Keefe, L.	VGF		$5.00
PAPERBACK LIBRARY	52 311	Battle For The Stars	1964	Hamilton, E.	AF		$5.00
PAPERBACK LIBRARY	53 332	What's Happening?	1966	Ianuzzi, J.N.	VG+		$6.00
PAPERBACK LIBRARY	52 338	World In Eclipse	1966	Dexter, W.	VGF		$6.00
PAPERBACK LIBRARY	52 357	Children Of The Void	1966	Dexter, W.	VG+		$6.00
PAPERBACK LIBRARY	56 383	Mike Mars Around The Moon	1966	Wollheim, D.A.	AF		$6.00
PAPERBACK LIBRARY	52 386	Dark Shadows #1 (2nd)	1967	Ross, M.	VG	TVTI	$3.00
PAPERBACK LIBRARY	52 392	Twin Planets	1967	High, P.E.	VGF+		$7.00
PAPERBACK LIBRARY	52 421	Dark Shadows #2	1967	Ross, M.	VG+	TVTI	$4.00
PAPERBACK LIBRARY	52 430	Abandon Galaxy	1967	Somers, B.*	VGF		$6.00
PAPERBACK LIBRARY	52 430	Abandon Galaxy	1967	Somers, B.*	VG		$5.00
PAPERBACK LIBRARY	54 438	Night Has A Thousand Eyes	1967	Woolrich, C.	VG		$7.00
PAPERBACK LIBRARY	52 469	The Torturer	1967	Saxon, P.	VG		$6.00

Paperback Lib. 65-281 VGF+ $25   Paperback Lib. 63-384 VG+ $47   Paperback Lib. 64-636 VGF $15   Paperback Lib. 76-928 VG+ $12

PUBLISHER	PUB. #	TITLE	DATE	AUTHOR	COND.	TYPE	PRICE
PAPERBACK LIBRARY	52 488	The Druid Stone	1967	Majors, S.*	VG		$6.00
PAPERBACK LIBRARY	52 508	Earthman, Go Home (Signed)	1964	Ellison, H.	VGF		$22.00 A
PAPERBACK LIBRARY	52 554	Beyond The Spectrum	1967	Thomas, M.	VG+		$6.00
PAPERBACK LIBRARY	53 566	The Rat Patrol #4	1967	King, D.	VG+	TVTI	$3.00
PAPERBACK LIBRARY	53 568	I Flew For The Fuhrer	1967	Knoke, H.	AF		$4.00
PAPERBACK LIBRARY	54 580	U-505	1967	Gallery, D.V.	AF		$7.00
PAPERBACK LIBRARY	52 584	Drums Of The Dark Gods	1967	Ballinger, W.A.	VGF-		$7.00
PAPERBACK LIBRARY	53 588	Slum Street, U.S.A.	1967	Farrell, J.T.	VGF		$6.00
PAPERBACK LIBRARY	54 596	Escape From Corregidor	1967	Whitcomb, E.D.	VGF		$4.00
PAPERBACK LIBRARY	52 608	Dark Shadows #5	1968	Ross, M.	VG+	TVTI	$4.00
PAPERBACK LIBRARY	53 628	The Rat Patrol #5	1968	King, D.	VG	TVTI	$3.00
PAPERBACK LIBRARY	53 675	The Billion Dollar Snatch	1968	Conway, T.	VG		$6.00
PAPERBACK LIBRARY	53 692	Wham, Bam, Thank You, Ma'am	1968	Conway, T.	VG+		$7.00
PAPERBACK LIBRARY	53 696	The Rat Patrol #6	1968	King, D.	VG+	TVTI	$6.00
PAPERBACK LIBRARY	52 726	Bonanza #1	1968	Owen, D.	VG+	TVTI	$6.00
PAPERBACK LIBRARY	53 727	Earthman, Go Home	1968	Ellison, H.	VGF+		$20.00 A
PAPERBACK LIBRARY	53 727	Earthman, Go Home	1968	Ellison, H.	VGF		$14.00
PAPERBACK LIBRARY	53 735	Come One, Come All	1968	Conway, T.	VG		$7.00
PAPERBACK LIBRARY	52 757	Bonanza #2	1968	Owen, D.	VG	TVTI	$6.00
PAPERBACK LIBRARY	52 816	Lisa	1965	Whitney, H.*	VG		$29.00 A
PAPERBACK LIBRARY	52 941	Terror On Planet Ionus	1966	Adler, A.	AF		$6.00
PAPERBACK LIBRARY	52 955	Step To The Stars	1966	Del Rey, L.	VGF		$6.00
PAPERBACK LIBRARY	54 962	The Lady Of The Shroud	1966	Stoker, B.	AF		$6.00
PAPERBACK LIBRARY	56 968	Mike Mars Astronaut	1966	Wollheim, D.A.	AF		$6.00
PAPERBACK LIBRARY	56 972	Mike Mars Flies The X-15	1966	Wollheim, D.A.	AF		$6.00
PAPERBACK LIBRARY	52 985	The Solarians	1966	Spinrad, N.	VG+		$5.00
PAPERBACK LIBRARY	62 9	Star Flight	1969	Tubb, E.C.	VGF		$6.00
PAPERBACK LIBRARY	64 15	Dark Don't Catch Me	1968	Packer, V.*	VGF		$6.00 A
PAPERBACK LIBRARY	62 39	Dark Shadows #7	1969	Ross, M.	VG	TVTI	$4.00
PAPERBACK LIBRARY	63 50	The Best Laid Plans	1969	Conway, T.	VG		$6.00
PAPERBACK LIBRARY	62 62	B. Collins In Funny Vein (5th)	1969		VG+	TVTI	$4.00
PAPERBACK LIBRARY	62 135	Dark Shadows #10	1969	Ross, M.	VG+	TVTI	$6.00
PAPERBACK LIBRARY	64 144	KKK	1969	Meilen, B.	VG+		$7.00
PAPERBACK LIBRARY	64 168	Why We March	1969	Soul Brother #44	VGF		$6.00
PAPERBACK LIBRARY	66 181	The Narrow Margin	1969	Wood, D.	VGF	MTI	$5.00
PAPERBACK LIBRARY	62 210	Barnabas Collins	1969	Frid, J.	VG+	TVTI	$5.00
PAPERBACK LIBRARY	62 212	Dark Shadows #11	1969	Ross, M.	VG	TVTI	$4.00
PAPERBACK LIBRARY	66 217	The Sexual Fetish	1969	Tralins, R.	VGF		$5.00
PAPERBACK LIBRARY	65 223	I Ain't Marchin' Anymore	1969	Rader, D.	VG+		$5.00
PAPERBACK LIBRARY	62 244	Dark Shadows #12	1969	Ross, M.	VG-	TVTI	$4.00
PAPERBACK LIBRARY	62 258	Dark Shadows #13	1970	Ross, M.	VG+	TVTI	$4.00
PAPERBACK LIBRARY	64 267	Death Of A Blue Eyed Soul Brother	1970	Johnson, B.B.	AF		$7.00
PAPERBACK LIBRARY	63 280	The Blow-Your-Mind Job	1970	Conway, T.	VG+		$7.00
PAPERBACK LIBRARY	65 281	The Romance Of Sorcery	1970	Rohmer, S.	VGF+		$25.00 A
PAPERBACK LIBRARY	63 296	Dark Shadows #15	1970	Ross, M.	VG+	TVTI	$4.00
PAPERBACK LIBRARY	63 318	Dark Shadows #16	1970	Ross, M.	VG+	TVTI	$7.00
PAPERBACK LIBRARY	63 321	Island Of Evil	1970	Daniels, D.	AF	TVTI	$8.00 A
PAPERBACK LIBRARY	64 343	Mother Of The Year	1970	Johnson, B.B.	AF		$7.00

Penguin 530 AF $8 (2nd)   Penguin 538 VG+ $7 (2nd)   Penguin 629 AF $16   Penguin 648 VGF $22

PUBLISHER	PUB. #	TITLE	DATE	AUTHOR	COND.	TYPE	PRICE
PAPERBACK LIBRARY	64 344	The Cunning Linguist	1970	Conway, T.	AF		$6.00
PAPERBACK LIBRARY	63 359	The Druid Stone	1970	Majors, S.*	F		$8.00
PAPERBACK LIBRARY	63 359	The Druid Stone	1970	Majors, S.*	VG		$6.00
PAPERBACK LIBRARY	63 384	Anti-Man	1970	Koontz, D.R.	VG+		$47.00 A
PAPERBACK LIBRARY	63 385	Dark Shadows #19	1970	Ross, M.	VG	TVTI	$3.00
PAPERBACK LIBRARY	64 388	That's Where The Cat's At	1970	Johnson, B.B.	VG		$4.00
PAPERBACK LIBRARY	63 419	Dark Shadows Book Of Vampires	1970	Anthology	VG	TVTI	$4.00
PAPERBACK LIBRARY	63 426	Black In Time	1970	Jakes, J.	VGF		$11.00 A
PAPERBACK LIBRARY	63 427	Dark Shadows #21	1970	Ross, M.	VG+	TVTI	$6.00
PAPERBACK LIBRARY	64 439	Turn The Other Sheik	1970	Conway, T.	VGF		$7.00
PAPERBACK LIBRARY	63 468	Dark Shadows #23	1970	Ross, M.	VG+	TVTI	$5.00
PAPERBACK LIBRARY	66 480	Quark #1	1970	Anthology	AF		$7.00
PAPERBACK LIBRARY	66 480	Quark #1	1970	Anthology	VG		$7.00
PAPERBACK LIBRARY	64 482	Bad Day For A Black Brother	1970	Johnson, B.B.	F		$7.00
PAPERBACK LIBRARY	63 515	Dark Shadows #25	1970	Ross, M.	VG+	TVTI	$7.00
PAPERBACK LIBRARY	66 530	Quark #2	1971	Anthology	VG+		$6.00
PAPERBACK LIBRARY	63 534	Dark Shadows #26	1971	Ross, M.	VG-	TVTI	$4.00
PAPERBACK LIBRARY	64 537	House Of Dark Shadows	1970	Ross, M.	VG+	MTI	$7.00
PAPERBACK LIBRARY	66 593	Quark #3	1971	Anthology	VGF		$7.00
PAPERBACK LIBRARY	64 604	Janis Joplin Her Life And Times	1971	Landau, D.	VGF+		$6.00 A
PAPERBACK LIBRARY	65 612	Across 110th	1971	Ferris, W.	F		$7.00
PAPERBACK LIBRARY	64 636	A Maze Of Death	1971	Dick, P.K.	VGF		$15.00
PAPERBACK LIBRARY	64 636	A Maze Of Death	1971	Dick, P.K.	AF-		$14.00 A
PAPERBACK LIBRARY	64 636	A Maze Of Death (2nd)	1973	Dick, P.K.	VGF+		$10.00
PAPERBACK LIBRARY	64 660	Sneak Preview	1971	Bloch, R.	VGF		$15.00
PAPERBACK LIBRARY	64 660	Sneak Preview	1971	Bloch, R.	VGF		$10.00
PAPERBACK LIBRARY	64 663	Dark Shadows #29	1971	Ross, M.	VG	TVTI	$5.00
PAPERBACK LIBRARY	64 663	Dark Shadows #29	1971	Ross, M.	VG	TVTI	$4.00
PAPERBACK LIBRARY	66 677	Defiance #3	1971	Anthology	VG		$7.00
PAPERBACK LIBRARY	66 897	Dealer	1972	Woodley, R.	VGF+		$7.00
PAPERBACK LIBRARY	64 963	The Blood Ring	1972	Robeson, K.	VGF		$5.00
PAPERBACK LIBRARY	78 77	An American Family	1973	Goulart, R.	AF	TVTI	$6.00
PAPERBACK LIBRARY	75 117	The Master	1973	Braly, M.	AF	MTI	$7.00
PAPERBACK LIBRARY	76 133	Rage	1973	Friedman, P.	VGF	MTI	$7.00
PAPERBACK LIBRARY	75 256	House Of Mystery #2	1973	Oleck, J.	AF		$10.00 A
PAPERBACK LIBRARY	78 295	Maryjane Tonight	1973	Caidin, M.	F		$7.00
PAPERBACK LIBRARY	76 494	McQ	1974	Edwards, A.	VGF	MTI	$7.00
PAPERBACK LIBRARY	75 611	The Purple Zombie	1974	Robeson, K.	AF		$8.00
PAPERBACK LIBRARY	75 677	The Werewolf Walks Tonight	1974	Avallone, M.	VGF		$7.00
PAPERBACK LIBRARY	79 827	M. Chambers: My Story (2nd)	1975	Chambers, M.	VG+		$7.00
PAPERBACK LIBRARY	76 833	Six Million Dollar Man #1	1975	Jahn, M.	VG+	TVTI	$5.00
PAPERBACK LIBRARY	76 835	Six Million Dollar Man #4	1975	Barbree, J.	VGF	TVTI	$6.00
PAPERBACK LIBRARY	76 836	Six Million Dollar Man #5	1975	Jahn, M.	AF	TVTI	$4.00
PAPERBACK LIBRARY	76 928	Bloodstalk (Vampirella #1)	1975	Goulart, R.	VG+		$12.00
PAPERBACK LIBRARY	76 928	Bloodstalk (Vampirella #1)	1975	Goulart, R.	VG+		$10.00
PAPERBACK LIBRARY	76 929	On Alien Wings (Vampirella #2)	1975	Goulart, R.	VG+		$8.00 A
PAPERBACK LIBRARY	76 929	On Alien Wings (Vampirella #2)	1975	Goulart, R.	VG+		$8.00
PAPERBACK LIBRARY	76 930	Deadwalk (Vampirella #3)	1976	Goulart, R.	VGF		$10.00

Pennant 16 VGF- $7 — Pennant 56 AF $12 — Pennant 64 VG $6 — Pennant 69 F $8

PUBLISHER	PUB. #	TITLE	DATE	AUTHOR	COND.	TYPE	PRICE
PAPERBACK LIBRARY	84 10	Defiance!	1976	Perkins, D.M.	VGF	MTI	$25.00 A
PAPERBACK LIBRARY	86 88	Blood Wedding (Vampirella #4)	1976	Goulart, R.	VGF		$10.00
PAPERBACK LIBRARY	88 295	Laverne And Shirley #2	1976	Steffanson, C.	VGF-	TVTI	$6.00
PAPERBACK LIBRARY	89 588	Telefon (4th)	1977	Wager, W.	VGF+	MTI	$8.00 A
PAPERBACK LIBRARY	89 794	Superman Quiz Book	1978	Nash, B.	VGF		$10.00
PAPERBACK LIBRARY	90 863	Dirty Harry #4	1982	Hartman, D.	VGF		$3.00
PARAGON	P 151	Male For Sale	1961	Goodman, D.	VGF		$7.00
PARAGON	P 153	Into Each Life	1961	Mencer, D.	VGF		$8.00
PARAGON	P 155	Strange Vengeance	1962	George, I.	AF		$8.00
PARAGON	P 161	Temptation	1962	Gavin, C.	VG+		$7.00
PEDIGREE	No#	Cabaret Splendide	n/d	Lamartne, G.	VG+		$27.00 A
PEDIGREE	No#	Criminal Files	n/d	Rowland, J.	VGF		$15.00 A
PENGUIN	509	The Pastures Of Heaven	1942	Steinbeck, J.	VG+		$10.00
PENGUIN	513	The Catalyst Club	1942	Dyer, G.	G+		$5.00
PENGUIN	517	Philosopher's Holiday	1943	Edman, E.	VG+		$8.00
PENGUIN	520	The Saga Of Billy The Kid	1942	Burns, W.N.	G-		$2.00
PENGUIN	525	Penguin Book Of Sonnets	1943	Anthology	VG+		$5.00
PENGUIN	530	The Ministry Of Fear (2nd)	1946	Greene, G.	AF	MTI	$8.00
PENGUIN	535	The Old Dark House (2nd)	1945	Priestley, J.B.	VG+		$8.00
PENGUIN	537	Out Of This World (2nd)	1944	Anthology	VG+		$6.00
PENGUIN	538	The Laughing Fox (2nd)	1946	Gruber, F.	VG+		$7.00
PENGUIN	540	My Name Is Aram	1944	Saroyan, W.	VGF		$10.00
PENGUIN	545	The Talking Clock (2nd)	1946	Gruber, F.	VGF+		$8.00
PENGUIN	545	The Talking Clock (2nd)	1946	Gruber, F.	VGF		$5.00 A
PENGUIN	551	Mr. Littlejohn	1944	Flavin, M.	VG-		$5.00
PENGUIN	559	Death Of A Saboteur	1945	Footner, H.	G		$2.00
PENGUIN	569	Conceived In Liberty	1945	Fast, H.	VGF		$7.00
PENGUIN	571	Death Down East	1945	Blake, E.	VGF		$7.00
PENGUIN	576	The Lovely Lady	1946	Lawrence, D.H.	VG+		$6.00
PENGUIN	591	Mildred Pierce	1946	Cain, J.M.	VG+		$8.00
PENGUIN	591	Mildred Pierce	1946	Cain, J.M.	VG		$5.00
PENGUIN	593	Handbook Of Politics	1946	Mellett, L.	VGF		$5.00
PENGUIN	604	Trio	1946	Baker, D.	VG		$5.00
PENGUIN	629	The King Is Dead On Queen St.	1947	Bonnamy, F.	AF		$16.00 A
PENGUIN	631	A Funeral In Eden	1947	McGuire, P.	VGF		$5.00 A
PENGUIN	647	Uncle Tom's Children	1947	Wright, R.	AF-		$12.00
PENGUIN	648	Deadly Weapon	1947	Miller, W.	VGF		$22.00 A
PENGUIN	650	American Beauty	1947	Ferber, E.	AF		$8.00
PENGUIN	651	Market For Murder	1947	Gruber, F.	VG		$5.00
PENGUIN	652	The New Quiz Book	1948	Morehead, A.H.	VG+		$7.00
PENGUIN	4454	False Starts	1977	Braly, M.	VG+		$8.00
PENGUIN	S 51	Must The War Spread?	1940	Pritt, D.N.	VG-		$4.00
PENGUIN	S 82	Aircraft Recognition (4th)	1943	Sneath, R.A.S.	VG+		$7.00
PENGUIN	S 201	What's That Plane (7th)	1943	Pitkin, W.	VG+		$7.00
PENGUIN	S 202	New Soldier's Handbook	1942	Anonymous	VG+		$8.00
PENGUIN	S 203	Guerilla Warfare	1942	Levy, Y.	VG+		$9.00
PENGUIN	S 209	Americans vs. Germans	1942	Anthology	VG		$6.00
PENGUIN	S 210	Modern Battle	1942	Thompson, P.W.	VG-		$6.00

Pennant Mystery 2 G $14   Perma P-118 VGF $20   Perma P-124 VG+ $12

PUBLISHER	PUB. #	TITLE	DATE	AUTHOR	COND.	TYPE	PRICE
PENGUIN	S 210	Modern Battle (4th)	1943	Thompson, P.W.	VG+		$8.00
PENGUIN	S 211	The Good Soldier Schweik (3rd)	1943	Hasek, J.	VG		$4.00
PENGUIN	S 212	Psychology For Fighting Man	1943	National Research	VG		$6.00
PENGUIN	S 216	A History Of The War	1943	Modley, R.	VG+		$5.00
PENGUIN	S 219	The Moon Is Down	1943	Steinbeck, J.	VGF		$10.00
PENGUIN	S 219	The Moon Is Down	1943	Steinbeck, J.	VG-		$7.00
PENGUIN	S 221	30 Seconds Over Tokyo	1944	Lawson, T.W.	VGF		$7.00
PENGUIN	S 227	This Is The Navy	1944	Anthology	VGF		$7.00
PENGUIN	S 229	Psychology for Serviceman	1945	National Research	VG-		$4.00
PENGUIN U.K.	No#	Penguin Parade 3	1938	Anthology	VGF		$5.00
PENGUIN U.K.	C 5	R. Browning - Poems (dust jkt.)	1938	Browning, R.	VGF		$8.00
PENGUIN U.K.	38	The Return (dust jkt.)	1935	De La Mare, W.	AF		$10.00
PENGUIN U.K.	68	With Mystics In Tibet (4th) (d.j.)	1938	David-Neel, A.	VGF		$20.00
PENGUIN U.K.	185	Confessions Of A Young Man (d.j.)	1939	Moore, G.	VGF		$10.00
PENGUIN U.K.	205	From Red Sea To Blue Nile (d.j.)	1939	Forbes, R.	VGF		$7.00
PENGUIN U.K.	527	Hashish	1946	Monfreid, H.D.	VGF		$10.00
PENGUIN U.K.	1096	The Little Sister (4th)	1961	Chandler, R.	VG		$5.00
PENNANT	P 1	Navajo Canyon	1953	Blackburn, T.W.	AF		$8.00
PENNANT	P 3	Epitaph For A Spy	1953	Ambler, E.	VG+		$7.00
PENNANT	P 5	In Those Days	1953	Fergusson, H.	AF		$7.00
PENNANT	P 7	Vanity Row	1953	Burnett, W.R.	VGF		$8.00
PENNANT	P 7	Vanity Row	1953	Burnett, W.R.	VG+		$6.00
PENNANT	P 8	Sunset Rider	1953	Stuart, M.	VGF		$6.00
PENNANT	P 11	A Time To Kill	1953	Household, G.	VGF+		$8.00
PENNANT	P 12	Warrant For A Wanton	1953	Gillian, M.	G		$3.00
PENNANT	P 13	Apache Desert	1953	Holmes, L.P.	AF		$8.00
PENNANT	P 16	Lily In Her Coffin	1953	Benson, B.	VGF-		$7.00 A
PENNANT	P 21	Border Graze	1953	Bennett, D.	VG+		$6.00
PENNANT	P 23	Man-Eaters Of Kumaon	1953	Corbett, J.	VG+		$7.00
PENNANT	P 24	Murder Won't Out	1953	Crouse, R.	VGF		$9.00
PENNANT	P 26	Santa Fe Passage	1953	Fisher, C.	VG+		$7.00
PENNANT	P 31	The Outlaw Years	1953	Coates, R.M.	VGF+		$7.00
PENNANT	P 32	Walls Rise Up	1953	Perry, G.S.	AF		$8.00
PENNANT	P 35	Walk The Dark Bridge	1954	O'Farrell, W.	AF		$10.00
PENNANT	P 35	Walk The Dark Bridge	1954	O'Farrell, W.	VG+		$8.00
PENNANT	P 41	The Bronze Mermaid	1954	Ernst, P.	VG+		$7.00
PENNANT	P 44	Adventures In Time And Space	1954	Anthology	VG		$7.00
PENNANT	P 50	One Way Ticket	1954	O'Brien, E.	VG		$6.00
PENNANT	P 50	One Way Ticket	1954	O'Brien, E.	VG		$4.00
PENNANT	P 51	Vaquero Of The Brush Country	1954	Dobie, J.F.	VGF-		$6.00
PENNANT	P 53	Toll Mountain	1954	McCaig, R.	AF		$8.00
PENNANT	P 53	Toll Mountain	1954	McCaig, R.	VGF		$7.00
PENNANT	P 55	Repeat Performance	1954	O'Farrell, W.	VGF		$7.00
PENNANT	P 56	Beyond Human Ken	1954	Anthology	AF		$12.00 A
PENNANT	P 56	Beyond Human Ken	1954	Anthology	VGF		$8.00

  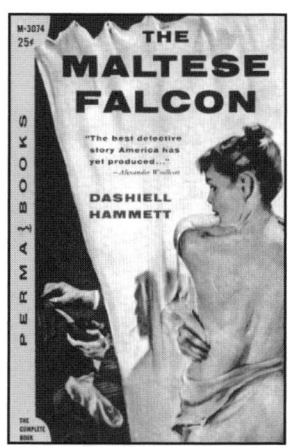

Perma M-3043 F $27   Perma M-3048 F $55   Perma M-3074 VGF $33

PUBLISHER	PUB. #	TITLE	DATE	AUTHOR	COND.	TYPE	PRICE
PENNANT	P 61	Argosy Book Of Sports Story	1954	Anthology	VGF		$6.00
PENNANT	P 64	The Stakes Are High	1954	Anthology	VG		$6.00
PENNANT	P 69	The Nester	1954	Daniels, J.S.	F		$8.00
PENNANT	P 75	The Altered Ego	1954	Sohl, J.	VGF		$8.00 A
PENNANT	P 75	The Altered Ego	1954	Sohl, J.	VG+		$8.00
PENNANT	P 75	The Altered Ego	1954	Sohl, J.	VG		$5.00
PENNANT	P 77	High Country	1955	Dawson, P.	VGF		$8.00
PENNANT	P 77	High Country	1955	Dawson, P.	VG+		$5.00
PENNANT	P 79	Code Three	1955	Fox, J.M.	AF		$10.00 A
PENNANT	P 79	Code Three	1955	Fox, J.M.	AF		$7.00 A
PENNANT MYSTERY	2	The Six Iron Spiders	n/d	Taylor, P.A.	G	Digest	$14.00
PERIOD	M 102	Sinners Don't Cry	1961	Dickson, R.C.	AF		$11.00 A
PERIOD	M 104	Filth For Sale!	1961	Savage, J.	VG+		$8.00
PERMA	P 23	Strange Customs Of Courtship	1949	Fielding, W.J.	VGF		$5.00
PERMA	P 108	Unconquered	1951	Swanson, N.H.	VG		$7.00
PERMA	P 112	The Well Of Loneliness	1951	Hall, R.	VGF		$18.00 A
PERMA	P 112	The Well Of Loneliness	1951	Hall, R.	VGF		$12.00
PERMA	P 112	The Well Of Loneliness	1951	Hall, R.	VG		$5.00
PERMA	P 116	Fear Is The Hunter	1951	Teilhet, H.T.	VG		$6.00
PERMA	P 117	In The Grip Of Terror	1951	Anthology	VGF		$11.00 A
PERMA	P 117	In The Grip Of Terror	1951	Anthology	VG+		$9.00
PERMA	P 117	In The Grip Of Terror	1951	Anthology	VG		$9.00
PERMA	P 117	In The Grip Of Terror	1951	Conklin, G.	G+		$5.00
PERMA	P 118	As Tough As They Come	1951	Anthology	VGF		$20.00 A
PERMA	P 118	As Tough As They Come	1951	Anthology	VGF		$17.00 A
PERMA	P 119	To Hell And Back	1951	Murphy, A.	VG+		$7.00
PERMA	P 122	New Stories For Men	1951	Anthology	VG+		$7.00
PERMA	P 124	Arrest The Saint!	1951	Charteris, L.	VG+		$12.00
PERMA	P 134	The Raging Tide	1951	Gann, E.K.	VG+	MTI	$4.00
PERMA	P 145	Beyond The End Of Time	1952	Anthology	VG		$7.00
PERMA	P 179	Big Old Sun	1952	Faherty, R.	AF		$8.00
PERMA	P 179	Big Old Sun	1952	Faherty, R.	VGF		$8.00
PERMA	P 186	Devil's Spawn	1952	Brown, W.	VG+		$10.00
PERMA	P 187	Murder, Inc.	1952	Feder, S.	VGF		$13.00 A
PERMA	P 187	Murder, Inc.	1952	Feder, S.	AF		$12.00
PERMA	P 187	Murder, Inc.	1952	Feder, S.	VGF		$10.00 A
PERMA	P 191	Beau Geste	1952	Wren, P.C.	VG+		$7.00
PERMA	P 194	Dark Memory	1953	Latimer, J.	VG+		$8.00
PERMA	P 194	Dark Memory	1953	Latimer, J.	VG		$5.00
PERMA	P 212	7 Arts (2nd)	1953	Anthology	VG+		$2.50
PERMA	P 213	New Voices	1953	Anthology	VGF		$2.50
PERMA	P 216	Toil Of The Brave	1953	Fletcher, I.	VGF		$7.00
PERMA	P 227	Swing The Big Eyed Rabbit	1953	McCoy, J.P.	AF		$7.00
PERMA	P 234	No Bugles Tonight	1953	Lancaster, B.	AF-		$6.00
PERMA	P 236	Shadow Of Tomorrow	1953	Anthology	VGF		$7.00

Perma M-3084 AF- $82

Perma M-3097 VGF $20

Perma M-3108 VG+ $15

PUBLISHER	PUB. #	TITLE	DATE	AUTHOR	COND.	TYPE	PRICE
PERMA	P 237	Salome	1953	Denker, H.	VGF		$9.00
PERMA	239	Women In Prison	1953	Henry, J.	AF		$14.00 A
PERMA	239	Women In Prison	1953	Henry, J.	VG		$7.00
PERMA	239	Women In Prison (2nd)	1953	Henry, J.	VGF+		$15.00 A
PERMA	244	The Tall Dolores	1953	Avallone, M.	AF		$21.00 A
PERMA	244	The Tall Dolores	1953	Avallone, M.	VG		$5.00
PERMA	244	The Tall Dolores (2nd)	1953	Avallone, M.	AF		$12.00
PERMA	P 267	Down & Out In Paris & London	1953	Orwell, G.	VGF		$6.00
PERMA	271	Range War	1954	Hopkins, T.J.	AF		$5.00 A
PERMA	277	With Murder For Some	1954	Huston, H.C.	VG-		$3.00
PERMA	279	The Lost World	1954	Doyle, A.C.	AF		$10.00
PERMA	P 286	The Condemned	1954	Pagano, J.	VG		$7.00
PERMA	289	The Spitting Image	1954	Avallone, M.	VG		$5.00
PERMA	289	The Spitting Image (2nd)	1954	Avallone, M.	VG		$7.00
PERMA	P 297	Flying Saucers From Outer Space	1954	Keyhoe, D.E.	VG		$5.00
PERMA	310	Against The Fall Of Night	1954	Clarke, A.C.	AF		$16.00
PERMA	310	Against The Fall Of Night	1954	Clarke, A.C.	VGF		$9.00 A
PERMA	M 3001	Texan-Killer (2nd)	1955	Austin, G.	VG+		$6.00
PERMA	M 3003	Spur To The Smoke	1954	Frazee, S.	VGF		$8.00
PERMA	M 3006	Boy Gang	1955	Kennedy, M.	VG+		$13.00 A
PERMA	M 3006	Boy Gang	1955	Kennedy, M.	VGF		$12.00 A
PERMA	M 3006	Boy Gang	1955	Kennedy, M.	VG		$8.00
PERMA	M 3007	The Desperate Hours (3rd)	1955	Hayes, J.	VG	MTI	$6.00
PERMA	M 3009	Honky-Tonk Woman	1955	Lomax, B.	AF		$8.00
PERMA	M 3009	Honky-Tonk Woman	1955	Lomax, B.	VG+		$7.00
PERMA	M 3011	The Stainless Steel Kimono	1955	Chaze, E.	AF		$10.00
PERMA	M 3011	The Stainless Steel Kimono	1955	Chaze, E.	AF		$7.00
PERMA	M 3022	The Big Boodle	1955	Sylvester, R.	AF-		$7.00
PERMA	M 3032	The Mean Streets	1956	Dewey, T.B.	VG		$14.00
PERMA	M 3036	Visa To Death	1956	Lacy, E.	VG+		$8.00
PERMA	M 3036	Visa To Death	1956	Lacy, E.	AF		$7.00 A
PERMA	M 3036	Visa To Death	1956	Lacy, E.	VG		$7.00
PERMA	M 3043	Red Harvest	1956	Hammett, D.	F		$27.00 A
PERMA	M 3043	Red Harvest	1956	Hammett, D.	AF		$24.00 A
PERMA	M 3043	Red Harvest	1956	Hammett, D.	VG+		$22.00 A
PERMA	M 3048	Live And Let Die	1956	Fleming, I.	F		$55.00 A
PERMA	M 3057	The Perma X-Word Puzzle Book	1956	Field, A.	F		$20.00 A
PERMA	M 3061	The Mugger	1956	McBain, E.*	VGF		$15.00
PERMA	M 3061	The Mugger	1956	McBain, E.*	VG+		$10.00
PERMA	M 3061	The Mugger	1956	McBain, E.*	G+		$6.00
PERMA	M 3062	The Pusher	1956	McBain, E.*	G+		$5.00
PERMA	M 3066	Murder Is Where You Find It	1956	Hansen, R.P.	VG+		$7.00
PERMA	M 3067	Pets - Including Women	1956	Anthology	VGF+		$6.00
PERMA	M 3070	Too Hot To Handle	1956	Fleming, I.	VGF		$71.00 A
PERMA	M 3074	The Maltese Falcon	1957	Hammett, D.	VGF		$33.00 A

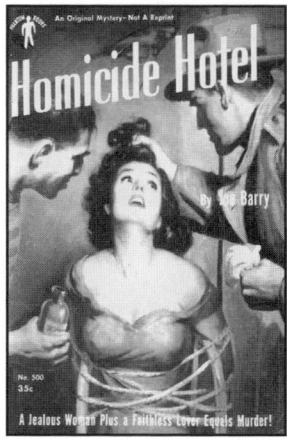

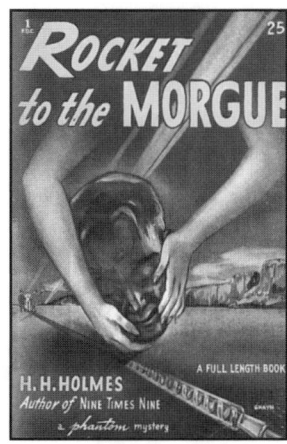

Phantom 500 VG+ $77   Phantom 508 VG $48   Phantom Mystery 1 VG+ $60

PUBLISHER	PUB. #	TITLE	DATE	AUTHOR	COND.	TYPE	PRICE
PERMA	M 3079	Unhappy Hooligan	1957	Palmer, S.	AF		$17.00 A
PERMA	M 3084	Diamonds Are Forever	1957	Fleming, I.	AF-		$82.00 A
PERMA	M 3096	Widow's Pique	1957	Treynor, B.	VGF		$5.00
PERMA	M 3097	Vanishing Ladies	1957	Marsten, R.	VGF		$20.00 A
PERMA	M 3103	The Saint Around The World	1958	Charteris, L.	AF		$44.00 A
PERMA	M 3106	Lead With Your Left	1958	Lacy, E.	VGF		$8.00
PERMA	M 3108	Killer's Choice	1957	McBain, E.*	VG+		$15.00 A
PERMA	M 3111	The Best From Manhunt	1958	Anthology	VG+		$23.00 A
PERMA	M 3111	The Best From Manhunt	1958	Anthology	VG+		$22.00 A
PERMA	M 3111	The Best From Manhunt	1958	Anthology	VG		$8.00
PERMA	M 3113	Killer's Payoff	1958	McBain, E.*	AF		$41.00 A
PERMA	M 3113	Killer's Payoff	1958	McBain, E.*	VG+		$12.00
PERMA	M 3113	Killer's Payoff	1958	McBain, E.*	VG		$8.00
PERMA	M 3117	Even The Wicked	1958	Marsten, R.	VGF		$24.00 A
PERMA	M 3118	Spearhead	1958	Davis, F.M.	AF		$5.00
PERMA	M 3119	Lady Killer	1958	McBain, E.*	VG		$5.00
PERMA	M 4024	The Well Of Loneliness (8th)	1955	Hall, R.	VGF		$9.00
PERMA	M 4056	South Sea Stories	1956	Maugham, W.S.	VG+		$4.00
PERMA	M 4057	Darien Venture	1956	Terry, C.V.	VG+		$6.00
PERMA	M 4085	Underworld U.S.A.	1957	Dinneen, J.F.	VGF		$8.00
PERMA	M 4088	Dracula	1957	Stoker, B.	VGF		$8.00
PERMA	M 4088	Dracula	1957	Stoker, B.	VG+		$7.00
PERMA	M 4103	The Royal Vultures	1958	Kolman, S.	VGF		$23.00 A
PERMA	M 4124	Imitation Of Life	1959	Hurst, F.	VG	MTI	$6.00
PERMA	M 4150	Killer's Wedge	1959	McBain, E.*	AF	TVTI	$43.00 A
PERMA	M 4150	Killer's Wedge	1959	McBain, E.*	VGF	TVTI	$11.00 A
PERMA	M 4161	Journey To Center Of Earth	1959	Verne, J.	VG	MTI	$6.00
PERMA	M 4166	Til Death	1960	McBain, E.*	F		$14.00
PERMA	M 4181	King's Ransom	1960	McBain, E.*	F		$46.00 A
PERMA	M 4181	King's Ransom	1960	McBain, E.*	VG+		$10.00
PERMA	M 4181	King's Ransom	1960	McBain, E.*	VG		$5.00
PERMA	M 4187	Give The Boys A Great Big Hand	1960	McBain, E.*	AF		$65.00 A
PERMA	M 4187	Give The Boys A Great Big Hand	1960	McBain, E.*	VG		$8.00
PERMA	M 4197	The World That Couldn't Be	1961	Anthology	VGF		$6.00
PERMA	M 4199	The Glass Key	1961	Hammett, D.	AF		$16.00
PERMA	M 4201	Red Harvest	1961	Hammett, D.	AF		$16.00
PERMA	M 4202	The Thin Man	1961	Hammett, D.	AF		$12.00
PERMA	M 4202	The Thin Man	1961	Hammett, D.	VG-		$3.00
PERMA	M 4218	The Heckler	1961	McBain, E.*	VGF		$49.00 A
PERMA	M 4218	The Heckler	1961	McBain, E.*	VG		$6.00
PERMA	M 4226	Out Of The Burning	1961	Freeman, I.H.	VGF-		$6.00 A
PERMA	M 4229	See Them Die	1961	McBain, E.*	VG+		$6.00
PERMA	M 4233	With A Madman Behind Me	1961	Powell, T.	VG+		$8.00
PERMA	M 4234	Hardly A Man Is Now Alive	1961	Ridgway, J.	VGF		$7.00
PERMA	M 4238	The Man Who Shot Liberty Valance	1962	Bellah, J.W.	VGF	MTI	$7.00

| Pike 101 VGF $42 | Pike 203 VG+ $93 | Playtime 626 AF $28 |

PUBLISHER	PUB. #	TITLE	DATE	AUTHOR	COND.	TYPE	PRICE
PERMA	M 4238	The Man Who Shot Liberty Valance	1962	Bellah, J.W.	G	MTI	$3.00
PERMA	M 4241	Moon Pilot	1962	Buckner, R.	VGF	MTI	$4.00
PERMA	M 4251	Start Screaming Murder	1962	Powell, T.	AF		$24.00 A
PERMA	M 4259	A Big Man, A Fast Man	1962	Appel, B.	VG+		$5.00
PERMA	M 4262	The Flintstones	1963	Hanna-Barbera	VG		$7.00
PERMA	M 4264	The Con Man	1962	McBain, E.*	VGF	TVTI	$8.00
PERMA	M 4266	The Mugger	1962	McBain, E.*	VG+	TVTI	$7.00
PERMA	M 4268	Cop Hater	1962	McBain, E.*	VGF	TVTI	$8.00
PERMA	M 4271	The Empty Hours	1963	McBain, E.*	VG		$8.00
PERMA	M 4272	The Hunter	1962	Stark, R.*	VG+		$8.00
PERMA	M 4272	The Hunter	1962	Stark, R.*	VG-		$3.00
PERMA	M 4279	Son Of Flubber	1963	Fuller, R.	VG+	MTI	$6.00
PERMA	M 4286	Anything But Saintly	1963	Deming, R.	VGF		$7.00
PERMA	M 4298	The Mourner	1963	Stark, R.*	AF		$34.00 A
PERMA	M 4298	The Mourner	1963	Stark, R.*	VG		$5.00
PERMA	M 4299	Runaway Black	1963	McBain, E.*	VG		$5.00
PERMA	M 4304	Ten Plus One	1964	McBain, E.*	VGF		$5.00
PERMA	M 5027	The Great Imposter (2nd)	1960	Crichton, R.	VG+	MTI	$5.00
PERMA	M 5094	The Hated One	1964	Tracy, D.	VGF		$7.00
PERMA	M 6002	Mysterious Island	1961	Verne, J.	VG	MTI	$4.00
PERMA	M 7508	Writing Fiction	1962	Cassill, R.V.	VGF+		$12.00
PHANTOM BOOKS	500	Homicide Hotel	1951	Barry, J.	VG+	Digest	$77.00 A
PHANTOM BOOKS	508	Swamp Kill	1952	Whittington, H.	VG	Digest	$48.00 A
PHANTOM BOOKS	510	Murder Doll	1952	Saber, R.O.	VG+	Digest	$40.00 A
PHANTOM BOOKS	513	Wake Up To Murder	1952	Keene, D.	VG	Digest	$82.00 A
PHANTOM MYSTERY	1	Rocket To The Morgue	1942	Holmes, H.H.*	VG+	Digest	$60.00 A
PIKE	101	Lost City Of The Damned	1961	Rivere, A.*	VGF		$42.00 A
PIKE	101	Lost City Of The Damned	1961	Rivere, A.*	VGF		$35.00 A
PIKE	101	Lost City Of The Damned	1961	Rivere, A.*	VG		$10.00
PIKE	102	Beatnik Ball	1961	Strick, M.	VG+		$30.00 A
PIKE	203	The Coming Of The Rats	1961	Smith, G.H.	VG+		$93.00 A
PIKE	208	Baroness Of Blood (signed)	1961	Smith, G.H.	AF		$27.00 A
PIKE	215	Scarlet Virgin	1962	Sheppard, D.	VG+		$19.00 A
PIKE	217	Love Goddess	1962	Hudson, J.*	VG+		$10.00
PILLAR	PB 806	Sin Mates	1963	Eliot, D.	VGF		$8.00
PILLAR	PB 810	Sin Census	1963	Holliday, D.	AF		$7.00
PILLAR	PB 812	Passion Plot	1963	Anderson, C.*	VGF+		$13.00 A
PILLAR	PB 814	Passion Spree	1963	Alden, B.	VG+		$6.00
PILLAR	PB 815	Lust Hop	1963	Marsh, A.	VGF		$9.00
PILLAR	PB 840	Shame Isle	1964	Marshall, A.*	VGF		$8.00
PILLAR	PB 845	Lust Stakes	1964	Marshall, A.*	VG+		$7.00
PILLAR	PB 849	Lust Set	1964	Elliott, D.*	AF		$8.00
PILLAR	PB 851	Adam's Eve	1964	Dexter, J.	VG+		$7.00
PINNACLE	P 1	The Executioner	1969	Pendleton, D.	VG+		$7.00
PINNACLE	43	The Alien Earth	1971	Elder, M.	VGF		$7.00

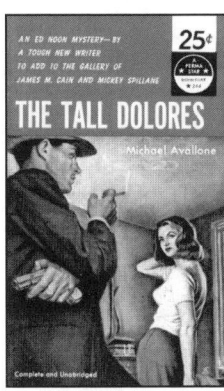
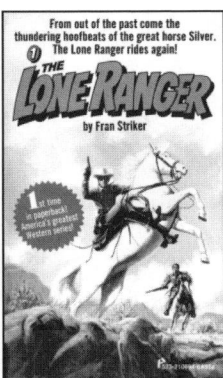

| Perma 244 AF $21 | Pinnacle 694 AF $18 | Pinnacle 40447 AF $14 | Playboy 16228 VGF $24 |

PUBLISHER	PUB. #	TITLE	DATE	AUTHOR	COND.	TYPE	PRICE
PINNACLE	200	The Hand Of Dracula	1973	Lory, R.	VGF		$6.00
PINNACLE	256	Dracula's Gold	1973	Lory, R.	AF-		$6.00
PINNACLE	299	Killinger! #1	1974	Palmer, P.K.	F		$4.00
PINNACLE	300	Killinger! #2	1974	Palmer, P.K.	F		$4.00
PINNACLE	394	Intimate Diary Of L. Lovelace	1974	Lovelace, L.	VGF		$20.00 A
PINNACLE	508	Dracula's Lost World	1974	Lory, R.	VG+		$5.00
PINNACLE	581	Dracula's Disciple	1975	Lory, R.	VG		$6.00
PINNACLE	629	Reminiscences Of Solar Pons #5	1975	Derleth, A.	VGF		$6.00
PINNACLE	633	The James Dean Story	1975	Martinetti, R.	VG+		$5.00
PINNACLE	694	The Lone Ranger #1	1975	Striker, F.	AF		$18.00 A
PINNACLE	695	The Private Life Of Sherlock Holmes	1975	Starrett, V.	VG-		$3.00
PINNACLE	732	The Lone Ranger #2	1975	Striker, F.	VGF		$15.00
PINNACLE	801	The Lone Ranger #3	1976	Striker, F.	AF		$18.00 A
PINNACLE	40447	Strange Eons	1979	Bloch, R.	AF		$14.00
PINNACLE	40447	Strange Eons	1979	Bloch, R.	VGF		$14.00
PINNACLE	40636	Solar Pons #6 (3rd)	1979	Derleth, A.	VGF		$5.00
PINNACLE	41505	Charlie Chan And The Curse..	1981	Avallone, M.	VG+	MTI	$4.00
PINNACLE	42226	The Hills Of Homicide	1983	L'Amour, L.	VGF		$7.00
PIRATE EDITIONS	No#	Steal This Book	1971	Hoffman, A.	VGF		$12.00
PLAYBOY	16194	The Pocket Playboy #1	1973	Anthology	VG+		$18.00 A
PLAYBOY	16205	The Pocket Playboy #2	1973	Anthology	VGF-		$24.00 A
PLAYBOY	16213	The Pocket Playboy #3	1973	Anthology	VGF		$26.00 A
PLAYBOY	16221	Playboy's Short Shorts #1 (2nd)	1974	Anthology	VGF		$6.00
PLAYBOY	16228	The Pocket Playboy #5	1974	Anthology	VGF		$24.00 A
PLAYBOY	16238	Playboy Photographer #1	1974	Posar, P.	VG		$8.00
PLAYBOY	16262	Playboy Photographer #2	1975	Hooker, D.	VG+		$10.00
PLAYBOY	16280	The Pocket Playboy #6	1975	Anthology	VGF-		$43.00 A
PLAYBOY	16751	Shadows	1980	Anthology	AF		$5.00
PLAYTIME	603	Bedroom Tramp	1962	Adams, B.	AF		$6.00
PLAYTIME	604	Moment Of Desire	1962	Bennett, F.	F		$7.00
PLAYTIME	606	Naked Streets	1962	Bennett, F.	AF		$10.00
PLAYTIME	609	The Golden Girls	1962	North, K.	VG+		$5.00
PLAYTIME	611	Escape Into Vice	1962	Bennett, F.	AF		$12.00
PLAYTIME	613	The Road Tramps	1962	North, K.	AF		$7.00
PLAYTIME	614	The Sexy Fraud	1962	Randolph, G.	F		$7.00
PLAYTIME	615	The Passionate Prude	1962	Weber, M.	VG+		$8.00
PLAYTIME	617	Night Clerk	1962	Hunter, W.	VG		$4.00
PLAYTIME	622	Edge Of Evil	1962	Steele, M.	AF		$10.00 A
PLAYTIME	623	Sex Goddess	1962	Randolph, G.	AF+		$9.00 A
PLAYTIME	625	The Way Of A Dame	1963	Bennett, F.	AF		$10.00 A
PLAYTIME	626	Gang Girls	1963	Crawford, R.	AF		$28.00 A
PLAYTIME	626	Gang Girls	1963	Crawford, R.	VG		$22.00 A
PLAYTIME	627	Road Show	1963	North, K.	AF		$10.00 A
PLAYTIME	630	No Holds Barred	1963	Weber, M.	AF		$7.00 A
PLAYTIME	633	School Of Desire	1963	North, K.	VGF		$7.00
PLAYTIME	636	The Jaded Sex	1963	Maxwell, B.	VGF		$8.00 A
PLAYTIME	639	Atomic Blonde	1963	Steele, M.	AF		$10.00
PLAYTIME	639	Atomic Blonde	1963	Steele, M.	VGF		$7.00

Pocket Books 82 VGF $14

Pocket Books 101 VGF $38

Pocket Books 111 VGF+ $25

PUBLISHER	PUB. #	TITLE	DATE	AUTHOR	COND.	TYPE	PRICE
PLAYTIME	641	The Drifter	1963	Holland, D.	VGF+		$7.00
PLAYTIME	642	Vice Row	1963	Bennett, F.	AF		$15.00 A
PLAYTIME	650	The Far Out Ones	1963	Holland, D.	VGF		$22.00 A
PLAYTIME	652	Undercover Job	1963	Daniels, B.	AF		$6.00 A
PLAYTIME	665	Beach Heat	1964	Woolfe, B.	F		$9.00
PLAYTIME	667	Campus Lust	1964	Swan, P.	F		$16.00 A
PLAYTIME	670	Hotel Hustler	1964	Lane, J.	F		$12.00
PLAYTIME	673	Whistle Them Willing	1964	Geis, R.E.	VG-		$5.00
PLAYTIME	675	Sex Scandal	1964	Stevens, G.	AF		$10.00
PLAYTIME	677	Campus Chippies	1964	Steele, M.	AF		$7.00
PLAYTIME	739	Sex Spy	1965	Weldon, R.	AF-		$10.00
PLAYTIME	739	Sex Spy	1965	Weldon, R.	VGF+		$8.00 A
PLAYTIME	760	G-String Girl	1965	Smith, G.	AF		$8.00
PLAYTIME	762	Bedroom Circus	1965	Joseph, G.	VGF		$8.00
PLAYTIME	765	Sex Society	1966	Davis, D.	AF		$7.00
PLAYTIME	770	Sex Substitute	1966	Linkletter, E.	VGF		$13.00 A
PLAYTIME	779	Night Of The Nymph	1966	Thompson, J.	AF		$7.00
PLAYTIME	785	Velvet Vice	1966	Miller, L.O.	VGF		$6.00
PLAYTIME	789	Bedroom Cheat	1966	Austin, W.	VGF		$7.00
PLAYTIME	797	The Sex Rally	1966	Monroe, E.	F		$12.00 A
PLAYTIME	798	Devil's Mistress	1966	Nemec, J.	AF		$7.00
PLEASURE READER	PR 104	Naked Portia	1967	Miller, M.	AF		$22.00 A
PLEASURE READER	PR 108	Lovers And Losers	1967	Williams, J.X.	VGF		$44.00 A
PLEASURE READER	PR 126	The Vice Vigilantes	1967	Miller, M.	AF		$9.00
PLEASURE READER	PR 128	Naked Before You	1967	Arana, R.	VGF+		$20.00 A
PLEASURE READER	PR 139	The Lust Crown	1967	Aldrich, C.	VG+		$25.00 A
PLEASURE READER	PR 156	Campus Sex Kitten	1968	Post, S.	VG+		$14.00 A
PLEASURE READER	PR 163	Maid Of Shame	1968	Marshall, A.*	VGF		$17.00
PLEASURE READER	PR 175	The Lust Assassin	1968	Lynn, D.	AF		$15.00 A
PLEASURE READER	PR 193	Harlot's Handyman	1968	Aldrich, C.	VG		$7.00
POCKET BOOKS	3	Shakespeare - 5 Tragedies (3rd)	1939	Shakespeare, W.	VG+		$10.00
POCKET BOOKS	4	Topper (2nd)	1939	Smith, T.	VG+	MTI	$15.00 A
POCKET BOOKS	7	Wuthering Heights (3rd)	1939	Bronte, E.	VGF+	MTI	$9.00
POCKET BOOKS	11	The Good Earth (3rd)	1939	Buck, P.S.	VG-		$4.00
POCKET BOOKS	16	Green Mansions	1939	Hudson, W.H.	G+		$8.00
POCKET BOOKS	18	Pinocchio	1939	Collidi, C.	VG+		$49.00 A
POCKET BOOKS	19	Abraham Lincoln (2nd)	1939	Charnwood, L.	VG+		$4.00
POCKET BOOKS	22	Swiss Family Robinson (5th)	1940	Wyss, J.D.	VGF+	MTI	$8.00
POCKET BOOKS	23	Autobiography Of Ben Franklin	1940	Franklin, B.	VG		$6.00
POCKET BOOKS	25	Treasure Island	1939	Stevenson, R.L.	VGF		$14.00 A
POCKET BOOKS	26	Elizabeth And Essex (3rd)	1940	Strachey, L.	VG+		$4.00
POCKET BOOKS	31	Hunchback Of Notre Dame I	1939	Hugo, V.	VG	MTI	$8.00
POCKET BOOKS	31	Hunchback Of Notre Dame I	1939	Hugo, V.	G	MTI	$5.00
POCKET BOOKS	32	Hunchback Of N. Dame II (2nd)	1940	Hugo, V.	VG	MTI	$8.00
POCKET BOOKS	32	Hunchback Of N. Dame II (3rd)	1940	Hugo, V.	VG	MTI	$8.00

Pocket Books 122 VGF $20   Pocket Books 126 AF $48   Pocket Books 214 VG+ $20

PUBLISHER	PUB. #	TITLE	DATE	AUTHOR	COND.	TYPE	PRICE
POCKET BOOKS	36	The Three Musketeers I	1940	Dumas, A.	G+		$6.00
POCKET BOOKS	37	The Three Musketeers II	1940	Dumas, A.	VG		$8.00
POCKET BOOKS	39	The Great Tales And Poems	1940	Poe, E.A.	G-		$3.00
POCKET BOOKS	39	Tales Of Myst. & Imagination (14th)	1946	Poe, E.A.	VG+		$5.00
POCKET BOOKS	45	The Light That Failed (3rd)	1940	Kipling, R.	VGF		$7.00
POCKET BOOKS	48	Scarlet Sister Mary (2nd)	1940	Peterkin, J.	VGF-		$9.00
POCKET BOOKS	49	Dr. Ehrlich's Magic Bullet (2nd)	1940	De Kruif, P.	VG+	MTI	$6.00
POCKET BOOKS	69	The 39 Steps	1940	Buchan, J.	VGF-		$20.00 A
POCKET BOOKS	71	The French Powder Mystery	1940	Queen, E.	VGF		$10.00
POCKET BOOKS	82	Captain Blood	1940	Sabatini, R.	VGF		$14.00 A
POCKET BOOKS	90	The Case Of The Sulky Girl	1941	Gardner, E.S.	G		$2.00
POCKET BOOKS	100	The General Died At Dawn	1941	Booth, C.	VGF		$14.00 A
POCKET BOOKS	101	It Walks By Night	1941	Carr, J.D.	VGF		$38.00 A
POCKET BOOKS	101	It Walks By Night	1941	Carr, J.D.	VGF		$35.00
POCKET BOOKS	102	The Philadelphia Story	1941	Barry, P.	VG+	MTI	$6.00
POCKET BOOKS	107	Pocket Book Of Etiquette	1941	Wilson, M.	VG		$4.00
POCKET BOOKS	111	Mr. Pinkerton Finds A Body	1941	Frome, D.	VGF+		$25.00 A
POCKET BOOKS	113	Enter A Murderer	1941	Marsh, N.	VGF		$13.00 A
POCKET BOOKS	122	The Simple Way Of Poison	1941	Ford, L.	VGF		$20.00 A
POCKET BOOKS	123	Dr. Jekyll And Mr. Hyde (2nd)	1941	Stevenson, R.L.	VG	MTI	$5.00
POCKET BOOKS	126	The Pocket Dictionary	1941	Pelo, W.J.	AF		$48.00 A
POCKET BOOKS	127	PB Of The War	1941	Anthology	G		$2.50
POCKET BOOKS	129	The Singapore Exile Murders	1941	Mason, V.W.	AF		$44.00 A
POCKET BOOKS	135	Long Remember	1942	Kantor, M.	AF		$11.00 A
POCKET BOOKS	138	TCOT Caretaker's Cat	1942	Gardner, E.S.	G		$2.00
POCKET BOOKS	141	The Saint-Fiacre Affair	1942	Simenon, G.	VGF		$9.00
POCKET BOOKS	143	The Man Who Came To Dinner	1942	Kaufman, G.S.	G	MTI	$3.00
POCKET BOOKS	147	The Royal Road To Romance	1942	Halliburton, R.	G		$3.00
POCKET BOOKS	154	The Red Badge Of Courage	1942	Crane, S.	VG+		$3.00
POCKET BOOKS	155	Hunger Fighters	1942	De Kruif, P.	AF-		$8.00
POCKET BOOKS	168	The Chinese Parrot	1942	Biggers, E.D.	VG		$6.00
POCKET BOOKS	170	Defense Will Not Win The War	1942	Kernan, W.T.	VGF		$5.00
POCKET BOOKS	181	The Pocket Cook Book	1942	Woody, E.	VG+		$7.00
POCKET BOOKS	191	Behind That Curtain	1942	Biggers, E.D.	VGF		$11.00 A
POCKET BOOKS	191	Behind That Curtain	1942	Biggers, E.D.	VG		$8.00
POCKET BOOKS	196	The Thin Man	1942	Hammett, D.	VG+		$7.00
POCKET BOOKS	205	Rebecca	1943	Du Maurier, D.	VG		$3.00
POCKET BOOKS	206	See Here Private Hargrove	1943	Hargrove, M.	VGF		$6.00
POCKET BOOKS	207	Charlie Chan Carries On	1943	Biggers, E.D.	VG		$4.00
POCKET BOOKS	212	Farewell, My Lovely (5th)	1943	Chandler, R.	VGF		$14.00
POCKET BOOKS	212	Farewell, My Lovely (6th)	1944	Chandler, R.	VG		$7.00
POCKET BOOKS	212	Farewell My Lovely (11th)	1945	Chandler, R.	VGF		$10.00
POCKET BOOKS	214	The PB Of Science Fiction	1943	Anthology	VG+		$20.00
POCKET BOOKS	214	The PB Of Science Fiction	1943	Anthology	VG		$17.00 A
POCKET BOOKS	214	The PB Of Science Fiction	1943	Anthology	VG		$11.00

Pocket Books 241 VG+ $12　　　　Pocket Books 295 AF $36　　　　Pocket Books 320 VG+ $25

PUBLISHER	PUB. #	TITLE	DATE	AUTHOR	COND.	TYPE	PRICE
POCKET BOOKS	217	The PB Of Home Canning	1943	Beveridge, E.	VG+		$4.00
POCKET BOOKS	221	Overture To Death (2nd)	1943	Marsh, N.	VG+		$6.00
POCKET BOOKS	232	A Coffin For Dimitrios (2nd)	1943	Ambler, E.	VGF		$6.00
POCKET BOOKS	236	The PB Of Father Brown (2nd)	1946	Chesterton, G.K.	VG+		$6.00
POCKET BOOKS	237	Trial By Fury	1943	Rice, C.	AF		$10.00
POCKET BOOKS	237	Trial By Fury	1943	Rice, C.	VG+		$8.00
POCKET BOOKS	241	Red Harvest	1943	Hammett, D.	VG+		$12.00
POCKET BOOKS	241	Red Harvest	1943	Hammett, D.	VG+		$10.00 A
POCKET BOOKS	241	Red Harvest	1943	Hammett, D.	VG		$8.00
POCKET BOOKS	245	The Four Of Hearts	1943	Queen, E.	AF		$8.00
POCKET BOOKS	245	The Four Of Hearts	1943	Queen, E.	VGF		$7.00
POCKET BOOKS	246	The Lady In The Morgue	1943	Latimer, J.	VG+		$6.00
POCKET BOOKS	246	The Lady In The Morgue	1943	Latimer, J.	G		$5.00
POCKET BOOKS	249	The Patriotic Murders	1943	Christie, A.	AF		$9.00
POCKET BOOKS	250	Destry Rides Again	1943	Brand, M.	AF		$12.00
POCKET BOOKS	252	TCOT Dangerous Dowager-11th	1946	Gardner, E.S.	AF		$7.00
POCKET BOOKS	253	Phantom Lady	1944	Irish, W.*	VGF+		$8.00 A
POCKET BOOKS	259	Halfway House	1944	Queen, E.	VGF		$7.00
POCKET BOOKS	259	Halfway House (variant ed.)	1944	Queen, E.	VG		$31.00 A
POCKET BOOKS	265	Official AAF Guide Book	1944	Anthology	G		$2.00
POCKET BOOKS	268	The Maltese Falcon (3rd)	1945	Hammett, D.	VG-		$6.00
POCKET BOOKS	269	Trent's Last Case (7th)	1945	Bentley, E.C.	VGF		$6.00
POCKET BOOKS	271	The Bride Wore Black (2nd)	1945	Woolrich, C.	VG+		$7.00
POCKET BOOKS	271	The Bride Wore Black (3rd)	1945	Woolrich, C.	VG		$7.00
POCKET BOOKS	276	The Story Pocket Book (2nd)	1945	Anthology	VG+		$5.00
POCKET BOOKS	278	Experiment Perilous	1944	Carpenter, M.	VGF		$5.00
POCKET BOOKS	283	Calamity Town	1945	Queen, E.	AF		$18.00 A
POCKET BOOKS	291	Complete Sayings Of Jesus	1945	Hinds, A. (ed.)	VGF		$6.00
POCKET BOOKS	295	The Dain Curse	1945	Hammett, D.	AF		$36.00 A
POCKET BOOKS	295	The Dain Curse	1945	Hammett, D.	G+		$3.00
POCKET BOOKS	319	Easy To Kill	1945	Christie, A.	VGF		$9.00 A
POCKET BOOKS	320	The High Window	1945	Chandler, R.	VG+		$25.00
POCKET BOOKS	320	The High Window	1945	Chandler, R.	VG+		$25.00 A
POCKET BOOKS	321	Chicken Every Sunday (dust jkt.)	1945	Taylor, R.	VG	MTI	$10.00
POCKET BOOKS	333	The Benson Murder Case (3rd)	1946	Van Dine, S.S.	VGF+		$7.00
POCKET BOOKS	358	Men Against The Sea	1946	Nordhoff, C.	VG+		$5.00
POCKET BOOKS	360	The Stephen Vincent Benet P.B.	1946	Benet, S.V.	VG+		$4.00
POCKET BOOKS	378	TCOT Perjured Parrot (8th)	1950	Gardner, E.S.	VGF		$6.00
POCKET BOOKS	384	The PB Of Ghost Stories	1947	Anthology	VGF		$10.00
POCKET BOOKS	389	The Lady In The Lake	1946	Chandler, R.	VGF		$30.00
POCKET BOOKS	389	The Lady In The Lake	1946	Chandler, R.	AF		$20.00
POCKET BOOKS	389	The Lady In The Lake	1946	Chandler, R.	VG+		$15.00
POCKET BOOKS	389	The Lady In The Lake (4th)	1947	Chandler, R.	VGF	MTI	$25.00
POCKET BOOKS	389	The Lady In The Lake (4th)	1947	Chandler, R.	VGF	MTI	$15.00
POCKET BOOKS	392	The PB Of Erskine Caldwell	1947	Caldwell, E.	VGF		$6.00

Pocket Books 425 AF $9	Pocket Books 426 VGF+ $14	Pocket Books 562 VGF $74

PUBLISHER	PUB. #	TITLE	DATE	AUTHOR	COND.	TYPE	PRICE
POCKET BOOKS	393	The Walsh Girls	1946	Janeway, E.	VG-		$3.00
POCKET BOOKS	396	Laugh With Leacock (w/errata slip)	1946	Leacock, S.	VGF		$25.00 A
POCKET BOOKS	397	The Pocket Atlantic	1946	Weeks, E.	VGF		$5.00
POCKET BOOKS	416	Bill Stern's Boxing Stories	1948	Stern, B.	VG		$6.00
POCKET BOOKS	425	The G-String Murders	1947	Lee, G.R.	AF		$9.00 A
POCKET BOOKS	426	Believe It Or Not #2	1948	Ripley	VGF+		$14.00 A
POCKET BOOKS	430	Good Night Sweet Prince	1947	Fowler, G.	VG+		$4.00
POCKET BOOKS	432	Malice Aforethought	1947	Iles, F.	AF		$8.00
POCKET BOOKS	440	Wife For Sale (7th)	1948	Norris, K.	AF		$6.00
POCKET BOOKS	444	The Unsuspected	1947	Armstrong, C.	VGF		$8.00
POCKET BOOKS	446	O. Henry Prize Stories	1947	Anthology	VGF		$6.00
POCKET BOOKS	448	Castle Skull	1947	Carr, J.D.	VG		$5.00
POCKET BOOKS	455	Treasure Of The Sierra Madre	1948	Traven, B.	VG+	MTI	$10.00
POCKET BOOKS	457	Pitcairn's Island	1947	Nordhoff, C.	AF		$6.00
POCKET BOOKS	472	Odd Man Out (3rd)	1947	Green, F.L.	VGF	MTI	$6.00
POCKET BOOKS	478	Death And The Gilded Man	1947	Dickson, C.*	VG		$4.00
POCKET BOOKS	485	The Hollow	1948	Christie, A.	VGF		$4.00
POCKET BOOKS	487	The Yukon Trail	1948	Raine, W.M.	VG		$3.00
POCKET BOOKS	515	Anna Karenina	1948	Tolstoy, L.	VG+	MTI	$10.00
POCKET BOOKS	519	Oliver Twist	1948	Dickens, C.	VG		$3.00
POCKET BOOKS	521	More Deaths Than One	1948	Fischer, B.	G+		$5.00
POCKET BOOKS	524	The Double Take	1948	Huggins, R.	G-		$3.00
POCKET BOOKS	555	Bill Stern's Football Stories	1948	Stern, B.	VG		$4.00
POCKET BOOKS	556	Anything Can Happen	1948	Papashvily, G.	VG+		$3.00
POCKET BOOKS	559	The Loves Of Carmen	1948	Merimee, P.	VG	MTI	$6.00
POCKET BOOKS	561	The D.A. Cooks A Goose	1943	Gardner, E.S.	VG+		$3.00
POCKET BOOKS	562	The Babe Ruth Story	1948	Ruth, B.	VGF		$74.00 A
POCKET BOOKS	570	Rendezvous In Black	1949	Woolrich, C.	AF-		$36.00 A
POCKET BOOKS	570	Rendezvous In Black	1949	Woolrich, C.	VG+		$12.00 A
POCKET BOOKS	571	Command Decision	1949	Haines, W.W.	AF	MTI	$7.00
POCKET BOOKS	573	Sundown Jim	1949	Haycox, E.	AF		$6.00
POCKET BOOKS	578	Pocket Book Of Old Masters	1949	Wechsler, H.J.	VGF		$6.00
POCKET BOOKS	584	King Of The Range	1949	Brand, M.	AF		$7.00
POCKET BOOKS	594	Deep West	1949	Haycox, E.	VGF		$5.00
POCKET BOOKS	608	Action By Night	1949	Haycox, E.	VGF+		$5.00
POCKET BOOKS	609	Valley Of Vanishing Men	1949	Brand, M.	AF		$7.00
POCKET BOOKS	610	West Of The Law	1949	Cody, A.	AF		$5.00
POCKET BOOKS	614	Love Is A Deadly Weapon	1949	Quentin, P.	VG		$4.00
POCKET BOOKS	621	The Shmoo	1949	Capp, A.	VG+		$17.00 A
POCKET BOOKS	624	Shoot The Works	1949	Ellington, R.	VG+		$6.00
POCKET BOOKS	626	Died In The Wool	1949	Marsh, N.	VGF		$6.00
POCKET BOOKS	632	Black Ivory	1949	Collins, N.	VGF		$7.00
POCKET BOOKS	633	My Late Wives	1949	Dickson, C.*	VG		$3.00
POCKET BOOKS	648	Disaster Trail	1949	Cody, A.	VG		$3.00
POCKET BOOKS	652	The Sea Chase	1949	Geer, A.	VG		$3.00

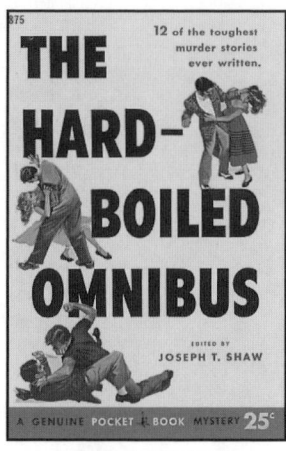

Pocket Books 823 VG+ $30   Pocket Books 833 VGF- $200   Pocket Books 875 VGF $34

PUBLISHER	PUB. #	TITLE	DATE	AUTHOR	COND.	TYPE	PRICE
POCKET BOOKS	672	Pilgrim's Inn	1950	Goudge, E.	VG+		$5.00
POCKET BOOKS	681	Rampart Street	1950	Webber, E.	AF		$10.00
POCKET BOOKS	695	Rhubarb	1950	Smith, H.A.	VGF		$6.00
POCKET BOOKS	696	The Big Sleep	1950	Chandler, R.	AF		$44.00 A
POCKET BOOKS	696	The Big Sleep	1950	Chandler, R.	VG		$15.00
POCKET BOOKS	696	The Big Sleep	1950	Chandler, R.	G		$5.00
POCKET BOOKS	696	The Big Sleep (3rd)	1950	Chandler, R.	VGF		$12.00
POCKET BOOKS	709	Halo In Brass	1950	Evans, J.*	VGF		$8.00 A
POCKET BOOKS	709	Halo In Brass	1950	Evans, J.*	VG		$4.00
POCKET BOOKS	723	The Hearth And Eagle	1950	Seton, A.	VGF		$5.00
POCKET BOOKS	746	Wilderness Nurse	1950	Marshall, M.M.	VG		$3.00
POCKET BOOKS	748	Call It Treason	1950	Howe, G.	AF		$5.00
POCKET BOOKS	748	Decision Before Dawn (3rd)	1951	Howe, G.	VG+	MTI	$6.00
POCKET BOOKS	750	The Little Sister	1950	Chandler, R.	VG		$27.00
POCKET BOOKS	750	The Little Sister	1950	Chandler, R.	VG+		$22.00
POCKET BOOKS	750	The Little Sister	1950	Chandler, R.	VG+		$15.00 A
POCKET BOOKS	750	The Little Sister	1950	Chandler, R.	G		$6.00
POCKET BOOKS	753	Crooked House	1950	Christie, A.	VGF		$10.00
POCKET BOOKS	753	Crooked House	1950	Christie, A.	VG		$6.00
POCKET BOOKS	771	The Brave Bulls	1951	Lea, T.	VGF		$5.00
POCKET BOOKS	776	The End Is Known	1951	Hall, G.H.	AF		$7.00
POCKET BOOKS	786	Very Cold For May	1951	McGivern, W.P.	AF		$12.00
POCKET BOOKS	792	TCOT Black-Eyed Blonde (2nd)	1951	Gardner, E.S.	AF		$6.00
POCKET BOOKS	801	Reprisal	1951	Gordon, A.	VG		$5.00
POCKET BOOKS	821	The Drowning Pool	1951	MacDonald, J.R.*	G+		$3.00
POCKET BOOKS	822	Cat Of Many Tails	1951	Queen, E.	AF		$8.00
POCKET BOOKS	823	Trouble Is My Business	1951	Chandler, R.	VG+		$30.00 A
POCKET BOOKS	823	Trouble Is My Business	1951	Chandler, R.	VGF		$27.00 A
POCKET BOOKS	833	Of Missing Persons	1951	Goodis, D.	VGF-		$200.00 A
POCKET BOOKS	833	Of Missing Persons	1951	Goodis, D.	VGF		$89.00 A
POCKET BOOKS	833	Of Missing Persons	1951	Goodis, D.	VGF+		$80.00
POCKET BOOKS	833	Of Missing Persons	1951	Goodis, D.	G		$18.00 A
POCKET BOOKS	846	Pick-Up On Noon Street	1952	Chandler, R.	VGF		$35.00 A
POCKET BOOKS	846	Pick-Up On Noon Street	1952	Chandler, R.	G		$6.00
POCKET BOOKS	870	Shield For Murder	1952	McGivern, W.P.	VG-		$5.00
POCKET BOOKS	875	The Hard-Boiled Omnibus	1952	Anthology	VGF		$34.00 A
POCKET BOOKS	886	TCOT Fan-Dancer's Horse	1952	Gardner, E.S.	AF		$7.00
POCKET BOOKS	894	Horns For The Devil	1952	Malley, L.	AF		$8.00
POCKET BOOKS	898	Cop	1952	Karney, J.	VG		$4.00
POCKET BOOKS	899	Naked Eye	1952	Cobean, S.	VG		$5.00
POCKET BOOKS	901	Murder For The Holidays	1952	Rigsby, H.	G		$3.00
POCKET BOOKS	904	Fear In The Night	1952	Schwartz, I.	VGF		$6.00
POCKET BOOKS	916	The Simple Art Of Murder	1952	Chandler, R.	VG+		$17.00
POCKET BOOKS	916	The Simple Art Of Murder	1952	Chandler, R.	VG		$8.00
POCKET BOOKS	920	Space Platform (2nd)	1953	Leinster, M.	VG+		$5.00

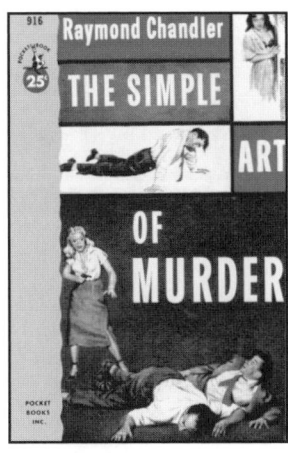

Pocket Books 916 VG+ $17   Pocket Books 971 VGF $25   Pocket Books 1222 VGF $7

PUBLISHER	PUB. #	TITLE	DATE	AUTHOR	COND.	TYPE	PRICE
POCKET BOOKS	934	Kill And Tell	1953	Rigsby, H.	VG+		$6.00
POCKET BOOKS	934	Kill And Tell	1953	Rigsby, H.	G		$3.00
POCKET BOOKS	943	Planet Of The Dreamers	1953	MacDonald, J.D.	VG+		$7.00
POCKET BOOKS	943	Planet Of The Dreamers	1953	MacDonald, J.D.	VG-		$6.00
POCKET BOOKS	946	River Of Rogues	1953	Giddings, A.	VGF		$5.00
POCKET BOOKS	947	The War Of The Worlds	1953	Wells, H.G.	VGF	MTI	$17.00 A
POCKET BOOKS	947	The War Of The Worlds	1953	Wells, H.G.	VG+	MTI	$7.00
POCKET BOOKS	960	Calendar Of Crime	1953	Queen, E.	AF		$6.00
POCKET BOOKS	961	The Crooked Frame	1953	McGivern, W.P.	AF		$10.00 A
POCKET BOOKS	964	Trespass	1953	Brown, E.	G+		$3.00
POCKET BOOKS	971	Marked For Murder	1953	MacDonald, J.R.*	VGF		$25.00 A
POCKET BOOKS	971	Marked For Murder	1953	MacDonald, J.R.*	VG		$7.00
POCKET BOOKS	975	Blood In Your Eye	1953	Wilmot, R.P.	VGF		$8.00
POCKET BOOKS	981	The Big Heat (3rd)	1957	McGivern, W.P.	VG+		$7.00
POCKET BOOKS	989	Sands Of Mars	1954	Clarke, A.C.	AF		$18.00 A
POCKET BOOKS	1020	Meet Me At The Morgue	1954	MacDonald, J.R.*	AF		$8.00
POCKET BOOKS	1020	Meet Me At The Morgue	1954	MacDonald, J.R.*	VG		$6.00
POCKET BOOKS	1024	The Barbarians (4th)	1957	Mason, F.	VGF		$5.00
POCKET BOOKS	1030	Rogue Cop	1954	McGivern, W.P.	AF		$12.00
POCKET BOOKS	1034	Walk Out On Death	1954	Armstrong, C.	AF		$8.00
POCKET BOOKS	1035	The Outlaw Of Eagle's Nest	1954	Field, P.	AF		$6.00 A
POCKET BOOKS	1036	A Pocket Full Of Rye	1954	Christie, A.	VGF		$6.00
POCKET BOOKS	1044	The Long Goodbye	1955	Chandler, R.	VGF		$40.00 A
POCKET BOOKS	1044	The Long Goodbye	1955	Chandler, R.	VGF		$25.00
POCKET BOOKS	1044	The Long Goodbye	1955	Chandler, R.	VG		$12.00
POCKET BOOKS	1044	The Long Goodbye	1955	Chandler, R.	VG-		$6.00
POCKET BOOKS	1044	The Long Goodbye (2nd)	1955	Chandler, R.	G+		$5.00
POCKET BOOKS	1045	Science Fiction Terror Tales	1955	Anthology	AF		$9.00
POCKET BOOKS	1055	I Die Possessed	1955	O'Sullivan, J.B.	VGF		$7.00
POCKET BOOKS	1059	Hero Driver	1955	Coppel, A.	VGF		$10.00
POCKET BOOKS	1062	Margin Of Terror	1955	McGivern, W.P.	F		$12.00
POCKET BOOKS	1062	Margin Of Terror	1955	McGivern, W.P.	AF-		$10.00
POCKET BOOKS	1070	The Victim Was Important	1955	Rayter, J.	G+		$3.00
POCKET BOOKS	1074	Invaders Of Earth	1955	Conklin, G.	AF		$10.00
POCKET BOOKS	1078	5 Against The House	1955	Finney, J.	G+		$2.00
POCKET BOOKS	1101	Cry, Coyote	1956	Frazee, S.	VGF+		$10.00
POCKET BOOKS	1105	Waterfront Cop	1956	McGivern, W.P.	F		$12.00
POCKET BOOKS	1105	Waterfront Cop	1956	McGivern, W.P.	VGF		$10.00
POCKET BOOKS	1105	Waterfront Cop	1956	McGivern, W.P.	VGF		$8.00
POCKET BOOKS	1107	TCOT Moth Eaten Mink	1956	Gardner, E.S.	AF		$6.00
POCKET BOOKS	1126	The Jungle Kids	1956	Hunter, E.	VGF+		$33.00 A
POCKET BOOKS	1126	The Jungle Kids (2nd)	1956	Hunter, E.	G+		$6.00
POCKET BOOKS	1129	6th PB Of Crossword Puzzles	1956	Farrar, M.P.	AF		$16.00 A
POCKET BOOKS	1136	Sinners And Shrouds	1956	Latimer, J.	VGF-		$44.00 A
POCKET BOOKS	1136	Sinners And Shrouds	1956	Latimer, J.	VG+		$8.00

Pocket Books 1261 AF $25

Pocket Books 2320 AF $22

Pocket Books 2846 VG+ $18

PUBLISHER	PUB. #	TITLE	DATE	AUTHOR	COND.	TYPE	PRICE
POCKET BOOKS	1145	Stab In The Dark	1957	Rayter, J.	AF		$27.00 A
POCKET BOOKS	1152	The Men From The Boys	1957	Lacy, E.	AF		$12.00
POCKET BOOKS	1156	The #7 File	1957	McGivern, W.P.	AF		$8.00
POCKET BOOKS	1191	Last Stage To Aspen	1958	Elston, A.V.	VGF		$5.00
POCKET BOOKS	1203	Two-Gun Rio Kid	1958	Davis, D.	F		$7.00 A
POCKET BOOKS	1204	The O.S.S. and I	1958	Morgan, W.J.	VG+		$6.00
POCKET BOOKS	1207	The Assault	1958	Matthews, A.R.	VGF		$6.00
POCKET BOOKS	1214	Dragnet: TCOT Crime King	1959	Deming, R.	VG	TVTI	$5.00
POCKET BOOKS	1215	Knocked For A Loop	1958	Rice, C.	AF		$8.00
POCKET BOOKS	1222	The Winds Of Time	1958	Oliver, C.	VGF		$7.00
POCKET BOOKS	1250	The Killer Is Mine	1959	Powell, T.	AF		$11.00 A
POCKET BOOKS	1261	Mark Kilby Solves A Murder	1959	Frazer, R.C.	AF		$25.00 A
POCKET BOOKS	1263	Wicked Women	1959	Anthology	VG+		$4.00
POCKET BOOKS	1272	Li'l Leaguer	1960	Liederman, A.	VGF+		$6.00
POCKET BOOKS	2250	Destry Rides Again (11th)	1954	Brand, M.	AF		$7.00
POCKET BOOKS	2283	Calamity Town	1955	Queen, E.	AF		$6.00
POCKET BOOKS	2320	The High Window	1955	Chandler, R.	AF		$22.00 A
POCKET BOOKS	2320	The High Window	1955	Chandler, R.	VG		$12.00
POCKET BOOKS	2468	TCOT Silent Partner	1956	Gardner, E.S.	AF		$6.00
POCKET BOOKS	2696	The Big Sleep	1958	Chandler, R.	AF		$15.00 A
POCKET BOOKS	2696	The Big Sleep	1958	Chandler, R.	VG		$8.00
POCKET BOOKS	2750	The Little Sister	1957	Chandler, R.	VG+		$12.00
POCKET BOOKS	2821	The Drowning Pool	1959	MacDonald, J.R.*	VG		$6.00
POCKET BOOKS	2823	Trouble Is My Business	1957	Chandler, R.	VG		$12.00
POCKET BOOKS	2846	Pick-Up On Noon Street	1956	Chandler, R.	VG+		$18.00
POCKET BOOKS	2846	Pick-Up On Noon Street	1956	Chandler, R.	VG+		$9.00
POCKET BOOKS	4001	The Little Sister	1963	Chandler, R.	VGF		$8.00
POCKET BOOKS	4002	Farewell My Lovely	1964	Chandler, R.	VGF		$10.00
POCKET BOOKS	4002	Farewell My Lovely	1964	Chandler, R.	VG		$7.00
POCKET BOOKS	4651	Towards Zero	1963	Christie, A.	AF		$5.00
POCKET BOOKS	4653	A Pocket Full Of Rye	1963	Christie, A.	VGF		$5.00
POCKET BOOKS	4656	The Body In The Library	1964	Christie, A.	F		$5.00
POCKET BOOKS	4657	Death Comes As The End	1964	Christie, A.	F		$5.00
POCKET BOOKS	4659	Remembered Death	1964	Christie, A.	F		$4.00
POCKET BOOKS	6001	TCOT Daring Decoy	1960	Gardner, E.S.	AF	TVTI	$10.00
POCKET BOOKS	6006	The Big Blackout	1960	Tracy, D.	VG		$6.00
POCKET BOOKS	6031	The Girl's Number Doesn't Answer	1960	Powell, T.	AF		$6.00
POCKET BOOKS	6047	The King Is Dead	1960	Queen, E.	VGF		$7.00
POCKET BOOKS	6053	The Fix	1961	Usher, J.	AF		$16.00 A
POCKET BOOKS	6053	The Fix	1961	Usher, J.	VG+		$8.00
POCKET BOOKS	6053	The Fix	1961	Usher, J.	VG		$5.00
POCKET BOOKS	6075	Killer On The Turnpike	1961	McGivern, W.P.	VG+		$6.00
POCKET BOOKS	6087	Black Is The Fashion For Dying	1961	Latimer, J.	AF		$10.00
POCKET BOOKS	6087	Black Is The Fashion For Dying	1961	Latimer, J.	G+		$5.00
POCKET BOOKS	6101	Savage Streets	1961	McGivern, W.P.	VG		$7.00

Pocket Books 4002 VGF $10   Pocket Books 6053 AF $16   Pocket Books 6101 VG $7

PUBLISHER	PUB. #	TITLE	DATE	AUTHOR	COND.	TYPE	PRICE
POCKET BOOKS	6114	Murder With Mirrors	1962	Christie, A.	VGF		$6.00
POCKET BOOKS	6143	Ripley's Believe It Or Not #8	1962	Ripley	AF		$7.00
POCKET BOOKS	6163	The 5th Galaxy Reader	1962	Anthology	AF		$6.00
POCKET BOOKS	6180	The Man With The Getaway Face	1963	Stark, R.*	VG-		$6.00
POCKET BOOKS	6202	Believe It Or Not #9	1963	Ripley	VGF		$7.00
POCKET BOOKS	43267	Twilight	1984	Nichols, L.*	G		$4.00
POCKET BOOKS	44112	Two For Texas	1982	Burke, J.L.	VG+		$30.00 A
POCKET BOOKS	45010	The Long Goodbye	1964	Chandler, R.	VGF		$7.00
POCKET BOOKS	48766	Six Science Fiction Plays	1976	Elwood, R.	VG+		$14.00
POCKET BOOKS	48766	Six Science Fiction Plays	1976	Elwood, R.	VG		$10.00
POCKET BOOKS	50019	Ax	1965	McBain, E.*	VGF		$7.00
POCKET BOOKS	50060	Nightcrawlers	1964	Addams, C.	AF		$7.00
POCKET BOOKS	50060	Nightcrawlers	1964	Addams, C.	VG+		$7.00
POCKET BOOKS	50061	Monster Rally	1965	Addams, C.	VG+		$5.00
POCKET BOOKS	50062	Homebodies	1965	Addams, C.	AF		$11.00 A
POCKET BOOKS	50063	Addams And Evil	1965	Addams, C.	VGF		$6.00
POCKET BOOKS	50063	Addams And Evil	1965	Addams, C.	VG		$5.00
POCKET BOOKS	50086	The Simple Art Of Murder (3rd)	1964	Chandler, R.	VG		$6.00
POCKET BOOKS	50118	The High Window	1965	Chandler, R.	VG		$6.00
POCKET BOOKS	50127	Trouble Is My Business	1965	Chandler, R.	VGF		$7.00
POCKET BOOKS	50149	The Jugger	1965	Stark, R.*	AF		$20.00 A
POCKET BOOKS	50149	The Jugger	1965	Stark, R.*	VG-		$5.00
POCKET BOOKS	50176	Pick-Up On Noon Street	1965	Chandler, R.	VG		$4.00
POCKET BOOKS	50177	Dead Man's Walk	1965	Prather, R.S.	VG		$5.00
POCKET BOOKS	50189	Mag. Men In Their Flying Machines	1965	Burke, J.	F	MTI	$7.00
POCKET BOOKS	50218	Harper	1966	MacDonald, R.*	VGF	MTI	$7.00
POCKET BOOKS	50230	The Lady In The Lake	1966	Chandler, R.	VG		$5.00
POCKET BOOKS	50243	Our Man Flint	1965	Pearl, J.	AF	MTI	$7.00
POCKET BOOKS	50292	The Meandering Corpse	1966	Prather, R.S.	AF		$6.00
POCKET BOOKS	50516	The Caper Of The Golden Bulls	1967	McGivern, W.P.	VG+	MTI	$6.00
POCKET BOOKS	50541	The Big Sleep	1967	Chandler, R.	VGF		$5.00
POCKET BOOKS	50548	The Long Ride Home	1967	Wolford, N.	VG+	MTI	$7.00
POCKET BOOKS	50560	The Hardboiled Dicks	1967	Anthology	VG+		$12.00
POCKET BOOKS	50560	The Hardboiled Dicks	1967	Anthology	VG		$10.00
POCKET BOOKS	50560	The Hardboiled Dicks	1967	Anthology	VGF		$9.00 A
POCKET BOOKS	50564	The Happiest Millionaire	1967	Biddle, C.D.	VG	MTI	$6.00
POCKET BOOKS	53136	Superluminal	1984	McIntyre, V.N.	AF		$11.00 A
POCKET BOOKS	55098	The Mahareeshi Says	1969	Boliska, A.	VGF		$6.00
POCKET BOOKS	62581	Enterprise: The 1st Adventure	1986	McIntyre, V.N.	VGF		$5.00
POCKET BOOKS	75020	The Well Of Loneliness	1966	Hall, R.	VGF		$6.00
POCKET BOOKS	75079	Buddwing	1965	Hunter, E.	AF		$7.00
POCKET BOOKS	75114	Nebula Award Stories 2	1968	Anthology	AF		$4.00
POCKET BOOKS	75138	Killer In The Rain	1965	Chandler, R.	VG+		$10.00
POCKET BOOKS	75138	Killer In The Rain	1965	Chandler, R.	VG		$6.00
POCKET BOOKS	75138	Killer In The Rain	1965	Chandler, R.	G+		$3.00

Pocket Books Jr. 48 AF $6

Pony 56 VGF $8

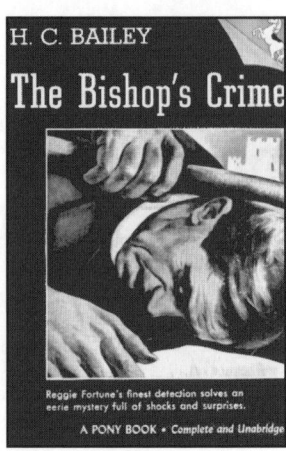

Pony 60 VG $7

PUBLISHER	PUB. #	TITLE	DATE	AUTHOR	COND.	TYPE	PRICE
POCKET BOOKS	75242	Go Down Dead	1968	Stevens, S.	VG		$6.00
POCKET BOOKS	75434	Marlowe	1969	Chandler, R.	VG+	MTI	$8.00
POCKET BOOKS	77024	Close Combat	1969	Ehrlich, J.	VGF		$5.00
POCKET BOOKS	77029	Bob Dylan	1968	Kramer, D.	VGF		$7.00
POCKET BOOKS	77232	M*A*S*H (5th)	1970	Hooker, R.	AF	MTI	$6.00
POCKET BOOKS	77337	The Scene	1971	Jahn, M.	VGF		$6.00
POCKET BOOKS	77428	Scorpion Reef	1972	Williams, C.	VG		$5.00
POCKET BOOKS	77504	I Gave At The Office	1972	Westlake, D.E.	VGF		$7.00
POCKET BOOKS	77506	The Big Bite	1973	Williams, C.	VGF		$7.00
POCKET BOOKS	77538	The Triumph Of Evil	1972	Kavanagh, P.*	VG+		$8.00
POCKET BOOKS	77728	Death Is A Ruby Light (Baroness #3)	1974	Kenyon, P.	AF		$8.00
POCKET BOOKS	77750	That Man Bolt!	1974	Crowcraft, P.	AF	MTI	$4.00
POCKET BOOKS	77762	Operation Doomsday (Baroness #5)	1974	Kenyon, P.	VGF		$8.00
POCKET BOOKS	77918	Hard-Core Murder (Baroness #4)	1974	Kenyon, P.	AF		$8.00
POCKET BOOKS	77938	Go Down Dead	1974	Stevens, S.	AF		$10.00
POCKET BOOKS	77938	Go Down Dead	1974	Stevens, S.	VG+		$8.00
POCKET BOOKS	77949	Sonic Slave (Baroness #6)	1974	Kenyon, P.	AF		$8.00
POCKET BOOKS	77961	Flicker Of Doom (Baroness #7)	1974	Kenyon, P.	VGF		$8.00
POCKET BOOKS	77961	Flicker Of Doom (Baroness #7)	1974	Kenyon, P.	VG+		$5.00
POCKET BOOKS	77962	Black Gold (The Baroness #8)	1975	Kenyon, P.	VGF		$8.00
POCKET BOOKS	77962	Black Gold (The Baroness #8)	1975	Kenyon, P.	AF		$7.00
POCKET BOOKS	78032	Revolution For Hell Of It	1970	Hoffman, A.	VG		$5.00
POCKET BOOKS	78343	The Night Stalker	1973	Rice, J.	VG+	TVTI	$7.00
POCKET BOOKS	78343	The Night Stalker	1973	Rice, J.	VG	TVTI	$5.00
POCKET BOOKS	78352	The Night Strangler	1974	Rice, J.	VGF	TVTI	$8.00
POCKET BOOKS	78391	Dead City	1974	Stevens, S.	VG		$5.00
POCKET BOOKS	78484	Rat Pack	1975	Stevens, S.	VGF		$8.00
POCKET BOOKS	78484	Rat Pack	1975	Stevens, S.	VG		$5.00
POCKET BOOKS	78887	No Direction Home	1975	Spinrad, N.	AF		$7.00
POCKET BOOKS	80241	S.W.A.T. #1 - Crossfire!	1975	Lynds, D.	AF	TVTI	$6.00
POCKET BOOKS	80542	Cross Of Frankenstein	1976	Myers, R.J.	AF		$7.00
POCKET BOOKS	80619	Felony Tank	1976	Braly, M.	VGF		$7.00
POCKET BOOKS	80741	Shake Him Till He Rattles	1976	Braly, M.	AF-		$6.00
POCKET BOOKS	80796	The Creation Of King Kong	1976	Bahrenburg, B.	VGF	MTI	$6.00
POCKET BOOKS	80915	The Key To Midnight	1979	Nichols, L.*	VG+		$14.00
POCKET BOOKS	80933	Sinbad & Eye Of The Tiger	1977	Hall, J.	VGF	MTI	$6.00
POCKET BOOKS	81446	The Incredible Hulk	1978	Lee, S.	VGF		$6.00
POCKET BOOKS	81447	Doctor Strange	1978	Lee, S.	VG+		$5.00
POCKET BOOKS	82044	Mayhem In Manhatten	1978	Wein, L.	AF		$7.00
POCKET BOOKS	82088	Marvel Novels #7 - Dr. Strange	1979	Rotsler	VGF		$6.00
POCKET BOOKS	82579	The Amazing Spider Man #3	1979	Lee, S.	VGF		$6.00
POCKET BOOKS	82784	The Eyes Of Darkness	1981	Nichols, L.*	VGF		$10.00
POCKET BOOKS	82784	The Eyes Of Darkness	1981	Nichols, L.*	VG+		$10.00
POCKET BOOKS	83026	Spider-Woman	1979	Lee, S.	VGF		$6.00
POCKET BOOKS JR.	J 36	Long Lash	1949	Shurtleff, B.	VGF+		$6.00

Popular Library 3 VG+ $22	Popular Library 6 VG+ $15	Popular Library 8 VG $17

PUBLISHER	PUB. #	TITLE	DATE	AUTHOR	COND.	TYPE	PRICE
POCKET BOOKS JR.	J 48	Buffalo Bill	1950	Garst, S.	AF		$6.00
POCKET BOOKS JR.	J 50	Tiger Roan	1950	Balch, G.	VG		$5.00
POCKET BOOKS JR.	J 51	The Kingdom Of Flying Men	1950	Litten, F.N.	VG+		$5.00
POCKET BOOKS JR.	J 52	Gridiron Challenge	1950	Scholz, J.	G		$3.00
POCKET BOOKS JR.	J 60	Buckskin Brigade	1950	Kjelgaard, J.	VGF		$6.00
POCKET BOOKS JR.	J 62	Yellowstone Scout	1951	Rush, W.M.	VG+		$6.00
POCKET BOOKS JR.	J 70	Shag (2nd)	1955	Hinkle, T.C.	VGF		$5.00
PONY	48	The Narrow Cell	1945	Clark, D.	VG		$7.00
PONY	50	The Wager	1946	Oursler, F.	VG		$6.00
PONY	56	Wanted: Someone Innocent	1946	Allingham, M.	VGF		$8.00
PONY	58	Salt River Ranny	1946	Nye, N.	VGF		$7.00
PONY	59	One Small Candle	1946	Roberts, C.	VG-		$5.00
PONY	60	The Bishop's Crime	1946	Bailey, H.C.	VG		$7.00
PONY	62	The Inconvenient Corpse	1946	Fenwick, E.P.	VG+		$7.00
PONY	63	Death And The Devil	1946	Whelton, P.	VG		$9.00
PONY	64	Mr. Fortune Wonders	1946	Bailey, H.C.	VG		$6.00
POPULAR LIBRARY	1	Saint Overboard	1943	Charteris, L.	VG		$14.00 A
POPULAR LIBRARY	2	Danger In The Dark	1943	Eberhart, M.G.	VG		$16.00
POPULAR LIBRARY	3	Crime Of Violence	1943	King, R.	VG+		$22.00 A
POPULAR LIBRARY	4	Murder In The Madhouse	1943	Latimer, J.	VG-		$8.00
POPULAR LIBRARY	5	Miss Pinkerton	1943	Rinehart, M.R.	G		$8.00
POPULAR LIBRARY	6	Three Bright Pebbles	1943	Ford, L.	VG+		$15.00 A
POPULAR LIBRARY	7	Death Demands An Audience	1943	Reilly, H.	VG		$12.00
POPULAR LIBRARY	8	Death For Dear Clara	1943	Patrick, Q.	VG		$17.00 A
POPULAR LIBRARY	8	Death For Dear Clara	1943	Patrick, Q.	VG		$14.00
POPULAR LIBRARY	9	The Eel Pie Murders	1943	Frome, D.	VG		$12.00
POPULAR LIBRARY	10	To Wake The Dead	1943	Carr, J.D.	VG+		$15.00
POPULAR LIBRARY	12	Death Sits On The Board	1943	Rhode, J.	VG+		$15.00
POPULAR LIBRARY	12	Death Sits On The Board	1943	Rhode, J.	VG-		$6.00
POPULAR LIBRARY	13	Valcour Meets Murder	1943	King, R.	VG		$20.00
POPULAR LIBRARY	15	The Third Eye	1943	White, E.L.	VGF		$20.00
POPULAR LIBRARY	16	The Dead Don't Care	1943	Latimer, J.	G+		$10.00
POPULAR LIBRARY	17	The House On The Roof	1943	Eberhart, M.G.	VG+		$12.00
POPULAR LIBRARY	17	The House On The Roof	1943	Eberhart, M.G.	VG		$12.00
POPULAR LIBRARY	18	Tragedy In The Hollow	1943	Croft, F.W.	VG+		$18.00
POPULAR LIBRARY	19	The Crooked Hinge	1943	Carr, J.D.	VG+		$15.00 A
POPULAR LIBRARY	22	Murder Masks Miami	1944	King, R.	VG		$14.00
POPULAR LIBRARY	23	S.S. Murder	1944	Patrick, Q.	VG+		$16.00
POPULAR LIBRARY	24	Reno Rendezvous	1944	Ford, L.	VG		$8.00
POPULAR LIBRARY	25	Out Of Order	1944	Taylor, P.A.	VGF		$16.00
POPULAR LIBRARY	26	Mr. Pinkerton Has The Clue	1944	Frome, D.	G-		$2.00
POPULAR LIBRARY	27	From This Dark Stairway	1944	Eberhart, M.G.	VG		$14.00
POPULAR LIBRARY	33	McKee Of Centre Street	1944	Reilly, H.	VG		$10.00 A
POPULAR LIBRARY	34	Mr. Pinkerton At Old Angel	1944	Frome, D.	VG		$6.00
POPULAR LIBRARY	55	Murder In The Willett Family	1945	King, R.	VG		$8.00

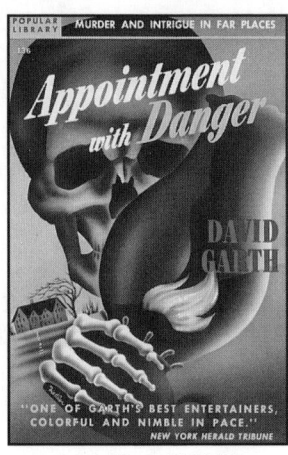

Popular Library 84 AF $25	Popular Library 129 VGF $39	Popular Library 136 AF $28

PUBLISHER	PUB. #	TITLE	DATE	AUTHOR	COND.	TYPE	PRICE
POPULAR LIBRARY	56	Dead For A Ducat	1945	Reilly, H.	VG+		$18.00 A
POPULAR LIBRARY	57	The Twelve Disguises	1945	Beeding, F.	AF-		$17.00
POPULAR LIBRARY	57	The Twelve Disguises	1945	Beeding, F.	G		$3.00
POPULAR LIBRARY	63	Sing A Song Of Homicide	1945	Langham, J.R.	VGF		$15.00 A
POPULAR LIBRARY	64	They Can't Hang Me	1945	Ronald, J.	VGF		$15.00
POPULAR LIBRARY	66	The Blind Side	1945	Wentworth, P.	VG		$8.00
POPULAR LIBRARY	69	The Listening House	1945	Seeley, M.	VG+		$8.00
POPULAR LIBRARY	69	The Listening House	1945	Seeley, M.	VG		$8.00
POPULAR LIBRARY	71	Hell Let Loose	1945	Beeding, F.	VG-		$5.00
POPULAR LIBRARY	75	She Faded Into Air	1946	White, E.L.	VG		$7.00
POPULAR LIBRARY	76	Fog	1946	Williams, V.	VG+		$8.00
POPULAR LIBRARY	78	Timbal Gulch	1946	Brand, M.	VG		$7.00
POPULAR LIBRARY	79	Rolling Stone	1946	Wentworth, P.	VG-		$6.00
POPULAR LIBRARY	80	The Golden Box	1946	Crane, F.	AF		$18.00
POPULAR LIBRARY	80	The Golden Box	1946	Crane, F.	VG		$8.00
POPULAR LIBRARY	81	Three Thirds Of A Ghost	1946	Fuller, T.	VG+		$20.00 A
POPULAR LIBRARY	82	The 24th Horse	1946	Pentecost, H.	AF		$10.00 A
POPULAR LIBRARY	82	The 24th Horse	1946	Pentecost, H.	VG+		$10.00
POPULAR LIBRARY	84	Challenge For Three	1946	Garth, D.	AF		$25.00 A
POPULAR LIBRARY	88	Romance In The First Degree	1946	Cohen, O.R.	VGF		$12.00
POPULAR LIBRARY	91	The Sea Hawk	1946	Sabatini, R.	VGF+		$12.00
POPULAR LIBRARY	94	The Mortal Storm	1946	Bottome, P.	VGF		$7.00
POPULAR LIBRARY	97	A Variety Of Weapons	1946	King, R.	VG+		$10.00
POPULAR LIBRARY	99	Dead Of The Night	1947	Rhode, J.	AF		$14.00
POPULAR LIBRARY	99	Dead Of The Night	1947	Rhode, J.	VG+		$8.00
POPULAR LIBRARY	99	Dead Of The Night	1947	Rhode, J.	VG		$7.00
POPULAR LIBRARY	103	The Phantom Canoe	1947	Mowery, W.B.	VGF		$10.00
POPULAR LIBRARY	103	The Phantom Canoe	1947	Mowery, W.B.	VG		$8.00
POPULAR LIBRARY	103	The Phantom Canoe	1947	Mowery, W.B.	VG		$7.00
POPULAR LIBRARY	106	Corpse With The Eerie Eye	1947	Walling, R.A.J.	VG		$7.00
POPULAR LIBRARY	108	The Yellow Violet	1947	Crane, F.	VGF		$20.00 A
POPULAR LIBRARY	110	Congo Song	1947	Cloete, S.	VG+		$10.00
POPULAR LIBRARY	116	The Red House	1947	Chamberlain, G.A.	VG	MTI	$5.00
POPULAR LIBRARY	118	The Flying U's Last Stand	1947	Bower, B.M.	VGF+		$10.00
POPULAR LIBRARY	119	Firebrand	1947	Gill, T.	VG+		$7.00
POPULAR LIBRARY	121	A Losing Game	1947	Crofts, F.W.	VG+		$8.00
POPULAR LIBRARY	123	A Question Of Proof	1947	Blake, N.	VG+		$8.00
POPULAR LIBRARY	128	The Voice Of The Pack	1947	Marshall, E.	VG+		$8.00
POPULAR LIBRARY	129	I Wake Up Screaming	1948	Fisher, S.	VGF		$39.00 A
POPULAR LIBRARY	132	Seven Keys To Baldpate	1948	Biggers, E.D.	VG+	MTI	$7.00
POPULAR LIBRARY	132	Seven Keys To Baldpate	1948	Biggers, E.D.	VG	MTI	$7.00
POPULAR LIBRARY	133	Advance Agent	1948	August, J.	VGF+		$8.00
POPULAR LIBRARY	134	Fighting Blood	1948	Young, G.	VGF		$11.00 A
POPULAR LIBRARY	136	Appointment With Danger	1948	Garth, D.	AF		$28.00 A
POPULAR LIBRARY	136	Appointment With Danger	1948	Garth, D.	VG		$5.00

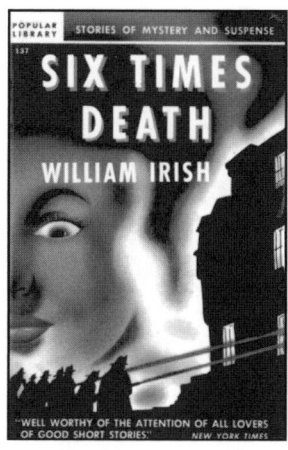

Popular Library 137 VG+ $30

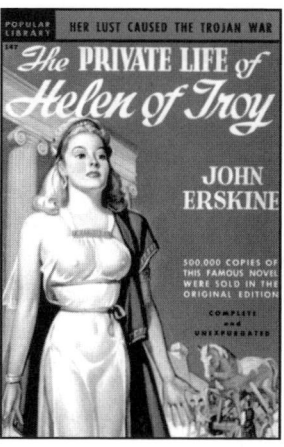

Popular Library 147 AF $91

Popular Library 155 VGF $38

PUBLISHER	PUB. #	TITLE	DATE	AUTHOR	COND.	TYPE	PRICE
POPULAR LIBRARY	137	Six Times Death	1948	Irish, W.*	VG+		$30.00
POPULAR LIBRARY	137	Six Times Death	1948	Irish, W.*	G		$8.00
POPULAR LIBRARY	144	Danger In Paradiise	1949	Cohen, O.R.	VG+		$17.00 A
POPULAR LIBRARY	147	The Private Life Of Helen Of Troy	1948	Erskine, J.	AF		$91.00 A
POPULAR LIBRARY	147	The Private Life Of Helen Of Troy	1948	Erskine, J.	VGF		$40.00 A
POPULAR LIBRARY	147	The Private Life Of Helen Of Troy	1948	Erskine, J.	VG-		$8.00
POPULAR LIBRARY	147	Private Life Of Helen Of Troy (2nd)	1948	Erskine, J.	VGF		$20.00 A
POPULAR LIBRARY	147	Private Life Of Helen Of Troy (2nd)	1948	Erskine, J.	VG		$15.00
POPULAR LIBRARY	147	Private Life Of Helen Of Troy (2nd)	1948	Erskine, J.	VG		$10.00
POPULAR LIBRARY	149	Hidden Blood	1948	Tuttle, W.C.	AF		$10.00
POPULAR LIBRARY	155	The Dreadful Night	1948	Williams, B.A.	VGF		$38.00 A
POPULAR LIBRARY	157	The Flying U Strikes	1948	Bower, B.M.	VG+		$7.00
POPULAR LIBRARY	158	The Strangled Witness	1948	Ford, L.	VGF-		$6.00
POPULAR LIBRARY	159	About The Murder Of Circus Queen	1948	Abbot, A.	VG-		$6.00
POPULAR LIBRARY	164	Lady In Peril	1948	Williams, B.A.	VG+		$9.00
POPULAR LIBRARY	164	Lady In Peril	1948	Williams, B.A.	VG+		$7.00
POPULAR LIBRARY	167	Pattern Of Murder	1948	Eberhart, M.G.	VG		$7.00
POPULAR LIBRARY	167	Pattern Of Murder	1948	Eberhart, M.G.	VG-		$5.00
POPULAR LIBRARY	168	Death And Taxes	1948	Dodge, D.	VG		$5.00
POPULAR LIBRARY	170	Omnibus Of American Humor	1949	Anthology	VG		$6.00
POPULAR LIBRARY	172	Pistol Pardners	1949	Raine, W.M.	VG+		$7.00
POPULAR LIBRARY	173	Death Is A Lovely Lady	1949	Fenisong, R.	VG-		$7.00
POPULAR LIBRARY	173	Death Is A Lovely Lady	1949	Fenisong, R.	G		$3.00
POPULAR LIBRARY	177	Some Day I'll Kill You	1949	Chambers, D.	VG+		$18.00 A
POPULAR LIBRARY	183	Gentle Annie	1949	Kantor, M.	VG+	MTI	$8.00
POPULAR LIBRARY	184	Marshall Of Sundown	1949	Gregory, J.	VG		$6.00
POPULAR LIBRARY	186	Cartoon Fun	1948	Anthology	G		$6.00
POPULAR LIBRARY	187	Selected Western Stories	1949	Anthology	VG+		$8.00
POPULAR LIBRARY	190	The Gay Bandit Of The Border	1949	Gill, T.	VG+		$7.00
POPULAR LIBRARY	192	Bodies Are Where You Find Them	1949	Halliday, B.	VG		$7.00
POPULAR LIBRARY	194	Death On Scurvy Street	1949	Williams, B.A.	VG+		$10.00
POPULAR LIBRARY	195	Ward 20	1949	Bellah, J.W.	VGF-		$20.00 A
POPULAR LIBRARY	195	Ward 20	1949	Bellah, J.W.	VG-		$4.00
POPULAR LIBRARY	196	There's Always Time To Die	1949	Cohen, O.R.	VG		$8.00
POPULAR LIBRARY	197	Pursuit Of A Parcel	1949	Wentworth, P.	VG		$10.00
POPULAR LIBRARY	200	Bats In The Belfry	1949	Matson, N.	VGF		$10.00
POPULAR LIBRARY	202	Shear The Black Sheep	1949	Dodge, D.	G+		$7.00
POPULAR LIBRARY	204	Arizona Jim	1949	Seltzer, C.A.	VG		$7.00
POPULAR LIBRARY	207	Reunion With Murder	1949	Fuller, T.	VG+		$7.00
POPULAR LIBRARY	208	Deputy At Snow Mountain	1949	Marshall, E.	VG+		$5.00
POPULAR LIBRARY	211	The Doll's Trunk Murder	1949	Reilly, H.	G		$7.00
POPULAR LIBRARY	211	The Doll's Trunk Murder	1949	Reilly, H.	G-		$5.00
POPULAR LIBRARY	212	Awake To Darkness	1949	McMullen, R.	VG		$7.00
POPULAR LIBRARY	215	The Silver Forest	1949	Williams, B.A.	VG+		$9.00
POPULAR LIBRARY	216	Cup Of Gold	1950	Steinbeck, J.	VGF		$20.00 A

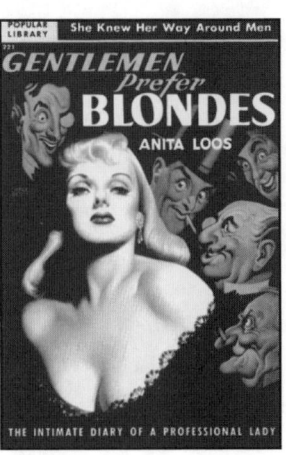

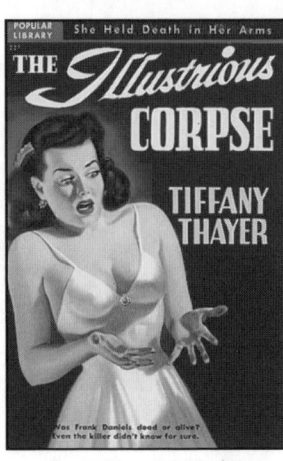

Popular Library 216 VGF $20   Popular Library 221 VGF $32   Popular Library 227 VG+ $39

PUBLISHER	PUB. #	TITLE	DATE	AUTHOR	COND.	TYPE	PRICE
POPULAR LIBRARY	216	Cup Of Gold	1950	Steinbeck, J.	VG+		$12.00
POPULAR LIBRARY	216	Cup Of Gold	1950	Steinbeck, J.	VG+		$8.00
POPULAR LIBRARY	217	Tales Of Chinatown	1950	Rohmer, S.	VG+		$27.00
POPULAR LIBRARY	218	The Pink Umbrella Murder	1950	Crane, F.	VGF		$16.00 A
POPULAR LIBRARY	218	The Pink Umbrella Murder	1950	Crane, F.	VG+		$15.00
POPULAR LIBRARY	219	Duke (8th)	1952	Ellson, H.	VGF		$7.00
POPULAR LIBRARY	220	The Damon Runyon Story	1950	Weiner, E.	VGF		$13.00 A
POPULAR LIBRARY	221	Gentlemen Prefer Blondes	1950	Loos, A.	VGF		$32.00 A
POPULAR LIBRARY	227	The Illustrious Corpse	1950	Thayer, T.	VG+		$39.00 A
POPULAR LIBRARY	228	The Sex Machine	1950	Mead, S.	VG+		$12.00
POPULAR LIBRARY	230	Focus	1950	Miller, A.	VG+		$10.00
POPULAR LIBRARY	230	Focus	1950	Miller, A.	VG		$8.00
POPULAR LIBRARY	233	Macamba	1950	Saher, L.V.	VGF+		$14.00
POPULAR LIBRARY	236	Pikes Peek Or Bust	1950	Wilson, E.	VG+		$7.00
POPULAR LIBRARY	237	Drums Of Destiny	1950	Bourne, P.	VGF		$27.00 A
POPULAR LIBRARY	237	Drums Of Destiny	1950	Bourne, P.	VG+		$10.00
POPULAR LIBRARY	238	She'll Be Dead By Morning	1950	Chambers, D.	VG		$7.00
POPULAR LIBRARY	243	Texas Breed	1950	Raine, W.M.	VG		$5.00
POPULAR LIBRARY	246	Murder By Latitude	1950	King, R.	VG+		$8.00
POPULAR LIBRARY	248	The Great Ones	1950	Ingersoll, R.	VG		$6.00
POPULAR LIBRARY	249	Twisted Trails	1950	Tuttle, W.C.	VG		$7.00
POPULAR LIBRARY	252	Bullets For The Bridegroom	1950	Dodge, D.	VG+		$15.00
POPULAR LIBRARY	254	The Pale Blonde Of Sands St.	1950	White, W.C.	VGF		$12.00 A
POPULAR LIBRARY	257	Whistle Stop	1950	Wolff, M.M.	VGF		$12.00 A
POPULAR LIBRARY	259	Murder In The Mews	1950	Reilly, H.	VG-		$7.00
POPULAR LIBRARY	260	The Edge Of Doom	1950	Brady, L.	VGF	MTI	$8.00
POPULAR LIBRARY	260	The Edge Of Doom	1950	Brady, L.	VG	MTI	$6.00
POPULAR LIBRARY	263	Murder At Cambridge	1950	Patrick, Q.	AF		$24.00 A
POPULAR LIBRARY	263	Murder At Cambridge	1950	Patrick, Q.	VG		$6.00
POPULAR LIBRARY	266	The Captain's Lady	1950	Heatter, B.	VGF		$8.00
POPULAR LIBRARY	271	Riders West	1950	Haycox, E.	VG+		$5.00
POPULAR LIBRARY	272	Trail's End	1950	Marshall, E.	VGF+		$11.00 A
POPULAR LIBRARY	273	The Big Eye	1950	Ehrlich, M.	VGF		$20.00
POPULAR LIBRARY	273	The Big Eye	1950	Ehrlich, M.	VGF		$18.00 A
POPULAR LIBRARY	273	The Big Eye	1950	Ehrlich, M.	G+		$7.00
POPULAR LIBRARY	274	They Move With The Sun	1950	Taylor, D.	VGF		$15.00 A
POPULAR LIBRARY	277	The Sure Thing	1950	Miller, M.	VGF+		$14.00
POPULAR LIBRARY	277	The Sure Thing	1950	Miller, M.	VG+		$8.00
POPULAR LIBRARY	278	The Hero	1950	Lampell, M.	VGF+		$12.00
POPULAR LIBRARY	278	The Hero	1950	Lampell, M.	VGF		$12.00
POPULAR LIBRARY	279	Shortgrass	1950	Evarts, H.G.	VGF		$16.00 A
POPULAR LIBRAR	283	Silence In Court	1950	Wentworth, P.	VGF		$17.00 A
POPULAR LIBRARY	284	Laura	1950	Caspary, V.	VG+		$8.00
POPULAR LIBRARY	285	The Curtain Never Falls	1950	Adams, J.	VGF		$12.00
POPULAR LIBRARY	286	Murder Of Clergyman's Mistress	1950	Abbot, A.	VG		$8.00

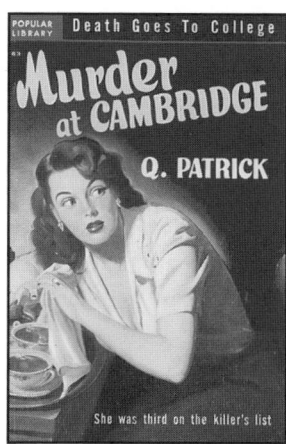

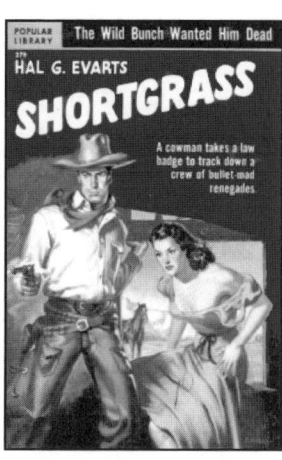

| Popular Library 263 AF $24 | Popular Library 272 VGF+ $11 | Popular Library 279 VGF $16 |

PUBLISHER	PUB. #	TITLE	DATE	AUTHOR	COND.	TYPE	PRICE
POPULAR LIBRARY	288	The Leather Pushers	1950	Witwer, H.C.	VGF-		$22.00 A
POPULAR LIBRARY	288	The Leather Pushers	1950	Witwer, H.C.	VGF		$14.00
POPULAR LIBRARY	291	The Wrath And The Wind	1950	Key, A.	VGF+		$10.00
POPULAR LIBRARY	293	The Hangman's Whip	1950	Eberhart, M.G.	VG		$15.00
POPULAR LIBRARY	294	The Two Worlds Of Johnny Truro	1950	Sklar, G.	VGF		$8.00
POPULAR LIBRARY	294	The Two Worlds Of Johnny Truro	1950	Sklar, G.	VG		$6.00
POPULAR LIBRARY	295	The Wolf That Fed Us	1950	Lowry, R.	AF		$12.00
POPULAR LIBRARY	295	The Wolf That Fed Us	1950	Lowry, R.	VGF		$8.00 A
POPULAR LIBRARY	296	The Dead Tree Gives No Shelter	1950	Scott, V.	VGF		$15.00 A
POPULAR LIBRARY	299	A Woman Of Samaria	1950	Ingles, J.W.	VG+		$7.00
POPULAR LIBRARY	299	A Woman Of Samaria	1950	Ingles, J.W.	VG-		$7.00
POPULAR LIBRARY	301	The Fifth Grave	1950	Latimer, J.	VGF		$20.00 A
POPULAR LIBRARY	301	The Fifth Grave	1950	Latimer, J.	G		$6.00
POPULAR LIBRARY	302	The Old Battle Ax	1950	Holding, E.S.	VGF		$27.00 A
POPULAR LIBRARY	302	The Old Battle Ax	1950	Holding, E.S.	VG		$8.00
POPULAR LIBRARY	306	The Haunted Hills	1951	Bower, B.M.	VG		$6.00
POPULAR LIBRARY	307	Her Life To Live	1951	Atkinson, O.	VG+		$18.00 A
POPULAR LIBRARY	310	Here Lies The Body	1951	Burke, R.	VG+		$9.00
POPULAR LIBRARY	311	Smoke Up The Valley	1951	Barrett, M.	AF		$13.00 A
POPULAR LIBRARY	312	Mamie Brandon	1951	Sheridan, J.	VGF		$15.00
POPULAR LIBRARY	314	Edge Of Beyond	1951	Hendryx, J.B.	VG+		$8.00
POPULAR LIBRARY	315	Check Your Wits	1951	Leopold, J.	VGF		$10.00 A
POPULAR LIBRARY	316	Tuesday To Bed	1951	Wickware, F.S.	VG+		$5.00 A
POPULAR LIBRARY	317	The Night Before Murder	1951	Fisher, S.	VG+		$29.00 A
POPULAR LIBRARY	318	The Deadly Dove	1951	King, R.	VGF		$37.00 A
POPULAR LIBRARY	318	The Deadly Dove	1951	King, R.	VGF		$22.00 A
POPULAR LIBRARY	319	My Forbidden Past	1951	Banks, P.	AF	MTI	$14.00
POPULAR LIBRARY	319	My Forbidden Past	1951	Banks, P.	G	MTI	$6.00
POPULAR LIBRARY	324	My Old Man's Badge	1951	Findley, F.	VG+		$13.00
POPULAR LIBRARY	324	My Old Man's Badge	1951	Findley, F.	VG+		$12.00 A
POPULAR LIBRARY	325	Murder By The Dozen	1951	Wiley, H.	VG		$8.00
POPULAR LIBRARY	325	Murder By The Dozen	1951	Wiley, H.	VG-		$8.00
POPULAR LIBRARY	326	Behind The Flying Saucers	1951	Scully, F.	VG+		$15.00
POPULAR LIBRARY	326	Behind The Flying Saucers	1951	Scully, F.	VGF		$14.00
POPULAR LIBRARY	327	Stranger And Alone	1951	Redding, J.S.	VG+		$8.00
POPULAR LIBRARY	327	Stranger And Alone	1951	Redding, J.S.	VG		$8.00
POPULAR LIBRARY	332	Don't Ever Love Me	1951	Cohen, O.R.	G+		$7.00
POPULAR LIBRARY	333	Lonesome Road	1951	Wentworth, P.	VGF		$27.00 A
POPULAR LIBRARY	335	Shadow Of A Hero	1951	Chase, A.	VG		$8.00
POPULAR LIBRARY	337	Ace In The Hole	1951	Gregory, J.	VG-		$8.00
POPULAR LIBRARY	340	Smart Guy	1951	MacHarg, W.	VGF		$10.00
POPULAR LIBRARY	340	Smart Guy	1951	MacHarg, W.	VG+		$10.00
POPULAR LIBRARY	343	While Murder Waits	1951	Esteven, J.	VGF+		$45.00 A
POPULAR LIBRARY	343	While Murder Waits	1951	Esteven, J.	VG+		$11.00 A
POPULAR LIBRARY	344	The Applegreen Cat	1951	Crane, F.	VG		$8.00

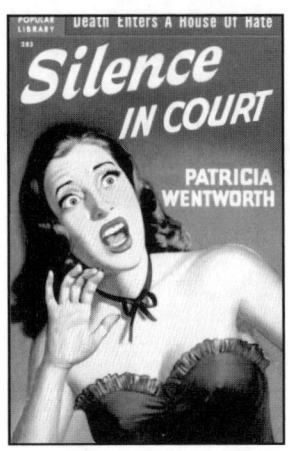

Popular Library 283 VGF $17   Popular Library 302 VGF $27   Popular Library 317 VG+ $29

PUBLISHER	PUB. #	TITLE	DATE	AUTHOR	COND.	TYPE	PRICE
POPULAR LIBRARY	347	Hoodlum	1951	Robertson, C.	VGF		$15.00
POPULAR LIBRARY	348	Adios O'Shaughnessy	1951	Tallman, R.	VG+		$7.00
POPULAR LIBRARY	351	Tonight Is Forever	1951	Mergendahl, C.	VG+		$10.00
POPULAR LIBRARY	355	I'll Be Right Home, Ma	1951	Denker, H.	VGF		$12.00
POPULAR LIBRARY	356	This Woman Is Mine	1951	Wolfson, P.J.	VGF		$9.00
POPULAR LIBRARY	356	This Woman Is Mine	1951	Wolfson, P.J.	VG		$7.00
POPULAR LIBRARY	357	How I Became A Girl Reporter	1951	Goldberg, H.	VGF-		$8.00
POPULAR LIBRARY	357	How I Became A Girl Reporter	1951	Goldberg, H.	VG+		$8.00
POPULAR LIBRARY	359	Beyond The Rio Grande	1951	Raine, W.M.	VGF		$6.00
POPULAR LIBRARY	360	The Silver Desert	1951	Haycox, E.	VG-		$5.00
POPULAR LIBRARY	361	Winter Kill	1951	Fisher, S.	VG		$15.00
POPULAR LIBRARY	362	Never Walk Alone	1951	King, R.	VGF		$18.00 A
POPULAR LIBRARY	362	Never Walk Alone	1951	King, R.	VG+		$17.00 A
POPULAR LIBRARY	362	Never Walk Alone	1951	King, R.	VG		$7.00
POPULAR LIBRARY	364	The Ringing Of The Glass	1951	Schoyer, P.	VG+		$8.00 A
POPULAR LIBRARY	365	Copperbelt	1951	Sligh, N.	VG		$6.00
POPULAR LIBRARY	366	Please Send Me Absolutely Free	1951	Leokum, A.	VG+		$8.00
POPULAR LIBRARY	368	Apache Crossing	1951	Ermine, W.	VGF		$8.00
POPULAR LIBRARY	368	Apache Crossing	1951	Ermine, W.	VG+		$6.00
POPULAR LIBRARY	371	The Strumpet Sea	1951	Williams, B.A.	VG		$7.00
POPULAR LIBRARY	374	Dark Drums	1951	Brown, W.	VGF		$8.00
POPULAR LIBRARY	374	Dark Drums	1951	Brown, W.	VG+		$8.00
POPULAR LIBRARY	375	Texas Sheriff	1951	Cunningham, E.	VG+		$16.00 A
POPULAR LIBRARY	377	Shadow Of Madness	1951	Pentecost, H.	VGF		$10.00
POPULAR LIBRARY	379	No Narrow Path	1951	Whitcomb, C.	VGF		$8.00
POPULAR LIBRARY	381	Heads Off At Midnight	1951	Beeding, F.	VG+		$12.00
POPULAR LIBRARY	384	Range Boss	1951	Young, G.	VG		$7.00
POPULAR LIBRARY	388	Hang My Wreath	1951	Weaver, W.	VGF		$7.00
POPULAR LIBRARY	389	This Way Out	1951	Ronald, J.	VG		$6.00
POPULAR LIBRARY	391	Mooney	1951	Meloney, W.B.	VGF		$8.00
POPULAR LIBRARY	393	The Bed She Made	1952	Waller, L.	VGF		$8.00
POPULAR LIBRARY	399	Whirlpool	1952	Henderson, J.L.	AF		$8.00
POPULAR LIBRARY	404	Divorce	1952	Bellah, J.W.	VGF		$12.00 A
POPULAR LIBRARY	407	Bonanza Gulch	1952	Stuart, M.	VGF+		$7.00
POPULAR LIBRARY	408	Waterfront	1952	Findley, F.	VG+		$5.00
POPULAR LIBRARY	409	One By One	1952	Nichols, F.	VGF		$10.00
POPULAR LIBRARY	409	One By One	1952	Nichols, F.	VG+		$7.00
POPULAR LIBRARY	412	The Spell	1952	Breuer, G.	VG+		$7.00
POPULAR LIBRARY	413	A Woman Of Forty	1952	Hall, D.	VGF		$9.00
POPULAR LIBRARY	413	A Woman Of Forty	1952	Hall, D.	VGF		$8.00
POPULAR LIBRARY	418	The Impudent Rifle	1952	Pearce, D.	VG+		$7.00
POPULAR LIBRARY	419	Lower Than Angels	1952	Karig, W.	VGF		$7.00
POPULAR LIBRARY	423	Johnny Bogan	1952	Baccante, L.	VG+		$7.00
POPULAR LIBRARY	428	The Train From Pittsburgh	1952	Farren, J.	VG+		$7.00
POPULAR LIBRARY	433	Bitter Fruit	1952	Packer, P.	VG+		$7.00

Popular Library 324 VG+ $13	Popular Library 343 VGF+ $45	Popular Library 404 VGF $12

PUBLISHER	PUB. #	TITLE	DATE	AUTHOR	COND.	TYPE	PRICE
POPULAR LIBRARY	434	So Deadly Fair	1952	Walker, G.	VG+		$5.00
POPULAR LIBRARY	435	The Lost Ones	1952	Javellana, S.	VGF		$8.00
POPULAR LIBRARY	438	At Sundown The Tiger	1952	Mannin, E.	VGF		$8.00
POPULAR LIBRARY	439	Rip Tide	1952	Wichelns, L.	VGF		$7.00
POPULAR LIBRARY	440	The Cruel Dawn	1952	Viazzi, A.	VGF		$7.00
POPULAR LIBRARY	443	Sweet And Deadly	1952	Chute, V.	VGF		$14.00
POPULAR LIBRARY	446	The Night And The Naked	1952	Merrick, G.	VGF		$8.00
POPULAR LIBRARY	447	Dragon's Island	1952	Williamson, J.	VGF		$14.00
POPULAR LIBRARY	451	Maharajah	1952	Cargoe, R.	VGF		$20.00 A
POPULAR LIBRARY	452	I'll Get Mine	1952	Scott, T.	AF		$43.00 A
POPULAR LIBRARY	473	Bluebeard's Seventh Wife	1952	Irish, W.*	VG+		$30.00
POPULAR LIBRARY	477	The Diary	1953	Ard, W.	VG		$8.00
POPULAR LIBRARY	485	Glitter	1953	Shiffrin, A.B.	VG+		$10.00
POPULAR LIBRARY	500	Time To Kill	1953	Spain, T.	VG+		$10.00
POPULAR LIBRARY	502	A Girl For Danny	1953	Ard, W.	G		$6.00
POPULAR LIBRARY	503	Rickey	1953	Calitri, C.	VGF-		$6.00
POPULAR LIBRARY	504	Joey Adams' Joke Book	1953	Adams, J.	VGF		$6.00
POPULAR LIBRARY	504	Joey Adams' Joke Book (2nd)	1953	Adams, J.	VG+		$4.00
POPULAR LIBRARY	526	You Can't Stop Me	1953	Ard, W.	G-		$3.00
POPULAR LIBRARY	528	Hooked	1953	Oursler, W.	VGF		$38.00 A
POPULAR LIBRARY	530	All The Way Down	1953	Chaber, M.E.	VG+		$5.00
POPULAR LIBRARY	535	Thunder In The Dust	1953	LeMay, A.	VG+		$7.00
POPULAR LIBRARY	536	Count Me In	1953	Nichols, F.	VG+		$10.00
POPULAR LIBRARY	549	Monkey On My Back	1954	Brown, W.	VG		$16.00
POPULAR LIBRARY	551	I Dive For Treasure	1954	Rieseberg, H.E.	VG+		$7.00
POPULAR LIBRARY	565	The Innocent At Large	1954	Langley, N.	VGF		$7.00
POPULAR LIBRARY	569	A Private Party	1954	Ard, W.	VGF		$12.00
POPULAR LIBRARY	569	A Private Party	1954	Ard, W.	VG+		$7.00
POPULAR LIBRARY	572	Country Girl	1954	McMullen, R.	VG		$6.00
POPULAR LIBRARY	578	Rainbow Road	1954	Steward, D.	VGF		$6.00
POPULAR LIBRARY	580	We Burn Like Candles	1954	Kavinoky, B.	VG+		$7.00
POPULAR LIBRARY	586	Devil Take Her	1954	Nichols, F.	VG+		$10.00
POPULAR LIBRARY	586	Devil Take Her	1954	Nichols, F.	VGF		$8.00
POPULAR LIBRARY	587	Dark Streets Of Paris	1954	Curtis, J.L.	VG+		$7.00
POPULAR LIBRARY	592	Teen-Age Gangs	1954	Kramer, D.	VGF		$15.00 A
POPULAR LIBRARY	598	The Innocent One	1954	Reach, J.	VG		$7.00
POPULAR LIBRARY	608	The Wrath And The Wind	1954	Key, A.	VG+		$7.00
POPULAR LIBRARY	618	Ten Roads To Hell	1954	Travers, R.	VGF		$13.00 A
POPULAR LIBRARY	639	Don't Come Crying To Me	1955	Ard, W.	VG+		$9.00
POPULAR LIBRARY	660	You Asked For It	1955	Fleming, I.	VG+		$65.00 A
POPULAR LIBRARY	660	You Asked For It	1955	Fleming, I.	VG+		$35.00 A
POPULAR LIBRARY	675	Cry Hard, Cry Fast	1955	MacDonald, J.D.	VGF		$66.00 A
POPULAR LIBRARY	675	Cry Hard, Cry Fast	1955	MacDonald, J.D.	VG+		$29.00 A
POPULAR LIBRARY	675	Cry Hard, Cry Fast	1955	MacDonald, J.D.	VG		$22.00
POPULAR LIBRARY	685	The Big Rumble	1955	Brown, W.	VG+		$22.00

Popular Library 675 VGF $66   Popular Library 737 VG+ $22   Popular Library 775 VGF $25   Popular Library 776 VGF $47

PUBLISHER	PUB. #	TITLE	DATE	AUTHOR	COND.	TYPE	PRICE
POPULAR LIBRARY	685	The Big Rumble	1955	Brown, W.	VG+		$20.00 A
POPULAR LIBRARY	685	The Big Rumble	1955	Brown, W.	VGF+		$18.00 A
POPULAR LIBRARY	690	The Long Watch	1955	Mirvish, R.F.	VGF		$5.00
POPULAR LIBRARY	697	Contrary Pleasure	1955	MacDonald, J.D.	G+		$5.00
POPULAR LIBRARY	697	Contrary Pleasure	1955	MacDonald, J.D.	G-		$5.00
POPULAR LIBRARY	706	Angel Face	1955	Nichols, F.	VG		$6.00
POPULAR LIBRARY	718	Carnival Girl	1956	Glendinning, R.	VG		$22.00 A
POPULAR LIBRARY	719	These Women	1956	D'Alessio, G.	VG		$6.00
POPULAR LIBRARY	723	Mr. Trouble	1956	Ard, W.	VG		$7.00
POPULAR LIBRARY	724	The Widow	1956	Simenon, G.	VGF		$7.00
POPULAR LIBRARY	725	I'll Fix You	1956	Ellson, H.	VGF		$16.00 A
POPULAR LIBRARY	725	I'll Fix You	1956	Ellson, H.	VG		$10.00
POPULAR LIBRARY	727	Revolt Of The Sinners	1956	Zatterin, U.	VGF		$6.00
POPULAR LIBRARY	737	You Live Once	1956	MacDonald, J.D.	VG+		$22.00 A
POPULAR LIBRARY	737	You Live Once	1956	MacDonald, J.D.	VG		$18.00
POPULAR LIBRARY	757	Duke	1956	Ellson, H.	VGF		$8.00
POPULAR LIBRARY	758	The Last Party	1956	Lowry, R.	AF		$12.00
POPULAR LIBRARY	775	Behold This Woman	1956	Goodis, D.	VGF		$25.00 A
POPULAR LIBRARY	776	This Is It	1956	Ellson, H.	VGF		$47.00 A
POPULAR LIBRARY	776	This Is It	1956	Ellson, H.	VG		$20.00
POPULAR LIBRARY	776	This Is It	1956	Ellson, H.	VG-		$13.00 A
POPULAR LIBRARY	780	Murder Makes Me Mad	1956	Findley, F.	VGF		$10.00 A
POPULAR LIBRARY	781	Take All You Can Get	1956	Fisher, S.	VGF		$30.00 A
POPULAR LIBRARY	782	The Hustlers	1956	Ross, S.	VG+		$10.00 A
POPULAR LIBRARY	782	The Hustlers	1956	Ross, S.	VG+		$9.00
POPULAR LIBRARY	787	The Dream Peddlers	1956	Miller, F.	VG		$24.00 A
POPULAR LIBRARY	830	The Empty Trap	1957	MacDonald, J.D.	VGF		$36.00 A
POPULAR LIBRARY	833	The Plundered Land	1958	Williams, C.	VGF		$6.00
POPULAR LIBRARY	1303	Bound Girl	1950	Webber, E.	VG		$7.00
POPULAR LIBRARY	1307	Her Life To Live	1951	Atkinson, O.	VG+		$9.00
POPULAR LIBRARY	1342	End Of Track	1952	Weaver, W.	VGF		$8.00
POPULAR LIBRARY	1375	Texas Sheriff	1952	Cunningham, E.	VGF		$7.00
POPULAR LIBRARY	1376	Trouble At Moon Dance	1952	Guthrie, A.B.	VGF		$7.00
POPULAR LIBRARY	1392	Jailbait (4th)	1952	Bernard, W.	VGF		$10.00
POPULAR LIBRARY	1392	Jailbait (4th)	1952	Bernard, W.	G		$6.00
POPULAR LIBRARY	1393	The Bed She Made	1952	Waller, L.	VG+		$7.00
POPULAR LIBRARY	1452	I'll Get Mine	1954	Scott, T.	AF		$20.00 A
POPULAR LIBRARY	1467	Shakedown	1948	Kerr, B.	AF		$12.00 A
POPULAR LIBRARY	1469	Hard To Get	1953	Gilbert, E.	VGF		$7.00
POPULAR LIBRARY	1562	I Take All	1954	Carson, R.	VG+		$5.00
POPULAR LIBRARY	1562	I Take All	1954	Carson, R.	VG-		$5.00
POPULAR LIBRARY	1592	Teen-Age Gangs	1955	Kramer & Karr	VG		$8.00
POPULAR LIBRARY	1606	The Departure	1955	Sherry, J.O.	VG		$5.00
POPULAR LIBRARY	1619	Naked To My Past	1955	Wakeman, F.	VG		$2.00
POPULAR LIBRARY	EB 4	Whispering Range	1953	Haycox, E.	VG		$7.00
POPULAR LIBRARY	EB 11	Macamba	1954	Van Saher, L.	AF-		$12.00 A
POPULAR LIBRARY	EB 11	Macamba	1954	Van Saher, L.	VG+		$7.00
POPULAR LIBRARY	EB 22	Born Of The Sun	1954	Wagner, G.	VG+		$7.00

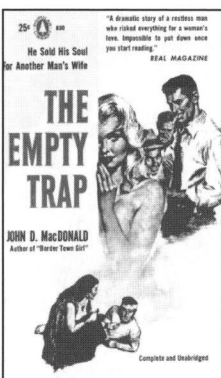

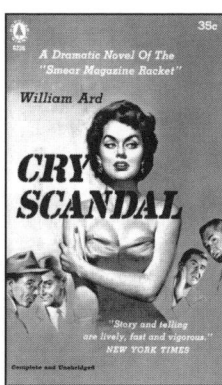

Popular Library 830 VGF $36   Popular Library 1452 AF $20   Popular Lib. EB11 AF- $12   Popular Lib. G236 AF $44

PUBLISHER	PUB. #	TITLE	DATE	AUTHOR	COND.	TYPE	PRICE
POPULAR LIBRARY	EB 26	The Eagle And The Wind	1954	Stover, H.E.	VG-		$7.00
POPULAR LIBRARY	EB 42	The Girl In The Red Jaguar	1955	Manor, J.	F		$11.00 A
POPULAR LIBRARY	EB 42	The Girl In The Red Jaguar	1955	Manor, J.	VG+		$6.00
POPULAR LIBRARY	EB 48	River Of Eyes	1955	Earl, L.	VGF		$10.00 A
POPULAR LIBRARY	EB 53	Fighting Indians Of The West	1955	Cooke, D.C.	AF		$6.00
POPULAR LIBRARY	EB 66	All Or Nothing	1956	Catto, M.	AF		$6.00
POPULAR LIBRARY	EB 93	Trail Town Marshall	1957	Ballard, T.	VGF		$6.00
POPULAR LIBRARY	EB 94	Duel In The Sun	1957	Busch, N.	VGF	MTI	$8.00
POPULAR LIBRARY	EB 96	Just So Far	1957	Miller, F.	AF		$7.00
POPULAR LIBRARY	G 101	The Nymph And The Lamp	1952	Raddall, T.H.	VGF		$8.00
POPULAR LIBRARY	G 102	From The Sea And The Jungle	1952	Carse, R.	VG+		$7.00
POPULAR LIBRARY	G 110	Congo Song	1952	Cloete, S.	VG		$7.00
POPULAR LIBRARY	G 111	The Forsaken	1952	Kormendi, F.	VGF		$8.00
POPULAR LIBRARY	G 115	The Naked Rich	1952	Connell, V.	VG		$7.00
POPULAR LIBRARY	G 116	Sword Of Fortune	1953	Gerson, N.B.	VGF		$8.00
POPULAR LIBRARY	G 120	The City Beyond	1953	Emerick, L.	VG+		$7.00
POPULAR LIBRARY	G 125	The Beach House	1953	Longstreet, S.	VG		$7.00
POPULAR LIBRARY	G 130	Tisa	1953	Moray, H.	G		$5.00
POPULAR LIBRARY	G 142	The Hot And The Cool	1954	Gilbert, E.	VG		$8.00
POPULAR LIBRARY	G 145	The Flesh Is Real (2nd)	1956	Shulman, I.	G		$7.00
POPULAR LIBRARY	G 146	Rumble On The Docks	1955	Paley, F.	VG		$6.00
POPULAR LIBRARY	G 146	Rumble On The Docks (2nd)	1956	Paley, F.	VG-		$6.00
POPULAR LIBRARY	G 187	The Quick And The Loving	1957	Irving, C.	VG+		$7.00
POPULAR LIBRARY	G 194	A Cry Of Children	1957	Burns, J.H.	VGF+		$7.00
POPULAR LIBRARY	G 196	Sisters Of The Night	1957	Stearn, J.	VGF		$6.00
POPULAR LIBRARY	G 223	The Sheriff's Son	1958	Raine, W.M.	VG+		$6.00
POPULAR LIBRARY	G 231	I Know My Love	1958	Nichols, F.	F		$14.00 A
POPULAR LIBRARY	G 236	Cry Scandal	1958	Ard, W.	AF		$44.00 A
POPULAR LIBRARY	G 240	Gun Hand	1958	Farrell, C.	AF		$6.00
POPULAR LIBRARY	G 243	Queen Of The East	1958	Baron, A.	AF		$8.00
POPULAR LIBRARY	G 248	The Deadly Reasons	1958	Radin, E.D.	AF		$8.00
POPULAR LIBRARY	G 248	The Deadly Reasons	1958	Radin, E.D.	AF		$7.00
POPULAR LIBRARY	G 260	Calendar Model	1958	Gale, G.	VGF		$8.00
POPULAR LIBRARY	G 261	Free Grass	1958	Haycox, E.	VG+		$5.00
POPULAR LIBRARY	G 276	Fury At Painted Rock	1958	Cook, W.	VGF-		$5.00
POPULAR LIBRARY	G 277	Don't Crowd Me	1958	Hunter, E.	VGF		$12.00
POPULAR LIBRARY	G 277	Don't Crowd Me	1958	Hunter, E.	AF		$8.00
POPULAR LIBRARY	G 287	I'll Get Mine	1958	Scott, T.	AF		$53.00 A
POPULAR LIBRARY	G 311	The Losers	1959	Irving, C.	AF-		$10.00 A
POPULAR LIBRARY	G 317	Dark Drums	1959	Brown, W.	VG+		$8.00
POPULAR LIBRARY	G 321	Jailbait	1959	Bernard, W.	F		$17.00 A
POPULAR LIBRARY	G 321	Jailbait	1959	Bernard, W.	VGF		$10.00 A
POPULAR LIBRARY	G 329	New York Call Girl	1959	Lowry, R.	AF		$12.00
POPULAR LIBRARY	G 333	That Randall Girl	1959	Edwards, S.	VGF		$7.00
POPULAR LIBRARY	G 346	I'll Get You Yet	1959	Howard, J.	VG		$6.00
POPULAR LIBRARY	G 352	The Tough Ones	1959	Anthology	F		$10.00 A
POPULAR LIBRARY	G 359	Violent Valley	1959	Ashburn, W.	VGF		$6.00
POPULAR LIBRARY	G 367	Rawhide Range	1959	Haycox, E.	VGF		$6.00

Popular Library G-532 AF $38   Popular Library PC-500 VGF $36   Popular Library SP-250 AF $71   Popular Lib. 50-8026 VGF+ $16

PUBLISHER	PUB. #	TITLE	DATE	AUTHOR	COND.	TYPE	PRICE
POPULAR LIBRARY	G 380	Marshal Of Sundown	1959	Gregory, J.	VG+		$6.00
POPULAR LIBRARY	G 386	A Matter Of Morals	1959	Gies, J.	AF		$7.00
POPULAR LIBRARY	G 388	Brush Rider	1959	Owen, D.	AF		$6.00
POPULAR LIBRARY	G 394	Beyond The Rio Grande	1959	Raine, W.M.	AF		$6.00
POPULAR LIBRARY	G 396	The Man From Texas	1959	Gregory, J.	AF		$6.00
POPULAR LIBRARY	G 403	The Untouchables	1960	Ness, E.	VG	TVTI	$6.00
POPULAR LIBRARY	G 421	Ramrod	1960	Short, L.	VGF		$6.00
POPULAR LIBRARY	G 426	Epitaph For An Enemy	1960	Barr, G.	VG+		$6.00
POPULAR LIBRARY	G 449	Tangerine	1960	De Rivoyre, C.	AF		$6.00
POPULAR LIBRARY	G 452	Too Hot For Hawaii	1960	Dewey, T.B.	VG-		$5.00
POPULAR LIBRARY	G 463	The Wilderness	1960	Vaughan, C.	VG		$6.00
POPULAR LIBRARY	G 486	The Adventures Of S. Holmes	1960	Doyle, A.C.	VGF		$6.00
POPULAR LIBRARY	G 499	The Man From Missouri	1960	Gruber, F.	AF		$7.00
POPULAR LIBRARY	G 507	You Kill Me	1961	MacDonald, J.D.	VG		$10.00
POPULAR LIBRARY	G 532	The Dead Beat	1961	Bloch, R.	AF		$38.00 A
POPULAR LIBRARY	G 532	The Dead Beat	1961	Bloch, R.	VG+		$8.00
POPULAR LIBRARY	G 541	Stay Away, Joe	1961	Cushman, D.	VG+		$6.00
POPULAR LIBRARY	G 552	TV Guide Roundup	1961	Anthology	VGF		$9.00
POPULAR LIBRARY	G 560	Donovan's Brain	1961	Siodmak, C.	AF		$6.00
POPULAR LIBRARY	K 6	The Haunting Of Hill House	1962	Jackson, S.	VG+	MTI	$7.00
POPULAR LIBRARY	K 18	Blood Runs Cold	1962	Bloch, R.	VGF		$23.00
POPULAR LIBRARY	K 18	Blood Runs Cold	1962	Bloch, R.	VG		$10.00
POPULAR LIBRARY	M 2054	Sangaree	1964	Slaughter, F.G.	VG+		$6.00
POPULAR LIBRARY	M 2073	The Moviegoer	1964	Percy, W.	F		$6.00
POPULAR LIBRARY	PC 500	Lady Chatterly's Daughter	1960	Lariar, L.	VGF		$36.00 A
POPULAR LIBRARY	PC 1003	Kiss Me, You Fool	1961	Anthology	AF		$32.00 A
POPULAR LIBRARY	PC 1027	The Lillies Of The Field	1963	Barrett, W.	VGF	MTI	$6.00
POPULAR LIBRARY	PC 1042	Station Six-Sahara	1964	Avallone, M.	AF	MTI	$6.00
POPULAR LIBRARY	PC 1048	36 Hours	1965	Hittleman, C.K.	VGF	MTI	$7.00
POPULAR LIBRARY	PC 1050	Bus Riley's Back In Town	1965	Hine, A.	VGF+	MTI	$8.00
POPULAR LIBRARY	PC 1050	Bus Riley's Back In Town	1965	Hine, A.	VGF	MTI	$6.00
POPULAR LIBRARY	SP 11	The Butchers	1957	Bishop, L.	VGF		$6.00
POPULAR LIBRARY	SP 100	Man Into Woman	1961	Hoyer, N.	VG		$7.00
POPULAR LIBRARY	SP 186	Anzio	1962	Thomas, W.V.	AF		$6.00
POPULAR LIBRARY	SP 245	Goodbye To Some	1963	Forbes, G.	AF		$7.00
POPULAR LIBRARY	SP 250	The Man In The High Castle	1964	Dick, P.K.	AF		$71.00 A
POPULAR LIBRARY	SP 250	The Man In The High Castle	1964	Dick, P.K.	VG+		$44.00 A
POPULAR LIBRARY	SP 294	Bullet Proof	1964	Dean, A.	VGF		$8.00
POPULAR LIBRARY	SP 352	The Shape Of Things	1965	Anthology	AF		$7.00
POPULAR LIBRARY	SP 400	I Spy	1965	Tiger, J.	VGF	TVTI	$6.00
POPULAR LIBRARY	SP 404	The Friendly Dead	1964	Gallant, T.G.	VGF+		$6.00
POPULAR LIBRARY	W 500	Fire Down Below	1957	Kent, S.	VG+	MTI	$7.00
POPULAR LIBRARY	50 8008	Madame X	1966	Avallone, M.	VG+	MTI	$5.00
POPULAR LIBRARY	50 8026	The Monkees	1966	Fawcette, G.	VGF+	TVTI	$16.00 A
POPULAR LIBRARY	60 2130	Hud	1965	McMurtry, L.	VGF	MTI	$6.00
POPULAR LIBRARY	60 2131	Spy Who Came In With The Gold	1965	Zeiger, H.A.	G		$6.00
POPULAR LIBRARY	60 2132	Kaleidoscope	1966	Avallone, M.	VG	MTI	$6.00
POPULAR LIBRARY	60 2180	I Spy #4	1967	Tiger, J.	VGF	TVTI	$6.00

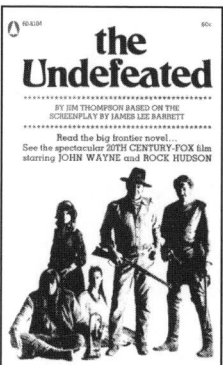

| Pop. Lib. 60-8104 VGF $65 | Pop. Lib. 445-325 VG+ $22 | Powell 121 VG+ $7 | Private Editions 384 AF $148 |

PUBLISHER	PUB. #	TITLE	DATE	AUTHOR	COND.	TYPE	PRICE
POPULAR LIBRARY	60 2236	The Secret Surrender	1967	Dulles, A.	VGF		$4.00
POPULAR LIBRARY	60 2244	Ironside	1967	Thompson, J.	VGF	TVTI	$27.00 A
POPULAR LIBRARY	60 2244	Ironside	1967	Thompson, J.	VGF	TVTI	$24.00
POPULAR LIBRARY	60 2244	Ironside	1967	Thompson, J.	VG	TVTI	$24.00 A
POPULAR LIBRARY	60 2244	Ironside	1967	Thompson, J.	VG-	TVTI	$20.00
POPULAR LIBRARY	60 2244	Ironside	1967	Thompson, J.	G	TVTI	$10.00
POPULAR LIBRARY	60 2256	Mannix	1968	Avallone, M.	VG	TVTI	$5.00
POPULAR LIBRARY	60 2289	The Man In The High Castle	1967	Dick, P.K.	VG		$5.00
POPULAR LIBRARY	60 2289	The Man In The High Castle	1967	Dick, P.K.	VG-		$5.00
POPULAR LIBRARY	60 2289	The Man In The High Castle	1967	Dick, P.K.	G+		$3.00
POPULAR LIBRARY	60 2299	The Dead Beat	1967	Bloch, R.	VG-		$5.00
POPULAR LIBRARY	60 2335	Danger Planet	1967	Sterling, B.*	VGF		$10.00 A
POPULAR LIBRARY	60 2399	Outlaws Of The Moon	1967	Hamilton, E.	AF		$6.00
POPULAR LIBRARY	60 2407	The Comet Kings	1967	Hamilton, E.	AF		$7.00
POPULAR LIBRARY	60 2430	Captain Future's Challenge	1967	Hamilton, E.	AF		$10.00 A
POPULAR LIBRARY	60 8045	Dragnet 1968	1967	Vowell, D.H.	VG+	TVTI	$6.00
POPULAR LIBRARY	60 8046	The Monkees Go Mod	1967	O'Connor, P.	VG+	TVTI	$7.00
POPULAR LIBRARY	60 8104	The Undefeated	1969	Thompson, J.	VGF	MTI	$65.00 A
POPULAR LIBRARY	60 8104	The Undefeated	1969	Thompson, J.	VG-	MTI	$22.00
POPULAR LIBRARY	60 8104	The Undefeated	1969	Thompson, J.	VG	MTI	$20.00
POPULAR LIBRARY	445 209	Games Singles Play	1974	Wayne, A.	VGF		$7.00
POPULAR LIBRARY	445 265	The Dean's Death (Columbo #2)	1975	Lawrence, A.	VGF	TVTI	$5.00
POPULAR LIBRARY	445 325	The Long Sleep	1975	Hill, J.*	VG+		$22.00 A
POPULAR LIBRARY	445 325	The Long Sleep	1975	Hill, J.*	VGF		$16.00
POPULAR LIBRARY	445 325	The Long Sleep	1975	Hill, J.*	VG		$8.00
POPULAR LIBRARY	445 326	By Dawn's Early Light (Columbo #4)	1975	Clement, H.	AF-	TVTI	$5.00
POPULAR LIBRARY	445 354	The Deadliest Game (Rockford #2)	1976	Jahn, M.	AF	TVTI	$6.00
POPULAR LIBRARY	445 394	Adventures Of Jules de Grandin	1976	Quinn, S.	VG		$5.00
POPULAR LIBRARY	445 428	Hellfire Files Of Jules de Grandin	1976	Quinn, S.	VG-		$5.00
POPULAR LIBRARY	445 514	The Japanese Mistress	1973	Neely, R.	VGF		$6.00
POPULAR LIBRARY	445 1471	Monkey On My Back	1972	Brown, W.	VG		$6.00
POPULAR LIBRARY	445 1524	Columbo	1972	Lawrence, A.	VGF-	TVTI	$5.00
POPULAR LIBRARY	445 1535	TV Guide Crosswords #4	1972		VGF		$7.00
POPULAR LIBRARY	445 1544	The Frankenstein Wheel	1972	Fairman, P.W.	VGF		$7.00
POPULAR LIBRARY	445 1558	Ghoul Lover	1972	Tralins, R.	AF		$8.00
POPULAR LIBRARY	445 1558	Ghoul Lover	1972	Tralins, R.	VGF		$6.00
POPULAR LIBRARY	445 1562	The Night Of The Wolf	1972	Long, F.B.	AF		$6.00
POPULAR LIBRARY	445 1572	Seven Tickets To Hell	1972	Williams, R.M.	VG+		$6.00
POPULAR LIBRARY	445 1577	The Marrow Eaters	1972	Moore, H.	AF		$7.00
POPULAR LIBRARY	445 1587	The Beast With Red Hands	1973	Stuart, S.	VGF+		$6.00
POPULAR LIBRARY	445 1593	The Hospital Horror	1973	Binder, O.O.	F		$8.00
POPULAR LIBRARY	445 1593	The Hospital Horror	1973	Binder, O.O.	F		$8.00
POPULAR LIBRARY	445 2474	Monster From Out Of Time	1970	Long, F.B.	F		$5.00
POPULAR LIBRARY	445 2485	Dr. Cyclops	1970	Anthology	VGF		$7.00
POPULAR LIBRARY	445 2563	Quicksand	1969	Land, M.	F		$4.00
POPULAR LIBRARY	445 2582	Garbo	n/d	Zierold, N.	VG+		$6.00
POPULAR LIBRARY	445 4006	Fear & Typewriter In The Sky	1977	Hubbard, L.R.	VGF	DBL	$8.00
POPULAR LIBRARY	445 8115	The Doctors	1970	Avallone, M.	VG	TVTI	$6.00

Private Eye 1-1 VGF $33   Prize Love Novel 24 AF $35   Pursuit 3 VG+ $24

PUBLISHER	PUB. #	TITLE	DATE	AUTHOR	COND.	TYPE	PRICE
POPULAR LIBRARY	445 8125	The Revolutionary	1970	Koningsberger, H.	VGF	MTI	$4.00
POPULAR LIBRARY	445 8146	Gunsmoke	1970	Stratton, C.	VGF	TVTI	$8.00
POPULAR LIBRARY	445 8194	Wit And Wisdom Of Archie Bunker	1971	Boe, E.	VGF	TVTI	$5.00
POPULAR LIBRARY	445 8274	F.S.Fitzgerald-In His Own Time	1971	Fitzgerald, F.S.	VGF		$5.00
POPULAR LIBRARY	445 8526	Nightmare Alley	1976	Gresham, W.L.	VG		$3.00
POWELL	PP 121	Swordmen Of Vistar	1969	Nuetzel, C.	VG+		$7.00
POWELL	PP 126	Murder Times 4	1969	Nuetzel, C.	AF		$22.00 A
POWELL	PP 149	Warriors Of Noomas	1969	Nuetzel, C.	VG-		$5.00
POWELL	PP 164	The Sundown Kid	1969	Brent, L.W.	VG+		$3.00
POWELL	PP 180	Trail-Blazers West	1969	Rayburn, D.	VG		$6.00
PRIORY	1039	Web Of Murder	n/d	Whittington, H.	VG+		$3.00
PRIORY	1070	Nightfall	n/d	Goodis, D.	G+		$3.00
PRIORY	1096	Play It Hard	n/d	Brewer, G.	VGF		$3.00
PRIORY	1127	The Squeeze	n/d	Brewer, G.	VG+		$3.00
PRIVATE EDITION	1	Nature Girl	1949	Stone, T.	VGF	Digest	$17.00 A
PRIVATE EDITIONS	PE 374	The Leather Girls	1966	Mujer, U.	F		$24.00 A
PRIVATE EDITIONS	PE 384	A Taste Of H	1966	Horn, A.	AF		$148.00 A
PRIVATE EDITIONS	PE 384	A Taste Of H	1966	Horn, A.	VG+		$137.00 A
PRIVATE EDITIONS	PE 384	A Taste Of H	1966	Horn, A.	G		$24.00
PRIVATE EDITIONS	PE 391	The Girl Habit	1966	James, H.A.	VG+		$20.00 A
PRIVATE EDITIONS	PE 391	The Girl Habit	1966	James, H.A.	AF		$15.00 A
PRIVATE EDITIONS	PE 393	Night Of The Firebird	1966	Hearde, B.	AF		$17.00 A
PRIVATE EDITIONS	PE 401	The Colonel's Wife (2nd)	1966	Weaver, D.	VG+		$7.00
PRIVATE EDITIONS	PE 405	Deny Me Not	1966	Fuchs, H.	AF		$7.00 A
PRIVATE EDITIONS	PE 413	Harlot's Holiday	1967	Dair, A.	VGF		$14.00 A
PRIVATE EDITIONS	PE 419	Passion's Puppet	1967	Phillips, V.	VGF		$41.00 A
PRIVATE EDITIONS	PE 419	Passion's Puppet	1967	Phillips, V.	AF-		$39.00 A
PRIVATE EDITIONS	PE 457	The Sexecutives	1968	Westermier, D.L.*	VG		$45.00 A
PRIVATE EYE	1 1	Private Eye 7/53	1953	Anthology	VGF	Digest	$33.00 A
PRIZE LOVE NOVEL	23	Night Club Angel	1949	Carter, R.	VGF	Digest	$14.00 A
PRIZE LOVE NOVEL	24	Time For Love	1949	Jacquin, L.	AF	Digest	$35.00 A
PRIZE MYSTERY	4	Hot Ice	1943	Casey, R.J.	VG+	Digest	$11.00
PRIZE MYSTERY	10	Murder On Safari	1944	Huxley, E.	VGF	Digest	$8.00 A
PRIZE MYSTERY	11	The Frightened Girl	1944	Crombie, M.	VGF	Digest	$11.00
PRIZE MYSTERY	12	The Third Degree	1944	Barry, J.	VGF	Digest	$10.00 A
PRIZE MYSTERY	20	Murder Is Forgetful	1946	Bogart, W.	VG-	Digest	$6.00
PRIZE WESTERN	39	Trouble Buster	1950	Sumner, E.	VG+	Digest	$8.00
PRIZE WESTERN	40	Guns Of Powder River	1950	Floren, L.	VG-	Digest	$5.00
PRODUCER	101	The Daughter Of Bonnie & Clyde	1971	Brent, L.W.	VG	MTI	$11.00 A
PURSUIT	1	Pursuit - 9/53	1953	Anthology	VGF	Digest	$46.00 A
PURSUIT	3	Pursuit - 3/54	1954	Anthology	VG+	Digest	$24.00 A
PURSUIT	3	Pursuit - 3/54	1954	Anthology	VG	Digest	$12.00
PURSUIT	12	Pursuit - 11/55	1955	Anthology	VG+	Digest	$15.00
PURSUIT	13	Pursuit - 1/56	1956	Anthology	VGF+	Digest	$15.00 A
PURSUIT	14	Pursuit - 3/56	1956	Anthology	VG	Digest	$34.00 A

| Pyramid 12 AF $30 | Pyramid 21 AF $15 (3rd) | Pyramid 23 VGF+ $20 |

PUBLISHER	PUB. #	TITLE	DATE	AUTHOR	COND.	TYPE	PRICE
PURSUIT	15	Pursuit - 5/56	1956	Anthology	VG	Digest	$34.00 A
PURSUIT	17	Pursuit - 9/56	1956	Anthology	VG	Digest	$20.00 A
PYRAMID	12	Reckless Passion	1949	Semple, G.	AF		$30.00 A
PYRAMID	20	Terror In Times Square	1950	Handley, A.	G+		$5.00
PYRAMID	21	Sin Street (3rd)	1952	Manners, D.	AF		$15.00
PYRAMID	22	The Dead Men Grin	1950	Fischer, B.	VG		$17.00 A
PYRAMID	23	Cry Shame!	1950	Everard, K.	VGF+		$20.00
PYRAMID	24	The Manatee	1950	Bruff, N.	VG+		$12.00
PYRAMID	26	Arizona Ranger	1951	Leslie, A.S.	VG		$5.00
PYRAMID	27	Sinful Cities	1951	De Leeuw, H.	VGF		$12.00
PYRAMID	27	Sinful Cities	1951	De Leeuw, H.	VG+		$8.00
PYRAMID	29	Stairway To Death	1951	Fischer, B.	VG+		$20.00
PYRAMID	30	Madeline	1951	Anonymous	VG+		$7.00
PYRAMID	31	Tough Town (2nd)	1952	Karney, J.	VGF		$10.00 A
PYRAMID	37	Farm Girl (2nd)	1952	Meloney, W.B.	G+		$5.00
PYRAMID	41	The House Of Madame Tellier	1952	De Maupassant, G.	VGF-		$12.00 A
PYRAMID	G 43	Teen-Age Vice!	1952	Cooper, C.R.	AF		$50.00 A
PYRAMID	G 43	Teen-Age Vice!	1952	Cooper, C.R.	VG		$7.00
PYRAMID	G 48	Cage Of Lust	1952	Seager, A.	VG+		$8.00
PYRAMID	G 48	Cage Of Lust	1952	Seager, A.	VG		$5.00
PYRAMID	49	A Diary Of Love	1952	Hutchins, M.	VG+		$5.00
PYRAMID	G 50	Yama, The Hell-Hole	1953	Kuprin, A.	VG		$6.00
PYRAMID	56	The Death Riders	1952	Cole, J.	VG-		$3.00
PYRAMID	58	Female Convict (2nd)	1953	Burns, V.E.	VG		$6.00
PYRAMID	63	Apache Devil	1952	Corle, E.	VG		$7.00
PYRAMID	G 64	The Heavenly Sinner	1952	Harre, E.	VG		$6.00
PYRAMID	66	Trigger Law	1952	Cole, J.	VG		$3.00
PYRAMID	73	Killer Country	1953	Cole, J.	VG+		$6.00
PYRAMID	G 77	Stella And Joe	1953	Cohen, L.	VG+		$7.00
PYRAMID	79	The Heel	1953	Rohde, W.	VG		$8.00
PYRAMID	82	Loves Of Goya	1953	Chapman, M.	VGF		$8.00
PYRAMID	90	Chicago Woman	1953	Saber, R.O.	AF		$12.00
PYRAMID	90	Chicago Woman (2nd)	1953	Saber, R.O.	VGF+		$10.00
PYRAMID	91	Land Grab	1953	Cole, J.	VGF		$6.00
PYRAMID	92	Road Show	1953	Tulley, J.	VG+		$27.00 A
PYRAMID	96	Mimi	1953	Taylor, R.W.	VG+		$7.00
PYRAMID	97	The Big Fake	1953	Forbes, M.	VG+		$10.00
PYRAMID	98	The Sea Tyrant	1953	Freuchen, P.	VG+		$8.00
PYRAMID	99	There Goes Shorty Higgins	1953	Karney, J.	VG+		$7.00
PYRAMID	100	Cellini	1953	Cellini	VGF-		$6.00
PYRAMID	102	African Mistress	1953	Royer, L.C.	VG+		$10.00
PYRAMID	104	Big Mike	1953	Givens, C.	VG		$6.00
PYRAMID	106	The Ordeal Of Private Heath	1953	Stuart, J.	VGF-		$6.00
PYRAMID	114	The Harem	1954	Royer, L.C.	VG+		$7.00
PYRAMID	115	Two Gun Deputy	1954	MacDonald, W.C.	VG+		$5.00

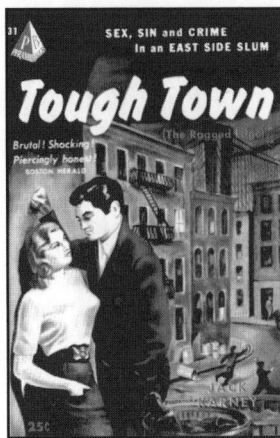

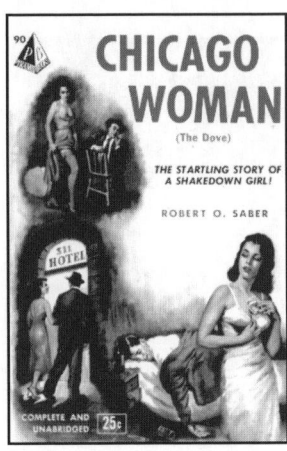

Pyramid 31 VGF $10 (2nd)   Pyramid 43 AF $50   Pyramid 90 AF $12

PUBLISHER	PUB. #	TITLE	DATE	AUTHOR	COND.	TYPE	PRICE
PYRAMID	118	Women On The Wall	1954	Anthology	VG-		$6.00
PYRAMID	119	The Great Balsamo	1954	Zolotow, M.	VGF		$10.00
PYRAMID	121	With Sirens Screaming	1954	Booth, E.	VG+		$7.00
PYRAMID	122	I Was A Drug Addict	1954	Street, L.	VGF		$110.00 A
PYRAMID	125	Bold Moment	1954	Johnson, V.H.	VGF+		$20.00 A
PYRAMID	126	The Junk Pusher	1954	Taylor, R.W.	VG		$44.00 A
PYRAMID	G 127	Teen-Age Vice	1954	Cooper, C.R.	VG+		$18.00
PYRAMID	G 127	Teen-Age Vice	1954	Cooper, C.R.	VG		$15.00
PYRAMID	G 129	Dark Brother	1954	Gordon, G.	VGF		$10.00
PYRAMID	130	A Diary Of Love	1954	Hutchins, M.	AF		$7.00
PYRAMID	130	A Diary Of Love	1954	Hutchins, M.	VGF		$7.00
PYRAMID	132	Jungle Heat	1954	Wilmer, D.*	VG+		$7.00
PYRAMID	134	Savage Triangle	1954	Royer, L.C.	VGF		$7.00
PYRAMID	136	A Night In Manilla	1954	Langdon, J.	VG-		$4.00
PYRAMID	138	His Father's Wife	1954	Keene, D.	AF		$60.00 A
PYRAMID	138	His Father's Wife	1954	Keene, D.	VG		$18.00
PYRAMID	G 145	Cage Of Lust	1955	Seager, A.	G+		$2.00
PYRAMID	151	The Proposition	1954	Collins, H.*	VG		$8.00
PYRAMID	153	Gunsmoke Trail	1955	Cole, J.	VG		$5.00
PYRAMID	156	Dangerous Game	1955	Anthology	AF		$20.00 A
PYRAMID	156	Dangerous Game	1955	Anthology	VG-		$3.00
PYRAMID	G 157	Shriek With Pleasure	1955	Howard, T.	VG		$5.00
PYRAMID	159	One Way Street	1955	Marino, N.	AF		$10.00
PYRAMID	G 161	Mademoiselle De Maupin	1955	Gautier, T.	VGF		$7.00
PYRAMID	164	Of A Strange Woman	1955	Burke, J.W.	VG+		$7.00
PYRAMID	164	Of A Strange Woman	1955	Burke, J.W.	VGF		$6.00
PYRAMID	165	Town Quarry	1955	Manners, M.	VGF		$6.00
PYRAMID	167	Texas Fury	1955	Cole, J.	VG+		$4.00
PYRAMID	G 170	Strange Friends	1955	Holk, A.	AF		$20.00 A
PYRAMID	171	Two-Gun Devil	1955	Cole, J.	VG		$5.00
PYRAMID	175	Madeline	1955	Anonymous	VGF		$8.00
PYRAMID	183	The World's Worst Women	1956	O'Donnell, B.	F		$15.00
PYRAMID	183	The World's Worst Women	1956	O'Donnell, B.	VG+		$9.00
PYRAMID	G 184	A Way Home	1956	Sturgeon, T.	VGF		$10.00
PYRAMID	G 189	Shadows Of Shame	1956	Taylor, J.	AF		$13.00 A
PYRAMID	193	Taking A Turn For The Nurse	1956	Kaz	VGF		$5.00
PYRAMID	R 202	The House Of Madame Tellier	1956	De Maupassant, G.	AF		$10.00
PYRAMID	G 206	Creep Into Thy Narrow Bed	1956	Bishop, L.	VG+		$7.00
PYRAMID	R 210	Women And Vodka	1956	Anthology	AF		$15.00 A
PYRAMID	R 210	Women And Vodka	1956	Anthology	VGF		$8.00
PYRAMID	R 211	Drinkers Of Darkness	1956	Hanley, G.	VG+		$7.00
PYRAMID	G 214	Tomorrow And Tomorrow	1956	Collins, H.*	AF		$22.00
PYRAMID	216	Outlaw Brand	1956	West, T.	AF		$8.00
PYRAMID	G 217	The Man From Paris	1956	Royer, J.C.	VG+		$5.00
PYRAMID	R 232	Woman Without Love	1956	Maruois, A.	VG+		$7.00

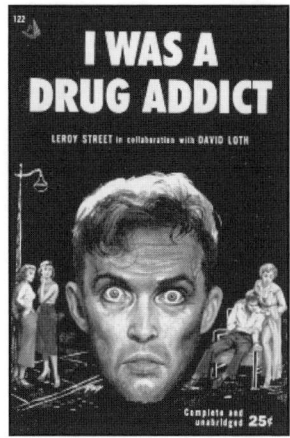
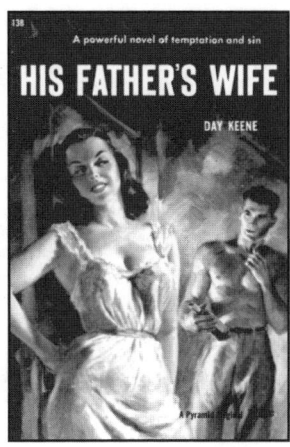

Pyramid 122 VGF $110		Pyramid 138 AF $60		Pyramid 156 AF $20

PUBLISHER	PUB. #	TITLE	DATE	AUTHOR	COND.	TYPE	PRICE
PYRAMID	G 234	Men Against The Stars	1957	Anthology	VG+		$8.00
PYRAMID	235	One For The Road	1957	Dietrich, R.*	VG+		$7.00
PYRAMID	235	One For The Road	1957	Dietrich, R.*	VG		$5.00
PYRAMID	G 242	Come See Them Die	1957	Hadley, H.	AF		$8.00
PYRAMID	R 246	Sex And Marriage	1957	Ellis, H.	VG+		$6.00
PYRAMID	G 247	The Synthetic Man	1957	Sturgeon, T.	VGF		$10.00
PYRAMID	G 252	Teen-Age Vice	1957	Cooper, C.R.	VGF		$29.00 A
PYRAMID	G 252	Teen-Age Vice	1957	Cooper, C.R.	VG+		$12.00 A
PYRAMID	G 260	The First Time	1957	Anthology	VG+		$8.00
PYRAMID	G 261	I Was A House Detective	1957	Sterling, S.	VGF		$8.00
PYRAMID	G 262	Twilight Men	1957	Tellier, A.	VGF		$15.00
PYRAMID	G 268	Impossible Greeting Cards	1957	Levinson, L.	VG+		$6.00
PYRAMID	G 271	The Young Punks	1957	Anthology	VG+		$55.00 A
PYRAMID	G 274	This Girl For Hire (2nd)	1957	Fickling, G.G.	AF		$10.00
PYRAMID	G 275	The Fuzzy Pink Nightgown	1957	Tate, S.	AF-	MTI	$6.00 A
PYRAMID	G 277	The Law Bringers	1957	Lomax, B.	F		$8.00
PYRAMID	R 281	Gestapo (2nd)	1957	Crankshaw, E.	VGF		$7.00
PYRAMID	G 284	The Name Is Chambers	1957	Kane, H.	VG-		$3.00
PYRAMID	R 290	Frankenstein	1957	Shelly, M.	VGF-		$6.00
PYRAMID	R 290	Frankenstein	1957	Shelly, M.	VG		$3.00
PYRAMID	G 292	You're Wrong, Delaney	1957	Shaw, C.	VG		$7.00
PYRAMID	G 295	The Daughter	1957	Markowitz, A.	AF		$7.00
PYRAMID	G 298	Hell Flower	1957	Smith, G.O.	VGF		$8.00 A
PYRAMID	G 298	Hell Flower	1957	Smith, G.O.	VGF-		$8.00
PYRAMID	G 298	Hell Flower	1957	Smith, G.O.	VG		$6.00
PYRAMID	G 301	She-Devil	1957	Hervey, H.	VG		$6.00
PYRAMID	G 309	Yaller Gal	1958	Lee, C.	VG+		$7.00
PYRAMID	G 311	Fury With Legs	1958	Lawrence, G.	VGF		$9.00 A
PYRAMID	G 311	Fury With Legs	1958	Lawrence, G.	VGF		$7.00
PYRAMID	G 315	City Limits	1958	Marino, N.	VG+		$7.00
PYRAMID	G 323	7 Days To Death	1958	Marric, J.J.	AF		$8.00
PYRAMID	G 326	House Of Dolls	1958	Tzetnik, K.	F		$12.00
PYRAMID	R 330	Hitler's Secret Service	1958	Schellenberg, W.	AF		$5.00
PYRAMID	G 332	The Skylark Of Space	1958	Smith, E.E.	AF		$9.00
PYRAMID	G 337	Operation Cicero	1958	Moyzisch, L.C.	VGF		$6.00
PYRAMID	G 339	Who?	1958	Budrys, A.	VG		$7.00
PYRAMID	G 342	Never The Same Again	1958	Tesch, G.	VG		$10.00
PYRAMID	G 344	A Gun For Honey	1958	Fickling, G.G.	VG		$9.00
PYRAMID	G 350	The Name Is Malone	1958	Rice, C.	VG+		$8.00
PYRAMID	G 357	Mr. Arkadin	1958	Welles, O.	F		$11.00 A
PYRAMID	G 357	Mr. Arkadin	1958	Welles, O.	AF		$11.00 A
PYRAMID	G 360	The Megstone Plot	1958	Garve, A.	VGF		$10.00
PYRAMID	G 368	The Man Of Cold Rages	1958	Park, J.*	VG		$10.00
PYRAMID	G 376	West Of The Pecos	1959	Evan, P.	F		$7.00
PYRAMID	G 377	Female Convict	1959	Burns, V.G.	VG-		$6.00

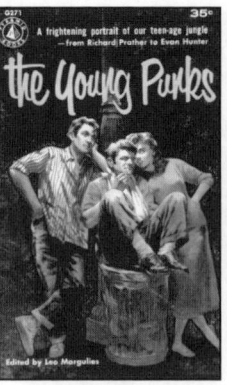

| Pyramid 214 AF $22 | Pyramid 252 VGF $29 | Pyramid 271 VG+ $55 | Pyramid 298 VGF $8 |

PUBLISHER	PUB. #	TITLE	DATE	AUTHOR	COND.	TYPE	PRICE
PYRAMID	G 379	The Spy	1959	Brome, V.	VG+		$5.00
PYRAMID	G 384	Whisper Of Love	1959	Flora, F.	VGF		$10.00
PYRAMID	G 385	The Survivor	1959	Ehle, J.	AF		$8.00
PYRAMID	G 387	The Dream And The Flesh	1959	Connell, V.	VGF		$12.00 A
PYRAMID	G 392	Baseball Stars Of 1959	1959	Robinson, R.	VG-		$6.00
PYRAMID	G 394	How Sharp The Point	1959	Wolfson, P.J.	G		$5.00
PYRAMID	G 399	The Beauty Makers	1959	Lamont, N.	VGF		$7.00
PYRAMID	G 400	The Husband	1959	Caspary, V.	AF		$14.00
PYRAMID	G 405	Al Capone	1959	Roeburt, J.	F	MTI	$12.00
PYRAMID	G 405	Al Capone	1959	Roeburt, J.	G	MTI	$3.00
PYRAMID	G 414	Born Innocent	1959	Burnham, C.B.	AF-		$11.00 A
PYRAMID	G 415	The Bride Is Much Too Beautiful	1959	Joyeux, O.	F	MTI	$17.00 A
PYRAMID	G 416	The Falling Torch	1959	Budrys, A.	AF		$10.00
PYRAMID	G 417	The Red Lily	1959	France, A.	VGF		$7.00
PYRAMID	R 419	The Divine Passion	1959	Fisher, V.	F		$15.00 A
PYRAMID	G 423	Make Mine Love	1959	Birren, F.	F		$10.00
PYRAMID	G 436	A Diary Of Love	1959	Hutchins, M.	AF		$8.00
PYRAMID	G 440	No Nice Girl	1959	Wilhelm, G.	VGF		$11.00 A
PYRAMID	G 441	Seeds Of Murder	1959	York, J.*	VG		$7.00
PYRAMID	G 446	The Magnificent Female	1959	St. Laurent, C.	AF		$10.00
PYRAMID	G 448	Dead In Bed	1959	Keene, D.	VGF		$27.00 A
PYRAMID	G 448	Dead In Bed	1959	Keene, D.	VG-		$5.00
PYRAMID	G 456	Hungry Men	1959	Anderson, E.	AF		$16.00 A
PYRAMID	G 457	The Big Bedroom	1959	Ronns, E.*	F		$14.00
PYRAMID	G 457	The Big Bedroom	1959	Ronns, E.*	AF		$10.00
PYRAMID	G 457	The Big Bedroom	1959	Ronns, E.*	VG+		$7.00
PYRAMID	G 462	Fire In My Blood	1959	Denisa	VGF		$30.00 A
PYRAMID	G 462	Fire In My Blood	1959	Denisa	VG+		$17.00
PYRAMID	G 464	Tough Cop	1959	Roeburt, J.	F		$10.00 A
PYRAMID	G 467	Gestapo	1959	Crankshaw, E.	VGF		$7.00
PYRAMID	G 469	Once More, With Feeling	1960	Pinchot, A.	VG+	MTI	$8.00
PYRAMID	R 472	The Golden Rooms	1960	Fisher, V.	VG+		$4.00
PYRAMID	G 478	I Always Wanted To Be Somebody	1960	Gibson, A.	F		$15.00
PYRAMID	G 479	Sam	1960	Coleman, L.	VG+		$15.00
PYRAMID	G 479	Sam	1960	Coleman, L.	AF		$12.00
PYRAMID	G 480	Space Prison	1960	Godwin, T.	VG+		$10.00
PYRAMID	R 486	D Day	1960	Howarth, D.	AF		$7.00
PYRAMID	G 488	Shadows Of Shame	1960	Taylor, J.	VG+		$6.00 A
PYRAMID	G 490	Comanche Crossing	1960	Peil, P.L.	AF		$8.00
PYRAMID	G 491	Old John's Woman	1960	Milburn, G.	VG+		$10.00
PYRAMID	G 497	Either Is Love	1960	Craigin, E.	F		$20.00
PYRAMID	G 497	Either Is Love	1960	Craigin, E.	VG+		$6.00
PYRAMID	G 499	Out Of Bounds	1960	Merril, J.	VG+		$7.00
PYRAMID	G 502	The Tomorrow People	1960	Merril, J.	VG+		$8.00
PYRAMID	G 509	The Time Of Desire	1960	Charbonneau, L.	AF		$9.00
PYRAMID	G 514	The Lost World (2nd)	1960	Doyle, A.C.	VG	MTI	$7.00
PYRAMID	G 516	Memoirs Of An Assassin	1960	Avner	VG		$5.00
PYRAMID	G 520	Kiss For A Killer	1960	Fickling, G.G.	VG+		$12.00

| Pyramid 339 VG $7 | Pyramid 419 F $15 | Pyramid 440 VGF $11 | Pyramid 448 VGF $27 |

PUBLISHER	PUB. #	TITLE	DATE	AUTHOR	COND.	TYPE	PRICE
PYRAMID	G 528	The Bomb	1960	Gigon, F.	VGF		$6.00
PYRAMID	G 530	The Incomplete Enchanter	1960	De Camp, L.S.	VG		$4.00
PYRAMID	G 531	Gunpoint	1960	Anthology	VG		$7.00
PYRAMID	G 538	Lover Man	1960	Anderson, A.	AF		$13.00 A
PYRAMID	G 538	Lover Man	1960	Anderson, A.	VG		$6.00
PYRAMID	G 544	Venus Plus X	1960	Sturgeon, T.	VGF		$8.00
PYRAMID	G 550	The Death Dealers	1960	Hirsch, P., ed.	F		$8.00
PYRAMID	G 551	Guns In The Valley	1960	Lehman, P.E.	F		$8.00
PYRAMID	G 559	The Lost Europeans	1960	Litvinoff, E.	AF		$7.00
PYRAMID	G 561	The Hanging Judge	1960	Fall, T.	AF		$6.00
PYRAMID	G 563	Blood On Boot Hill	1960	Welles, K.	AF		$26.00 A
PYRAMID	G 578	Journey Into Violence	1961	Whittington, H.	VG+		$42.00 A
PYRAMID	G 579	The Insidious Dr. Fu Manchu	1961	Rohmer, S.	F		$25.00 A
PYRAMID	G 580	Diary Of A Nun	1961	De Mejo, O.	VG+		$6.00
PYRAMID	G 582	Pyramid Crosswords #3	1961	Luzzatto, J.	VG+		$10.00 A
PYRAMID	G 583	The War Between The Mates	1961	Anthology	F		$6.00 A
PYRAMID	R 587	Dr. Goebbels	1961	Manvell, R.	AF		$6.00
PYRAMID	G 590	The Unexpected	1961	Anthology	VGF		$8.00
PYRAMID	G 590	The Unexpected	1961	Anthology	VG+		$8.00
PYRAMID	G 592	The First Time	1961	Anthology	VGF		$7.00
PYRAMID	G 609	Prison Girl	1961	Brown, W.	G		$6.00
PYRAMID	G 615	Orbit Unlimited	1961	Anderson, P.	AF		$10.00 A
PYRAMID	R 616	The Spy	1961	Brome, V.	VGF+		$7.00
PYRAMID	G 617	The Bad Girls	1961	Clifton, B.	VG		$10.00
PYRAMID	G 617	The Bad Girls	1961	Clifton, B.	VG+		$7.00 A
PYRAMID	R 620	Clark Gable	1961	Carpozi, G.	VGF		$8.00
PYRAMID	G 622	Voyage To The Bottom Of The Sea	1961	Sturgeon, T.	VG+	MTI	$8.00
PYRAMID	G 623	Blood And Honey	1961	Fickling, G.G.	F		$23.00 A
PYRAMID	G 624	The Green Rain (2nd)	1961	Tabori, P.	AF		$7.00
PYRAMID	R 625	Concentration Camp	1961	Heimler, E.	AF		$6.00
PYRAMID	R 640	War Fish	1961	Grider, G.	AF		$7.00
PYRAMID	G 641	The Return Of Dr. Fu-Manchu	1961	Rohmer, S.	VGF		$6.00
PYRAMID	G 641	The Return Of Dr. Fu-Manchu	1961	Rohmer, S.	VG		$6.00
PYRAMID	G 642	Six By Heinlein	1961	Heinlein, R.A.	AF		$6.00
PYRAMID	G 648	Yaller Gal	1961	Lee, C.	VGF		$15.00
PYRAMID	G 654	Tomorrow And Tomorrow	1961	Collins, H.*	VGF+		$7.00
PYRAMID	G 656	The Loner (2nd)	1961	Smith, J.W.	VGF		$7.00
PYRAMID	G 658	The Planet Strappers	1961	Gallun, R.Z.	VGF		$7.00
PYRAMID	G 665	The Ghoul Keepers	1961	Anthology	VGF		$8.00
PYRAMID	G 665	The Ghoul Keepers	1961	Anthology	VGF		$7.00
PYRAMID	G 665	The Ghoul Keepers	1961	Anthology	VG+		$5.00
PYRAMID	F 675	Basketball Stars Of 1962	1961	Mokray, W.G.	AF		$8.00
PYRAMID	F 675	Basketball Stars Of 1962	1961	Mokray, W.G.	VG		$3.00
PYRAMID	F 680	The Young Nurses	1961	Whittington, H.	VG+		$16.00 A
PYRAMID	F 680	The Young Nurses	1961	Whittington, H.	G-		$7.00
PYRAMID	F 688	The Hand Of Fu-Manchu	1962	Rohmer, S.	VGF		$6.00
PYRAMID	G 690	Crossword Puzzle Book #2	1962	Luzzatto, J.	VGF+		$28.00 A
PYRAMID	G 690	Crossword Puzzle Book #2	1962	Luzzatto, J.	VG		$10.00

Pyramid 480 VG+ $10   Pyramid 578 VG+ $42   Pyramid 617 VG $10   Pyramid 622 VG+ $8

PUBLISHER	PUB. #	TITLE	DATE	AUTHOR	COND.	TYPE	PRICE
PYRAMID	N 695	Japanese Inn	1962	Statler, O.	VG+		$6.00
PYRAMID	F 710	Baseball Stars Of 1962	1962	Robinson, R.	VG+		$5.00
PYRAMID	F 712	House Of Evil	1962	Trinian, J.	VGF		$11.00 A
PYRAMID	F 719	Private Eyeful	1962	Kane, H.	AF		$8.00
PYRAMID	R 736	The Music Man	1962	Wilson, M.	VGF	MTI	$6.00
PYRAMID	F 740	The Mark Of Fu Manchu	1962	Rohmer, S.	VGF		$6.00
PYRAMID	F 750	The Divorcees	1962	Martin, K.	AF		$7.00
PYRAMID	F 752	The Flesh	1962	Royer, L.C.	VGF		$7.00
PYRAMID	F 753	Five Weeks In A Balloon	1962	Verne, J.	VG+	MTI	$5.00
PYRAMID	F 760	Calling Dr. Dare-Kill	1962	Tupper, B.	VGF		$6.00
PYRAMID	F 774	Space Prison	1962	Godwin, T.	VG		$3.00
PYRAMID	F 782	The Hands Of Love	1962	Hutchins, M.	AF		$8.00
PYRAMID	R 787	Cleopatra	1962	Gardner, J.K.	VG+		$7.00
PYRAMID	F 804	The Drums Of Fu Manchu	1962	Rohmer, S.	VG		$4.00
PYRAMID	F 809	Swamp Girl	1962	Wall, E.	VG+		$8.00
PYRAMID	F 809	Swamp Girl	1962	Wall, E.	VGF		$7.00
PYRAMID	F 812	Power Of Positive Drinking	1963	Peel, N.L.	VGF		$7.00 A
PYRAMID	F 839	Bogey Men	1963	Bloch, R.	AF		$17.00 A
PYRAMID	F 839	Bogey Men	1963	Bloch, R.	VGF		$14.00
PYRAMID	F 841	Either Is Love	1963	Craigin, E.	AF		$7.00
PYRAMID	G 853	The Last Notch	1963	Gant, M.	VG+		$5.00
PYRAMID	F 861	By The She	1963	Hirsch, P., ed.	AF-		$14.00 A
PYRAMID	R 877	Two	1963	Jourdan, E.	VGF+		$7.00
PYRAMID	F 902	Fighting Generals	1963	Anthology	VGF		$6.00
PYRAMID	R 906	Dark Death	1963	Gilbert, A.	AF		$6.00
PYRAMID	F 914	Mister And Mistress	1963	Hirsch, P., ed.	VGF		$14.00 A
PYRAMID	R 942	Fifth Wife	1963	Gowen, V.	AF		$6.00
PYRAMID	F 945	Basketball Stars Of 1964	1964	Mokray, W.G.	VG		$6.00
PYRAMID	F 974	Sturgeon In Orbit	1964	Sturgeon, T.	VG		$6.00
PYRAMID	R 984	A Case For Mr Crook	1964	Gilbert, A.	AF		$6.00
PYRAMID	R 1003	The Trail Of Fu Manchu	1964	Rohmer, S.	F		$5.00
PYRAMID	R 1015	Ten Years To Doomsday	1964	Anderson, C.	AF		$8.00
PYRAMID	R 1041	After The Verdict	1964	Gilbert, A.	AF		$6.00
PYRAMID	R 1043	The Time Tunnel	1964	Leinster, M.	VG+		$7.00
PYRAMID	F 1044	Two On The Isle	1964	Hirsch, P., ed.	VGF		$7.00 A
PYRAMID	R 1068	Voyage To Bottom Of Sea (4th)	1967	Sturgeon, T.	VG	TVTI	$6.00
PYRAMID	R 1081	Fighting Marines	1964	Anthology	VG+		$7.00
PYRAMID	R 1085	A Rocket For The Toff	1964	Creasey, J.	AF		$5.00
PYRAMID	R 1086	The Toff In New York	1964	Creasey, J.	AF		$5.00
PYRAMID	R 1097	A Knife For The Toff	1964	Creasey, J.	F		$5.00
PYRAMID	R 1107	And Death Came Too	1964	Gilbert, A.	AF		$6.00
PYRAMID	F 1113	Laugh 'Til You Bust	1964	Hirsch, P., ed.	VGF+		$20.00 A
PYRAMID	R 1121	Leave It To The Toff	1965	Creasey, J.	F		$5.00
PYRAMID	R 1122	African Mistress	1965	Royer, L.C.	VG+		$7.00
PYRAMID	R 1125	Worlds Of The Weird	1965	Anthology	VGF		$8.00
PYRAMID	R 1134	Model For The Toff	1965	Creasey, J.	AF		$5.00
PYRAMID	R 1139	Tales In A Jugular Vein	1965	Bloch, R.	VG		$7.00
PYRAMID	R 1139	Tales In A Jugular Vein	1965	Bloch, R.	G		$5.00

Pyramid 680 VG+ $16   Pyramid 861 AF- $14   Pyramid 2482 VGF $15   Pyramid 3967 VG+ $8

PUBLISHER	PUB. #	TITLE	DATE	AUTHOR	COND.	TYPE	PRICE
PYRAMID	R 1150	Murder Comes Home	1965	Gilbert, A.	AF		$6.00
PYRAMID	R 1162	City Under The Sea	1965	Fairman, P.W.	AF	TVTI	$6.00
PYRAMID	R 1183	Space Lords	1965	Smith, C.	VGF		$5.00
PYRAMID	R 1192	The Spell Of Seven	1965	De Camp, L.S.	AF		$30.00 A
PYRAMID	R 1192	The Spell Of Seven	1965	De Camp, L.S.	VGF		$12.00
PYRAMID	R 1193	Fighting Aces	1965	Anthology	VGF		$6.00
PYRAMID	R 1194	Poison For The Toff	1965	Creasey, J.	F		$5.00
PYRAMID	R 1219	Great Spy Novels	1965	Anthology	VG		$5.00
PYRAMID	R 1229	The Addams Family	1965	Sharkey, J.	G	TVTI	$6.00
PYRAMID	R 1247	Skull Of The Marquis De Sade	1965	Bloch, R.	VGF+		$11.00
PYRAMID	R 1247	Skull Of The Marquis De Sade	1965	Bloch, R.	VG		$8.00
PYRAMID	R 1247	Skull Of The Marquis De Sade	1965	Bloch, R.	G		$4.00
PYRAMID	R 1257	The Addams Family Strikes Back	1965	Miksch, W.F.	G	TVTI	$7.00
PYRAMID	R 1258	A Question Of Murder	1965	Gilbert, A.	AF		$6.00
PYRAMID	R 1269	Out For The Kill	1965	Gilbert, A.	AF		$6.00
PYRAMID	R 1270	Paingod	1965	Ellison, H.	VGF		$15.00
PYRAMID	R 1270	Paingod	1965	Ellison, H.	VGF		$12.00
PYRAMID	R 1270	Paingod	1965	Ellison, H.	VG		$6.00
PYRAMID	T 1274	The Quiller Memorandum	1966	Hall, A.	AF		$6.00
PYRAMID	R 1291	Operation N	1966	Daniels, N.	VGF		$7.00
PYRAMID	R 1303	The Mask Of Fu Manchu	1966	Rohmer, S.	VGF		$6.00
PYRAMID	R 1339	Girl On The Prowl	1965	Fickling, G.G.	VG+	TVTI	$7.00
PYRAMID	R 1354	Bombshell	1965	Fickling, G.G.	VG	TVTI	$4.00
PYRAMID	R 1355	Dig A Dead Doll	1965	Fickling, G.G.	VG+	TVTI	$4.00
PYRAMID	R 1356	Girl On The Loose	1965	Fickling, G.G.	VG+	TVTI	$4.00
PYRAMID	R 1358	A Gun For Honey	1965	Fickling, G.G.	VG+	TVTI	$5.00
PYRAMID	R 1360	This Girl For Hire (5th)	1965	Fickling, G.G.	VG	TVTI	$4.00
PYRAMID	X 1466	The Warriors	1966	Yurik, S.	VG		$5.00
PYRAMID	R 1498	Treasury Of Terror	1966	Anthology	VG+		$10.00
PYRAMID	X 1586	The Legion Of Time	1967	Williamson, J.	VGF		$5.00
PYRAMID	X 1611	I Have No Mouth And Must Scream	1967	Ellison, H.	VG-		$5.00
PYRAMID	X 1634	The Cometeers	1967	Williamson, J.	VGF		$5.00
PYRAMID	X 1657	One Against The Legion	1967	Williamson, J.	VGF		$6.00
PYRAMID	R 1664	The Invaders	1967	Laumer, K.	VGF	TVTI	$8.00
PYRAMID	R 1664	The Invaders	1967	Laumer, K.	AF	TVTI	$7.00
PYRAMID	X 1679	Lost In Space	1967	Van Arnam, D.	VG	TVTI	$4.00
PYRAMID	X 1689	The Invaders #2	1967	Laumer, K.	AF	TVTI	$8.00
PYRAMID	R 1711	The Invaders #3	1967	Bernard, R.	VGF	TVTI	$8.00
PYRAMID	X 1730	The Butterfly Kid	1967	Anderson, C.	AF		$10.00 A
PYRAMID	X 1774	Re-Enter Fu Manchu	1968	Rohmer, S.	VG+		$6.00
PYRAMID	X 1790	Hooked	1968	Anthology	G-		$3.00
PYRAMID	X 1798	Wild In The Streets	1968	Thom, R.	VG+	MTI	$7.00
PYRAMID	X 1850	The Swimmer	1968	Perry, E.	AF	MTI	$7.00
PYRAMID	X 1863	With Six You Get Eggroll	1968	Bagni, G.	VG+	MTI	$7.00
PYRAMID	X 1889	Playback	1968	Chandler, R.	VG		$7.00
PYRAMID	X 1912	Great Stories Of Korean War	1968	Anthology	AF		$4.00
PYRAMID	X 1942	Survival	1969	Anthology	VG-		$5.00
PYRAMID	X 1996	Joanna	1969	Sarne, M.	F	MTI	$10.00

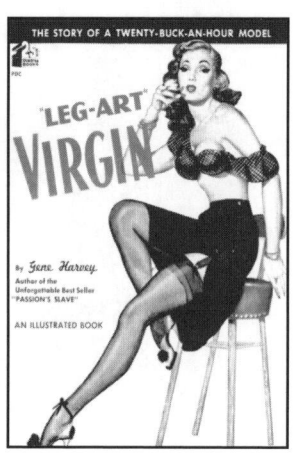

| Quarter Books 60 VG+ $30 | Quarter Books 74 AF- $108 | Quick Reader 121 VGF $44 |

PUBLISHER	PUB. #	TITLE	DATE	AUTHOR	COND.	TYPE	PRICE
PYRAMID	T 2002	Slaves	1969	Killens, J.O.	VG+	MTI	$4.00
PYRAMID	T 2009	Listen, White Man	1969	Anthology	G		$4.00
PYRAMID	T 2019	The Real 007	1969	Wharton, B.	VG-		$5.00
PYRAMID	T 2034	Eight Men	1969	Wright, R.	VG+		$7.00
PYRAMID	T 2048	Futures Unlimited	1969	Anthology	AF		$7.00
PYRAMID	T 2048	Futures Unlimited	1969	Anthology	VG+		$6.00
PYRAMID	X 2079	Mutiny In Space	1969	Davidson, A.	VGF		$5.00
PYRAMID	T 2084	Change Of Mind	1969	Stratton, C.	VG	MTI	$4.00
PYRAMID	T 2133	The Spell Of Seven	1969	Anthology	AF		$6.00
PYRAMID	X 2166	The Insidious Dr. Fu Manchu	1970	Rohmer, S.	VGF		$5.00
PYRAMID	T 2257	Blood On The Ivy	1970	Ellison, H.	AF		$10.00
PYRAMID	T 2259	Then Came Bronson #3	1970	Stratton, C.	VG+	TVTI	$7.00
PYRAMID	T 2264	The Comedians	1970	Thomey, T.	AF		$7.00
PYRAMID	V 2277	The Movement	1970	Garbo, N.	VG		$5.00
PYRAMID	X 2289	Ensicklopedia	1970	Simon, J., (ed.)	VGF		$5.00
PYRAMID	N 2384	The Necrophiles	1971	Gurney, D.	AF		$7.00
PYRAMID	T 2393	The Space Magicians	1971	Anthology	AF		$7.00
PYRAMID	T 2416	Ghostly By Gaslight	1971	Anthology	VGF		$7.00
PYRAMID	T 2466	The Yngling	1971	Dalmas, J.	AF		$5.00
PYRAMID	T 2482	Peter Max Paper Airplane Book	1971	Max, P.	VGF		$15.00
PYRAMID	T 2482	Peter Max Paper Airplane Book	1971	Max, P.	VG-		$7.00
PYRAMID	T 2638	I Have No Mouth And Must Scream	1972	Ellison, H.	VG+		$6.00
PYRAMID	N 3108	Charley Varrick	1973	Reese, J.	AF	MTI	$7.00
PYRAMID	V 3339	Mafia: Operation Hijack	1974	Romano, D.	VG		$6.00
PYRAMID	V 3444	Mafia: Operation Hitman	1974	Romano, D.	VG		$5.00
PYRAMID	N 3478	The Black Master (Shadow #2)	1974	Grant, M.*	VG		$7.00
PYRAMID	N 3554	The Shadow #3 (Signed)	1974	Grant, M.*	VG+		$15.00 A
PYRAMID	N 3554	The Shadow #3	1974	Grant, M.*	VG+		$8.00
PYRAMID	N 3557	Hands In The Dark (Shadow #4)	1975	Grant, M.*	VGF+		$12.00
PYRAMID	N 3597	The Shadow - Shadow #1, (3rd)	1975	Grant, M.*	VGF		$6.00
PYRAMID	N 3699	The Crime Cult (The Shadow #6)	1975	Grant, M.*	AF		$7.00
PYRAMID	N 3700	Double Z (The Shadow #5)	1975	Grant, M.*	VGF		$8.00
PYRAMID	A 3746	Weird Heroes #1	1975	Anthology	VG+		$6.00
PYRAMID	A 3791	The Other Glass Teat	1975	Ellison, H.	VGF+		$27.00 A
PYRAMID	M 3798	Love Ain't Nothing But . . .	1975	Ellison, H.	VG+		$16.00
PYRAMID	N 3875	The Red Menace (Shadow #7)	1975	Grant, M.*	VGF+		$9.00
PYRAMID	N 3875	The Red Menace (Shadow #7)	1975	Grant, M.*	VG		$5.00
PYRAMID	N 3876	Mox (The Shadow #8)	1975	Grant, M.*	AF		$11.00
PYRAMID	N 3876	Mox (The Shadow #8)	1975	Grant, M.*	VG		$7.00
PYRAMID	N 3877	The Romanoff Jewels (Shadow #9)	1975	Grant, M.*	VGF		$9.00
PYRAMID	N 3877	The Romanoff Jewels (Shadow #9)	1975	Grant, M.*	VG		$7.00
PYRAMID	V 3883	Spider Kiss	1975	Ellison, H.	VGF		$9.00 A
PYRAMID	V 3931	The Deadly Streets	1975	Ellison, H.	VGF		$14.00
PYRAMID	N 3966	The Silent Seven (Shadow #10)	1975	Grant, M.*	VGF		$9.00
PYRAMID	N 3967	Kings Of Crime (Shadow #11)	1976	Grant, M.*	VG+		$8.00

| Rainbow 111 AF $90 | Rainbow 121 VG $75 | Readers Choice 22 AF $50 |

PUBLISHER	PUB. #	TITLE	DATE	AUTHOR	COND.	TYPE	PRICE
PYRAMID	N 3968	Shadowed Millions (Shadow #12)	1976	Grant, M.*	VGF+		$9.00
PYRAMID	V 4030	The Drums Of Fu Manchu	1976	Rohmer, S.	AF		$6.00
PYRAMID	A 4034	Quest Of The Gypsy (W.H. #3)	1976	Goulart, R.	VGF		$7.00
PYRAMID	A 4035	Nightshade (Weird Heroes #4)	1976	Anthology	VG+		$4.00
PYRAMID	M 4037	Weird Heroes #6	1977	Anthology	VG		$6.00
PYRAMID	A 4044	Weird Heroes #2	1977	Anthology	VG+		$4.00
PYRAMID	V 4053	The Shadow Of Fu Manchu	1976	Rohmer, S.	AF		$6.00
PYRAMID	V 4205	Green Eyes (The Shadow #13)	1977	Grant, M.*	VG		$7.00
PYRAMID	V 4206	The Creeping Death (Shadow #14)	1977	Grant, M.*	VG		$7.00
PYRAMID	V 4207	Gray Fist (The Shadow #15)	1977	Grant, M.*	VGF+		$20.00 A
PYRAMID	V 4278	The Shadow's Shadow (#16)	1977	Grant, M.*	VGF		$20.00 A
PYRAMID	PR 11	The Moonstone	1958	Collins, W.	AF		$6.00
PYRAMID	PG 13	The Sky Block	1958	Frazee, S.	VG+		$5.00 A
PYRAMID	PR 15	The Lost World	1958	Doyle, A.C.	VG+		$7.00
PYRAMID FICTION ILLUST.	2	Starfawn	1976	Preiss, B.	VGF	Digest	$4.00
QUARTER BOOKS	19	Bed Time Girl	1949	Clayford, J.	VGF	Digest	$40.00
QUARTER BOOKS	22	Unfaithful!	1949	Gordon, L.	VG+	Digest	$27.00 A
QUARTER BOOKS	25	Wanted Dead Or Alive!	1949	Leinster, M.	VG	Digest	$20.00
QUARTER BOOKS	26	Respectable Harlot	1949	Clayford, J.	AF	Digest	$37.00 A
QUARTER BOOKS	29	Immoral!	1949	Gordon, L.	AF	Digest	$17.00 A
QUARTER BOOKS	32	Careless!	1949	Clayford, J.	VG	Digest	$16.00
QUARTER BOOKS	37	Love Cheat	1949	Gordon, L.	VG	Digest	$38.00 A
QUARTER BOOKS	39	Frenchy	1949	Bellamy, H.	VG	Digest	$17.00
QUARTER BOOKS	49	Affairs Of A Burlesque Queen	1949	Higgins, R.	VGF	Digest	$40.00 A
QUARTER BOOKS	51	Wild Passion	1949	Wright, W.E.	VGF	Digest	$40.00 A
QUARTER BOOKS	52	Three Naked Souls	1949	Sloane, R.	VG+	Digest	$14.00
QUARTER BOOKS	60	Room And Dame	1950	Foster, G.	VG+	Digest	$30.00 A
QUARTER BOOKS	62	Everybody Loves Irene	1950	Williams, W.	AF	Digest	$40.00 A
QUARTER BOOKS	63	One Night With Diane	1950	Jones, H.	G	Digest	$8.00
QUARTER BOOKS	65	Passionate Pick-Up	1950	Dupperault, D.	VGF	Digest	$45.00 A
QUARTER BOOKS	74	"Leg-Art" Virgin	1950	Harvey, G.	AF-	Digest	$108.00 A
QUARTER BOOKS	75	The Sins Of Allie-May	1950	Quandt, A.L.	VG	Digest	$15.00
QUARTER BOOKS	77	Red-Light Babe	1950	Duperrault, D.	VGF+	Digest	$21.00 A
QUARTER BOOKS	81	Fast, Loose And Lovely	1950	Bligh, N.	VG+	Digest	$40.00 A
QUARTER BOOKS	82	Illicit Pleasure	1950	Gaddis, P.	VGF	Digest	$23.00
QUARTER BOOKS	83	Four Men And A Dame	1951	Stonebraker, F.	VG	Digest	$16.00
QUARTER BOOKS	84	Born To Be Bad	1951	Bligh, N.	VG+	Digest	$24.00
QUARTER BOOKS	84	Born To Be Bad	1951	Bligh, N.	G	Digest	$6.00
QUARTER BOOKS	86	Girl On The Make	1951	Sherman, J.	VG+	Digest	$33.00 A
QUARTER BOOKS	93	Thrill Me - Suzy	1951	Sherman, J.	VG+	Digest	$14.00 A
QUICK READER	107	The Florentine Dagger	1943	Hecht, B.	VGF		$8.00 A
QUICK READER	108	Webster's Pocket Dictionary	1943		AF		$11.00 A
QUICK READER	108	Webster's Pocket Dictionary	1943		VG+		$8.00 A
QUICK READER	109	Bushido	1943	Pernikoff, A.	VGF		$12.00 A
QUICK READER	114	Crime And Punishment	1944	Dosytoyevsky, F.	VG		$10.00

Readers Choice 31 VG+ $17   Reader's League No# VG+ $22   Red Dagger 29 VG+ $10

PUBLISHER	PUB. #	TITLE	DATE	AUTHOR	COND.	TYPE	PRICE
QUICK READER	117	Count Bruga	1944	Hecht, B.	VGF		$13.00 A
QUICK READER	121	The Curve Of The Catenary	1944	Rinehart, M.R.	VGF		$44.00 A
QUICK READER	122	Wuthering Heights	1944	Bronte, E.	VG		$10.00
QUICK READER	127	Celebrated Stories Into Movies	1944	Anthology	VG+		$8.00 A
QUICK READER	128	Cat And Mouse	1944	Pentecost, H.	VG		$8.00
QUICK READER	132	I'll Be Glad When You're Dead	1945	Lyon, D.	VG+		$10.00 A
QUICK READER	136	Gulliver's Travels	1945	Swift, J.	VG+		$19.00 A
QUICK READER	137	Bedside Bedlam	1945	Anthology	VG+		$9.00 A
QUICK READER	139	One Side Please	1945	Anthology	AF		$17.00 A
QUICK READER	143	Great Comedies	1945	Anthology	VGF		$16.00 A
QUICK READER	145	The Dead Man's Tale	1945	Pentecost, H.	VG+		$15.00 A
QUICK READER	145	The Dead Man's Tale	1945	Pentecost, H.	VGF		$12.00 A
QUILL	3922	The Killer Inside Me	1984	Thompson, J.	AF		$10.00 A
R. & L. LOCKER	No#	Lady Throw Me A Curve	1950	Ross, G.	VG+	Digest	$25.00 A
R.W.	No# 1	The Vice Czar Murders	n/d	Charles, F.	VGF-	Digest	$28.00 A
RAINBOW	105	Four Dames Named "Sin"	1951	Reed, M.	AF	Digest	$33.00 A
RAINBOW	105	Four Dames Named "Sin"	1951	Reed, M.	G	Digest	$7.00
RAINBOW	111	Walk The Evil Street	1952	Wade, D.	AF	Digest	$90.00 A
RAINBOW	115	Carnival Of Passion	1952	Munroe, V.	VG	Digest	$20.00 A
RAINBOW	116	She Walks By Night	1952	Wade, D.	VG-	Digest	$9.00
RAINBOW	117	Bedroom In Hell	1952	Daniels, N.A.	VG	Digest	$22.00
RAINBOW	119	Joy Ride!	1952	Treat, R.	VG	Digest	$14.00
RAINBOW	119	Joy Ride!	1952	Treat, R.	G+	Digest	$12.00
RAINBOW	121	Seven Hungry Men!	1952	White, L.	VG	Digest	$75.00 A
RAINBOW	126	She-Devil	1952	Turner, R.	VGF	Digest	$37.00 A
RAINBOW (Colonial)	101	Complete Bedside Joke Book	1953	Stackman, H.	G+	Digest	$5.00
RAM	RC 545	The Underground Press	1969	Angleman, J.	VGF		$7.00
RAPTURE	103	God Of Lust	1964	Saxon, V.	AF		$20.00 A
RAPTURE	202	Hungry Virgin	1967	Weldon, R.	VG+		$40.00 A
RAPTURE	238	Sex Worshippers	1968	Laurence, J.	VGF		$12.00
RAVEN	705	Suddenly It's Sin	1962	Craig, D.W.	VG+		$10.00
READERS CHOICE	4	The Powder Burner	1950	Robertson, F.C.	VG+		$12.00 A
READERS CHOICE	7	Shoe The Wild Mare	1950	Fowler, G.	VG		$5.00 A
READERS CHOICE	8	Green Light For Death	1950	Kane, F.	VG		$10.00
READERS CHOICE	14	Trouble Shootin' Man	1950	Robertson, F.C.	VG+	Digest	$8.00
READERS CHOICE	16	Murder '97	1950	Gruber, F.	VGF	Digest	$22.00 A
READERS CHOICE	21	Don't Wait For Love	1950	Greig, M.	VG+	Digest	$16.00
READERS CHOICE	22	The Hussy	n/d	Grainger, B.	AF	Digest	$50.00
READERS CHOICE	27	Sinful Bargain	n/d	Valbeck, M.	AF	Digest	$50.00
READERS CHOICE	31	Farm Girl	1951	Lange, A.D.	VG+	Digest	$17.00 A
READERS CHOICE	35	Wild Oats	n/d	Rockey, H.	AF	Digest	$50.00
READERS CHOICE	36	Strange Love	1952	Glemser, B.	VGF	Digest	$23.00 A
READERS CHOICE	37	They Call It Sin	1952	Eagan, A.	VG		$7.00
READERS CHOICE	38	Death Is My Lover	1952	Brock, S.	VG		$7.00
READERS CHOICE	39	Lover Boy	1952	Hayden, E.R.	VG+		$12.00

| Red Seal 12 VGF $30 | Red Seal 24 VGF $19 | Regency RB-311 AF $33 | Saber 7 AF $109 |

PUBLISHER	PUB. #	TITLE	DATE	AUTHOR	COND.	TYPE	PRICE
READERS CHOICE	39	Lover Boy	1952	Hayden, E.R.	VGF		$8.00 A
READER'S LEAGUE	No#	PB Of American Short Stories	1943	Anthology	VG+		$11.00 A
READER'S LEAGUE	No#	Phantom Lady	1942	Irish, W.*	VG		$5.00 A
READER'S LEAGUE	No#	TCOT Substitute Face	1942	Gardner, E.S.	VGF		$13.00 A
READER'S LEAGUE	No#	The Four Of Hearts	1942	Queen, E.	VG+		$22.00 A
READER'S LEAGUE	No#	The PB Of Crossword Puzzles	1943	Petherbridge, M.	VG+		$24.00 A
READERS LIBRARY	No#	Weeping Is For Women	1940	Chidsey, D.B.	VG+	Digest	$15.00 A
RED CIRCLE	3	Leg Artist	1949	Harvey, G.	VGF		$58.00 A
RED CIRCLE	3	Leg Artist	1949	Harvey, G.	VG-		$15.00
RED CIRCLE	13	Carnival Of Love	1949	Scott, A.	VG		$15.00
RED DAGGER	23	Kill At Dusk	1946	Ketchum, P.	G+	Digest	$3.00
RED DAGGER	25	Murder From The Mind	1947	Laing, P.	G	Digest	$5.00
RED DAGGER	29	Blood On The Beach	1947	Holley, H.	VG+	Digest	$10.00 A
RED SEAL	9	This Woman	1952	Idell, A.	VGF		$14.00 A
RED SEAL	10	Naked In The Streets	1952	Johnson, R.	AF-		$10.00 A
RED SEAL	12	City of Women	1952	Morgan, N.	VGF		$30.00 A
RED SEAL	12	City Of Women	1952	Morgan, N.	VGF		$22.00
RED SEAL	13	The Sea Waifs	1952	Vail, J.	VG+		$7.00
RED SEAL	16	The Golden Sorrow	1952	Pratt, T.	VGF+		$11.00 A
RED SEAL	23	The Magnificent Moll	1952	Gonzales, J.	VGF		$13.00 A
RED SEAL	24	One For Hell	1952	Davis, J.M.	VGF		$19.00 A
RED SEAL	26	This Too, Is Love	1953	Ross, S.	VGF-		$15.00
RED SEAL	26	This Too, Is Love	1953	Ross, S.	VGF		$14.00 A
RED SEAL	27	Love Isn't For Now	1953	Vail, J.	AF		$16.00 A
RED SEAL	28	Mississippi Flame	1953	Johnson, R.	VGF		$12.00
RED SEAL	29	Fare Thee Well	1953	Spafford, R.	VG		$7.00
RED SEAL (MODERN AGE)	17	Daring Young Man (dust jkt.)	1937	Saroyan, W.	VG-		$8.00
RED SEAL (MODERN AGE)	21	Blood Of The Conquerors (dust jkt.)	1937	Fergusson, H.	VG		$9.00
RED SEAL (MODERN AGE)	37	Burton, Arabian Nights (dust jkt.)	1938	Downey, F.	VG+		$14.00
REED NIGHTSTAND	3015	More Than A Tango	1973	Holliday, D.	AF		$13.00 A
REED NIGHTSTAND	3023	The Tainted One	1973	Longman, M.*	VGF		$12.00 A
REGAL	RN 1132	A Trace Of Sin	1967	Bortell, E.	AF		$6.00
REGENCY	RB 101	Firebug	1961	Bloch, R.	VGF+		$32.00 A
REGENCY	RB 101	Firebug	1961	Bloch, R.	VG		$11.00 A
REGENCY	RB 106	Memos From Purgatory	1961	Ellison, H.	VG+		$62.00 A
REGENCY	RB 107	The Man Nobody Knows	1961	Traven, B.	AF		$44.00 A
REGENCY	RB 109	Weed	1961	Cooper, C.L.	VGF-		$82.00 A
REGENCY	RB 109	Weed	1961	Cooper, C.L.	VG+		$33.00 A
REGENCY	RB 110	Some Will Not Die	1961	Budrys, A.	AF		$50.00 A
REGENCY	RB 113	With The 11th Commandment	1962	Del Rey, L.	VG		$11.00 A
REGENCY	RB 114	Panic!	1962	Alexander, D.	G+		$5.00
REGENCY	RB 116	The Dark Messenger	1962	Cooper, C.L.	VG+		$22.00 A
REGENCY	RB 118	Fire And The Night	1962	Farmer, P.J.	VGF-		$25.00 A
REGENCY	RB 118	Fire And The Night	1962	Farmer, P.J.	VG+		$13.00 A
REGENCY	RB 301	Philosopher Of Evil	1962	Drummond, W.	AF-		$25.00 A
REGENCY	RC 308	Crimes And Chaos	1962	Davidson, A.	VG+		$16.00 A
REGENCY	RB 308	Crimes And Chaos	1962	Davidson, A.	VG		$10.00
REGENCY	RB 309	You Will Never Be The Same	1963	Smith, C.	VGF		$30.00 A

Rex Stout's Mystery 8 VG+ $17   Rocket Stories 1-2 VG+ $17   Romantic Novels No# F $25

PUBLISHER	PUB. #	TITLE	DATE	AUTHOR	COND.	TYPE	PRICE
REGENCY	RB 311	The Gilded Witch	1963	Webb, J.	AF		$33.00 A
REGENCY	RB 312	Women Of The Swastika	1963	Vetter, H.	VG+		$17.00 A
REGENCY	RB 316	Hack Number 777	1963	Bunin, E.	VGF		$7.00 A
REGENCY	RB 319	KKK	1963	Haas, B.	VGF		$20.00 A
REGENCY	RB 319	KKK	1963	Haas, B.	VGF		$13.00 A
REGENCY	RB 321	The Expatriates	1963	Reynolds, M.	VG+		$15.00 A
REGENCY	RB 324	No Law But Their Own	1963	Millard, J.	VGF		$11.00 A
REGENCY	RB 324	No Law But Their Own	1963	Millard, J.	AF		$10.00 A
REGENCY	RB 324	No Law But Their Own	1963	Millard, J.	G+		$5.00
RENDEZVOUS READER	RR 108	Strange Sin	1962	Robinson, G.D.	VGF		$7.00
RETAIL DISTRIBUTORS	No#	World's Champs	1958	Bromberg, L.	VG		$8.00
RETAIL DISTRIBUTORS	No#	World's Champs	1958	Bromberg, L.	VG+		$7.00
REX STOUT	1	Rex Stout's Myst. Quarterly	1945	Anthology	G	Digest	$6.00
REX STOUT	6	Rex Stout's Myst. 10/46	1946	Anthology	VGF+	Digest	$28.00 A
REX STOUT	6	Rex Stout's Myst. 10/46	1946	Anthology	VG+	Digest	$20.00 A
REX STOUT	8	Rex Stout's Myst. 5/47	1947	Anthology	VG+	Digest	$17.00 A
ROBERT EDWARDS	No#	48 Current Short Stories	n/d	Anthology	VG+	Digest	$16.00 A
ROBERTS & VINTNER	No#	Hell Of A Dame	1960	Janson, H.	VG-	Digest	$5.00
ROCKET STORIES	1 2	Rocket Stories 7/53	1953	Anthology	VG+	Digest	$17.00 A
ROMANTIC NOVELS	No#	Dance Hall Girl	1952	Lawrence, A.	G+	Digest	$12.00 A
ROMANTIC NOVELS	No#	The Loves Of A Harlot	1952	Brown, B.	F	Digest	$25.00 A
ROYAL GIANT	14	Matador	1953	Steen, M.	VGF		$10.00 A
ROYAL GIANT	18	Allan Quartermain	1953	Haggard, H.R.	VGF	DBL	$36.00 A
		King Solomon's Mines		Haggard, H.R.		MTI	
ROYAL GIANT	19	Trek East	1953	Mundy, T.	G		$6.00
ROYAL GIANT	20	High Priest Of California	1953	Willeford, C.	VG+	DBL	$150.00 A
		Full Moon		Mundy, T.			
ROYAL GIANT	20	High Priest Of California	1953	Willeford, C.	VG+	DBL	$123.00 A
ROYAL GIANT	20	High Priest Of California	1953	Willeford, C.	VG+	DBL	$109.00 A
ROYAL GIANT	20	High Priest Of California	1953	Willeford, C.	G	DBL	$42.00
ROYAL GIANT	22	Gozanga's Woman	1953	Jakes, J.	VG+	DBL	$19.00 A
		Affair In Araby		Mundy, T.			
ROYAL GIANT	27	Confessions Of A Psychiatrist	1954	Nixon, H.L.	VG	DBL	$14.00
		The Woman He Wanted		Winston, D.			
ROYAL GIANT	28	The Unnatural Son	1954	Twain, M.	VG+	DBL	$12.00
		A Connecticut Yankee in King Arthur's Court		Twain, M.			
ROYAL GIANT	28	The Unnatural Son	1954	Twain, M.	VG	DBL	$8.00
ROYAL GIANT	29	The Way Of All Flesh	1954	Butler, S.	VGF		$16.00 A
ROYAL LINE	RL 101	Love Queen's Remake	1964	Hunt, G.	AF		$12.00
ROYAL LINE	RL 105	The Twilight Lust	1965	Arden, V.	VG+		$7.00
ROYAL LINE	RL 109	Lust Be A Lady Tonight	1965	Marsh, S.	VGF		$7.00
SABER	SA 2	Karla	1957	Wade, V.	VG+		$7.00
SABER	SA 5	Love Princess	1958	Hitt, O.	VG		$8.00
SABER	SA 7	I Am A Lesbian	1958	Sela, L.	AF		$109.00 A
SABER	SA 7	I Am A Lesbian	1958	Sela, L.	VG+		$24.00 A

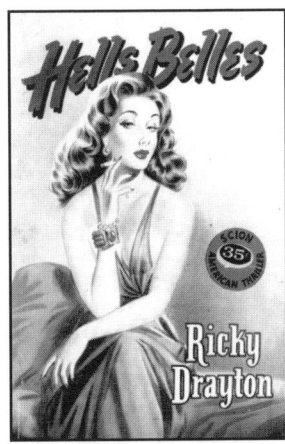

Royal Giant 14 VGF $10   Royal Giant 20 VG+ $150   Scion No# VGF $38

PUBLISHER	PUB. #	TITLE	DATE	AUTHOR	COND.	TYPE	PRICE
SABER	SA 7	I Am A Lesbian (2nd)	1959	Sela, L.	VGF		$34.00 A
SABER	SA 8	Never Enough	1958	Woolfe, B.	VG+		$8.00
SABER	SA 12	Deception	1959	Spruill, J.	AF		$10.00
SABER	SA 13	Camera Bait	1960	Sela, L.	AF		$12.00
SABER	SA 13	Camera Bait	1960	Sela, L.	VG+		$10.00
SABER	SA 14	The Right Bed	1959	Walters, L.	VG		$7.00
SABER	SA 17	Ruthless Fraternity	1960	Marmor, A.	VG+		$8.00
SABER	SA 19	The Odd Switch	1961	Parker, L.	VG+		$8.00
SABER	SA 22	Two Of A Kind	1962	Hampton, B.	VGF		$10.00
SABER	SA 23	Hutch Creek Girl	1962	Gooch, M.S.	VG		$8.00
SABER	SA 25	The Way Of The Flesh (3rd)	1965	Wayne, C.	VGF+		$8.00
SABER	SA 49	The Women Were Willing	1963	Abbott, S.	F		$12.00 A
SABER	SA 54	Strands Of Lust	1964	Woolfe, B.	VGF		$8.00
SABER	SA 56	We Poor Sinners	1964	Devon, J.	VGF		$8.00
SABER	SA 58	House Of The Damned	1964	Harvey, J.	AF		$10.00
SABER	SA 63	Sexmates	1964	Weldon, R.	VGF		$10.00
SABER	SA 66	She Offered Her Body	1964	Moore, J.	AF		$10.00
SABER	SA 86	Pay Off The Damned	1965	DiSpaldo, A.	VG+		$7.00
SABER	SA 89	Woman In The Window	1965	Moore, J.	VGF+		$19.00 A
SABER	SA 90	Immorality In Three Dimensions	1965	Palmer, D.	F		$10.00
SABER	SA 94	In Rooms Of Sin	1965	Madigan, K.	VG+		$7.00
SABER	SA 95	Switch Partners	1964	Harris, F.G.	AF		$20.00 A
SABER	SA 98	Lust Empire	1965	Vaughan, R.	AF		$12.00 A
SABER	SA 101	Country Sinners	1965	Parker, B.L.	VGF		$9.00
SABER	SA 102	Stacy	1965	Summers, E.	AF		$10.00
SABER	SA 103	The Devil's Wrath	1965	Lucas, M.	VG+		$8.00
SABER	SA 104	Confessions Of A Woman Immoral	1965	Vanson, B.	F		$22.00 A
SABER	SA 105	Her Soul Went First	1965	Moore, J.	AF		$15.00 A
SABER	SA 106	Youth Against Obscenity	1965	Nevins, R.	VGF+		$11.00 A
SABER	SA 110	School Of The Damned	1967	Lucas, M.	AF		$10.00
SABER	SA 119	Offbeat Love	1968	Lucas, M.	AF		$12.00 A
SABER	SA 122	Sex By Appointment	1968	Koby, D.	VG+		$7.00
SABER	SA 123	It's Orgy Time!	1968	Palmer, D.	AF		$15.00 A
SABER	SA 124	Sinner's Paradise	1969	Reed, T.	VG+		$8.00
SABER	SA 127	Sex Among Searchers	1968	Craig, S.	VG		$6.00
SABER	SA 129	Patterns Of Lust	1968	Reed, T.	AF		$12.00 A
SABER	SA 135	Swingers In Danger	1968	Palmer, D.	AF		$14.00
SABER	SA 139	Expensive Passions	1968	Nelms, P.	AF		$11.00 A
SABER	SA 146	The Swap Set	1969	Harris, F.G.	F		$9.00 A
SABER	SA 149	So Wild The Flesh	1969	Corbin, M.	VGF		$7.00
SABER	SA 156	The Unwilling Switchers	1969	Martin, A.	AF		$9.00 A
SABER	SA 183	Rude Awakening	1970	Elwood, P.	VG+		$17.00 A
SABER	SA 240	Halls Of MacIverson	1972	Overton, J.	VG+		$8.00
SABER	SA 278	The Champ And The Star	1972	Dee, D.	VGF		$7.00
SABER	SAR 4	Naked Return	1963	McIntosh, G.	VG+		$7.00

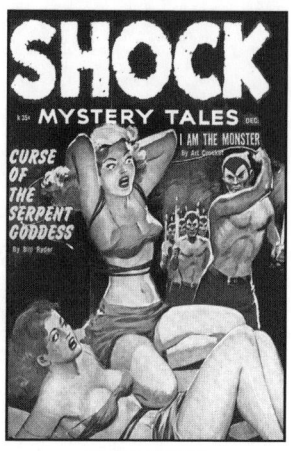

Scion No# VG+ $32　　　Samuel Lowe No# VGF $24　　　Shock 2-1 AF $82

PUBLISHER	PUB. #	TITLE	DATE	AUTHOR	COND.	TYPE	PRICE
SABER READER	1 1	Call Girl	1963	Lewis, B.	VGF		$11.00 A
SABER READER	2 1	Saber Reader 2-1	1963	Anthology	AF	DBL	$31.00 A
SABER TROPIC*		*See TROPIC					
SAINT DET./MYST. MAG.	1 4	The Saint Detective Mag. 10/53	1953	Anthology	VGF	Digest	$8.00
SAINT DET./MYST. MAG.	1 5	The Saint Detective Mag. 1/54	1954	Anthology	VG+	Digest	$8.00
SAINT DET./MYST. MAG.	2 2	The Saint Detective Mag. 7/54	1954	Anthology	VG+	Digest	$8.00
SAINT DET./MYST. MAG.	6 2	The Saint Detective Mag. 8/56	1956	Anthology	AF	Digest	$8.00
SAINT DET./MYST. MAG.	17 1	The Saint Mystery Mag. 7/62	1962	Anthology	AF	Digest	$10.00
SAINT DET./MYST. MAG.	18 5	The Saint Mystery Mag. 5/63	1963	Anthology	VG	Digest	$7.00
SAINT DET./MYST. MAG.	20 3	The Saint Mystery Mag. 3/64	1964	Anthology	AF	Digest	$7.00
SAINT DET./MYST. MAG.	21 2	The Saint Mystery Mag. 9/64	1964	Anthology	VG+	Digest	$8.00
SAINT DET./MYST. MAG.	25 6	The Saint Mystery Mag. 10/67	1967	Anthology	VG+	Digest	$5.00
SAINT MYSTERY LIBRARY	119	Witness To Death	1959	Brown, W.	VG+		$12.00
SAINT MYSTERY LIBRARY	120	Murder Set To Music	1959	Brown, F.	VG+		$13.00
SAINT MYSTERY LIBRARY	120	Murder Set To Music	1959	Brown, F.	VG		$7.00
SAINT MYSTERY LIBRARY	121	The Frightened Millionaire	1959	Rice, C.	VGF		$8.00
SAINT MYSTERY LIBRARY	122	Murder Made In Moscow	1959	Anthology	VG+		$8.00
SAINT MYSTERY LIBRARY	124	Death Stops At Tourist Camp	1959	Ford, L.	VG		$5.00
SAINT MYSTERY LIBRARY	127	Murder Seeks An Agent	1960	Brown, W.	VG+		$8.00
SAINT MYSTERY LIBRARY	127	Murder Seeks An Agent	1960	Brown, W.	VG		$7.00
SAINT NOVEL	K 101	The Saint Steps In	1963	Charteris, L.	AF	TVTI	$12.00
SAINT NOVEL	K 104	The Avenging Saint	1964	Charteris, L.	VGF	TVTI	$7.00
SAINT NOVEL	K 107	Enter The Saint	1964	Charteris, L.	VG+	TVTI	$4.00
SAINT NOVEL	K 110	Alias The Saint	1964	Charteris, L.	VGF	TVTI	$8.00
SAINT NOVEL	K 113	The Saint vs. Scotland Yard	1964	Charteris, L.	VG	TVTI	$5.00
SAINT NOVEL	K 114	The Saint And Mr. Teal	1964	Charteris, L.	VG+	TVTI	$7.00
SAMUEL LOWE	No#	Stories From Dickens	1948	Thorndike, R.P.	VGF	Digest	$11.00
SAMUEL LOWE	No#	Stories From Scott	1948	Thorndike, R.P.	VGF	Digest	$8.00
SAMUEL LOWE	No#	The Vanishing Redhead	1948	Anonymous	VGF	Digest	$24.00 A
SATAN PRESS	104	The Seeker	1965	Trainer, R.	AF		$16.00
SATAN PRESS	107	Black Water Nymph	1965	Morgan, H.	AF		$18.00 A
SATAN PRESS	107	Black Water Nymph	1965	Morgan, H.	AF		$14.00
SATAN PRESS	111	Just For Kicks	1965	Powell, D.	AF		$16.00 A
SATAN PRESS	122	Sexpionage	1966	Woods, J.	VGF		$22.00
SATELLITE	1 2	Satellite Sci-Fi - 12/56	1956	Anthology	AF	Digest	$10.00
SATELLITE	2 5	Satellite Sci-Fi - 6/58	1958	Anthology	VGF	Digest	$6.00
SCHOLASTIC	T 782	The Great Doctors (2nd)	1971	Silverberg, R.	VG+		$3.00
SCHOLASTIC	TK 2227	Silent Running	1972	Thompson, H.	VGF	MTI	$8.00
SCHOLASTIC	TK 2227	Silent Running	1972	Thompson, H.	VG+	MTI	$8.00
SCIENCE-FANTASY	2 4	Science-Fantasy Spring 1952	1952	Anthology	VG	Digest	$7.00
SCIENCE-FANTASY	2 5	Science-Fantasy Autumn 1952	1952	Anthology	VG	Digest	$7.00
SCI-FI ADV. (Royal)	1 2	Sci-Fi Adventures - 2/57	1957	Anthology	VGF	Digest	$8.00
SCI-FI ADVENTURES	1 1	Sci-Fi Adventures - 11/52	1952	Anthology	VGF	Digest	$8.00
SCI-FI ADVENTURES	1 2	Sci-Fi Adventures - 2/57	1957	Anthology	VG	Digest	$6.00
SCI-FI ADVENTURES	1 6	Sci-Fi Adventures - 12/56	1956	Anthology	VGF	Digest	$8.00

Signet 690 VG+ $20   Signet 726 VG+ $10   Signet 756 VG+ $20   Signet 768 VG+ $20

PUBLISHER	PUB. #	TITLE	DATE	AUTHOR	COND.	TYPE	PRICE
SCI-FI DIGEST	1 1	Science Fiction Digest	1954	Anthology	VG+	Digest	$7.00
SCI-FI FORTNIGHTLY	3	Gold Men Of Aureus	1951	Sheldon, R.	VG	Digest	$20.00 A
SCI-FI STORIES	1	Science Fiction Stories #1	1953	Anthology	VGF	Digest	$18.00 A
SCI-FI STORIES	2	Science Fiction Stories #2	1954	Anthology	VG	Digest	$10.00
SCION	No#	A Dame Doles Death	n/d	Perrelli, N.	VGF	Digest	$38.00 A
SCION	No#	Hell's Belles	1953	Drayton, R.	VGF	Digest	$38.00 A
SCION	No#	Jittery Dame	1953	Vogel, H.	VG+	Digest	$25.00 A
SCION	No#	Killer Bait	1953	Linton, D.	VG	Digest	$35.00 A
SCION	No#	Magnetic Brain	1953	Gridban, V.	VGF-	Digest	$22.00 A
SCION	No#	Moons For Sale	1953	Gridban, V.	VG+	Digest	$16.00 A
SCION	No#	Some Get It	1953	Shannon, B.	VG	Digest	$44.00 A
SCION	No#	The Red Insects	1951	Statten, V.	VG+	Digest	$32.00 A
SCION	No#	The Sun Makers	1950	Statten, V.	VG+	Digest	$11.00 A
SCION	No#	Was She Poison	1953	Linton, D.	VGF-	Digest	$44.00 A
SCORPION	103	Hollywood Nymph	1964	Rivers, S.	VG		$13.00 A
SCORPION	108	Nobody Loves A Tramp	1964	Blake, A.	VG+		$9.00 A
THE SEVEN SEAS	1 1	The Seven Seas - Winter 1953	1953	Anthology	AF	Digest	$22.00 A
THE SEVEN SEAS	1 1	The Seven Seas - Winter 1953	1953	Anthology	VG	Digest	$8.00
THE SHADOW	48 3	The Shadow - 11/44	1944	Anthology	VG+	Digest	$38.00 A
THE SHADOW	49 3	The Shadow - 5/45	1945	Anthology	VG+	Digest	$32.00 A
THE SHADOW	49 5	The Shadow - 7/45	1945	Anthology	VG+	Digest	$29.00 A
THE SHADOW	50 1	The Shadow - 9/45	1945	Anthology	VG+	Digest	$45.00 A
THE SHADOW	50 5	The Shadow - 1/46	1946	Anthology	VG+	Digest	$40.00 A
THE SHADOW	51 1	The Shadow - 3/46	1946	Anthology	VG+	Digest	$56.00 A
THE SHADOW	52 4	The Shadow - 12/46	1946	Anthology	VGF	Digest	$57.00
THE SHADOW	52 5	The Shadow - 1/47	1947	Anthology	G-	Digest	$14.00
THE SHADOW	53 5	Shadow Mystery - Dec./Jan. 1948	1948	Anthology	VG	Digest	$40.00 A
SHELL SCOTT	1 1	Shell Scott Myst. Mag. 2/66	1966	Anthology	VG	Digest	$8.00
SHELL SCOTT	1 1	Shell Scott Myst. Mag. 2/66	1966	Anthology	VG+	Digest	$10.00
SHELL SCOTT	1 2	Shell Scott Myst. Mag. 3/66	1966	Anthology	VGF	Digest	$10.00
SHELL SCOTT	1 4	Shell Scott Myst. Mag. 5/66	1966	Anthology	VG	Digest	$10.00
SHOCK	1 1	Shock 5/60	1960	Anthology	AF	Digest	$24.00 A
SHOCK	2 1	Shock Mystery Tales - 12/61	1961	Anthology	AF	Digest	$82.00 A
SHOCK	2 4	Shock Mystery Tales - 7/62	1962	Anthology	AF	Digest	$83.00 A
SHORT STORIES	1990	Short Stories - 10/53	1953	Anthology	VG+	Digest	$9.00
SHORT STORIES	1992	Short Stories - 12/53	1953	Anthology	VGF+	Digest	$20.00 A
SHORT STORIES	1997	Short Stories - 7/54	1954	Anthology	VG+	Digest	$10.00
SHORT STORIES	2010	Short Stories - 12/57	1957	Anthology	VGF+	Digest	$9.00 A
SHORT STORIES	2013	Short Stories - 6/58	1958	Anthology	VGF+	Digest	$10.00
SHREWESBURY	No#	The Murders In The Rue Morgue	n/d	Poe, E.A.	VG+		$6.00
SIGNET	647	Uncle Tom's Children	1949	Wright, R.	VGF		$6.00 A
SIGNET	667	The Pinkerton Case Book	1948	Hynd, A.	VGF		$8.00 A
SIGNET	668	The Dim View	1948	Heatter, B.	VG		$4.00
SIGNET	670	They Shoot Horses, Don't They?	1948	McCoy, H.	VGF		$18.00 A
SIGNET	670	They Shoot Horses, Don't They?	1948	McCoy, H.	VG+		$14.00
SIGNET	677	Guilty Bystander	1948	Miller, W.	VG		$6.00
SIGNET	680	Past All Dishonor (6th)	1949	Cain, J.M.	VGF		$7.00
SIGNET	683	The Lost Weekend	1948	Jackson, C.	AF		$11.00 A

Signet 769 VGF $40   Signet 981 AF- $11   Signet 1076 VGF $27   Signet 1131 VGF $76

PUBLISHER	PUB. #	TITLE	DATE	AUTHOR	COND.	TYPE	PRICE
SIGNET	690	No Pockets In A Shroud	1948	McCoy, H.	VG+		$20.00
SIGNET	696	The Snake Pit (2nd)	1948	Ward, M.J.	VGF	MTI	$7.00
SIGNET	699	I, The Jury (5th)	1949	Spillane, M.	AF		$8.00
SIGNET	705	A Woman In The House (3rd)	1949	Caldwell, E.	VGF		$6.00
SIGNET	707	The Honest Dealer	1949	Gruber, F.	VG+		$10.00
SIGNET	715	The Fall Of Valor	1949	Jackson, C.	VGF		$10.00
SIGNET	720	The Butterfly	1949	Cain, J.M.	AF		$13.00
SIGNET	720	The Butterfly	1949	Cain, J.M.	VG+		$9.00
SIGNET	720	The Butterfly (3rd)	1949	Cain, J.M.	VGF		$8.00
SIGNET	722	Uneasy Street	1949	Miller, W.	G+		$4.00
SIGNET	726	The Whispering Master	1949	Gruber, F.	VG+		$10.00
SIGNET	726	The Whispering Master	1949	Gruber, F.	VG-		$6.00
SIGNET	729	Stranger In Town (4th)	1949	Hunt, H.	VGF		$7.00
SIGNET	730	The Body In The Bed (3rd)	1949	Ballinger, B.S.	VGF		$7.00
SIGNET	734	Meet The Girls (3rd)	1949	Farrell, J.T.	VG+		$5.00
SIGNET	736	Draw The Curtain Close	1949	Dewey, T.B.	AF		$25.00 A
SIGNET	738	Nightmare Alley	1949	Gresham, W.L.	AF-		$27.00 A
SIGNET	738	Nightmare Alley	1949	Gresham, W.L.	G		$4.00
SIGNET	738	Nightmare Alley (3rd)	1950	Gresham, W.L.	G		$6.00
SIGNET	748	Mistress Glory (2nd)	1949	Morley, S.	AF		$8.00
SIGNET	754	Kiss Tomorrow Good-Bye	1949	McCoy, H.	VGF		$55.00 A
SIGNET	754	Kiss Tomorrow Good-Bye	1949	McCoy, H.	AF		$26.00 A
SIGNET	754	Kiss Tomorrow Good-Bye	1949	McCoy, H.	VG+		$20.00 A
SIGNET	755	An American Tragedy	1949	Dreiser, T.	VGF		$7.00
SIGNET	756	If He Hollers Let Him Go	1949	Himes, C.B.	VG+		$20.00 A
SIGNET	759	Everybody Does It	1949	Cain, J.M.	AF	MTI	$57.00 A
SIGNET	761	Country Place	1950	Petry, A.	VGF		$8.00
SIGNET	765	Murder All Over	1950	Adams, C.F.	VG+		$8.00
SIGNET	766	Appointment In Samarra	1950	O'Hara, J.	VG		$7.00
SIGNET	768	Dark Encounter	1950	Hunt, H.	VG+		$20.00 A
SIGNET	769	Margaret	1950	Slade, C.	VGF		$40.00 A
SIGNET	773	The City And The Pillar	1950	Vidal, G.	VGF		$7.00
SIGNET	781	The Outer Edges	1950	Jackson, C.	G+		$6.00
SIGNET	784	Double Indemnity	1950	Cain, J.M.	VG		$10.00
SIGNET	791	My Gun Is Quick (31st)	1955	Spillane, M.	G		$2.00
SIGNET	802	Knock On Any Door	1950	Motley, W.	VG		$7.00
SIGNET	811	The Moth	1950	Cain, J.M.	VGF		$10.00
SIGNET	811	The Moth (4th)	1951	Cain, J.M.	AF		$8.00
SIGNET	812	Beyond The Moon	1950	Hamilton, E.	VGF		$7.00
SIGNET	827	A Job Of Murder	1950	Gruber, F.	VG		$8.00
SIGNET	830	Night Unto Night	1950	Wylie, P.	VG+		$7.00
SIGNET	833	The Flesh Was Cold	1951	Fischer, B.	VG		$10.00
SIGNET	839	Limbo Tower	1951	Gresham, W.L.	VG		$6.00
SIGNET	839	Limbo Tower	1951	Gresham, W.L.	G+		$5.00
SIGNET	840	The Sheltering Sky	1951	Bowles, P.	VGF		$8.00
SIGNET	841	Black Boy	1951	Wright, R.	VGF		$15.00
SIGNET	855	The Snow Was Black	1951	Simenon, G.	VGF		$8.00 A
SIGNET	857	Meg	1951	Keogh, T.	VG+		$5.00 A

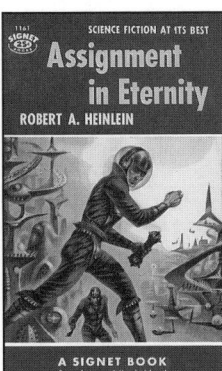

| Signet 1151 AF $8 | Signet 1161 VGF $8 | Signet 1185 AF $8 | Signet 1216 AF $30 |

PUBLISHER	PUB. #	TITLE	DATE	AUTHOR	COND.	TYPE	PRICE
SIGNET	879	No Luck For A Lady	1951	Mahannah, F.	VG		$6.00
SIGNET	884	I Should Have Stayed Home	1951	McCoy, H.	VG		$12.00
SIGNET	884	I Should Have Stayed Home	1951	McCoy, H.	VG-		$12.00
SIGNET	892	The Silent Dust	1951	Fischer, B.	VG+		$11.00 A
SIGNET	892	The Silent Dust	1951	Fischer, B.	VGF		$8.00 A
SIGNET	894	Cornbread Aristocrat (2nd)	1952	Garner, C.	VGF		$7.00
SIGNET	902	Contraband	1951	Adams, C.F.	VGF		$19.00 A
SIGNET	902	Contraband	1951	Adams, C.F.	G		$7.00
SIGNET	908	Murder Charge	1951	Miller, W.	G		$5.00
SIGNET	909	Butcher's Dozen	1952	Martin, J.B.	VGF+		$20.00 A
SIGNET	915	The Big Kill	1951	Spillane, M.	VG		$8.00
SIGNET	919	The Delicate Prey	1952	Bowles, P.	VG+		$5.00
SIGNET	928	Deadly Weapon	1952	Miller, W.	VGF+		$6.00 A
SIGNET	936	Sabotage	1952	Adams, C.F.	VG+		$8.00
SIGNET	942	Pressure	1952	Coe, C.F.	AF		$13.00 A
SIGNET	942	Pressure	1952	Coe, C.F.	VG+		$8.00
SIGNET	949	The Kiss-Off	1952	Heyes, D.	AF		$20.00 A
SIGNET	950	Only the Dead Know Brooklyn	1952	Wolfe, T.	VG+		$7.00
SIGNET	959	The Revolt Of Mamie Stover (11th)	1956	Huie, W.B.	VGF	MTI	$11.00 A
SIGNET	959	The Revolt Of Mamie Stover (7th)	1956	Huie, W.B.	VG	MTI	$7.00
SIGNET	974	Who Walk In Darkness	1952	Brossard, C.	VG+		$7.00
SIGNET	976	The Temptress	1952	Marshall, R.	AF		$7.00
SIGNET	977	The Unvanquished	1952	Faulkner, W.	AF		$7.00
SIGNET	981	The Lonely Hearts Murders	1952	Brown, W.	AF-		$11.00 A
SIGNET	988	Stripped For Murder	1953	Fischer, B.	VG		$10.00
SIGNET	993	Act Of Passion	1953	Simenon, G.	VG		$5.00
SIGNET	1000	Kiss Me, Deadly	1953	Spillane, M.	VG+		$12.00
SIGNET	1000	Kiss Me, Deadly	1953	Spillane, M.	VG-		$5.00
SIGNET	1001	The Catcher In The Rye	1953	Salinger, J.D.	VGF		$12.00
SIGNET	1001	The Catcher In The Rye	1953	Salinger, J.D.	VG+		$10.00
SIGNET	1015	The Song Of The Whip	1953	Evans, E.	AF		$8.00
SIGNET	S 1017	Scalpel	1953	McCoy, H.	VG-		$5.00
SIGNET	1020	The Grass Harp	1953	Capote, T.	VGF		$8.00
SIGNET	1027	The Devil's Passkey	1953	Shannon, J.	AF		$13.00 A
SIGNET	1027	The Devil's Passkey	1953	Shannon, J.	VGF		$8.00
SIGNET	1033	My Life In Crime	1953	Martin, J.B.	VG+		$7.00
SIGNET	1034	I Take This Woman	1953	Simenon, G.	VG		$6.00
SIGNET	1035	To End The Night	1953	Gaby, A.	VGF		$7.00
SIGNET	1044	Tomorrow, The Stars	1953	Anthology	VGF		$5.00
SIGNET	1050	Pistol Pete	1953	Eaton, F.	VGF		$6.00
SIGNET	1056	The Mistress	1953	Branner, H.C.	AF		$8.00
SIGNET	1057	No Head For Her Pillow	1953	Taylor, S.S.	VGF		$8.00
SIGNET	1060	Riddle Me This	1953	Roscoe, M.	VGF+		$22.00 A
SIGNET	1060	Riddle Me This	1953	Roscoe, M.	VG+		$10.00
SIGNET	1064	The Descent	1953	Peters, F.	AF		$6.00
SIGNET	1076	The Big Sin	1953	Webb, J.	VGF		$27.00 A
SIGNET	1084	Deadlier Than The Male	1953	Gunn, J.	VG		$5.00
SIGNET	1088	Young Man With A Horn	1953	Baker, D.	VG		$7.00

Signet 1225 VGF $12　　　Signet 1256 VGF $20　　　Signet 1276 VGF $11　　　Signet 1310 AF $67

PUBLISHER	PUB. #	TITLE	DATE	AUTHOR	COND.	TYPE	PRICE
SIGNET	1089	Guilty Bystander	1954	Miller, W.	VGF		$6.00 A
SIGNET	1092	It Depends On What You Mean...	1954	Monsarrat, N.	AF		$7.00
SIGNET	S 1094	Amazon Head Hunters	1954	Cotlow, L.	VGF+		$7.00
SIGNET	1103	The Sunburned Corpse	1954	Knight, A.	VG+		$7.00
SIGNET	1112	The Double Shuffle	1954	Chase, J.H.	VG+		$7.00
SIGNET	1112	The Double Shuffle	1954	Chase, J.H.	VG		$6.00
SIGNET	1119	Murder, Madness And The Law	1954	Cohen, L.H.	AF		$10.00 A
SIGNET	1119	Murder, Madness And The Law	1954	Cohen, L.H.	VGF		$8.00
SIGNET	S 1123	The Street	1954	Petry, A.	AF		$10.00
SIGNET	1124	Belle	1954	Simenon, G.	F		$20.00
SIGNET	1124	Belle	1954	Simenon, G.	VGF		$12.00
SIGNET	1124	Belle	1954	Simenon, G.	VG+		$10.00
SIGNET	1129	Pajama	1954	Bissell, R.	AF		$7.00
SIGNET	S 1131	Cancel All Our Vows	1955	MacDonald, J.D.	VGF		$76.00 A
SIGNET	S 1148	The Wild Palms / The Old Man	1954	Faulkner, W.	VGF	DBL	$7.00
SIGNET	1149	The Naked Angel	1955	Webb, J.	VG		$7.00
SIGNET	1151	Mafia	1954	Reid, E.	AF		$8.00 A
SIGNET	1151	Mafia	1954	Reid, E.	VGF		$8.00
SIGNET	1152	Galatea	1954	Cain, J.M.	F		$16.00 A
SIGNET	1159	The Scattered Seed	1954	Engstrand, S.	VG		$5.00
SIGNET	1161	Assignment In Eternity	1954	Heinlein, R.A.	VGF		$8.00 A
SIGNET	1172	A Private Stair	1955	Loughlin, D.	VG+		$7.00
SIGNET	1173	The Spider In The Cup	1955	Hales, N.	VGF		$5.00
SIGNET	1180	Fatal Step	1955	Miller, W.	G		$5.00
SIGNET	1185	Room Clerk	1955	Gold, H.	AF		$8.00
SIGNET	1188	The Strangled Stripper	1955	Simenon, G.	VGF		$27.00 A
SIGNET	1193	River In My Blood	1955	Bissell, R.	VG		$6.00
SIGNET	1196	Mean As Hell	1955	Harkey, D.	AF		$8.00
SIGNET	S 1215	Lost Island	1955	McInnis, G.	VG		$3.00
SIGNET	1216	Slice Of Hell	1955	Roscoe, M.	AF		$30.00 A
SIGNET	1216	Slice Of Hell	1955	Roscoe, M.	VG		$6.00
SIGNET	1225	The Last Kill	1955	Wells, C.	VGF		$12.00
SIGNET	1225	The Last Kill	1955	Wells, C.	VGF		$9.00 A
SIGNET	D 1229	Moby Dick	1955	Melville, H.	VGF	MTI	$7.00
SIGNET	1233	The Damned Lovely	1955	Webb, J.	VG		$6.00
SIGNET	1235	Killer's Choice	1955	Miller, W.	AF		$10.00
SIGNET	1241	To Find A Killer	1955	White, L.	VG+		$7.00
SIGNET	1241	To Find A Killer	1955	White, L.	VG-		$6.00
SIGNET	1241	To Find A Killer	1955	White, L.	G		$5.00
SIGNET	1243	The Body In The Bed	1955	Ballinger, B.S.	VG+		$6.00
SIGNET	S 1245	Satchmo	1955	Armstrong, L.	VG+		$18.00
SIGNET	1247	So Cold, My Bed	1955	Taylor, S.S.	VG+		$15.00
SIGNET	1248	Insector Maigret And The Killers	1955	Simenon, G.	VGF		$20.00 A
SIGNET	S 1252	Goodbye To Berlin (3rd)	1956	Isherwood, C.	AF	MTI	$7.00
SIGNET	1255	The Unholy Three	1955	Auchincloss, L.	VGF		$10.00
SIGNET	1256	The Bleeding Scissors	1955	Fischer, B.	VGF		$20.00
SIGNET	1267	Margaret	1956	Slade, C.	VG		$10.00
SIGNET	1267	Margaret	1956	Slade, C.	VG		$10.00

  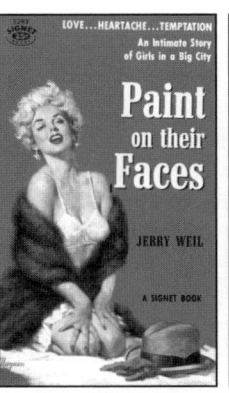 

Signet 1316 VGF $10   Signet 1368 VGF- $23   Signet 1393 VG+ $15   Signet 1399 AF $20

PUBLISHER	PUB. #	TITLE	DATE	AUTHOR	COND.	TYPE	PRICE
SIGNET	1268	Stopover For Murder	1956	Mahannah, F.	VG-		$7.00
SIGNET	1270	Calamity Fair	1956	Miller, W.	G		$5.00
SIGNET	1276	I'll Kill You Next	1956	Knight, A.	VGF		$11.00 A
SIGNET	S 1282	I, Robot	1956	Asimov, I.	VG+		$6.00
SIGNET	1286	The Big Steal	1956	Basinsky, E.	VG+		$10.00
SIGNET	1286	The Big Steal	1956	Basinsky, E.	VG+		$8.00
SIGNET	1301	The Secret Of Mary Magdalene	1956	Ilton, P.	VG+		$6.00
SIGNET	1310	The Killing	1956	White, L.	AF	MTI	$67.00 A
SIGNET	1310	The Killing	1956	White, L.	VG+	MTI	$10.00
SIGNET	1316	The Glass Play-Pen	1956	Fadiman, E.	VGF		$10.00 A
SIGNET	1316	The Glass Play-Pen	1956	Fadiman, E.	VGF		$8.00
SIGNET	1319	The Tooth And The Nail	1956	Ballinger, B.S.	AF		$10.00 A
SIGNET	1322	Stone Cold Blonde	1956	Knight, A.	VGF+		$9.00 A
SIGNET	S 1334	Baby Doll	1956	Williams, T.	VGF+	MTI	$8.00
SIGNET	1335	The Living Idol	1956	Switzer, R.	AF	MTI	$26.00 A
SIGNET	1338	New York's Underworld	1956	Simenon, G.	VG+		$6.00
SIGNET	S 1346	Operation: Outer Space	1957	Leinster, M.	AF		$7.00
SIGNET	1347	Girl Running	1956	Knight, A.	VGF		$7.00
SIGNET	1349	French Girls Are Vicious	1956	Farrell, J.T.	AF		$6.00 A
SIGNET	1350	Office Wife	1957	Weil, J.	VGF		$10.00
SIGNET	1358	One Tear For My Grave	1956	Roscoe, M.	VG+		$7.00
SIGNET	D 1368	1,000,000 Delinquents	1957	Fine, B.	VGF-		$23.00
SIGNET	D 1368	1,000,000 Delinquents	1957	Fine, B.	VGF		$16.00 A
SIGNET	D 1368	1,000,000 Delinquents	1957	Fine, B.	VG		$7.00 A
SIGNET	1374	An Act Of Violence	1957	Fadiman, E.	VGF		$7.00
SIGNET	1378	Flight Into Terror	1957	White, L.	VG+		$10.00
SIGNET	1378	Flight Into Terror	1957	White, L.	VG		$7.00
SIGNET	1393	Paint On Their Faces	1957	Weil, J.	VG+		$15.00
SIGNET	1393	Paint On Their Faces	1957	Weil, J.	VG		$12.00
SIGNET	1395	Murder For Madame	1957	Knight, A.	VGF		$7.00
SIGNET	1399	Last Days Of Sodom & Gomorrah	1957	Ilton, P.	AF		$20.00 A
SIGNET	1399	Last Days Of Sodom & Gomorrah	1957	Ilton, P.	VG+		$9.00
SIGNET	1405	The Private Eye	1957	Adams, C.	VGF		$7.00
SIGNET	S 1409	The Prince And The Showgirl	1957	Rattigan, T.	AF-	MTI	$16.00 A
SIGNET	S 1409	The Prince And The Showgirl	1957	Rattigan, T.	VGF	MTI	$10.00
SIGNET	S 1409	The Prince And The Showgirl	1957	Rattigan, T.	VG	MTI	$10.00
SIGNET	S 1409	The Prince And The Showgirl	1957	Rattigan, T.	VG-	MTI	$5.00
SIGNET	1414	Flint	1957	Dodge, G.	VG+		$40.00 A
SIGNET	1414	Flint	1957	Dodge, G.	VG+		$32.00 A
SIGNET	1434	The Tight Corner	1957	Ross, S.	VG+		$7.00
SIGNET	1440	Coral Comes High	1957	Hunt, G.P.	F		$4.00
SIGNET	1442	The House Next Door	1957	White, L.	VGF		$13.00
SIGNET	1445	Love's Lovely Counterfeit	1957	Cain, J.M.	VGF		$15.00
SIGNET	1445	Love's Lovely Counterfeit	1957	Cain, J.M.	VG		$7.00
SIGNET	1448	Find My Killer	1957	Wellman, M.	G+		$5.00
SIGNET	S 1453	Tip On A Dead Jockey	1957	Shaw, I.	AF	MTI	$10.00
SIGNET	T 1454	Marjorie Morningstar	1957	Wouk, H.	AF	MTI	$7.00
SIGNET	1461	Wild Town	1957	Thompson, J.	VG		$55.00 A

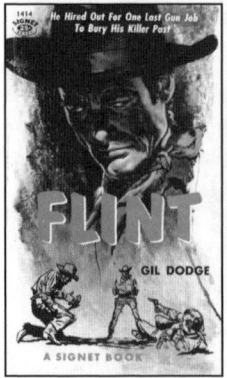

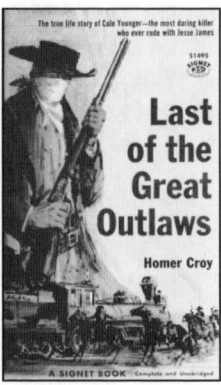

Signet 1414 VG+ $40　　　Signet 1445 VGF $15　　　Signet 1461 VG $55　　　Signet 1495 AF $8

PUBLISHER	PUB. #	TITLE	DATE	AUTHOR	COND.	TYPE	PRICE
SIGNET	1461	Wild Town	1957	Thompson, J.	VG-		$36.00 A
SIGNET	S 1467	A Walk In The Sun	1957	Brown, H.	VG		$3.00
SIGNET	1472	Kill Once, Kill Twice	1957	Hunt, K.	VGF		$8.00
SIGNET	1474	The Flesh Was Cold	1957	Fischer, B.	AF		$14.00 A
SIGNET	1474	The Flesh Was Cold	1957	Fischer, B.	VGF		$10.00
SIGNET	1475	Death In The Fifth Position	1957	Box, E.*	AF		$7.00
SIGNET	1482	Guilty Bystander	1958	Miller, W.	VGF		$7.00
SIGNET	1482	Guilty Bystander	1958	Miller, W.	VG		$6.00
SIGNET	1484	Death Likes It Hot	1958	Box, E.*	AF		$7.00
SIGNET	S 1485	Pylon	1958	Faulkner, W.	AF	MTI	$10.00
SIGNET	1489	Sing, Boy, Sing	1958	Vincent, R.	VG+	MTI	$6.00
SIGNET	1489	Sing, Boy, Sing	1958	Vincent, R.	G+	MTI	$5.00
SIGNET	S 1495	Last Of The Great Outlaws	1958	Croy, H.	AF		$8.00
SIGNET	S 1499	Cat Man	1958	Hoagland, E.	AF		$10.00 A
SIGNET	S 1501	The Long Hot Summer	1958	Faulkner, W.	VGF	MTI	$5.00
SIGNET	1502	Desire Under The Elms	1958	O'Neill, E.	F	MTI	$7.00
SIGNET	AE 1508	The Running Man	1982	Bachman, R.*	VG+		$20.00
SIGNET	S 1512	The Invisible Flag	1958	Bamm, P.	AF		$6.00
SIGNET	S 1513	The Barbarian & The Geisha	1958	Payne, R.	AF	MTI	$10.00
SIGNET	1528	The Nightwalkers	1958	Cross, B.	VG+		$7.00
SIGNET	D 1529	A Streetcar Named Desire	1958	Williams, T.	VG+	MTI	$6.00
SIGNET	D 1530	No Time For Sergeants	1958	Hyman, M.	VGF	MTI	$7.00
SIGNET	S 1533	Branded West	1958	Anthology	VG+		$6.00
SIGNET	1541	The Restless Gun	1958	Hickok, W.	VG+	TVTI	$6.00
SIGNET	S 1544	The Puppet Masters	1958	Heinlein, R.A.	VGF		$6.00
SIGNET	S 1557	The Wild Bunch	1958	Horan, J.D.	VGF+		$7.00
SIGNET	S 1563	From Russia, With Love	1958	Fleming, I.	VG+		$16.00
SIGNET	S 1563	From Russia, With Love	1958	Fleming, I.	VG		$16.00
SIGNET	1573	Kill A Wicked Man	1958	Hunt, K.	AF		$8.00
SIGNET	S 1579	Not Yet...	1958	Torres, T.	AF		$7.00
SIGNET	1582	The Doll's Smile	1958	Boros, E.	AF		$7.00
SIGNET	1586	TCOT Strangled Starlet	1958	Chase, J.H.	AF		$7.00
SIGNET	S 1590	Cat On A Hot Tin Roof	1958	Williams, T.	AF	MTI	$7.00
SIGNET	S 1593	The Demolished Man	1959	Bester, A.	VG		$6.00
SIGNET	S 1609	Separate Tables	1959	Rattigan, T.	AF	MTI	$7.00
SIGNET	S 1613	Nobody Cries For Me	1959	Harris, S.	VG+		$6.00
SIGNET	D 1619	On The Road	1958	Kerouac, J.	VG+		$33.00 A
SIGNET	D 1619	On The Road	1958	Kerouac, J.	VG+		$15.00
SIGNET	D 1619	On The Road	1958	Kerouac, J.	VG		$9.00
SIGNET	D 1619	On The Road	1958	Kerouac, J.	VG		$8.00
SIGNET	1636	The Whispering Master	1959	Gruber, F.	AF		$7.00
SIGNET	1646	Dormitory Women	1959	Cassill, R.V.	VG		$6.00
SIGNET	S 1652	Beat Beat Beat	1959	Brown, W.F.	VGF		$8.00
SIGNET	S 1652	Beat Beat Beat	1959	Brown, W.F.	VG		$7.00
SIGNET	1654	The Loving And The Dead	1959	Brown, C.	AF		$5.00
SIGNET	1662	Kiss Her Goodbye	1959	Miller, W.	VG+		$7.00
SIGNET	1663	Walk Softly, Witch	1959	Brown, C.	AF		$8.00
SIGNET	1665	Cancel All Our Vows	1959	MacDonald, J.D.	G-		$4.00

Signet 1563 VG+ $16	Signet 1619 VG+ $33	Signet 1670 VG+ $42	Signet 2034 VG $82

PUBLISHER	PUB. #	TITLE	DATE	AUTHOR	COND.	TYPE	PRICE
SIGNET	S 1670	Doctor No	1959	Fleming, I.	VG+		$42.00 A
SIGNET	S 1670	Doctor No	1959	Fleming, I.	G+		$8.00
SIGNET	1674	The Passionate	1959	Brown, C.	AF		$12.00
SIGNET	1675	Trail Of The Restless Gun	1959	Hickok, W.	VG+	TVTI	$6.00
SIGNET	1677	The Silver Tombstone Mystery	1959	Gruber, F.	AF		$6.00
SIGNET	D 1679	They Came To Cordura	1959	Swarthout, G.	F	MTI	$10.00
SIGNET	D 1679	They Came To Cordura	1959	Swarthout, G.	VGF	MTI	$7.00
SIGNET	1687	Violent Streets	1959	Kramer, D.	VG		$7.00
SIGNET	1688	Wake Up With A Stranger	1959	Flora, F.	VG+		$15.00 A
SIGNET	1688	Wake Up With A Stranger	1959	Flora, F.	AF		$10.00
SIGNET	D 1693	Let No Man Write My Epitaph	1959	Motley, W.	VGF	MTI	$8.00 A
SIGNET	S 1701	Son Of Mad	1959	Gaines, W.M.	VG+		$10.00
SIGNET	1707	Invitation To Violence	1959	White, L.	AF		$27.00 A
SIGNET	1707	Invitation To Violence	1959	White, L.	VG+		$7.00
SIGNET	S 1712	Entry E	1959	Frede, R.	AF		$7.00
SIGNET	1713	The Wanton	1959	Brown, C.	AF		$5.00
SIGNET	D 1718	The Dharma Bums	1959	Kerouac, J.	VG+		$22.00 A
SIGNET	D 1718	The Dharma Bums	1959	Kerouac, J.	VG+		$17.00
SIGNET	S 1719	Galactic Cluster	1959	Blish, J.	VGF		$6.00
SIGNET	S 1719	Galactic Cluster	1959	Blish, J.	VGF		$5.00
SIGNET	1723	Live And Let Die	1959	Fleming, I.	F		$64.00 A
SIGNET	D 1727	Breakfast At Tiffany's (4th)	1961	Capote, T.	VGF-	MTI	$5.00
SIGNET	1738	The Dame	1959	Brown, C.	AF		$5.00
SIGNET	S 1762	Casino Royale	1960	Fleming, I.	AF		$31.00 A
SIGNET	S 1762	Casino Royale	1960	Fleming, I.	AF		$23.00
SIGNET	S 1762	Casino Royale	1960	Fleming, I.	VG+		$14.00
SIGNET	1764	The Desired	1960	Brown, C.	AF		$7.00
SIGNET	S 1769	Islands In The Sky	1960	Clarke, A.C.	VGF		$5.00
SIGNET	D 1771	Scalpel	1960	McCoy, H.	VGF		$7.00
SIGNET	S 1776	The Alamo	1960	Tinkle, L.	AF	MTI	$7.00
SIGNET	S 1788	Visit To A Small Planet	1960	Vidal, G.	VG	MTI	$6.00
SIGNET	D 1793	The Mountain Road	1960	White, T.E.	AF	MTI	$7.00
SIGNET	S 1797	A Real Cool Cat	1960	Weil, J.	AF		$19.00 A
SIGNET	S 1812	The Beach Bums	1960	Owen, J.	AF		$7.00
SIGNET	S 1822	Goldfinger	1960	Fleming, I.	VGF		$31.00 A
SIGNET	S 1822	Goldfinger	1960	Fleming, I.	G		$7.00
SIGNET	S 1850	Moonraker	1960	Fleming, I.	AF		$53.00 A
SIGNET	S 1850	Moonraker	1960	Fleming, I.	VG+		$22.00 A
SIGNET	S 1850	Moonraker	1960	Fleming, I.	VGF		$17.00
SIGNET	S 1850	Moonraker	1960	Fleming, I.	VG		$13.00
SIGNET	D 1865	Naked In Babylon	1960	Davis, G.	AF		$5.00
SIGNET	D 1869	The Case Against A. Eichman	1960	Zeiger, H.A.	VG+		$6.00
SIGNET	D 1875	Errol And Me	1960	Rice, C.	VGF		$9.00
SIGNET	S 1894	The Girl In The Gold Leather Dress	1961	Morhaim, V.K.	VGF		$10.00
SIGNET	S 1894	The Girl In The Gold Leather Dress	1961	Morhaim, V.K.	AF		$8.00
SIGNET	S 1894	The Girl In The Gold Leather Dress	1961	Morhaim, V.K.	VGF		$8.00
SIGNET	T 1900	Sanctuary	1961	Faulkner, W.	VGF+	MTI	$7.00
SIGNET	S 1911	Fatal Step	1961	Miller, W.	VGF		$7.00

Signet 2995 VGF $18   Signet 3874 AF $7   Signet 7645 AF $155   Signet 8754 VGF $51

PUBLISHER	PUB. #	TITLE	DATE	AUTHOR	COND.	TYPE	PRICE
SIGNET	S 1919	The Ever-Loving Blues	1961	Brown, C.	AF		$7.00
SIGNET	S 1948	For Your Eyes Only	1961	Fleming, I.	VG		$16.00
SIGNET	S 1988	The Deadly Sex	1961	Webb, J.	VGF		$6.00
SIGNET	D 2019	Summer And Smoke	1961	Williams, T.	VGF	MTI	$7.00
SIGNET	S 2034	The Transgressors	1961	Thompson, J.	VG		$82.00 A
SIGNET	D 2046	Limbo Tower	1962	Gresham, W.L.	AF		$7.00
SIGNET	T 2085	Knock On Any Door	1962	Motley, W.	VG		$7.00
SIGNET	D 2095	Sweet Bird Of Youth	1962	Williams, T.	VGF	MTI	$7.00
SIGNET	S 2205	The Hundred-Dollar Girl	1962	Gault, W.C.	VG		$11.00
SIGNET	D 2210	Period Of Adjustment	1962	Williams, T.	VGF	MTI	$7.00
SIGNET	D 2245	Last Days Sodom & Gomorrah	1962	Ilton, P.	AF		$7.00
SIGNET	P 2354	The S.O. Bees	1963	Dwiggins, D.	VGF		$6.00
SIGNET	P 2423	The Best Man	1964	Vidal, G.	AF	MTI	$7.00
SIGNET	D 2427	The Americanization Of Emily	1964	Huie, W.B.	F	MTI	$6.00
SIGNET	G 2435	Call For The Dead	1964	LeCarre, J.	VGF		$6.00
SIGNET	P 2486	633 Squadron	1964	Smith, F.E.	VGF	MTI	$5.00
SIGNET	G 2505	Death In The 5th Position	1964	Box, E.*	AF		$5.00
SIGNET	P 2536	My Fair Lady	1964	Lerner, A.J.	AF	MTI	$6.00
SIGNET	D 2547	Planet Of The Apes	1964	Boulle, P.	AF		$17.00 A
SIGNET	G 2551	Trinity In Violence	1964	Kane, H.	VGF		$7.00
SIGNET	T 2566	Von Ryan's Express	1965	Westheimer, D.	VGF	MTI	$6.00
SIGNET	P 2595	The Primitive (2nd)	1965	Himes, C.	AF-		$6.00
SIGNET	P 2607	Nerve	1965	Francis, D.	AF		$5.00 A
SIGNET	P 2639	Nightmare Alley	1965	Gresham, W.L.	AF		$11.00 A
SIGNET	P 2639	Nightmare Alley	1965	Gresham, W.L.	F		$8.00
SIGNET	P 2664	The Ballad Of Cat Ballou	1965	Chanslor, R.	VGF	MTI	$8.00
SIGNET	D 2669	Moll Flanders	1965	Defoe, D.	VGF	MTI	$7.00
SIGNET	D 2674	The Spy In The Jungle	1966	Ballinger, B.S.	F		$7.00
SIGNET	P 2712	You Only Live Twice	1965	Fleming, I.	VGF	MTI	$7.00
SIGNET	D 2820	The Spy In Bangkok	1965	Ballinger, B.S.	VG+		$5.00
SIGNET	D 2836	The Wild Wild West	1966	Wormser, R.	VGF	TVTI	$7.00
SIGNET	P 2839	Where The Spies Are	1966	Leasor, J.	VG	MTI	$6.00
SIGNET	D 2899	The Spy At Angkor Wat	1966	Ballinger, B.S.	F		$7.00
SIGNET	D 2921	The Big Night	1966	Ellin, S.	F		$5.00
SIGNET	D 2939	Batman	1966	Kane, F.	VGF	TVTI	$8.00
SIGNET	D 2939	Batman	1966	Kane, F.	VG+	TVTI	$7.00
SIGNET	D 2939	Batman	1966	Kane, F.	G+	TVTI	$3.00
SIGNET	D 2944	The Key To Nicholas Street	1966	Ellin, S.	F		$5.00
SIGNET	D 2949	The Twisted Thing	1966	Spillane, M.	VGF		$8.00
SIGNET	P 2960	The James Bond Dossier	1966	Amis, K.	VG+		$5.00
SIGNET	D 2995	Batman vs. Fearsome Foursome	1966	Lyon, W.	VGF	MTI	$18.00 A
SIGNET	D 2995	Batman vs. Fearsome Foursome	1966	Lyon, W.	VG	MTI	$5.00 A
SIGNET	D 3012	The Girl From UNCLE	1966	Avallone, M.	AF	TVTI	$7.00
SIGNET	D 3012	The Girl From UNCLE	1966	Avallone, M.	VGF+	TVTI	$6.00
SIGNET	P 3028	The Hare In March	1966	Packer, V.*	VG+		$8.00
SIGNET	P 3028	The Hare In March	1966	Packer, V.*	VG		$7.00
SIGNET	Q 3036	A Spaniard In The Works	1967	Lennon, J.	VG	DBL	$7.00
SIGNET	D 3042	The Girl From UNCLE #2	1966	Avallone, M.	AF	TVTI	$6.00

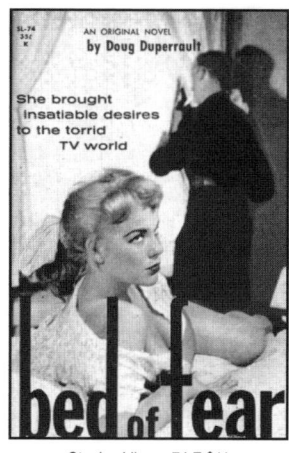

Stanley Library 74 F $11   Star Books 38 VG+ $7   Star Books 751 VG $15

PUBLISHER	PUB. #	TITLE	DATE	AUTHOR	COND.	TYPE	PRICE
SIGNET	D 3045	Man From UNCLE's ABC Of Esp.	1966	Hill, J.	AF	TVTI	$7.00
SIGNET	P 3108	Sandra Rifkin's Jewels	1966	Doliner, R.	F		$7.00
SIGNET	P 3112	The Naked Runner	1967	Clifford, F.	VGF	MTI	$7.00
SIGNET	T 3219	Luv	1967	Schisgal, M.	AF	MTI	$7.00
SIGNET	P 3221	The Body Lovers	1967	Spillane, M.	VG+		$7.00
SIGNET	T 3234	The Night Action	1967	Reeves, B.D.	VGF	MTI	$6.00
SIGNET	P 3374	Easy Go	1968	Lange, J.*	AF		$14.00
SIGNET	P 3374	Easy Go	1968	Lange, J.*	VGF		$8.00
SIGNET	P 3425	Swing Low, Sweet Harriet	1968	Baxt, G.	VGF		$5.00
SIGNET	W 3442	The Marihuana Papers (3rd)	1968	Anthology	VG		$7.00
SIGNET	T 3453	The Hippies	1968	Wolfe, B.H.	G-		$3.00
SIGNET	Q 3471	Down These Mean Streets	1968	Thomas, P.	VGF		$5.00
SIGNET	Q 3505	Red-Dirt Marijuana	1968	Southern, T.	VG		$5.00
SIGNET	P 3516	Viva Mad!	1968	Aragones, S.	VGF		$6.00
SIGNET	AE 3605	The Door To December	1985	Paige, R.*	VG+		$9.00 A
SIGNET	P 3622	Hawaii Five-O	1968	Avallone, M.	VG	TVTI	$6.00
SIGNET	T 3625	God Save The Mark	1968	Westlake, D.E.	VG+	MTI	$6.00
SIGNET	Q 3632	Yellow Submarine	1968	Wilk, M.	VG+	MTI	$8.00
SIGNET	T 3660	Game Of Survival	1968	Meaker, M.	VG-		$5.00
SIGNET	T 3732	The Gap	1968	Lorber, R.	VGF		$7.00
SIGNET	P 3742	Death To My Beloved	1969	Neely, R.	AF		$6.00
SIGNET	T 3746	Zero Cool	1969	Lange, J.*	VGF		$10.00
SIGNET	Q 3761	True Grit (10th)	n/d	Portis, C.	VG	MTI	$6.00
SIGNET	T 3768	Gore And Igor	1969	Levin, M.	VG+		$6.00
SIGNET	P 3797	Krakatoa, East Of Java	1969	Avallone, M.	VG+	MTI	$8.00
SIGNET	P 3799	Heist Me Higher	1969	Ballinger, B.S.	VGF		$6.00
SIGNET	T 3800	Do Androids Dream . . . ?	1969	Dick, P.K.	VG		$12.00
SIGNET	T 3812	Time Out Of Mind	1969	Boulle, P.	F		$7.00
SIGNET	Q 3854	Last Summer	1969	Hunter, E.	VG	MTI	$7.00
SIGNET	T 3856	The Chicago Riots	1969	Anthology	VG+		$5.00
SIGNET	P 3874	The Damsel	1969	Stark, R.*	AF		$7.00
SIGNET	P 3874	The Damsel	1969	Stark, R.*	G+		$5.00
SIGNET	N 4002	Bored Of The Rings	1969	Beard, H.N.	VG		$7.00
SIGNET	Q 4007	The Chairman (5th)	1969	Kennedy, J.R.	AF	MTI	$7.00
SIGNET	Y 4026	Easy Rider	1969	Southern, T.	AF	MTI	$6.00
SIGNET	Q 4082	Gaily, Gaily	1969	Hecht, B.	AF	MTI	$5.00
SIGNET	P 4096	The Doomsday Bag	1969	Avallone, M.	VGF		$6.00
SIGNET	T 4214	Grave Descend	1970	Lange, J.*	VGF-		$6.00
SIGNET	Q 4229	Countdown 2	1970	Anthology	VG		$7.00
SIGNET	Q 4237	Fool's Parade	1970	Grubb, D.	VG+		$6.00
SIGNET	T 4464	Jigsaw	1970	McBain, E.*	VGF		$6.00
SIGNET	t 4490	Death Dives Deep	1971	Avallone, M.	VGF		$5.00
SIGNET	Q 4515	And The Deep Blue Sea	1971	Williams, C.	VG		$5.00
SIGNET	Q 4642	Fool's Parade (2nd)	1971	Grubb, D.	VG	MTI	$6.00
SIGNET	Y 4766	The Walter Syndrome	1971	Neely, R.	VGF		$5.00

Stork 6 VG+ $40

Sundown Reader 611 VG+ $82

Super-Science Fiction 3-3 AF $40

PUBLISHER	PUB. #	TITLE	DATE	AUTHOR	COND.	TYPE	PRICE
SIGNET	Q 4802	Adios Scheherazade	1971	Westlake, D.E.	VGF+		$9.00 A
SIGNET	Q 5338	The Mechanic	1971	Carlino, L.J.	VG+	MTI	$6.00
SIGNET	Y 5664	Pat Garrett And Billy The Kid	1973	Wurlitzer, R.	AF	MTI	$7.00
SIGNET	J 5672	Again, Dangerous Visions Vol. 1	1973	Ellison, H.	VGF		$6.00
SIGNET	J 5673	Again, Dangerous Vis. 2 (Signed)	1973	Anthology	VG		$12.00
SIGNET	Y 5828	Every Little Crook And Nanny	1974	Hunter, E.	VGF		$15.00
SIGNET	Y 5828	Every Little Crook And Nanny	1974	Hunter, E.	VGF		$12.00
SIGNET	Y 6358	The Real Cool Killers	1975	Himes, C.	VGF		$7.00
SIGNET	W 6390	The Killing Of Sharon Tate (3rd)	1975	Schiller, L.	VGF		$6.00
SIGNET	Y 6506	The Crazy Kill	1975	Himes, C.	VG-		$5.00
SIGNET	W 7645	Rage	1977	Bachman, R.*	AF		$155.00 A
SIGNET	Y 7841	The Mad World Of W.M. Gaines	1978	Jacobs, F.	AF		$10.00
SIGNET	W 7928	Runaway Black	1978	McBain, E.*	VGF		$5.00
SIGNET	E 8525	The Tolkien Quiz Book	1979	Andrews, B.	VGF		$6.00
SIGNET	J 8754	The Long Walk	1979	Bachman, R.*	VGF		$51.00 A
SIGNET	J 8754	The Long Walk	1979	Bachman, R.*	VG		$20.00
SIGNET	J 8754	The Long Walk	1979	Bachman, R.*	VG		$17.00
SIGNET	E 9668	Roadwork	1981	Bachman, R.*	VG		$11.00 A
SIGNET	E 9966	The Voice Of The Night	1981	Coffey, B.*	VG+		$11.00 A
SIGNET	E 9966	The Voice Of The Night	1981	Coffey, B.*	VG		$10.00
SIGNET KEY	Ks 360	Rockets And Outer Space	1958	Ley, W.	VG		$6.00
SLEUTH	1 1	Sleuth Mystery Mag. 10/58	1958	Anthology	AF-	Digest	$20.00 A
SLEUTH	1 2	Sleuth Mystery Mag. 12/58	1958	Anthology	VGF	Digest	$17.00 A
SOFTCOVER LIBRARY*		*See BEACON					
SPACE SCI-FI	1 1	Space Science Fiction 5/52	1952	Anthology	VGF-	Digest	$8.00
SPACE TRAVEL	5 4	Space Travel - 7/58	1958	Anthology	VGF	Digest	$5.00
SPACEWAY	3 1	Spaceway Sci-Fi - 4/55	1955	Anthology	VG	Digest	$4.00
SPARTAN LINE	SL 152	Final Desire	1967	Thorpe, F.L.	VG+		$6.00
SPHERE	4683	Conan The Freebooter	1976	Howard, R.E.	VGF		$6.00
SPHERE	4687	Conan The Conqueror	1976	Howard, R.E.	AF		$6.00
SPHERE	4731	Conan The Wanderer (3rd)	1976	Howard, R.E.	VGF		$5.00
SPHERE	29572	Game Players Of Titan	1969	Dick, P.K.	VG		$7.00
SPICY LIBRARY	400	Doctor Sex	1967	Kingsley, T.	AF		$8.00
SPORT MAGAZINE LIBRARY	1	Johnny Unitas	1960	Fitzgerald, E.	VGF		$5.00
SPORT MAGAZINE LIBRARY	6	Willie Mays	1961	Hano, A.	VGF		$8.00
SPOTLIGHT	308	Night Riders	1967	Davis, D.	VG+		$7.00
SPOTLIGHT	326	Bluebeard's Bed	1968	Ellis, V.	VG		$7.00
STANLEY LIBRARY	SL 67	The Oldest Profession	1958	Campbell, J.	VGF		$16.00
STANLEY LIBRARY	SL 67	The Oldest Profession	1958	Campbell, J.	VG+		$16.00 A
STANLEY LIBRARY	SL 72	Strictly For The Boys	1959	Whittington, H.	AF		$55.00 A
STANLEY LIBRARY	SL 74	Bed Of Fear	1959	Duperrault, D.	F		$11.00 A
STAR	1	Christopher Lee's 'X' Certificate	1975	Anthology	AF		$4.00
STAR	No#	Weird Legacies	1977	Anthology	VGF		$25.00 A
STAR (Adult)	EC 1136	The Young College Professor	1972	McCade, M.	VGF		$8.00
STAR (Adult)	EC 1137	A Blonde Girl Named Lynn	1972	Akins, K.	VGF		$15.00 A

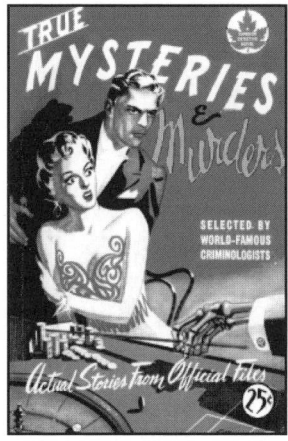

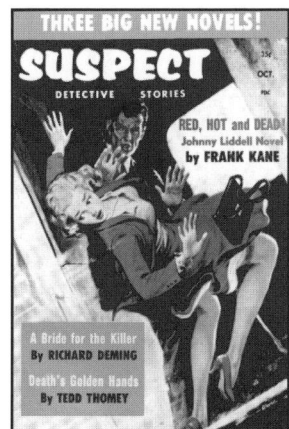

Superior Detective No# VG $33   Sure Fire Detective 2-1 AF $32   Suspect 1-5 VGF $33

PUBLISHER	PUB. #	TITLE	DATE	AUTHOR	COND.	TYPE	PRICE
STAR BOOKS	6	Flaming Guns	1950	Arthur, B.	VGF	Digest	$18.00 A
STAR BOOKS	9	Border Wolves	1950	Joscelyn, A.	VG+	Digest	$14.00 A
STAR BOOKS	13	Gun-Thunder Valley	1951	Joscelyn, A.	VG+	Digest	$6.00
STAR BOOKS	15	The Long Trail North	1951	Floren, L.	VG	Digest	$6.00
STAR BOOKS	19	Duel On The Range	1951	Arthur, B.	VG+	Digest	$6.00
STAR BOOKS	29	Duel At Killman Creek	1951	Joscelyn, A.	VG	Digest	$5.00
STAR BOOKS	30	Texas Outlaw	1952	Joscelyn, A.	VG+	Digest	$7.00
STAR BOOKS	38	Gun-Law On The Range	1952	Arthur, B.	VG+	Digest	$7.00
STAR BOOKS	751	Baby Sitter	1955	Quandt, A.L.	VG	Digest	$15.00 A
STAR NOVELS	762	Backwoods Hussy	1956	Whitney, H.*	VG	Digest	$38.00 A
STARDUST READER	SR 103	Mistress Of Lust	1965	Pagano, H.	F		$7.00
STARTLING MYSTERY	1 4	Startling Mystery-Spring '67	1967	Anthology	VG+	Digest	$8.00
STORK	6	The Sins Of Donna Kenyon	1950	Carter, R.	VG+	Digest	$40.00 A
STORK	8	Two Sinners	1950	Jackquin, L.	VGF	Digest	$16.00 A
STRANGE	1 1	Strange - 3/52	1952	Anthology	VG+	Digest	$35.00 A
STRANGE	1 2	Strange - 5/52	1952	Anthology	VG+	Digest	$23.00 A
STRANGE	1 3	Strange - 7/52	1952	Anthology	VG+	Digest	$12.00
SUN VOLUME	SV 101	The Big Passion Game	1964	Bontempo, R.	AF-		$6.00
SUNDOWN READER	SR 501	Shame Shop	1964	Hudson, D.	AF		$8.00
SUNDOWN READER	SR 510	Gatefold Girls	1964	Allison, C.	AF		$10.00
SUNDOWN READER	SR 517	Lust Bent	1964	Bellmore, D.	G		$3.00
SUNDOWN READER	SR 521	Orgy Voyage	1964	Allison, C.	AF-		$15.00
SUNDOWN READER	SR 527	The Procurer	1964	Shay, A.	VGF		$8.00
SUNDOWN READER	SR 528	Passion Doll	1964	Marshall, A.*	VG+		$8.00
SUNDOWN READER	SR 529	Harpy Town	1965	Hudson, D.	AF		$8.00
SUNDOWN READER	SR 530	Sally's Sinners	1965	Dexter, J.	VG+		$5.00
SUNDOWN READER	SR 532	Lust Finale	1965	Elliott, D.*	AF		$10.00
SUNDOWN READER	SR 533	Luster's Revolt	1965	Allison, C.	AF		$12.00
SUNDOWN READER	SR 534	Passion Killer	1964	Elliott, D.*	AF		$9.00
SUNDOWN READER	SR 536	Mob Doll	1965	Holliday, D.	VGF		$7.00
SUNDOWN READER	SR 538	Halls Of Sin	1965	Shaw, A.*	VG		$5.00
SUNDOWN READER	SR 542	The Sin Fishers	1965	Dexter, J.	AF		$7.00
SUNDOWN READER	SR 544	Casino Trollop	1965	Marshall, A.*	VGF		$8.00
SUNDOWN READER	SR 551	Dice Dame	1965	Calvano, T.	AF		$6.00
SUNDOWN READER	SR 554	Lust Bust	1965	Marshall, A.*	AF		$8.00
SUNDOWN READER	SR 555	Shame Lane	1965	Hudson, D.	VGF		$12.00
SUNDOWN READER	SR 562	Lez	1965	Bellmore, D.	VGF		$16.00 A
SUNDOWN READER	SR 563	Passion Profiteer	1965	Allison, C.	F		$14.00
SUNDOWN READER	SR 564	The Sin Samplers	1965	Dexter, J.	VGF		$6.00
SUNDOWN READER	SR 565	Passion Hotshot	1965	Marshall, A.*	VG+		$7.00
SUNDOWN READER	SR 568	The Sin Smugglers	1965	Calvano, T.	VG-		$4.00
SUNDOWN READER	SR 575	Passion Misfit	1965	Calvano, T.	AF		$7.00
SUNDOWN READER	SR 576	Remembered Sin	1965	Dexter, J.	VG		$5.00
SUNDOWN READER	SR 577	Double Sindemnity	1965	Dexter, J.	AF		$7.00
SUNDOWN READER	SR 579	Sin Defector	1966	Aldrich, C.	VGF		$7.00

Terror 4 VGF $22

Thrilling Novels 22 VG+ $7

Toby No# VG+ $17

PUBLISHER	PUB. #	TITLE	DATE	AUTHOR	COND.	TYPE	PRICE
SUNDOWN READER	SR 581	Passion Prodigal	1965	Hudson, D.	AF		$7.00
SUNDOWN READER	SR 583	The Flesh Gig	1966	Dexter, J.	VGF		$7.00
SUNDOWN READER	SR 587	Harridan	1966	Calvano, T.	AF		$7.00
SUNDOWN READER	SR 589	Lust Cat	1966	Elliott, D.*	AF		$7.00
SUNDOWN READER	SR 593	The Shames Of Adam	1966	Dexter, J.	AF		$7.00
SUNDOWN READER	SR 595	Make Me Cry	1966	Marshall, A.*	AF		$7.00
SUNDOWN READER	SR 601	Sinners Circle	1966	Marshall, A.*	AF		$10.00
SUNDOWN READER	SR 609	Sin On Salary	1966	Hudson, D.	VGF		$8.00
SUNDOWN READER	SR 610	The Violent Vixen	1966	Marshall, A.*	AF		$12.00
SUNDOWN READER	SR 611	Parisian Passions	1966	Wood, E., Jr.	VG+		$82.00 A
SUNDOWN READER	SR 614	Substitute Sinners	1966	Dexter, J.	VGF		$8.00
SUNDOWN READER	SR 619	Sin's Child	1966	Calvano, T.	VG+		$5.00
SUNDOWN READER	SR 621	Look-Alike Lovers	1966	Dexter, J.	VGF		$8.00
SUNDOWN READER	SR 622	The Cellar Sinners	1966	Williams, J.X.	VGF+		$13.00 A
SUPER-SCIENCE FICTION	1 6	Super-Science Fiction - 10/57	1957	Anthology	VG+	Digest	$8.00
SUPER-SCIENCE FICTION	2 3	Super-Science Fiction - 4/58	1958	Anthology	G	Digest	$3.00
SUPER-SCIENCE FICTION	2 5	Super-Science Fiction - 8/58	1958	Anthology	VGF	Digest	$20.00 A
SUPER-SCIENCE FICTION	2 6	Super-Science Fiction -10/58	1958	Anthology	VGF	Digest	$22.00 A
SUPER-SCIENCE FICTION	3 1	Super-Science Fiction -12/58	1958	Anthology	VG+	Digest	$32.00 A
SUPER-SCIENCE FICTION	3 3	Super-Science Fiction - 4/59	1959	Anthology	AF	Digest	$40.00 A
SUPER-SCIENCE FICTION	3 3	Super-Science Fiction - 4/59	1959	Anthology	VGF+	Digest	$14.00 A
SUPER-SCIENCE FICTION	3 4	Super-Science Fiction - 6/59	1959	Anthology	AF	Digest	$40.00 A
SUPER-SCIENCE FICTION	3 5	Super-Science Fiction - 8/59	1959	Anthology	AF	Digest	$40.00 A
SUPER-SCIENCE FICTION	3 6	Super-Science Fiction - 10/59	1959	Anthology	AF	Digest	$35.00
SUPERIOR	No#	Jam-Session Slayer	n/d	Anthology	VG	Digest	$55.00 A
SUPERIOR DETECTIVE	No#	True Mysteries & Murders	1945	Anonymous	VG	Digest	$33.00 A
SUPERIOR REPRINT	M 641	Family Affair	1944	Shriber, I.S.	VG		$5.00
SUPERIOR REPRINT	M 646	The Love Nest And Other Stories	1945	Lardner, R.	G		$4.00
SUPERIOR REPRINT	M 655	The Mighty Blockhead	1945	Gruber, F.	G+		$5.00
SURE FIRE	1 3	Sure Fire Detective - 4/57	1957	Anthology	VGF	Digest	$50.00 A
SURE FIRE	1 6	Sure Fire Detective - 12/57	1957	Anthology	AF	Digest	$59.00 A
SURE FIRE	2 1	Sure Fire Detective - 2/58	1958	Anthology	AF	Digest	$32.00 A
SURE FIRE	2 2	Sure Fire Detective - 4/58	1958	Anthology	VGF	Digest	$42.00 A
SURE FIRE	2 3	Sure Fire Detective - 7/58	1958	Anthology	AF	Digest	$30.00 A
SURE FIRE	2 3	Sure Fire Detective - 7/58	1958	Anthology	VG-	Digest	$13.00
SUSPECT	1 1	Suspect Det. Stories 11/55	1955	Anthology	AF	Digest	$17.00 A
SUSPECT	1 2	Suspect Det. Stories 2/56	1956	Anthology	VGF	Digest	$39.00 A
SUSPECT	1 4	Suspect Det. Stories 8/56	1956	Anthology	VG+	Digest	$20.00
SUSPECT	1 4	Suspect Det. Stories 8/56	1956	Anthology	VG	Digest	$14.00 A
SUSPECT	1 5	Suspect Det. Stories 10/56	1956	Anthology	VGF	Digest	$33.00 A
SUSPENSE	1 1	Suspense - Spring 1951	1951	Anthology	VG+	Digest	$10.00
SUSPENSE	1 2	Suspense - Summer 1951	1951	Anthology	VG-	Digest	$8.00
SUSPENSE	1 3	Suspense - Fall, 1951	1951	Anthology	VG	Digest	$8.00
SUSPENSE	1 4	Suspense - Winter 1952	1952	Anthology	VG	Digest	$8.00
SUSPENSE (U.K.)	1 5	Suspense (British) 12/58	1958	Anthology	VGF	Digest	$9.00 A

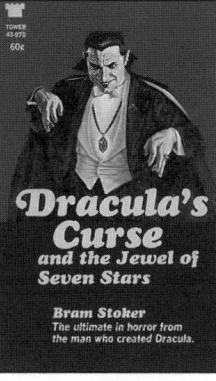

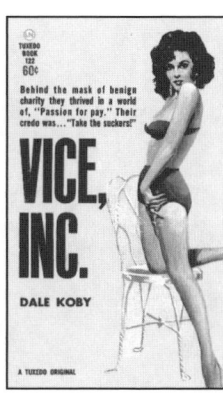

Tower 42-407 VG+ $7   Tower 43-970 VGF $28   Tropic 945 VG+ $12   Tuxedo 122 VGF $12

PUBLISHER	PUB. #	TITLE	DATE	AUTHOR	COND.	TYPE	PRICE
SUSPENSE NOVEL	1	Strange Pursuit	1951	De Mexico, N.R.	VGF-	Digest	$15.00
TAB	TX 137	Revolt On Alpha C	1959	Silverberg, R.	VG	Digest	$7.00
TALES OF FRIGHTENED	1 1	Tales Of The Frightened	1957	Anthology	VG+	Digest	$32.00
TALES OF FRIGHTENED	1 2	Tales Of The Frightened 8/57	1957	Anthology	VGF	Digest	$12.00
TALES OF THE SEA	1 1	Tales Of The Sea - Spring '53	1953	Anthology	VG+	Digest	$20.00 A
TECH MYSTERY	No#	Murder Man	n/d	Bogart, W.	VG	Digest	$8.00
TECH MYSTERY	1	The Candle	n/d	Hopkins, L.C.	VG+	Digest	$13.00 A
TECH MYSTERY	2	Murder Is My Racket	n/d	Leitfred, R.H.	VGF	Digest	$11.00 A
TECH WESTERN	2	Rainbow Trail	n/d	Shappiro, H.	VG+	Digest	$7.00
TEMPO	T 6	Invaders Of Earth	1962	Anthology	AF		$8.00
TEMPO	T 10	The Red Car	1962	Stanford, D.	VG+		$6.00
TEMPO	T 28	Secret Of The Martian Moons	1963	Wollheim, D.A.	VGF		$6.00
TEMPO	T 39	Great Stories Of Space Travel (2nd)	1965	Anthology	AF		$5.00
TEMPO	T 48	Sleep In Thunder	1964	Lacy, E.	AF		$16.00 A
TEMPO	T 48	Sleep In Thunder	1964	Lacy, E.	VGF		$15.00
TEMPO	T 62	Life Under The Pharaohs	1964	Cottrell, L.	AF		$6.00
TEMPO	5368	The Best Of Creepy	1971	Anthology	VGF-		$6.00
TEMPO	7494	The Shadow	n/d	Gibson, W.B.	VG+		$9.00
TEMPO	17155	Flash Gordon #4	1980		F		$11.00 A
TERROR	1	Terror Detective Story - 10/56	1956	Anthology	G+	Digest	$15.00
TERROR	4	Terror Detective Story - 4/57	1957	Anthology	VGF	Digest	$22.00 A
THREE STAR	101	In The Lion's Den	1965	Cotton, J.	VG		$6.00
THREE STAR	104	Ian Fleming's Incredible Creation	1965	Antony, P.	AF		$20.00
THREE-BOOK WESTERN	1 2	3-Book Western - 5/57	1957	Anthology	VG+	Digest	$13.00
THREE-BOOK WESTERN	1 2	3-Book Western - 5/57	1957	Anthology	AF	Digest	$10.00
THRILLER NOVEL CLASSIC	3	The Yellow Strangler	1942	Robertson, C.	VG+	Digest	$11.00 A
THRILLER NOVEL CLASSIC	3	The Yellow Strangler	1942	Robertson, C.	VG+	Digest	$7.00
THRILLER NOVEL CLASSIC	27	Assignment To Death	1944	Leonard, C.L.	VG	Digest	$7.00
THRILLING NOVELS	16	Cow Country Law	n/d	Robertson, F.C.	VG	Digest	$6.00
THRILLING NOVELS	17	Man To Man	n/d	Gregory, J.	VG	Digest	$6.00
THRILLING NOVELS	17	Man To Man	n\d	Gregory, J.	G+	Digest	$5.00
THRILLING NOVELS	20	Rustlers' Valley	n/d	Mulford, C.E.	VG-	Digest	$7.00
THRILLING NOVELS	20	Rustlers' Valley	n/d	Mulford, C.E.	VG	Digest	$6.00
THRILLING NOVELS	22	Hot Lead Trail	n/d	Seltzer, C.A.	VG+	Digest	$7.00
THRILLING NOVELS	30	Thorson Of Thunder Gulch	n/d	Fox, N.A.	VGF	Digest	$17.00
TOBY	No#	Escape	1953	Anthology	VG	Digest	$9.00
TOBY	No#	You'll Die Now	1953	Drennen, R.	VG+	Digest	$17.00 A
TOR	No#	Treachery On Mongo (1982)	1982	King Features	VG		$6.00
TOWER	43 167	Felony Tank	1961	Braly, M.	AF		$7.00
TOWER	43 167	Felony Tank	1961	Braly, M.	VG-		$5.00
TOWER	42 406	The Organization	1964	Demaris, O.	VGF		$8.00
TOWER	42 407	Before I Die	1964	White, L.	VG+		$7.00
TOWER	44 429	The Hard Sell	1964	Costigan, L.	VG		$4.00
TOWER	43 430	Catherine The Great	1964	Matthews, K.*	VG+		$13.00 A
TOWER	43 461	Time To Come	1965	Anthology	VGF		$7.00
TOWER	43 473	The Buccaneers	1965	Kemp, P.K.	AF		$8.00
TOWER	42 502	Five Day Nightmare	1965	Brown, F.	AF		$25.00 A
TOWER	43 572	Cave Of The Chinese Skeletons	1965	Seward, J.	AF-		$9.00 A

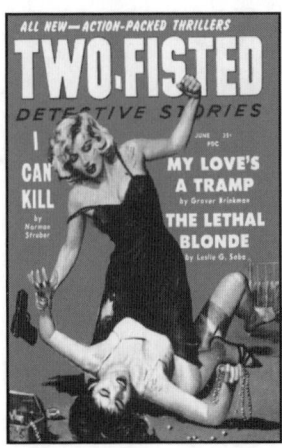

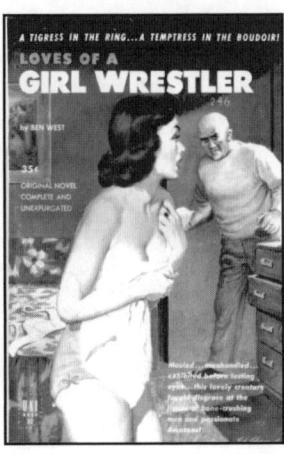

Two-Fisted Detective 1-1 VGF+ $45   Uni Book 15 VGF- $36   Uni Book 32 VG $25

PUBLISHER	PUB. #	TITLE	DATE	AUTHOR	COND.	TYPE	PRICE
TOWER	43 619	The Summer Ghosts	1966	Lykiard, A.	AF		$4.00
TOWER	42 621	The Doomsday Planet	1966	Vincent, H.	VGF		$5.00
TOWER	42 671	There Oughta Be A Law	1966	Shorten, H.	VG+		$4.00
TOWER	42 672	Noman	1966		VGF		$14.00 A
TOWER	42 674	Menthor	1966		AF		$11.00 A
TOWER	44 688	The Frightened Women	1966	Gelinas, N.J.	VG-		$3.00
TOWER	43 823	The Two Mrs. Carrolls	1967	Arvonen, H.	G	MTI	$5.00
TOWER	43 925	Before I Die	1968	White, L.	VG-		$5.00
TOWER	43 970	Dracula's Curse	1968	Stoker, B.	VGF	DBL	$28.00 A
		The Jewel Of The Seven Stars		Stoker, B.			
TOWER	44 126	To Russia With L.U.S.T.	1968	Gray, R.	VG		$6.00
TOWER	44 171	South Of The Bordello	1969	Gray, R.	VG-		$7.00
TOWER	43 246	Bloch And Bradbury	1969	Bloch, Bradbury	AF		$5.00 A
TOWER	44 266	Black Harvest	1969	Tyrone, W.S.	VGF		$4.00
TOWER	95 23	Up Against The War	1970	Woodstone, N.S.	VGF		$7.00
TOWER	51572	Death To A Downbeat	1980	Brown, C.	VGF		$5.00
TOWER	51780	The Seduction	1982	Houston, D.	VG+	MTI	$7.00
TRAPPED	1 1	Trapped - 6/56	1956	Anthology	VGF	Digest	$24.00 A
TRAPPED	1 4	Trapped - 12/57	1957	Anthology	VGF+	Digest	$42.00 A
TRAPPED	2 2	Trapped - 8/57	1957	Anthology	G+	Digest	$10.00
TRAPPED	3 5	Trapped - 2/59	1959	Anthology	VG+	Digest	$24.00
TRAPPED	4 3	Trapped - 10/59	1959	Anthology	AF	Digest	$51.00 A
TRAPPED	5 1	Trapped - 8/60	1960	Anthology	VGF	Digest	$27.00 A
TRAPPED	7 2	Trapped - 11/62	1962	Anthology	VGF	Digest	$15.00 A
TREASURY OF GREAT SF	1	Treasury Of Great Sci-Fi	1964	Anthology	VG+	Digest	$22.00 A
TRIPLE NICKLE	2	Davy Crockett And Danger . . .	1955	Wilson, N.	VGF	Digest	$15.00
TROPHY	401	Smile, Brother, Smile	1946	Anthology	VG	Digest	$38.00
TROPIC	901	Devil's Playmates	1962	Mead, E.	AF		$5.00 A
TROPIC	902	Bartered Sin	1962	Savage, M.	VGF		$7.00 A
TROPIC	903	Girls Of Chance	1962	Sands, N.	VGF+		$12.00 A
TROPIC	906	Carnal Frenzy	1963	Coulter, A.	AF		$14.00 A
TROPIC	907	Wings Of Sin	1963	Howley, C.	AF		$11.00 A
TROPIC	908	Patterns Of Passion	1963	Jackson, L.	AF		$23.00 A
TROPIC	914	Frustrations Of Judy	1965	Harris, F.G.	VGF		$20.00 A
TROPIC	914	Frustrations Of Judy	1965	Harris, F.G.	VGF		$14.00 A
TROPIC	920	Sex In White	1966	Marchand, K.	VGF+		$10.00
TROPIC	921	Sin Moved In	1966	Rand, R.	VGF		$7.00 A
TROPIC	922	Patterns Of Sin	1966	Patrick, D.	VGF		$10.00
TROPIC	923	Female Spoilers	1966	Harris, F.G.	VGF		$10.00
TROPIC	924	A Virgin In Their Midst	1966	Horn, A.	F		$17.00 A
TROPIC	928	Sex Racket	1966	Lucas, M.	VGF		$10.00
TROPIC	929	Nurse On The Beach	1966	Fletcher, M.	VGF+		$10.00
TROPIC	932	Wanton In White	1966	Fletcher, M.	VGF		$10.00
TROPIC	939	The Flesh Is Wild	1966	Moore, J.	AF		$12.00 A
TROPIC	945	The Sin Goddess	1967	Harris, F.G.	VG+		$12.00 A

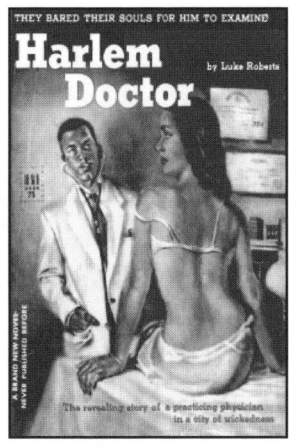

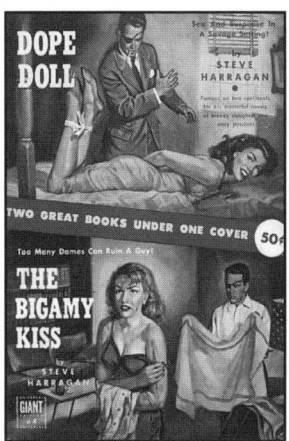

Uni Book 75 VG $20	Universal Giant 4 VGF $50	Value Book 104 VG $6

PUBLISHER	PUB. #	TITLE	DATE	AUTHOR	COND.	TYPE	PRICE
TROPIC	947	Lyrics Of Love	1967	French, A.	VGF+		$12.00 A
TRUE CRIME DETECTIVE	2 1	True Crime Det.-Winter 1952	1952	Anthology	VGF	Digest	$7.00
TRUE CRIME DETECTIVE	2 3	True Crime Det.-Summer, 1952	1952	Anthology	VG+	Digest	$7.00
TRUE CRIME DETECTIVE	3 2	True Crime Det. - Spring 1953	1953	Anthology	AF	Digest	$7.00
TRUE CRIME DETECTIVE	3 4	True Crime Det. - Fall 1953	1953	Anthology	VGF	Digest	$7.00
TUXEDO	101	Congo Lust	1961	Tralins, B.	VGF		$22.00 A
TUXEDO	107	Law Of Lust	1962	Tralins, B.	AF		$11.00 A
TUXEDO	108	Naked Sin	1962	Robinson, G.D.	AF		$13.00 A
TUXEDO	109	Campus Mistress	1962	Du Herson, E.	VGF		$8.00 A
TUXEDO	113	Passion Trip	1962	Robinson, G.D.	AF		$8.00
TUXEDO	114	Sin Lens	1962	Koby, D.	AF		$16.00 A
TUXEDO	117	Warped Passions	1962	Marmor, A.	VGF		$10.00
TUXEDO	118	What Every Man Wants	1962	Robbins, R.	VGF		$8.00
TUXEDO	119	Film Strip	1962	Morgan, M.X.	VG+		$8.00
TUXEDO	120	Sex Merry-Go-Round	1962	Moore, J.	AF		$25.00 A
TUXEDO	122	Vice, Inc.	1962	Koby, D.	VGF		$12.00
TUXEDO	122	Vice, Inc.	1962	Koby, D.	AF-		$10.00
TWO BOOK MYSTERY	1 2	Two Book Mystery - 6/46	1946	Anthology	VG	Digest	$15.00
TWO-FISTED	1 1	Two-Fisted Detective - 6/59	1959	Anthology	VGF+	Digest	$45.00 A
TWO-FISTED	1 2	Two-Fisted Detective - 7/59	1959	Anthology	AF	Digest	$22.00 A
TWO-FISTED	1 3	Two-Fisted Detective - 9/59	1959	Anthology	AF-	Digest	$24.00 A
TWO-FISTED	1 3	Two-Fisted Detective - 9/59	1959	Anthology	VGF	Digest	$16.00 A
TWO-FISTED	1 3	Two-Fisted Detective - 9/59	1959	Anthology	VGF-	Digest	$14.00
TWO-FISTED	1 4	Two-Fisted Detective - 11/59	1959	Anthology	AF	Digest	$34.00 A
TWO-FISTED	1 4	Two-Fisted Detective - 11/59	1959	Anthology	VG+	Digest	$29.00 A
TWO-FISTED	1 4	Two-Fisted Detective - 11/59	1959	Anthology	AF	Digest	$26.00 A
TWO-FISTED	1 5	Two-Fisted Detective - 1/60	1960	Anthology	VGF	Digest	$44.00 A
TWO-FISTED	1 6	Two-Fisted Detective - 3/60	1960	Anthology	AF	Digest	$41.00 A
TWO-FISTED	2 3	Two-Fisted Detective - 10/60	1960	Anthology	VGF	Digest	$34.00 A
TWO-FISTED	2 3	Two-Fisted Detective - 10/60	1960	Anthology	VG	Digest	$15.00
TWO-FISTED	2 4	Two-Fisted Detective - 1/61	1961	Anthology	VGF	Digest	$24.00 A
U.S. CRIME	1 1	U.S. Crime - 12/7/51	1951	Anthology	VG	Digest	$7.00
UNI	No#	Die, Lover	n/d	Whittington, H.	VGF		$5.00
UNI	No#	Homicidal Lady	n/d	Keene, D.	VGF		$4.00
UNI	No#	So Dead, My Lovely	n/d	Keene, D.	VG-		$3.00
UNI	No#	Swing Low, Swing Dead	n/d	Gruber, F.	VG+		$3.00
UNI	No#	To Kiss Or Kill	n/d	Keene, D.	VG-		$3.00
UNI BOOK	3	Unfaithful Wives	1950	Gaddis, P.	VGF	Digest	$7.00
UNI BOOK	9	Warped Women	1951	Pritchard, J.	VGF	Digest	$82.00 A
UNI BOOK	13	Torment	1951	Meeker, R.	VG+	Digest	$15.00
UNI BOOK	14	Stripper!	1951	Williams, W.	VGF	Digest	$13.00
UNI BOOK	15	The Thing That Made Love	1951	Reed, D.V.	VGF-	Digest	$36.00 A
UNI BOOK	15	The Thing That Made Love	1951	Reed, D.V.	G	Digest	$10.00
UNI BOOK	16	Raw Passion	1951	Martin, C.	VG+	Digest	$15.00
UNI BOOK	18	Love Cheat	1951	Arthur, W.	VG	Digest	$25.00 A

Vega V-8 VGF $8   Vega V-23 VGF $8   Vega VSF-7 AF $14   Vega VW-112 VG $7

PUBLISHER	PUB. #	TITLE	DATE	AUTHOR	COND.	TYPE	PRICE
UNI BOOK	21	Hideaway	1952	Gaddis, P.	VG	Digest	$9.00
UNI BOOK	23	Sin Ship	1952	Pritchard, J.	G	Digest	$4.00
UNI BOOK	28	Unleashed Woman	1952	Jordan, G.	G	Digest	$10.00
UNI BOOK	31	Doctor Prescott's Secret	1952	Gaddis, P.	G+	Digest	$8.00
UNI BOOK	32	Loves Of A Girl Wrestler	1952	West, B.	VG	Digest	$25.00 A
UNI BOOK	35	Slave Ship	1952	Drake, H.B.	VG	Digest	$20.00 A
UNI BOOK	35	Slave Ship	1952	Drake, H.B.	VG	Digest	$17.00
UNI BOOK	36	Hoyden Of The Hills	1952	Lawrence, A.	VG+	Digest	$17.00 A
UNI BOOK	36	Hoyden Of The Hills	1952	Lawrence, A.	VG	Digest	$12.00
UNI BOOK	38	Secrets Of A Co-Ed	1952	West, B.	G-	Digest	$5.00
UNI BOOK	43	The Queer Sisters	1952	Harragan, S.	VG-	Digest	$12.00
UNI BOOK	44	Sin Is A Redhead	1952	Harragan, S.	VGF+	Digest	$33.00 A
UNI BOOK	45	Bad Sister	1953	Wall, E.	G	Digest	$5.00
UNI BOOK	47	Kiss Of The Damned	1953	Harragan, S.	G-	Digest	$4.00
UNI BOOK	57	Three Bad Girls	1953	Harragan, S.	AF	Digest	$29.00 A
UNI BOOK	63	Passion In The Pines	1953	Woodford, J.	VGF+	Digest	$24.00 A
UNI BOOK	64	Cuban Heel	1953	Harragan, S.	VG	Digest	$25.00 A
UNI BOOK	65	Hill Billy In High Heels	1953	Bogar, J.	VG	Digest	$7.00
UNI BOOK	69	Confessions Of A Chinatown Moll	1953	Bogar, J.	VG	Digest	$47.00 A
UNI BOOK	70	Wild Oats	1953	Whittington, H.	G	Digest	$10.00
UNI BOOK	73	Cabin Fever	1954	Hitt, O.	G	Digest	$6.00
UNI BOOK	75	Harlem Doctor	1953	Roberts, L.	VG	Digest	$20.00 A
UNI BOOK	78	Out Of Bounds	1954	Matthews, E.L.	VG	Digest	$8.00
UNIQUE	UB 105	Hypnotize	1966	Cole, D.	VG		$17.00 A
UNIQUE	UB 108	Tight Fit	1966	Gardner, K.	VGF		$14.00
UNIQUE	UB 124	Ship Master	1967	Dixon, A.	VGF		$8.00
UNIQUE	UB 126	Stranger In Town	1968	D'Orque, R.	VGF		$8.00
UNIQUE	UB 154	A Lesson In Eros	1968	Parker, J.	VGF-		$8.00
UNIQUE	UB 154	A Lesson In Eros	1968	Parker, J.	VG+		$7.00
UNIQUE	UB 155	Lady Butler	1968	Nelson, R.	VGF+		$14.00 A
UNIVERSAL GIANT	1	Prime Sucker	1952	Whittington, H.	VG	DBL	$20.00
		The Hussy		Williams, I.			
UNIVERSAL GIANT	1	Prime Sucker	1952	Whittington, H.	G+	DBL	$16.00
UNIVERSAL GIANT	2	Paprika	n/d	Stroheim, E.V.	VG+		$9.00 A
UNIVERSAL GIANT	3	His Majesty O'Keefe	1953	Klingman, L.	VG+		$9.00
UNIVERSAL GIANT	4	Dope Doll	1953	Harragan, S.	VGF	DBL	$50.00 A
		The Bigamy Kiss		Harragan, S.			
UNIVERSAL GIANT	7	Savage Mistress	1953	Hartt, J.	VGF	DBL	$8.00 A
		Concubine		Dean, E.			
UNIVERSAL GIANT	8	The Lusty Land	1953	Taylor, V.	VG	DBL	$9.00
		Forbidden Fruit		Lucas, C.			
UNIVERSAL GIANT	9	Aphrodite's Lover	1953	MacArthur, A.	VGF	Digest	$17.00
UNIVERSAL GIANT	11	The Queen's Warrant	1953	Mundy, T.	VGF	DBL	$11.00 A
		Paths Of Glory		Cobb, H.			
UNIVERSAL LIBRARY	UL 49	Green Mansions (dust jkt.)	n/d	Hudson, W.H.	VG	MTI	$19.00 A
UNIVERSAL ROMANCE	No#	Any Man's Woman	n/d	Barr, C.	VG+	Digest	$17.00
UNIVERSE	4	Universe Sci-Fi 3/54	1954	Anthology	VGF+	Digest	$6.00
UNIVERSE	5	Universe Sci-Fi 5/54	1954	Anthology	VG+	Digest	$6.00

Venus 114 VGF $33

Venus 131 VG $42

Vital No#1 VG+ $27

PUBLISHER	PUB. #	TITLE	DATE	AUTHOR	COND.	TYPE	PRICE
UNIVERSE	6	Universe Sci-Fi 7/54	1954	Anthology	VGF	Digest	$5.00
UNIVERSE	9	Universe Sci-Fi 1/55	1955	Anthology	VG+	Digest	$6.00
UNIVERSITY CIRCLE	No#	The Ecstasy Drugs	1966	Bischoff, W.H.	VG		$7.00
UNSOLVED MURDERS	1 1	Unsolved Murders 6/54	1954	Anthology	VGF	Digest	$12.00 A
UPTOWN	703	The Sex Life Of The Gods	1962	Knerr, M.	AF-		$30.00 A
UPTOWN	703	The Sex Life Of The Gods	1962	Knerr, M.	VG+		$16.00 A
VALUE BOOK	101	The Young Adventurer	n/d	Alger, H.	VG+		$7.00
VALUE BOOK	102	Strive And Succeed	n/d	Alger, H.	G+		$5.00
VALUE BOOK	103	Do And Dare	n/d	Alger, H.	VG+		$7.00
VALUE BOOK	104	Brave And Bold	n/d	Alger, H.	VG		$6.00
VALUE BOOK	105	Making His Way	n/d	Alger, H.	VGF		$7.00
VANGUARD SCI. FI.	1 1	Vanguard Sci-Fi - 6/58	1958	Anthology	VGF-	Digest	$7.00
VANITAS	V 4402	Alligator (2nd)	1963	FI*M*NG, I.	VG+		$13.00 A
VEGA	V 1	The Animal Urge	1960	Woolfe, B.	VGF-		$8.00
VEGA	V 4	Joy Killer	1960	Brandon, R.	AF		$7.00
VEGA	V 4	Joy Killer	1960	Brandon, R.	VG+		$6.00
VEGA	V 5	Burden Of Guilt	1960	Spears, F.	VGF		$8.00
VEGA	V 6	Executive Bed	1960	Harvey, L.	VGF		$11.00 A
VEGA	V 6	Executive Bed	1960	Harvey, L.	VGF		$8.00
VEGA	V 7	The Takers	1960	Stacy, J.	VG+		$8.00
VEGA	V 7	The Takers	1960	Stacy, J.	VGF		$7.00
VEGA	V 8	Included Out	1960	Gooch, M.S.	VGF		$8.00
VEGA	V 9	Murder's For The Birds	1961	Miller, F.S.	VGF		$8.00
VEGA	V 9	Murder's For The Birds	1961	Miller, F.S.	VG		$8.00
VEGA	V 10	The Opposite Six	1961	Turni, M.	VGF		$8.00
VEGA	V 14	Destination: Death	1961	Bishop, G.	VG+		$7.00
VEGA	V 16	Frame Up	1962	Gregory, S.	VGF		$8.00
VEGA	V 17	Vice Town	1962	Willie, E.	VGF		$8.00
VEGA	V 18	The Suspected Four	1962	Roberts, W.L.	VGF		$8.00
VEGA	V 19	Knock On Any Head	1962	Miller, F.S.	VGF-		$8.00
VEGA	V 20	All For One	1962	Marmor, J.	VGF		$10.00
VEGA	V 21	Hayseed	1962	Moore, H.L.	VGF		$8.00
VEGA	V 21	Hayseed	1962	Moore, H.L.	VG+		$7.00
VEGA	V 23	The River Is Cold	1962	Rimel, D.	VGF		$8.00 A
VEGA	V 24	The Suckers	1962	Fullilove, J.	VGF		$8.00
VEGA	V 25	Savage Summer	1962	Vance, G.	VGF		$7.00
VEGA	V 26	The Pagans Three	1963	Gilman, W.	AF		$8.00
VEGA	V 27	Reaching High	1963	Strand, B.	AF		$10.00
VEGA	V 38	The Devastating Urge	1964	Randolph, D.	VGF		$8.00
VEGA	V 46	Sin-Drome	1965	Howe, A.A.	AF		$10.00
VEGA	V 48	Lust Versus Sanity	1966	Ringo, J.	VGF		$7.00
VEGA	V 52	Young And Willing	1967	Lucas, M.	VG+		$10.00
VEGA	V 53	New Girl In Town	1967	Rand, R.	VGF		$35.00 A
VEGA	V 64	Judd And The Three Widows	1969	Barstow, L.	VGF		$15.00 A
VEGA	V 71	Sex Has No Private Hour	1970	Knight, R.	VG+		$7.00

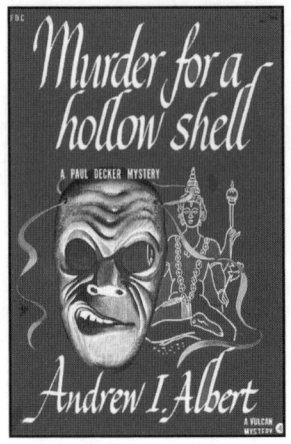

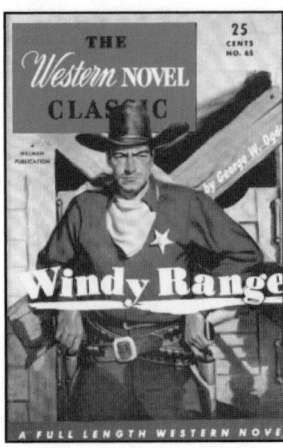

Vulcan 4 VG+ $15   Web Detective 2-6 AF $22   Western Novel Classic 65 VG+ $5

PUBLISHER	PUB. #	TITLE	DATE	AUTHOR	COND.	TYPE	PRICE
VEGA	VSF 7	The Planet Seekers	1963	Barton, E.	AF		$14.00 A
VEGA	VSF 7	The Planet Seekers	1963	Barton, E.	AF		$12.00 A
VEGA	VSF 9	Suspension	1963	Fane, B.	VG-		$7.00
VEGA	VSF 10	The Return	1963	Torro, P.	VGF-		$6.00
VEGA	VW 102	Trail Of Vengeance	1962	Clark, A.	VG		$10.00
VEGA	VW 103	War At Bluestem Basin	1962	Nemec, J.	VGF		$12.00 A
VEGA	VW 111	Come A-Smokin'	1964	Nye, N.C.	AF		$22.00 A
VEGA	VW 112	Storm Ross	1964	Howe, A.A.	VG		$7.00
VEGA	VW 114	Where The Big Gun Rides	1964	Fonville, J.	VG		$6.00
VEGA	VW 115	Sudden Rage At War Rim	1964	Ryerson, M.	VG+		$14.00 A
VEGA MYSTERY READER	1	Vega Mystery Reader #1	1963	Anthology	F		$33.00 A
VEGA MYSTERY READER	1	Vega Mystery Reader #1	1963	Anthology	VG+		$8.00 A
VENICE	VB 313	Bizarre World Of The Peeping Tom	1967	Riordan, J.	AF		$7.00
VENICE	VB 417	Main Street, U.S.A.	1969	Lord, B.	VG		$3.00
VENUS BOOKS	101	Girl With No Past	1950	Gaddis, P.	VGF	Digest	$22.00 A
VENUS BOOKS	101	Girl With No Past	1950	Gaddis, P.	VG	Digest	$7.00
VENUS BOOKS	104	Beach Party	1950	Gaddis, P.	VGF	Digest	$30.00 A
VENUS BOOKS	105	Take My Love!	1950	Gaddis, P.	VG+	Digest	$16.00
VENUS BOOKS	106	Over Night	1950	Bligh, N.	VG+	Digest	$22.00
VENUS BOOKS	109	Lover Boy	1950	Bellamy, H.	VGF	Digest	$22.00 A
VENUS BOOKS	109	Lover Boy	1950	Bellamy, H.	VG	Digest	$9.00
VENUS BOOKS	111	Pick-Up Alley	1950	Quandt, A.L.	VG	Digest	$14.00
VENUS BOOKS	114	Confessions Of A Carnival Dancer	1951	Harvey, G.	VGF	Digest	$33.00 A
VENUS BOOKS	116	One Wild Night!	1951	Gaddis, P.	VGF	Digest	$30.00 A
VENUS BOOKS	119	No Time For Marriage	1951	Charlson, D.	VGF-	Digest	$27.00 A
VENUS BOOKS	120	The Naked Night	1951	Bligh, N.	VG+	Digest	$17.00 A
VENUS BOOKS	122	Pleasure At Midnight	1951	Gaddis, P.	VG	Digest	$12.00
VENUS BOOKS	124	She Couldn't Be Good!	1951	Harvey, G.	VGF	Digest	$43.00 A
VENUS BOOKS	128	She Had What It Takes	1951	Welles, K.	VG-	Digest	$25.00 A
VENUS BOOKS	131	Tough Doll	1951	Gaddis, P.	VG	Digest	$42.00 A
VENUS BOOKS	131	Tough Doll	1951	Gaddis, P.	VG	Digest	$25.00 A
VENUS BOOKS	133	She Tried To Be Good	1951	Stonebraker, F.	VG	Digest	$22.00
VENUS BOOKS	148	Remembered Moment	1952	Bligh, N.	VG+	Digest	$14.00
VENUS BOOKS	153	Sailor's Weekend	1952	Harrison, W.*	VG	Digest	$24.00
VENUS BOOKS	157	Women's Doctor	1953	Haskell, F.	VG+	Digest	$12.00
VENUS BOOKS	168	Backwoods Girl	1954	Gaddis, P.	VG-	Digest	$8.00
VENUS BOOKS	171	Beach Girl	1954	Sherman, J.	VG	Digest	$27.00 A
VENUS BOOKS	175	Young Sinners	1954	Manning, J.	VG	Digest	$45.00 A
VENUS BOOKS	187	Backwoods Girl	1954	Gaddis, P.	VG	Digest	$16.00
VENUS BOOKS	196	Cabin Hostess	1954	Gaddis, P.	VG	Digest	$33.00 A
VENUS BOOKS	198	Hollywood Starlet	1954	Hall, R.	VG+	Digest	$11.00 A
VENUS VOLUME	102	The Wild Practice Of Love	1964	Massey, C.	AF		$7.00
VERDICT	1 1	Verdict - 6/53	1953	Anthology	G	Digest	$12.00
VERDICT	1 2	Verdict - 7/53	1953	Anthology	VGF-	Digest	$23.00 A
VERDICT	1 2	Verdict - 7/53	1953	Anthology	VG+	Digest	$16.00

White Circle 54 VG $27　　　White Circle 80 VGF $7　　　White Circle 469 VGF $7　　　White Circle 515 VG+ $7

PUBLISHER	PUB. #	TITLE	DATE	AUTHOR	COND.	TYPE	PRICE
VERDICT CRIME	1 1	Verdict Crime Det. - 8/56	1956	Anthology	VGF	Digest	$12.00
VEST-POCKET	VP 102	Playpet	1962	Hitt, O.	VG		$25.00 A
VITAL	No# 1	Empire Of Crime	1945	Carter, N.	VG+	Digest	$27.00 A
VITAL	No# 2	Murder Unlimited	1945	Carter, N.	AF	Digest	$19.00 A
VITAL	No# 3	Death Has Green Eyes!	1946	Carter, N.	VG+	Digest	$30.00
VITAL	No# 4	Park Avenue Murder!	1946	Carter, N.	VG+	Digest	$25.00
VOLITANT	V 750	Sir! Droll Stories	1967	Anthology	AF		$7.00
VORTEX	1 1	Vortex Science Fiction	1953	Anthology	VGF	Digest	$6.00
VORTEX	1 2	Vortex Science Fiction	1953	Anthology	VGF	Digest	$6.00
VULCAN	No# 1	The Maori Murder Case	1944	Albert, A.I.	G	Digest	$7.00
VULCAN	No# 2	Death Meets The Deadline	1944	George, D.R.	VG	Digest	$15.00 A
VULCAN	No# 2	Death Meets The Deadline	1944	George, D.R.	VG+	Digest	$12.00 A
VULCAN	4	Murder For A Hollow Shell	1945	Albert, A.I.	VG+	Digest	$15.00 A
VULCAN	5	TCOT Phantom Fingerprints	1945	Crossen, K.	VG	Digest	$8.00
VULCAN	6	Curtain Call For Murder	1945	Yates, P.	VG	Digest	$10.00
WARNER*		* See PAPERBACK LIBRARY					
WEB DETECTIVE	1 6	Web Detective Stories 9/58	1958	Anthology	AF	Digest	$15.00 A
WEB DETECTIVE	2 6	Web Detective Stories 3/60	1960	Anthology	AF	Digest	$22.00 A
WEB DETECTIVE	3 2	Web Detective Stories 8/60	1960	Anthology	VGF	Digest	$14.00 A
WEB TERROR	4 1	Web Terror Stories 8/62	1962	Anthology	AF	Digest	$55.00 A
WEB TERROR	4 1	Web Terror Stories 8/62	1962	Anthology	VGF	Digest	$23.00 A
WEB TERROR	4 2	Web Terror Stories 3/63	1963	Anthology	AF	Digest	$34.00
WEB TERROR	4 2	Web Terror Stories 3/63	1963	Anthology	AF	Digest	$31.00 A
WEB TERROR	4 2	Web Terror Stories 3/63	1963	Anthology	VGF	Digest	$25.00 A
WEB TERROR	4 3	Web Terror Stories 11/63	1963	Anthology	VGF	Digest	$24.00 A
WEB TERROR	4 3	Web Terror Stories 11/63	1963	Anthology	VG	Digest	$7.00
WEB TERROR	4 4	Web Terror Stories 4/64	1964	Anthology	VGF+	Digest	$18.00 A
WEB TERROR	4 5	Web Terror Stories 8/64	1964	Anthology	AF	Digest	$33.00
WEB TERROR	4 6	Web Terror Stories 11/64	1964	Anthology	VGF	Digest	$24.00 A
WEB TERROR	5 1	Web Terror Stories 2/65	1965	Anthology	VG-	Digest	$7.00
WEB TERROR	5 2	Web Terror Stories 6/65	1965	Anthology	AF	Digest	$33.00
WEE HOURS	WH 512	Dealer's Luck	1967	Parker, J.	VG+		$10.00 A
WEE HOURS	WH 515	A Study Of Wife Swapping	1967	Gilmore, R.	F		$8.00 A
WEE HOURS	WH 516	Screen Test	1966	Dean, A.	AF		$12.00 A
WEE HOURS	WH 517	Pickup	1967	Parker, J.	AF		$15.00
WEE HOURS	WH 521	Lady Peeper	1967	Drake, D.	VGF		$8.00
WEE HOURS	WH 526	Backstage Trio	1967	Davis, A.	VG+		$12.00 A
WEE HOURS	WH 544	Reserved For Three	1967	Barrows, P.	VGF		$7.00
WEE HOURS	WH 547	One Way Trip	1967	Sands, N.	VGF		$13.00 A
WEIRD MYSTERY	2	Weird Mystery - Winter 1970	1970	Anthology	VGF+	Digest	$17.00 A
WEIRD TALES	45 4	Weird Tales - 9/53	1953	Anthology	VGF	Digest	$17.00
WEIRD TALES	46 1	Weird Tales - 3/54	1954	Anthology	VGF	Digest	$16.00
WEIRD TALES	46 2	Weird Tales - 5/54	1954	Anthology	VGF	Digest	$16.00
WEIRD TALES	46 3	Weird Tales - 7/54	1954	Anthology	VG+	Digest	$8.00
WEIRD TALES	46 4	Weird Tales - 9/54	1954	Anthology	VG	Digest	$12.00
WEST IN ACTION	2	The Western Trail	1948	Leinster, M.	VG	Digest	$7.00
WESTERN	1 3	Western Magazine - 12/55	1955	Anthology	VG+	Digest	$20.00 A
WESTERN	2 1	Western Magazine - 3/56	1956	Anthology	AF	Digest	$12.00

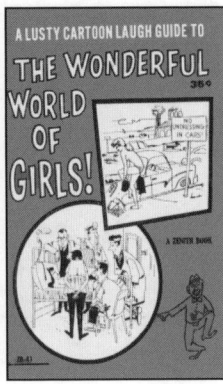

Wisdom House 109 VG $7　　　Zenith 4 VG+ $18　　　Zenith 29 VG $12　　　Zenith 41 VG $18

PUBLISHER	PUB. #	TITLE	DATE	AUTHOR	COND.	TYPE	PRICE
WESTERN	4 1	Western Magazine - 7/57	1957	Anthology	VG+	Digest	$13.00
WEST. NVL. OF THE MONTH	11	Brand Of The Outlaw	1942	Lehman, P.E.	VG+	Digest	$6.00
WESTERN NOVEL CLASSIC	63	Horsethief Creek	1946	Lomax, B.	VG+	Digest	$6.00
WESTERN NOVEL CLASSIC	65	Windy Range	1946	Ogden, G.W.	VG+	Digest	$5.00
WESTERN NOVEL CLASSIC	67	Sudden Takes Charge	1946	Strange, O.	VG	Digest	$5.00
WESTERN NOVEL CLASSIC	85	Black River Ranch	1948	Westland, L.	VG	Digest	$5.00
WESTERN NOVEL CLASSIC	90	Gunsmoke Galoot	1948	Ernenwein, L.	VG	Digest	$5.00
WESTERN NOVEL CLASSIC	92	Bury Me Not	1948	Bosworth, A.R.	VGF	Digest	$7.00
WESTERN NOVEL CLASSIC	98	The Shootin' Sheriff	1949	Riley, T.	VG	Digest	$5.00
WESTERN NOVEL CLASSIC	112	Room For The Rolling M	1951	Sinclair, B.W.	VG+	Digest	$7.00
WHITE CIRCLE	No#	Belt Of Suspicion	1942	Wakefield, R.	VGF		$15.00
WHITE CIRCLE	No#	This Man Is Dangerous	1942	Cheyney, P.	VG		$9.00 A
WHITE CIRCLE	54	No Sleep At All	1943	Warren, J.	VG		$27.00 A
WHITE CIRCLE	59	Dangerous Curves	1943	Cheyney, P.	G+		$5.00
WHITE CIRCLE	60	Six Feet Of Dynamite	1943	Gray, B.	VG		$7.00
WHITE CIRCLE	67	No Murder Of Mine	1943	Campbell, A.	VG-		$6.00
WHITE CIRCLE	69	The Vanishing Corpse	1943	Gilbert, A.	VG		$5.00
WHITE CIRCLE	71	Slippery Staircase	1943	Lorac, E.C.R.	VG+		$11.00 A
WHITE CIRCLE	80	The Ridin' Fool	1943	Curran, T.	VGF		$7.00
WHITE CIRCLE	88	The Last Bullet	1944	Curran, T.	VGF		$7.00
WHITE CIRCLE	88	The Last Bullet	1946	Curran, T.	G+		$6.00
WHITE CIRCLE	99	Kitty	1944	Marshall, R.	VG	MTI	$5.00
WHITE CIRCLE	112	The Man From Peace River (2nd)	1944	Reid, W.O.	VGF		$7.00
WHITE CIRCLE	213	Literary Lapses	1945	Leacock, S.	VG		$5.00
WHITE CIRCLE	219	Dangerous Curves	1945	Cheyney, P.	VGF		$12.00
WHITE CIRCLE	224	The Nutmeg Tree	1946	Sharp, M.	VG-		$5.00
WHITE CIRCLE	263	Restless Beauty	1946	Ames, J.	VG		$6.00
WHITE CIRCLE	313	Duchess Hotspur	1947	Marshall, R.	VG+		$7.00
WHITE CIRCLE	332	El Caid	1947	Sheridan, C.	VG+		$6.00
WHITE CIRCLE	422	Exit Only	1949	Maddock, S.	VG		$7.00
WHITE CIRCLE	CD 469	The Lady In Question	1950	Shann, R.	VGF		$7.00
WHITE CIRCLE	CD 501	Special Delivery	1951	Gielgud, V.	VG		$6.00
WHITE CIRCLE	CD 506	No Duty On A Corpse	1951	Murray, M.	VG		$8.00
WHITE CIRCLE	CD 515	Cat And Mouse	1951	Brand, C.	VG+		$7.00
WHITMAN	746	War Planes	1940	Walker, J.B.	VGF		$42.00 A
WING BOOK	104	Queen Of The Kooch Dancers	1965	Feld, H.	AF		$44.00 A
WISDOM HOUSE	G 1	The Day The Communists . . .	1961	Moore, I.	VG+		$8.00
WISDOM HOUSE	G 2	God In Hollywood	1961	Canfield, A.	G+		$6.00
WISDOM HOUSE	W 104	The Life And Loves Of Lana Turner	1961	Wright, J.	AF		$8.00 A
WISDOM HOUSE	W 104	The Life And Loves Of Lana Turner	1961	Wright, J.	G		$7.00
WISDOM HOUSE	W 109	Splendors Of Love	1962	Thompson, J.B.	VG		$7.00
WIZARD	410	Ring For Service	1967	Hanson, L.	VGF		$10.00
WONDER STORIES	45 1	Wonder Stories 1957	1957	Anthology	VG+	Digest	$23.00 A
WONDER STORIES	45 2	Wonder Stories	1963	Anthology	VGF	Digest	$35.00
WONDER STORIES	45 2	Wonder Stories	1963	Anthology	VG+	Digest	$20.00 A
WORLDS BEYOND	1 1	World's Beyond - 12/50	1950	Anthology	VG+	Digest	$25.00 A
WORLDS OF FANTASY	1 1	Worlds Of Fantasy	1968	Anthology	VG-	Digest	$5.00
WORLD OF IF	1	The First World Of If	1957	Anthology	VG+	Digest	$18.00

Zane Grey's Western 7-10 AF $10   Zenith 35 AF- $50   Zephyr 41 VGF $17

PUBLISHER	PUB. #	TITLE	DATE	AUTHOR	COND.	TYPE	PRICE
WORLDS OF TOMORROW	1	Worlds Of Tomorrow	1963	Anthology	VG+	Digest	$7.00
ZANE GREY'S WESTERN	5 10	Zane Grey's Western - 12/51	1951	Anthology	VG	Digest	$6.00
ZANE GREY'S WESTERN	6 7	Zane Grey's Western - 9/52	1952	Anthology	VGF	Digest	$8.00
ZANE GREY'S WESTERN	6 8	Zane Grey's Western - 10/52	1952	Anthology	AF	Digest	$10.00
ZANE GREY'S WESTERN	6 10	Zane Grey's Western - 12/52	1952	Anthology	AF	Digest	$13.00 A
ZANE GREY'S WESTERN	6 11	Zane Grey's Western - 1/53	1953	Anthology	AF	Digest	$10.00
ZANE GREY'S WESTERN	6 12	Zane Grey's Western - 2/53	1953	Anthology	VG+	Digest	$7.00
ZANE GREY'S WESTERN	7 1	Zane Grey's Western - 3/53	1953	Anthology	AF	Digest	$10.00
ZANE GREY'S WESTERN	7 10	Zane Grey's Western - 1/54	1954	Anthology	AF	Digest	$10.00
ZEBRA	126	Worms Of The Earth	1975	Howard, R.E.	VGF		$5.00
ZEBRA	2987	Rest In Peace	1990	MacLane, J.*	AF		$7.00
ZEBRA	3212	Just Before Dark	1990	MacLane, J.*	VGF		$7.00
ZENITH	ZB 1	The Sisters	1958	Jackson, C.	VGF		$15.00 A
ZENITH	ZB 1	The Sisters	1958	Jackson, C.	AF		$13.00 A
ZENITH	ZB 2	All Over Town	1958	Milburn, G.	VGF		$8.00
ZENITH	ZB 2	All Over Town	1958	Milburn, G.	VG		$6.00
ZENITH	ZB 4	Die Screaming	1958	Pagano, J.	VG+		$18.00 A
ZENITH	ZB 5	Best Cartoons From Argosy	1958	Anthology	AF		$9.00 A
ZENITH	ZB 6	The Oral Roberts Reader	1958	Roberts, O.	VG		$7.00
ZENITH	ZB 7	The Girl From Hateville	1958	Brewer, G.	VGF		$55.00 A
ZENITH	ZB 8	Adventure In Paradise	1958	Anthology	AF		$8.00 A
ZENITH	ZB 10	Rawhiders	1958	Roan, T.	VGF		$12.00 A
ZENITH	ZB 12	The Rascal's Guide	1959	Anthology	AF		$20.00 A
ZENITH	ZB 13	The Three Legions	1959	Solon, G.	VGF		$8.00
ZENITH	ZB 14	The People Maker	1959	Knight, D.	VGF		$7.00
ZENITH	ZB 14	The People Maker	1959	Knight, D.	VG		$6.00
ZENITH	ZB 16	Lysistrata	1959	Flora, F.	VGF		$10.00 A
ZENITH	ZB 17	Death Of The Party	1958	Fenisong, R.	AF		$15.00
ZENITH	ZB 18	Blonde Bait	1959	Lacy, E.	VG		$14.00 A
ZENITH	ZB 24	Moran's Woman	1959	Keene, D.	VG		$66.00 A
ZENITH	ZB 29	Sweet And Deadly	1959	MacDonald, P.	VG		$12.00
ZENITH	ZB 30	Strangers On Friday	1959	Whittington, H.	G+		$15.00
ZENITH	ZB 33	The Gray Flannel Shroud	1959	Slesar, H.	VG+		$22.00 A
ZENITH	ZB 33	The Gray Flannel Shroud	1959	Slesar, H.	AF		$17.00 A
ZENITH	ZB 33	The Gray Flannel Shroud	1959	Slesar, H.	VG		$5.00
ZENITH	ZB 35	Man Crazy	1960	Harrison, W.*	AF-		$50.00 A
ZENITH	ZB 39	The Blonde On Borrowed Time	1960	Sanborn, B.X.	G		$6.00
ZENITH	ZB 40	Corpus Earthling	1960	Charbonneau, L.	VGF		$8.00
ZENITH	ZB 41	The Wonderful World Of Girls	1960	Anthology	VG		$18.00
ZENITH	ZB 43	The Hot Sands Of Hell	1960	Landon, C.	VG	MTI	$7.00
ZENITH	ZB 44	The Black Satin Jungle	1960	Frame, B.	VG+		$18.00
ZEPHYR	7	Tortilla Flat (dust jkt.)	1946	Steinbeck, J.	AF		$15.00 A
ZEPHYR	41	The Long Valley (dust jkt.)	1946	Steinbeck, J.	VGF		$17.00 A
ZEPHYR	148	The Big Sleep (dust jkt.)	1947	Chandler, R.	VGF		$48.00 A
ZEPHYR	162	The Lady In The Lake (dust jkt.)	1947	Chandler, R.	VGF		$67.00 A

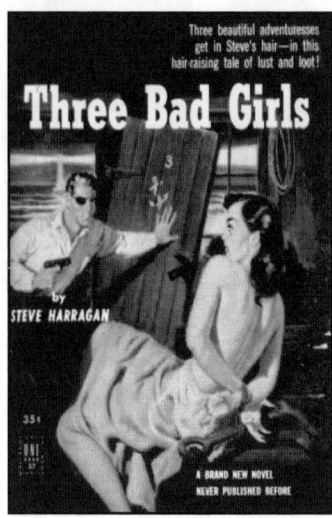

Uni Book 57 (1953)

Beacon B155 (1957)

Popular Detective 9/48

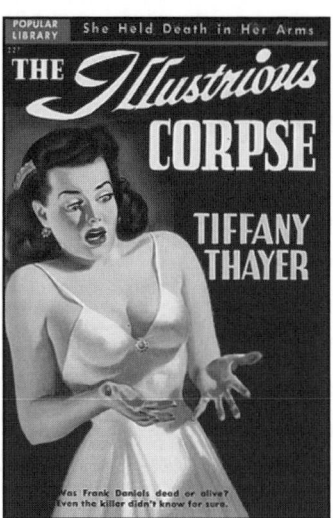

Popular Library 227 (1950)

Two examples of cover art re-use

APPENDIX A
AUTHOR PSEUDONYMS

In the preceding listings, an asterisk following the author's name indicates that the name is a pseudonym that appears on the following list. This is not a comprehensive list of all the pseudonyms that can be found the listings, but it includes most that are important to paperback collectors.

PSEUDONYM	TRUE AUTHOR
Addams, Kay	Orrie Hitt
Aldrich, Ann	Marijane Meaker
Ames, Clyde	Clyde Allison (1)
Anderson, Clyde	Clyde Allison (1)
Axton, David	Dean R. Koontz
Bachman, Richard	Stephen King
Beauchamp, Loren	Robert Silverberg
Box, Edgar	Gore Vidal
Buchanan, Jack	Joe Lansdale and others
Cannon, Curt	Evan Hunter
Carter, Ashley	Harry Whittington
Challon, David	Robert Silverberg
Coffey, Brian	Dean R. Koontz
Collins, Hunt	Evan Hunter
Cooper, Jefferson	Gardner F. Fox
Davidson, John	Charles Nuetzel
Dickson, Carter	John Dickson Carr
Dietrich, Robert	Howard E. Hunt
Duke, Will	William C. Gault
Dwyer, Deanna	Dean R. Koontz
Dwyer, K.R.	Dean R. Koontz
Elliott, Don	Robert Silverberg and others
Emerson, Jill	Lawrence Block
Evans, John	Howard Browne
Evans, Lesley	Lawrence Block
Evans, Tabor	Harry Whittington and others
Fair, A.A.	Erle Stanley Gardner
Gardner, Miriam	Marion Zimmer Bradley
Grant, Maxwell	Walter Gibson
Grantland, Keith	Charles Beaumont
Harrison, Chip	Lawrence Block
Harrison, Whit	Harry Whittington
Hill, John	Dean R. Koontz (2)
Holland, Kel	Harry Whittington
Holmes, H.H.	Anthony Boucher
Hudson, Jan	George H. Smith
Irish, William	Cornell Woolrich
Ives, Morgan	Marion Zimmer Bradley
Kavanagh, Paul	Lawrence Block
Kay, Cameron	Gore Vidal

1) Clyde Allison's true name is William Knoles
2) This only applies to Popular Library #445-325, *The Long Sleep*

PSEUDONYM	TRUE AUTHOR
Kendricks, James	Gardner F. Fox
Kenton, Maxwell	Terry Southern
Knight, David	Richard S. Prather
Lange, John	Michael Crichton
Lee, William	William S. Burroughs
Longman, Marlene	Robert Silverberg
Lord, Sheldon	Lawrence Block and others
MacCargo, J.T.	Peter Rabe
MacDonald, John Ross	Kenneth Millar
MacDonald, Ross	Kenneth Millar
MacLane, Jack	Bill Crider
Majors, Simon	Gardner F. Fox
Malaponte, Marco	Peter Rabe
Mara, Bernard	Brian Moore
Marshall, Alan	Donald Westlake and others
Matthews, Kevin	Gardner F. Fox
Mayo, Jim	Louis L'Amour
McBain, Ed	Evan Hunter
Morgan, Claire	Patricia Highsmith
Morse, Benjamin, M.D.	Lawrence Block
Myers, Harriet K.	Harry Whittington
Nichols, Leigh	Dean R. Koontz
Noone, Edwina	Michael Avallone
Packer, Vin	Marijane Meaker
Paige, Richard	Dean R. Koontz
Park, Jordan	C.M. Kornbluth
Richards, Wm.	Day Keene
Rivere, Alec	Charles Nuetzel
Ronns, Edward	Edward Aarons
Sanders, W. Franklin	Charles Willeford
Scotland, Jay	John Jakes
Shaw, Andrew	Lawrence Block and others
Shepard, Shep	Harry Whittington
Somers, Bart	Gardner F. Fox
Stark, Richard	Donald Westlake
Sterling, Brett	Edmond Hamilton
Stevens, Blaine	Harry Whittington
Stuart, Clay	Harry Whittington
Swenson, Peggy	Richard E. Geis
Weaver, Nicky	Orrie Hitt
Wells, John Warren	Lawrence Block
West, Edwin	Donald Westlake
West, Owen	Dean R. Koontz
Westermier, D.L.	Ed Wood Jr.
Whitney, Hallam	Harry Whittington
Wilmer, Dale	Wade Miller (3)
Wolfe, Aaron	Dean R. Koontz
Woodward, L.T., M.D.	Robert Silverberg
York, Jeremy	John Creasey

3) Wade Miller was actually a collaboration of Bob Wade and Bill Miller

APPENDIX B
ADDITIONAL RESOURCES

MAGAZINES:

PAPERBACK PARADE – Highly recommended, a digest size magazine that has covered the entire paperback collecting field since 1986. It features informative articles on paperback authors, publishers, cover artists, and events. Each issue also includes news, letters, and ads of interest to collectors. Always well illustrated. Published four times per year and available by mail at $8 for a single issue or $35 for a five issue subscription. For information visit www.gryphonbooks.com or write to: Gryphon Books/Paperback Parade, PO Box 209, Brooklyn, NY 11228-0209.

FIRSTS The Book Collector's Magazine – The premier magazine in its field, *Firsts* is a valuable resource for book collectors of all types. Paperback collectors are not neglected—recent articles have featured such subjects as the Dell mapbacks and popular paperback authors such as Richard Matheson, Raymond Chandler, David Goodis, and others. Another useful feature is the Collector's Calendar, which lists upcoming book shows. Published ten times per year and available at independent bookstores throughout the country or by subscription. For more information contact Firsts Magazine, P.O. Box 65166, Tucson, AZ 85728 Telephone: (520) 529-1355. Or visit www.firsts.com.

PAPER COLLECTORS' MARKETPLACE – This monthly magazine covers collectable paper items of all types, including paperbacks. It consists primarily of classified and display ads, although each issue also has one or two feature articles. Interesting, and fun to peruse. For more information write to Paper Collectors' Marketplace, PO Box 128, Scandinavia, WI 54977-0128 or call (715) 467-2379.

ILLUSTRATION – A new magazine dedicated to vintage era American illustration art as seen on paperbacks, pulps, magazines, and comic books. The magazine features profiles and checklists of leading artists, outstanding reproductions of classic vintage cover art, and other regular features. For more information write to Illustration Magazine, 540 Wooddell Court, Kirkwood, MO 63122, or visit www.illustration-magazine.com.

BOOKS:

Several of the following books are out of print, but can be found at libraries or obtained from used book dealers:

Paperbacks U.S.A. by Piet Schreuders – Blue Dolphin Books, 1981
The classic book on the mass-market paperback, written by an avid collector and true paperback devotee. The book has a strong emphasis on cover art and artists and also covers paperback history, how paperbacks are produced, vintage publishers, and more. Many illustrations, including thirty-two pages in color.

The Great American Paperback by Gary Lupoff – Collectors Press, 2001

This attractive new coffee table book features hundreds of color illustrations of classic vintage paperbacks and digests, as well as information on many of the popular paperback genres and vintage era publishers.

The Movie Tie-In Book by Moe Wadle – Nostalgia Press, 1994

A comprehensive list of movie tie-in paperbacks published from 1939 to 1980. The most extensive guide of its kind—over 2750 books are listed in alphabetical order by title. Listing information includes author, publisher, publisher's number, movie stars, and more. Many illustrations.

TV Tie-Ins by Kurt Peer – TV Books, 1999

Subtitled *A Bibliography of American TV Tie-In Paperbacks*. This useful and interesting reference covers over 1400 TV tie-in paperbacks. The books are indexed by author, by publisher, and by the name of the show.

The Mushroom Jungle by Steve Holland – Zardoz Books, 1993

British paperbacks are often considered highly desirable by American collectors, particularly the sensational digest format books published in the decade following World War II by England's "mushroom" publishers (so called because they sprang up so quickly). This book tells the story of these publishers and their books. Well illustrated with hundreds of cover reproductions.

Two Bit Culture by Kenneth C, Davis – Houghton Mifflin, 1984

An interesting and well researched history of the mass-market paperback and its contribution to the American way of life. Appropriately subtitled *The Paperbacking of America*, the book covers paperback development from the advent of Pocket Books, through the early 1980s.

Under Cover by Thomas L. Bonn – Penguin, 1982

Subtitled *An Illustrated History of American Mass-Market Paperbacks*. A brief and readable history of the paperback from its early forerunners, such as the dime novels of the 1800s, through the vintage era, and into the 1970s.

BOOK SHOWS:

Book shows and fairs are one of the best ways to buy, sell, and learn about collectable books, including vintage paperbacks. Check your newspaper or talk to local book dealers to find out about shows in your area. Three shows are of special interest to paperback collectors:

The New York Collectable Paperback and Pulp Fiction Expo, now in its fourteenth year, is held annually each fall and brings together collectors and dealers from across the country. In addition to the opportunity to buy, sell, trade, and "window shop," the Expo features book signings by prominent paperback authors and cover artists. For more information write to Gryphon Books, P.O. Box 209, Brooklyn, NY 11228, or visit www.gryphonbooks.com.

The Paperback Collectors Show and Sale is a Los Angeles area show held annually in the spring. This is another very popular show. Like the New York Expo, it is national in scope and also attracts participants from Canada, England, and Europe. The show always features a large line-up of special guests. In recent years guests have included authors Robert Bloch, Ray Bradbury, Ann Bannon and Richard Prather, and artists such as Kelly Freas. For more information contact show co-sponsor Tom Lesser at (818) 349-3844.

The Windy City Pulp and Paperback Show is a new two-day show held annually in March in the Chicago area. Although only two years old, the show has already outgrown its original venue. The Windy City show features both vintage paperbacks and pulp magazines. Added attractions include special guests, an auction of key items consigned by the various dealers, and a pulp film festival. For more information visit the show's web site at www.pulpshow.com or write to P.O. Box 45495, Madison, WI 53744

THE INTERNET:

The Internet is quickly becoming a major source of information about vintage paperbacks and it can also be a good way to buy and sell. Web sites now display thousands of images of vintage paperbacks along with basic bibliographic information on the books. The auction site Ebay recently created a separate category for vintage paperbacks, and additionally, there are now hundreds of on-line book sellers offering vintage paperbacks at fixed prices.

A word of caution is appropriate, though—Internet sellers are free to ask any price they like for a paperback, and in some cases, usually due to inexperience or overreaching, sellers set prices that are far too high to be sustained by actual demand. Other sellers, however, may see these asking prices and use them as benchmarks to set their own prices for the same books. In this way, an unrealistically high price can become the standard Internet price for a book, even though no actual sales have been made at that level. Overpricing of this type is most likely to occur with relatively scarce paperbacks. Additionally, in light of rising reports of Internet fraud, you should proceed with some caution if you have not had any prior dealings with a particular seller.

SUPPLIES:

Paperback bags, both plastic and mylar, as well as storage boxes can be obtained from Bags Unlimited. For their annual catalog write to Bags Unlimited, 7 Canal Street, Rochester, NY 14608-1910 or call (800) 767-2247. Comic book shops and used book stores often carry paperback supplies also.

VINTAGE PAPERBACK AUCTIONS AND SALES LISTS:

Write to:

Modern Age Books
P.O. Box 325
East Lansing, MI 48826

APPENDIX C
PAPERBACK REPAIR

It can be very tempting to try to improve the condition of books in your collection but as a general rule you should resist the temptation. Attempted repairs can easily backfire and leave the book worse than before. For example, attempts to re-color scuffs and scratches using felt-tip markers will almost always be noticeable and considered a serious defect. The same is true of almost all attempts to re-glue loose cover lamination, or to re-bind a book to correct uneven pages. Similarly, you should never try to repair a paperback with invisible tape. There are some relatively safe and effective repair techniques though.

To remove dirt and grime from paperback covers, soap and water is usually a safe method. Use a soft cloth dampened with warm water and, if necessary, apply a small amount of hand soap or mild detergent to the cloth. Lightly scrub the cover until the dirt is gone and then remove any excess soap and dirt with a damp part of the cloth. Thoroughly dry the book with a cloth or a Kleenex. The whole process should take no more than fifteen seconds and in that time the moisture will not damage a typical paperback—however, this method should not be used on books that do not have glossy water resistant covers (such as most digests).

White erasers labeled "non-abrasive" are now readily available in office supply stores and these are very effective for removing pencil and grease pencil from paperback covers and pages, and are somewhat effective on ball-point pen. These non-abrasive erasers are so superior to regular pink erasers that you should not even try using a regular eraser. Even with the non-abrasiveness, though, excessive rubbing will damage a book, so always exercise moderation.

Very small precise repairs to spines can be made with an archival type acid-free glue stick. These can also be found at most office supply stores. Use a pocket knife to apply a small amount of the glue to the problem area.

For removing price stickers or tape from covers and pages, rubber cement thinner is very effective. This solvent can be obtained from art supply dealers and it will soften and remove almost any adhesive that has not completely dried out and hardened. Like other solvents, it is extremely fast drying so when applying it to a sticker you may need to cover it with something to give it time to penetrate. Usually a minute or two is sufficient but old stickers may require more time. Rubber cement thinner applied with a soft cloth can also be somewhat effective at removing magic marker from laminated or coated book covers.

Folded or curled page corners can be flattened by moistening the pages and then pressing the book. This is a very easy and effective technique. Use a damp sponge or cloth and lightly moisten the problem area on each page. If the entire book is waved, you may have to moisten every page. Unfold the corners (if necessary) and then press the book under a weight for a day or two. You should work quickly so the pages do not completely dry out before you get to the pressing stage. If a book is only slightly warped, it can often be satisfactorily flattened simply by pressing it under a moderate weight for a few weeks.

As a final tip, cellophane tape used like a lint roller is very effective for lifting off the dust and dirt that often accumulates on a book's page tops.

The information throughout this book was obtained primarily from the author's direct examination of vintage paperbacks. The outside source most frequently consulted for historical information was the magazine *Publishers Weekly*. Also helpful were the publications listed below.

Avallone, Michael. "How Can You Put Your Name on Books Like That? Or Make Mine Midwood!" *Paperback Parade*, no. 32, (1993): 48–62.

Bonn, Thomas, L. *Under Cover: An Ilustrated History of American Mass Market Paperbacks*. New York: Penguin Books, 1982.

Cole, John Y., ed. *Books in Action: The Armed Services Editions*. Washington, D.C.: The Center for the Book, Library of Congress, 1984.

Crider, Allen Billy, ed. *Mass Market Publishing in America*. Boston: G.K. Hall & Co., 1982.

Davis, Kenneth C. *Two-Bit Culture*. Boston: Houghton Mifflin, 1984.

Harbottle, Philip and Stephen Holland. *British Science Fiction Paperbacks and Magazines 1949–1956: An Annotated Bibliography and Guide*. San Bernardino: Borgo Press, 1994.

Hecklemann, Charles N. "An Interview with Charles N. Hecklemann (Part 2)," interview by Gary Lovisi. *Paperback Parade*, no. 35, (1993): 15–28.

Holland, Steve. *The Mushroom Jungle: A History of Postwar Paperback Publishing*. England: Zeon Books, 1993.

Jamieson, John. *Editions for the Armed Services, Inc.: A History*. New York: Editions for the Armed Services, Inc., 1948.

Kurian, George Thomas. *The Directory of American Book Publishing: From Founding Fathers to Today's Conglomerates*. New York: Simon and Schuster, 1975.

Lesser, Robert. *Pulp Art*. New York: Gramercy Books, 1997.

Lyles, William H. *Putting Dell on the Map: A History of the Dell Paperbacks*. Westport, Conn.: Greenwood Press, 1983.

———. *Dell Paperbacks, 1942 to Mid-1962: A Catalog Index*, Westport, Conn.: Greenwood Press, 1983.

Madison, Charles A. *Book Publishing in America*. New York: McGraw-Hill, 1966.

Williams, William Emrys. *The Penguin Story*. London: Penguin Books, 1956.

Miller, Stephen T., and William G. Contento. S*cience Fiction, Fantasy, & Weird Fiction Magazine Index (1890–2000)*. Oakland, Cal.: Locus Press, 2001.

Petersen, Clarence. *The Bantam Story*. New York: Bantam Books, 1975.

Schick, Frank L. *The Paperbound Book in America: The History of Paperbacks and Their European Background*. New York: R.R. Bowker Co., 1958.

Schreuders, Piet. *Paperbacks, U.S.A.: A Graphic History, 1939–1959*. San Diego: Blue Dolphin, 1981.

Shimkin, Leon. "An Interview with Leon Shimkin," interview conducted by Michael S. Barson. *Paperback Quarterly* 4, no. 4 (Winter 1981): 5–9.

Tebbel, John. *A History of Book Publishing in the United States*. Vol. 2, *The Expansion of an Industry, 1865–1919*. New York: R.R. Bowker Co., 1975.

———. *A History of Book Publishing in the United States*. Vol. 4, *The Great Change, 1940–1980*. New York: R.R. Bowker Co., 1981.

Tuck, Donald H. *The Encyclopedia of Science Fiction and Fantasy*, Vol. 3, *Miscellaneous*. Chicago: Advent, 1982.

Weybright, Victor. *The Making of a Publisher*. New York: Reynal & Company, 1967.

Avon T-165

Bantam 743

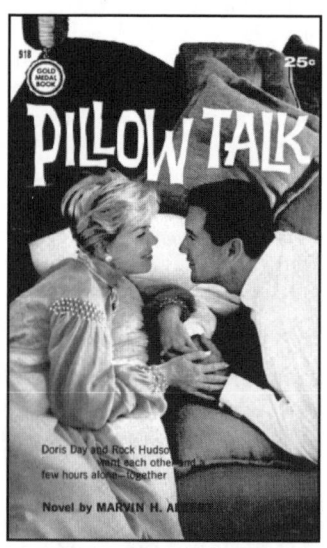

Gold Medal 918

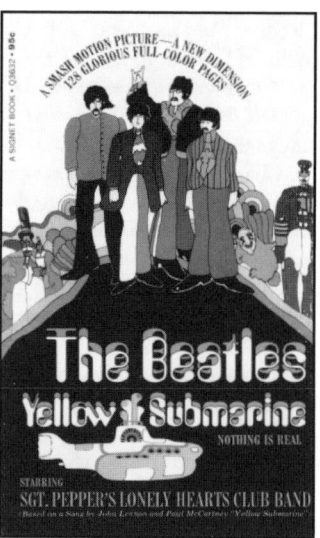

Signet 3632

Four movie tie-in (MTI) paperbacks

The following index can be used to find all the listed books by any particular author. As an additional reference aid, when an author has two or more different books appearing on the same page in the listings, the number of such different books is shown in parenthesis following the page number. If the same book has multiple listings, it is only counted once for purposes of the parenthesis numbering system, except when the listings for the book run to a second page, in which case it is counted once for each page. Authors with the same last name and first initial are distinguished in the index by their first names, even though only first initials appear in the listings. Finally, as in the listings, an asterisk following an author's name indicates that the name is a pseudonym identified in Appendix A.